American Philosophical Society

Transactions of the American Philosophical Society

Volume 21

American Philosophical Society

Transactions of the American Philosophical Society
Volume 21

ISBN/EAN: 9783337237486

Printed in Europe, USA, Canada, Australia, Japan

Cover: Foto ©Andreas Hilbeck / pixelio.de

More available books at **www.hansebooks.com**

AMERICAN PHILOSOPHICAL SOCIETY

HELD AT PHILADELPHIA

FOR PROMOTING USEFUL KNOWLEDGE

VOLUME XXI—NEW SERIES

PHILADELPHIA
PUBLISHED BY THE SOCIETY
1908

CONTENTS OF VOL. XXI.

ARTICLE I.

ARTICLE II.

ARTICLE III.

ARTICLE IV.

ARTICLE V.

TRANSACTIONS

OF THE

AMERICAN PHILOSOPHICAL SOCIETY

HELD AT PHILADELPHIA

FOR PROMOTING USEFUL KNOWLEDGE

VOLUME XXI—NEW SERIES

PART I

ARTICLE I—*The Morphology of the Skull of the Pelycosaurian Genus Dimetrodon.* By E. C. Case

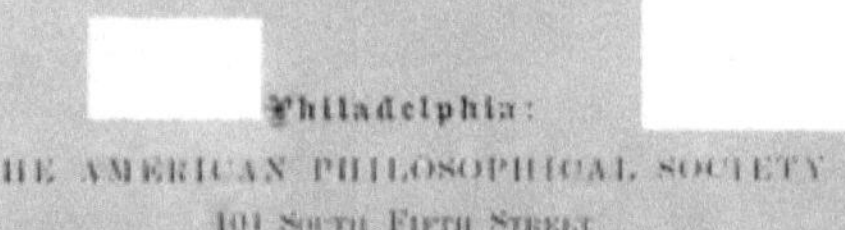

Philadelphia:
THE AMERICAN PHILOSOPHICAL SOCIETY
104 SOUTH FIFTH STREET
1905

TRANSACTIONS

OF THE

AMERICAN PHILOSOPHICAL SOCIETY.

ARTICLE I.

THE MORPHOLOGY OF THE SKULL OF THE PELYCOSAURIAN GENUS DIMETRODON.

[Plates 1-7.]

BY E. C. CASE.

(Read October 7, 1904.)

The following description is based on four skulls in the collection of the University of Chicago, bearing the numbers 1, 114, 1001 and 1002, in the collection of vertebrate fossils of that University. All four of the skulls were discovered and collected by the author of this paper, the first two in the summer of 1896 and the last two in the summer of 1903. All are from practically the same horizon, the Permian beds of Texas, in Archer and Baylor Counties. Numbers 1 and 114 have already been pretty fully described by the author (Baur and Case, '99, '03), and only such portions are here redescribed as are necessary to supplement the material afforded by specimens 1001 and 1002. The last two consist of singularly perfect skulls, showing the complete anatomy of the temporal arches, a region which, by reason of its fragility, is almost always destroyed in the process of fossilization. The two skulls were accompanied by considerable portions of the skeleton in both cases, but were preserved in a very different manner. Number 1001 was discovered in a soft, friable shale, carrying much gypsum and many impressions of ferns, with a considerable quantity of lignite. The nature of the matrix caused the bones to be badly broken and in some parts rotted by the gypsum, but all were preserved in place, and the skull and lower jaws were continuous with the skeleton. The processes of collection and preparation have been very tedious, but when once the bones were joined they could be cleaned from the clay by simple washing with a soft sponge, so that all the most minute details of structure and sculpture are clearly made out.

Specimen No. 1002 was preserved in a compact red clay, and the bones were covered with a hard scale of calcareous material, which was removed with comparative ease, leaving the bones hard and perfect. This skull is unique in the perfection of its preservation, the only portions missing being the temporal arches, in part, of the left side and the median portion of the epipterygoids. The skull lay on its side, and all the bones are joined in their natural relations. The whole skull has been crushed slightly from the sides, so that it is seemingly more narrow than it really is. The bones of the top of the skull have been slightly broken and the palate has been pushed slightly downward, but on the whole the skull has been so little changed from its natural condition in life that it is easily restored.

The four specimens are evidently of the same genus, *Dimetrodon*, of the *Pelycosauria* but do not belong to the same species; it is impossible to state their specific position exactly in the present state of our knowledge, but the specimen numbered 1 has been described (Baur and Case, '99) as *Dimetrodon incisivus*: number 114 as *Dimetrodon* (*Embolophorus*) *dollovianus* (Case, '03); number 1001 is undetermined but stands very close to number 1; number 1002 is almost certainly *Dimetrodon gigas*. No attempt will be made in this paper to point out specific distinctions, the object being solely to give an accurate account of the skull of the genus *Dimetrodon* as an example of the skull of the *Pelycosauria* in general. The restored skull is made up almost entirely from the skull of *D. gigas* (No. 1002) and may be accepted as a very accurate account of the skull of that species, as so little has been used from other sources.

In the original descriptions of specimens 1 and 114 (Baur and Case, '99; Case, '03) an error was made in considering the articular region of the lower jaw as the articular region of the skull proper: this led to an unfortunate series of comparisons and speculations which must be in large part abandoned as based on false assumptions. Notable among these was direct comparison of the *Pelycosauria* with the *Theriodonts* of South Africa (*Cynognathus* and *Gomphognathus*); this error was due to the supposed depression of the quadrate bone and its almost complete disappearance under the suspensorial bones, a condition very close to that of the African forms: the demonstration that this condition is not found in the *Pelycosaurs* removes them from any possible connection with the *Theriodonts* though newly discovered structures place them, probably, rather nearer to the *Therocephalia* of Broom ('03). The error here cited has already been corrected in two papers (Case, '04, '04').

The discovery of the elevated condition of the quadrate region shows that the restoration of the skull previously published (Baur and Case, '99) was too short in the posterior portion and that the orbit was much nearer to the middle of the skull. The elevated facial region while it is one of the most characteristic features of the skull was not carried to the extent figured by Cope in his restoration of the closely related genus *Naosaurus* ('92).

Below is a detailed description of the skull in which it will be seen that in most particulars it bears a striking likeness to the skull of *Sphenodon* so that in most parts the two can be compared directly.

The *quadrate*, Pl. V, fig. 1: This is a thin plate of bone of considerable vertical extent reaching nearly half the height of the posterior portion of the skull, but not reaching such a great antero-posterior length as the same bone in *Sphenodon*. The articular portion consists of two condyles elongate in the antero-posterior direction and with their main axes converging slightly as they advance so that all motion of the jaws was rigidly limited to the vertical plane. The outer condyle is the more slender and lies almost in the plane of the upper portion of the bone; posteriorly it extends beyond the main part of the bone as a prominent process with its upper face flattened into a sort of shelf to which is attached the lower end of the quadrato-jugal. The inner condyle is stouter and is offset from the body of the bone. The posterior edge of the quadrate is rounded and gives attachment through its length to the quadrato-jugal, but just above where the quadrato-jugal joins the upper surface of the inner condyle the two are separated by a good sized foramen, the *foramen quadratum*. This foramen serves as an important landmark in the skull; it is not present in the *Cotylosauria*; it is probably present in the primitive *Archosauria* (= *Diaptosauria*, Osborn) although it has been demonstrated only in the *Pelycosauria* and *Rhynchocephalia vera*; it is present in the *Theropodous Dinosaurs*, the *Ichthyosaurs* and the *Phytosaurs*; it is absent in the *Crocodilia*, the *Pterosaurs* and the *Squamata*.

The posterior end of the pterygoid overlaps the quadrate on the inner side, the lower edge extends back almost to the posterior limit of the bone and is attached to the inner side of the inner condyle.

The *quadrato-jugal*: The quadrato-jugal occupies a relatively unimportant position in the skull. It is a very thin plate of bone, with its lower end and posterior edge attached to the quadrate as described above. The upper end becomes very sharp and is wedged in between the prosquamosal and squamosal and comes in contact with the parietal. It is separated from any contact with the jugal by the descending process of the prosquamosal, as described below, and in turn it separates the prosquamosal from the squamosal, thus occupying a unique position among the reptiles. The position of the quadrato-jugal is not anomalous, however, for if the upper end were withdrawn from contact with the parietal by shortening, the prosquamosal and squamosal would come in contact, and a union of the two would produce the bone called squamosal or squamosal + prosquamosal in *Sphenodon*.

The *prosquamosal*: The prosquamosal has the position usually assigned to the quadrato-jugal: that is, it connects the jugal and the quadrate. It would have been taken for the quadrato-jugal in the present specimens if the presence of the *foramen quadratum* had not indicated the true position of the quadrato-jugal. (The significance of the position of the prosquamosal is discussed in the description of the temporal region below.) The prosquamosal joins the jugal in about the middle of the inferior temporal arch, the two bones narrowing somewhat as they approach, so the edges of the inferior arch are concave both above and below. Posteriorly the prosquamosal widens, so that it has an upper and lower process and the bone becomes roughly T-shaped. The lower three quarters of the posterior edge join the quadrato-jugal and the upper quarter joins the anterior edge of the posterior process of the postorbital to form the posterior edge of the superior temporal vacuity. There is a little doubt as to whether the prosquamosal joins the edge of the quadrato-jugal directly or passes under it, articulating with the lower surface, and finally articulates with the edge of the quadrate near the quadrato-jugal. The specimen No. 1002 seems to indicate the latter condition on one side.

The bones forming the edges of the superior temporal vacuity are approximated so the vacuity is very small.

In the crushed specimens the sides of the upper vacuity are very close together and it seems that they must have been so in life. The edges of the bones where they would meet are very thin and it is possible that they did meet over the vacuity in specimen 1001, although there could have been no articulation even in this case. It is impossible to say positively whether this is an appearing or a disappearing vacuity but the former seems to be the most probable from all considerations. In *Diopeus* the most primitive member of the *Clepsydropidae*, the superior vacuity is very small or absent. In specimen 1001 there is a strong rugosity of the lower ends of the parietal which covers the vacuity but this I am inclined to regard as pathological.

From the foregoing it will be seen that so far from the quadrate region of the skull being depressed and approaching the *Theriodont* type with any relation to the development of the mammalian skull it is elevated and of the most primitive character and in connection with all the other specializations of the skeleton of the American *Pelycosauria* (*Clepsydropidae*) indicates rather the approaching culmination of a side branch of the primitive stem than the true progress of the *Sauromammalian* mutation which was seemingly accomplished in Africa. It is not proven however, as Osborn suggests, that the *Gomphodontia* were descended from forms with primitively a single arch (*Synapsida*) for the possible affinity of the *Pelycosauria* and *Theromorphia*, the last the acknowledged ancestors of the *Theriodonts*, shows that the ancestors of the two groups may have been common and have had two arches, at least potentially.

The determination of the composition of the temporal arches and the identification of the *foramen quadratum* in the *Pelycosauria* enables certain comparisons to be made that shed some light on the possible history of the development of the temporal region in general. Baur has claimed that the squamosal of *Sphenodon* is the united prosquamosal and squamosal of the *Lacertilia* and has cited the condition of *Sapheosaurus* to prove this; on the other hand the evidence of embryology is negative or even against this idea, for Howse and Swinnerton have shown that there is but a single center of ossification in the developing squamosal of *Sphenodon* ('01), a fact admitted by Baur ('94), and Parker has shown that there is but a single center of ossification for the squamosal of the *Crocodilia*.

In the specimens of *Dimetrodon* here described we have the most perfect example of the skull of the primitive *Archosauria* (= *Diaptosauria*, Osborn) known; it is unfortunate that the specimens should be of the most specialized members of the group but a comparison with a less perfect skull of a more generalized member of the same family, *Diopeus* (Case, '03) shows that the primitive condition has remained largely unaffected by minor changes. As shown in the figures, the prosquamosal of the *Pelycosauria* occupies the position of the quadrato-jugal in higher forms, *i. e.*, it connects the jugal and the quadrate region; it articulates with the postorbital above and the quadrato-jugal behind, and is separated from the squamosal by the union of the quadrato-jugal and the parietal. It is evident that the shortening of the quadrato-jugal and its withdrawal from contact with the parietal would permit the meeting and possible union of the squamosal and prosquamosal; if the two bones united it would produce the exact condition of the skull of *Sphenodon*, for all the other bones have the same relations in the two forms and the *Sphenodon* has a forward prolongation of the squamosal which is exactly the same in form and relations as the separate prosquamosal of the *Pelycosauria*. This with the separate condition of the two bones in *Sapheosaurus* and in the *Ichthyosauria* would seem to establish the primitive freedom of the bones beyond question were it not for the antagonistic embryological evidence; because of this it seems best to present the case in full.

Concerning the region, Baur said ('94, p. 321): "Es handelt sich nun darum, zu zeigen, dass das squamosum von Sphenodon in der That aus 2 Elementen besteht. Der jüngste von 6 schädeln, den ich vor mir habe (Condylis-occipitalis-Praemax, 25 mm.) zeigt keine andeutung von 2 elementen; dagegen scheint bei Sapheosaurus (Sauranodon) aus dem lithographischen Schiefer von Cirin das squamosum durch 2 stücke vertreten zu sein." He then cites Lortet's description of the skull ('93) as incorrect, and Boulenger's remarks on Lortet's description ('93) to support his own contention as to the separate nature of the elements. Boulenger said "The bones described as the posterior portions of the parietals appear to be the supratemporals (= prosquamosals), distinct from the squamosals."

In the *Ichthyosaurs* the two bones are always separate.

In the *Dinosaurs, Phytosaurs, Crocodilia* and *Pterosaurs* there is one less element in the temporal complex; the absent bone belongs to the lower arch, and, judging from its relations, could be either the quadrato-jugal or the prosquamosal; that it is the latter is shown by the presence of the quadrate foramen, for it is hardly possible that such a fenestra as the quadrate foramen, carrying no vessels, should survive a series of changes involving the disappearance of the quadrato-jugal and the assumption of its position by the prosquamosal. If the above reasoning is correct the foramen quadratum assumes a considerable morphological importance, as it marks definitely the posterior bone of the lower arch as the quadrato-jugal. From a consideration of the position of the quadrato-jugal in the *Pelycosauria* and *Sphenodon* and a comparison with the position of the same bone in the *Crocodilia, Dinosauria* and *Pterosauria* it is easily seen that the forward growth of the quadrato-jugal to unite with the jugal may have pushed up the prosquamosal and excluded it from the lower arch. In the *Dinosauria* in general, and especially in the *Theropodous Dinosaurs*, which are the most primitive, and very similar in most points of skull structure to the *Pelycosaurs* (the *Theropodous Dinosaurs* are the only ones which possess the quadrate foramen), we find the same sort of an anterior process of the squamosal as occurs in *Sphenodon*. The steps seem perfect from one condition in the *Pelycosauria* to the other in the *Sphenodon* and *Theropodous Dinosaurs*.

In the *Dinosauria* where the quadrate foramen is missing, the *Sauropoda* and *Predentata*, the *Crocodilia* and *Pterosauria* it is safe to assume that the same bone has disappeared as in the forms where the steps can be traced.

Although the present specimens give no positive evidence concerning the disappearance of the lower arch in the *Squamata* it suggests very forcibly one thought. The foramen quadratum is in its inception in the *Pelycosauria* (it does not occur in the *Cotylosauria* or in the primitive Pelycosaurians, *Diopeus* (Case, '03') and is much larger in *Sphenodon*; it seems possible that the same process of fenestration which developed the superior and inferior temporal vacuities may have increased the size of the foramen quadratum after the exclusion of the prosquamosal from the lower arch, until the quadrato-jugal was loosened from the quadrate and disappeared in the ligament that represents the inferior arch in the *Lacertilia*.

The *parietal:* The parietal has a broadened horizontal upper portion which unites by strong suture with the frontal, postorbital and the parietal of the opposite side but does not join the postfrontal. The pineal foramen lies in about the middle of this horizontal portion and completely posterior to the orbits. The descending portion of the bone curves sharply outward and downward and joins the quadrato-jugal as described above.

The *squamosal:* The squamosal lies largely on the posterior and inner (toward the median line) side of the parietal. Its lower end is widened and overhangs the distal end of the opisthotic exactly as in the *Sphenodon* but in larger degree. The relations of the parietal and squamosal are rather peculiar: the squamosal forms the posterior side of the parietal arch and reaches almost to the median line of the skull thus forming the major portion of the posterior aspect of the upper part of the skull. in the *Sphenodon* the parietal forms the posterior portion of the skull in the median and does not pass under the squamosal till about the middle of the parietal arch. This gives the squamosal an appearance of greater prominence on the back of the Pelycosaurian skull but the bones have essentially the same relations in both forms.

The cranial region is formed by a single complex bone composed of the closely coössified basioccipital, supraoccipital, exoccipital, opisthotic and petrosal; in none of the specimens are there well defined sutures separating these bones so that they must have united early in life. Figures 2 and 3, Pl. V show this region in specimen 1 where it was found disarticulated and complete; the same region in the other specimens has been somewhat crushed but show enough to make it evident that they are of the same character as specimen 1. The following description is taken from a previous paper discussing specimen 1. (Case, '04.)

"The occipital region closely resembles that of *Sphenodon*. The condyle is formed by the exoccipitals and basioccipital. The exoccipitals meet in the median line above, excluding the supraoccipital from any part in the foramen magnum. Laterally they join the expanded proximal ends of the opisthotics. The supraoccipital is a triangular plate inclined forward as it ascends and joining by the base of the triangle the parietals above. Laterally it joins the opisthotics and inferiorly the exoccipitals. The opisthotics are expanded proximally, joining the supraoccipital and exoccipitals. Distally they are elongated outwards, backwards and downwards. The lower edge of the proximal end is marked by a notch which, in union with similar notches in the basioccipital and petrosal form the fenestra ovalis. The opisthotics remained free during life or until advanced age. This feature is found only in turtles, *Ichthyosaurus* and the young *Sphenodon*. It has been noticed in young lizards before leaving the egg.* The basioccipital forms the lower portion of the condyle and lies between the exoccipitals and opisthotics. The lower surface is trough-like for its posterior half and supported a posterior extension of the basisphenoid. Laterally a slight notch forms the inner wall of the fenestra ovalis. Anterior to the horizontal, trough-like portion the inferior surface rises sharply; the angle thus formed is marked by a large foramen of unknown function, perhaps the hypophysis passes into the interior of the basioccipital, Pl. V, Fig. 3. The petrosals join the opisthotics, exoccipitals and the basioccipital, but the sutures are not distinguishable. The lower part of the anterior edges were continued forward as long processes, the anterior inferior processes of Siebenrock.† These are partially destroyed in the specimen. A deep notch in the anterior edge of the petrosals just above the origin of these processes, the *incisura otosphenoidea* Sieb., marks the point of exit from the brain cavity of the fifth pair of nerves (trigeminus). The superior end of the anterior edge is separated from the supraoccipital by a notch which is continued on the sides of the bone as a shallow, short groove. The posterior edge contributes the last portion to the walls of the fenestra ovalis.

"The basisphenoid remained free. The posterior edge is greatly thickened vertically and its lower edge stood well away from the basioccipital. The otic region and the posterior edge of the basisphenoid were covered with a large mass of cartilage. The lower surface of the basisphenoid is excavated by a deep pit, Pl. V, Fig. 4, which opens on the posterior as well as the inferior surface of the bone and divides the posterior into two parts. The upper edge of the posterior surface, forming the base of the pit, was continued backward as a spout-like process articulating with the lower surface of basioccipital. The anterior edge is extended forward as a parasphenoid rostrum originating between the short and stout pterygoid processes.

"The foramina penetrating these bones are remarkably similar in position to those penetrating the same bones in *Sphenodon*. The condylar foramen transmitting the twelfth pair (hypoglossus) penetrates the exoccipital just anterior to the edge of foramen magnum. Its outer end opens in a notch (the *incisura venæ jugularis* Sieb.) in the side of the exoccipital. A little below and further forward a second and much smaller foramen opens in the same notch; this may transmit either the ninth or tenth pair of nerves or a minor blood vessel. Passing forward the notch deepens and is very soon converted into a foramen by the adjacent portion of the opisthotic. This is the *foramen venæ jugularis* of Siebenrock and transmits the jugular vein and either the

* Siebenrock, F.: Das Skelet der Lacerta Simonyi Steind. und der Lacertiden familie überhaupt; Sitzunberichten der kaiserl. Akademie der Wissenschaften in Wien. Mathm. Naturwiss. Classe., ciii, Abth. 1, April, 1894.

† Siebenrock, F.: Zur Osteologie des Hatteria-Kopfes, ibid., Bd. cii, Abth. 1, June, 1893.

ninth or tenth nerves or both of them. In *Sphenodon* the foramen transmits not only these but the twelfth pair as well, the nerves being separated from the vein by very thin walls of bone and may be separated from each other or have a common canal. The opening of the twelfth pair into the notch which forms the beginning of the jugular foramen is then very similar to the condition found in *Sphenodon*.

FIG. 1. Lateral view of the cast of the brain cavity of the *Dimetrodon incisivus*, specimen No. 1. *Cb.*, cerebellum; *Ty.*, cast of the otic cavity; *Hy.*, hypophysis; *Ju.*, cast of jugular foramen. 5, 7, 12, casts of the foramina for the corresponding cranial nerves.

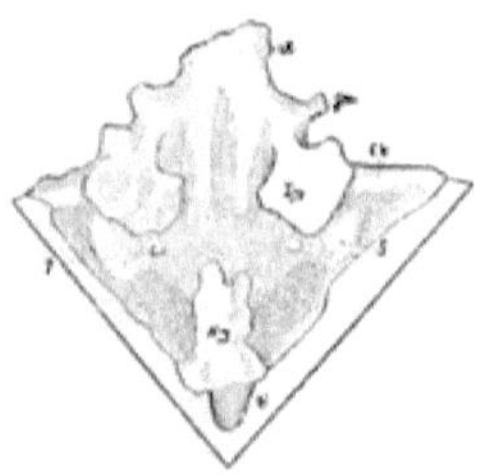

FIG. 2. Inferior view of the same cast. Lettering as in Fig. 1.

"The fenestra ovalis is a single opening leading by a very short canal directly into the brain cavity, a character found in fishes and the amphibian *Menopoma* and existing imperfectly in some recent reptilia, as the turtles. The same thing is described by Cope as existing in another Permian reptile, from the same horizon as the present specimen, but belonging to a separate family, the *Diadectidæ*, and his order *Cotylosauria*.

"The foramina for the seventh (facial) pair of nerves appear on the outer surface of the petrosal just anterior to the fenestra ovalis. They are located relatively a little further back than in *Sphenodon*. On the inner face of the same bone the foramina appear at the side of the base of the brain cavity a little anterior to their external opening. They are located just anterior to a slight ridge which defines the limits of the tympanic cavity. In *Sphenodon* this is about the point of location of a foramen common to the seventh and eighth nerves, which, however, almost immediately divides, the posterior branch penetrating the inner wall of the tympanic cavity and leading the auditory nerve to the inner ear.

"The foramen for the fifth (trigeminus) nerve is completed from the incisura otosphenoidea by the membranous wall of the anterior portion of the brain case, as in *Sphenodon* and many lizards.

"A cast of the brain cavity shows fairly well all parts posterior to the fifth pair of nerves, and the hypophysis anterior to them. As is well known, the brain in the reptilia does not fill the brain cavity, but is supported by a mass of connective tissue carrying lymph and fat masses; so a cast of the brain cavity does not give an exact copy of the brain. However, many points can be brought out by such a cast.

"If the cast be held with the short terminal portion of the medulla horizontal, the lower surface pitches downward at a sharp angle to a point anterior to the tympanic region, and then ascends as sharply to the point of origin of the hypophysis. The superior surface is horizontal and arched from side to side to a point over the tympanic cavity and there turns upward at an angle of 45°. The angle thus produced is marked by a low, narrow ridge running across the cast and marking the position on the brain of a narrow and elevated cerebellum, Fig. 1 *Cb.*, such as occurs in *Sphenodon*. This region was probably the seat of a large amount of connective tissue, and it is probable that the upper surface of the medulla descended at as sharp an angle as the lower. This would make still more marked the resemblance to *Sphenodon* and to the cast figured by Cope. This sharp bend of the medulla downward is not found in other forms, though in the brain of *Chelonia* and some lacertilia a bend is apparent.

"The sides of the medulla show most posteriorly the beginning of the twelfth nerves, Figs. 1 and 2 (12), anterior to these the cast of the jugular foramen, Figs. 1 and 2 *Ju.*, and finally the large casts of the tympanic cavity, Figs. 1 and 2 *Ty.*

"Anterior to the tympanic casts a sharp constriction marks the ridge defining the limits of the tympanic cavity, and then a sharp outswelling the point of exit of the trigeminus nerve, Figs. 1 and 2 (5). Near where these leave the body of the cast a small stub on each side marks the origin of the seventh pair, Figs. 1 and 2 (7).

"The hypophysis is the most interesting feature of the brain. Descending between the anterior inferior process of the petrosal and turning posteriorly, it occupies a small notch in the posterior edge of the upper surface of the basisphenoid and then passes directly into the body of the basioccipital through the foramen mentioned. In the *Crocodilia* a somewhat similar condition exists."

Some additional points have been made out from specimens 1001 and 1002. The distal ends of the opisthotics rest on or close to the upper edges of the quadrates and are overlapped by the squamosals. On the left side of the cranial region of specimen 1002 the median portion of the stapes is preserved; it shows that the stapes was a slender rod extending from the foramen to the quadrate just beneath the opisthotic, unfortunately neither end is preserved. Cope speaks of both a columella auris and a stapes but there is no evidence of more than a single bone in these specimens. The semicircular canals of both sides are fairly well preserved and show the presence of a large ampullar space (*ampullenraum* Siebenrock) and well developed semicircular canals. A displaced portion of the petrosal shows the penetration of the canals into its body.

The *jugal*: The jugal forms the lower half of the orbital rim. The orbital edge is widened by the development of a strong, sharp ridge on the outer side of the bone so that the socket is bordered on the lower side by a shelf of at least a centimeter in width. The lower part of the bone is very thin and the edges are without thickening rugosities. On the inner side of the jugal a strong ridge extends obliquely downwards and forwards from the orbit to the antero-inferior angle of the bone, here it leaves the

FIG. 3. View of the inner side of the skull opposite the posterior end of the maxillary showing the mode of articulation of jugal, palatine, maxillary and transverse; *pt*. transverse. Specimen No. 1002.

bone and extends as a sessile process with a bifurcate end; into the bifurcation of the end articulates the upper end of the transverse, figure 3. The articulation with the maxillary is by a close interdigitating suture which locks the bones very closely together.

The bones of the top of the skull have already been described from specimens number 1 and 114 and the separate elements figured but in the specimen 1001 the top of the skull is preserved on one side without distortion and the bones can be seen in their natural relations. Figures 1 and 1*a*, Pl. VI.

The *postorbital*: The postorbital consists of a flat anterior portion and two posterior branches. One of the posterior branches extends downwards to join the jugal and form the upper half of the posterior rim of the orbit, it passes inside of the jugal and so forms much more of the orbital rim than appears on the exterior. The second, upper, posterior process passes backward to join the prosquamosal and form the upper edge of the inferior temporal vacuity. The anterior portion joins the postfrontal and parietal, its outer edge is thickened and rugose and forms the posterior portion of the superorbital ridge.

The *postfrontal*: The postfrontal is a quadrangular bone which articulates with postorbital and frontal, its outer edge carries forward the rugose superorbital ridge.

The roof of the orbit formed by the postorbital, postfrontal, frontal and prefrontal is rounded and vaulted so that its capacity is much increased inwardly. From the inner edges of the lower side of the postorbital and prefrontal, ridges extend inward in a curve, these are continued inward on the lower surfaces of the frontal and postfrontal until they finally meet on the median line of the skull completing a perfect semicircle. This truss-like ridge surrounding the vaulted roof of the orbit adds greatly to the strength of the skull.

The *lachrymal*: The lachrymal is not well shown in any of the specimens nor is there a lachrymal foramen. In some of the specimens there is evidence of a faint suture on the anterior edge of the orbit indicating the possible presence of a distinct bone but it is impossible to trace the suture out upon the facial portion of the skull. Howse and Swinnerton in their discussion of the development of *Sphenodon* say that there is no trace of a lachrymal in that form, it may be very possible that it did not develop in the *Pelycosauria*, certainly if it did it very early coalesced with the surrounding bones.

The *frontal*: The frontal is an elongate bone lying horizontally in the skull, near the posterior end a process extends outward to the orbital rim forming the middle of the edge. The union of the bones of the two sides gives a distinct cruciform arrangement in the middle of the skull roof. The articulations of the bone are best shown in Figure 1, Pl. VI.

The *prefrontal*: The prefrontal forms the superior anterior angle of the orbit and extends forward between the nasal and frontal above and the maxillary and lachrymal (?) below. The posterior portion of the bone is bent at right angles on the antero-posterior axis, so that the upper portion of the bones is horizontal and the lower vertical. The horizontal portion forms a part of the roof of the skull and the anterior part of the superorbital ridge. On the vertical portion a strong ridge carries forward onto the facial region the superorbital ridge. Beneath the posterior end of this ridge and just anterior to the orbit is a deep pit. The presence of this ridge and pit is one of the characteristic features of the *Pelycosaurian* skull.

The *nasal*: The nasals are elongate bones occupying the median line of the skull and extending from a point just anterior to the orbits to the anterior nares in front.

The *septo-maxillary*: Anterior to the nasal and forming the posterior edge of the narial opening is a singular bone, the septo-maxillary. These bones are of peculiar form, difficult of description, but indicated in figures 1, Pls. II and IV. Each bone is bent at right angles, so that the lower half forms the floor of the posterior half of the nares and the upper half its posterior edge. The two bones of the opposite side meet in the median line. Of the vertical portion, the inner part is only one-half so high as the outer, so that while the outer part extends to the top of the nares, the inner part reaches up only one-half the height. This forms a dam across the posterior part of the nares, so that the air in entering must first pass upward and over the dam and then downward into the mouth. On the outer side of the septo-maxillary a short

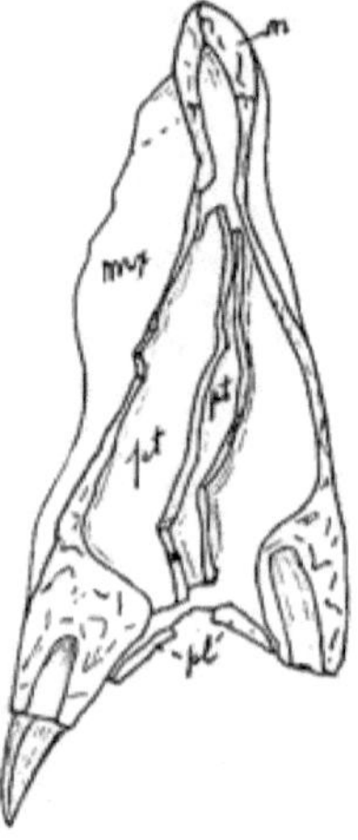

Fig. 4. Cross section through the facial region of the skull of *D. gigas*, No. 1002, opposite the middle of the palate. Showing the thinness of the facial bones and the alveolar edge. *n.*, nasal; *mx.*, maxillary; *pt.*, vertical plates of pterygoids; *pl.*, palatines; *pv.*, prevomer.

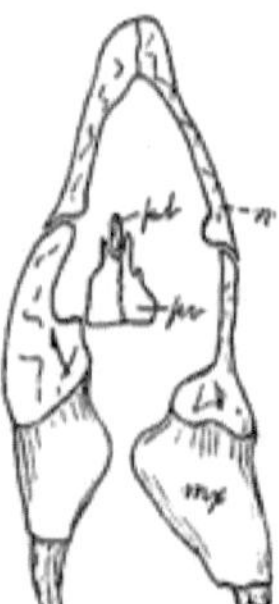

Fig. 5. Section of same opposite the middle of the diastemal notch. Letterings as in Fig. 4.

process at the posterior inferior angle of the nares divides two foramina which pass between the septo-maxillary and the maxillary to the interior of the skull. Their function is entirely problematical.

The *premaxillaries*: The premaxillaries are heavy rounded bones uniting in the median line by a wide sutural area. The lower edge is thickened for the reception of the tooth sockets, and the outer surface of the edge is marked by deep pits and rugosities. The suture between the premaxillary and maxillary terminates below in the middle of the diastemal notch. Superiorly the premaxillaries send upward and backward long processes, which pass between the nasals and form the upper portion of the nares. The premaxillaries always carry large tusks and smaller teeth; the tusks lie near the median line in the fore part of the bone, but their number seems to be variable in the different species.

The *maxillaries:* The maxillaries are peculiar in their great vertical extent forming the greater portion of the elevated facial region. The upper portion is remarkably thin, never exceeding 2 mm., even in the largest specimen, while the edge of the bone carrying the teeth may reach a thickness of two and three centimeters. The thinness of the upper portion of the maxillary is shared by the adjacent bones, the nasals, prefrontal, jugal and lachrymal; so that this part of the skull is almost always shattered in the processes of fossilization and lost. Specimen 1002 is the only one I know in which the facial region is perfect. The lower edge of the bone is very abruptly widened into a thick dentigerous border, Figs. 4 and 5, which is in strong contrast to the weak upper portion of the facial region. The width of this border is greatest opposite the enlarged canine near the anterior end of the maxillary and decreases in width toward the posterior end of the bone as the teeth become smaller. In the diastemal notch there seems to be no great widening of the edge, even in the forms where teeth are present in the notch. The posterior end of the bone articulates with the jugal, as described above. The outer surface of the bone on the lower edge is marked with pits and rugosities.

The teeth are lenticular in form with distinct fore and aft cutting edges which are strongly serrate. The roots of the teeth are implanted in distinct sockets which may reach a depth as great as the length of the tooth beyond the outer edge of the bone; the outer edge of the bone extends much farther down than the inner so that a good bit of the length of the tooth after it leaves the socket rests against this edge. The root of the tooth is hollow and its inner end is open so that it is evident that the teeth were replaced by absorption of the root and continued growth of new teeth; this process is seen in actual progress in some places. In specimen 114 there are two large canines in the maxillary and in the others but one, this is possibly a case of where one canine has failed to fall out as the other develops. The number of maxillary teeth is variable but does not exceed twenty in any of the specimens. Teeth develop in the diastemal arch in some forms of the *Pelycosauria* and not in others, but this seems to be a developmental feature, as teeth occur in the more primitive *Diopeus*, in the notch but are absent in *Dimetrodon* and *Naosaurus*, the most specialized.

The *transverse:* Heretofore the transverse has not been recognized in any specimen but in numbers 1001 and 1002 its presence and relations are readily seen. On the inner side of the jugal as described above and shown in figure 3 a strong ridge extends forward and receives into its bifurcated end the upper end of the transverse. from this point the transverse extends straight downward on the anterior and outer face of the outer process of the pterygoid; its lower edge fuses with the pterygoid so that it is impossible to describe its lower limit exactly but it does not extend very far down on the pterygoid. The anterior edge of the transverse unites with the posterior end of the maxillary so that it is held firmly in its position.

The *pterygoid:* The pterygoid as repeatedly described has a distinct tripartite form, consisting of an anterior horizontal portion, a median vertical process and a posterior portion which joins the quadrate. The form of the bone is best shown in figures 6 and 7, Pl. V, which are from specimen 1.

The anterior plate is separated from the maxillary by the palatine and the transverse, the bones join the pterygoid directly so that there are no palatine vacuities in the posterior part of the palate. The anterior processes come very close together in the median line but it is impossible to say whether they are united throughout their length or not; it seems probable that there was a space between the posterior portions but the anterior parts come close together. From the inner edges of the anterior portions of the pterygoids vertical plates extend upward in the skull forming a median septum in the lower part of the nasal region. Anteriorly these plates unite and below they pass into the prevomers; the suture between the plates and prevomers is visible anteriorly but posteriorly it disappears. (Figs. 4 and 5, and Pl. IV, Fig. 1, pt.) Similar vertical plates on the inner edge of the pterygoids of *Protorosuchus fergusi* Broom. See Fig. 7*a*, page 26. The median portions of the anterior processes were covered with small teeth that were in part, at least, implanted in shallow sockets.

The median external process is a stout projection with a flat external face which formed a buttress for the lower jaw such as occurs in the *Crocodilia* and in *Sphenodon;* it stands much nearer the surface of the skull than in the forms mentioned so that its outer face is in almost the same plane as the side of the skull. The upper and anterior portion of the external face of this process is certainly formed by the transverse and it is marked by a sculpture of fine lines. The lower edge of the process is rounded and carries a row of teeth in sockets; the number and size of these teeth vary and so seem to be of value in specific determination.

The posterior process is a broad plate standing nearly vertically in the skull but inclining inward somewhat at the top. At the point of departure from the median process it is of less vertical extent and stouter but as it passes back it becomes very thin and plate-like. It joins the quadrate as described above and from its upper surface rises the epipterygoid.

The *epipterygoid:* The epipterygoid is the only bone that does not have a complete representation in one of the four skulls. In number 1002 the lower ends are still in contact with the pterygoid but the upper part is lost, it seems that the bone articulated loosely by the intervention of cartilage much as in *Sphenodon*. The form was that of a slender flattened pillar.

The *palatine:* The palatines are slender plates closely attached to both the maxillaries and pterygoids. The attachment to the maxillary is very firm, a vertical expansion of the bone is applied to the inner side of the alveolar edge and from this springs the horizontal plate. The bone reaches from the posterior end of the maxillary to a point opposite the canine tooth. The anterior end forms the posterior edge of the posterior nares.

The *basi-sphenoid:* The form of the basi-sphenoid is best shown in figures 4 and 5, Pl. V, the posterior end is swollen and articulates with the basi-occipital; there is evidence of the presence of considerable cartilage in this region during life. On the lower surface there is a deep pit and near the anterior end two strong articular faces. The anterior end terminates in a strong, median, vertical plate.

The deep pit excavating the lower surface of the basisphenoid is in all probability the lower opening of the eustachian tubes. In most reptilian forms the tubes pass into the pharynx in the neighborhood of the basioccipital-basisphenoid suture and anterior to the fenestra ovalis. In the crocodilia and the aglossal batrachians they have a common opening into the mouth. In the present form the tubes probably penetrated the large mass of cartilage covering the otic region and the posterior end of the basisphenoid and found a common opening in the deep pit described. It is difficult to imagine the use of such an extensive cavity in the basisphenoid, but in the *Teleosauria* an equally large cavity is found roofed over with bone. Anterior to this pit two foramina penetrate the lower surface of the basisphenoid bone and on its upper surface a large foramen appears just posterior to the origin of the parasphenoid rostrum. Through the pair on the lower surface the internal carotid arteries enter the bone and through the upper it gains access to the brain cavity by way of the pituitary fossa. On either side of the single foramen a pair of small foramina carry branches of the internal carotid. All of these foramina are very similar in position to the same ones in *Sphenodon*.

The two articular faces near the anterior end are the basipterygoid processes; there are no corresponding articular faces on the pterygoid and it is evident from the specimen 1002 where the bones of the palatal surface of the skull are little disturbed that they did not articulate with the pterygoids on their inner side opposite the external processes, as at first supposed, but much further back. It is probable that there was a large mass of cartilage between the basipterygoid processes and the pterygoid comparable to the *meniscus pterygoideus* described by Howse and Swinnerton in the developing *Sphenodon* skull.

The *parasphenoid:* From between the basipterygoid process extends anteriorly a vertical, compressed plate (Fig. 2. Pl. VII. and Figs. 4 and 5, Pl. V) which extends directly upward in the median line of the skull. The point of union of this plate and the basisphenoid is marked on the upper edge by a deep notch. It has been shown by Parker, Siebenrock, Howse and Swinnerton and others that the basisphenoid of the adult reptiles is a compound bone formed of the true cartilaginous basisphenoid and a dermal ossification which is the parasphenoid of the amphibians. In embryonic and even in early postembryonic life in *Sphenodon* (according to Siebenrock) the suture between the two is traceable. In the forms with a cartilaginous interorbital septum (*Crocodilia, Lacertilia* and *Chelonia*) the cartilaginous presphenoid is not ossified and the parasphenoid extends as a slender styliform process from the anterior end of the basisphenoid beneath the cartilaginous interorbital septum and supports in embryonic life the membranous floor of the pituitary space. There is no doubt that the anterior process of the basisphenoid in the *Pelycosauria*, as in the *Lacertilia* and *Rhynchocephalia vera*, is the remnant of the parasphenoid united to the basisphenoid and not the presphenoid as first described by Baur and Case ('99).

The *ethmoid:* Instead, however, of the parasphenoid process of the *Pelycosauria* ending as a slender rod in the floor of the pituitary space it extends upward as a strong slender plate and unites above with a second plate which is in contact with the lower surface of the frontal bones. The suture between the parasphenoid and this plate is closed but its position is marked by a low ridge showing the point of coossification. The upper edge of the upper plate is planted firmly against the under side of the frontals and there seems to be ample evidence of a direct sutural union but as the region is somewhat crushed it is possible that the plate did not quite touch the frontal in life but was connected with it by cartilage and that it has been forced into close contact by the accidents of fossilization; however it may be, the relations of the bone would not be altered. The anterior edge of the plate is irregular and very thin showing that it passed gradually into the cartilage of the interorbital septum in front. The upper portion of the posterior edge is thin but the inferior posterior angle is thickened and rounded, there is a deep notch between this angle and the parasphenoid below and this notch marks the position of the escape of the second pair of cranial nerves. There is no trace of either orbito- or ali-sphenoid ossification, as remarked above.

A plate identical in position and relations with this one has recently (Broom, '04) been demonstrated in *Lystrosaurus* (*Ptychognathus*), see Fig. 6. In the *Crocodilia*, *Lacertilia* and *Chelonia* the interorbital septum is cartilaginous, and in the *Ophidia* the osseous septum is formed in a very different manner, by the extension of the brain case forward and the downward development of the frontal bones to meet the parasphenoid without any intervening ossification of a median septum.

In the young *Sphenodon* there is a very complete cartilaginous septum which is double in the region of the nasal and oral capsules, but in the orbital region is single and reaches upward toward the frontal, from the upper surface of the parasphenoid. This plate is called by Howse and Swinnerton the presphenoid cartilage, but the presphenoid is a basi-cranial bone, and in the chondrocranium is that portion of the

FIG. 6. Median section of the skull of *Lystrosaurus* (*Ptychognathus*) *latirostris* Owen. After Broom. *bo.*, basi-occipital; *bs.*, basi-sphenoid; *eth.*, ethmoid; *fr.*, frontal; *fm.*, foramen magnum; *n.*, nasal; *p.*, parietal; *pp.*, preparietal; *pf.*, pineal foramen, *pmx.*, premaxillary; *pt.*, pterygoid; *vo.*, vomer.

cartilage anterior to the pituitary region. It is evident that the whole of the cartilage called by Howse and Swinnerton the presphenoid cannot be true presphenoid, but that the anterior portion at least must belong to the interorbital septum, the ethmoidal complex.

The developing chondrocranium of the different orders of reptiles is, in all the essentials of the relationships of the parasphenoid bone and presphenoid and septal cartilages, the same; so that it is evident that the median plate of the skull of the *Pelycosauria* here described is an ossification of the median septum of the skull directly connected below with the parasphenoid bone, *i. e.*, the ethmoid.

The *vomers*: Sutton ('84) and Broom ('02) have demonstrated that the bones known as vomers in the fishes, amphibians and reptiles are not homologous with the bone known as vomer in the mammals, but they are separate ossifications of the palatine region of the skull.

It is impossible to reproduce the argument of Sutton's paper because of its length, but the main points made are as follows: He first shows that the parasphenoid of the adult Pike and the vomer of the human fœtus at birth have essentially the same relations, and that in an earlier stage of the human fœtus, before the roof of the mouth has closed, all the resemblance between the positions of the two bones is even more striking. He shows that in the history of the development of reptiles from amphibians the increased ossification of the basi-cranial bones does away with the need of a well developed parasphenoid bone to support the floor of the brain case. He then demonstrates the complex origin of the maxillary bone in the mammals and comes to the following conclusions:

"It is now evident that for morphological purposes the superior maxillary consists of four distinct portions—

"(*a*) The premaxillary region in relation with the ethmo-vomerine cartilage and the naso-palatine nerve.

"(*b*) A prepalatine portion forming a platform for the support of the anterior end of the vomer.

"(*c*) A maxillary center situate to the inner side of the superior maxillary division of the fifth nerve.

"(*d*) The malar piece lying outside this nerve and supporting the maxillary bone." He concludes that the prepalatine centers are the homologues of the vomers of the amphibians because—

1. They are membrane-formed bones.

2. The bone in each case underlies the anterior end of the vomer and parasphenoid, respectively.

3. Although in the Pike the so-called vomer is median and single, nevertheless in Lepidosteus, Rana, Menobranchus and many other (*reptiles*) forms, the bones so called are double.

4. In their relation to the premaxillæ and palate bones they fulfill the required anatomical conditions.

In his work on the origin of the mammalian vomer Broom ('03), after a careful and full discussion of the relations of the bones, gives the following conclusion, p. 354: "In the large majority of the reptilian orders the so-called "vomers" are undoubtedly homologous with the prevomers of the lizard. This is the case in the Ophidia, Rhynocephalia, Plesiosauria, Ichthyosauria, Pelycosauria, Dinosauria and Pareiasauria. In the Theriodontia and Anomodontia the bone which has been referred to as the vomer is the true homologue of the mammalian vomer, and this is almost certainly also the case in the Chelonia." He then, following the same line of argument, proceeds to demonstrate that the parasphenoid of the *Amphibia* is the homologue of the mammalian vomer.

In comparing the median section of the skull of the *Dimetrodon* with that of *Lystrosaurus* (*Ptychognathus*), Fig. 6, it is evident that the separate vomer of the Anomodont skull is absent in the *Pelycosauria*, but it seems probable that the parasphenoid plate still attached to the anterior end of the basi-sphenoid can be nothing but the developing vomer, thus furnishing ample proof of the theory of the origin of the mammalian vomer as proposed by Sutton and Broom.

Broom has already shown (:03") that the most primitive of the African forms, *Proterosuchus* of the *Therocephalia*, has a true median vomer (parasphenoid) correlated with vertical plates rising from the inner edge of the pterygoids exactly as in the *Pelycosauria*. This median plate is present in the mammals and in the *Gomphodontia*, it is just as certainly absent in all other reptiles; it seems safe to predict that when the anatomy of the *Theriodonts* is known that a complete series connecting the *Gomphodonts* with the *Therocephalia* will be shown to have this median plate.

The *prevomers:* The specimen number 1002 is of especial value in preserving the thin median plates of the skull. It clearly shows the presence of paired prevomers. The prevomers (Broom :03") are rather stout rods of bones extending from the middle of the premaxillaries backward and downward in a curve to a point opposite the end of the palatine. Their form and relations are shown in Figs. 1 and 2, Pl. VII, and Fig. 1, Pl. IV. The curvature of the lower surface makes a vaulted roof to the mouth in the anterior portion. In about the middle of their course they are free from the bones on the sides leaving a cavity which forms the posterior nares; the sides of the prevomers at this point are marked by a prominent rugosity of the edge. Superiorly and posteriorly the prevomers join the vertical pterygoid plates; superiorly the upper edges diverge and receive between them the united plates, posteriorly they shade indefinitely into the plates so that it is impossible to fix the exact limits of the bones.

The *lower jaw:* In specimen 1001 the lower jaws are preserved almost perfectly; the coronoid which was a small splint bone seems to be lost from both sides. The posterior portion of the jaw becomes very high by the development of the posterior bones as vertical plates and from the inner side of this region the articular region projects as an almost sessile process made up of various processes from the angular, surangular and prearticular (splenial); for this reason the posterior portion of the jaw is almost always shattered in the ground and the more solid articular region is the most commonly preserved. It was such an isolated mass which was interpreted by Baur and Case as the articular region of the skull.

Figs. 1 and 1a, Pl. III, shows the lower jaws and the articular region in detail.

The *articular:* The articular is a flattened disc-like bone completely enclosed on all sides but the superior. The upper surface bears two cotyli corresponding to the condyles of the quadrate. On the under side of the articular the posterior ends of the prearticular (splenial) and the angular meet in the median line and furnish the main support of the articular region; between the articular and angular is slipped the posterior end of the surangular, this appears largely on the upper surface and forms the inner side of the pedicle supporting the articular and its main attachment to the main portion of the jaw. On the outer side of the upper surface the prearticular appears and the articular sends a process forward for a short distance between this bone and the surangular. There is a deep pit extending backward and inward along the line of the articular-surangular suture. From the posterior edge of the articular in specimen 1001 a curious short curved process extends inward and upward.

The main portion of the bone is best understood from figures. The articular pedicle is crushed down, in the natural condition it stood out almost at right angles from the jaw.

The *surangular* passes directly into a broad plate forming the posterior portion of the upper half of the bone; it rises rapidly as it passes forward to meet the rising end of the dentary. There are impressions on the adjoining ends of these two bones indicating the loss of an element, the coronoid.

The *angular* forms the lower portion of the posterior half of the jaw; it is rather wide and continues the lower edge of the jaw as far downward as the coronoid carried the superior edge upward. It extends forward past the middle of the jaw forming a good portion of the outer surface of the jaw.

The *prearticular* extends forward between the angular and surangular till it meets the splenial.

The *splenial* is relatively narrow, covering the upper half of the inner face of the jaw and extending as far forward as the symphasis of the jaw but does not take part in the symphasis.

The *dentary* carries a variable number of teeth in the different species, there are always one or two enlarged tusks near the anterior end, corresponding to the incisor tusks of the premaxillary above but none that correspond to the canine tusk.

It is impossible to pass from the discussion of the skull of the *Pelycosauria* without speaking of its relations to certain of the more primitive reptiles of the African region; it has been shown in the first part of this paper that there can be no relation as previously supposed between the more specialized African which are ancestral to the Promammalia and the Pelycosauria but there is a group of very primitive forms which show a very decided resemblance to the *Pelycosaurs*.

In the prosecution of his valuable work on the Permian reptiles of South Africa Broom has divided the original group *Theriodontia* into two groups, the Therocephalia and Theriodontia ('03). These groups are characterized as follows:

THEROCEPHALIA.

"Medium sized reptiles, with temporal region supported by a single lateral arch. Post frontals usually absent (present in Scylacosaurus), postorbitals and squamosals

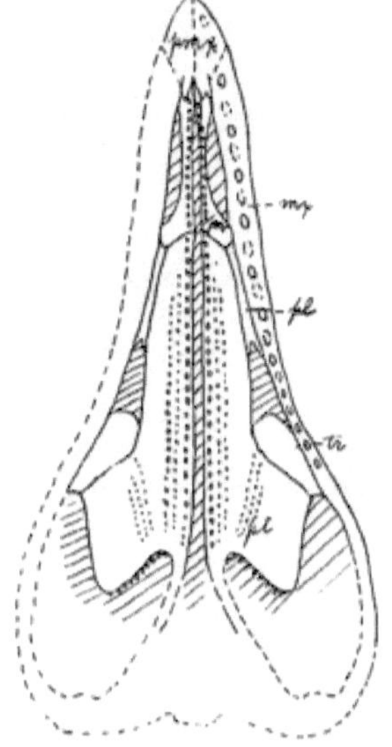

Fig. 7. The palate of *Prolycosuchus fergusi*, Broom after Broom.

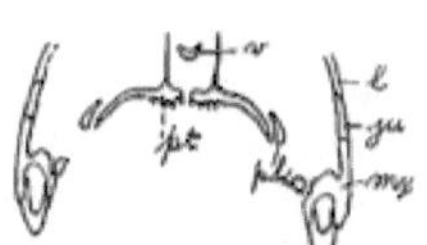

Fig. 7a. Cross section through the skull of *P. fergusi* after Broom.

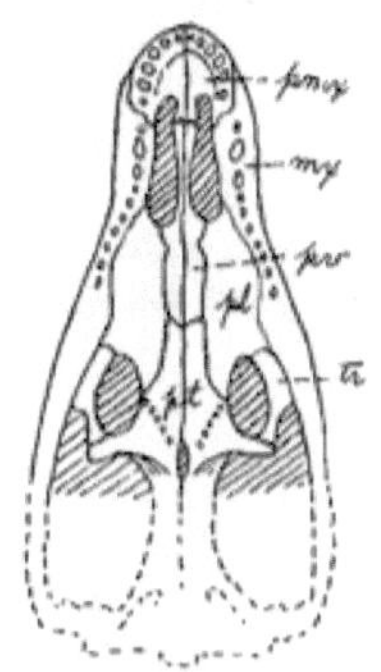

Fig. 8. The palatal region of *Scylacosaurus sclateri*, Broom after Broom.

present, supratemporals and quadrato-jugals absent. A well developed quadrate. Palate a slight modification of the Rhynchocephalian type. Teeth on the pterygoids in Scylacosaurus and Ælurosaurus. Maxillary and premaxillary differentiated as in mammals into incisors, canines and molars. Occasionally more than one pair of canines; molars simple. Scapula without an acromion process; probably a cleithrum. Manus and pes unknown." Including *Scylacosaurus*, *Ælurosaurus*, *Ictidosuchus*, *Deuterosaurus*, *Rhopalodon*, *Titanosuchus*, and *Gorgonops*.

THERIODONTIA.

Medium sized reptiles, with temporal region supported by a single lateral arch. No distinct postfrontals, supratemporals or quadrato-jugals. Quadrate rudimentary. A secondary palate formed by the maxillaries and palatines. Prevomers small. True vomer large. Transpalatines usually absent. Occipital condyle double. No teeth in palate. Scapula with a distinct acromion. Phalangeal formula 2, 3, 3, 3, 3."

Including *Lycosaurus*, *?Cynodraco*, *Cynognathus*, *Galesaurus*, *Gomphognathus*, *Microgomphodon*, *Trirachodon*, and *Diademodon*.

A glance will show the resemblance that, except for the condition of the temporal arches, exists between the *Therocephalia* and the *Pelycosauria*. In Figures 7 and 8 are shown the palate of *Scylacosaurus* and *Proterosuchus* drawn after Broom showing the remarkable similarity of the palate in these genera to the *Pelycosauria*. This resemblance Dr. Broom regards as a common inheritance in the two groups from a Cotylosaurian ancestor, but it is to be observed that the genus *Gorgonops* is the only one in which the condition of the arches is known and in this the temporal region is completely roofed over; the presence of a primitively single arch in the forms otherwise most closely related to the *Pelycosauria* is unknown from observation. Should the genera, *Scylacosaurus*, *Proterosuchus*, *Ælurosaurus* or any of them prove to have an arrangement of the temporal bones indicating the Rhynchocephalian type, even though the temporal vacuities are very poorly developed or even not open the extremely primitive origin of the single arched ancestor of the mammalia as assumed in Osborn's *Synapsida* and *Diapsida* must be subject to some revision.

State Normal School,
Milwaukee, Wis.

References.

Baur, G., '94. Bemerkung ueber die Osteologie der Schläfengegend der höhern Wirbeltiere. Anat. Anzeig., Bd. X, No. 10, p. 321.

Baur, G., and Case, E. C., '99. The History of the Pelycosauria with a Description of the Genus Dimetrodon, Cope. Trans. Am. Phil. Soc., N. S. Vol. XX, pp. 1-58.

Boulenger, G. A., '93. On some newly described Jurassic and Cretaceous Lizards and Rhynocephalians. Anns. Mag. Nat. Hist. March, pp. 204-210.

Broom, R., '03. On the classification of the Theriodonts and their Allies. Rep. South African As. Ad. Sc. 1903.

'03'. On the Mammalian and Reptilian Vomerine Bones. Proc. Linn. Soc. New South Wales, pt. 4.

'03''. On a new Reptile (*Proterosuchus fergusi*) from the Karoo Beds of Tarkastad, South Africa. Anns. South Af. Mus., Vol. IV, Art. 7, p. 159.

'04. On some points in the anatomy of the Anomodont skull. Records of the Albany Museum. Vol. 1, No. 11, p. 75, Pl. IV, Fig. 5.

Case, E. C., '97. On the Foramina perforating the Cranial region of a Permian Reptile and on a Cast of its Brain Cavity. Am. Jnl. Sc., Vol. III, p. 321.

'03. The osteology of Embolophorous dollovianus, Cope, with an attempted restoration. Jnl. Geol., Vol. XI, p. 1.

'03'. The structure and relationships of the American Pelycosauria. Am. Naturalist, Vol. XXXVII, No. 434, p. 85.

'04. A remarkably preserved specimen of a Pelycosaur collected during the last summer in Texas. Sc., Feb. 12, p. 253.

'04'. The Osteology of the skull of the Pelycosaurian genus, Dimetrodon. Jnl. Geol., Vol. XII, May–June, pp. 304-311.

Cope, E. D., '92. On the homologies of the Posterior Cranial Arches in the Reptilia. Trans. Am. Phil. Soc., Vol. XVII, p. 11.

Lortet, L., '93. Les Reptiles fossiles du Bassin du Rhone. Arch. Mus. d'Hist. Nat. Lyon, Vol. V, p. 41.

Howes, G. B., and Swinnerton, H. H., '93. On the Development of the Skeleton of the Tuatara, *Sphenodon punctatus*, with remarks on the Egg, on the Hatching and on the Hatched young. Trans. Zool. Soc. London, Vol. XVI, pp. 1-86.

Sutton, J. Bland, '84. Observations on the Parasphenoid, the Vomer, and the Palato-pterygoid arcade. Proc. Zool. Soc., p. 566.

Description of Plates.

Plate I.

Fig. 1. Right side of skull of *Dimetrodon* sp. near *incisivus*, Cope. Specimen 1001.

Fig. 1*a*. Explanation. *f.*, frontal; *ju.*, jugal; *mx.*, maxillary; *n.*, nasal; *orb.*, orbit; *p.*, parietal; *ptf.*, postfrontal; *prf.*, prefrontal; *pf.*, parietal foramen; *psq.*, prosquamosal; *q.*, quadrate; *qf.*, quadrate foramen; *qj.*, quadrato-jugal.

Plate II.

Fig. 1. Left side of skull of *Dimetrodon gigas*, Cope. Specimen 1002.

Fig. 1*a*. Explanation. Lettering as in Fig. 1*a*, Pl. I. *pmx.*, premaxillary; *sm.*, septo-maxillary; *l.*, lachrymal; *pt.*, pterygoid.

Plate III.

Fig. 1. Inner side of the left side of the lower jaw of skull shown in Pl. I.

Fig. 2. Outer side of right side of the jaw of same specimen.

Figs. 1*a* and 2*a*. Explanation. *art.*, articular; *ang.*, angular; *dent.*, dentary; *pre-art.*, pre articular, *sp.*, splenial; *s. ang.*, surangular.

Plate IV.

Fig. 1. Skull of *Dimetrodon gigas* with the left side removed showing the bones of the median axis. Specimen 1002.

Fig. 1*a*. Explanation. *bo.*, basi-occipital; *ep.*, epipterygoid; *mx.*, maxillary of right side; *n.*, nasal; *pv.*, prevomer, *pt.*, vertical plates of the pterygoids; *pl.*, palatine; *pas.* parasphenoid; *pt.*, pterygoid; *pf.*, prefrontal; *pmx.*, premaxillary; *sm.*, septo-maxillary; *e.*, ethmoid.

Plate V.

Fig. 1. Inner side of the quadrate region of specimen 1001. *pt.*, posterior end of pterygoid, *q.*, quadrate; *qj.*, quadrato-jugal; *qf.*, quadrate foramen.

Fig. 2. Posterior view of the occipital region of specimen 1, *Dimetrodon incisivus*.

Fig. 3. Lower view of the same.

Fig. 4. Lower view of the basi-sphenoid of the same specimen.

Fig. 5. Lateral view of the same.

Fig. 6. Lateral view of the pterygoid of the same specimen.

Fig. 7. Lower view of the pterygoid of the same.

Plate VI.

Fig. 1. Top of the skull of specimen 1001.

Fig. 1*a*. Explanation. Lettering as in Pl. I., Fig. 1*a*.

Fig. 2. Restoration of the skull of *Dimetrodon gigas*. Lettering as in Pl. I.

Plate VII.

Fig. 1. Restoration of the palate of *Dimetrodon gigas*. Specimen 1002.

Fig. 2. Restoration of the median section of the same skull.

Fig. 3. Restoration of the posterior view of the same skull. Lettering of all as in previous figures. *eth.*, ethmoid, *po.*, paroccipital. The arrow of Fig. 2 shows the course of the nares.

NOTICE

Preceding volumes of the New Series can be obtained at the Hall of the Society. Price, five dollars each.

A few complete sets of the Transactions, New Series, Vols. I—XX, are on sale. Price, one hundred dollars.

TRANSACTIONS

OF THE

AMERICAN PHILOSOPHICAL SOCIETY

HELD AT PHILADELPHIA

FOR PROMOTING USEFUL KNOWLEDGE

VOLUME XXI—NEW SERIES

PART II

ARTICLE II—*On the Construction of Isobaric Charts for High Levels in the Earth's Atmosphere and their Dynamic Significance.* By J. W. Sandström

Philadelphia:
THE AMERICAN PHILOSOPHICAL SOCIETY
104 South Fifth Street
1906

ARTICLE II.

ON THE CONSTRUCTION OF ISOBARIC CHARTS FOR HIGH LEVELS IN THE EARTH'S ATMOSPHERE AND THEIR DYNAMIC SIGNIFICANCE.

(Plate VIII.)

BY J. W. SANDSTRÖM, STOCKHOLM, SWEDEN.

(Read April 14, 1905.)

I. INTRODUCTION.

The construction of isobaric charts for high levels has been attempted by several investigators in dynamic meteorology. I will here only mention:

(*a*) Teisserenc de Bort's attempt to draw such charts over the whole earth based on the isobars and isotherms at sealevel, the observed direction of motion of the clouds, and an assumed probable diminution of temperature with altitude;

(*b*) Koeppen's graphic presentation of such charts based on the isobars and isoterms at sealevel, and

(*c*) Hergesell's construction of similar charts on the basis of the results of the international balloon ascensions.

From the relation of the isobaric charts for sealevel to the dynamics of the lower atmospheric strata, the analogous relation of the isobaric charts for higher levels to the dynamics of the upper strata has been correctly appreciated. Indeed from the charts already drawn we have succeeded in explaining many of the phenomena of the upper layers of the atmosphere, for example, the general circulation from West to East * and the movements of the clouds in the upper portions of cyclones.†

My attempts to apply Bjerknes' theory of solenoids ‡ to dynamic meteorology have led me also to the construction of isobaric charts for higher levels. This theory requires, however, that such charts be drawn on level surfaces of gravity and not on surfaces of equal elevation above sealevel. In the following pages I shall show how such charts can be constructed from meteorological observations obtained by means of kites and balloons in the free air.

* L. Teisserenc de Bort: Étude sur la circulation generale de l'atmosphere. Annales du Bureau Central Meteorologique de France, 1885, Tome 4.

† W. Koeppen: Ueber die Gestalt der Isobaren in ihrer Abhängung von Seehöhe u. Temperaturvertheilung. Met. Zeit., 1888, p. 476.

‡ See Bjerknes, in Monthly Weather Review, 1900, October, pp. 434-443. December, pp. 532-535. Sandström: On the Application of Prof. V. Bjerknes' Theory, in Memoirs Royal Swedish Academy, 1900, vol. 33.

I shall then draw auxiliary charts that show the differences of pressure for any vertical line between sealevel and the higher levels; by a simple graphic superposition of these charts upon the isobaric charts drawn in the ordinary way for sealevel we shall obtain the isobaric charts for the various higher levels. It is necessary to proceed in this way in the construction because the kite and balloon stations are too far apart from each other to allow us to draw the upper isobars directly from the results obtained from the ascensions. On the other hand these kite and balloon results suffice quite well for drawing the charts of differences, because the differences change but little from place to place.

Furthermore, Bjerknes' theory leads to the construction of yet another kind of charts, namely those which represent the lines of intersection of any given isobaric surface with the level surfaces of gravity, and which are thus a kind of topographic charts of the different isobaric surfaces. These charts, which are closely related to the isobaric maps, are like those constructed by the superposition of difference-charts based on the observations made at fixed meteorological stations combined with those made by means of kites and balloons.

If the isobaric chart for any level not too far removed from sealevel is compared with the chart of isobars at sealevel, both charts will be found to show nearly the same type of isobars, and one can scarcely learn more from both together than from the chart for sealevel alone. In such a case, however, the difference-chart furnishes a much more effective means of discovering the relation between these two isobaric charts. Now it has been found that such difference-charts are very closely related to the Bjerknes' solenoids, so that indeed, the number and positions of the solenoids in the atmosphere are fully presented by these difference-charts. I shall therefore in this essay consider equally the difference-charts, the isobaric maps, and the topographic charts of isobaric surfaces.

I shall first construct the level surfaces of gravity in the atmosphere and then calculate the mutual positions of the isobaric surfaces and the level surfaces of gravity under both static and dynamic conditions. Thus all the aids necessary for the construction of the above-mentioned maps will be obtained. Finally I shall show how Bjerknes' theory is to be applied to these charts.

I would express my warmest thanks to the United States Weather Bureau for the abundant observational data so kindly sent me. I also owe many thanks to Professor V. Bjerknes for his interest and many good suggestions and the support which he has given me during the progress of my work.

II. The Level Surfaces of Gravity.

We first consider the level surfaces of gravity because, by reason of their absolutely fixed positions with relation to the earth, they are specially adapted to serve as coördinate planes in the atmosphere. Let it be remarked in passing, that all the burdensome corrections in meteorological work arising from the variations of gravity with elevation and geographical latitude disappear * if once for all we introduce level surfaces of gravity as the coördinate planes in place of surfaces of equal elevation above sealevel.

The level surfaces of gravity are surfaces which are at every point perpendicular to the direction of the gravitational force.† A fundamental property of the level surfaces of gravity results directly from this definition, viz.: no work is necessary to shift a mass from any point in a level surface to any other point in the same surface. Further it also follows that the same amount of work must be performed to transfer a mass from any given level surface to any other given level surface, quite independently of the path along which the transfer takes place. We shall make use of this property in the construction of our system of level surfaces in the atmosphere by choosing the surface of sealevel [*i. e.*, the geodesist's spheroid], as our zero-surface and distributing the other surfaces in such a way that it will always require just one unit of work to raise the unit of mass from one level surface to the surface next above it. As unit of mass we choose 1 pound (English) and as unit of work one $\frac{\text{pound} \times \text{mile}^2}{\text{hour}^2}$.

To raise one pound through the vertical distance of one mile requires a number g of units of work, if by g we indicate the acceleration of gravity in mile/hour². If

* This does not refer to the reduction of the mercurial barometer to normal gravity, because this is to be considered as an instrumental correction.

† Note by the Editor: This is the so-called "apparent gravity" or the attraction of the earth as diminished by the distance from the earth's center and also by the centrifugal force due to the diurnal rotation of the globe.

Let the term *geoid* apply to the natural irregular surface of the earth and the term *spheroid* to the ideal regular surface of the geodesist which coincides nearly with sealevel and is necessarily a level surface. The observed values of acceleration of apparent gravity made at points on the surface of the geoid are usually reduced vertically downward to a point on the ideal spheroid by some one of several formulæ, and the collation of all such reduced values shows that for this spheroid in general

$$g = 32.172\,6\,(1 - 0.002\,59 \cos 2\varphi).$$

For a point on the geoid surface, h in feet, or H in meters, above this spheroid apparent gravity diminishes by distance but increases by the attraction of the intervening earth, as represented altogether by the factor $\left(1 - \frac{5}{4} \cdot \frac{H}{R}\right)$, *i. e.*,

$$(1 - 0.000\,000\,059\,7h) \quad \text{or} \quad (1 - 0.000\,000\,196H).$$

For a point in the atmosphere, z in feet or Z in meters, above the geoid surface apparent gravity diminishes by increase of distance only, or by the factor $(1 - 2z/R)$, *i. e.*, $(1 - 0.000\,000\,095\,7z)$ or $(1 - 0.000\,000\,314Z)$. Hence starting from the geoid surface we may say that apparent gravity increases with descent by the factor $\left(1 - \frac{5}{4} \cdot \frac{H}{R}\right)$, but decreases with ascent by the factor $(1 - 2z/R)$.

however, g be expressed in feet/second^2 units as is customarily done, then we find that in order to raise one pound a vertical distance of one foot the expression

$$0.464\,876 \times g \times \frac{\text{pound} \times \text{mile}^2}{\text{hour}^2}$$

represents the amount of work which must be performed. Therefore every foot of vertical distance will be intersected by 0.464 876 × g level surfaces of gravity. At the Equator, where gravity equals 32.089 $\frac{\text{feet}}{\text{sec.}^2}$, there will be 0.464 876 × 32.089 = 14.917 such planes; and at either pole, where gravity equals 32.256, there will be 0.464 876 × 32.256 = 14.995 such planes to every foot of vertical rise. These figures hold true near sealevel, while at greater heights the level surfaces will lie somewhat farther apart. The level surfaces are thus seen to constitute closed surfaces at approximately one-fifteenth foot intervals from one another, enclosing the earth and showing a polar flattening similar to that of the ocean surface.

In order to distinguish the individual surfaces of this system they are numbered as follows: sealevel is numbered zero (0); the plane standing about one-fifteenth foot above zero is numbered one (1); the plane standing about two-fifteenths foot above zero is numbered two (2) and so onward. Thus the surface numbered ten (10) has an elevation of about two-thirds foot; number 100 an elevation of about 6⅔ feet; the planes numbered 1 000, 10 000, 100 000, etc., have respectively heights of about 67, 669, 6 690 feet, etc., above sealevel. The true elevations above sealevel of these level surfaces are somewhat greater at the Equator and somewhat less at the poles, than the average values here given.

If now these level surfaces of gravity are to be used as coördinate surfaces in the atmosphere instead of the surfaces of equal elevation above sealevel, then instead of expressing the elevation of any point in feet above sealevel we must state the ordinal number of the level surface in which it lies. The transformation from "feet above sealevel" to the ordinal number of the level surface of gravity may be easily performed by means of a table showing the relation between the two numbers. Such a table should be calculated for every locality where the elevations of kites, balloons or clouds are measured, and in the following paragraphs I show how such a table may be calculated.

Designate the elevation above sealevel of the point by z, and the ordinal number of the level surface in which it lies by V. Then V is equal to the number of level surfaces included between the given point and sealevel. V also expresses the work required to be done in order to raise a unit mass from sealevel to the position of the given point, for it always requires one unit of work to raise a unit mass from one surface to the next higher one. Now this total quantity of work required is equal to

$$\int_0^{z_1} g \cdot dz$$

where by dz we designate an element of the vertical line from the point to sealevel and by g designate the acceleration of gravity for this element. We thus obtain the following relation between V, g, and z:

$$V = \int_0^{z_1} g \cdot dz \qquad (1)$$

where the integration is to be carried out along the vertical line joining the point with sealevel. The distribution of gravity along the vertical and above the surface of the earth is given by the well known formula

$$g = g_0(1 - 0.000\,000\,095\,7(z - z_0)), \qquad (2)$$

where z_0 represents the elevation of the earth's surface above sealevel, and g_0 is the acceleration of gravity at the earth's surface. If z represents depth below the earth's surface then g at this depth is given by the formula

$$g = g_0(1 + 0.000\,000\,059\,7(z_0 - z)). \qquad (3)$$

Here and in what follows, by the earth's surface in the neighborhood of a meteorological station is always meant the level of the barometer of the station, or the level from which cloud-altitudes, kite-altitudes and the like are calculated [*i. e.*, the so-called "station level" of the United States Weather Bureau].

The ordinal number V_0 of the gravity surface which coincides with the surface of the earth at the station is obtained by substituting equation (3) in equation (1) and integrating from sealevel up to the surface of the earth. We thus find

$$V_0 = 0.464\,876 \times g_0 \times z_0(1 + 0.000\,000\,029\,85 z_0). \qquad (4)$$

For example, to find V_0 for the kite-station at Omaha, Nebr., we substitute the altitude above sealevel, $z_0 = 1\,241$ feet, and the acceleration of gravity at the earth's surface at Omaha, $g_0 = 32.160$ foot/sec.^{2}, in formula (4); whence we have

$$V_0 = 0.464\,876 \times 32.160 \times 1\,241(1 + 0.\,000\,000\,029\,85 \times 1\,241)$$
$$= 18\,550.$$

There are thus seen to be 18 550 level surfaces of gravity between sealevel and the level of the barometer of the kite-station at Omaha; or work to the amount of

$$18\,550 \,\frac{\text{pound} \times \text{mile}^2}{\text{hour}^2}$$

must be performed in order to raise one pound from sealevel to the level of the station barometer in Omaha. From now on the numbers of these level surfaces of gravity will be expressed in even tens, since the heights are not measured closer than to one foot.

If now we substitute in (1) the value of gravity obtained from (2) and continue the integration from the surface of the earth up to the elevation z above sealevel, we obtain the ordinal number V of the level surface that passes through the point at the elevation z. We find

$$V = V_0 + 0.464\,876 g_0 (z - z_0)(1 - 0.000\,000\,047\,85(z - z_0))$$

where $z - z_0$ is the elevation of the point above the earth's surface. If this elevation, $z - z_0$, be represented by z_1 then we have

$$V = V_0 + 0.464\,876 g_0 z_1 (1 - 0.000\,000\,047\,85 z_1). \qquad (5)$$

The calculation of V is much simplified by using the small Table 1, which contains the value of the quantity $0.464\,876 \times z_1(1 - 0.000\,000\,047\,85 z_1)$ for each 1 000 feet of elevation above the earth's surface.

TABLE 1.

$0.464\,876 \times z_1(1 - 0.000\,000\,047\,85 z_1)$.

z_1	$(V - V_0)/g_0$
1 000 ft.	464.85
2 000	929.66
3 000	1 394.43
4 000	1 859.15
5 000	2 323.82
6 000	2 788.46
7 000	3 253.04
8 000	3 717.58
9 000	4 182.08
10 000	4 646.54

Thus to calculate V for Omaha, we must, according to formula (5) multiply the values given in Table 1 by $g_0 = 32.160$ and then add the quantities thus obtained to $V_0 = 18\,550$. We thus obtain the values given in Table 2.

TABLE 2.

GRAVITY-POTENTIAL TABLE FOR OMAHA, NEBR.

z_1	V
1 000 ft.	33 500
2 000	48 448
3 000	63 395
4 000	78 340
5 000	93 285
6 000	108 227
7 000	123 168
8 000	138 107
9 000	153 046
10 000	167 983

By linear interpolation in this Table we obtain Table 3 which we may designate as the gravity-potential table for Omaha, since V is identical with the potential of gravity according to (1). In other words by taking the derivative of that formula we find

$$\frac{dV}{dz} = g.$$

TABLE 3.

TABLE OF GRAVITY POTENTIALS FOR OMAHA, NEBR.

z	0	10	20	30	40	50	60	70	80	90
0	18550	18700	18850	19000	19150	19300	19450	19600	19750	19900
100	20050	20190	20340	20490	20640	20790	20940	21090	21240	21390
200	21540	21690	21840	21990	22140	22290	22440	22590	22740	22890
300	23040	23180	23330	23480	23630	23780	23930	24080	24230	24380
400	24530	24680	24830	24980	25130	25280	25430	25580	25730	25880
500	26030	26170	26320	26470	26620	26770	26920	27070	27220	27370
600	27520	27670	27820	27970	28120	28270	28420	28570	28720	28870
700	29020	29160	29310	29460	29610	29760	29910	30060	30210	30360
800	30510	30660	30810	30960	31110	31260	31410	31560	31710	31860
900	32010	32150	32300	32450	32600	32750	32900	33050	33200	33350
1000	33500	33650	33800	33950	34100	34250	34400	34550	34700	34850
1100	35000	35140	35290	35440	35590	35740	35890	36040	36190	36340
1200	36490	36640	36790	36940	37090	37240	37390	37540	37690	37840
1300	37990	38130	38280	38430	38580	38730	38880	39030	39180	39330
1400	39480	39630	39780	39930	40080	40230	40380	40530	40680	40830
1500	40980	41120	41270	41420	41570	41720	41870	42020	42170	42320
1600	42470	42620	42770	42920	43070	43220	43370	43520	43670	43820
1700	43970	44110	44260	44410	44560	44710	44860	45010	45160	45310
1800	45460	45610	45760	45910	46060	46210	46360	46510	46660	46810
1900	46960	47100	47250	47400	47550	47700	47850	48000	48150	48300
2000	48450	48600	48750	48900	49050	49200	49350	49500	49650	49800
2100	49940	50090	50240	50390	50540	50690	50840	50990	51140	51290
2200	51440	51590	51740	51890	52040	52190	52340	52490	52640	52790
2300	52930	53080	53230	53380	53530	53680	53830	53980	54130	54280
2400	54430	54580	54730	54880	55030	55180	55330	55480	55630	55780
2500	55920	56070	56220	56370	56520	56670	56820	56970	57120	57270
2600	57420	57570	57720	57870	58020	58170	58320	58470	58620	58770
2700	58910	59060	59210	59360	59510	59660	59810	59960	60110	60260
2800	60410	60560	60710	60860	61010	61160	61310	61460	61610	61760
2900	61900	62050	62200	62350	62500	62650	62800	62950	63100	63250
3000	63400	63550	63700	63850	64000	64150	64300	64450	64600	64740
3100	64890	65040	65190	65340	65490	65640	65790	65940	66090	66240
3200	66390	66540	66690	66840	66990	67140	67280	67430	67580	67730
3300	67880	68030	68180	68330	68480	68630	68780	68930	69080	69230
3400	69380	69530	69670	69820	69970	70120	70270	70420	70570	70720
3500	70870	71020	71170	71320	71470	71620	71770	71920	72070	72210
3600	72360	72510	72660	72810	72960	73110	73260	73410	73560	73710
3700	73860	74010	74160	74310	74460	74610	74750	74900	75050	75200
3800	75350	75500	75650	75800	75950	76100	76250	76400	76550	76700
3900	76850	77000	77140	77290	77440	77590	77740	77890	78040	78190
4000	78340	78490	78640	78790	78940	79090	79240	79390	79540	79690
4100	79840	79980	80130	80280	80430	80580	80730	80880	81030	81180
4200	81330	81480	81630	81780	81930	82080	82230	82380	82530	82680
4300	82830	82970	83120	83270	83420	83570	83720	83870	84020	84170
4400	84320	84470	84620	84770	84920	85070	85220	85370	85520	85670
4500	85820	85960	86110	86260	86410	86560	86710	86860	87010	87160
4600	87310	87460	87610	87760	87910	88060	88210	88360	88510	88660
4700	88810	88950	89100	89250	89400	89550	89700	89850	90000	90150
4800	90300	90450	90600	90750	90900	91050	91200	91350	91500	91650
4900	91800	91940	92090	92240	92390	92540	92690	92840	92990	93140

P.P.	
1	10
2	30
3	40
4	60
5	70
6	90
7	100
8	120
9	130

TABLE 3 (*Concluded*).

TABLE OF GRAVITY POTENTIALS FOR OMAHA, NEBR.

z_1	0	10	20	30	40	50	60	70	80	90
5000	93290	93440	93590	93740	93890	94040	94190	94340	94490	94630
5100	94780	94930	95080	95230	95380	95530	95680	95830	95980	96130
5200	96280	96430	96580	96730	96880	97030	97170	97320	97470	97620
5300	97770	97920	98070	98220	98370	98520	98670	98820	98970	99120
5400	99270	99420	99560	99710	99860	100010	100160	100310	100460	100610
5500	100760	100910	101060	101210	101360	101510	101660	101810	101960	102100
5600	102250	102400	102550	102700	102850	103000	103150	103300	103450	103600
5700	103750	103900	104050	104200	104350	104500	104640	104790	104940	105090
5800	105240	105390	105540	105690	105840	105990	106140	106290	106440	106590
5900	106740	106890	107030	107180	107330	107480	107630	107780	107930	108080
6000	108230	108380	108530	108680	108830	108980	109130	109280	109430	109570
6100	109720	109870	110020	110170	110320	110470	110620	110770	110920	111070
6200	111220	111370	111520	111670	111820	111970	112110	112260	112410	112560
6300	112710	112860	113010	113160	113310	113460	113610	113760	113910	114060
6400	114210	114360	114500	114650	114800	114950	115100	115250	115400	115550
6500	115700	115850	116000	116150	116300	116450	116600	116750	116900	117040
6600	117190	117340	117490	117640	117790	117940	118090	118240	118390	118540
6700	118690	118840	118990	119140	119290	119440	119580	119730	119880	120030
6800	120180	120330	120480	120630	120780	120930	121080	121230	121380	121530
6900	121680	121830	121970	122120	122270	122420	122570	122720	122870	123020
7000	123170	123320	123470	123620	123770	123920	124070	124220	124370	124510
7100	124660	124810	124960	125110	125260	125410	125560	125710	125860	126010
7200	126160	126310	126460	126610	126760	126910	127050	127200	127350	127500
7300	127650	127800	127950	128100	128250	128400	128550	128700	128850	129000
7400	129150	129300	129440	129590	129740	129890	130040	130190	130340	130490
7500	130640	130790	130940	131090	131240	131390	131540	131690	131840	131980
7600	132130	132280	132430	132580	132730	132880	133030	133180	133330	133480
7700	133630	133780	133930	134080	134230	134380	134520	134670	134820	134970
7800	135120	135270	135420	135570	135720	135870	136020	136170	136320	136470
7900	136620	136770	136910	137060	137210	137360	137510	137660	137810	137960
8000	138110	138260	138410	138560	138710	138860	139010	139160	139310	139450
8100	139600	139750	139900	140050	140200	140350	140500	140650	140800	140950
8200	141100	141250	141400	141550	141700	141850	141990	142140	142290	142440
8300	142590	142740	142890	143040	143190	143340	143490	143640	143790	143940
8400	144090	144240	144380	144530	144680	144830	144980	145130	145280	145430
8500	145580	145730	145880	146030	146180	146330	146480	146630	146780	146920
8600	147070	147220	147370	147520	147670	147820	147970	148120	148270	148420
8700	148570	148720	148870	149020	149170	149320	149460	149610	149760	149910
8800	150060	150210	150360	150510	150660	150810	150960	151110	151260	151410
8900	151560	151710	151850	152000	152150	152300	152450	152600	152750	152900
9000	153050	153200	153350	153500	153650	153800	153950	154100	154240	154390
9100	154540	154690	154840	154990	155140	155290	155440	155590	155740	155890
9200	156040	156190	156330	156480	156630	156780	156930	157080	157230	157380
9300	157530	157680	157830	157980	158130	158280	158420	158570	158720	158870
9400	159020	159170	159320	159470	159620	159770	159920	160070	160220	160370
9500	160520	160660	160810	160960	161110	161260	161410	161560	161710	161860
9600	162010	162160	162310	162460	162610	162750	162900	163050	163200	163350
9700	163500	163650	163800	163950	164100	164250	164400	164550	164700	164840
9800	164990	165140	165290	165440	165590	165740	165890	166040	166190	166340
9900	166490	166640	166790	166930	167080	167230	167380	167530	167680	167830

P.P.	
1	10
2	30
3	40
4	60
5	70
6	90
7	100
8	120
9	130

The dimension or "dimensional equation" of the quantity V is obtained from formula (1), and in fact this quantity is expressed in terms of $\frac{\text{distance}^2}{\text{time}^2}$, that is to say the dimension for work done upon a unit mass. In Table 3 the unit for V is chosen as one $\frac{\text{mile}^2}{\text{hour}^2}$ in order that the velocities resulting from the solenoids may be expressed in $\frac{\text{mile}}{\text{hour}}$. In order to obtain from Table 3 the value of V at any given elevation, *e. g.*, 3 487 feet, above the level of the station barometer at Omaha, we proceed as follows. First in the principal Table 3 we seek the value of V corresponding to $z = 3\,480$ feet, viz., 70 570; then by the aid of the small auxiliary table of proportional parts we find for $z = 7$ feet the additional portion of $V = 100$ and thus the complete $V = 70\,670$ for $z = 3\,487$ feet. Consequently work amounting to 70 670 $\frac{\text{mile}^2}{\text{hours}^2}$ must be performed in order to raise the unit mass from sealevel to the altitude of 3 487 feet above the station barometer at Omaha, or we may say that there are 70 670 level surfaces of gravity between sealevel and the point standing 3 487 feet above the Omaha station barometer.

This method for the calculation of V can be applied at all stations where g_0 has been previously determined by pendulum observations. At points where no such measurements of g_0 have been made the following well-known formula for the calculation of gravity at the earth's surface must be employed,

$$g_0 = 32.1726(1 - 0.002\,59 \cos 2\lambda)(1 - 0.000\,000\,059\,7\, z_0). \qquad (6)$$

TABLE 4.

THE ACCELERATION OF GRAVITY AT SEALEVEL.

Latitude.	0°	1°	2°	3°	4°	5°	6°	7°	8°	9°
0°	32.089	32.089	32.089	32.090	32.090	32.091	32.091	32.092	32.092	32.093
10	.094	.095	.096	.098	.099	.100	.102	.104	.105	.107
20	.109	.111	.113	.115	.117	.119	.121	.124	.126	.128
30	.131	.133	.136	.139	.141	.144	.147	.150	.152	.155
40	.158	.161	.164	.167	.170	.173	.176	.178	.181	.184
50	.187	.190	.193	.196	.198	.201	.204	.206	.209	.212
60	.214	.217	.219	.222	.224	.226	.228	.231	.233	.235
70	.236	.238	.240	.242	.243	.245	.246	.247	.249	.250
80	.251	.252	.253	.253	.254	.255	.255	.255	.256	.256

TABLE 5.

DECREASE OF GRAVITY WITH ELEVATION ABOVE SEALEVEL.

Elevation.	Decrease.
1 000 ft.	−0.002
2 000	−0.004
3 000	−0.006
4 000	−0.008
5 000	−0.010
6 000	−0.012
7 000	−0.013
8 000	−0.015
9 000	−0.017
10 000	−0.019

Table 4 shows the acceleration of gravity at sealevel, and Table 5 the decrease in the acceleration of gravity with elevation above sealevel calculated according to formula (6). To find the value of g at the surface of the earth, for instance at Omaha, by the aid of these tables one first seeks in Table 4 for the value of g at sealevel for the latitude of Omaha ($\lambda = 41° 16'$) and finds it to be 32.162. From this value one then subtracts the correction 0.002 given in Table 5 for the elevation ($z = 1\,241$ feet) above sealevel; hence the value 32.160 for g at the surface of the earth [*i. e.*, the geoid] at Omaha.

When one would consider the influence of the topography of the earth's surface on the dynamic meteorological processes he constructs charts having lines of equal values of V_0 instead of contour lines of equal elevation above sealevel. Such charts of lines of V_0 may be easily constructed from the contour charts by means of Table 6, which gives the elevations above sealevel of the lines $V_0 = 10\,000$, $V_0 = 20\,000$, etc., to $V_0 = 150\,000$, for each 10° of latitude, north or south.

TABLE 6.

ELEVATIONS ABOVE SEALEVEL OF THE V_0 SURFACES FOR EACH TEN DEGREES OF LATITUDE.

V_0	0°	10°	20°	30°	40°	50°	60°	70°	80°	90°
10000	670	670	670	669	669	668	668	667	667	667
20000	1341	1341	1340	1339	1338	1337	1336	1335	1334	1334
30000	2011	2011	2010	2009	2007	2005	2003	2002	2001	2001
40000	2682	2681	2680	2678	2676	2673	2671	2669	2668	2668
50000	3352	3352	3350	3348	3345	3342	3339	3337	3335	3335
60000	4023	4022	4020	4017	4014	4010	4007	4004	4002	4002
70000	4693	4692	4690	4687	4683	4679	4675	4672	4670	4669
80000	5364	5363	5360	5357	5352	5347	5343	5339	5337	5336
90000	6034	6033	6031	6026	6021	6016	6011	6007	6004	6003
100000	6705	6704	6701	6696	6690	6684	6679	6674	6671	6670
110000	7375	7374	7371	7366	7360	7353	7347	7342	7338	7337
120000	8046	8045	8041	8036	8029	8022	8015	8009	8006	8005
130000	8717	8715	8711	8706	8698	8690	8683	8677	8673	8672
140000	9388	9386	9382	9375	9367	9359	9351	9345	9341	9339
150000	10058	10057	10052	10045	10037	10028	10019	10012	10008	10006

Such a map for North America, constructed by the aid of this table, is shown in Pl. VIII. The curves of V_0 on this map show that by reason of gravitation it always requires the performance of work amounting to 10 000 $\frac{\text{mile}^2}{\text{hour}^2}$ in order to raise the unit mass from a point on one curve to any point on the curve next above.

III. The Relative Positions of the Isobaric Surfaces and the Level Surfaces of Gravity under Static Conditions.

The well-known condition for atmospheric equilibrium is that the isobaric surfaces and the level surfaces of gravity shall coincide. If this condition is fulfilled then we may express the pressure p as a function of the gravity-potential only; and conversely can write the gravity-potential V as a function of the pressure only. In the following pages pressure considered as a function of gravity-potential will be represented by p_V, and gravity-potential considered as a function of pressure will be represented by V_p. The values of these functions are obtained by integrating the differential equation for the barometric determination of heights.* Since it is convenient to perform these integrations at first for special intervals, the following expressions are introduced:

$$\mathrm{E}_{p_1}^{p_0} = V_{p_1} - V_{p_0} \tag{7}$$

$$\Pi_{V_1}^{V_0} = p_{V_0} - p_{V_1}. \tag{8}$$

According to the above given definitions the quantities V_{p_0} and V_{p_1} are equal to the number of level surfaces of gravity expressed in $\frac{\text{mile}^2}{\text{hour}^2}$ units lying between sealevel and the isobaric surfaces p_0 and p_1 respectively; and $\mathrm{E}_{p_1}^{p_0}$ is the number of level surfaces between the two isobaric surfaces p_0 and p_1. The quantities p_{V_0} and p_{V_1} are the numbers of isobaric surfaces lying between sealevel and the two level surfaces of gravity numbered V_0 and V_1 respectively. $\Pi_{V_1}^{V_0}$ represents the number of isobaric surfaces lying between the two level surfaces of gravity V_0 and V_1. In all this we imagine the existence in the atmosphere of an isobaric surface for each inch of the column of a mercurial barometer [under standard gravity].

To calculate $\mathrm{E}_{p_1}^{p_0}$ we start with the equation of condition for dry air, viz.:

$$\frac{pv}{T} = \frac{p_0 v_0}{T_0} \tag{9}$$

and with the differential equation for the barometric measurement of altitudes, viz.:

* Note by the Editor: All barometric readings and isobars refer to absolute pressures as indicated by the mercurial column reduced to standard temperature, gravity, etc.

$$g\,dz = -v\,dp. \tag{10}$$

By solving (9) for v and substituting in (10) we obtain

$$g\,dz = -\frac{p_0 v_0}{T_0} \times T \times \frac{dp}{p}. \tag{11}$$

But from (1) we see that

$$dV = g\,dz,$$

and if we substitute this in (11) we have

$$dV = -\frac{p_0 v_0}{T_0} \cdot T \cdot \frac{dp}{p}. \tag{12}$$

By integrating formula (12) from $p = p_0$ to $p = p_1$ we obtain

$$V_{p_1} - V_{p_0} = \frac{p_0 v_0}{T_0} \int_{p_1}^{p_0} T \cdot \frac{dp}{p} \tag{13}$$

or by substituting from equation (7)

$$E_{p_0}^{p_1} = \frac{p_0 v_0}{T_0} \int_{p_1}^{p_0} T \cdot \frac{dp}{p}. \tag{14}$$

In the calculation of $H_{V_0}^{V_1}$ we may start with equation (12). First solving for $\frac{dp}{p}$ and then integrating from $V = V_0$ to $V = V_1$ we obtain

$$\log \text{nat.} \frac{p_{V_1}}{p_{V_0}} = -\frac{T_0}{p_0 v_0} \int_{V_0}^{V_1} \frac{dV}{T}$$

or

$$p_{V_0} - p_{V_1} = p_{V_0}\left(1 - e^{-\frac{T_0}{p_0 v_0} \int_{V_0}^{V_1} \frac{dV}{T}}\right) \tag{15}$$

whence by (8) we find

$$H_{V_0}^{V_1} = p_{V_0}\left(1 - e^{-\frac{T_0}{p_0 v_0} \int_{V_0}^{V_1} \frac{dV}{T}}\right). \tag{16}$$

Now by substituting the values

$$p_0 = 2.4934 \times 32.1726 \times 846.728,$$

$$v_0 = 1/0.080\,259,$$

$$T_0 = 459.4 + 32.0 = 491.4,$$

in equation (14) we obtain the following expression

$$E_{p_0}^{p_1} = \frac{2.4934 \times 32.1726 \times 846.728}{0.080259 \times 491.4} \int_{p_1}^{p_0} T \frac{dp}{p}. \tag{17}$$

The dimension of this expression is most readily found when it is written in the following form

$$E_{p_0}^{p_1} = 2.4934 \times 32.1726 \times \frac{846.728}{0.080\ 529} \int_{p_1}^{p_0} \frac{T}{491.4} \cdot \frac{dp}{p}.$$

In this expression the quantity 2.4934 is the height in feet of the mercurial column for a pressure of one atmosphere, and hence it has the dimension, foot. The number 32.1726 is the acceleration of gravity at sealevel at latitude 45° and has the dimension $\frac{\text{foot}}{\text{second}^2}$. The quotient $\frac{846.728}{0.080\ 529}$ is the ratio of the densities of mercury and air and has the dimension zero. The two remaining quotients, $\frac{T}{491.4}$ and $\frac{dp}{p}$ are also non-dimensional. Therefore the dimension of the whole expression is $\frac{\text{foot}^2}{\text{second}^2}$. In order to convert this into $\frac{\text{mile}^2}{\text{hour}^2}$ it must be multiplied by 0.464 876. Furthermore $\frac{dp}{p}$ may be replaced by 2.302 59 d (log p) by introducing Briggsian instead of natural logarithms and we then write (17) in the form

$$E_{p_0}^{p_1} = 1\ 837.3 \int_{p_1}^{p_0} (t + 459.4)\, d(\log p) \qquad (18)$$

where t indicates degrees Fahrenheit, but p may be of any system of units since $d(\log p)$ is non-dimensional.

By treating equation (16) in a similar way we obtain

$$H_{E_0}^{E_1} = p_{E_0}\left(1 - 10^{-\frac{1}{1837.3}\int_{E_0}^{E_1} \frac{dE}{t+459.4}}\right). \qquad (19)$$

Moist air has a somewhat greater specific volume than dry air at the same temperature and pressure; but by applying an appropriate correction to the temperature, the Mariotte-Gay-Lussac law and formulas (18) and (19) can be made applicable to moist air also. To determine this correction we start with the equation of condition for moist air, viz.:

$$\frac{v(p - 0.377rf)}{T} = \frac{p_0 v_0}{T_0}$$

where r = relative humidity and f = tension of saturated water-vapor at the temperature T. We have now to apply such a correction to T that the equation may be written in the Mariotte-Gay-Lussac form and yet give a true value of v. We therefore write

$$p \cdot \frac{v}{T_v} = p_0 \cdot \frac{v_0}{T_0}$$

where T_r expresses the corrected temperature. By eliminating e from these last two equations it is found that

$$T_r = \frac{pT}{p - 0.377r \cdot f}.$$

By subtracting T from both members this gives the correction

$$T_r - T = \frac{0.377r \cdot f \cdot T}{p - 0.377r \cdot f},$$

which by translating the above temperatures from the absolute to the Fahrenheit scale, may be written

$$t_r - t = \frac{0.377r \cdot f \cdot (t + 459.4)}{p - 0.377r \cdot f}, \tag{20}$$

where t_r is the "virtual temperature" of Guldberg and Mohn on the Fahrenheit scale. For purposes of tabulation we make $r = 1$ in equation (20), thus obtaining as the correction for saturated air

$$t_1 - t = \frac{0.377f \cdot (t + 459.4)}{p - 0.377f}.$$

Table 7 gives $t_1 - t$ for each inch of the mercurial barometer and each Fahrenheit degree. In order to derive $t_r - t$ from $t_1 - t$ and r, the approximate formula

$$t_r - t = r(t_1 - t)$$

suffices. Table 8 gives $t_r - t$ for each five per cent. of relative humidity and each half degree of the quantity $t_1 - t$.

TABLE 7.

THE VALUES OF $t_1 - t$.

t Temp. °F.	p = Pressure in Inches.													t Temp. °F.
	19.0	20.0	21.0	22.0	23.0	24.0	25.0	26.0	27.0	28.0	29.0	30.0	31.0	
0	0.5	0.5	0.5	0.5	0.5	0.5	0.5	0.5	0.5	0.5	0.5	0.5	0.5	0
10	0.5	0.5	0.5	0.5	0.5	0.5	0.5	0.5	0.5	0.5	0.5	0.5	0.5	10
20	1.0	1.0	1.0	1.0	1.0	1.0	1.0	1.0	0.5	0.5	0.5	0.5	0.5	20
30	1.5	1.5	1.5	1.5	1.5	1.5	1.0	1.0	1.0	1.0	1.0	1.0	1.0	30
35	2.0	2.0	2.0	2.0	1.5	1.5	1.5	1.5	1.5	1.5	1.5	1.5	1.5	35
40	2.5	2.5	2.0	2.0	2.0	2.0	2.0	2.0	1.5	1.5	1.5	1.5	1.5	40
45	3.0	3.0	2.5	2.5	2.5	2.5	2.5	2.0	2.0	2.0	2.0	2.0	2.0	45
50	3.5	3.5	3.5	3.0	3.0	3.0	3.0	2.5	2.5	2.5	2.5	2.5	2.0	50
51	4.0	3.5	3.5	3.5	3.0	3.0	3.0	3.0	2.5	2.5	2.5	2.5	2.5	51
52	4.0	3.5	3.5	3.5	3.5	3.0	3.0	3.0	2.0	2.5	2.5	2.5	2.5	52
53	4.0	4.0	3.5	3.5	3.5	3.5	3.0	3.0	3.0	3.0	2.5	2.5	2.5	53
54	4.0	4.0	4.0	3.5	3.5	3.5	3.5	3.0	3.0	3.0	3.0	2.5	2.5	54
55	4.5	4.0	4.0	4.0	3.5	3.5	3.5	3.0	3.0	3.0	3.0	3.0	2.5	55
56	4.5	4.5	4.0	4.0	4.0	4.0	3.5	3.5	3.0	3.0	3.0	3.0	3.0	56
57	4.5	4.5	4.5	4.0	4.0	4.0	4.0	3.5	3.5	3.0	3.0	3.0	3.0	57
58	5.0	4.5	4.5	4.5	4.0	4.0	4.0	4.0	3.5	3.5	3.5	3.0	3.0	58
59	5.0	5.0	4.5	4.5	4.5	4.0	4.0	4.0	3.5	3.5	3.5	3.5	3.0	59
60	5.5	5.0	5.0	4.5	4.5	4.5	4.0	4.0	3.5	3.5	3.5	3.5	3.5	60
61	5.5	5.0	5.0	5.0	4.5	4.5	4.5	4.0	4.0	4.0	3.5	3.5	3.5	61
62	6.0	5.5	5.0	5.0	5.0	4.5	4.5	4.0	4.0	4.0	4.0	3.5	3.5	62
63	6.0	5.5	5.5	5.0	5.0	5.0	4.5	4.5	4.0	4.0	4.0	4.0	3.5	63
64	6.0	6.0	5.5	5.5	5.0	5.0	4.5	4.5	4.5	4.0	4.0	4.0	4.0	64
65	6.5	6.0	6.0	5.5	5.5	5.0	5.0	4.5	4.5	4.5	4.0	4.0	4.0	65
66	6.5	6.5	6.0	6.0	5.5	5.5	5.0	5.0	4.5	4.5	4.5	4.0	4.0	66
67	7.0	6.5	6.5	6.0	6.0	5.5	5.5	5.0	5.0	4.5	4.5	4.5	4.0	67
68	7.0	7.0	6.5	6.5	6.0	5.5	5.5	5.5	5.0	5.0	4.5	4.5	4.5	68
69	7.5	7.0	7.0	6.5	6.0	6.0	5.5	5.5	5.5	5.0	5.0	4.5	4.5	69
70	7.5	7.5	7.0	6.5	6.5	6.0	6.0	5.5	5.5	5.5	5.0	5.0	5.0	70
71	8.0	7.5	7.5	7.0	6.5	6.5	6.0	6.0	5.5	5.5	5.5	5.0	5.0	71
72	8.5	8.0	7.5	7.0	7.0	6.5	6.5	6.0	6.0	5.5	5.5	5.5	5.0	72
73	8.5	8.5	8.0	7.5	7.0	7.0	6.5	6.5	6.0	6.0	5.5	5.5	5.5	73
74	9.0	8.5	8.0	8.0	7.5	7.0	7.0	6.5	6.5	6.0	6.0	5.5	5.5	74
75	—	9.0	8.5	8.0	7.5	7.5	7.0	7.0	6.5	6.5	6.0	6.0	5.5	75
76	—	9.0	8.5	8.5	8.0	7.5	7.5	7.0	7.0	6.5	6.5	6.0	6.0	76
77	—	9.5	9.0	8.5	8.5	8.0	7.5	7.5	7.0	7.0	6.5	6.5	6.0	77
78	—	10.0	9.5	9.0	8.5	8.0	8.0	7.5	7.5	7.0	7.0	6.5	6.5	78
79	—	10.0	9.5	9.5	9.0	8.5	8.0	8.0	7.5	7.5	7.0	7.0	6.5	79
80	—	—	—	9.5	9.0	9.0	8.5	8.0	8.0	7.5	7.5	7.0	7.0	80
81	—	—	—	10.0	9.5	9.0	9.0	8.5	8.0	8.0	7.5	7.5	7.0	81
82	—	—	—	10.5	10.0	9.5	9.0	8.5	8.5	8.0	8.0	7.5	7.5	82
83	—	—	—	10.5	10.0	10.0	9.5	9.0	8.5	8.5	8.0	8.0	7.5	83
84	—	—	—	11.0	10.5	10.0	9.5	9.5	9.0	8.5	8.5	8.0	8.0	84
85	—	—	—	—	—	10.5	10.0	9.5	9.5	9.0	8.5	8.5	8.0	85
86	—	—	—	—	—	11.0	10.5	10.0	9.5	9.5	9.0	8.5	8.5	86
87	—	—	—	—	—	11.0	11.0	10.5	10.0	9.5	9.0	9.0	8.5	87
88	—	—	—	—	—	11.5	11.0	10.5	10.5	10.0	9.5	9.0	9.0	88
89	—	—	—	—	—	12.0	11.5	11.0	10.5	10.0	10.0	9.5	9.0	89

TABLE 7 (*Continued*).

THE VALUES OF t_1-t.

t Temp. °F.	p Pressure in Inches. 19.0	20.0	21.0	22.0	23.0	24.0	25.0	26.0	27.0	28.0	29.0	30.0	31.0	t Temp. °F.
90	—	—	—	—	—	—	—	11.5	11.0	10.5	10.0	10.0	9.5	90
91	—	—	—	—	—	—	—	12.0	11.5	11.0	10.5	10.5	10.0	91
92	—	—	—	—	—	—	—	12.5	12.0	11.5	11.0	10.5	10.5	92
93	—	—	—	—		—	—	12.5	12.0	12.0	11.5	11.0	10.5	93
94	—	—	—	—	—	—	—	13.0	12.5	12.0	11.5	11.5	11.0	94
95	—	—	—	—	—	—	—	—	—	12.5	12.0	11.5	11.5	95
96	—	—	—	—	—	—	—	—	—	13.0	12.5	12.0	11.5	96
97	—	—	—	—	—	—	—	—	—	13.5	13.0	12.5	12.0	97
98	—	—	—	—	—	—	—	—	—	14.0	13.5	13.0	12.5	98
99	—	—	—	—	—	—	—	—	—	14.5	14.0	13.5	13.0	99

TABLE 8.

THE VALUES OF t_1-t.

t_1-t °Fahr.	Percentage of Relative Humidity. 0	5	10	15	20	25	30	35	40	45	50	55	60	65	70	75	80	85	90	95	100	t_1-t °Fahr.
0.5	0.0	0.0	0.0	0.0	0.0	0.0	0.0	0.0	0.0	0.0	0.5	0.5	0.5	0.5	0.5	0.5	0.5	0.5	0.5	0.5	0.5	0.5
1.0	0.0	0.0	0.0	0.0	0.0	0.5	0.5	0.5	0.5	0.5	0.5	0.5	0.5	0.5	0.5	1.0	1.0	1.0	1.0	1.0	1.0	1.0
1.5	0.0	0.0	0.0	0.0	0.5	0.5	0.5	0.5	0.5	0.5	1.0	1.0	1.0	1.0	1.0	1.0	1.5	1.5	1.5	1.5	1.5	1.5
2.0	0.0	0.0	0.0	0.5	0.5	0.5	0.5	0.5	1.0	1.0	1.0	1.0	1.0	1.5	1.5	1.5	1.5	1.5	2.0	2.0	2.0	2.0
2.5	0.0	0.0	0.5	0.5	0.5	0.5	1.0	1.0	1.0	1.0	1.5	1.5	1.5	1.5	2.0	2.0	2.0	2.0	2.5	2.5	2.5	2.5
3.0	0.0	0.0	0.5	0.5	0.5	1.0	1.0	1.0	1.0	1.5	1.5	1.5	2.0	2.0	2.0	2.0	2.5	2.5	2.5	3.0	3.0	3.0
3.5	0.0	0.0	0.5	0.5	0.5	1.0	1.0	1.0	1.5	1.5	2.0	2.0	2.0	2.5	2.5	2.5	3.0	3.0	3.0	3.5	3.5	3.5
4.0	0.0	0.0	0.5	0.5	1.0	1.0	1.0	1.5	1.5	2.0	2.0	2.0	2.5	2.5	3.0	3.0	3.0	3.5	3.5	4.0	4.0	4.0
4.5	0.0	0.0	0.5	0.5	1.0	1.0	1.5	1.5	2.0	2.0	2.5	2.5	2.5	3.0	3.0	3.5	3.5	4.0	4.0	4.5	4.5	4.5
5.0	0.0	0.5	0.5	1.0	1.0	1.5	1.5	2.0	2.0	2.5	2.5	3.0	3.0	3.5	3.5	4.0	4.0	4.5	4.5	5.0	5.0	5.0
5.5	0.0	0.5	0.5	1.0	1.0	1.5	1.5	2.0	2.0	2.5	3.0	3.0	3.5	3.5	4.0	4.0	4.5	4.5	5.0	5.0	5.5	5.5
6.0	0.0	0.5	0.5	1.0	1.0	1.5	2.0	2.0	2.5	2.5	3.0	3.5	3.5	4.0	4.0	4.5	5.0	5.0	5.5	5.5	6.0	6.0
6.5	0.0	0.5	0.5	1.0	1.5	1.5	2.0	2.5	2.5	3.0	3.5	3.5	4.0	4.0	4.5	5.0	5.0	5.5	6.0	6.0	6.5	6.5
7.0	0.0	0.5	0.5	1.0	1.5	2.0	2.0	2.5	3.0	3.0	3.5	4.0	4.0	4.5	5.0	5.5	5.5	6.0	6.5	6.5	7.0	7.0
7.5	0.0	0.5	1.0	1.0	1.5	2.0	2.5	2.5	3.0	3.5	4.0	4.0	4.5	5.0	5.5	5.5	6.0	6.5	7.0	7.0	7.5	7.5
8.0	0.0	0.5	1.0	1.0	1.5	2.0	2.5	3.0	3.0	3.5	4.0	4.5	5.0	5.0	5.5	6.0	6.5	7.0	7.0	7.5	8.0	8.0
8.5	0.0	0.5	1.0	1.5	1.5	2.0	2.5	3.0	3.5	4.0	4.5	4.5	5.0	5.5	6.0	6.5	7.0	7.0	7.5	8.0	8.5	8.5
9.0	0.0	0.5	1.0	1.5	2.0	2.5	2.5	3.0	3.5	4.0	4.5	5.0	5.5	6.0	6.5	7.0	7.0	7.5	8.0	8.5	9.0	9.0
9.5	0.0	0.5	1.0	1.5	2.0	2.5	3.0	3.5	4.0	4.5	5.0	5.0	5.5	6.0	6.5	7.0	7.5	8.0	8.5	9.0	9.5	9.5
10.0	0.0	0.5	1.0	1.5	2.0	2.5	3.0	3.5	4.0	4.5	5.0	5.5	6.0	6.5	7.0	7.5	8.0	8.5	9.0	9.5	10.0	10.0
10.5	0.0	0.5	1.0	1.5	2.0	2.5	3.0	3.5	4.0	4.5	5.5	6.0	6.5	7.0	7.5	8.0	8.5	9.0	9.5	10.0	10.5	10.5
11.0	0.0	0.5	1.0	1.5	2.0	3.0	3.5	4.0	4.5	5.0	5.5	6.0	6.5	7.0	7.5	8.5	9.0	9.5	10.0	10.5	11.0	11.0
11.5	0.0	0.5	1.0	1.5	2.5	3.0	3.5	4.0	4.5	5.0	6.0	6.5	7.0	7.5	8.0	8.5	9.5	10.0	10.5	11.0	11.5	11.5
12.0	0.0	0.5	1.0	2.0	2.5	3.0	3.5	4.0	5.0	5.5	6.0	6.5	7.0	8.0	8.5	9.0	9.5	10.0	11.0	11.5	12.0	12.0
12.5	0.0	0.5	1.5	2.0	2.5	3.0	4.0	4.5	5.0	5.5	6.5	7.0	7.5	8.0	9.0	9.5	10.0	10.5	11.5	12.0	12.5	12.5
13.0	0.0	0.5	1.5	2.0	2.5	3.5	4.0	4.5	5.0	6.0	6.5	7.0	8.0	8.5	9.0	10.0	10.5	11.0	11.5	12.5	13.0	13.0
13.5	0.0	0.5	1.5	2.0	2.5	3.5	4.0	4.5	5.5	6.0	7.0	7.5	8.0	9.0	9.5	10.0	11.0	11.5	12.0	13.0	13.5	13.5
14.0	0.0	0.5	1.5	2.0	3.0	3.5	4.0	5.0	5.5	6.5	7.0	7.5	8.5	9.0	10.0	10.5	11.0	11.5	12.5	13.0	14.0	14.0

Example: During a kite ascension made at Omaha on Sept. 23, 1898, at 11.25 A. M., 75th meridian standard time, there was observed $p = 24.20$ inches, $t = 68°$ F., $r = 51$ per cent.

Table 7, for $p = 24.20$ inches and $t = 68°$ F., gives $t_1 - t = 5°.5$; and

Table 8, for $t_1 - t = 5°.5$ and $r = 51$ per cent., gives $t_v - t = 3°.0$. The virtual temperature is thus found to be $68° + 3° = 71°$ F.

Formulæ (18) and (19) can be made valid for moist air if t_v be substituted for t in them, and they then read

$$E_{p_1}^{p_0} = 1\,837.3\int_{p_1}^{p_0}(t_v + 459.4)\,d(\log p), \tag{21}$$

$$\Pi_{V_0}^{V_1} = p_{V_0}\left(1 - 10^{-\frac{1}{1837.3}\int_{V_0}^{V_1}\frac{dV}{t_v + 459.4}}\right). \tag{22}$$

The condition for atmospheric equilibrium may be so formulated that the number $\Pi_{V_0}^{V_1}$ of isobaric surfaces contained between two level surfaces, $V = V_0$ and $V = V_1$ is everywhere the same. From equation (22) it appears that this is the case when t_v can be expressed as a function of V alone, *i. e.*, when the surfaces of equal values of t_v coincide with the level surfaces of gravity. Whence it appears that in an atmosphere in the condition of static equilibrium the surfaces of equal values of t_v, as well as the isobaric surfaces, coincide with the level surfaces of gravity.

The values of $E_{p_1}^{p_0}$ and of $\Pi_{V_0}^{V_1}$ may be easily tabulated if we restrict ourselves once for all to a small number of limiting values of p_0 and p_1 as well as of V_0 and V_1. For example, we choose respectively every half-inch of barometric pressure and every 10 000th level surface of gravity, that is to say we compute the following values:

$$E_{30.0}^{30.5}\quad E_{29.5}^{30.0}\quad E_{29.0}^{29.5}\quad E_{28.5}^{29.0}\quad E_{28.0}^{28.5}\ \text{etc.},$$

$$\Pi_{0}^{10\,000}\quad \Pi_{10\,000}^{20\,000}\quad \Pi_{20\,000}^{30\,000}\quad \Pi_{30\,000}^{40\,000}\ \text{etc.}$$

For such small intervals the average values of t_v may be readily found by graphic interpolation. When these values are substituted in (21) and (22) and the latter are then integrated we obtain:

$$E_{p_1}^{p_0} = 1\,837.3(t_v + 459.4)\log\frac{p_0}{p_1} \tag{23}$$

and

$$\Pi_{V_0}^{V_1} = p_{V_0}\left(1 - 10^{-\frac{V_1 - V_0}{1837.3(t_v + 459.4)}}\right). \tag{24}$$

From equation (23) are obtained the following:

$E^{[illegible]} = 12.966(t_v + 459.4)$ $E^{[illegible]} = 14.920(t_v + 559.4)$ $E^{[illegible]} = 17.535(t_v + 459.4)$

$E^{[illegible]} = 13.186(t_v + 459.4)$ $E^{[illegible]} = 15.206(t_v + 459.4)$ $E^{[illegible]} = 17.929(t_v + 459.4)$

$E^{[illegible]} = 13.410(t_v + 459.4)$ $E^{[illegible]} = 15.498(t_v + 459.4)$ $E^{[illegible]} = 18.340(t_v + 459.4)$

$E^{[illegible]} = 13.640(t_v + 459.4)$ $E^{[illegible]} = 15.804(t_v + 459.4)$ $E^{[illegible]} = 18.773(t_v + 459.4)$

$E^{[illegible]} = 13.877(t_v + 459.4)$ $E^{[illegible]} = 16.116(t_v + 459.4)$ $E^{[illegible]} = 19.230(t_v + 459.4)$

$E^{[illegible]} = 14.122(t_v + 459.4)$ $E^{[illegible]} = 16.445(t_v + 459.4)$ $E^{[illegible]} = 19.703(t_v + 459.4)$

$E^{[illegible]} = 14.375(t_v + 459.4)$ $E^{[illegible]} = 16.788(t_v + 459.4)$ $E^{[illegible]} = 20.204(t_v + 459.4)$

$E^{[illegible]} = 14.640(t_v + 459.4)$ $E^{[illegible]} = 17.148(t_v + 459.4)$ $E^{[illegible]} = 20.736(t_v + 459.4)$

From equation (24) there results

$$\Pi_{V}^{V+10\,000} = p_V \left\{1 - 10^{-\frac{10\,000}{E(t_v + 459.4)}}\right\}.$$

Table 9 contains the values of $E^{[illegible]} \cdots E^{[illegible]}$ for each whole degree Fahrenheit of the virtual temperature between the limits $t_v = 15°$ and $t_v = 99°$.

Table 10 contains the values of $\Pi_{V}^{V+10\,000}$ as a function of p_V and t_v for every tenth of an inch of barometric pressure between the limits $p_V = 19.0$ inches and $p_V = 30.9$ inches and for every ten degrees of the Fahrenheit scale.

In calculating the value of p_V those level surfaces of gravity that lie beneath the surface of the earth are of course to be excluded. We compute first the pressure for the first level surface above the ground that is a whole multiple of 10 000. For example, in Omaha this would be $V = 20\,000$ since the station-barometer there is in the level surface 18 550. If we substitute $V_0 = 18\,550$ and $V_1 = 20\,000$ in (24) we obtain the difference in pressure between the level surface of gravity $V = 20\,000$ and the station-barometer at Omaha, viz.:

$$\Pi_{18\,550}^{20\,000} = p_{18\,550} - p_{20\,000}$$

$$= p_{18\,550} \left\{1 - 10^{-\frac{1\,450}{E(t_v + 459.4)}}\right\},$$

Table 11 contains these values of $\Pi_{18\,550}^{20\,000}$ expressed as a function of the pressure $p_{18\,550}$ recorded by the station-barometer at Omaha, and the mean virtual temperature, t_v between $V = 18\,550$ and $V = 20\,000$.

TABLE 9

Temp. °F	E[illegible]	E[illegible]	E[illegible]	E[illegible]	E[illegible]	E[illegible]	E[illegible]	E[illegible]	E[illegible]	E[illegible]	E[illegible]	E[illegible]	E[illegible]	E[illegible]	E[illegible]	E[illegible]	E[illegible]	E[illegible]	E[illegible]	E[illegible]	E[illegible]	E[illegible]	E[illegible]	E[illegible]
15	9830	9580	9350	9120	8910	8700	8510	8330	8140	7970	7800	7650	7500	7350	7210	7090	6950	6820	6700	6580	6470	6360	6260	6150
16	9860	9600	9370	9140	8930	8720	8530	8340	8160	7990	7820	7660	7510	7360	7220	7090	6960	6830	6720	6600	6480	6380	6270	6170
17	9880	9620	9390	9160	8940	8740	8540	8350	8180	8000	7810	7680	7530	7380	7240	7110	6980	6840	6730	6610	6490	6390	6280	6180
18	9900	9640	9410	9180	8960	8760	8560	8370	8190	8020	7830	7700	7540	7400	7260	7120	6990	6860	6740	6620	6510	6400	6300	6190
19	9920	9660	9430	9200	8980	8780	8580	8390	8210	8040	7870	7710	7560	7410	7270	7140	7010	6870	6760	6640	6520	6420	6310	6210
20	9940	9680	9450	9220	9000	8800	8600	8410	8230	8050	7890	7730	7570	7430	7290	7150	7020	6890	6770	6650	6540	6430	6320	6220
21	9960	9700	9470	9240	9020	8810	8620	8420	8240	8070	7900	7750	7590	7440	7300	7170	7030	6900	6790	6660	6550	6440	6340	6230
22	9980	9720	9490	9260	9040	8830	8630	8440	8260	8090	7920	7760	7610	7460	7320	7180	7050	6920	6800	6680	6570	6460	6350	6240
23	10000	9740	9500	9280	9060	8850	8650	8460	8280	8110	7930	7780	7620	7470	7330	7200	7060	6930	6810	6690	6580	6470	6370	6260
24	10020	9770	9520	9290	9080	8870	8670	8480	8300	8120	7950	7790	7640	7490	7350	7210	7080	6950	6830	6710	6590	6480	6380	6270
25	10040	9790	9540	9310	9090	8890	8690	8490	8310	8140	7970	7810	7650	7500	7360	7230	7090	6960	6840	6720	6610	6500	6390	6280
26	10060	9810	9560	9330	9110	8910	8710	8510	8330	8160	7980	7830	7670	7520	7380	7240	7110	6970	6860	6730	6620	6510	6400	6300
27	10080	9830	9580	9350	9130	8920	8720	8530	8350	8170	8000	7840	7690	7540	7390	7260	7120	6990	6870	6750	6630	6520	6420	6310
28	10100	9850	9600	9370	9150	8940	8740	8550	8360	8190	8020	7860	7700	7550	7410	7270	7140	7000	6880	6760	6650	6540	6430	6320
29	10120	9870	9620	9390	9170	8960	8760	8560	8380	8210	8030	7870	7720	7570	7430	7290	7150	7020	6900	6780	6660	6550	6440	6340
30	10150	9890	9640	9410	9190	8980	8780	8580	8400	8220	8050	7890	7730	7580	7440	7300	7170	7030	6910	6790	6670	6570	6460	6350
31	10170	9910	9660	9430	9210	9000	8790	8600	8420	8240	8070	7910	7750	7600	7450	7320	7180	7050	6930	6800	6690	6580	6470	6360
32	10190	9930	9680	9450	9230	9020	8810	8620	8430	8260	8080	7920	7760	7610	7470	7330	7200	7060	6940	6820	6700	6590	6480	6370
33	10210	9950	9700	9470	9240	9030	8830	8630	8450	8270	8100	7940	7780	7630	7480	7350	7210	7070	6950	6830	6720	6610	6500	6390
34	10230	9970	9720	9490	9260	9050	8850	8650	8470	8290	8120	7950	7800	7640	7500	7360	7220	7090	6970	6840	6730	6620	6511	6400
35	10250	9990	9740	9510	9280	9070	8870	8670	8480	8310	8130	7970	7810	7660	7510	7370	7240	7100	6980	6860	6740	6630	6520	6410
36	10270	10010	9760	9530	9300	9090	8880	8690	8500	8320	8150	7990	7830	7670	7530	7390	7250	7120	7000	6870	6760	6650	6540	6430
37	10290	10030	9780	9540	9320	9110	8900	8700	8520	8340	8170	8000	7840	7690	7540	7400	7270	7130	7010	6890	6770	6660	6550	6440
38	10310	10050	9800	9560	9340	9130	8920	8720	8540	8360	8180	8020	7860	7710	7560	7420	7280	7150	7020	6900	6780	6670	6560	6450
39	10330	10070	9820	9580	9360	9140	8940	8740	8550	8370	8200	8040	7880	7720	7570	7430	7300	7160	7040	6910	6800	6680	6570	6460
40	10350	10090	9840	9600	9380	9160	8960	8760	8570	8390	8210	8050	7890	7740	7590	7450	7310	7180	7050	6930	6810	6700	6590	6480
41	10370	10110	9860	9620	9400	9180	8970	8770	8590	8400	8230	8070	7910	7750	7610	7460	7330	7190	7070	6940	6820	6710	6600	6490
42	10390	10130	9880	9640	9410	9200	8990	8790	8600	8420	8250	8090	7920	7770	7620	7480	7340	7200	7080	6960	6840	6720	6610	6500
43	10410	10150	9900	9660	9430	9220	9010	8810	8620	8440	8260	8100	7940	7780	7640	7490	7360	7220	7100	6970	6850	6740	6630	6520
44	10440	10170	9920	9680	9450	9240	9030	8830	8640	8460	8280	8120	7950	7800	7650	7510	7370	7230	7110	6980	6870	6750	6640	6530
45	10460	10190	9940	9700	9470	9250	9050	8840	8660	8470	8300	8130	7970	7810	7670	7520	7380	7250	7120	7000	6880	6760	6650	6540
46	10480	10210	9960	9720	9490*	9270	9060	8860	8670	8490	8310	8150	7980	7830	7680	7540	7400	7260	7140	7010	6890	6780	6670	6560
47	10500	10230	9980	9740	9510	9290	9080	8880	8690	8510	8330	8160	8000	7850	7700	7550	7420	7280	7150	7030	6910	6790	6680	6570
48	10520	10250	10000	9760	9530	9310	9100	8900	8710	8530	8350	8180	8020	7860	7710	7570	7430	7290	7170	7040	6920	6800	6690	6580
49	10540	10270	10020	9780	9550	9330	9120	8910	8730	8540	8360	8200	8030	7880	7730	7580	7440	7300	7180	7050	6930	6820	6710	6590
50	10560	10290	10040	9790	9560	9350	9140	8930	8740	8560	8380	8210	8050	7890	7740	7600	7460	7320	7200	7070	6950	6830	6720	6610
51	10580	10310	10060	9810	9580	9360	9150	8950	8760	8580	8400	8230	8060	7910	7760	7610	7470	7330	7210	7080	6960	6850	6730	6620
52	10600	10330	10080	9830	9600	9380	9170	8970	8780	8590	8410	8240	8080	7920	7770	7630	7490	7350	7220	7090	6970	6860	6750	6630
53	10620	10350	10100	9850	9620	9400	9190	8980	8790	8610	8430	8260	8100	7940	7790	7640	7500	7360	7240	7110	6980	6870	6760	6650
54	10640	10370	10120	9870	9640	9420	9210	9000	8810	8630	8440	8280	8110	7950	7800	7660	7520	7380	7250	7120	7000	6880	6770	6660
55	—	10390	10140	9890	9660	9440	9230	9020	8830	8640	8460	8290	8130	7970	7820	7670	7530	7390	7270	7140	7020	6900	6790	6670
56	—	10410	10150	9910	9680	9460	9240	9040	8840	8660	8480	8310	8140	7980	7830	7690	7550	7410	7280	7150	7030	6910	6800	6690
57	—	—	10170	9930	9700	9470	9260	9060	8860	8680	8490	8330	8160	8000	7850	7700	7560	7420	7290	7160	7040	6920	6810	6700
58		—	10190	9950	9710	9490	9280	9070	8880	8690	8510	8340	8180	8020	7860	7720	7580	7430	7310	7180	7060	6940	6820	6710
59		—	10210	9970	9730	9510	9300	9090	8890	8710	8530	8350	8190	8030	7880	7730	7590	7450	7320	7190	7070	6950	6840	6720

TABLE 9 (*Concluded*).

t_0 Temp °F	$E^{+19.0}_{-19.5}$	$E^{+19.5}_{-20.0}$	$E^{+20.0}_{-20.5}$	$E^{+20.5}_{-21.0}$	$E^{+21.0}_{-21.5}$	$E^{+21.5}_{-22.0}$	$E^{+22.0}_{-22.5}$	$E^{+22.5}_{-23.0}$	$E^{+23.0}_{-23.5}$	$E^{+23.5}_{-24.0}$	$E^{+24.0}_{-24.5}$	$E^{+24.5}_{-25.0}$	$E^{+25.0}_{-25.5}$	$E^{+25.5}_{-26.0}$	$E^{+26.0}_{-26.5}$	$E^{+26.5}_{-27.0}$	$E^{+27.0}_{-27.5}$	$E^{+27.5}_{-28.0}$	$E^{+28.0}_{-28.5}$	$E^{+28.5}_{-29.0}$	$E^{+29.0}_{-29.5}$	$E^{+29.5}_{-30.0}$	$E^{+30.0}_{-30.5}$	$E^{+30.5}_{-31.0}$
60				9990	9750	9530	9310	9110	8910	8730	8540	8370	8210	8060	7890	7750	7610	7460	7340	7210	7090	6970	6850	6740
61				10010	9770	9550	9330	9130	8930	8740	8560	8390	8220	8060	7910	7760	7620	7480	7350	7230	7100	6980	6870	6750
62					9790	9570	9350	9140	8950	8760	8580	8400	8240	8080	7920	7780	7630	7490	7360	7230	7110	6990	6880	6760
63					9810	9580	9370	9160	8960	8780	8590	8420	8250	8090	7940	7790	7650	7510	7380	7250	7120	7010	6890	6780
64					9830	9600	9390	9180	8980	8790	8610	8440	8250	8110	7950	7810	7660	7520	7390	7260	7140	7020	6900	6790
65						9620	9400	9200	9000	8810	8630	8450	8280	8120	7970	7820	7680	7530	7410	7280	7150	7030	6920	6800
66						9640	9420	9210	9020	8830	8640	8470	8300	8140	7990	7840	7690	7550	7430	7290	7170	7050	6930	6810
67							9440	9230	9030	8840	8660	8490	8320	8150	8000	7850	7710	7560	7440	7300	7180	7060	6940	6830
68							9460	9250	9050	8860	8670	8500	8330	8170	8020	7870	7720	7580	7450	7320	7190	7070	6960	6840
69							9480	9270	9070	8880	8690	8520	8350	8190	8030	7880	7740	7590	7460	7330	7210	7090	6970	6850
70								9290	9080	8890	8710	8530	8370	8200	8050	7900	7750	7610	7480	7340	7220	7110	6980	6870
71								9300	9100	8910	8720	8550	8380	8220	8060	7910	7770	7620	7490	7360	7230	7120	7000	6880
72									9120	8930	8740	8570	8400	8230	8080	7930	7780	7640	7510	7370	7250	7130	7010	6890
73									9140	8950	8760	8590	8410	8250	8090	7940	7800	7650	7520	7390	7260	7140	7020	6910
74									9150	8960	8770	8600	8430	8260	8110	7960	7810	7660	7530	7400	7270	7150	7040	6920
75										8980	8790	8620	8440	8290	8120	7970	7830	7680	7550	7410	7290	7170	7050	6930
76										9000	8810	8630	8460	8290	8140	7990	7840	7690	7560	7430	7300	7180	7060	6940
77											8820	8650	8480	8310	8150	8000	7850	7710	7570	7440	7320	7200	7080	6950
78											8840	8660	8490	8330	8170	8020	7870	7720	7590	7460	7330	7210	7090	6970
79											8860	8680	8510	8340	8180	8030	7880	7740	7600	7470	7340	7220	7100	6980
80												8700	8520	8360	8200	8050	7900	7750	7620	7480	7360	7240	7120	7000
81												8710	8540	8370	8210	8060	7910	7760	7630	7500	7370	7250	7130	7010
82													8550	8390	8230	8070	7930	7780	7650	7510	7380	7260	7140	7020
83													8570	8400	8240	8080	7940	7790	7660	7520	7400	7280	7160	7040
84													8580	8420	8260	8110	7950	7810	7680	7540	7410	7290	7170	7050
85														8430	8270	8120	7970	7820	7690	7550	7420	7300	7180	7060
86														8450	8290	8140	7990	7840	7700	7570	7440	7310	7190	7070
87															8300	8150	8000	7850	7720	7580	7450	7330	7210	7090
88															8320	8170	8020	7870	7730	7590	7470	7340	7220	7100
89															8330	8180	8030	7880	7750	7610	7480	7350	7230	7110
90																8200	8040	7890	7760	7620	7490	7370	7250	7130
91																8210	8050	7900	7770	7640	7500	7380	7260	7140
92																	8070	7920	7780	7650	7520	7390	7270	7150
93																	8080	7940	7800	7660	7530	7410	7280	7170
94																	8100	7950	7810	7680	7550	7420	7300	7180
95																		7970	7830	7690	7560	7430	7310	7190
96																		7980	7840	7710	7570	7450	7330	7200
97																			7860	7720	7590	7460	7340	7220
98																			7870	7730	7600	7470	7350	7230
99																			7890	7750	7620	7490	7370	7240

Table 10.

The Values of $\Pi_r^{r+10\,000} = p_r - p_{r+10\,000}$

p_r	t. 0°	10°	20°	30°	40°	50°	60°	70°	80°	90°	100°
19.0	0.511	0.501	0.490	0.480	0.471	0.462	0.453	0.444	0.436	0.429	0.421
.1	.514	.503	.493	.483	.473	.464	.455	.447	.439	.431	.423
.2	.517	.506	.495	.485	.476	.467	.458	.449	.441	.433	.425
.3	.519	.509	.498	.488	.478	.469	.460	.451	.443	.435	.427
.4	.522	.511	.501	.490	.481	.471	.462	.454	.446	.438	.430
19.5	.525	.514	.503	.493	.483	.474	.465	.456	.448	.440	.432
.6	.527	.516	.506	.495	.486	.476	.467	.458	.450	.442	.434
.7	.530	.519	.508	.498	.488	.479	.470	.461	.453	.444	.436
.8	.533	.522	.511	.501	.491	.481	.472	.463	.455	.447	.439
.9	.536	.524	.513	.503	.493	.484	.474	.465	.457	.449	.441
20.0	0.538	0.527	0.516	0.506	0.496	0.486	0.477	0.468	0.459	0.451	0.443
.1	.541	.530	.519	.508	.498	.488	.479	.470	.462	.453	.445
.2	.544	.532	.521	.511	.501	.491	.482	.472	.464	.456	.447
.3	.546	.535	.524	.513	.503	.493	.484	.475	.466	.458	.450
.4	.549	.538	.526	.516	.506	.496	.486	.477	.469	.460	.452
20.5	.552	.540	.529	.518	.508	.498	.489	.479	.471	.462	.454
.6	.554	.543	.531	.521	.510	.501	.491	.482	.473	.465	.456
.7	.557	.545	.534	.523	.513	.503	.493	.484	.475	.467	.459
.8	.560	.548	.537	.526	.515	.505	.496	.487	.478	.469	.461
.9	.562	.551	.539	.528	.518	.508	.498	.489	.480	.472	.463
21.0	0.565	0.553	0.542	0.531	0.520	0.510	0.501	0.491	0.482	0.474	0.465
.1	.568	.556	.544	.533	.523	.513	.503	.494	.485	.476	.467
.2	.570	.559	.547	.536	.525	.515	.505	.496	.487	.478	.470
.3	.573	.561	.550	.538	.528	.518	.508	.498	.489	.481	.472
.4	.576	.564	.552	.541	.530	.520	.510	.501	.492	.483	.474
21.5	.579	.567	.555	.544	.533	.522	.513	.503	.494	.485	.476
.6	.581	.569	.557	.546	.535	.525	.515	.505	.496	.487	.478
.7	.584	.572	.560	.549	.538	.527	.517	.508	.498	.490	.481
.8	.587	.574	.562	.551	.540	.530	.520	.510	.501	.492	.483
.9	.589	.577	.565	.554	.543	.532	.522	.512	.503	.494	.485
22.0	0.592	0.580	0.568	0.556	0.545	0.535	0.524	0.515	0.505	0.496	0.487
.1	.595	.582	.570	.559	.548	.537	.527	.517	.508	.499	.490
.2	.597	.585	.573	.561	.550	.539	.529	.519	.510	.501	.492
.3	.600	.588	.575	.564	.553	.542	.532	.522	.512	.503	.494
.4	.603	.590	.578	.566	.555	.544	.534	.524	.515	.505	.496
22.5	.605	.593	.581	.569	.558	.547	.536	.526	.517	.508	.498
.6	.608	.596	.583	.571	.560	.549	.539	.529	.519	.510	.501
.7	.611	.598	.586	.574	.563	.552	.541	.531	.521	.512	.503
.8	.614	.601	.588	.576	.565	.554	.544	.533	.524	.514	.505
.9	.616	.603	.591	.579	.567	.556	.546	.536	.526	.517	.507
23.0	0.619	0.606	0.593	0.581	0.570	0.559	0.548	0.538	0.528	0.519	0.509
.1	.622	.609	.596	.584	.572	.561	.551	.540	.531	.521	.512
.2	.624	.611	.599	.586	.575	.564	.553	.543	.533	.523	.514
.3	.627	.614	.601	.589	.577	.566	.555	.545	.535	.526	.516
.4	.630	.617	.604	.592	.580	.569	.558	.547	.537	.528	.518
23.5	.632	.619	.606	.594	.582	.571	.560	.550	.540	.530	.521
.6	.635	.622	.609	.597	.585	.573	.563	.552	.542	.532	.523
.7	.638	.624	.611	.599	.587	.576	.565	.554	.544	.535	.525
.8	.640	.627	.614	.602	.590	.578	.567	.557	.547	.537	.527
.9	.643	.630	.617	.604	.592	.581	.570	.559	.549	.539	.529

TABLE 10.—*Continued.*

THE VALUES OF $\Pi_r^{r+10000} = p_r - p_{r+10000}$

p_r	t = 0°	10°	20°	30°	40°	50°	60°	70°	80°	90°	100°
24.0	0.646	0.632	0.619	0.607	0.595	0.583	0.572	0.561	0.551	0.541	0.532
.1	.649	.635	.622	.609	.597	.586	.575	.564	.554	.544	.534
.2	.651	.638	.624	.612	.600	.588	.577	.566	.556	.546	.536
.3	.654	.640	.627	.614	.602	.590	.579	.568	.558	.548	.538
.4	.657	.643	.630	.617	.605	.593	.582	.571	.560	.550	.540
24.5	.659	.646	.632	.619	.607	.595	.584	.573	.563	.553	.543
.6	.662	.648	.635	.622	.610	.598	.586	.575	.565	.555	.545
.7	.665	.651	.637	.624	.612	.600	.589	.578	.567	.557	.547
.8	.667	.653	.640	.627	.615	.603	.591	.580	.570	.559	.549
.9	.670	.656	.642	.629	.617	.605	.594	.582	.572	.562	.552
25.0	0.673	0.659	0.645	0.632	0.620	0.608	0.596	0.585	0.574	0.564	0.554
.1	.675	.661	.648	.635	.622	.610	.598	.587	.577	.566	.556
.2	.678	.664	.650	.637	.624	.612	.601	.589	.579	.569	.558
.3	.681	.667	.653	.640	.627	.615	.603	.592	.581	.571	.560
.4	.684	.669	.655	.642	.629	.617	.606	.594	.583	.573	.563
25.5	.686	.672	.658	.645	.632	.620	.608	.596	.586	.575	.565
.6	.689	.675	.660	.647	.634	.622	.610	.599	.588	.578	.567
.7	.692	.677	.663	.650	.637	.625	.613	.601	.590	.580	.569
.8	.694	.680	.666	.652	.639	.627	.615	.603	.593	.582	.571
.9	.697	.682	.668	.655	.642	.629	.617	.606	.595	.584	.574
26.0	0.700	0.685	0.671	0.657	0.644	0.632	0.620	0.608	0.597	0.587	0.576
.1	.702	.688	.673	.660	.647	.634	.622	.610	.600	.589	.578
.2	.705	.690	.676	.662	.649	.637	.625	.613	.602	.591	.580
.3	.708	.693	.679	.665	.652	.639	.627	.615	.604	.593	.583
.4	.710	.696	.681	.667	.654	.642	.629	.617	.606	.596	.585
26.5	.713	.698	.684	.670	.657	.644	.632	.620	.609	.598	.587
.6	.716	.701	.686	.672	.659	.646	.634	.622	.611	.600	.589
.7	.718	.704	.689	.675	.662	.649	.637	.625	.613	.602	.591
.8	.721	.706	.691	.678	.664	.651	.639	.627	.616	.605	.594
.9	.724	.709	.694	.680	.667	.654	.641	.629	.618	.607	.596
27.0	0.727	0.711	0.697	0.683	0.669	0.656	0.614	0.632	0.620	0.609	0.598
.1	.729	.714	.699	.685	.672	.659	.646	.634	.622	.611	.600
.2	.732	.717	.702	.688	.674	.661	.648	.636	.625	.614	.602
.3	.735	.719	.704	.690	.676	.663	.651	.639	.627	.616	.605
.4	.737	.722	.707	.693	.679	.666	.653	.641	.629	.618	.607
27.5	.740	.725	.710	.695	.681	.668	.656	.643	.632	.620	.609
.6	.743	.727	.712	.698	.684	.671	.658	.646	.634	.623	.611
.7	.745	.730	.715	.700	.686	.673	.660	.648	.636	.625	.614
.8	.748	.733	.717	.703	.689	.676	.663	.650	.639	.627	.616
.9	.751	.735	.720	.705	.691	.678	.665	.653	.641	.629	.618
28.0	0.753	0.738	0.722	0.708	0.694	0.680	0.668	0.655	0.643	0.632	0.620
.1	.756	.740	.725	.710	.696	.683	.670	.657	.645	.634	.622
.2	.759	.743	.728	.713	.699	.685	.672	.660	.648	.636	.625
.3	.762	.746	.730	.715	.701	.688	.675	.662	.650	.638	.627
.4	.764	.748	.733	.718	.704	.690	.677	.664	.652	.641	.629
28.5	.767	.751	.735	.720	.706	.693	.679	.667	.655	.643	.631
.6	.770	.754	.738	.723	.709	.695	.682	.669	.657	.645	.633
.7	.772	.756	.740	.726	.711	.697	.684	.671	.659	.647	.636
.8	.775	.759	.743	.728	.714	.700	.687	.674	.662	.650	.638
.9	.778	.762	.746	.731	.716	.702	.689	.676	.664	.652	.640

TABLE 10.—*Concluded.*

THE VALUES OF $\Pi_V^{V+10\,000} = p_V - p_{V+10\,000}$

p_V	t_v 0°	10°	20°	30°	40°	50°	60°	70°	80°	90°	100°
29.0	0.780	0.764	0.748	0.733	0.719	0.705	0.691	0.678	0.666	0.654	0.642
.1	.783	.767	.751	.736	.721	.707	.694	.681	.668	.656	.645
.2	.786	.769	.753	.738	.724	.710	.696	.683	.671	.659	.647
.3	.788	.772	.756	.741	.726	.712	.699	.685	.673	.661	.649
.4	.791	.775	.759	.743	.729	.714	.701	.688	.675	.663	.651
29.5	.794	.777	.761	.746	.731	.717	.703	.690	.678	.666	.653
.6	.797	.780	.764	.748	.733	.719	.706	.692	.680	.668	.656
.7	.799	.783	.766	.751	.736	.722	.708	.695	.682	.670	.658
.8	.802	.785	.769	.753	.738	.724	.710	.697	.685	.672	.660
.9	.805	.788	.771	.756	.741	.727	.713	.699	.687	.675	.662
30.0	0.807	0.791	0.774	0.758	0.743	0.729	0.715	0.702	0.689	0.677	0.665
.1	.810	.793	.777	.761	.746	.731	.718	.704	.691	.679	.667
.2	.813	.796	.779	.763	.748	.734	.720	.706	.694	.681	.669
.3	.815	.798	.782	.766	.751	.736	.722	.709	.696	.684	.671
.4	.818	.801	.784	.769	.753	.739	.725	.711	.698	.686	.673
30.5	.821	.804	.787	.771	.756	.741	.727	.713	.701	.688	.676
.6	.823	.806	.789	.774	.758	.744	.730	.716	.703	.690	.678
.7	.826	.809	.792	.776	.761	.746	.732	.718	.705	.693	.680
.8	.829	.812	.795	.779	.763	.748	.734	.720	.707	.695	.682
.9	.832	.814	.797	.781	.766	.751	.737	.723	.710	.697	.684

TABLE 11.

THE VALUES OF $\Pi_{18\,550}^{20\,000} = p_{18\,550} - p_{20\,000}$

$p_{18\,550}$	t_v 0°	10°	20°	30°	40°	50°	60°	70°	80°	90°	100°
	Inch.	Inch.	Inch.	Inch.	Inch.	Inch.	Inch.	Inch.	Inch.	Inch.	Inch.
24.0	0.095	0.093	0.091	0.089	0.087	0.085	0.084	0.082	0.081	0.079	0.078
25.0	.099	.097	.095	.093	.091	.089	.087	.086	.084	.083	.081
26.0	.103	.100	.098	.096	.094	.093	.091	.089	.087	.086	.084
27.0	.107	.104	.102	.100	.098	.096	.094	.093	.091	.089	.087
28.0	.111	.108	.106	.104	.102	.100	.098	.096	.094	.092	.091
29.0	.115	.112	.110	.108	.105	.103	.101	.099	.097	.096	.094
30.0	.119	.116	.113	.111	.109	.107	.105	.103	.101	.099	.097
31.0	.122	.120	.117	.115	.113	.110	.108	.106	.104	.102	.100

As an illustration of the way in which Tables 9, 10 and 11 are to be used let it be supposed that the following values of t_v have been deduced from balloon observations made during static atmospheric conditions:

Between V = 18 550 and V = 20 000, t_v = 67.0
" V = 20 000 " V = 30 000, t_v = 69.5
" V = 30 000 " V = 40 000, t_v = 73.0
" V = 40 000 " V = 50 000, t_v = 74.0
" V = 50 000 " V = 60 000, t_v = 73.5

Between	$V = 60\,000$	and	$V = 70\,000$, $t_r = 71.5$
"	$V = 70\,000$	"	$V = 80\,000$, $t_r = 70.5$
"	$V = 80\,000$	"	$V = 90\,000$, $t_r = 69.5$
"	$V = 90\,000$	"	$V = 100\,000$, $t_r = 68.0$
"	$V = 100\,000$	"	$V = 110\,000$, $t_r = 65.0$
"	$V = 110\,000$	"	$V = 120\,000$, $t_r = 62.0$

Assume further that the mercurial barometer at the level surface, $V = 18\,550$, shows a pressure of 28.496 inches.

Table 11 for $p_{18\,550} = 28.496$ and $t_r = 67.0$ gives $p_{18\,550} - p_{20\,000} = 0.098$ inch. Therefore the pressure at the level surface $V = 20\,000$ equals $28.496 - 0.098 = 28.398$ inch. For $p_{20\,000} = 28.398$ and $t_r = 69.5$ Table 10 gives $H^{30\,000}_{20\,000} = 0.666$, so that $p_{30\,000} = 28.398 - 0.666 = 27.732$ inches. Again when $p_{30\,000} = 27.732$ and $t_r = 73.0$ Table 10 gives $H^{40\,000}_{30\,000} = 0.645$, whence $p_{40\,000} = 27.732 - 0.645 = 27.087$. Proceeding upward in this same manner, the following values of $H^{V}_{V'}$ and p_V are obtained:

$H^{30\,000}_{20\,000} = 0.666$ inch	$p_{20\,000} = 28.398$ inches
$H^{40\,000}_{30\,000} = 0.645$ "	$p_{30\,000} = 27.732$ "
$H^{50\,000}_{40\,000} = 0.629$ "	$p_{40\,000} = 27.087$ "
$H^{60\,000}_{50\,000} = 0.614$ "	$p_{50\,000} = 26.458$ "
$H^{70\,000}_{60\,000} = 0.603$ "	$p_{60\,000} = 25.844$ "
$H^{80\,000}_{70\,000} = 0.590$ "	$p_{70\,000} = 25.241$ "
$H^{90\,000}_{80\,000} = 0.577$ "	$p_{80\,000} = 24.651$ "
$H^{100\,000}_{90\,000} = 0.565$ "	$p_{90\,000} = 24.074$ "
$H^{110\,000}_{100\,000} = 0.555$ "	$p_{100\,000} = 23.509$ "
$H^{120\,000}_{110\,000} = 0.545$ "	$p_{110\,000} = 22.954$ "
	$p_{120\,000} = 22.409$ "

From these values of pressure and the corresponding values of t_r already given, may be obtained graphically the mean value of t_r for each pair of the isobaric surfaces $p = 28.5$ in., 28.0 in., 27.5 in., etc., as follows:

Between	$p = 28.5$	and	$p = 28.0$, $t_r = 68.0$
"	$p = 28.0$	"	$p = 27.5$, $t_r = 71.0$
"	$p = 27.5$	"	$p = 27.0$, $t_r = 73.0$
"	$p = 27.0$	"	$p = 26.5$, $t_r = 74.0$
"	$p = 26.5$	"	$p = 26.0$, $t_r = 73.5$
"	$p = 26.0$	"	$p = 25.5$, $t_r = 72.0$
"	$p = 25.5$	"	$p = 25.0$, $t_r = 71.0$
"	$p = 25.0$	"	$p = 24.5$, $t_r = 70.0$

Between $p = 24.5$ and $p = 24.0$, $t_r = 69.5$
" $p = 24.0$ " $p = 23.5$, $t_r = 67.5$
" $p = 23.5$ " $p = 23.0$, $t_r = 65.0$
" $p = 23.0$ " $p = 22.5$, $t_r = 62.5$

For these values of t, Table 9 gives the following:

$E^{28.0}_{28.5} = 7\ 450$	$E^{26.0}_{26.5} = 8\ 100$	$E^{24.0}_{24.5} = 8\ 700$
$E^{27.5}_{28.0} = 7\ 620$	$E^{25.5}_{26.0} = 8\ 230$	$E^{23.5}_{24.0} = 8\ 850$
$E^{27.0}_{27.5} = 7\ 800$	$E^{25.0}_{25.5} = 8\ 380$	$E^{23.0}_{23.5} = 9\ 000$
$E^{26.5}_{27.0} = 7\ 960$	$E^{24.5}_{25.0} = 8\ 530$	$E^{22.5}_{23.0} = 9\ 150$

Finally, to calculate the quantities $V_{31.0}$, $V_{30.5}$, $V_{30.0}$, $V_{29.5}$ etc., we must first determine the number V_{p_1} of level surfaces of gravity lying between sealevel and the first of the isobaric surfaces just named which the balloon meets as it rises into the air. This number consists of two parts, viz., V_0 = the number of level surfaces lying between sealevel and the station-barometer, and $E^{p_1}_{p_0}$ = the number of level surfaces lying between the station-barometer for which the pressure is p_0, and the isobaric surface $p = p_1$. V_0 is a constant and has already been computed for Omaha so that it only remains to obtain the quantity $E^{p_1}_{p_0}$. To accomplish this we use formula (23), written in the following form:

$$E^{p_1}_{p_0} = 1837.3 \times 509.4 \times \log\frac{p_0}{p_1} + 1837.3(t_r - 50^\circ \text{ F.}) \log\frac{p_0}{p_1}.$$

By writing

$$1837.3 \times 509.4 \times \log\frac{p_0}{p_1} = (E^{p_1}_{p_0})_{50}$$

this equation may be written

$$E^{p_1}_{p_0} = (E^{p_1}_{p_0})_{50} + \frac{t_r - 50^\circ \text{ F.}}{509.4} (E^{p_1}_{p_0})_{50}.$$

Table 12 contains the values of $(E^{p_1}_{p_0})_{50}$ considered as a function of p_1 and p_0.

Table 13 contains the values of the expression $\frac{t_r - 50}{509.4} (E^{p_1}_{p_0})_{50}$ considered as a function of $(E^{p_1}_{p_0})_{50}$ and t_r. Of course the difference $p_0 - p_1$ never exceeds 0.5 inch.

In the illustrative example for Omaha, $p_0 = 28.496$, $p_1 = 28.0$, and $t_r = 68.0$, whence from Table 12 $(E^{p_1}_{p_0})_{50} = 7\ 130$, and from Table 13, $\frac{t_r - 50}{509.4} (E^{p_1}_{p_0})_{50} = + 250$. Thus the number of level surfaces lying between the station-barometer and the 28.0-inch isobaric surface equals $7\ 130 + 250 = 7\ 380$. The number V_0 of level surfaces lying between sealevel and the isobaric surface of the station-barometer is 18 550. The total number of level surfaces of gravity included between sealevel and the isobaric surface of 28.0 inches, is therefore $V_{28.0} = 25\ 930$.

If the value $E^{27.5}_{28.0} = 7\ 620$, viz., the number of level surfaces of gravity previously found to lie between the isobaric surfaces $p = 28.0$ and $p = 27.5$, be added to the value 25 930 just found for $V'_{28.0}$, then we obtain the quantity $V'_{27.5} = 33\ 550$, or the total number of level surfaces of gravity lying between sealevel and the isobaric surface $p = 27.5$ inches. Again by adding $E^{27.0}_{27.5} = 7\ 800$ to $V'_{27.5} = 33\ 550$, we obtain $V'_{27.0} = 41\ 350$; by repeating this process the following values of V'_p result:

$V'_{28.0} = 25\ 930$	$V'_{26.0} = 57\ 410$	$V'_{24.0} = 91\ 250$
$V'_{27.5} = 33\ 550$	$V'_{25.5} = 65\ 640$	$V'_{23.5} = 100\ 100$
$V'_{27.0} = 41\ 350$	$V'_{25.0} = 74\ 020$	$V'_{23.0} = 109\ 100$
$V'_{26.5} = 49\ 310$	$V'_{24.5} = 82\ 550$	$V'_{22.5} = 118\ 250$

Under static equilibrium in the atmosphere the values of $\Pi^{p}_{p_0}$, p_0, $E^{p}_{p_0}$, and V'_p are constants at all points and at all times. Therefore a single balloon ascension, worked up in the manner just described, would suffice to determine for all time the relative positions of the isobaric surfaces and the level surfaces of gravity throughout the whole mass of static atmosphere.

Table 12.

The Values of $(E_{p_0}^{p_1})_{45}$, or the Number of level Surfaces between p_0 the Station Pressure and p_1 the proximate Isobaric Surface.

p_1 = *24.5 Inches.*

p_0	0	1	2	3	4	5	6	7	8	9
24.5	0	170	330	500	660	830	990	1160	1320	1490
.6	1660	1820	1990	2150	2320	2480	2650	2810	2980	3140
.7	3300	3470	3630	3800	3960	4130	4290	4450	4620	4780
.8	4950	5110	5270	5440	5600	5770	5930	6090	6260	6420
.9	6580	6750	6910	7070	7230	7400	7560	7720	7890	8050

p_1 = *25.0 Inches.*

p_0	0	1	2	3	4	5	6	7	8	9
25.0	0	160	320	490	650	810	970	1140	1300	1460
.1	1620	1780	1950	2110	2270	2430	2590	2750	2920	3080
.2	3240	3400	3560	3720	3880	4040	4210	4370	4530	4690
.3	4850	5010	5170	5330	5490	5650	5810	5970	6130	6290
.4	6450	6610	6770	6930	7090	7250	7410	7570	7730	7890

p_1 = *25.5 Inches.*

p_0	0	1	2	3	4	5	6	7	8	9
25.5	0	160	320	480	640	800	960	1110	1270	1430
.6	1590	1750	1910	2070	2230	2380	2540	2700	2860	3020
.7	3180	3330	3490	3650	3810	3970	4120	4280	4440	4600
.8	4750	4910	5070	5230	5380	5540	5700	5850	6010	6170
.9	6330	6480	6640	6800	6950	7110	7270	7420	7580	7740

p_1 = *26.0 Inches.*

p_0	0	1	2	3	4	5	6	7	8	9
26.0	0	160	310	470	620	780	940	1090	1250	1400
.1	1560	1720	1870	2030	2180	2340	2490	2650	2800	2960
.2	3110	3270	3420	3580	3730	3890	4040	4200	4350	4510
.3	4660	4820	4970	5130	5280	5440	5590	5740	5900	6050
.4	6210	6360	6510	6670	6820	6970	7130	7280	7440	7590

p_1 = *26.5 Inches.*

p_0	0	1	2	3	4	5	6	7	8	9
26.5	0	150	310	460	610	770	920	1070	1220	1380
.6	1530	1680	1840	1990	2140	2290	2450	2600	2750	2900
.7	3060	3210	3360	3510	3660	3820	3970	4120	4270	4420
.8	4580	4730	4880	5030	5180	5330	5480	5640	5790	5940
.9	6090	6240	6390	6540	6690	6840	6990	7150	7300	7450

p_1 = *27.0 Inches.*

p_0	0	1	2	3	4	5	6	7	8	9
27.0	0	150	300	450	600	750	900	1050	1200	1350
.1	1500	1650	1800	1950	2100	2250	2400	2550	2700	2850
.2	3000	3150	3300	3450	3600	3750	3900	4040	4190	4340
.3	4490	4640	4790	4940	5090	5240	5380	5530	5680	5830
.4	5980	6130	6270	6420	6570	6720	6870	7010	7160	7310

p_1 = *27.5 Inches.*

p_0	0	1	2	3	4	5	6	7	8	9
27.5	0	150	300	440	590	740	890	1030	1180	1330
.6	1480	1620	1770	1920	2060	2210	2360	2500	2650	2800
.7	2950	3090	3240	3390	3530	3680	3820	3970	4120	4260
.8	4410	4560	4700	4850	4990	5140	5290	5430	5580	5720
.9	5870	6020	6160	6310	6450	6600	6740	6890	7030	7180

TABLE 12.—*Concluded.*

THE VALUES OF $(E_{p_0}^{p_1})_{\pm c}$, OR THE NUMBER OF LEVEL SURFACES BETWEEN p_0 THE STATION PRESSURE, AND p_1 THE PROXIMATE ISOBARIC SURFACE.

p_0	0	1	2	3	4	5	6	7	8	9
					p_1 = 28.0 Inches.					
28.0	0	150	290	440	580	730	870	1010	1160	1300
.1	1450	1590	1740	1880	2030	2170	2320	2460	2600	2750
.2	2890	3040	3180	3330	3470	3610	3760	3900	4040	4190
.3	4330	4480	4620	4760	4910	5050	5190	5340	5480	5620
.4	5770	5910	6050	6190	6340	6480	6620	6770	6910	7050
					p_1 = 28.5 Inches.					
28.5	0	140	280	430	570	710	850	1000	1140	1280
.6	1420	1570	1710	1850	1990	2130	2280	2420	2560	2700
.7	2840	2980	3130	3270	3410	3550	3690	3830	3970	4110
.8	4260	4400	4540	4680	4820	4960	5100	5240	5380	5520
.9	5660	5810	5950	6090	6230	6370	6510	6650	6790	6930
					p_1 = 29.0 Inches.					
29.0	0	140	280	420	560	700	840	980	1120	1260
.1	1400	1540	1680	1820	1960	2100	2240	2380	2510	2650
.2	2790	2930	3070	3210	3350	3490	3630	3770	3910	4040
.3	4180	4320	4460	4600	4740	4880	5010	5150	5290	5430
.4	5570	5710	5840	5980	6120	6260	6400	6530	6670	6810
					p_1 = 29.5 Inches.					
29.5	0	140	280	410	550	690	830	960	1100	1240
.6	1380	1510	1650	1790	1920	2060	2200	2340	2470	2610
.7	2750	2880	3020	3160	3290	3430	3570	3700	3840	3980
.8	4110	4250	4390	4520	4660	4790	4930	5070	5200	5340
.9	5470	5610	5750	5880	6020	6150	6290	6420	6560	6700
					p_1 = 30.0 Inches.					
30.0	0	140	270	410	540	680	810	950	1080	1220
.1	1350	1490	1620	1760	1890	2030	2160	2300	2430	2570
.2	2700	2840	2970	3100	3240	3370	3510	3640	3780	3910
.3	4040	4180	4310	4450	4580	4710	4850	4980	5120	5250
.4	5380	5520	5650	5780	5920	6050	6190	6320	6450	6590
					p_1 = 30.5 Inches.					
30.5	0	130	270	400	530	670	800	930	1060	1200
.6	1330	1460	1600	1730	1860	1990	2130	2260	2390	2520
.7	2660	2790	2920	3050	3190	3320	3450	3580	3710	3850
.8	3980	4110	4240	4370	4510	4640	4770	4900	5030	5160
.9	5300	5430	5560	5690	5820	5950	6080	6220	6350	6480
					p_1 = 31.0 Inches.					
31.0	0	130	260	390	520	660	790	920	1050	1180
.1	1310	1440	1570	1700	1830	1960	2090	2220	2350	2480
.2	2610	2740	2870	3000	3130	3260	3390	3520	3650	3780
.3	3910	4040	4170	4300	4430	4560	4690	4820	4950	5080
.4	5210	5340	5470	5600	5730	5860	5990	6120	6250	6370

TABLE 13.

THE VALUES OF $\frac{L-50}{502.4}\left(E^{r_s}_{r_s}\right)_{ss}$ FOR VALUES OF L AND $\left(E^{r_s}_{r_s}\right)_{ss}$.

$\left(E^{r_s}_{r_s}\right)_{ss}$	L 0°	10°	20°	30°	40°	50°	60°	70°	80°	90°	100°
0	0	0	0	0	0	0	0	0	0	0	0
100	−10	−10	−10	0	0	0	0	0	10	10	10
200	−20	−20	−10	10	0	0	0	10	10	20	20
300	−30	−20	−20	−10	−10	0	10	10	20	20	30
400	−40	−30	−20	−20	−10	0	10	20	20	30	40
500	−50	−40	−30	−20	−10	0	10	20	30	40	50
600	−60	−50	−40	−20	−10	0	10	20	40	50	60
700	−70	−50	−40	−30	−10	0	10	30	40	50	70
800	−80	−60	−50	−30	−20	0	20	30	50	60	80
900	−90	−70	−50	−40	−20	0	20	40	50	70	90
1000	−100	−80	−60	−40	−20	0	20	40	60	80	100
1100	−110	−90	60	−40	−20	0	20	40	60	90	110
1200	−120	−90	−70	−50	−20	0	20	50	70	90	120
1300	−130	−100	−80	−50	−30	0	30	50	80	100	130
1400	−140	−110	−80	−60	−30	0	30	60	80	110	140
1500	−150	−120	−90	−60	−30	0	30	60	90	120	150
1600	−160	−130	−90	−60	−30	0	30	60	90	130	160
1700	−170	−130	−100	−70	−30	0	30	70	100	130	170
1800	−180	−140	−110	−70	−40	0	40	70	110	140	180
1900	−190	−150	−110	−70	−40	0	40	70	110	150	190
2000	−200	−160	−120	−80	−40	0	40	80	120	160	200
2100	−210	−160	−120	80	−40	0	40	80	120	160	210
2200	−220	−170	−130	−90	−40	0	40	90	130	170	220
2300	−230	−180	−140	−90	−50	0	50	90	140	180	230
2400	−240	−190	−140	−90	−50	0	50	90	140	190	240
2500	−250	−200	−150	−100	−50	0	50	100	150	200	250
2600	−260	−200	−150	−100	−50	0	50	100	150	200	260
2700	−270	210	−160	−110	−50	0	50	110	160	210	270
2800	−270	−220	−160	−110	−50	0	50	110	160	220	270
2900	−280	−230	−170	−110	−60	0	60	110	170	230	280
3000	−290	−240	−180	−120	−60	0	60	120	180	240	290
3100	−300	−240	−180	−120	−60	0	60	120	180	240	300
3200	−310	−250	−190	−130	−60	0	60	130	190	250	310
3300	−320	−260	−190	−130	−60	0	60	130	190	260	320
3400	−330	−270	−200	−130	−70	0	70	130	200	270	330
3500	−340	−270	−210	−140	−70	0	70	140	210	270	340
3600	−350	280	−210	−140	−70	0	70	140	210	280	350
3700	−360	−290	−220	−150	−70	0	70	150	220	290	360
3800	−370	−300	−220	−150	−70	0	70	150	220	300	370
3900	−380	−310	−230	−150	−80	0	80	150	230	310	380
4000	−390	−310	−240	−160	−80	0	80	160	240	310	390
4100	−400	−320	240	−160	−80	0	80	160	240	320	400
4200	−410	−330	250	170	−80	0	80	170	250	330	410
4300	−420	−340	−250	−170	−80	0	80	170	250	340	420
4400	−430	−350	260	−170	−90	0	90	170	260	350	430
4500	−440	−350	−270	−180	−90	0	90	180	270	350	440
4600	−450	−360	−270	−180	−90	0	90	180	270	360	450
4700	−460	−370	−280	−180	90	0	90	180	280	370	460
4800	−470	−380	−280	−190	−90	0	90	190	280	380	470
4900	−480	−380	−290	−190	−100	0	100	190	290	380	480

TABLE 13.—*Concluded.*

THE VALUES OF $\frac{t_c - 50}{500.4}\left(E\right)_{..}$ FOR VALUES OF t_c AND $\left(E\right)_{..}$

$(E)_{..}$	$t_c = 0°$	10°	20°	30°	40°	50°	60°	70°	80°	90°	100°
5000	−490	−390	−290	−200	−100	0	100	200	290	390	490
5100	−500	−400	−300	−200	−100	0	100	200	300	400	500
5200	−510	−410	−310	−200	−100	0	100	200	310	410	510
5300	−520	−420	−310	−210	−100	0	100	210	310	420	520
5400	−530	−420	−320	−210	−110	0	110	210	320	420	530
5500	−540	−430	−320	−220	−110	0	110	220	320	430	540
5600	−550	−440	−330	−220	−110	0	110	220	330	440	550
5700	−560	−450	−340	−220	−110	0	110	220	340	450	560
5800	−570	−460	−340	−230	−110	0	110	230	340	460	570
5900	−580	−460	−350	−230	−120	0	120	230	350	460	580
6000	−590	−470	−350	−240	−120	0	120	240	350	470	590
6100	−600	−480	−360	−240	−120	0	120	240	360	480	600
6200	−610	−490	−370	−240	−120	0	120	240	370	490	610
6300	−620	−490	−370	−250	−120	0	120	250	370	490	620
6400	−630	−500	−380	−250	−130	0	130	250	380	500	630
6500	−640	−510	−380	−260	−130	0	130	260	380	510	640
6600	−650	−520	−390	−260	−130	0	130	260	390	520	650
6700	−660	−530	−390	−260	−130	0	130	260	390	530	660
6800	−670	−530	−400	−270	−130	0	130	270	400	530	670
6900	−680	−540	−410	−270	−140	0	140	270	410	540	680
7000	−690	−550	−410	−280	−140	0	140	280	410	550	690
7100	−700	−560	−420	−280	−140	0	140	280	420	560	700
7200	−710	−570	−420	−280	−140	0	140	280	420	570	710
7300	−720	−570	−430	−290	−140	0	140	290	430	570	720
7400	−730	−580	−440	−290	−150	0	150	290	440	580	730
7500	−740	−590	−440	−290	−150	0	150	290	440	590	740
7600	−750	−600	−450	−300	−150	0	150	300	450	600	750
7700	−760	−600	−450	−300	−150	0	150	300	450	600	760
7800	−770	−610	−460	−310	−150	0	150	310	460	610	770
7900	−780	−620	−470	−310	−150	0	150	310	470	620	780

IV. THE RELATIVE POSITIONS OF THE ISOBARIC SURFACES AND THE LEVEL SURFACES OF GRAVITY UNDER DYNAMIC CONDITIONS.

Experience has shown that the formula for static barometric conditions, viz.,

$$dp = \rho dV,$$

also obtains very closely indeed for the actual dynamic conditions. In the succeeding pages I shall assume this formula to hold true since thereby the calculations are simplified and more clearly apprehended.

The primary cause of all atmospheric movements consists in the fact that on account of the unequal heating of the atmosphere the surfaces of equal values of t, do not coincide with the level surfaces of gravity. The immediate consequence is that the number of isobaric surfaces included between two level surfaces of gravity, as well as the number of the level surfaces included between any pair of isobaric surfaces, can not be everywhere the same, as is the case under static conditions, but on the contrary all the isobaric surfaces are in a state of continuous movement and deformation relative to the level surfaces of gravity, as is well known from the study of daily synoptic weather maps.

Therefore, in order to find the relative positions of the isobaric surfaces and the level surfaces of gravity under dynamic conditions, the quantities $H_{p_0}^{p}$, p_0, $E_{p_0}^{p}$, and V_p must be calculated along every vertical in the atmosphere and for every instant. The practical carrying out of this problem would require the sending up simultaneously from a number of stations, kites or balloons carrying self-registers, by means of whose records the four above-mentioned quantities for the verticals at the stations can be calculated. The values thus obtained for these quantities can then be entered on synoptic charts and graphically interpolated, just as is now done, daily, for the barometric readings observed at the meteorological stations and reduced to sealevel.

The kite- and balloon-ascensions heretofore executed may be classed under four types, viz.: ascents reaching great altitudes by means of sounding balloons, as at Trappes, near Paris; ascents in manned balloons, such as are made in Germany; ascents to great heights by means of kites, as at Blue Hill, Mass., and Trappes; and finally the kite-ascents carried out by the Weather Bureau from a large number of specially equipped kite-stations, *e. g.*, the 17 kite-stations of 1898. In coöperation with the manned balloon ascents in Germany, frequent simultaneous ascents of manned and unmanned balloons are carried out at many other European stations (*i. e.*, the international balloon-ascensions). These international balloon-ascensions in Europe and the kite-ascensions made by the U. S. Weather Bureau in America, are especially adapted to synoptic presentation of the four quantities $E_{p_0}^{p}$, $H_{p_0}^{p}$, p_0 and V_p in the atmosphere, because the pressure may be calculated from them along a number of verticals in the atmosphere for the same moment of time. In the present paper I shall work up only the observations with kites executed by the U. S. Weather Bureau.

For the purpose of synoptical study of the Weather Bureau kite-observations it is very desirable that they be carried out at those hours for which the daily weather maps are made, viz., at 8 A. M. and at 8 P. M., 75th meridian time. Since, however, the wind-conditions often made it impracticable to send up the kite at so early or so late an hour, therefore the observations made at any time during the day must be extrapolated to 8 A. M. or to 8 P. M. The rules for this extrapolation can be deduced only after the proper study of all the kite-observations heretofore made.

Because of our ignorance of these rules I have in the succeeding calculations interpolated to 8 A. M. only those observations obtained from ascents between 6 A. M. and 11 A. M.

The extrapolation of the observations to 8 A. M. or to 8 P. M. and the calculation of the values of the four quantities $H^{\prime\prime}_{8}$, p_r, $E^{\prime\prime}_{8}$, V_p, can be most advantageously performed by the kite-observers immediately upon reeling in the kite. The results may be readily concentrated to two or three numbers and thus easily telegraphed to the Central Office. As an illustrative example I proceed to show how the kite-ascension at Omaha, Nebr., on 23 Sept., 1898, should be worked up. In Table 14 the figures for pressure (p), temperature (t), and relative humidity (r), are taken from the corresponding curves of the self-recording meteorograph at the kite, while the heights (h) are calculated trigonometrically from the length of the kite-line of steel wire and the angular elevation of the kite. The values of t_r are deduced from p, t and r; and the values of V from the observed elevations, in the manner already described.

TABLE 14.

KITE OBSERVATIONS WITH THE VALUES OF t_r AND V, AT OMAHA, SEPT. 23, 1898.

Time.*	p	t	r	h	t_r	V
	Inch.	° F.	Per cent.	Feet.	° F.	
7^{30} a. m.	28.50	63.0	88	0	66.5	18550
8^{06}	27.35	69.5	82	1467	74.0	40490
8^{19}	27.10	70.0	79	1742	74.5	44590
11^{15}	24.80	68.0	51	4453	71.0	85110
11^{45}	24.20	68.0	30	5111	69.5	94940
11^{59}	23.75	65.0	18	5739	66.0	104340
12^{20} p. m.	23.40	64.0	12	6224	64.5	114580
12^{26}	23.15	62.0	11	6541	62.5	116310
12^{47}	23.00	61.5	10	6780	62.0	119880
12^{58}	22.90	61.0	10	6965	61.5	121750
1^{10}	24.10	70.0	5	5131	70.5	95240
1^{38}	24.25	71.0	4	4960	71.5	92690
3^{58}	25.10	69.0	50	3736	72.0	74400
4^{18}	25.32	70.0	58	3487	73.5	70680
4^{19}	——	73.0	60	2963	77.0	62840
4^{30}	26.30	77.0	70	2405	82.5	54500
4^{58}	26.90	81.0	66	1638	86.0	43010
5^{30}	28.40	87.0	53	0	92.0	18550

Using the values of t_r in Table 14, as abscissæ and the corresponding values of V as ordinates, the points in Fig. 1 are plotted and then a curve drawn through them which gives the values of t_r at the elevation of every level surface of gravity both for the ascent and the descent, by direct reading. By the aid of this (t_r, V)-curve and the observations made at 8 A. M. at the station, the observer or kite official should

* 75th meridian time or $1^h\ 24^m$ faster than Omaha local mean solar time.

next proceed to construct upon the same set of coördinates by extrapolation, the curve showing the value of t_v at each level surface of the station-vertical, for 8 A. M. This curve for our example, and as drawn on the same coördinate plane, is shown in Fig. 2,

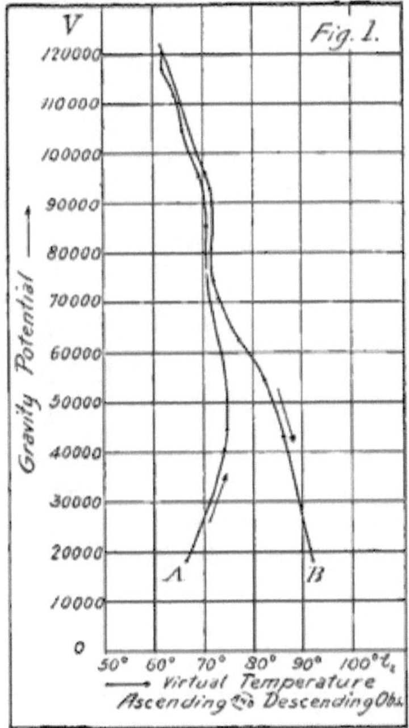

Fig. 1. The curves of virtual temperatures at Omaha for each value of the gravity potential as calculated from kite records for September 23, 1898. Ascending curve *A*, descending curve *B*.

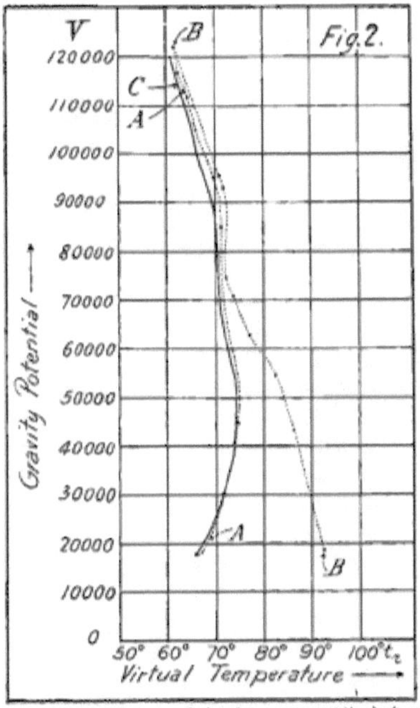

Fig. 2. The curves of virtual temperatures at Omaha from Fig. 1 with the interpolated curve *C* for the hour of the synoptic map, or 8 a. m., 75th meridian time, September 23, 1898.

where the 8 A. M. extrapolated (t_v, V)-curve is given as the heavy line (C) together with the curves in dotted lines, obtained directly from the observations of the day as already shown in Fig. 1. From the extrapolated (t_v, V)-curve of Fig. 2 for 8 A. M. may now be read off the following values for the average virtual temperatures (t_v) at 8 A. M. of the day in question.

Between $V = 18\,550$ and $V = 20\,000$, $t_v = 67°.0$
" $V = 20\,000$ " $V = 30\,000$, $t_v = 69°.5$
" $V = 30\,000$ " $V = 40\,000$, $t_v = 73°.0$
" $V = 40\,000$ " $V = 50\,000$, $t_v = 74°.0$
" $V = 50\,000$ " $V = 60\,000$, $t_v = 73°.5$
" $V = 60\,000$ " $V = 70\,000$, $t_v = 71°.5$
" $V = 70\,000$ " $V = 80\,000$, $t_v = 70°.5$
" $V = 80\,000$ " $V = 90\,000$, $t_v = 69°.5$
" $V = 90\,000$ " $V = 100\,000$, $t_v = 68°.0$
" $V = 100\,000$ " $V = 110\,000$, $t_v = 65°.0$
" $V = 110\,000$ " $V = 120\,000$, $t_v = 62°.0$

We may further assume that the air pressure shown by the station barometer at 8 A. M. equalled 28.496 inches of mercury.*

Now, if the barometric formula for static conditions be assumed as sufficiently exact for the assumed dynamic conditions, then the calculation of the four quantities $H_{V_0}^{V_1}$, p_V, $E_{p_0}^{p_1}$ and V_p, will be carried on in exactly the same way for the vertical through Omaha, Nebr., on 23 Sept., 1898, 8 A. M., 75th meridian time, as though the atmosphere had been in a static condition on that day. We might therefore here make use of the tables given in the chapter on static conditions. In order to avoid unnecessary repetition, the values just given for t_v for Omaha, 23 Sept., 1893, 8 A. M., 75th meridian time, have been used as the basis for this illustration of static conditions. The following values were found by the method previously described:

$H_{18\,550}^{20\,000} = 0,098$	$p_{18\,550} = 28.496$
$H_{20\,000}^{30\,000} = 0,666$	$p_{20\,000} = 28.398$
$H_{30\,000}^{40\,000} = 0,645$	$p_{30\,000} = 27.732$
$H_{40\,000}^{50\,000} = 0,629$	$p_{40\,000} = 27.087$
$H_{50\,000}^{60\,000} = 0,614$	$p_{50\,000} = 26.458$
$H_{60\,000}^{70\,000} = 0,603$	$p_{60\,000} = 25.844$
$H_{70\,000}^{80\,000} = 0,590$	$p_{70\,000} = 25.241$
$H_{80\,000}^{90\,000} = 0,577$	$p_{80\,000} = 24.651$
$H_{90\,000}^{100\,000} = 0,565$	$p_{90\,000} = 24.074$
$H_{100\,000}^{110\,000} = 0,555$	$p_{100\,000} = 23.509$
$H_{110\,000}^{120\,000} = 0,545$	$p_{110\,000} = 22.954$
	$p_{120\,000} = 22.409$

* This station-pressure is to be reduced to standard gravity since this reduction is considered as one of the instrumental corrections, see pp. 33 and 42. The correction to a self-registering aneroid should include this item. — C. A.

Here the quantities $p_{18\,550}$, $p_{20\,000}$, etc., are the barometric pressures at the level surfaces $V = 18\,550$, $V = 20\,000$, etc. From the (t_v, V)-curve for 8 A. M. in Fig. 2, we find corresponding values of t_v for the same level surfaces as follows:

For $V_{18\,550}$ $p = 28.496$, $t_v = 67.0$
for $V_{20\,000}$ $p = 28.398$, $t_v = 67.5$
for $V_{30\,000}$ $p = 27.732$, $t_v = 71.0$
for $V_{40\,000}$ $p = 27.087$, $t_v = 74.0$
for $V_{50\,000}$ $p = 26.458$, $t_v = 74.0$
for $V_{60\,000}$ $p = 25.844$, $t_v = 72.5$
for $V_{70\,000}$ $p = 25.241$, $t_v = 71.0$
for $V_{80\,000}$ $p = 24.651$, $t_v = 70.0$
for $V_{90\,000}$ $p = 24.074$, $t_v = 69.0$
for $V_{100\,000}$ $p = 23.509$, $t_v = 66.0$
for $V_{110\,000}$ $p = 22.954$, $t_v = 63.5$
for $V_{120\,000}$ $p = 22.409$, $t_v = 61.0$

By plotting the above values of p and t_v as a system of coördinates in which p is ordinate and the corresponding value of t_v is abscissa, a curve is obtained which shows

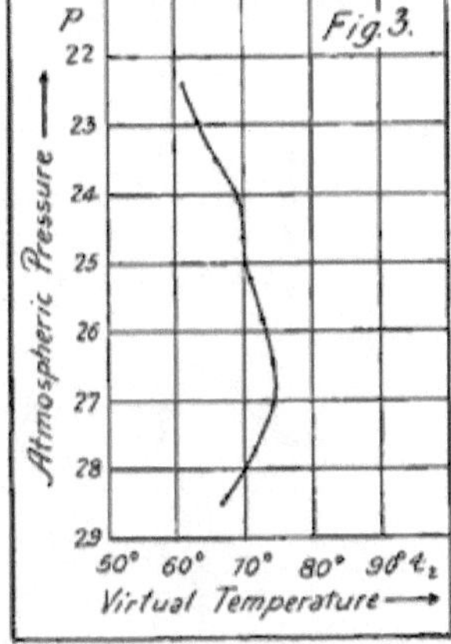

Fig. 3. The (p, t_v)-curve of virtual temperatures at Omaha for each value of atmospheric pressure as calculated for 8 a. m., 75th meridian time, from the kite record of September 23, 1898.

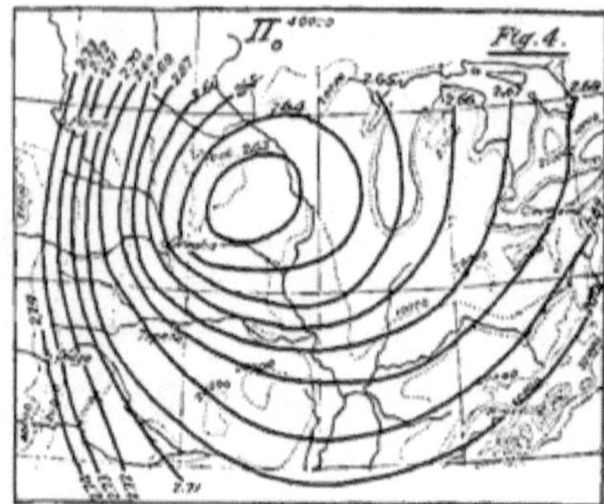

Fig. 4. Chart of $\Pi_0^{40\,000}$ for 8 a. m., September 23, 1898, or lines of equal differences of barometric pressure between sea level and the 40000 potential surface of gravity as telegraphed from all stations to the Central Office.

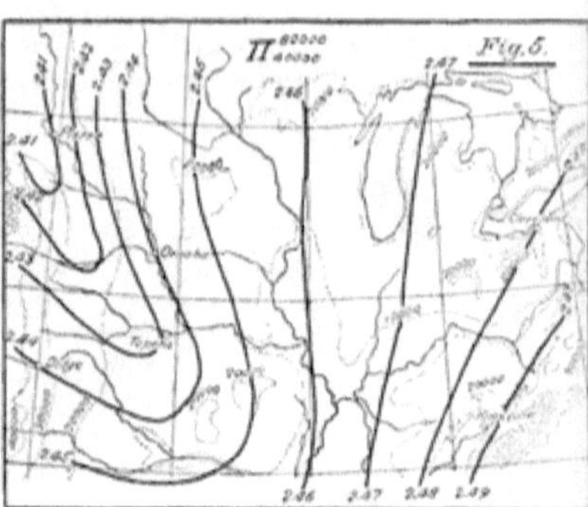

Fig. 5. Chart of $\Pi_{40\,000}^{80\,000}$ for 8 a. m., September 23, 1898, or lines of equal differences of barometric pressure between the 40 000 and 80 000 potential surfaces of gravity as telegraphed to the Central Office.

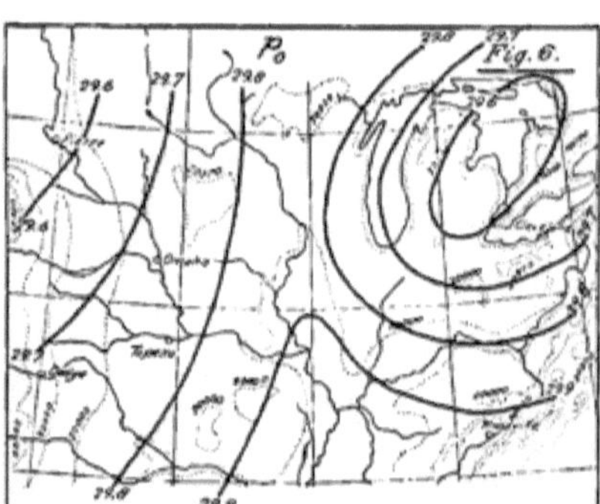

Fig. 6. Chart of p_0 or isobars for sea level for 1898, September 23, 8 a. m., as observed and telegraphed.

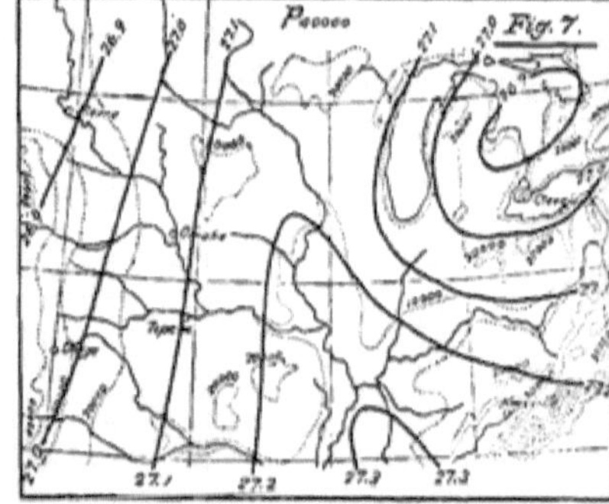

Fig. 7. Chart of $p_{40\,000}$ for 1898, September 23, 8 a. m., or isobars at the 40 000 level surface as deduced from the isobars for sea level by subtracting the numbers on Fig. 4 from those on Fig. 6.

the value of t_r in every isobaric surface above Omaha for 23 Sept., 1898, 8 A. M. This curve is shown in Fig. 3.

From this curve the following average values of t_r are easily read off:

Between	$p = 28.196$	and	$p = 28.000$	$t_r = 68.0$
"	$p = 28.0$	"	$p = 27.5$	$t_r = 71.0$
"	$p = 27.5$	"	$p = 27.0$	$t_r = 73.0$
"	$p = 27.0$	"	$p = 26.5$	$t_r = 74.0$
"	$p = 26.5$	"	$p = 26.0$	$t_r = 73.5$
"	$p = 26.0$	"	$p = 25.5$	$t_r = 72.0$
"	$p = 25.5$	"	$p = 25.0$	$t_r = 71.0$
"	$p = 25.0$	"	$p = 24.5$	$t_r = 70.0$
"	$p = 24.5$	"	$p = 24.0$	$t_r = 69.5$
"	$p = 24.0$	"	$p = 23.5$	$t_r = 67.5$
"	$p = 23.5$	"	$p = 23.0$	$t_r = 65.0$
"	$p = 23.0$	"	$p = 22.5$	$t_r = 62.5$

For these values of t_r and p we obtain from Table 9

$E^{28.0}_{28.196} = 7\,380$	$E^{26.0}_{26.5} = 8\,100$	$E^{24.0}_{24.5} = 8\,700$
$E^{27.5}_{28.0} = 7\,620$	$E^{25.5}_{26.0} = 8\,230$	$E^{23.5}_{24.0} = 8\,850$
$E^{27.0}_{27.5} = 7\,800$	$E^{25.0}_{25.5} = 8\,380$	$E^{23.0}_{23.5} = 9\,000$
$E^{26.5}_{27.0} = 7\,960$	$E^{24.5}_{25.0} = 8\,530$	$E^{22.5}_{23.0} = 9\,150$

and, by the aid of Tables 12 and 13, the following values

$V'_{28.0} = 25\,930$	$V'_{26.0} = 57\,110$	$V'_{24.0} = 91\,250$
$V'_{27.5} = 33\,550$	$V'_{25.5} = 65\,640$	$V'_{23.5} = 100\,100$
$V'_{27.0} = 41\,350$	$V'_{25.0} = 74\,020$	$V'_{23.0} = 109\,100$
$V'_{26.5} = 49\,310$	$V'_{24.5} = 82\,550$	$V'_{22.5} = 118\,250$

By bringing together the preceding results we may arrange a convenient tabular form as in Table 15 for working up the results of a kite ascension at a kite-station. As an example I have collected in this Table 15, the results already worked out for the observations at Omaha, 23 Sept., 1898.

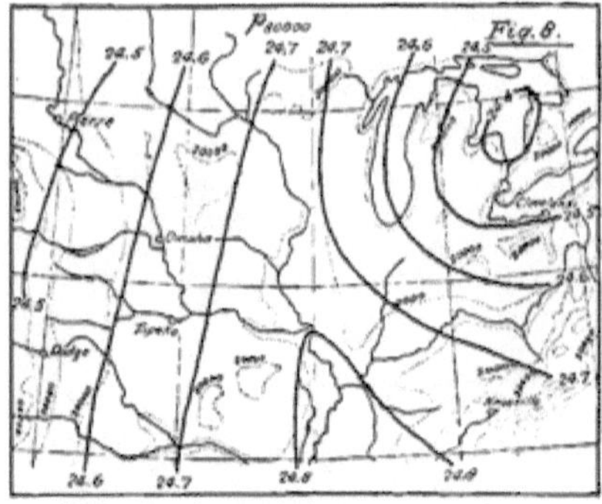

Fig. 8. Chart of $p_{80\,000}$ for 1898, 8 a. m., September 23, or isobars at the level surface 80 000 as deduced from the isobars for 40 000 by subtracting the numbers on Fig. 5 from those on Fig. 7.

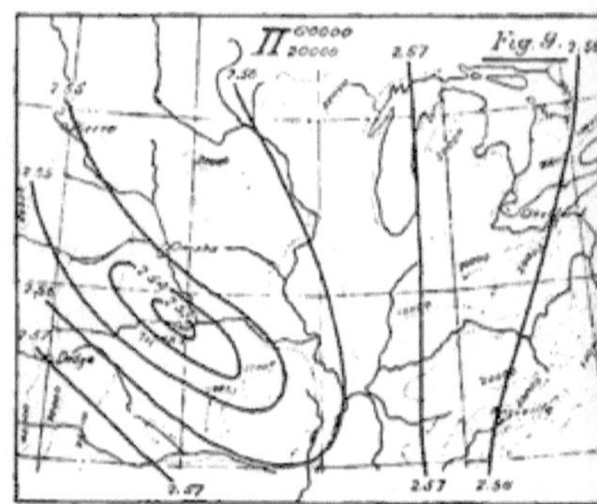

Fig. 9. Chart of $\Pi^{60\,000}_{20\,000}$ for 1898, September 23, 8 a. m., or lines of equal differences of barometric pressure between the 60 000 and the 20 000 potential surfaces of gravity.

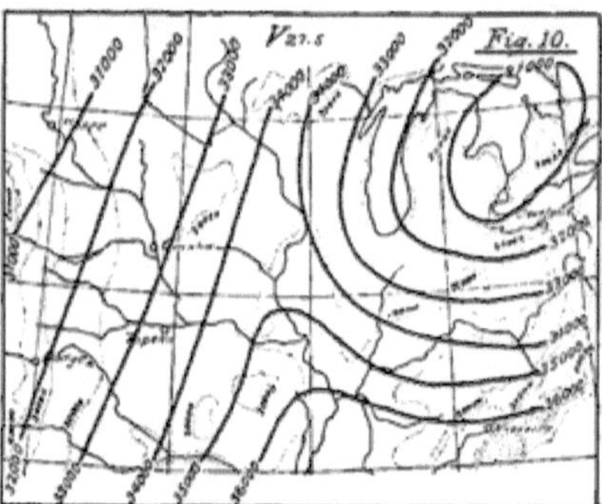

Fig. 10. Chart of $V_{27.5}$ for 8 a. m., September 23, 1898, or chart of the level lines on the isobaric surface 27.5 inches as telegraphed.

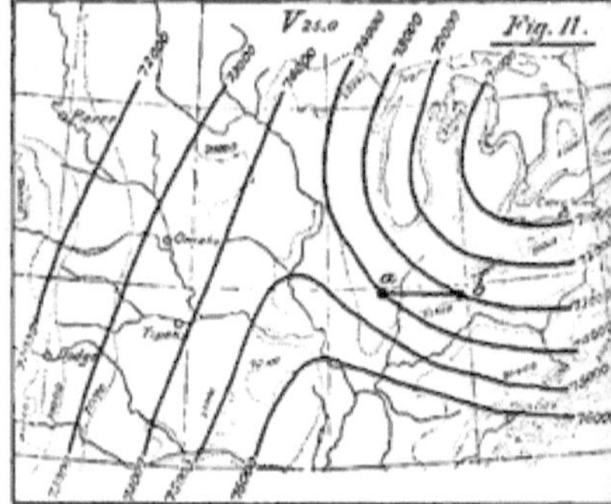

Fig. 11. Chart of $V_{25.0}$ for 8 a. m., September 23, 1898, or chart of the level lines on the isobaric surface 25.0 inches as deduced by adding the numbers on Fig. 12 to those on Fig. 10.

TABLE 15.

FORM FOR THE DYNAMIC COMPUTATIONS BASED ON KITE OBSERVATIONS.
OMAHA, NEBRASKA, SEPT. 23, 1898.

1	Computation of t_o and V.									Computation of $B^{t}_{t_o}$ and p_V.					1
2	1	2	3	4	5	6	7	8	9	10	11	12	13	14	2
3	Time.*	Bar.	Temp.	t_1-t	r	t_2-t	t_o	z	V	V	t_o	$B^{t}_{t_o}$	p_V	t_o	3
	h m	Inch.	°	°		°	°	feet					Inch.	°	
4	8:00 a. m.	28.496	63.5	4.0	88	3.5	67	0	18 550	18 550	67.0	0.698<	28.496	67	4
5	7:50	28.50	63	4.0	88	3.5	66.5	0	18 550	20 000	69.5	0.686<	28.298	67.5	5
6	8:06	27.35	69.5	5.5	82	4.5	74	1467	40 490	30 000	73.0	0.645<	27.732	71	6
7	8:19	27.10	70	5.5	79	4.5	74.5	1742	44 590	40 000	71.0	0.629<	27.087	74	7
8	11:25	24.80	68	5.5	51	3.0	71	4153	85 110	50 000	73.5	0.614<	26.458	74	8
9	11:45	24.20	68	5.5	30	1.5	69.5	5111	94 940	60 000	71.5	0.603<	25.844	72.5	9
10	11:54	23.75	65	5.0	18	1.0	66	5739	104 340	70 000	70.5	0.590<	25.241	71	10
11	12:13 p. m.	23.40	64	5.0	12	0.5	64.5	6224	111 580	80 000	69.5	0.577<	24.651	70	11
12	12:25	23.15	62	5.0	11	0.5	62.5	6541	116 310	90 000	68.0	0.565	24.074	69	12
13	12:47	23.00	61.5	4.5	10	0.5	62	6780	119 880	100 000	65.0	0.555<	23.509	66	13
14	12:57	22.90	61	4.5	10	0.5	61.5	6905	121 750	110 000	62.0	0.545<	22.954	63.5	14
15	1:44	24.10	70	6.0	5	0.5	70.5	5431	95 240	120 000			22.400	61	15
16	1:57	24.25	71	6.5	4	0.5	71.5	4960	92 690						16
17	3:56	25.10	69	5.5	50	3.0	72	3736	74 400						17
18	4:16	25.32	70	6.0	58	3.5	73.5	3487	70 080						18
19	4:25		73	6.5	60	4.0	77	2963	62 840						19
20	4:39	26.30	77	7.5	70	5.5	82.5	2405	54 500						20
21	4:54	26.90	81	8.0	66	5.0	86	1638	43 040						21
22	5:25	28.40	87	9.5	53	5.0	92	0	18 550						22

* All records are kept on 75th meridian time which is 1h 24m faster than Omaha local mean solar time.

TABLE 15.—*Continued.*

FORM FOR THE DYNAMIC COMPUTATIONS BASED ON KITE OBSERVATIONS.
OMAHA, NEBRASKA, SEPT. 23, 1898.

1	Computation of $B^{p_1}_{p_o}$ and V_p.					Values of t_V in sets.					1
2	15	16	17	18	19	20	21	22	23	24	2
3	p	t_o	$B^{p_1}_{p_o}$	V_p	t_o	V	Time.	t_o	Time.	t_o	3
	Inch.	°					h m	°	h m	°	
4	28.496	68	7 380<	18 550	67.0	0	—	—	—	—	4
5	28.0	71	7 620<	25 930	69.5	10 000	—	—	—	—	5
6	27.5	73	7 800<	33 550	72	20 000	7:32 a. m.	67	5:23 p. m.	91.5	6
7	27.0	74	7 960<	41 350	74	30 000	7:57	71	5:10	89.5	7
8	26.5	73.5	8 100<	49 310	74	40 000	8:06	71	4:58	87.0	8
9	26.0	72	8 240<	57 410	73	50 000	8:45	71.5	4:48	84.0	9
10	25.5	71	8 380<	65 640	71.5	60 000	9:34	73.5	4:29	79.0	10
11	25.0	70	8 530<	74 020	70	70 000	10:22	71.5	4:12	73.5	11
12	24.5	69.5	8 700<	82 550	70	80 000	11:08	71.0	3:23	72.0	12
13	24.0	67.5	8 850<	91 250	68.5	90 000	11:36	70.5	2:12	72.0	13
14	23.5	65	9 000<	100 100	66	100 000	11:40	67	1:39	69.0	14
15	23.0	62.5	9 150<	109 100	63.5	110 000	12:10 p. m.	65	1:30	66.0	15
16	22.5			118 250	61.5	120 000	12:50	62	1:13	62.0	16
17						130 000	1:00	60	1:00	60.0	17
18											18
19											19
20											20
21											21
22											22

In this schematic presentation, the various columns as numbered have the following significance:

No. 1 contains the moments of observation. All time records are uniformly in 75th meridian time.

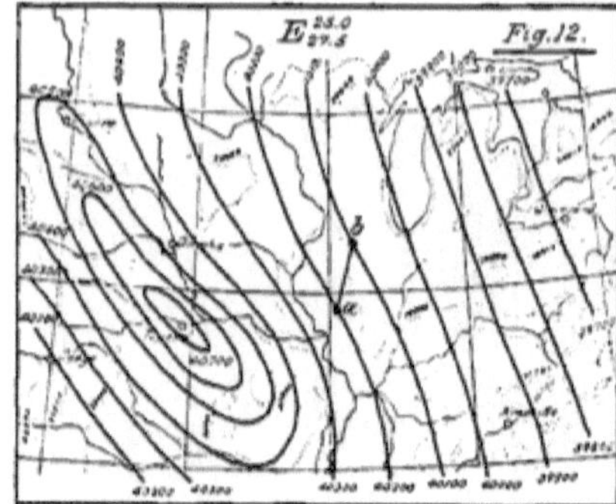

Fig. 12. Chart of $E^{25.0}_{27.5}$ for 8 a. m., September 23, 1898, or the number of solenoids in the layer of atmosphere over any place between the isobaric surfaces 27.5 and 25.0 as computed and telegraphed; showing the tendency of the air at any place to maintain a vertical circulation.

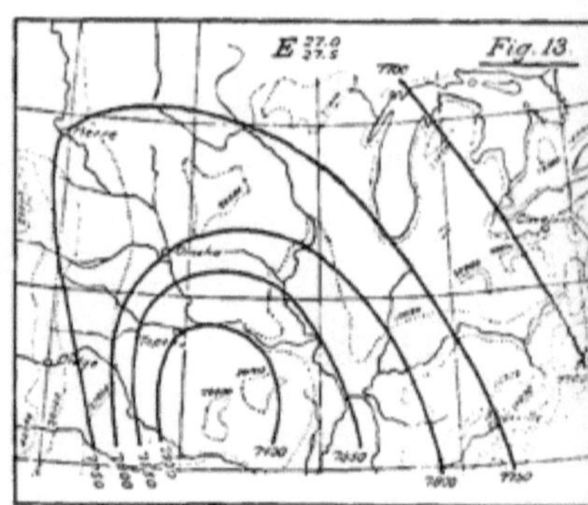

Fig. 13. Chart of $E^{27.0}_{27.5}$ for 8 a. m., September 23, 1898, or th number of solenoids in the layer of atmosphere between the isobars 27. and 27.5 above any place.

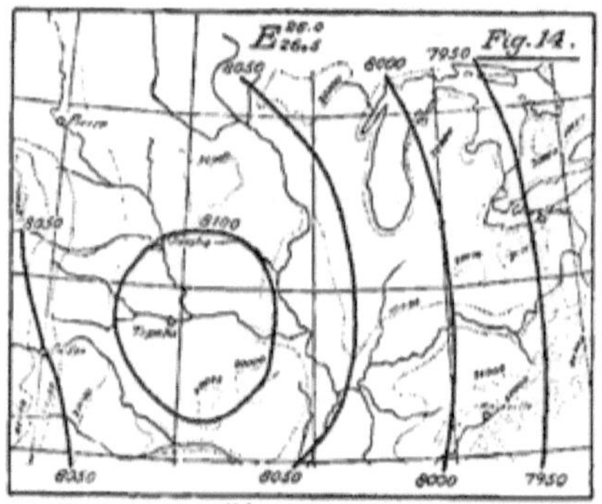

Fig. 14. Chart of $E^{26.0}_{26.5}$ for 8 a. m., September 23, 1898, or the number of solenoids in the layer of atmosphere between the isobars 26.0 and 26.5 above any place.

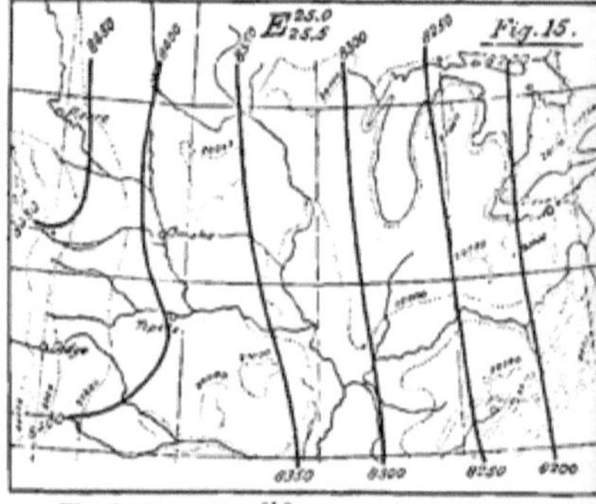

Fig. 15. Chart of the $E^{25.0}_{25.5}$ for 8 a. m., September 23, 1898, or th number of solenoids in the layer of atmosphere between the isobars 25. and 25.5 above any place.

Nos. 2 and 3, respectively, the pressure and temperature registered at these hours [the local pressure expressed in inches of mercury under standard gravity.—C. A.].

No. 4, the values of $(t_1 - t)$ for these pressures and temperatures as obtained from Table 7.

No. 5, the registered relative humidities.

No. 6, the values of $(t_v - t)$ deduced from Table 8, for the data in columns 4 and 5.

No. 7, the t_v or the sum of the $(t_v - t)$ in column 6 and the temperatures t in column 3.

No. 8, the observed elevations computed trigonometrically.

No. 9, the values of the gravity potentials V obtained from No. 8 by means of Table 3.

From the t_v and V in columns 7 and 9 the (t_v, V) curve of Fig. 1 is constructed and along side of it the corresponding extrapolated curve for 8 A. M. as in Fig. 2. From the (t_v, V) curve for 8 A. M. we read off the mean values of t_v for the intervals $V = 18\,550$ to $V = 20\,000$, $V = 20\,000$ to $V = 30\,000$, etc., and proceed to the following columns:

No. 10, the ordinal numbers of the level surfaces of gravity.

No. 11, the mean values of t_v for the intervals between the surfaces of column No. 10.

No. 12, the values of H_1^2 for the average t_v as given by Tables 10 and 11.

No. 13, the value of p_V for each level surface obtained by successive algebraic additions of H_1^2 to the reading of the station-barometer at 8 A. M.

No. 14, contains the values of t_v for the level surfaces, $V = 18\,550$, $V = 20\,000$, etc. at 8 A. M., obtained directly from the extrapolated (t_v, V)-curve of Fig. 2.

From the values of p_V and t_v given in columns 13 and 14, the curve of Fig. 3 is constructed and from this the mean value of t_v for each half-inch of barometric change is read off.

No. 15, contains the barometric pressure for each of these half-inch intervals.

No. 16 gives the corresponding mean values of t_v.

No. 17 gives the values of $E_{p_2}^{p_1}$ for these t_v-values, obtained by aid of Tables 9, 12 and 13.

No. 18 contains the values of V_p, that result from successive additions of the values in column 17 [to the value of V_p for the level surface that contains the station barometer.—C. A.].

From the curves in Figs. 2 and 3 there may also be determined the values of t_v for the isobaric surfaces at 8 A. M., and for the level surfaces of gravity at the moments when the kite passed through them.

No. 19 contains the values of t_v at 8 A. M. read off from the curve of Fig. 3 and corresponding to the isobaric surfaces given in column 15.

No. 20 gives the ordinal number for each 10 000th level surface of gravity.

Nos. 21 and 23 give the times when the kite passed through each of the surfaces given in column 20, ascending and descending respectively.

These times of passage through the level surfaces as given in columns 21 and 23 may readily be obtained graphically as follows: The times given in column 1 are plotted as abscissæ and the values of V in column 5 as ordinates. Then the (Time, V)-curve is drawn through the points thus plotted and from this curve the time of the moment of intersection for each 10 000th level surface of gravity may be read off directly.

Nos. 22 and 24 give the values of t, at each passage through the level surfaces of column 20; these values having been read from the curves for the kite ascension shown in Fig. 2.

Preparation of Synoptical Charts at the Central Station.

For synoptic study at the central station it is sufficient to telegraph only some of the most important of the quantities above calculated, *e.g.*, the quantities $\Pi_0^{10\,000}$, $\Pi_{10\,000}^{20\,000}$, $\Pi_{20\,000}^{30\,000}$, $V_{27.5}$, $E_{27.5}^{25.0}$ and $E_{25.0}^{22.5}$. The value of $\Pi_0^{10\,000}$ is obtained by subtracting $p_{10\,000} = 27.087$ from the reading of the station-barometer reduced to sealevel, or $p_0 = 29.74$, whence results the difference, $\Pi_0^{10\,000} = 2.653$. In the same way are obtained the values $\Pi_{10\,000}^{20\,000} = 27.087 - 24.651 = 2.436$, and $\Pi_{20\,000}^{30\,000} = 24.651 - 22.409 = 2.242$. The value of $V_{27.5} = 33\,550$ is taken directly from column 18 of Table 15. The values of $E_{27.5}^{25.0} = 40\,470$, and $E_{25.0}^{22.5} = 44\,230$ are the differences $V_{25.0} - V_{27.5}$ and $V_{22.5} - V_{25.0}$ respectively. The numbers to be telegraphed to the central station are therefore 2.653, 2.436, 2.242, 33 550, 40 470 and 44 230. For telegraphic purposes these numbers may be shortened by dropping the first and the last figures of each, so that we have to telegraph only the abbreviated numbers 65, 44, 24, 355, 047 and 423. These may be combined into three groups of five figures each, as for example 65 355, 44 047, 24 423.*

Now assume that all the kite-stations where ascensions were made with registering instruments during the forenoon of 23 Sept., 1898, had worked up their observations according to the foregoing method and sent telegraphic reports to the central office. Then these telegrams as received would have read somewhat as follows:

23 SEPT., 1898, 8 A. M., 75TH MERIDIAN TIME.

Cleveland, O.	68 135	48 963	....
Dodge City, Kan.	74 193	44 016	22 446
Knoxville, Tenn.	70 635	49 993	....
Omaha, Nebr.	65 355	44 047	24 423
Pierre, S. D.	73 076	41 054	....
Topeka, Kan.	68 363	43 074	....

* This contraction for economy in European telegraphy would be advantageously replaced in America by our usage of short cipher code words or syllables. — C. A.

At the central office of the Weather Bureau by means of these numbers charts can be drawn presenting synoptically the values of $H_0^{40\,000}$, $H_{40\,000}^{60\,000}$, $p_{40\,000}$, $p_{60\,000}$, $E_{27.5}^{25.0}$, $V_{27.5}$ and $V_{25.0}$. The first step is to separate the figures of the telegrams and to supply the missing figures, with the following result:

23 Sept., 1898, 8 A. M.

Obs. Station.	$H_0^{40\,000}$	$H_{40\,000}^{60\,000}$	$H_{60\,000}^{120\,000}$	$V_{27.5}$	$E_{27.5}^{25.0}$	$E_{25.0}^{22.5}$
Cleveland, O.	2.68	2.48	—	31 350	39 630	—
Dodge City, Kans.	2.74	2.44	2.22	31 930	40 160	44 460
Knoxville, Tenn.	2.70	2.49	—	36 350	39 930	—
Omaha, Nebr.	2.65	2.44	2.24	33 550	40 470	44 230
Pierre, So. Dak.	2.73	2.41	—	30 760	40 540	—
Topeka, Kans.	2.68	2.43	—	33 630	40 740	—

The second step is to enter these values at the appropriate stations on a series of skeleton maps. The sketch map forming Fig. 4 on page 67 gives a synoptic map of the quantity $H_0^{40\,000}$. Fig. 5, page 67, shows a similar map for the quantity $H_{40\,000}^{60\,000}$. The maps, Figs. 4 and 5 and curves have been drawn just as the isobars for sealevel are drawn on the usual isobaric maps. The three maps following, viz., Figs. 6, 7, 8, pages 67, 69, show the quantities p_0, $p_{40\,000}$, $p_{60\,000}$ respectively. The map for p_0, Fig. 6, is copied directly from the Weather Bureau map of barometric pressure reduced to sealevel. The $p_{40\,000}$ map, Fig. 7, which is a map of the isobars at the level surface $V = 40\,000$, is constructed graphically by superposition of the p_0 chart, Fig. 6, and the $H_0^{40\,000}$ chart, Fig. 4, making use of the relation

$$p_{40\,000} = p_0 - H_0^{40\,000}.$$

The $p_{60\,000}$ map, Fig. 8, page 69, is constructed in an analogous way by superposing Figs. 5 and 7, using the relation

$$p_{60\,000} = p_{40\,000} - H_{40\,000}^{60\,000}.$$

The synoptic map of the values $H_{20\,000}^{60\,000}$ forming Fig. 9, of page 69, will be discussed later.

Fig. 10, on page 71, shows the synoptic distribution of the quantity $V_{27.5}$, *i. e.*, the number of level surfaces of gravity between sealevel and the isobaric surface for $p = 27.5$ inches; it is constructed from the telegraphed values of $V_{27.5}$ superposed on the map of isobars for sealevel. The last map on page 69, Fig. 11, shows the distribution of the values of $V_{25.0}$, *i. e.*, the number of level surfaces between sealevel and the isobaric surface $p = 25.0$. It is constructed by superposing Fig. 10 for $V_{27.5}$ and Fig. 12 for $E_{27.5}^{25.0}$ using the relation

$$V_{25.0} = V_{27.5} + E_{27.5}^{25.0}.$$

The first map on page 71, viz., Fig. 12, presents a synoptic view of the values of the quantity $E^{2.0}_{29.5}$ and is constructed from the telegraphed values of $E^{2.0}_{29.5}$ in a manner analogous to the chart of H_0^{5000}, page 67, Fig. 4. The remaining maps on page 71, viz., Figs. 13, 14, 15, present synoptic views of the distribution of the quantities $E^{29.0}_{29.5}$, $E^{29.0}_{30.5}$ and $E^{31.0}_{30.5}$ respectively, and will be discussed later.

The distribution of pressure under the prevailing dynamic conditions in the atmosphere is thus presented on the one hand by p_V charts, showing the isobars on the level surfaces of gravity, and on the other hand by V_p charts, showing the level lines of gravity on the isobaric surfaces. These two systems of charts taken together present a very clear picture of the relative positions of the isobaric surfaces and of the level surfaces of gravity. From kite observations and by the aid of the tables accompanying this memoir, isobars on the level surfaces of gravity can be constructed for much smaller intervals, *i. e.*, for the level surfaces of $V=0$, $V=10\,000$, $V=20\,000$, $\cdots V=180\,000$, as also level lines on the isobaric surfaces of $p=31$, $p=30.5$, $p=30.0 \cdots p=19.0$. The charts on pages 67, 69, 71, however, suggest that such intervals are much too small. In fact, the charts for $p_{5\,000}$, $p_{10\,000}$ and p_0 show nearly the same characteristics; and the same is true of the charts for $V_{30.0}$ and $V_{29.5}$. It is obviously superfluous to draw charts for such small intervals that the types are nearly identical. On the other hand the interval must not be too large since then the features would differ so much that it would be difficult or impossible to follow the continuity of the change in the type with increasing elevation. We must learn through experience what intervals are to be chosen as best suited to our studies, and to the condition of the atmosphere.

I have chosen the isobaric map drawn for sealevel as the base for the p_V- and V_p-maps, because the values of atmospheric pressures as telegraphed from permanent observing stations are, without exception, reduced to sealevel. But when one wishes to construct maps for the free atmosphere, it is quite superfluous to first reduce the pressure to sealevel, and then re-reduce it upwards from sealevel to a higher one. The rational way would be to reduce the pressures observed at the permanent stations, not to sealevel but to the nearest level surface of gravity for which a p_V-map is to be constructed, and then use the value of p_V thus obtained in constructing the corresponding p_V-map. In an analogous way the number of level surfaces of gravity lying between the level of the station-barometer and the nearest isobaric surface adopted for mapping values of V_p, might be calculated; whence by adding the values of V_0, the values of V_p for the isobaric surface in question could be determined and be used in constructing the proper V_p-map. The values of p_V and V_p obtained from the kite-observations would thus serve in constructing their respective maps for the free air and the values of H^{V}_{V} and E^{p}_{p} could be used in the manner already described, for superposition on the p_V- and V_p-maps. By the foregoing method of procedure, however, no isobaric charts at sealevel would be obtained for those regions where the stations are at considerable altitudes above sealevel.

V. The Dynamic Significance of the Charts of p_V, V_p; E^p_V and H^p_V.

The following conclusions are deduced on the distinct assumption that the earth does not rotate and that friction does not exist. I defer to a later paper the consideration of the influence of the rotation of the earth and of friction upon the dynamic processes of the atmosphere. In this section I shall consider only the primary cause of all atmospheric movements, in other words the want of uniformity as to temperature and humidity. This is that which has the power to set up a movement in an atmosphere otherwise at rest relative to the earth, whereas the earth's rotation and the friction do not possess such power.

Significance of p_V-maps.—The dynamic significance of the p_V-maps, namely, the maps of the isobars on the different level surfaces of gravity, is already familiar enough through the daily use of the maps of the isobars at sealevel. I would only here call attention to the fact that in order to obtain the acceleration of the particles of air the pressure-gradient must be divided by the appropriate density of the air. Consequently, in the higher levels where the air has a less density, the same gradient of pressure will produce a much greater velocity than it would at sealevel.

Significance of V_p-maps.—The dynamic significance of the V_p-maps (which may be called topographic charts of isobaric surfaces, or maps showing the intersections of an isobaric surface by successive level surfaces of equal values of gravity), is seen from the fact that an air-particle moving on such an isobaric surface experiences the same acceleration as if it were confined to that surface and subject only to the force of gravity. Therefore, if we assume that an air-particle moves from a to b on the $V_{25.0}$-chart (see Fig. 11, page 69), and during this movement remains in the isobaric surface, $p = 25.0$, then the acceleration of the particle may be found by dividing the difference in gravity-potential at the points a and b by the length of the path of the particle or the distance between a and b. Now the gravity-potential at a equals $V_a = 74\,000 \frac{\text{mile}^2}{\text{hour}^2}$, and at b equals $V_b = 73\,000 \frac{\text{mile}^2}{\text{hour}^2}$, so that the difference in gravity-potential at the two points is $V_a - V_b = 1\,000 \frac{\text{mile}^2}{\text{hour}^2}$. The distance between a and b is approximately 140 miles, whence the acceleration of the particle of air is seen to be $\frac{1\,000}{140} = 7.14 \frac{\text{mile}}{\text{hour}^2}$. It is easy to calculate the velocity v_1 of the air-particle, when it arrives at b, from the velocity v_a it had at a and the difference in gravity-potential, $V_a - V_b$, by the aid of the well known formula

$$\frac{v_1^2 - v_0^2}{2} = V_a - V_b.$$

Thus if it be assumed that the velocity v_0 at the point a be $10\,\frac{\text{mile}}{\text{hour}}$ and that $V_a - V_b = 1\,000\,\frac{\text{mile}^2}{\text{hour}^2}$ then the velocity v_1 of the particle on arriving at b is obtained by solving the equation

$$v_1^2 = 10^2 + 2 \times 1\,000 = 2\,100$$

$$v_1 = \sqrt{2\,100} = 45{,}8\,\frac{\text{mile}}{\text{hour}}.$$

This method of using the map for calculating the acceleration of an air-particle from the length of its path and the difference in gravity-potential, and for calculating the velocity of the particle from the difference in gravity-potential and the initial velocity, may also be used when we consider relative movements, since the component of acceleration due to the Earth's rotation always acts in a direction at right angles to the path of the particle and thus has no effect upon the acceleration along this path.

The calculations have been carried out for a particle which always remains in the same isobaric surface. They are, however, equally applicable to particles moving within a slight distance from the given isobaric surface, because these surfaces, which lie very close to one another, have almost mutually parallel directions, and thus intersect very nearly the same number of level surfaces of gravity.

Comparison of V_p- and p_V-maps.— It seems to me that from a dynamic point of view the V_p-maps possess certain advantages over the p_V-maps. These advantages arise, partly, from the fact that the acceleration and the square of the velocity of a particle may be read directly from the V_p-maps without taking into consideration the density of the air, whereas the pressure-gradients obtained from the p_V-maps must first be divided by the density of the air in order to obtain these quantities. When we limit ourselves to purely qualitative considerations these advantages appear yet more striking; for the accelerations are directly proportional to the number of lines [between any two points] on the V_p charts and quite independent of altitude in the atmosphere. On the other hand, if the p_V-maps for two different levels show the same number of lines [within the same distance], then the air-particles at the higher level have the greater acceleration. It is thus seen that the V_p-maps for different levels are completely comparable with one another, while the p_V-maps are not.

Significance of $E_{p_s}^{p_s}$-maps. — The dynamic significance of the $E_{p_s}^{p_s}$-maps, Figs. 12–15, results from a principle in hydrodynamics recently stated by Prof. V. Bjerknes,* and I would first recall this principle. According to Lord Kelvin's definition, the circulation of a closed curve made up of atmospheric particles, consists of the sum of the tangential components of the velocity of every particle around the whole curve. If the velocity of a particle of the curve be designated by u, and the tangential component of this velocity along the curve by u_t, then the circulation "C" is expressed by the integral

$$C = \int u_t \delta s$$

where "δs" is a longitudinal element of the curve and the integration is to be carried out completely around the whole of the closed curve. This "circulation" is an expression for the rotatory movement of the atmosphere, for wherever the velocity of the air has a potential, there all closed curves have no "circulation"; and conversely, the more intense is the rotatory movement of the air so much the greater is the "circulation" of the closed curves.

By means of the integral just cited, the "circulation" of a closed curve in the atmosphere may be determined from simultaneous observations of the direction and velocity of the wind at different points on the curve. Bjerknes has given a theorem for calculating the increase or decrease of the "circulation" during a unit of time, by using the observations of pressure, temperature and humidity at points along the curve. If then we have the four elements — wind, pressure, temperature and relative humidity observed at any moment of time, for various points along a closed curve in the atmosphere we may calculate the "circulation" of that curve not only for the moment of observation, but also for a series of instants both preceding and following that moment. The theorem may be mathematically formulated as follows:

$$\frac{dC}{dt} = -\int v dp = A. \qquad (25)$$

Here dC/dt is the increase of circulation C in a unit of time; v is the specific volume of a particle of air on the curve, and p is the pressure prevailing at this particle. The integration is to be carried out around the whole closed curve and will give A = the number of solenoids,† enclosed within the closed curve. The law may then be stated as follows.

* See V. Bjerknes. "The dynamic principle of circulatory movements in the atmosphere." — *Monthly Weather Review*, Oct., 1900, p. 434.

† A solenoid is a tubular figure in the atmosphere arising from the intersections of surfaces of equal pressure, or isobaric surfaces, with surfaces of equal specific volume, or isosteric surfaces. The unit solenoid is found between two isobaric surfaces differing by the unit of pressure and two isosteric surfaces differing by the unit of specific volume.

The increase of circulation per unit of time, in a closed atmospheric curve made up of air-particles is equal to the total number of unit solenoids embraced within that curve.

Now the number and position of the solenoids in the atmosphere may be obtained in a very simple way from the $E^{25.0}_{27.5}$ maps. Thus we choose any two points a and b on any two of the lines of such a map as the $E^{25.0}_{27.5}$ map shown in Fig. 12, page 71. Imagine verticals falling from these points in the atmosphere to corresponding points on the isobaric surfaces $p=27.5$ and 25.0 which vertical lines we will designate also by the letters a and b. The lower ends of these verticals are connected by the line a–b, which lies wholly in the isobaric surface 25.0 and the upper ends are connected by the line a–b which lies wholly in the isobaric surface $p=27.5$. Thus is obtained a closed curve in the atmosphere consisting of two vertical portions aa and bb, and two isobaric portions, ab and ba. The number of solenoids within this closed curve may be determined by carrying out the integration $\int v dp$ around the whole curve. Now along the two isobaric portions ab and ba of the curve, both $v dp$ and $\int v dp$, are equal to zero so it only becomes necessary to perform the integration along the two verticals aa and bb. The integral along aa may be represented by $\left(\int_{25.0}^{27.5} v\cdot dp\right)_a$ and the integral along bb by $\left(\int_{25.0}^{27.5} v\cdot dp\right)_b$, then by virtue of equation (25) we have

$$A=\left(\int_{25.0}^{27.5} v\cdot dp\right)_a-\left(\int_{25.0}^{27.5} v\cdot dp\right)_b \tag{26}$$

which integral may be simplified by making use of the barometric formula *

$$dV=-v\cdot dp.$$

By integrating both sides of this latter formula along the vertical aa we find that

$$V_{25.0}-V_{27.5}=\left(\int_{25.0}^{27.5} v\cdot dp\right)_a.$$

If by $(E^{25.0}_{27.5})_a$ we designate the number of level surfaces of gravity lying between the 27.5- and 25.0-isobaric surfaces along the vertical a, then we may write

$$\left(\int_{25.0}^{27.5} v\cdot dp\right)_a=(E^{25.0}_{27.5})_a.$$

Whence from (7) we have

$$(V_{25.0}-V_{27.5})_a=(E^{25.0}_{27.5})_a.$$

Analogously we find that

$$\left(\int_{25.0}^{27.5} v\cdot dp\right)_b=(E^{25.0}_{27.5})_b.$$

* See equations (1) and (10).

By substituting these into (26) there results

$$A = (E_{27.5}^{25.0})_a - (E_{27.5}^{25.0})_b \qquad (27)$$

This formula holds true for any two points a and b on the $E_{27.5}^{25.0}$-map and for the corresponding closed curves in the atmosphere. For the points a and b shown on the $E_{27.5}^{25.0}$-map (Fig. 12) of page 71 we have $(E_{27.5}^{25.0})_a = 40\,200\ \frac{\text{mile}^2}{\text{hour}^2}$ and $(E_{27.5}^{25.0})_b = 40\,100\ \frac{\text{mile}^2}{\text{hour}^2}$, so that by equation 27, $A = 100\ \frac{\text{mile}^2}{\text{hour}^2}$. If now we move the points a and b of this map at will along the curves 40 200 and 40 100 respectively, and imagine the closed curve consisting of the verticals a and b, and the connecting lines lying in the isobaric surfaces of $p = 27.5$ and $p = 25.0$ as moving in a corresponding manner, then we see that during this movement the quantities $(E_{27.5}^{25.0})_a$ and $(E_{27.5}^{25.0})_b$, always retain the values 40 200 and 40 100 just calculated for them. Therefore the closed curve, even during its movement, always encloses 100 solenoids. We therefore conclude that the tubular structure in the atmosphere, bounded by vertical walls through the curves 40 200 and 40 100 and by the isobaric surfaces of $p = 27.5$ and $p = 25.0$, encloses exactly 100 unit solenoids whose courses must lie parallel to the curves 40 200 and 40 100. By a series of analogous operations we are led to the conclusion that there are always 100 solenoids between each pair of adjacent curves on the $E_{27.5}^{25.0}$-map (Fig. 12, page 71).

According to Bjerknes' theory these solenoids tend to set up a rotational movement in the atmosphere. The direction of this rotation is expressed by the rule that the air tends to rise where $E_{27.5}^{25.0}$ is large, and to sink where $E_{27.5}^{25.0}$ is small. Thus the movement resulting from the solenoid system of the chart of $E_{27.5}^{25.0}$, page 71, Fig. 12, is an ascending one in the vicinity of Pierre and Topeka, and a descending one in the outer portions of the region shown on the map.

Returning to the closed curve in the atmosphere indicated at ab in Fig. 12, we know first of all that it embraces 100 solenoids. Therefore from the preceding theorem we know that the increase of circulation along this closed curve is at the rate of 100 $\frac{\text{mile}^2}{\text{hour}^2}$ per hour, and that it is directed upward along the vertical a and downward along the vertical b. If this increase in the circulation be divided by the length of the line ab, which from measurement is seen to amount to 125 miles, then, according to the definition of circulation, we obtain a mean tangential acceleration of 0.8 $\frac{\text{mile}}{\text{hour}^2}$ for the air-particles composing the curve. In other words, if we assume that the air was originally at rest, and if we leave out of consideration the influences of friction and the earth's rotation, then this solenoid-system would have produced a mean velocity of 0.8 $\frac{\text{mile}}{\text{hour}}$ along the curve by the end of the first hour. At the end of the second hour the mean velocity would be 1.6 $\frac{\text{mile}}{\text{hour}}$; at the end of the third hour 2.4 $\frac{\text{mile}}{\text{hour}}$ and so on. By carrying out a number of such numerical calculations on the $E^{p_1}_{p_0}$-map one will soon become so familiar with the dynamic significance of its lines that a glance at the chart will suffice to recognize and read the accelerations indicated by it.

The $E^{27.5}_{25.0}$-map may be constructed directly from the values telegraphed to the central office; but after the complete results of the kite-observations at the different stations have been received by mail these maps may be constructed for much thinner strata in the atmosphere. Then, for instance, the layer of air between the isobaric surfaces for $p = 27.5$ and $p = 25.0$ can be subdivided into five strata whose dynamic condition can be presented by charts for $E^{27.5}_{27.0}$, $E^{27.0}_{26.5}$, $E^{26.5}_{26.0}$, $E^{26.0}_{25.5}$, $E^{25.5}_{25.0}$. On page 71 only three of these latter maps have been drawn, viz., for $E^{27.5}_{27.0}$ as Fig. 13; $E^{26.5}_{26.0}$ as Fig. 14; and $E^{26.0}_{25.5}$ as Fig. 15. From Fig. 13 it is seen that in the layer of air between the isobaric surfaces of 27.5 and 27.0, the maximum ascensive tendency is southeast of Topeka. The $E^{26.5}_{26.0}$-map, Fig. 14, shows that in the layer between the 26.5 and the 26.0 isobaric surfaces the air has its maximum ascensive tendency just over Topeka. The $E^{26.0}_{25.5}$-map of Fig. 15 shows the maximum ascensive tendency to be above Pierre and Dodge City. If we neglect this shift of the center of ascension toward the northwest then we find that the solenoids as drawn for the thinner strata have nearly the same characters as those drawn for the larger interval of the $E^{27.5}_{25.0}$-map. It suffices, therefore, to construct $E^{p_1}_{p_0}$-maps for thicker strata or greater intervals by aid of the telegraphic reports and afterward for smaller intervals by means of the more complete reports by mail. In this way very brief condensed telegraphic reports may be made to do good service.

The general expression for the number of solenoids within a closed curve consisting of two verticals a and b, and two curves lying in the isobaric surfaces $p = p_0$ and $p = p_1$, is

$$A = (E^{p_1}_{p_0})_a - (E^{p_1}_{p_0})_b \tag{28}$$

This may be deduced in exactly the same way as the special formula equation (27). It follows from equation (28) that each of the tubular-shaped figures in the atmosphere bounded by the isobaric surfaces $p = p_1$ and $p = p_0$, and the vertical walls, passing through the curves drawn on such a map, contains a number of solenoids equal to the number obtained by subtracting the numbers belonging to those latter curves. Hence it follows that in the maps forming Figs. 13, 14 and 15 of page 71 designated as E[illegible], E[illegible], E[illegible], there are always 50 solenoids between each pair of adjacent curved lines.

Significance of $H_{V_0}^{V_1}$-maps.—The dynamic significance of the charts of $H_{V_0}^{V_1}$ results from a second principle enunciated by Bjerknes.* If the velocity of the air be indicated by u, and the density of the air by ρ, then $\bar{u} = \rho u$ expresses the amount of the so-called specific quantity of motion of the air. The tangential component u_t of this quantity, when integrated along a closed curve, we call the "moment-circulation" of that curve. By moment-solenoid we designate the tubular figure formed in the atmosphere by surfaces of equal density (isodense surfaces) and by level surfaces of gravity, when these surfaces are constructed for each unit difference of density and of gravity potential, respectively. If we further assume that the barometric formula for static conditions also holds true under dynamic conditions, then Bjerknes' second theorem may be stated somewhat as follows:

The increase, during a unit of time, of the moment-circulation of a closed curve consisting of particles of air in the atmosphere, is equal to the number of moment-solenoids enclosed by that curve. We designate the moment-circulation of the closed curve by $\bar{C}$ and the number of enclosed moment-solenoids by $\bar{A}$; then this theorem is expressed by the formula

$$\frac{d\bar{C}}{dt} = \bar{A} = \int \rho d V \tag{29}$$

where integration is to be carried out along the whole closed curve. Now the numbers and positions of the moment-solenoids are readily determined from the $H_{V_0}^{V_1}$-maps. To demonstrate this let the closed atmospheric curve be composed of two lines ab and ab, lying in the level-surfaces of gravity $V = V_0$ and $V = V_1$ respectively, and of the two verticals aa and bb, joining the ends of these two lines. Then $\rho d V$, and $\int \rho d V$, each equal zero along the lines ab in the level surfaces and it only becomes necessary to carry out the integration along the verticals aa and bb.

Thus we obtain

$$\frac{d\bar{C}}{dt} = \left(\int_{V_0}^{V_1} \rho d V\right)_a - \left(\int_{V_0}^{V_1} \rho d V\right)_b. \tag{30}$$

By the aid of the static barometric formula

$$dp = -\rho d V$$

the above integrals may be transformed. The integration of this formula along the vertical aa gives

$$\left(\int_{V_0}^{V_1} \rho d V\right)_a = (p_{V_0} - p_{V_1})_a$$

* V. Bjerknes—"On the formation of circulatory movements and vortices in frictionless fluids."—*Christiania, Videnskabsselskabets Skriften*, 1898, No. 5.

but

$$(p_{V_0} - p_{V_1})_a = (\Pi^{V_0}_{V_1})_a$$

hence

$$\left(\int_{V_1}^{V_0} \rho\, dV\right)_a = (\Pi^{V_0}_{V_1})_a .$$

In an analogous way,

$$\left(\int_{V_1}^{V_0} \rho\, dV\right)_b = (\Pi^{V_0}_{V_1})_b .$$

Then by substitutions in (30) we have

$$A = (\Pi^{V_0}_{V_1})_a - (\Pi^{V_0}_{V_1})_b . \tag{31}$$

The number of moment-solenoids, A, has therefore the same dimensions as a pressure, *i. e.*,

$$\frac{\text{mass}}{\text{length, time}^2}$$

or its equivalent,

$$\text{density} \times \frac{\text{length}^2}{\text{time}^2} .$$

If the specific gravity, ρ_0, of water at its maximum density be selected as our unit of density, then

$$\text{a pressure of 1 inch of the mercurial column} = 16.945 \times \rho_0 \times \frac{\text{mile}^2}{\text{hour}^2}$$

If we choose the density of air, ρ_1, at 32° F. and 1 atmosphere of pressure as the unit of density, then

$$\text{a pressure of 1 inch of the mercurial column} = 13\,105 \times \rho_1 \times \frac{\text{mile}^2}{\text{hour}^2}$$

Finally if $\rho_2 = 0.169\,45\ \rho_0$ be chosen as unit of density, then

$$\text{a pressure of 1 inch of the mercurial column} = 100 \times \rho_2 \times \frac{\text{mile}^2}{\text{hour}^2}$$

Therefore a closed curve composed of two verticals *aa* and *bb*, and two lines, *ab* and *ab* lying in the level surfaces $V = V_0$ and $V = V_1$ respectively, for which curve we have $A = (\Pi^{V_0}_{V_1})_a - (\Pi^{V_0}_{V_1})_b = 1$ inch of the mercurial barometer column, embraces 16.945 moment-solenoids of the $\rho_0 \cdot \frac{\text{mile}^2}{\text{hour}^2}$ -system of dimensions; or 13 105 moment-solenoids of the $\rho_1 \cdot \frac{\text{mile}^2}{\text{hour}^2}$ -system, or 100 moment-solenoids of the $\rho_2 \cdot \frac{\text{mile}^2}{\text{hour}^2}$ -system.

On the $\Pi^{V_0}_{V_1}$-chart, see pages 67, 69. Figs. 4, 5, 9, curves for each 0.01 inch difference of pressure have been drawn. Therefore each of the tubular figures in the atmosphere bounded by vertical walls through any two adjacent curves of these maps, and by the two level surfaces of gravity, $V = V_0$ and $V = V_1$, embraces

$$0.16945\ \rho_0\ \frac{\text{mile}^2}{\text{hour}^2}\ \text{moment-solenoids,}$$

or

$$131.05\ \rho_1\ \frac{\text{mile}^2}{\text{hour}^2}\ \text{moment-solenoids,}$$

or

$$1 \times \rho_2\ \frac{\text{mile}^2}{\text{hour}^2}\ \text{moment-solenoids}$$

according to the standard unit that we adopt.

These moment-solenoids tend to direct the specific quantity of motion upward at places where $\Pi^{V_1}_{V_0}$ is small, and downward at points where $\Pi^{V_1}_{V_0}$ is large. Accordingly, the air lying between the level surfaces $V = 0$ and $V = 40\,000$ (see Fig. 4) will be pushed upward most strongly in the region northeastward from Omaha. The $\Pi^{60\,000}_{40\,000}$-map (see Fig. 9) shows the greatest ascensive tendency to be over Topeka, and the $\Pi^{80\,000}_{40\,000}$-map (see Fig. 5) shows the greatest upward force to be westward from Pierre.

With the aid of these $\Pi^{V_1}_{V_0}$-maps such numerical examples showing the specific quantity of motion can be computed, just as corresponding examples for the velocity were computed from the $E^{V_1}_{V_0}$-maps. It seems to me, however, that from a dynamical point of view the specific quantity of motion is a less convenient quantity than the velocity. Probably the $\Pi^{V_1}_{V_0}$-charts will only be used in working on certain special problems, such as the comparison of movements in media of such different densities, as the air and the ocean; or when one wishes to calculate the mass of air transported by the winds.

VI.

Concluding Remarks.

The connection of the charts that we have here drawn for the higher atmospheric strata with the dynamics of the atmosphere must be clear from the preceding pages. It is to be expected that upon such maps we may easily and naturally present our observations and experience as to atmospheric movements and therefore, it would seem to promise good results if the daily weather-predictions could be based upon such maps. At least this latter is practicable in so far as it would require not more than an hour to work up the data necessary for the telegraphic reports from the kite stations. Certainly within one and a half hours after the descent of the last kite these maps could be drawn and finished at the central office of the Weather Bureau.

On the other hand, practical difficulties will certainly be experienced, through occasional inability to make kite ascensions at the proper hour of the day at a sufficient number of stations. But it is to be expected that better results will be attained as the technique of kite-flying develops. In any case it is very desirable that kite-observations be supplemented by observations of another character. Such supplementary observations are indeed supplied by the measurements of cloud heights and cloud velocities. But in order to utilize these we must make use of the Bjerknes theorem of circulation as perfected by taking into account the earth's rotation. I hope soon to return to the consideration of cloud-observations as supplementary to the high-level charts, and also to the consideration of the importance of such charts in weather prediction.

APPENDIX.

FORMULÆ AND TABLES IN THE METRIC SYSTEM (DATED OCTOBER, 1902).*

It is easy to convert the formulæ and tables of the preceding memoir from English into metric measures by using the following relations:

$$\text{Velocity, } 1\ \frac{\text{mile}}{\text{hour}} = 0.447\ 032\ \frac{\text{meter}}{\text{second}}.$$

$$\text{Acceleration of velocity, } 1\ \frac{\text{mile}}{\text{hour}^2} = 0.000\ 124\ 175\ 5\ \frac{\text{meter}}{\text{second}^2}.$$

$$\text{Circulation, } 1\ \frac{\text{mile}^2}{\text{hour}} = 719.415\ \frac{\text{meter}^2}{\text{second}}.$$

$$\text{Acceleration of circulation, } 1\ \frac{\text{mile}^2}{\text{hour}^2} = 0.199\ 837\ 5\ \frac{\text{meter}^2}{\text{second}^2}.$$

The formulæ of this memoir thus become converted respectively into the following, where the units are the meter, the second of mean solar time and the degree centigrade:

(2) $g = g_o(1 - 0.000\ 000\ 314(z - z_o))$.

(3) $g = g_o(1 + 0.000\ 000\ 196(z_o - z))$.

(4) $V_o = g_o z_o(1 + 0.000\ 000\ 098 z_o)$.

(5) $V = V_o + g_o z_1(1 - 0.000\ 000\ 157 z_1)$.

(6) $g_o = 9.80604(1 - 0.00259 \cos 2\lambda)(1 - 0.000\ 000\ 196 z_o)$.

(17) $$E^{p_1}_{p_0} = \frac{0.760 \times 9.80604 \times 13.59593}{0.001293052 \times 273} \int_{p_1}^{p_0} T \frac{dp}{p}.$$

(18) $$E^{p_1}_{p_0} = 660.9 \int_{p_1}^{p_0} (t + 273) d(\log p).$$

(19) $$\Pi^{r_1}_{r_0} = p_{r_0}\left(1 - 10^{-\frac{1}{660.9}\int_{r_0}^{r_1}\frac{dr}{t+273}}\right).$$

(20) $$t_r - t = \frac{0.377 rf(t + 273)}{p - 0.377 rf}.$$

* In order to meet any possible question of priority or responsibility it is proper to say that this memoir by J. W. Sandström was received by Professor Cleveland Abbe in April, 1902, with permission to translate and publish: the appendix in metric measures was received in October, 1902. The translation by Dr. Cleveland Abbe, junior, was finished during 1903, and was read by Professor Abbe at the annual meeting of the American Philosophical Society, April, 1905. — C. A.

(21) $$E_{p_0}^{p_1} = 660.9\int_{p_1}^{p_0}(t_v + 273)\,d(\log p).$$

(22) $$\Pi_{V_0}^{V_1} = p_{V_0}\left(1 - 10^{-\frac{1}{660.9}\int_{V_0}^{V_1}\frac{dV}{t_v+273}}\right).$$

(23) $$E_{p_0}^{p_1} = 660.9(t_v + 273)\log\frac{p_0}{p_1}.$$

(24) $$\Pi_{V_0}^{V_1} = p_{V_0}\left(1 - 10^{-\frac{V_1-V_0}{660.9(t_v+273)}}\right).$$

From formula (23) it results that

E = 7.267 (t_v + 273°)	E = 9.731 (t_v + 273°)
E = 7.456 (")	E = 10.072 (")
E = 7.654 (")	E = 10.438 (")
E = 7.864 (")	E = 10.832 (")
E = 8.086 (")	E = 11.257 (")
E = 8.320 (")	E = 11.717 (")
E = 8.569 (")	E = 12.216 (")
E = 8.832 (")	E = 12.759 (")
E = 9.113 (")	E = 13.352 (")
E = 9.411 (t_v + 273°)	E = 14.004 (t_v + 273°)

If we put $V_1 = V_0 + 2\,000$ then from equation (24) we get

$$\Pi_{V_0}^{V_0+2000} = p_{V_0}\left(1 - 10^{-\frac{2000}{660.9(t_v+273)}}\right).$$

The other equations will not be changed by the introduction of the metric system of measures.

In the following pages are given the most important metric tables, numbered the same as the corresponding tables in English measures in the preceding memoir:

Table 1 in the Metric System.

$z_1\,(1-0.000000157\,z_1)$.

z_1 = altitude =	1000	2000	3000	4000	5000	6000	7000	8000	9000	10000 meters
$(V-V_a)/g_a$ =	999.8	1999.4	2998.6	3997.5	4996.1	5994.4	6992.4	7990.0	8987.3	9984.3

Table 4 in the Metric System.

The Acceleration of Gravity at Sealevel in Meters per Second.

Geographic Latitude λ.	0°	1°	2°	3°	4°	5°	6°	7°	8°	9°
0°	9.7806	9.7807	9.7807	9.7808	9.7809	9.7810	9.7812	9.7814	9.7816	9.7819
10	9.7822	9.7825	9.7828	9.7832	9.7836	9.7840	9.7845	9.7850	9.7855	9.7860
20	9.7866	9.7872	9.7878	9.7884	9.7891	9.7897	9.7904	9.7911	9.7919	9.7926
30	9.7934	9.7941	9.7949	9.7957	9.7965	9.7974	9.7982	9.7990	9.7999	9.8008
40	9.8016	9.8025	9.8034	9.8043	9.8052	9.8060	9.8069	9.8078	9.8087	9.8096
50	9.8105	9.8113	9.8122	9.8130	9.8139	9.8147	9.8156	9.8164	9.8172	9.8180
60	9.8187	9.8195	9.8202	9.8210	9.8217	9.8224	9.8230	9.8237	9.8243	9.8249
70	9.8255	9.8261	9.8266	9.8271	9.8276	9.8280	9.8285	9.8288	9.8292	9.8296
80	9.8299	9.8302	9.8305	9.8307	9.8309	9.8311	9.8312	9.8313	9.8314	9.8314

Table 5 in the Metric System.

Decrease of Gravity with Altitude above Sealevel.

Altitude in meters	1000	2000	3000	4000	5000	6000	7000	8000	9000	10000
Decrease of g	−0.0019	−0.0038	−0.0058	−0.0077	−0.0096	−0.0115	−0.0135	−0.0154	−0.0173	−0.0192

TABLE 6 IN THE METRIC SYSTEM.

THE ALTITUDES IN METERS ABOVE SEALEVEL OF THE LEVEL SURFACES OF GRAVITY.

V_0	λ Geographic Latitude.										V_0
	0°	10°	20°	30°	40°	50°	60°	70°	80°	90°	
	Meter.	Meter.	Meter.	Meter.	Meter.	Meter.	Meter.	Meter.	Meter.	Meter.	
0	0	0	0	0	0	0	0	0	0	0	0
1000	102.2	102.2	102.2	102.1	102.0	101.9	101.8	101.8	101.7	101.7	1000
2000	204.5	204.5	204.4	204.2	204.1	203.9	203.7	203.6	203.5	203.4	2000
3000	306.7	306.7	306.6	306.3	306.1	305.8	305.5	305.3	305.2	305.2	3000
4000	409.0	408.9	408.7	408.4	408.1	407.7	407.4	407.1	406.9	406.9	4000
5000	511.2	511.1	510.9	510.6	510.1	509.7	509.2	508.9	508.7	508.6	5000
6000	613.5	613.4	613.1	612.7	612.2	611.6	611.1	610.7	610.4	610.3	6000
7000	715.8	715.7	715.3	714.8	714.2	713.6	712.9	712.5	712.2	712.0	7000
8000	818.0	817.9	817.5	816.9	816.3	815.5	814.8	814.3	813.9	813.8	8000
9000	920.3	920.2	919.7	919.1	918.3	917.4	916.7	916.1	915.6	915.5	9000
10000	1022.5	1022.4	1021.9	1021.2	1020.3	1019.4	1018.6	1017.9	1017.4	1017.3	10000
11000	1124.8	1124.6	1124.1	1123.3	1122.4	1121.3	1120.4	1119.7	1119.2	1119.0	11000
12000	1227.1	1226.9	1226.3	1225.5	1224.4	1223.3	1222.3	1221.5	1220.9	1220.7	12000
13000	1329.3	1329.1	1328.5	1327.6	1326.5	1325.3	1324.2	1323.3	1322.7	1322.5	13000
14000	1431.6	1431.4	1430.7	1429.7	1428.5	1427.2	1426.0	1425.1	1424.4	1424.2	14000
15000	1533.9	1533.6	1532.9	1531.9	1530.6	1529.2	1527.9	1526.9	1526.2	1526.0	15000
16000	1636.1	1635.9	1635.1	1634.0	1632.6	1631.2	1629.8	1628.7	1627.9	1627.7	16000
17000	1738.4	1738.1	1737.4	1736.1	1734.7	1733.1	1731.7	1730.5	1729.7	1729.4	17000
18000	1840.7	1840.4	1839.6	1838.3	1836.8	1835.1	1833.6	1832.3	1831.4	1831.2	18000
19000	1943.0	1942.7	1941.8	1940.4	1938.8	1937.1	1935.5	1934.1	1933.2	1932.9	19000
20000	2045.3	2044.9	2044.0	2042.6	2040.9	2039.0	2037.3	2035.9	2035.0	2034.7	20000
21000	2147.6	2147.2	2146.2	2144.7	2143.0	2141.0	2139.2	2137.7	2136.8	2136.5	21000
22000	2249.9	2249.5	2248.5	2246.9	2245.0	2243.0	2241.1	2239.6	2238.6	2238.2	22000
23000	2352.1	2351.8	2350.7	2349.1	2347.1	2345.0	2343.0	2341.4	2340.3	2340.0	23000
24000	2454.4	2454.0	2452.9	2451.2	2449.2	2446.9	2444.9	2443.2	2442.1	2441.7	24000
25000	2556.7	2556.3	2555.1	2553.4	2551.2	2548.9	2546.8	2545.0	2543.9	2543.5	25000
26000	2659.0	2658.6	2657.4	2655.5	2653.3	2650.9	2648.7	2646.9	2645.7	2645.3	26000
27000	2761.3	2760.9	2759.6	2757.7	2755.4	2752.9	2750.6	2748.7	2747.5	2747.0	27000
28000	2863.6	2863.1	2861.9	2859.9	2857.5	2854.9	2852.5	2850.5	2849.3	2848.8	28000
29000	2965.9	2965.4	2964.1	2962.0	2959.6	2956.9	2954.4	2952.4	2951.0	2950.6	29000
30000	3068.2	3067.6	3066.3	3064.2	3061.6	3058.9	3056.3	3054.2	3052.8	3052.4	30000

Table 7 in the Metric System.

The Values of $t_1 - t$ for any Pressure and Temperature and saturated Air.

Temp. Cent. t	400	420	440	460	480	500	520	540	560	580	600	620	640	660	680	700	720	740	760	780	800	Temp. Cent. t
	Barometric Pressure in mm.																					
−30°	0.1	0.1	0.1	0.1	0.1	0.1	0.1	0.1	0.1	0.1	0.1	0.1	0.1	0.1	0.1	0.0	0.0	0.0	0.0	0.0	0.0	−30°
−20	0.2	0.2	0.2	0.2	0.2	0.2	0.2	0.2	0.2	0.2	0.2	0.2	0.2	0.2	0.1	0.1	0.1	0.1	0.1	0.1	0.1	−20
−15	0.4	0.3	0.3	0.3	0.3	0.3	0.3	0.3	0.3	0.3	0.3	0.2	0.2	0.2	0.2	0.2	0.2	0.2	0.2	0.2	0.2	−15
−10	0.5	0.5	0.5	0.5	0.4	0.4	0.4	0.4	0.4	0.4	0.4	0.4	0.3	0.3	0.3	0.3	0.3	0.3	0.2	0.2	0.2	−10
− 8	0.6	0.6	0.6	0.6	0.5	0.5	0.5	0.5	0.5	0.4	0.4	0.4	0.4	0.4	0.4	0.4	0.4	0.3	0.3	0.3	0.3	− 8
− 6	0.7	0.7	0.7	0.7	0.6	0.6	0.6	0.6	0.5	0.5	0.5	0.5	0.5	0.5	0.4	0.4	0.4	0.4	0.4	0.3	0.3	− 6
− 4	0.9	0.8	0.8	0.8	0.7	0.7	0.7	0.6	0.6	0.6	0.6	0.6	0.5	0.5	0.5	0.5	0.5	0.5	0.5	0.5	0.4	− 4
− 2	1.0	1.0	0.9	0.9	0.8	0.8	0.8	0.7	0.7	0.7	0.7	0.6	0.6	0.6	0.6	0.6	0.6	0.6	0.5	0.5	0.5	− 2
0	1.2	1.1	1.1	1.0	1.0	0.9	0.9	0.9	0.8	0.8	0.8	0.8	0.7	0.7	0.7	0.7	0.7	0.6	0.6	0.6	0.6	0
1	1.3	1.2	1.2	1.1	1.1	1.0	1.0	0.9	0.9	0.9	0.9	0.8	0.8	0.8	0.8	0.7	0.7	0.7	0.7	0.6	0.6	1
2	1.4	1.3	1.2	1.2	1.1	1.1	1.1	1.0	1.0	0.9	0.9	0.9	0.9	0.8	0.8	0.8	0.8	0.7	0.7	0.7	0.7	2
3	1.5	1.4	1.3	1.3	1.2	1.2	1.1	1.1	1.1	1.0	1.0	1.0	0.9	0.9	0.9	0.8	0.8	0.8	0.8	0.8	0.7	3
4	1.6	1.5	1.5	1.4	1.3	1.3	1.2	1.2	1.1	1.1	1.1	1.0	1.0	1.0	0.9	0.9	0.9	0.9	0.8	0.8	0.8	4
5	1.7	1.6	1.6	1.5	1.4	1.4	1.3	1.3	1.2	1.2	1.1	1.1	1.1	1.0	1.0	1.0	1.0	0.9	0.9	0.9	0.8	5
6	1.8	1.7	1.7	1.6	1.5	1.5	1.4	1.4	1.3	1.3	1.2	1.2	1.2	1.1	1.1	1.1	1.0	1.0	1.0	0.9	0.9	6
7	2.0	1.9	1.8	1.7	1.7	1.6	1.5	1.5	1.4	1.4	1.3	1.3	1.2	1.2	1.2	1.1	1.1	1.1	1.0	1.0	1.0	7
8	2.1	2.0	1.9	1.9	1.8	1.7	1.6	1.6	1.5	1.5	1.4	1.4	1.3	1.3	1.3	1.2	1.2	1.1	1.1	1.1	1.0	8
9	2.3	2.2	2.1	2.0	1.9	1.8	1.8	1.7	1.6	1.6	1.5	1.5	1.4	1.4	1.3	1.3	1.3	1.2	1.2	1.2	1.1	9
10	2.5	2.3	2.2	2.1	2.0	2.0	1.9	1.8	1.7	1.7	1.6	1.6	1.5	1.5	1.4	1.4	1.4	1.3	1.3	1.3	1.2	10
11	2.6	2.5	2.4	2.3	2.2	2.1	2.0	1.9	1.9	1.8	1.8	1.7	1.6	1.6	1.5	1.5	1.5	1.4	1.4	1.3	1.3	11
12	2.8	2.7	2.6	2.5	2.4	2.3	2.2	2.1	2.0	1.9	1.9	1.8	1.8	1.7	1.7	1.6	1.6	1.5	1.5	1.4	1.4	12
13	3.0	2.9	2.8	2.6	2.5	2.4	2.3	2.2	2.2	2.1	2.0	1.9	1.9	1.8	1.8	1.7	1.7	1.6	1.6	1.5	1.5	13
14	3.3	3.1	3.0	2.8	2.7	2.6	2.5	2.4	2.3	2.2	2.2	2.1	2.0	2.0	1.9	1.8	1.8	1.7	1.7	1.7	1.6	14
15	3.5	3.3	3.2	3.0	2.9	2.8	2.7	2.6	2.5	2.4	2.3	2.2	2.2	2.1	2.0	2.0	1.9	1.9	1.8	1.8	1.7	15
16	3.7	3.5	3.4	3.2	3.1	3.0	2.9	2.8	2.7	2.6	2.5	2.4	2.3	2.2	2.2	2.1	2.1	2.0	2.0	1.9	1.8	16
17	4.0	3.8	3.6	3.5	3.3	3.2	3.1	3.0	2.8	2.7	2.6	2.6	2.5	2.4	2.3	2.3	2.2	2.1	2.1	2.0	2.0	17
18	4.3	4.1	3.9	3.7	3.5	3.4	3.3	3.2	3.0	2.9	2.8	2.7	2.7	2.6	2.5	2.4	2.4	2.3	2.2	2.2	2.1	18
19	4.6	4.3	4.1	4.0	3.8	3.6	3.5	3.4	3.2	3.1	3.0	2.9	2.8	2.8	2.7	2.6	2.5	2.4	2.4	2.3	2.2	19
20	4.9	4.6	4.4	4.2	4.1	3.9	3.7	3.6	3.5	3.3	3.2	3.1	3.0	2.9	2.9	2.8	2.7	2.6	2.5	2.5	2.4	20
21	5.2	5.0	4.7	4.5	4.3	4.2	4.0	3.8	3.7	3.6	3.5	3.3	3.2	3.1	3.0	3.0	2.9	2.8	2.7	2.6	2.5	21
22	5.6	5.3	5.0	4.8	4.6	4.4	4.3	4.1	3.9	3.8	3.7	3.6	3.4	3.3	3.2	3.2	3.1	3.0	2.9	2.8	2.7	22
23	5.9	5.7	5.4	5.1	4.9	4.7	4.5	4.4	4.2	4.1	3.9	3.8	3.7	3.6	3.5	3.4	3.3	3.2	3.1	3.0	2.9	23
24			5.7	5.5	5.2	5.0	4.9	4.7	4.5	4.3	4.2	4.0	3.9	3.8	3.7	3.6	3.5	3.4	3.3	3.2	3.1	24
25				5.9	5.6	5.4	5.2	5.0	4.8	4.6	4.5	4.3	4.2	4.1	3.9	3.8	3.7	3.6	3.5	3.4	3.3	25
26						5.7	5.5	5.3	5.1	4.9	4.8	4.6	4.5	4.3	4.2	4.1	4.0	3.8	3.7	3.6	3.5	26
27							5.9	5.6	5.4	5.3	5.1	4.9	4.7	4.6	4.5	4.3	4.2	4.1	4.0	3.9	3.8	27
28									5.8	5.6	5.4	5.2	5.1	4.9	4.8	4.6	4.5	4.4	4.3	4.1	4.0	28
29										5.9	5.7	5.6	5.4	5.2	5.1	4.9	4.8	4.6	4.5	4.4	4.3	29
30												5.9	5.7	5.5	5.4	5.2	5.1	4.9	4.8	4.7	4.5	30
31														5.9	5.7	5.6	5.4	5.2	5.1	5.0	4.8	31
32																5.9	5.7	5.6	5.4	5.3	5.2	32
33																		5.9	5.8	5.6	5.5	33
34																				6.0	5.8	34
	400	420	440	460	480	500	520	540	560	580	600	620	640	660	680	700	720	740	760	780	800	

Table 8 in the Metric System.

The Values of $t_r - t$ for any Value of $t_1 - t$ and Relative Humidity.

Relative Humidity.	t_1-t.															Relative Humidity.
	0.2	0.4	0.6	0.8	1.0	1.2	1.4	1.6	1.8	2.0	2.2	2.4	2.6	2.8	3.0	
10%	0.0	0.0	0.1	0.1	0.1	0.1	0.1	0.2	0.2	0.2	0.2	0.2	0.3	0.3	0.3	10%
20	0.0	0.1	0.1	0.2	0.2	0.2	0.3	0.3	0.4	0.4	0.4	0.5	0.5	0.6	0.6	20
30	0.1	0.1	0.2	0.2	0.3	0.4	0.4	0.5	0.5	0.6	0.7	0.7	0.8	0.8	0.9	30
40	0.1	0.2	0.2	0.3	0.4	0.5	0.6	0.6	0.7	0.8	0.9	1.0	1.0	1.1	1.2	40
50	0.1	0.2	0.3	0.4	0.5	0.6	0.7	0.8	0.9	1.0	1.1	1.2	1.3	1.4	1.5	50
60	0.1	0.2	0.4	0.5	0.6	0.7	0.8	1.0	1.1	1.2	1.3	1.4	1.6	1.7	1.8	60
70	0.1	0.3	0.4	0.6	0.7	0.8	1.0	1.1	1.3	1.4	1.5	1.7	1.8	2.0	2.1	70
80	0.2	0.3	0.5	0.6	0.8	1.0	1.1	1.3	1.4	1.6	1.8	1.9	2.1	2.2	2.4	80
90	0.2	0.4	0.5	0.7	0.9	1.1	1.3	1.4	1.6	1.8	2.0	2.2	2.3	2.5	2.7	90
100	0.2	0.4	0.6	0.8	1.0	1.2	1.4	1.6	1.8	2.0	2.2	2.4	2.6	2.8	3.0	100

Relative Humidity.	t_1-t.															Relative Humidity.
	3.2	3.4	3.6	3.8	4.0	4.2	4.4	4.6	4.8	5.0	5.2	5.4	5.6	5.8	6.0	
10%	0.3	0.3	0.4	0.4	0.4	0.4	0.4	0.5	0.5	0.5	0.5	0.5	0.6	0.6	0.6	10%
20	0.6	0.7	0.7	0.8	0.8	0.8	0.9	0.9	1.0	1.0	1.0	1.1	1.1	1.2	1.2	20
30	1.0	1.0	1.1	1.1	1.2	1.3	1.3	1.4	1.4	1.5	1.6	1.6	1.7	1.7	1.8	30
40	1.3	1.4	1.4	1.5	1.6	1.7	1.8	1.8	1.9	2.0	2.1	2.2	2.2	2.3	2.4	40
50	1.6	1.7	1.8	1.9	2.0	2.1	2.2	2.3	2.4	2.5	2.6	2.7	2.8	2.9	3.0	50
60	1.9	2.0	2.2	2.3	2.4	2.5	2.6	2.8	2.9	3.0	3.1	3.2	3.4	3.5	3.6	60
70	2.2	2.4	2.5	2.7	2.8	2.9	3.1	3.2	3.4	3.5	3.6	3.8	3.9	4.1	4.2	70
80	2.6	2.7	2.9	3.0	3.2	3.4	3.5	3.7	3.8	4.0	4.2	4.3	4.5	4.6	4.8	80
90	2.9	3.1	3.2	3.4	3.6	3.8	4.0	4.1	4.3	4.5	4.7	4.9	5.0	5.2	5.4	90
100	3.2	3.4	3.6	3.8	4.0	4.2	4.4	4.6	4.8	5.0	5.2	5.4	5.6	5.8	6.0	100

Table 9 in the Metric System.

The Values of $E^{b_0}_{b}$.

t_c	E^{780}_{800}	E^{760}_{780}	E^{740}_{760}	E^{720}_{740}	E^{700}_{720}	E^{680}_{700}	E^{660}_{680}	E^{640}_{660}	E^{620}_{640}	E^{600}_{620}	E^{580}_{600}	E^{560}_{580}	E^{540}_{560}	E^{520}_{540}	E^{500}_{520}	E^{480}_{500}	E^{460}_{480}	E^{440}_{460}	E^{420}_{440}	E^{400}_{420}	t_c
°C.																					°C.
−20	1839	1886	1936	1990	2046	2105	2168	2234	2306	2381	2462	2548	2641	2740	2848	2964	3091	3228	3378	3543	−20
−19	1846	1894	1944	1997	2054	2113	2177	2243	2315	2390	2472	2558	2651	2751	2859	2976	3103	3241	3391	3557	−19
−18	1853	1901	1952	2005	2062	2122	2185	2252	2324	2400	2481	2568	2662	2762	2871	2988	3115	3254	3405	3571	−18
−17	1860	1909	1959	2013	2070	2130	2194	2261	2333	2409	2491	2578	2672	2773	2882	3000	3127	3266	3418	3585	−17
−16	1868	1916	1967	2021	2078	2138	2202	2270	2342	2419	2501	2589	2683	2784	2893	3011	3140	3279	3431	3599	−16
−15	1875	1924	1975	2029	2086	2147	2211	2279	2351	2428	2511	2599	2693	2795	2904	3023	3152	3292	3445	3613	−15
−14	1882	1931	1982	2037	2094	2155	2219	2287	2360	2437	2520	2609	2703	2805	2916	3035	3164	3305	3458	3627	−14
−13	1889	1939	1990	2045	2102	2163	2228	2296	2369	2447	2530	2619	2714	2816	2927	3046	3176	3317	3472	3641	−13
−12	1897	1946	1998	2053	2110	2172	2237	2305	2378	2456	2540	2629	2724	2827	2938	3058	3188	3330	3485	3655	−12
−11	1904	1953	2005	2060	2119	2180	2245	2314	2388	2466	2550	2639	2735	2838	2949	3070	3201	3343	3498	3669	−11
−10	1911	1961	2013	2068	2127	2188	2254	2323	2397	2475	2559	2649	2745	2849	2961	3082	3213	3356	3512	3683	−10
−9	1918	1968	2021	2076	2135	2196	2262	2332	2406	2485	2569	2659	2756	2860	2972	3093	3225	3368	3525	3697	−9
−8	1926	1976	2028	2084	2143	2205	2271	2340	2415	2494	2579	2669	2766	2870	2983	3105	3237	3381	3538	3711	−8
−7	1933	1983	2036	2092	2151	2213	2279	2349	2424	2503	2588	2679	2777	2881	2994	3117	3249	3394	3552	3725	−7
−6	1940	1991	2044	2100	2159	2221	2288	2358	2433	2513	2598	2689	2787	2892	3006	3128	3262	3407	3565	3739	−6
−5	1948	1998	2051	2108	2167	2230	2296	2367	2442	2522	2608	2699	2797	2903	3017	3140	3274	3419	3578	3753	−5
−4	1955	2006	2059	2115	2175	2238	2305	2376	2451	2532	2618	2709	2808	2914	3028	3152	3286	3432	3592	3767	−4
−3	1962	2013	2067	2123	2183	2246	2314	2385	2461	2541	2627	2719	2818	2925	3039	3164	3298	3445	3605	3781	−3
−2	1969	2021	2074	2131	2191	2255	2322	2393	2470	2550	2637	2729	2829	2935	3051	3175	3311	3458	3618	3795	−2
−1	1977	2028	2082	2139	2199	2263	2331	2402	2479	2560	2647	2740	2839	2946	3062	3187	3323	3470	3632	3809	−1
0	1984	2035	2090	2147	2207	2271	2339	2411	2488	2569	2657	2750	2850	2957	3073	3199	3335	3483	3645	3823	0
1	1991	2043	2097	2155	2216	2280	2348	2420	2497	2579	2666	2760	2860	2968	3084	3210	3347	3496	3658	3837	1
2	1998	2050	2105	2163	2224	2288	2356	2429	2506	2588	2676	2770	2870	2979	3096	3222	3359	3509	3672	3851	2
3	2006	2058	2113	2170	2232	2296	2365	2438	2515	2597	2686	2780	2881	2990	3107	3234	3372	3521	3685	3865	3
4	2013	2065	2120	2178	2240	2305	2374	2446	2524	2607	2696	2790	2891	3000	3118	3246	3384	3534	3699	3879	4
5	2020	2073	2128	2186	2248	2313	2382	2455	2533	2616	2705	2800	2902	3011	3129	3257	3396	3547	3712	3893	5
6	2027	2080	2135	2194	2256	2321	2391	2464	2543	2626	2715	2810	2912	3022	3141	3269	3408	3560	3725	3907	6
7	2035	2088	2143	2202	2264	2330	2399	2473	2552	2635	2725	2820	2923	3033	3152	3281	3420	3573	3739	3921	7
8	2042	2095	2151	2210	2272	2338	2408	2482	2561	2644	2734	2830	2933	3044	3163	3292	3433	3585	3752	3935	8
9	2049	2103	2158	2218	2280	2346	2416	2491	2570	2654	2744	2840	2944	3055	3174	3304	3445	3598	3765	3949	9
10	2057	2110	2166	2226	2288	2355	2425	2499	2579	2663	2754	2850	2954	3065	3186	3316	3457	3611	3779	3963	10
11	2064	2118	2174	2233	2296	2363	2434	2508	2588	2673	2764	2860	2964	3076	3197	3328	3469	3624	3792	3977	11
12	2071	2125	2181	2241	2305	2371	2442	2517	2597	2682	2773	2871	2975	3087	3208	3339	3482	3636	3805	3991	12
13	2078	2132	2189	2249	2313	2380	2451	2526	2606	2692	2783	2881	2985	3098	3220	3351	3494	3649	3819	4005	13
14	2086	2140	2197	2257	2321	2388	2459	2535	2615	2701	2793	2891	2996	3109	3231	3363	3506	3662	3832	4019	14
15	2093	2147	2204	2265	2329	2396	2468	2544	2625	2710	2803	2901	3006	3120	3242	3374	3518	3675	3845	4033	15
16	2100	2155	2212	2273	2337	2404	2476	2552	2634	2720	2812	2911	3017	3130	3253	3386	3530	3687	3859	4047	16
17	2107	2162	2220	2281	2345	2413	2485	2561	2643	2729	2822	2921	3027	3141	3265	3398	3543	3700	3872	4061	17
18	2115	2170	2227	2288	2353	2421	2494	2570	2652	2739	2832	2931	3037	3152	3276	3410	3555	3713	3885	4075	18
19	2122	2177	2235	2296	2361	2429	2502	2579	2661	2748	2841	2941	3048	3163	3287	3421	3567	3726	3899	4089	19
20	2129	2185	2243	2304	2369	2438	2511	2588	2670	2757	2851	2951	3058	3174	3298	3433	3579	3738	3912	4103	20
21	2136	2192	2250	2312	2377	2446	2519	2597	2679	2767	2861	2961	3069	3185	3310	3445	3592	3751	3925	4117	21
22	2144	2200	2258	2320	2385	2454	2528	2605	2688	2776	2871	2971	3079	3195	3321	3457	3604	3764	3939	4131	22
23	2151	2207	2266	2328	2393	2463	2536	2614	2697	2786	2880	2981	3090	3206	3332	3468	3616	3777	3952	4145	23
24	2158	2214	2273	2336	2402	2471	2545	2623	2707	2795	2890	2991	3100	3217	3343	3480	3628	3789	3966	4159	24
25	2166	2222	2281	2343	2410	2479	2554	2632	2716	2804	2900	3001	3111	3228	3355						25
26	2173	2229	2289	2351	2418	2488	2562	2641	2725	2814	2910	3012	3121	3239	3366						26
27	2180	2237	2296	2359	2426	2496	2571	2650	2734	2823	2919	3022	3131	3250	3377						27
28	2187	2244	2304	2367	2434	2504	2579	2658	2743	2833	2929	3032	3142	3260	3388						28
29	2195	2252	2312	2375	2442	2513	2588	2667	2752	2842	2939	3042	3152	3271	3400						29
30	2202	2259	2319	2383	2450	2521	2596	2676	2761	2852											30
31	2209	2267	2327	2391	2458	2529	2605	2685	2770	2861											31
32	2216	2274	2334	2399	2466	2538	2614	2694	2779	2870											32
33	2224	2282	2342	2406	2474	2546	2622	2703	2789	2880											33
34	2231	2289	2350	2414	2482	2554	2631	2711	2798	2889											34
35	2238	2296	2357	2422	2490																35
36	2246	2304	2365	2430	2499																36
37	2253	2311	2373	2438	2507																37
38	2260	2319	2380	2446	2515																38
39	2762	2326	2388	2454	2523																39
	E^{780}_{800}	E^{760}_{780}	E^{740}_{760}	E^{720}_{740}	E^{700}_{720}	E^{680}_{700}	E^{660}_{680}	E^{640}_{660}	E^{620}_{640}	E^{600}_{620}	E^{580}_{600}	E^{560}_{580}	E^{540}_{560}	E^{520}_{540}	E^{500}_{520}	E^{480}_{500}	E^{460}_{480}	E^{440}_{460}	E^{420}_{440}	E^{400}_{420}	

TABLE 10 IN THE METRIC SYSTEM.

THE VALUES OF $\prod_{P_0}^{P_0-100}$.

P_0	−20°	−15°	−10°	−5°	0°	5°	10°	15°	20°	25°	30°	35°	40°	P_0
mm.														mm.
400	10.87	10.66	10.46	10.27	10.08	9.90	9.73	9.56						400
410	11.14	10.93	10.72	10.52	10.33	10.15	9.97	9.80						410
420	11.41	11.19	10.98	10.78	10.58	10.40	10.21	10.04						420
430	11.68	11.46	11.24	11.04	10.84	10.64	10.46	10.28						430
440	11.95	11.72	11.50	11.29	11.09	10.89	10.70	10.52						440
450	12.22	11.99	11.77	11.55	11.34	11.14	10.94	10.76	10.58					450
460	12.50	12.26	12.03	11.81	11.59	11.39	11.19	11.00	10.81					460
470	12.77	12.52	12.29	12.06	11.84	11.63	11.43	11.23	11.05					470
480	13.04	12.79	12.55	12.32	12.10	11.88	11.67	11.47	11.28					480
490	13.31	13.06	12.81	12.58	12.35	12.13	11.92	11.71	11.52					490
500	13.58	13.32	13.07	12.83	12.60	12.38	12.16	11.95	11.75	11.56				500
510	13.85	13.59	13.33	13.09	12.85	12.62	12.40	12.19	11.99	11.79				510
520	14.13	13.86	13.60	13.35	13.10	12.87	12.65	12.43	12.22	12.02				520
530	14.40	14.12	13.86	13.60	13.36	13.12	12.89	12.67	12.46	12.25				530
540	14.67	14.39	14.12	13.86	13.61	13.37	13.13	12.91	12.69	12.48				540
550	14.94	14.66	14.38	14.12	13.86	13.61	13.38	13.15	12.93	12.71	12.50			550
560	15.21	14.92	14.64	14.37	14.11	13.86	13.62	13.39	13.16	12.94	12.73			560
570	15.48	15.19	14.90	14.63	14.36	14.11	13.86	13.63	13.40	13.17	12.96			570
580	15.76	15.46	15.17	14.89	14.62	14.36	14.11	13.86	13.63	13.40	13.18			580
590	16.03	15.72	15.43	15.14	14.87	14.60	14.35	14.10	13.87	13.64	13.41			590
600	16.30	15.99	15.69	15.40	15.12	14.85	14.59	14.34	14.10	13.87	13.64	13.42		600
610	16.57	16.25	15.95	15.66	15.37	15.10	14.84	14.58	14.34	14.10	13.87	13.65		610
620	16.84	16.52	16.21	15.91	15.62	15.35	15.08	14.82	14.57	14.33	14.10	13.87		620
630	17.11	16.79	16.47	16.17	15.88	15.59	15.32	15.06	14.81	14.56	14.32	14.09		630
640	17.39	17.05	16.73	16.43	16.13	15.84	15.57	15.30	15.04	14.79	14.55	14.32		640
650	17.66	17.32	17.00	16.68	16.38	16.09	15.81	15.54	15.28	15.02	14.78	14.54	14.31	650
660	17.93	17.59	17.26	16.94	16.63	16.34	16.05	15.78	15.51	15.25	15.00	14.76	14.53	660
670	18.20	17.85	17.52	17.20	16.88	16.58	16.30	16.02	15.75	15.48	15.23	14.99	14.75	670
680	18.47	18.12	17.78	17.45	17.14	16.83	16.54	16.25	15.98	15.72	15.46	15.21	14.97	680
690	18.74	18.39	18.04	17.71	17.39	17.08	16.78	16.49	16.22	15.95	15.69	15.43	15.19	690
700	19.02	18.65	18.30	17.97	17.64	17.33	17.02	16.73	16.45	16.18	15.91	15.66	15.41	700
710	19.27	18.92	18.56	18.22	17.89	17.57	17.27	16.97	16.69	16.41	16.14	15.88	15.63	710
720	19.56	19.19	18.83	18.48	18.14	17.82	17.51	17.21	16.92	16.64	16.37	16.11	15.85	720
730	19.83	19.45	19.09	18.74	18.40	18.07	17.75	17.45	17.16	16.87	16.60	16.33	16.07	730
740	20.10	19.72	19.35	18.99	18.65	18.32	18.00	17.69	17.39	17.10	16.82	16.55	16.29	740
750	20.37	19.99	19.61	19.25	18.90	18.56	18.24	17.93	17.63	17.33	17.05	16.78	16.51	750
760	20.65	20.25	19.87	19.51	19.15	18.81	18.48	18.17	17.86	17.56	17.28	17.00	16.73	760
770	20.92	20.52	20.13	19.76	19.40	19.06	18.73	18.41	18.10	17.80	17.51	17.22	16.95	770
780	21.19	20.78	20.39	20.02	19.66	19.31	18.97	18.65	18.33	18.03	17.73	17.45	17.17	780
790	21.46	21.05	20.66	20.28	19.91	19.55	19.21	18.88	18.57	18.26	17.96	17.67	17.39	790
	−20°	−15°	−10°	−5°	0°	5°	10°	15°	20°	25°	30°	35°	40°	

(Column heading: Virtual Temperature in Centigrade.)

TABLE 11 IN THE METRIC SYSTEM.

VALUES OF $\prod_{760}^{680}$ FOR OMAHA; WHERE $\lambda = 41° 16'$ N.; $z_0 = 378.2$ METERS, $g_0 = 9.8020$ MET./SEC.^{2} WHENCE $V_0 = 3\,707$ MET./SEC.^{2}.

P_{vvv}	−20° C.	−10° C.	0° C.	10° C.	20° C.	30° C.	40° C.	P_{vvv}
680	2.74	2.63	2.54	2.45	2.37	2.28	2.21	680
690	2.78	2.67	2.57	2.48	2.40	2.32	2.24	690
700	2.82	2.71	2.61	2.52	2.44	2.35	2.28	700
710	2.86	2.75	2.65	2.56	2.47	2.39	2.31	710
720	2.90	2.79	2.69	2.59	2.51	2.42	2.34	720
730	2.94	2.83	2.72	2.63	2.54	2.45	2.37	730
740	2.98	2.86	2.76	2.66	2.58	2.49	2.41	740
750	3.02	2.90	2.80	2.70	2.61	2.52	2.44	750
760	3.06	2.94	2.83	2.74	2.64	2.55	2.47	760
770	3.10	2.98	2.87	2.77	2.68	2.59	2.50	770

(Column heading: θ = Virtual Temperature.)

Table 12 in the Metric System.

The Values of $\left(E^{p_1}_{p_0}\right)_{t_0=0°C.}$ or the Number of Level Surfaces between p_0 and p_1 when $t_0 = 0°$ C.

p_1	p_0	0	1	2	3	4	5	6	7	8	9
mm.	mm.										
400	400	0	196	391	585	780	973	1167	1359	1552	1744
	410	1935	2126	2316	2506	2696	2885	3073	3261	3449	3636
420	420	0	186	372	558	743	927	1111	1295	1478	1661
	430	1843	2025	2207	2389	2570	2750	2930	3109	3288	3467
440	440	0	178	355	532	709	885	1061	1237	1412	1587
	450	1761	1935	2108	2281	2454	2627	2799	2971	3142	3313
460	460	0	170	340	509	678	847	1015	1183	1351	1518
	470	1685	1852	2018	2184	2349	2514	2679	2844	3008	3172
480	480	0	163	325	488	650	812	973	1134	1295	1456
	490	1616	1775	1935	2094	2253	2411	2569	2727	2885	3042
500	500	0	157	313	469	624	779	934	1089	1244	1398
	510	1552	1705	1858	2011	2164	2316	2468	2620	2771	2922
520	520	0	150	301	451	600	750	899	1048	1196	1345
	530	1493	1640	1788	1935	2082	2228	2375	2521	2667	2812
540	540	0	145	290	434	578	722	866	1009	1152	1295
	550	1438	1580	1722	1864	2006	2147	2288	2429	2569	2710
560	560	0	140	279	419	558	696	835	973	1111	1249
	570	1387	1524	1661	1798	1935	2071	2207	2343	2479	2614
580	580	0	135	270	404	539	673	807	940	1073	1206
	590	1339	1472	1605	1737	1869	2001	2132	2264	2395	2526
600	600	0	130	261	391	521	650	780	909	1038	1167
	610	1295	1424	1552	1680	1807	1935	2062	2189	2316	2443
620	620	0	126	252	378	504	629	755	880	1005	1129
	630	1254	1378	1502	1626	1750	1873	1996	2119	2242	2365
640	640	0	122	244	366	488	610	731	852	973	1094
	650	1215	1335	1456	1576	1696	1815	1935	2054	2173	2292
660	660	0	119	237	355	474	592	709	827	944	1061
	670	1178	1295	1412	1528	1645	1761	1877	1992	2108	2224
680	680	0	115	230	345	460	574	688	802	916	1030
	690	1144	1257	1371	1484	1597	1710	1822	1935	2047	2159
700	700	0	112	224	335	446	558	669	780	890	1001
	710	1111	1222	1332	1442	1552	1661	1771	1880	1989	2099
720	720	0	109	217	326	434	542	650	758	866	973
	730	1081	1188	1295	1402	1509	1616	1722	1829	1935	2041
740	740	0	106	211	317	422	528	633	738	843	947
	750	1052	1156	1260	1365	1469	1572	1676	1780	1883	1987
760	760	0	103	206	309	411	514	616	718	821	923
	770	1024	1126	1228	1329	1430	1531	1632	1733	1834	1935
780	780	0	100	201	301	401	501	601	700	800	899
	790	998	1097	1196	1295	1394	1493	1591	1689	1788	1886

TABLE 13 IN THE METRIC SYSTEM.

THE VALUES OF $\frac{t_0}{273} \cdot (E_{p_0}^{m})_{(t_0=0°\,C.)}$

$E_{p_0(t_0=0°\,C.)}^{m}$	t_0 −20	−15	−10	−5	0	5	10	15	20	25	30	35	40	$E_{p_0(t_0=0°\,C.)}^{m}$
0	0	0	0	0	0	0	0	0	0	0	0	0	0	0
100	− 7	− 5	4	− 2	0	2	4	5	7	9	11	13	15	100
200	15	11	7	4	0	4	7	11	15	18	22	26	29	200
300	22	16	11	5	0	5	11	16	22	27	33	38	41	300
400	29	22	15	7	0	7	15	22	29	37	44	51	59	400
500	37	− 27	− 18	− 9	0	9	18	27	37	46	55	64	73	500
600	44	33	22	11	0	11	22	33	44	55	66	77	88	600
700	51	38	26	13	0	13	26	38	51	64	77	90	103	700
800	59	44	29	15	0	15	29	44	59	73	88	103	117	800
900	66	49	33	16	0	16	33	49	66	82	99	115	132	900
1000	− 73	− 55	− 37	18	0	18	37	55	73	92	110	128	147	1000
1100	81	60	40	20	0	20	40	60	81	101	121	141	161	1100
1200	88	66	44	22	0	22	44	66	88	110	132	154	176	1200
1300	95	71	48	24	0	24	48	71	95	119	143	167	190	1300
1400	103	77	51	26	0	26	51	77	103	128	154	179	205	1400
1500	110	− 82	55	27	0	27	55	82	110	137	165	192	220	1500
1600	117	88	59	29	0	29	59	88	117	147	176	205	234	1600
1700	125	93	62	31	0	31	62	93	125	156	187	218	249	1700
1800	132	99	66	33	0	33	66	99	132	165	198	231	264	1800
1900	139	104	70	35	0	35	70	104	139	174	209	244	278	1900
2000	−147	−110	− 73	37	0	37	73	110	147	183	220	256	293	2000
2100	154	115	77	38	0	38	77	115	154	192	231	269	308	2100
2200	161	121	81	40	0	40	81	121	161	201	242	282	322	2200
2300	168	126	84	42	0	42	84	126	168	211	253	295	337	2300
2400	176	132	88	44	0	44	88	132	176	220	264	308	352	2400
2500	−183	−137	− 92	−46	0	46	92	137	183	229	275	321	366	2500
2600	190	143	95	48	0	48	95	143	190	238	286	333	381	2600
2700	198	148	99	49	0	49	99	148	198	247	297	346	396	2700
2800	205	154	103	51	0	51	103	154	205	256	308	359	410	2800
2900	212	159	106	53	0	53	106	159	212	266	319	372	425	2900
3000	−220	165	−110	55	0	55	110	165	220	275	330	385	440	3000
3100	227	170	114	57	0	57	114	170	227	284	341	397	454	3100
3200	234	176	117	59	0	59	117	176	234	293	352	410	469	3200
3300	242	181	121	60	0	60	121	181	242	302	363	423	484	3300
3400	249	187	125	62	0	62	125	187	249	311	374	436	498	3400
	−20	−15	−10	−5	0	5	10	15	20	25	30	35	40	

NOTICE

Preceding volumes of the New Series can be obtained at the Hall of the Society. Price, five dollars each.

A few complete sets of the Transactions. New Series, Vols. I—XX, are on sale. Price, one hundred dollars.

TRANSACTIONS

OF THE

AMERICAN PHILOSOPHICAL SOCIETY

HELD AT PHILADELPHIA

FOR PROMOTING USEFUL KNOWLEDGE

VOLUME XXI—NEW SERIES

PART III

ARTICLE III.—*Chromosomes in the Spermatogenesis of the Hemiptera Heteroptera.* By *Thos. H. Montgomery, Jr.*

Philadelphia:
THE AMERICAN PHILOSOPHICAL SOCIETY
104 SOUTH FIFTH STREET
1906

ARTICLE III.

CHROMOSOMES IN THE SPERMATOGENESIS OF THE HEMIPTERA HETEROPTERA.*

By Thos. H. Montgomery, Jr.

The present paper treats of the behavior of the chromosomes in forty species of the Hemiptera, whereby especial attention is given to their number and form in the maturation mitoses, and to the changes of the modified chromosomes. Then there are treated from broader points of view, the modified chromosomes, chromosome difference, and the facts of the number of chromosomes. This is an amplification and correction of earlier researches of mine (1898, 1901*a*, 1901*b*, 1904*a*) upon the same species; and the preparations studied were the same as those previously used.

Certain phenomena treated in those earlier papers are not discussed in the present one, such as the conditions of the plasmosomes (nucleoli), and the relations of the modified chromosomes in the rest stage of the spermatogonium.

I have felt it necessary to introduce a new nomenclature, indicated in a preliminary note (1906), for the different kinds of chromosomes. Since the discovery of peculiarly modified chromosomes in certain of the insects a great variety of names has been proposed for them, and most of these suffer from a quite unnecessary length. My own earlier terms "heterochromosome" and "chromatin nucleolus" were cumbersome, and "accessory chromosome" and "heterotropic chromosome" sin equally in this regard, while "special chromosome" and "idiochromosome" are no way self-explanatory. Therefore for the sake of uniformity but more especially simplicity in writing I here employ the following nomenclature:

Chromosome, the original term of Waldeyer (1888), to be retained as a convenient collective word for each separate mass of chromatin and linin. When there are no marked differences in the behavior of the several chromosomes of a cell, all may be given this name. But when chromosomes of different behavior occur, they are distinguished as follows:

(1) *Autosome* (*autosoma*), the non-aberrant chromosomes that I have previously called *ordinary chromosomes*.

(2) *Allosome* (*allosoma*), any chromosome that behaves differently from the autosomes, and is a modification of the latter. This term is much more concise than my

* Contributions from the Zoological Laboratory of the University of Texas, no. 72.

earlier one, *heterochromosome*, and etymologically has the same significance. Two main kinds of allosomes are now known in spermatogenetic cycles, and these are:

(*a*) *Monosome* (*monosoma*), an allosome that is unpaired in the spermatogonium, *i. e.*, without a correspondent mate there. Heretofore these have been named variously: *accessory chromosomes* (McClung), *chromosomes spéciaux* (de Sinéty), *chromosomes x* and *unpaired chromosomes* (Montgomery), *heterotropic* and *differential chromosomes* (Wilson).

(*b*) *Diplosome* (*diplosoma*), allosomes that occur in pairs in the spermatogonium. These have been previously denominated: *small chromosomes* (Paulmier), *chromatin nucleoli* (Montgomery), *idiochromosomes* and *m-chromosomes* (Wilson).

I regret to have to add new names to the cytological dictionary, for there is already somewhat of a chaos of them. But these seem to be about as simple and uniform as could be invented, and I trust that their convenient brevity will insure their adoption by fellow investigators.

Wilson's recent series of "Studies on Chromosomes" has brought out two new and important points with regard to the allosomes. One is that the diplosomes (his idiochromosomes) of certain Hemiptera conjugate in the second spermatocytes and there divide reductionally. This phenomenon had been entirely overlooked by me; my oversight was due in part to the fact that in most of the species I did not examine the spermatogenesis beyond the stages of the first maturation mitosis; and in greater part to the fact that I was influenced by the thought that when there is an even number of chromosomes in the spermatogonium there must be exactly half that number of bivalent chromosomes in the first spermatocytes. And yet in certain species (*Euschistus tristigmus*, *Oncopeltus*, *Zaitha*), I showed that diplosomes may be univalent in the first spermatocytes and divide there separately. Now I am able to confirm Wilson's discovery for quite a number of species. His second and more valuable conclusion is that when there is a single monosome in the spermatogenesis, it is always represented by a pair in the ovogenesis; and Miss Stevens and he have enlarged upon this phenomenon to partially explain sex-determination. Further, Wilson has found the occurrence of a monosome in certain Coreids where I had overlooked it, and even in *Anasa* where his own student, Paulmier, had not found it.

The present paper then is an attempt to reconcile these differences of observation, on the basis of a fuller and more complete study of all of my old material. It seemed clearest to present the facts gained for each species separately, then in conclusion to bring them together under certain generalizations.

The term "reduction division" is here used to express the separation of entire chromosomes from each other in an anaphase of division; or, in the case of a monosome, of its passage without division to one of the daughter cells. In reality such processes are not acts of division at all, but rather ones of separation, yet it seems best to retain the long-accustomed terminology for them. And by "equational division" is meant any division of a univalent chromosome: this is always along the length of an elongate element, and then probably always an equal halving; in the case of a rounded chromosome it is practically impossible to determine the plane of the division, except by an analysis of the changes of the chromosome in the early prophases, when it can be demonstrated that even rounded chromosomes divide in a plane along which they were previously elongated.

Farmer and Moore (1905) have introduced the term "maiotic phase," "to cover the whole series of nuclear changes included in the two divisions that were designated as heterotype and homotype by Flemming." But the older word "maturation period" need not be given up, provided we recognize that one of the maturation mitoses is always reductional.

Finally, by the term "safraninophilous" I indicate that an element stains red after the use of the triple stain of Hermann, safranine, gentian violet and orange G; and would again insist on the point that for the study of the allosomes this stain is in a number of ways preferable to the iron haematoxyline method.

I. Observations.

PENTATOMIDÆ.

1. Euschistus variolarius Pal. Beauv.

Spermatogonic Divisions. — Pole views of the equatorial plate stage show in most cases 14 chromosomes; the two smallest are not quite equal in volume and are the diplosomes (*Di, di*, Plate IX, Figs. 3, 4); the twelve others are autosomes which compose 6 pairs of graduated volumes (*A, a–F, f*). But in one case there were clearly 15, and this was illustrated in Fig. 3 of my preceding paper (1901*b*); that earlier figure erroneously showed 16 because I had mistaken one of the longest for 2. And now I find two clear cases each with 16 chromosomes (Figs. 1, 2); the additional elements are the ones marked *G, g*. In both of these cells it will be noted that the components of the pair *G, g* do not lie in the same plane, but that one is placed immediately below the other, which would be a reason to conclude that the two are the precociously separated halves of a single one. These differences in number are puzzling, and I have been unable to explain them satisfactorily. But perhaps they are to be interpreted as follows: the usual number of chromosomes is 14, but occasionally there is present an additional one which divides before the others, and thereby gives the appearance of a totality of 16. It was on the basis of cases of this kind that I had previously decided that the normal number is 16, whereas I now find that the usual number is 14. Whenever all the chromosomes lie with their long axes in the plane of the equator their arrangement in pairs of like components may be readily made out.

Growth Period. — In the synapsis the 12 autosomes conjugate to form 6 bivalent ones as I previously described in some detail (1898, 1901*b*). The diplosomes also always unite then end to end. At first each diplosome may become more or less irregularly bent (Fig. 5), later becoming more spherical. After the synapsis period they are at first in intimate contact, each is a little longer than wide with a slight constriction around the middle (Fig. 6, *Di, di*): this probably represents a longitudinal split of each. The two may lie parallel or slightly divergent, or frequently with their long axes making a right angle. When they are so placed a small space is seen between them, and this I erroneously described in 1898 as a vacuole within a single element; now I can decide that no such vacuole is formed, and that the diplosomes swell but little in size during the growth period. Though the two may often be so near together as to appear to form an apparent single sphere, they never seem to actually fuse, for a line of separation can always be found.

First Maturation Division. — The behavior of the autosomes was described in full in the papers already referred to. In the late prophase, just before the dissolution of the nuclear membrane, or at that time, the diplosomes separate. After they separate each may continue to show the longitudinal split (Fig. 8) or may not (Fig. 9); in the latter case there is, that is to say, a temporary closure of the split, just as happens regularly with the autosomes. In the monaster stage are found 8 elements, and all of these are shown on lateral view in Fig. 10. Six of them are bivalent autosomes and these divide reductionally. But each of the two smallest chromosomes is a univalent diplosome, and their division is probably through the plane of their earlier longitudinal split. Each second spermatocyte receives 6 univalent autosomes, and half of each of the diplosomes.

Second Maturation Mitosis. — In the equator of the spindle (Figs. 11, 12) all the 6 autosomes become placed with their constrictions (longitudinal splits) in the plane of the equator, and they all divide equationally. But the two diplosomes conjugate in the middle of the chromosomal plate where they compose a bivalent element with components of unequal volume (*Di, di*), and this double element divides reductionally. Consequently each spermatid receives 7 chromosomes, whereby half the spermatids get the larger diplosome (Fig. 13) and half the smaller (Fig. 14).

Literature. — In my previous papers, 1898, 1901*b*, I made the serious mistake of failing to note the separation of the diplosomes just before the first maturation division, their equational division there, and their conjugation and separation in the second mitosis. In my first paper on this species the spermatogonial number of chromosomes was correctly given, while in the later paper I was misled by one of the unusual cases, here described, of 16 chromosomes in the equator of the spindle.

2. Euschistus tristigmus Say.

Spermatogonic Divisions. — Always 14 chromosomes (Plate IX, Fig. 15), 3 (*di, F, f*) being noticeably smaller than the others. When these elements lie suitably 12 of them are seen to compose 6 pairs (*A, a–F, f*) each pair with components of approximately equal volume and form; these are the maternal and paternal autosomes. There remain two elements, *Di* and *di*, one of which is the smallest of all, the other larger than this and also larger than either component of the smallest autosome pair; these two elements of such different volumes are the diplosomes.

Growth Period. — The autosomes unite to form 6 bivalent ones as previously described by me. The diplosomes also unite regularly and remain so during the earlier part of the growth period (*Di, Di*, Fig. 16), but they later separate.

First Maturation Division. — There are always 8 elements (Figs. 17, 18). 6 of these are bivalent autosomes (*A, a–F, f*), and these divide reductionally. And 2 are the separated and univalent diplosomes (*Di, di*) which also divide and hence equationally. A pole view of a daughter chromosomal plate of the ensuing anaphase (Fig. 19) before the chromosomes have taken their place in the equator of the second spindle shows the two diplosomes unconstricted, and each of the six autosomes with a constriction that is the longitudinal split.

Second Maturation Division. — In the equator of the spindle (Fig. 20) are seen the 6 autosomes dividing along the line of the longitudinal split; but the two diplosomes have conjugated end to end and form a bivalent element with unequal components that divides reductionally. Each spermatid receives 7 chromosomes, half of them receiving the larger (Fig. 22) and half the smaller diplosome (Fig. 21).

In this species each chromosome pair can be followed with great certainty during all its changes, thanks to the marked differences in volume of the different pairs; and this I have illustrated upon the figures by correspondence in the lettering.

Literature. — My first account was entirely correct (1901*b*), and I described how the diplosomes divide separately in the first maturation mitosis. But I failed to notice their conjugation in the second spermatocytes. Wilson's account of this and the preceding species is correct.

3. Podisus spinosus Dall.

Spermatogonic Divisions. — There are 16 chromosomes in the equator of the spindle (Plate IX, Fig. 23). Fourteen of them make up 7 pairs (*A, a–G, g*), and the pairs form a gradated series. The 2 others are the diplosomes which are of unequal volumes, one of them (*Di*) being the smallest of all the chromosomes while the other (*di*) is as large as the components of the smallest autosome pair.

Growth Period. — The 14 autosomes conjugate to form 7 bivalent ones. The diplosomes likewise become apposed and during the synapsis stage and a part of the later portion of the growth period this bivalent diplosome is placed against the nuclear membrane and is composed of a larger and a smaller element in close contact (Fig. 24, *Di, di*), but usually, as in the figure, a narrow line of separation is to be seen between the two.

First Maturation Division. — In the late prophases the diplosomes separate, and are apart from each other in the equatorial plate (Fig. 25); the smallest element there is the smaller diplosome (*Di*), but which element represents the larger it would be difficult to determine from the size relations. Each diplosome divides in the plane of its transverse constriction, which can represent nothing else than a longitudinal split. Each of the 7 bivalent autosomes divides reductionally.

Second Maturation Division. — In the center of the spindle the diplosomes conjugate end to end; Fig. 26 shows a pole view of all the chromosomes, and in the center can be seen a smaller diplosome placed at the end of a larger (*Di, di*); lateral views (Fig. 27) show clearly this bivalent diplosome with its unequal components. This bivalent element divides reductionally, while all the 7 autosomes divide equationally.

Literature. — My preceding account (1901*b*) was entirely correct except that I failed to note the unequal volumes of the diplosomes and the phenomenon of their being separate in the first maturation monaster: I had figured and described the second maturation monaster in mistake for the first. Wilson (1905*a*) was the first to show the conjugation of the diplosomes in the second spermatocyte, and their reductional division there.

4. Mormidea lugens Fabr.

Spermatogonic Division. — There are apparently 14 chromosomes in the spindle (Plate IX, Fig. 28); this is a redrawing of Fig. 31 of my preceding paper (1901*b*) in which I had erroneously represented each of the two largest elements *A, a* as two. There are 6 autosome pairs, *A, a–F, f*, which show gradations in volumes; only in regard to the supposed pair *E, e* am I undecided whether it is a single or two chromosomes. The two smallest bodies are the diplosomes (*Di, di*) and are unequal in size.

Growth Period. — There are formed in the early growth period 6 bivalent autosomes, and one bivalent diplosome. In the earlier stages the latter is composed of two of unequal volume placed end to end. Later stages show a much larger, ovoid diplosome containing one large or several smaller vacuoles; I could not decide whether this is the whole bivalent diplosome or only one of its components.

First Maturation Division. — Pole views of the equatorial plate (Fig. 29) show always 8 elements, 6 of which must be bivalent autosomes. Two elements are much smaller, and judging by their size relations in the spermatogonia these must be the diplosomes (*Di*, *di*); if this conclusion be correct, then the bivalent diplosome must have separated into its two elements in the prophases of this mitosis. The chromosomes are very regularly arranged; a large autosome forms the center of a circle composed of the five other autosomes and the two diplosomes.

Second Maturation Division. — Pole views show apparently only seven elements in the spindle (Fig. 30); but the central one is really bivalent, made up of the two diplosomes placed end to end; probably this bivalent diplosome undergoes a reduction here, but I cannot say so with certainty because my slides contained only a few of these stages.

Literature. — Previously (1901*b*) I was mistaken in supposing there to be 16 chromosomes in the spermatogonia; I did not describe the second maturation division.

5. Cosmopepla carnifex Fabr.

Spermatogonic Divisions. — There are 14 autosomes which compose 7 pairs of gradated sizes (*A*, *a*–*G*, *g*, Plate IX, Fig. 31); and two diplosomes, one of which (*Di*) is the smallest element of all, while the other is much larger and rod-shaped (*di*).

Growth Period. — The 14 autosomes conjugate to produce 7 bivalent ones. The 2 diplosomes also first unite end to end, then more closely side to side; each of them becomes longitudinally split, and their changes appear to be exactly as described for *Euschistus variolarius*.

First Maturation Division. — In the late prophases (Fig. 32) the diplosomes separate, each is bipartite, and they enter into the spindle apart from each other. Both of them divide, therefore equationally, while the 7 bivalent autosomes divide reductionally. On pole views it is difficult to recognize which are the diplosomes (Fig. 33), but on lateral aspects (Fig. 34) they may be recognized as being the two smallest elements and the only ones that are not tetrads.

Second Maturation Division. — Just before the arrangement of the chromosomes in the plane of the equator the unequal diplosomes conjugate in the middle of the equatorial plate to form a bivalent element, hence one sees either 8 bodies (Fig. 35) in which case the smaller diplosome is hidden from view by the larger, or 9 (Fig. 36) when one of the diplosomes is seen below the other. The 7 autosomes divide equationally, but the diplosomes without dividing pass into opposite daughter cells (spermatids). Each spermatid (Fig. 37) shows on pole view 8 chromosomes, a circle of 7 autosomes around a central diplosome; half the spermatids receive the larger diplosome, and half the smaller.

Literature. — I had originally erroneously stated there were 18 chromosomes in the spermatogonia, and had failed to note that the diplosomes enter separately into the equatorial plate of the first maturation monaster.

6. Nezara hilaris Say.

Spermatogonic Divisions. — In the equatorial plate (Plate IX, Fig. 38) there are 14 chromosomes; 12 are autosomes that compose 6 pairs of gradated volumes (*A, a–F, f*), while the two smallest are apparently not quite equal in volume (*Di, di*) and are the diplosomes.

Growth Period. — The diplosomes conjugate and remain in close contact during the growth period (Fig. 39, *Di, di*). From the late synapsis stage on each appears plainly constricted, which is probably to be interpreted as a longitudinal splitting.

There were no later stages upon my slides.

Literature. — In the former paper (1901*b*) I was mistaken in supposing there to be 16 chromosomes in the spermatogonia. Wilson (1905*a*) presents observations upon the later stages, and shows that the diplosomes divide separately and equationally in the first maturation division, but conjugate and separate reductionally in the second; but he is mistaken in saying that the diplosomes are of equal volume.

7. Brochymena sp.

Spermatogonic Division. — Pole views of the equatorial plate (Plate IX, Figs. 40, 41) show 14 chromosomes, of which 12 (*A, a–F, f*) form 6 pairs of graduated volumes in which the two members of each pair are approximately equal in form and volume: while the remaining pair consists of one element (*Di*) that is the smallest of all and of another (*di*) that is constricted and is larger than either of the components of the autosome pair, *F, f*.

Growth Period. — The twelve autosomes unite to form 6 bivalent ones. The diplosomes also conjugate, and each becomes constricted as in *Euschistus variolarius*.

First Maturation Division. — Late in the prophase the diplosomes separate and enter into the chromosomal plate apart from each other (*Di, di*, Figs. 42, 43). These divide equationally, but the 6 bivalent autosomes reductionally.

Second Maturation Division. — Here there are 6 univalent autosomes that divide equationally (Figs. 44, 45, *A–F*). But the diplosomes conjugate in the center of the equator and this bivalent element (*Di*, *di*), with components of very unequal volume, divides reductionally. Accordingly each spermatid receives 6 autosomes and one of the two diplosomes.

This is another species where the particular chromosome pairs may be recognized with great precision in each cell generation, as one finds by comparing the correspondingly lettered elements in the figures.

Literature. — I previously (1901*b*) concluded there were 16 instead of 14 chromosomes in the spermatogonia, for I was misled into counting two constricted elements as two each. Further I did not notice that the diplosomes enter separately into the plate of the first maturation mitosis, and did not describe the following mitosis. Wilson (1905*a*) described and figured this process correctly.

8. Perillus confluens H.-S.

Spermatogonic Divisions. — There are 14 chromosomes (Plate IX, Fig. 46) of which 12 form 6 gradated pairs of autosomes (*A, a–F, f*); while the two smallest elements (*Di*, *di*) are not of quite equal volume and are diplosomes as the later history shows.

Growth Period. — Six bivalent autosomes are formed. The diplosomes also conjugate but later in the synapsis stage than in the other Pentatomids. Subsequently each becomes constricted, and they lie close together and at the same time against the plasmosome (Fig. 47).

First Maturation Division. — In the late prophases the diplosomes separate and lie in the chromosomal plate near each other (Fig. 48, *Di*, *di*); each divides through the plane of its previous constriction. Fig. 49 shows a daughter chromosomal plate of the early anaphase of this mitosis; 6 show a line of division and they are univalent autosomes with the reopening longitudinal split, while the two that show no such constriction are the autosomes.

Second Maturation Division. — On pole view of the spindle (Fig. 50) are seen 7 elements of which the central one is really bivalent, formed by the conjugation of the two univalent diplosomes (*Di*, *di*). Fig. 51 represents a lateral view of the same stage but showing only 6 of the 7 elements; the one with the two components of unequal volume is the bivalent diplosome. This diplosome divides reductionally, the autosomes equationally; consequently each spermatid (Fig. 52) receives 7 elements, namely, 6 autosomes and one of the two diplosomes.

Literature. — My previous description was erroneous in stating there to be 16 chromosomes in the spermatogonia, and in failing to note that the diplosomes lie separate in the first maturation monaster. I did not describe the second maturation mitosis.

9. Cœnus delius Say.

Spermatogonic Divisions. — In the equator of the spindle there are 14 chromosomes (Plate IX, Figs. 53, 54). Ten of these compose 5 pairs of gradated sizes, each pair with components of equal volume (*A, a–E, e*). Of the remaining 4 I take 2 (*F, f*) to be another pair of autosomes, though they are not quite equal; while 2 others still more unequal in size (*Di, di*) are probably the diplosomes judging from the later history of the chromosomes in the spermatocytes. That all of these elements become halved in the anaphase is shown by the recurrence of the number 14 in a daughter chromosomal plate (Fig. 55).

Growth Period. — The two very unequal diplosomes may be either united during the growth period, which appears more frequent, or they may be separated.

First Maturation Division. — Eight chromosomes enter into the spindle, and were all shown on lateral view in Fig. 64 of my earlier paper (1901*b*). They are 6 bivalent autosomes that divide reductionally, and 2 separated diplosomes that divide equationally. A pole view of a daughter chromosomal plate of the early anaphase is shown in Fig. 56; the 6 bipartite elements are univalent autosomes with the reopening longitudinal split, and the two unipartite bodies in the center are the diplosomes (*Di, di*).

Second Maturation Mitosis. — The two diplosomes conjugate in the center of the equatorial plate (Figs. 57, 58), and in the anaphase separate from each other without dividing, while the 6 autosomes divide equationally.

Literature. — My previous account (1901*b*) was incorrect in stating 16 to be the number of spermatogonial chromosomes, and in considering the diplosomes to divide reductionally in the first maturation mitosis; then I did not follow the spermatogenesis beyond this point. Wilson has given a full account of the whole process, and my present observations corroborate his in every particular, except that I find the two diplosomes to be by no means always regularly separated from each other in the growth period as Wilson describes.

10. Trichopepla semivittata Say.

Spermatogonic Divisions. — Fig. 59, Plate IX, is a careful redrawing of the chromosomal plate illustrated in Fig. 65 of my earlier paper (1901*b*). It shows distinctly 15 elements, while the small protuberance *Z* attached to the chromosome *a* may be a sixteenth. From the phenomena of the growth period there are to be concluded at least 16 chromosomes for the spermatogonium, in agreement with my former description. Twelve, which compose a series of gradated pairs (*A, a–F, f*), are probably autosomes, while two remaining elements of very unequal volume (*Di*, *di*) are probably correspondent to the two larger diplosomes of the later stages. The minute body lettered *Z* is probably another diplosome and so also the one lettered *Y*. All the chromosomes are characterized by rather uneven and irregular outlines.

Growth Period. — Twelve autosomes unite to form 6 bivalent ones as shown by the phenomena of the subsequent prophases. The two larger diplosomes (*Di*, *di*, Figs. 60–63) usually lie close together in the earlier growth period, but separate from each other either soon after or else not until the late prophases. When in contact their long axes may be parallel, but more usually they are crossed. At an early stage each becomes distinctly split along its length, but this usually closes soon after it becomes well marked, which is associated with the phenomenon that each diplosome swells in size and becomes more spherical ; just before the following mitosis this split reappears on each as a transverse constriction. Besides these two larger diplosomes more minute ones are to be seen during the growth period, and despite their small size may be easily distinguished by their deep stain from the pale autosomes. It is very difficult to decide exactly what their number is, though in most cases 3 or 4 such bodies can be found. Generally two minutest ones of equal volume (*K*, Figs. 61, 63) lie upon the surface of the largest plasmosome (*Pl*), while 1 or 2 slightly larger ones (*x*, Figs. 62, 63) are situated elsewhere in the nucleus and sometimes in contact with smaller plasmosomes. The 2 smallest, those upon the largest plasmosome designated by the letter *K*, are always close together and of equal size, therefore they are probably (longitudinal?) division products of a single one ; while the two others are usually widely separated and of unequal size. These four smallest diplosomes of the growth period may be represented by three minute elements in the spermatogonium : we found in that stage (Fig. 59) one minute element (*Y*) and another probably separate element (*Z*), and there might be still another in this chromosomal plate but hidden from view. Accordingly, judging from the phenomena of the growth period, there must be at least 4 diplosomes represented in the spermatogonium, that is, a total of 16 chromosomes, if not indeed 5 diplosomes.

First Maturation Mitosis. — There are always at least 8 distinct elements in the spindle, which are : 6 bivalent autosomes of very different volumes (*A*, *a*–*F*, *f*, Fig. 65) which undergo a reduction division ; and two univalent diplosomes (*Di*, *di*) which divide presumably equationally, and represent the diplosomes so lettered in the preceding stages. The minute diplosomes are rarely found in the equatorial plate, but in two cases, one of them shown in Fig. 64, a pair of small bodies (*x*) placed close together were found ; they do not appear to divide with the other chromosomes and seem afterwards to move out into the cytoplasm ; they may represent the small elements marked *K* and *x* of Figs. 61–63, and the elements *Z* and *Y* of the spermatogonium (Fig. 59).

Second Maturation Division. — On pole view of the spindle (Plate X, Fig. 67) are seen 7 chromosomes, the central one of which is bivalent and represents the two larger diplosomes placed end to end as lateral views evince (Fig. 66, *Di, di*); this bivalent chromosome divides reductionally, the 6 autosomes probably equationally. In the spermatids (Fig. 68) there are always 7 chromosomes, half of the spermatids containing the larger and half the smaller component of the larger diplosome pair.

Literature. — My previous account was entirely correct, except that I failed to note that the larger diplosomes divide equationally in the first maturation mitosis. Wilson (1905*a*) described the second maturation mitosis correctly, but could not follow the history of the smallest diplosomes any more satisfactorily than I have been able to do in either of my accounts.

14. Eurygaster alternatus Say.

Growth Period. — There are two diplosomes of very different volumes (*Di, di*, Plate X, Fig. 69); this figure shows also three whole bivalent autosomes. In the earlier period these are usually, not always, placed end to end. Each is at first elongate, in the postsynapsis undergoes a split through its length, and for a considerable time retains this fissure in this position; later each half of each diplosome rounds up so that the whole appears to be transversely constricted, but this constriction is the same as the earlier split. There is no complete rest stage.

First Maturation Division. — There are always 7 chromosomes (Fig. 70); the two smallest (*Di, di*) are the diplosomes that come to lie separately in the equator and divide equationally; their precise location in the chromosomal plate is variable. The others are 5 bivalent autosomes that divide reductionally as may be ascertained with great certainty from the examination of the earlier stages; and when seen from the flat surface each shows the longitudinal split parallel to the long axis. In the succeeding anaphase this split opens up as in the other Hemiptera.

Second Maturation Mitosis. — Pole views (Fig. 72) show apparently only 6 chromosomes, but the central one is really bivalent, composed of the two diplosomes (*Di, di*) placed end to end; a lateral view shows this bivalent element more distinctly (Fig. 73). The diplosomes divide reductionally, the autosomes equationally, so that each spermatid receives 6 elements.

Though there were no spermatogonic mitoses upon my preparations, there can be little doubt that the chromosomes there would consist of 10 autosomes and 2 diplosomes.

Literature. — My previous very brief account was correct so far as it went.

12. Peribalus limbolaris Stal.

Spermatogonic Divisions. — There are 14 chromosomes (Plate X, Fig. 74); 12 of them make up 6 well marked pairs of autosomes (*A, a–F, f*), and all of these are elongate; the two remaining are very unequal in volume (*Di, di*), are rounded, are the smallest of all, and are the diplosomes. The gradation in size of the autosome pairs is very marked.

Growth Period. — During the greater part of the growth period there appears to be only one diplosome in the spermatocytes, and it usually is of rounded form and contains one or several vacuoles; whether this single one represents both diplosomes of the spermatogonia, or only the larger one of them, I could not positively determine. Towards the close of this period, however, two separated ones of very dissimilar volume are occasionally found (Fig. 75, *Di, di*). During the synapsis, unlike the conditions in the other Pentatomids, these are not safraninophilous but stain violet like the plasmosomes of which there are usually two or three in each nucleus, and for this reason it is then difficult to determine the diplosomes.

First Maturation Mitosis. — In the equator of the spindle are present always 8 chromosomes (Figs. 76, 77); the two smallest are the diplosomes which have entered the spindle separately and divide there equationally; they are dyads. The 6 larger elements are bivalent autosomes, each of which appears as a tetrad with distinct components when seen from its flattened surface (Fig. 77); the longitudinal split of these is parallel to their long axes, the same position as it held in all the earlier stages, and accordingly in this first maturation mitosis the autosomes divide reductionally. A pole view of one of the daughter chromosome plates, from the early anaphase, is illustrated in Fig. 79; the diplosomes (*Di, di*) can be readily distinguished from the autosomes by being unipartite and smaller.

Second Maturation Division. — Pole views show apparently only 7 elements (Fig. 78); but the central one is seen to be composed of two placed the one immediately above the other (*Di, di*), which are the now conjugated diplosomes. This bivalent diplosome is more easily recognized upon side view (Fig. 80), and divides reductionally, *i. e.*, the larger diplosome (*di*) passes into one spermatid and the smaller diplosome (*Di*) into the other, while the 6 autosomes divide through the plane of their longitudinal splits.

Literature. — I had erroneously (1901*b*) stated the number of spermatogonial chromosomes to be 16, and was consequently led into concluding that there is a bivalent diplosome dividing reductionally in the first spermatocyte division.

NABIDÆ.

13. Nabis annulatus Reut.

On my preparations there were no stages of the spermatogonia or earlier portion of the growth period.

First Maturation Mitosis. — Very early prophases show 6 autosomes in the form of long loops which are evidently to be considered tetrads with a very wide longitudinal split. Besides these there is apposed to a plasmosome (*Pl*, Plate X, Fig. 81) a still larger body (*Di*), safraninophilous, of uneven contours, which the later history shows to be a number of allosomes in close juxtaposition. Later the 6 autosomes shorten and condense, and then each appears to consist of two parallel univalent elements each longitudinally split, as illustrated by those marked *a* in Figs. 81–83; each of these gradually condenses into a tetrad composed of four parallel rods, whereas in most other Hemiptera the univalent elements come to lie end to end; further, the longitudinal split remains open instead of closing temporarily. In these later prophases the safraninophilous body (*Di*, Fig. 81) separates into 4 allosomes, while the plasmosome to which it is attached gradually dissolves (Figs. 82, 83). Two of these compact allosomes are quadripartite (*Di. 2*), and each of these is therefore probably, and the later history confirms this decision, a bivalent, longitudinally split chromosome; these are the ones lettered *Di. 2, di. 2* and *Di. 3, di. 3* in Figs. 82, 83 and 85. Each is, that is to say, a bivalent diplosome with its components in close contact and with these components of approximately equal volume. But the remaining pair of allosomes consist of the largest and the smallest respectively, and are very unlike in volume, while each is a dyad and not a tetrad (*Di. 1, di. 1*, Figs. 82–85). These relations cannot be determined as long as these bodies are in close contact, but very clearly as soon as they become separate. These three pairs of diplosomes are readily distinguished from the autosomes by their dense and rounded form and their strong affinity for the safranine stain. There are accordingly three pairs of diplosomes in the spermatocyte, two of them tetrads, and one pair with widely separated components of unequal volume.

Pole views of the first maturation monaster show always 10 chromosomes (Fig. 86). Eight of these are clearly quadripartite, as can be readily determined when the pole view is slightly oblique as that of the figure given, and these must correspond to the 8 tetrads of the prophases, namely, to the 6 bivalent autosomes, and to the 2 bivalent diplosomes marked *Di. 2, di. 2* and *Di. 3, di. 3*; which two, however, are these particular diplosomes, cannot be determined with certainty in the stage of the equatorial plate. The two remaining elements are not tetrads but dyads, they are of unequal volumes (*Di. 1, di. 1*, Figs. 86–88), and clearly represent the third pair of diplosomes of the preceding prophases; they are respectively the largest and the smallest elements of the chromosomal plate. Each tetrad is composed of 4 parallel rods, shown in their length in Fig. 86, and from end in Figs. 87, 88; their long axes always lie in the plane of the equator. But in the case of the two dyads, the larger (*di. 1*) may have its long axis in this plane (Fig. 88), but more frequently is inclined to it (Fig. 87); while the smaller dyad (*Di. 1*) is composed of two spherules, one on either side of the equatorial plane. All these chromosomes are large, and their parts can be made out with unusual facility. Each of these 10 elements divides so that each second spermatocyte receives 10, *i. e.*, a portion of each of them. Whether this is a reductional or an equational division of the 8 tetrads it would be exceedingly difficult to determine, since each, as in the case of *Ascaris*, is in the form of four parallel rods; but I conceive that these 8 bivalent elements differ from those of other Hemiptera only in having their univalent components placed side to side instead of end to end, and that therefore their division may well be, as is certainly the case in the other Hemiptera, reductional. A pole view of one daughter chromosomal plate in the early anaphase is shown in Fig. 89; here are 8 bipartite elements, the daughters of the former 8 tetrads, and 2 unipartite ones (*Di. 1, di. 1*), the division products of the 2 earlier dyads.

Second Maturation Mitosis. — The 8 bipartite elements, which are 6 autosomes and 2 of the diplosomes, take positions with their long axes in the plane of the equator (Figs. 90, 91), and all of them divide so that the components of each become separated into opposite spermatids; this is probably an equational division. But the unipartite diplosomes *Di. 1* and *di. 1* never lie in the equator, but one is always near one spindle pole and the other near the opposite pole; this was invariably the case with every one of these stages found. Accordingly, the smaller diplosome, *Di. 1*, passes wholly into one spermatid, the larger diplosome, *Di. 1*, into the other spermatid. Fig. 92 shows the chromosomes of a spermatid that has received the smaller one, and Fig. 93 a spermatid that has gotten the larger, these diplosomes being recognizable among the other chromosomes by their form as well as by their deeper stain.

In the spermatocytes there are accordingly 6 autosomes that divide in both maturation mitoses; 2 probably bivalent diplosomes each of which divides as do the autosomes; but one pair of diplosomes, that one characterized by very unequal components, each component dividing separately (so probably equationally) in the first mitosis, but their daughter products, without conjugating, passing without division into opposite spermatids in the second mitosis.

The 6 quadripartite autosomes are probably, by analogy with the phenomena of the other Hemiptera, bivalent in the spermatocytes, and so are probably the 2 quadripartite diplosomes; the large and small diplosomes are undoubtedly univalent. Therefore we can postulate for the spermatogonium with a high degree of certainty: 12 autosomes, and 6 diplosomes, the components of only one of these diplosome pairs being very unequal in volume.

Literature. — My preceding account (1901*a*), which did not extend beyond the first maturation mitosis, was entirely correct except for the conclusion that the spermatocyte had four bivalent diplosomes. My preparations of *Corizus ficus*, another member of the same family, had faded to such a degree that I could not test the correctness of my account of it (1901*b*).

COREIDÆ.

14. Harmostes reflexulus Say.

Spermatogonic Divisions. — There are 13 chromosomes. One unpaired element (Plate X, Figs. 94, 95, *Mo*) is the monosome, and it is not the largest. The 2 smallest are the diplosomes (*Di, di*) and are not quite equal in volume. The remaining 10 are autosomes and are seen to compose 5 readily recognizable pairs (*A, a–E, e*); what is to be noted in them is that the two components of each pair seem to be of slightly different form and volume, as is seen most clearly in the case of the pair *A, a*; and perhaps in each pair the larger element may be the maternal one and the smaller the paternal. The components of the 2 or 3 largest pairs are regularly transversely constricted.

Growth Period. — The 10 autosomes conjugate to form 5 bivalent ones. The monosome (*Mo*, Figs. 96–99) remains safraninophilous during this whole period. In the synapsis (Fig. 96) it becomes elongated and concomitantly more or less bent, thereby showing a great variety of forms; frequently it is attenuated at the ends and thicker at the middle. In the early postsynapsis (Fig. 97) it becomes longitudinally split so that the halves sometimes widely diverge from each other and at the same time it becomes less dense and more or less granular, though to much less extent than the autosomes (Fig. 98). In the rest stage, which is complete (Fig. 99), this split becomes more or less closed; and then the monosome (*Mo*) has usually a rod shape, shorter than in the synapsis stage, with its arms parallel; throughout the growth period it lies against the nuclear membrane. I could not distinguish the diplosomes in the earlier part of the growth period before the plasmosome arises. In the rest stage the latter (*Pl*, Fig. 99) is a large body near the center of the nucleus. Quite generally there are attached to its surface about 3 or 4 small safraninophilous bodies; the 2 larger that may or may not be in contact I take to be the diplosomes (*Di, di*);

the smaller ones (x) are bodies represented in neither the spermatogonic nor the spermatocytic mitoses. In the case figured (Fig. 99) the bivalent diplosome has each component longitudinally split.

First Maturation Division. — In the early prophases (Figs. 100, 101) a bivalent diplosome (*Di*, *di*) is frequently to be seen lying near the monosome (*Mo*), which might indicate that previously it had been in contact with it, from which it would appear possible that when the diplosomes are not discernible in the preceding rest period it is because they may be closely applied against the monosome. The diplosomes seem not to increase in size during the growth period. In these prophases the longitudinal split of the monosome again appears.

In the chromosomal plate (Figs. 102, 103) there are always present 1 bivalent diplosome (*Di*, *di*) that divides reductionally, and 1 monosome (*Mo*) that divides through the plane of its longitudinal split. There may be either 5 bivalent autosomes (Fig. 102, *A*, *a–E*, *e*) all of which divide reductionally: or 4 bivalent autosomes (*A*, *a–C*, *c*, *E*, *e*, Fig. 103) and 2 univalent ones (*D*, *d*); in the latter case the 2 univalent ones are regularly of the same form and volume, and therefore are evidently ones that had either failed to conjugate or, more probably, ones that had precociously separated from each other after conjugation, and which in this mitosis pass without division into opposite daughter cells, *i. e.*, divide reductionally as do the other autosomes. The longitudinal split is well marked upon one or two of the larger autosomes.

Second Maturation Division. — Here there are always 7 elements (Fig. 104, where one of the autosomes has not yet taken its place in the equator of the spindle). The smallest, the diplosome (*Di*), regularly divides, and so do the 5 autosomes, all of these equationally. But the monosome (*Mo*) shows no sign of any division and passes bodily over into one of the spermatids. The latter show correspondingly either 6 chromosomes (Fig. 105) or 7 (Fig. 106), the monosome being absent in the former case; the minute element in each spermatid is a diplosome.

Literature. — My preceding accounts (1901*a*, *b*) were correct in the main, stated the spermatogonial number of chromosomes accurately, the variation in number in the first maturation spindle, and the behavior of the monosome in the maturation divisions. But what escaped me then was that the large allosome of the growth period is the monosome and not the bivalent diplosome.

15. Corizus alternatus Say.

Spermatogonic Divisions. — There are 13 chromosomes (Plate X, Fig. 107). The smallest elements, of slightly different volume, are the diplosomes (*Di*, *di*). Then 5 pairs of autosomes (*A*, *a–E*, *e*); of these the largest pair (*A*, *a*) is composed of 2 relatively enormous elements, one of which is approximately straight and apparently a little more voluminous, while the other is horseshoe-shaped. Finally there is a single chromosome without a corresponding mate, therefore a monosome (*Mo*).

Growth Period. — In the synapsis stage the 10 autosomes become longitudinally split and conjugate to form 5 bivalent ones. But 3 of the chromosomes differ in preserving their safraninophilous stain and dense structure; from the later history of these there can be no question that the largest (*Mo*, Figs. 108–111) is the monosome, the 2 smaller the diplosomes (*Di, di*). The monosome increases somewhat in volume and in the postsynapsis (Figs. 109, 110) is rod-shaped, sometimes bent, and undergoes a longitudinal splitting; in the rest stage, that is complete (Fig. 111), it becomes more rounded and then shows either no trace of this split, or else only a mere sign of it in the form of an indentation at either end; it may or may not lie against the nuclear membrane. The diplosomes are unequal in volume as in the spermatogonium, and undergo but slight increase in mass during the growth period. In the postsynapsis each (*Di, di*, Fig. 109) becomes bipartite, which is evidently a longitudinal splitting, and they remain so during the remainder of the growth period. The spermatocytes contain each several large plasmosomes (*Pl*, Figs. 110, 111), and the diplosomes, and less frequently the monosome, may be in contact with these.

First Maturation Division. — In the prophases there are 5 bivalent autosomes (*A, a–E, e*, Figs. 114–116), each longitudinally split. One of them, by far the largest (*A, a*), is in the earlier stages the single one that is regularly ring shaped (Fig. 112), with a distinct longitudinal split in each arm of the ring; this ring gradually opens until it first becomes an angle (Fig. 113), then straight (Figs. 114–116), the longitudinal split still continuing in the axis of each arm (univalent constituent). By the gradual condensation of the autosomes (Fig. 116) their longitudinal splits become more or less closed, but even in the metaphase it is sometimes clearly indicated (Plate XI, Fig. 118), and is then always parallel to the long axis of the chromosome. No animal shows more decisively than this one that the first maturation mitosis separates whole univalent chromosomes. The monosome can be recognized as a large dyad (*Mo*, Figs. 114–116). The diplosomes (*Di, di*, Figs. 114–116) do not conjugate until the later prophases, apparently usually not until the nuclear membrane has disappeared; in them the longitudinal split becomes temporarily closed as in the case of the autosomes, but the monosome continues to show it distinctly.

There are in the spindle almost invariably 7 elements (Plate XI, Figs. 117, 118); in a few cases 8 are to be seen on pole aspect, which is then due, as in *Harmostes*, to a precocious division of two of the bivalent elements, but here usually of the bivalent diplosome. There is a central bivalent diplosome (*Di, di*) and around it a circle composed of 5 bivalent autosomes and the univalent monosome (*Mo*, Fig. 117); the latter can be recognized on pole view by its lesser depth, and on lateral view (Fig. 118) by its quadratic form. The constrictions of the autosomes seen on pole view mark their longitudinal splits, as is very clearly proven by the earlier history of these chromosomes. The bivalent diplosome and autosomes divide reductionally, the monosome equationally. Fig. 119 reproduces a daughter plate of chromosomes from the early anaphase; the monosome (*Mo*) can be recognized as being the only element that shows no longitudinal split.

Second Maturation Division. — Here again there are always 7 elements (Plate XI, Figs. 120, 121), the smallest being a diplosome (*Di*), and the one that is rounded without having any constriction the monosome (*Mo*). The diplosome and the 5 autosomes always divide, but the monosome passes wholly over into one of the spermatids; this is shown clearly by the anaphase shown in Fig. 122, where at one spindle pole are 7 elements and at the other only 6.

Literature. — My preceding description (1901*a*) was incorrect in giving 14 as the normal number of chromosomes; this was because I had counted into the chromosomal plate elements of an adjacent cell. Further, I had entirely overlooked the presence of a monosome, and had not described the second maturation mitosis.

16. Corizus lateralis Say.

No spermatogonic divisions were found.

Growth Period. — My preparations had faded considerably so that I could not make out the diplosomes with any certainty. But the largest allosome present is the monosome and it becomes longitudinally split.

First Maturation Division. — There are 7 elements (Plate XI, Fig. 123): 5 bivalent autosomes and 1 bivalent diplosome (*Di*, *di*, with components of dissimilar volume) that divide reductionally; and 1 roundish element, the monosome (*Mo*), that also divides but equationally.

Second Maturation Division. — Again 7 elements: 5 autosomes and 1 diplosome (*di*) that divide again, and a rounded monosome (*Mo*) that passes into one spermatid without division, as shown in all lateral views of the anaphase (Fig. 125).

The whole spermatogenesis seems very similar to that of the preceding species, and we may conclude with considerable certainty that there will be found in the spermatogonia: 10 autosomes, 2 diplosomes and 1 monosome.

Literature. — My earlier account (1901*b*) was in the main correct, and though I did not decide for the presence of a monosome I noted that one of the chromosomes of the first maturation mitosis differed in form from the others, "for it is not more than half the volume of the other five, and sometimes it does not appear dumbell-shaped."

17. Chariesterus antennator Fabr.

There were no spermatogonic divisions suitable for study.

Growth Period. — In the synapsis and later stages (a complete rest stage was not observed) there are in each nucleus two compact, safraninophilous bodies, close to the nuclear membrane: a plasmosome was not found. The smaller of these bodies (*Di, di*, Plate XI, Fig. 126) is regularly constricted, and by analogy with the relations in other members of the family is probably a bivalent diplosome, and its later history is in accord with this assumption. The larger safraninophilous body is longitudinally split (*Mo*), and corresponds to the monosome of the later stages.

First Maturation Division. — Pole views of the chromosomal plate show in most cases (14 out of 18) 13 elements (Fig. 127). The central is always the smallest, and very likely is a bivalent diplosome (*Di, di*); its two components are of approximately the same size. Around it is a circle of 11 autosomes, and just outside of the latter an element (*Mo*), the monosome, lying with its long axis in the equator while the autosomes are perpendicular to it. In 4 out of the 18 clear pole views examined there appeared to be 14 elements (Fig. 128); these are to be interpreted, as in *Harmostes*, that one of the bivalent autosomes has its univalent components precociously separated; and in all such cases illustrated by Fig. 128 there lie near each other two elements of equal volume (*M*), each of which is of less depth than any other of the autosomes. The autosomes and the diplosome divide reductionally, the monosome through the plane of its longitudinal split (Fig. 129).

Second Maturation Division. — Here there are always 13 elements (Fig. 130). The smallest is a diplosome (*di*), 11 others are autosomes, and all these divide equationally. But the monosome passes without division into one of the spermatids. This is shown distinctly in two daughter chromosomal plates of the early anaphases of the same cell, the drawings made accordingly at different focusses (Figs. 131, 132); in each there is a diplosome recognizable by its very small size, but only one shows the monosome (*Mo*, Fig. 131). And in later anaphases on lateral views (Fig. 133) are to be seen regularly an element, the monosome, in one spermatid that is not found in the other. Half the spermatids receive, accordingly, 13 elements, and half 12.

Judging from the relations during these maturation mitoses the number of chromosomes in the spermatogonia would be: 1 monosome, 2 diplosomes, 22 autosomes, a total of 25.

Literature. — My preceding observations (1901*b*) were correct, and though I did not distinguish a monosome in the growth period of the spermatocytes, I called attention to the fact that one of the chromosomes of the first maturation mitosis is different in form from the others, and left the question open whether it might be univalent there (so be a monosome). The subsequent mitosis was not described.

18. Protenor belfragei Hagl.

The previous account given by me (1904b) was detailed and entirely correct, and Wilson has recently corroborated it. I have simply to add to it that all the autosomes of the spermatogonium can be grouped into pairs (*A*, *a–E*, *e*, Plate XI, Fig. 134), that the diplosomes there are slightly unequal in volume (*Di*, *di*), and that the monosome (*Mo*) is by far the largest element. Another figure (135) is given of these elements in the growth period. The monosome becomes always longitudinally split in the synapsis period (*Mo*, Fig. 135), and its division in the first maturation mitosis is along the plane of this split and not, as I had previously interpreted it, transverse to its long axis.

19. Alydus pilosulus H. S.

Spermatogonic Division. — Four clear pole views showed in each case 13 elements, namely (Plate XI, Fig. 136): 5 pairs of autosomes *A*, *a–E*, *e* of remarkably different volumes and forms; 2 unequal diplosomes (*Di*, *di*), the smallest of all; and 1 monosome (*Mo*).

Growth Period. — In the growth period there is a single safraninophilous body of considerable size, that from its singularity and later behavior is undoubtedly the monosome (*Mo*, Figs. 137, 138), and from the early synapsis on increases to at least twice its original volume, as shown by comparison of the figures. In the postsynapsis it becomes longitudinally split, lies regularly against the nuclear membrane and frequently also against a plasmosome. The diplosomes are apparently not distinguishable during the growth period, and therefore it is probable that they undergo much the same changes as the autosomes except for their later conjugation.

First Maturation Division. — In the prophases the diplosomes (*Di*, *di*, Fig. 139) become compact ahead of the autosomes, and reappear as two rounded bodies that do not conjugate until the nuclear membrane disappears. The monosome (*Mo*) is to be distinguished from them by its larger size. The autosomes are longitudinally split and bivalent. In the equatorial plate (Fig. 140) there are always 7 elements: 5 bivalent autosomes that divide reductionally, and a bivalent diplosome (*Di*, *di*) that divides in the same manner as may be readily determined on the basis of its two components being dissimilar in volume. The monosome (*Mo*) divides lengthwise. The bivalent diplosome is always central, the monosome most excentric. In a number of cases two of the larger autosomes were found closely applied side to side and in the preceding late prophases this is also sometimes the case.

Second Maturation Division. — Again 7 elements are found (Fig. 141), the smallest of which is the diplosome, the nonconstricted one the monosome (*Mo*). All of these divide except the monosome which passes wholly over into one of the spermatids, as shown clearly in the anaphase illustrated in Fig. 142 where one daughter plate shows 7 and the other only 6 elements. The monosome frequently lags behind the others in reaching the spindle pole (Fig. 143).

Literature. — My preceding account (1901*b*) was very brief, I overlooked the monosome entirely and erroneously gave 14 chromosomes as the normal number. Wilson (1905e, 1906) has correctly emended my observations and has given a good series of figures, but he failed to note that the diplosomes are unequal in size.

20. Alydus eurinus Say.

My earlier accounts (1901*b*, 1905 p. 191) were correct, except that I failed to note that the allosome of the growth period (*Mo*, Plate XI, Fig. 145) is the odd chromosome, *i. e.*, the monosome, and not a bivalent diplosome; there is no trace during the growth period of the very minute diplosomes. The monosome is rather ovoid in the synapsis period, but it later becomes more elongate and longitudinally split (this split shows usually simply as an indentation at either end, but sometimes as a fine clear line along the whole length). Its division in the first maturation mitosis (Fig. 147) is in the line of this split, therefore equational. A daughter chromosomal plate of this division is reproduced in Fig. 148; the monosome is the only element that appears unconstricted, while all the others, including the small central diplosome (*Di*), show a constriction that is the longitudinal split reopening for the next mitosis. In the second mitosis there are again 7 elements, all of which divide except the monosome (*Mo*) that passes without division into one of the spermatids. In the spermatogonium (Fig. 144) the 13 chromosomes make up 5 pairs of autosomes (*A*, *a–E*, *e*) one pair of diplosomes (*Di*, *di*), and the monosome (*Mo*). The whole spermatogenesis is quite similar to that of the preceding form.

21. Anasa tristis De Geer.

Spermatogonic Divisions. — In seven very clear pole views 21 chromosomes could be counted. These are (Plate XI, Fig. 151): 2 small rounded bodies, not quite equal in size, the diplosomes (*Di*, *di*); a longest unpaired one that is sometimes constricted, the monosome (*Mo*); and a series of 9 pairs of autosomes (*A*, *a–I*, *i*).

Growth Period. — The large allosome of the growth period is the monosome (*Mo*, Figs. 152–155), which remains compact and safraninophilous. It is irregularly elongate during the synapsis (Fig. 152) and in the later postsynapsis (Fig. 155) shows a split along its length which, as is the case also with the autosomes, is widest at its middle; this split becomes temporarily closed a little later. The diplosomes (*Di, di*, Figs. 153, 154) remain very small during the growth period but retain their red stain and dense structure; usually but not always they are close together, and like the monosome lie against the nuclear membrane. There is always one large plasmosome (Figs. 154, 155, *Pl*) and frequently one or two smaller ones.

First Maturation Mitosis. — In the spindle there are 11 elements so placed that within a circle of 9 autosomes is the bivalent diplosome (*Di, di*, Fig. 156), and outside of this circle the univalent monosome (*Mo*) which lies with its long axis in the equatorial plane; the annular constrictions of the autosomes found upon pole views mark their longitudinal splits. All of these are shown on lateral view in Fig. 157, and 6 of them in Fig. 158. The 9 autosomes divide reductionally, and so does the bivalent diplosome because its parts that separate from each other are unequal in volume and in the preceding stages we found this dissimilarity characteristic of the two. The monosome, however, lies with its long axis in the plane of the equator (Figs. 157, 158, *Mo*), and divides through its length.

Second Maturation Division. — Here again there are 11 elements (Fig. 159), but grouped differently from those of the preceding division in that there are usually 2 within a circle of 9. They are 1 univalent diplosome (*Di*), 9 univalent autosomes, and the half of the monosome. The autosomes and the diplosome divide again and equationally (Fig. 160), but the monosome (*Mo*, Figs. 160, 161) passes undivided into one of the spermatids and usually lags behind the others in reaching the spindle pole.

Literature. — Paulmier's monographic account of the spermatogenesis of this species (1899) was in the main a very correct one, save that he stated the normal number of chromosomes to be 22, and consequently identified the allosome of the growth period and the chromosome that does not divide in the second maturation mitosis with the minute diplosomes. I (1901*b*) followed Paulmier in these mistakes, and because the monosome of the spermatogonium is constricted counted it as two. Wilson (1905*c*, 1906), in whose laboratory Paulmier's work was done, was the first to correct these errors, and to trace the history of the monosome distinct from that of the diplosomes. But Wilson failed to note that the diplosomes are not quite of the same size, and that they may be distinctly recognized during the greater part of the growth period.

22. Anasa sp. (from California).

Spermatogonic Divisions. — In every case there are 21 elements in the spindle (Plate XI, Fig. 164). These are: 2 diplosomes of unequal volume (*Di, di*); 1 monosome that appears to be regularly constricted (*Mo*); and 9 pairs of autosomes (*A*, *a–I*, *i*).

Oogonic Divisions. — On the only two clear pole views upon my preparations there were exactly 22 elements. A careful comparison shows that the odd one of the spermatogonia, the monosome (*Mo*, Fig. 164), is represented in the ovogonia (Figs. 162, 163) by a pair of elements (*Mo*, *mo*); each component of this ovogonic pair is of about the same volume as the single monosome of the spermatogonia. In the ovogonia there are also a pair of diplosomes of dissimilar volumes.

Growth Period. — The monosome and the diplosomes show the same behavior as in the preceding species, and the longitudinal split of the monosome is very distinct.

First Maturation Division. — Pole views show 11 elements, in the center the bivalent diplosome (*Di*, *di*, Fig. 165) and a bivalent autosome, then a circle of 8 bivalent autosomes, and outside of the latter the monosome (*Mo*). All of these divide reductionally except the monosome (*Mo*, Fig. 166) that divides equationally.

My preparations contained no second maturation mitoses, but probably the monosome will be found to behave in them as it does in *Anasa tristis*.

Literature. — My earlier account (1901*b*) was erroneous in stating the spermatogonic number of chromosomes to be 22; because the monosome there is regularly constricted I was misled into counting it as two. And that led to the farther mistake of concluding the allosome of the growth period to be the bivalent diplosome.

23. Anasa armigera Say.

Spermatogonic Divisions. — On the only two clear pole views of chromosomal plates 21 elements could be counted (Plate XI, Fig. 167); here the monosome is the only one that is somewhat constricted (*Mo*) and is not the largest; then there are 2 very small diplosomes (*Di*, *di*) of nearly equal size, and 9 pairs of autosomes (*A*, *a–I*, *i*).

Growth Period. — The staining of my single preparation was not favorable for determining the behavior of the diplosomes, but the large allosome must be the monosome on account of its similarity to that of the other species of this genus.

First Maturation Division. — There are 11 elements, all shown in Fig. 168. The smallest is the bivalent diplosome (*Di*, *di*), while the monosome can be recognized by its unipartite appearance (*Mo*). I have seen stages no later than this metaphase, but it is sufficient to show that the autosomes and the diplosomes divide reductionally.

Literature. — My previous very brief account (1901*b*) made the same mistakes as I had made for the other species of the genus. In the figure then given of the spermatogonic chromosomes (Fig. 77, 1901*b*) I had counted the constricted one just to the left of the two diplosomes as two whereas it is really but a single monosome: my drawing was more correct than my reasoning.

21. Metapodius terminalis Dall.

Spermatogonic Divisions.—Two pole views of the chromosomes are shown in Plate XI, Figs. 169, 170. Each shows 2 very minute elements which are unequal in size and are the diplosomes (*Di, di*). Then there is one unpaired, constricted element, the monosome (*Mo*). The remainder are 9 pairs of autosomes (*A. a–I. i*).

Growth Period.—Throughout this period there is a dense safraninophilous body of considerable size close to the nuclear membrane (*Mo*, Plate XII, Figs. 171–173): it is ovoid in the synapsis, more elongate in the postsynapsis, ovoid again in the (incomplete) rest stage: it never appears double as if formed by the conjugation of two elements, nor any at any period shows clearly a longitudinal split. This is probably the monosome because it is far too large to be the bivalent diplosome. No sign at all of the diplosomes is to be seen; this may be either on account of their very small size, or perhaps on account of their not retaining a compact form. The 18 autosomes conjugate end to end to form 9 bivalent ones.

First Maturation Division.—In the prophases (Fig. 174) reappear the diplosomes (*Di, di*) as a pair of small rounded bodies, not attached together until the time of disappearance of the nuclear membrane. In the spindle the 11 elements show a very regular disposition (Figs. 176, 177) like that of *Anasa tristis*, with the bivalent diplosome in the center and the monosome (*Mo*) excentric. All these elements are shown on side view in Fig. 175: there the diplosome is seen to have its components of dissimilar volume, and to divide reductionally as do the 9 bivalent autosomes. But the monosome (*Mo*, Fig. 175), when examined in profile, is seen to be placed with its long axis in the plane of the equator and to divide through its length. As the daughter chromosomes separate in the anaphase (Fig. 178) a constriction upon each marks the reopening of the longitudinal split; but the monosome (*Mo*) does not show this constriction, and upon pole views of a daughter plate (Fig. 179) appears simply ovoid while all the others are dumbbell-shaped.

Second Maturation Division.—In the spindle the chromosomes are again differently arranged (Fig. 180), they are 11 in number; the diplosome (*di*) can be recognized by its small size, the monosome (*Mo*) by its small depth. All of these divide again except the monosome which passes without division into one of the spermatids (*Mo*, Figs. 181, 182).

Literature.—In my previous brief account (1901*b*) I did not describe the second maturation division, gave the number of spermatogonic chromosomes as 22 (counting the constricted monosome as 2), and in the growth period confused the monosome with the diplosomes.

LYGÆIDÆ.

25. Œdancala dorsalis Say.

Spermatogonic Division.—The spindle contains 13 elements (Plate XII, Fig. 183). These are: 2 diplosomes of approximately equal volume, the smallest of all (*Di, di*); 1 monosome (*Mo*), the only unpaired element; and 5 pairs of autosomes (*A*, *a*–*E*, *e*) of which the pairs are to be recognized rather by peculiarities in form than in size.

Growth Period.—Up to the late postsynapsis the allosomes cannot be distinguished from the autosomes, that is, they neither remain dense and compact nor do they continue safraninophilous. It is, accordingly, probable that until then the allosomes undergo changes parallel to those of the autosomes, except, as will appear from the later history, the monosome remains a single element and the diplosomes probably do not conjugate, while the 10 autosomes go to compose 5 longitudinally split bivalent chromosomes. Throughout there is a large plasmosome (*Pl*, Figs. 184, 185), lying usually against the nuclear membrane. The growth period is closed by an almost complete rest stage (Fig. 185), one in which the chromosomal boundaries cannot be well distinguished. Just before this rest stage there becomes visible a safraninophilous double body (*Mo*, Fig. 184) placed almost invariably upon the plasmosome; we shall find that this is the monosome. It reappears first in the form of a pair of rods, each finely granular, which are to be considered the split halves of the monosome because they are of equal length and volume; at this stage the two are more or less curved so that together they bound an oval space. They soon become compacter with smooth surfaces, and appear as two shorter parallel rods (*Mo*, Fig. 185). No trace of the diplosomes is to be seen, *i. e.*, they do not stain differently from the autosomes.

First Maturation Division.—In the early prophases the plasmosome dissolves without a visible remnant. The monosome (*Mo*, Figs. 186, 187) has the form of two short, thick rods, which may be parallel but are more frequently divergent. The autosomes now commence to stain with saffranine (Figs. 186, 187), and they compose 5 bivalent elements in which each univalent component is longitudinally split: this split gradually narrows up to the stage of the metaphase. And now reappear for the first time the diplosomes (*Di, di*, Figs. 186, 187) as two very small elements, each in structure and stain like a miniature univalent autosome; they are not in contact with each other in any part of the prophase, but are more or less widely separated; sometimes each appears longitudinally split (Fig. 187). By their size relations there can be no doubt which of these various nuclear structures are the diplosomes and which is the monosome. In the late prophases (Fig. 188) the monosome (*Mo*) changes form so that each of its halves becomes spherical; the diplosomes (*Di, di*) become compact and shorter, and though they are usually near together appear never to actually conjugate; and the 5 bivalent autosomes shorten and condense into short tetrads.

In the spindle the diplosomes never form a bivalent element in the equator but always lie on either side and at some distance from this plane (*Di*, *di*, Fig. 190). A pole view of the equatorial plane shows, accordingly, only 6 chromosomes (Fig. 189), which are the univalent monosome (*Mo*), recognizable by its lesser depth, and 5 autosomes; the constrictions seen on end views of the latter are their longitudinal splits. The monosome is a dyad, while the autosomes are tetrads, as shown on lateral views (Fig. 190). In the anaphase (Fig. 191) each daughter cell receives one of the diplosomes (*Di*, *di*), a half of the monosome (*Mo*), while the 5 autosomes divide reductionally and their daughter components as they separate show each the reopening longitudinal split.

Second Maturation Mitosis. — Pole views (Fig. 192) of the spindle show 7 elements all in one plane; the smallest is a diplosome (*Di*) while the monosome (*Mo*) may be distinguished from the autosomes by its lesser depth; a lateral view of the same stage is given in Fig. 193, where the monosome is readily marked by its unconstricted form. Each of the autosomes divides equationally and so does the diplosome. But the monosome passes without dividing into one of the spermatids (*Mo*, Fig. 194). A pole view of any spermatid shows a circle of 5 autosomes around a minute central diplosome (Fig. 195): and half of the spermatids show just beneath this chromosomal plate a monosome.

Literature. — I had described (1901*b*) this spermatogenesis in the main correctly, only I failed to decide whether what I called the "odd chromosome" divided in the second maturation division and failed to notice that it is the larger allosome of the growth period; but later (1905) I showed that the monosome does not divide in this mitosis.

26. Oncopeltus fasciatus Dall.

My preceding account, a rather detailed one, of the spermatogenesis of this species was entirely correct. Of the 16 chromosomes of the spermatogonia I demonstrated that 2 are diplosomes, that these are distinguishable during the growth period, and very frequently separated from each other there, and that they enter the chromosomal plate of the first maturation mitosis separately and that each divides by itself. All that is to be corrected is my former interpretation that each of these is in the spermatogonium already bivalent, and that the division of each in the spermatocytes is to be considered reductional; now I find no good reason for such a view, and judge the latter division to be an equational one of the diplosomes. There is to be added to that former account the description of the

Second Maturation Division. — A pole view of a daughter chromosomal plate of the first maturation mitosis (Plate XII, Fig. 196) shows 9 elements; the 2 central rounded ones are the univalent diplosomes, and outside of them is a circle of 7 univalent diplosomes the constriction of each being its longitudinal split. As these come to arrange themselves in the equator of the second spindle there appear to be only 8 instead of 9 of them: this is because the univalent diplosomes have conjugated in the centre to form a bivalent one (Fig. 197). This bivalent element can be recognized only by its central position because its components are of equal volume (*Di*, *di*, Fig. 198). Each of the 7 autosomes divides equationally, but the bivalent diplosome divides reductionally. And each spermatid exhibits always exactly 8 elements of which the central one is a diplosome (Fig. 199).

27. Peliopelta abbreviata Uhler.

Spermatogonic Division. — There were on my preparations only two fairly clear pole views of the equatorial plate (Plate XII, Figs. 200, 201), and in each of these the elements were more or less obliquely placed. There are in all 14 chromosomes, 10 of which are noticeably larger and 4 considerably smaller. The following history shows that these 4 smaller ones are diplosomes, which compose a larger pair (*Di. 2*, *di. 2*) and a smaller pair (*Di. 1*, *di. 1*).

Growth Period. — From the synapsis stage (Fig. 202) there are in each nucleus, besides the long loops of the bivalent autosomes, 2 large dense bodies of equal volume; and when the autosomes become longitudinally split each of these becomes constricted at its middle point (*Di. 2*, *di. 2*, Fig. 203). By their size relations these are evidently the same as the pair of larger diplosomes of the spermatogonia, for they are much too large to correspond to the smaller pair. They may be apposed (Fig. 202) or may be separated (Fig. 203). The smaller diplosomes could not be distinguished with certainty at this time, whence it is likely that they undergo changes like the autosomes do, or at least do not remain dense and safraninophilous. The 10 large autosomes join end to end to form bivalent elements, and each becomes longitudinally split; they are then mostly in the form of a U or a V and the split in the arm of each remains narrow and never opens up widely.

First Maturation Division. — In the prophases condense 5 large tetrads, which are the bivalent autosomes; a single one of them is drawn in Fig. 204, and 4 in Fig. 205, they being the bodies that are not lettered; these may condense so as to appear nearly solid and very massive, but frequently the point of junction of the univalent elements continues recognizable as well as the longitudinal split in each of the latter, and this split is always parallel to the long axis. Next in size to these are 2 elements

(*Di. 2, di. 2*) alike in volume, each transversely constricted and the two never in close contact; each of these is then a dyad, not a tetrad, therefore is univalent and the two correspond to the larger pair of diplosomes of the earlier stages. Then there become clearly distinguishable a pair of much smaller bodies (*Di. 1, di. 1*, Figs. 204, 205) which correspond to the smallest chromosomes of the spermatogonium, and are a smaller pair of diplosomes; in the earlier prophases (Fig. 204) each of them is longitudinally split, and they may or may not be in mutual contact. Therefore there are in the prophases: 5 bivalent autosomes, 2 larger univalent diplosomes, and 2 smaller univalent diplosomes, 9 bodies in all.

In the equator of the spindle there may be the same number of elements, or there may be only 8 (Figs. 205, 206). This results because the smallest diplosomes may be joined end to end (as in Figs. 206, 207, *Di. 1, di. 1*) or be placed side by side (Fig. 208, *Di. 1, di. 1*); in either case, however, a whole one of these passes without division into one of the daughter cells, which amounts to a reduction division of the pair, and to each appear to be attached mantle fibres from only one spindle pole. The 2 larger diplosomes (*Di. 2, di. 2*, Figs. 206–208), which are recognizable by being dyads of equal volume and next in order of size, remain separated from each other, and each by dividing along the plane of its previous constriction divides equationally. The remaining, largest, chromosomes are all tetrads (the unlettered ones of Figs. 206–208), and these divide reductionally, because each divides transversely to its long axis. Each second spermatocyte receives accordingly 5 whole autosomes, a whole diplosome of the smaller pair, and a half of each larger diplosome, a total of 8 elements.

Second Maturation Division.—Here there are on pole views (Fig. 209) always only 7 chromosomes visible, 5 larger and two much smaller. The five largest are clearly the autosomes. The two smaller must then correspond to the 3 diplosomes that each second spermatocyte receives, *i. e.*, one of them must be bivalent. Lateral views (Fig. 210, which shows all the elements) demonstrate that each of the smaller elements is composed of two parts of equal volumes. Therefore there could not have taken place a conjugation of a large with a small diplosome, but two diplosomes of equal volumes must have conjugated. Now since we found that the second spermatocyte receives only one diplosome of the smaller pair, but a half of each of the larger, and since the latter were of equal volume, it is these larger ones that must conjugate, come to lie the one immediately above the other, in the second spindle. Accordingly, of the 6 elements shown in Figs. 209 and 210, the 5 largest are univalent autosomes, the smallest (*di. 1*) is one univalent diplosome of the smaller pair, while the next smallest, the central one, is bivalent (*Di. 2, di. 2*). This explanation suffices to make clear the change in number from 8 to 7 in conjunction with the persisting size relations.

Stages later than that of Fig. 240 were not found; but from the form and position of the chromosomes there it is probable that the 5 autosomes divide equationally, that the small diplosome (*Di. 1*) divides in the same way, but that the bivalent diplosome (*Di. 2, di. 2*) divides reductionally.

Accordingly, there are two pairs of diplosomes: in the maturation mitoses the larger of them divide first equationally then reductionally, the smaller first reductionally then equationally, so that the phenomena of division are reversed in the two pairs.

Literature. — In my preceding account (1901c) the spermatogonial number of chromosomes was erroneously given as 16, since I had counted two of the larger constricted ones as two each; and the contrasted behavior of the two diplosome pairs was overlooked because the second maturation mitosis was not studied.

28. Ischnodemus falicus Say.

Spermatogonic Division. — On the clearest pole view (Plate XII, Fig. 211) 15 elements could be counted. There must, however, be 16 present at this stage as will be shown by the later ones. Further, 4 must be diplosomes, of which the two marked *Di. 2, di. 2* must be the larger pair of diplosomes and *Di. 1* be one component of a smaller pair. The 12 largest bodies are certainly autosomes.

Growth Period. — Six bivalent autosomes are found in the form of V's or, as frequently, parallel rods, that is, they may conjugate end to end or side to side; each becomes longitudinally split. Sharply distinguishable from these during the whole growth period are 2 deep-staining, compact bodies, markedly different in volume, attached to the nuclear wall (*Di. 2, di. 2*, Figs. 212–214). These are the larger pair of diplosomes and represent the two similarly lettered ones in the spermatogonium (Fig. 211). They are rarely in contact with each other so that it may be that they do not conjugate. The larger of them (*di. 2*, Fig. 214) becomes longitudinally split, this split continuing up to the following mitosis; the smaller one is elongate, but only in rare cases does it show signs of division (*Di. 2*, Fig. 213). Towards the close of the growth period, which is not a rest stage, a large irregular plasmosome is developed (*Pl.*, Fig. 214), to which one or the other of the large diplosomes is frequently attached.

First Maturation Division. — In the early prophases reappear the pair of small diplosomes (*Di. 1, di. 1*, Fig. 215); they are not connected and each is at first a small bent rod with uneven contours and a longitudinal split. Each condenses and shortens, the split still maintained (*Di. 1, di. 1*, Figs. 216–219), and they usually do not conjugate until the stage of the equatorial plate. The pair of larger diplosomes are recognizable by their greater size (*Di. 2, di. 2*). Then there are in each nucleus 6 bivalent autosomes (Figs. 215–219, all of them shown in Fig. 217), which are much larger than any of the 4 diplosomes; they are at first of very diverse forms, inasmuch as each may have its univalent components meeting at an angle, or placed side by side, or more or less twisted around each other; the longitudinal split may be narrow for its whole length, or may be widest at the middle. These generally condense so that in each the univalent components come to lie in one line and the longitudinal split becomes obscured (Fig. 219).

On pole views of the monaster stage (Figs. 221, 222) are seen always 9 elements. The 6 largest are the bivalent autosomes (those that are not lettered), the smallest one, which is usually central in position, is bivalent being the pair of small diplosomes (*Di. 1, di. 1*) the components of which may lie one above the other or else side by side. The 2 remaining elements are those marked *Di. 2, di. 2*; they are unequal in volume and are placed apart from each other upon the periphery of the chromosomal plate; these are the elements of the larger diplosome pair, each of them univalent. A lateral view of the spindle (Fig. 220) shows the small bivalent diplosome (*Di. 1, di. 1*), the separated univalent diplosomes of the larger pair (*Di. 2, di. 2*), and 3 of the 6 autosomes. The 6 autosomes and the small bivalent diplosome divide reductionally as can be told from their position within the spindle; but each large diplosome by dividing separately undergoes an equation division; each second spermatocyte receives, accordingly, 6 univalent autosomes, one whole univalent component of the smaller diplosome pair, and a half of each component of the larger diplosome pair.

Second Maturation Division. — Pole views of the equatorial plate (Fig. 224) show only 8 elements, and not 9 as in the preceding mitosis. The six largest are the autosomes, and the very smallest is clearly the small diplosome (*Di. 1*). The element lettered *di. 2* must therefore be composed of two elements, in order to account for the apparent reduction in number in the second spermatocyte; and it is indeed bivalent, the composite of the components of the larger diplosome pair, for on lateral aspect of the spindle (Fig. 223) this chromosome is found to be composed of 2 bodies of dissimilar volumes placed end to end (*Di. 2, di. 2*), and we found that the diplosomes of the larger pair were characterized by this dissimilarity in volume. From the position of all these elements in the spindle it becomes evident that all the autosomes divide again, so equationally, and that the small diplosome (*Di. 1*) does the same; but that the bivalent larger diplosome divides reductionally in that its larger component passes into one spermatid and its smaller one into another. Only one good pole view of a spermatid was found (Fig. 225); this showed 7 elements which from their size are to be considered the 6 autosomes and the smaller component of the larger diplosome pair, while the element of the smaller diplosome pair was not visible (though it must be present on account of its division foreshadowed in the case shown in Fig. 223).

Literature. — In my preceding account (1901*b*) I did not find the diplosomes in the spermatogonic monaster, and did not describe the second maturation division; but I was correct in concluding that there are one bivalent and two univalent diplosomes in the first maturation monaster.

29. Cymus angustatus Stål.

My preparations showed neither spermatogonic mitoses nor pole views of the first maturation division, and their staining was unsuitable for determining the phenomena of the growth period.

Second Maturation Division. — Pole views show 14 elements, one of them (*di. 1*, Fig. 226, Plate XII), very minute and probably a univalent diplosome. Lateral views of the spindle demonstrate that one of the larger elements is composed of two bodies of unequal size placed end to end (*Di. 2, di. 2*, Fig. 228); in one case these two lay side by side (Fig. 227), and each seemed to be connected with only one spindle fibre. This is probably a bivalent diplosome destined to undergo a reductional division. The 13 other elements would seem to divide equationally or at least into equal parts.

While not much can be definitely decided from this stage alone, yet the phenomena show similarity to those of *Peliopelta* and *Ischnodemus*. That is, in the first spermatocyte there might well be 15 elements, one more than in the second; and these would be 12 autosomes that divide reductionally, a small bivalent diplosome dividing in the same manner, and a larger pair of diplosomes each component of which would divide by itself and these two then conjugate in the daughter cell. In the second spermatocyte there is certainly one bivalent element that divides reductionally, and it shows close resemblance to the bivalent diplosome of the same stage in *Ischnodemus*.

Literature. — My preceding observations (1901*b*) stated nothing definite. My preparations of *Cymus luridus*, of which a brief description was given by me (1901*a*), were not favorable for study.

TINGITIDÆ.

30. Tingis clavata Stål.

No spermatogonic divisions were seen.

Growth Period. — The iron-hæmatoxylin stain of the slides was too deep for clearly distinguishing allosomes, but, in addition to a large, somewhat irregular body that is probably a plasmosome, may be found one or two dense bodies of different volumes that may be diplosomes.

First Maturation Division. — Pole views show in most cases 7 elements (Plate XIII, Fig. 229), a circle of 6 around a central one. On side view all of these appear dumb-bellshaped (Fig. 230) except the central one which is composed of parts of unequal volumes (*Di, di*); these parts are placed usually end to end but sometimes side by side. This central one is probably a bivalent diplosome and divides reductionally, while the 6 others are probably bivalent autosomes that also divide. In two pole views out of a considerable number seen 8 elements were found; this happens because sometimes the components of one of the autosomes may be separated, as the two bodies marked *M* in Fig. 231.

Second Maturation Division. — There are regularly 7 elements present, namely, 6 autosomes and either the larger (*di*, Fig. 232) or the smaller diplosome (*Di*, Fig. 233). In a single case, manifestly an abnormality, 8 elements were present, both diplosomes being in the same cell (*Di, di*, Fig. 234). All 7 elements divide, presumably equationally, and 7 elements are always present in the spermatids (Fig. 235), half of the spermatids containing a division product of the larger and half of them a division product of the smaller spermatid.

Literature. — In my earlier description (1901*a*) I noted that one of the chromosomes of the first maturation mitosis is characterized "in having its two components of very unequal volume," but I failed to follow its behavior in this and the following mitosis.

PHYMATIDÆ.

31. Phymata sp. (*P. wolffii* Stal.?).

I can add little to my former account (1901*b*), and find that the chromosomes are too crowded in the second spermatocytes to be counted with precision. But in the spermatogonium I now think there are 29 and not 30 elements as I had previously described, for one is much longer than any of the others (*Mo*, Fig. 237, Plate XIII), and this I had originally counted as two. This unique chromosome was to be seen in all three of the distinct pole views. Therefore there is a possibility that a monosome is present in this species.

REDUVIIDÆ.

32. Acholla multispinosa de G.

Spermatogonic Division. — Pole views show exactly 32 chromosomes (Plate XIII, Fig. 238), of which 8 are 4 minute pairs of diplosomes.

Growth Period. — The 4 pairs of diplosomes can be recognized throughout the growth period, and were described in some detail in my previous paper; they lie on the surface of the plasmosome (*Pl*, Fig. 239), and as in the spermatogonium the pairs are of slightly different sizes.

First Maturation Division.—The bivalent diplosomes, 4 in number, are readily distinguished by their small size and lie always upon the periphery of the chromosomal plate; most frequently 3 lie close together, the 4th some distance off from them (Fig. 241); or they may all be near each other (Fig. 242), or 2 may be situated at one place and 2 at another. These diplosomes with the 12 bivalent autosomes are all illustrated on lateral aspect in Fig. 240, and all these elements divide, probably reductionally.

Second Maturation Division—Pole views of the spindle show again 16 elements but in different arrangement in that the 4 diplosomes now lie in the center (Figs. 243, 244). Lateral views show that all of these are bipartite, and therefore they all probably divide again though their number could not be counted in the spermatids. There is certainly no conjugation of any of the diplosomes in the second spermatocytes, and no evidence at any stage of the presence of a monosome.

Literature.—My earlier observations (1901 *b*) were entirely correct, and I have to add to them simply the account of the second spermatocytes.

33. Sinea diadema Fabr.

My earlier observations were essentially correct, and the three pairs of diplosomes of the rest stage of the spermatocyte are shown in Plate XIII, Fig. 245, attached to the plasmosome (*Pl*). Another pole view of a first maturation monaster is presented in Fig. 246, the 3 bivalent diplosomes readily distinguishable by their small volumes. Of the 13 autosomes three are always close together and so form a regular complex (*A*, *a*, *B*, *b*, *C*, *c*), just as I previously described; but now I find no reason to consider the central one of this complex quadrivalent, for there is no good evidence that it is anything else than an unusually large bivalent autosome and it does not behave differently from the others during the preceding growth period. This central one of the complex is always the largest and a very evident tetrad (*B*, *b*, Figs. 247, 248); close to one end of it is a smaller bivalent autosome (*A*, *a*), and close to its other end a still smaller one (*C*, *c*); these size relations are always the same. All the elements of this mitosis are shown on lateral view in Fig. 247; the 3 smallest are the bivalent diplosomes and they are of slightly different volumes. All 16 elements divide reductionally, so that each second spermatocyte receives a univalent component of each. The complex of the 3 autosomes *A*, *a*, and *B*, *b*, and *C*, *c* divides more tardily than the others, as shown by the successive stages of Figs. 248–250, and in these anaphases the lateral autosomes (*A*, *a* and *C*, *c*) become separated from the large middle one (*B*, *b*).

There were no clear cases of second maturation mitoses. But judging from the composition and behavior of the elements in the first spermatocytes, there would be in the spermatogonium: 6 univalent diplosomes and 26 univalent autosomes.

34. Prionidus cristatus Linn.

My former account (1901*b*) was correct in the main.

A new drawing of a spermatogonic monaster is given (Plate XIII, Fig. 251). Of the 26 chromosomes 2 are much larger (*A, a*) and 2 much smaller (*L, l*) than the others. All these are found on careful inspection to be arrangeable into a series of pairs, *A, a–M, m*, in which the two components of each pair are of approximately equal volume except the 2 marked *K, k*. There is probably no monosome because the number is an equal one.

In the complete rest stage of the spermatocytes are found 3 or 4 safraninophilous bodies (Fig. 252, *Di. 1, Di. 2, Di. 3*) attached to the surface of a large, more or less central, plasmosome (*Pl*). They are of unequal volumes; and when there are 3 of them each appears bipartite, while when there are 4 the 2 smallest are each unipartite. Perhaps, as in *Sinea*, these relations are to be interpreted as 3 bivalent diplosomes, the smallest of which may sometimes have its parts separated.

BELOSTOMATIDÆ.

35. Zaitha sp.

Spermatogonic Division. — In all of eight clear pole views 24 chromosomes were counted (Plate XIII, Fig. 253). They are of very different volumes, 4 being much larger and 2 much smaller than any of the others. They make up 11 pairs gradated both in form and size (*A, a–K, k*), all these being autosomes; and 1 pair of 2 unequal components (*Di, di*) that correspond to the diplosomes of the later stages. The 4 largest autosomes are about equal in length, but 2 of them (*A, a*) are thicker than the others (*B, b*). The 2 smallest elements (*K, k*), are always slightly different in volume.

Growth Period. — This terminates with a complete rest stage of short duration. In it is found a single spherical plasmosome (*Pl*, Fig. 254), and attached to its surface either 2 or 3 smaller rounded bodies, *Di. 1, di. 1*. The most frequent condition is that figured, and these smaller bodies probably represent the unequal diplosomes of the spermatogonium, the bipartite nature of the larger being due to a splitting. The amount of cytoplasm is relatively great and it contains towards the end of the growth period, besides one or a few small yolk spherules (*Yk*), 3 or 4 rather dense bodies (*bl*) more or less spherical in form, staining like the cytoplasm; they are variable in position and size but are usually close to the nucleus. Each one has a considerable resemblance in form and size to the single idiozome body of *Peripatus*; and they are probably masses of idiozome substance, well defined and few in number, whereas in most of the Hemiptera this substance is usually more or less diffused in a zone concentric to the nucleus. In the synapsis stage there is a single large mass of this substance at the distal pole of the nucleus.

First Maturation Division. — There are always 13 elements (Fig. 256), one more than half the number in the spermatogonium, therefore 2 of them must be univalent and the others bivalent. They show rather a dense grouping. The largest 2 (*A, a–B, b*) correspond to the 2 largest pairs of the spermatogonium, and are usually placed in the middle of the chromosomal plate; 2 smallest elements always lie on the periphery, the smaller of which (*K, k*) probably represents the smallest pair of the spermatogonium. All divide in this mitosis so that the second spermatocyte receives also 13 chromosomes.

Second Maturation Division. — Here the chromosomes are grouped differently in the spindle (Fig. 258), namely, as a circle of 11 around a central pair. The latter is composed of a smaller (*Di*) and a larger (*di*) body placed one above the other, and these move apart into opposite spermatids before the other chromosomes divide (Fig. 257); these 2 are obviously the unequal elements of the spermatogonia, and each of them must have undergone an equational division in the preceding mitosis and have been univalent there. The smaller component of this bivalent diplosome, *Di*, is next larger than the smallest of the autosomes, *K, k*, while the larger, *di*, is, counting from the smallest, the fourth in size of all the elements; these size relations probably hold true for the preceding division, and by means of it we can determine which elements of the former chromosomal plate (Fig. 256) are these elements *Di* and *di*. Each of the 11 autosomes divides, so that each spermatid receives 12 elements in all; this is to be determined from the form of the chromosomes and their position in the spindle (Fig. 257), for they are too densely crowded in the spermatids to be determined there.

Literature. — My preceding account (1901*b*) was entirely correct, except that by a slip of the pen I stated that the second spermatocyte receives only 11 chromosomes; I did not describe the second maturation mitosis.

HYDROBATIDÆ.

36. Hygrotrechus sp.

Spermatogonic Division. — There were only four good pole views. In three of them 20 elements could be counted, but in the fourth, which was the clearest because the chromosomes were most fully separated, 21 were found (Plate XIII, Fig. 259). Twenty of these are seen to form 10 pairs (*A, a–J, j*), which vary to considerable extent in both form and volume; but the very smallest (*Mo*) has no mate in size, and is therefore a monosome.

Growth Period. — This terminates in a complete rest stage (Fig. 260). There is a large plasmosome (*Pl*) attached to which is either a single body or a pair of bodies of like volume (*Mo*); the latter condition is to be explained as a monosome divided equationally into two parts, because these later join to compose the monosome of the maturation mitoses, and more particularly because in the earlier growth period these are represented by a single one. This monosome, respectively its halves, swells considerably in size during the growth period, and while continuing dense it does not remain safraninophilous. No bodies were found that represented diplosomes.

First Maturation Division. — In the prophases the plasmosome disappears; Fig. 261 reproduces a late prophase and shows all the chromosomes. Each autosome is bivalent, composed of 2 univalent ones placed more usually end to end, more rarely side to side, and each univalent element when viewed from its flattened surface shows a split along its axis which is evidently the same as the earlier longitudinal split of the postsynapsis stage. This split gradually closes, though never completely, as the autosomes condense and retains its position parallel to the length of the autosome. Besides these autosomes there are 2 much smaller bodies (*Mo*), which are alike in size and each, so far as I could determine, is unipartite; at this stage they are frequently not separated but apposed, and probably represent the halves of the monosome.

Pole views of the equatorial plate (Figs. 266, 267) show 11 elements, one more than half the number in the spermatogonium; on strict pole view 10 of them, the autosomes, always seem bipartite, while the smallest one, the monosome (*Mo*), appears unipartite; seen from the side (Fig. 262) the 10 autosomes are found to be tetrads, while the monosome (*Mo*) is a dyad. This monosome divides and apparently through the plane where its halves had previously come together, therefore equationally. The 10 tetrads, the bivalent autosomes, are so nearly quadratic in outline that it is difficult to decide how they divide, but there is no reason to hold that they do not divide reductionally. As a result each second spermatocyte receives also 11 elements.

Second Maturation Division. — The chromosomes evince no great constancy in their arrangement in the spindle (Figs. 266, 267), the monosome may be recognized by its lesser depth (*Mo*). Side views (Fig. 265) show that 10 are always bipartite with their constrictions placed in the equator; these are the autosomes and there can be no question that all of them divide. But the smallest element, the monosome (*Mo*), is spherical, and placed usually a little above or below the plane of the autosomes; I have not drawn its mantle fiber attachments because I was unable to ascertain them. Only one clear pole view of a daughter plate of chromosomes of this mitosis was seen

(Fig. 268), and that showed 10 elements. But from its unipartite appearance in the spindle, and from its situation a little out of the plane of the autosomes, there can be little doubt that the monosome passes undivided into one of the spermatids.

Literature. — My former description (1901) was incorrect in concluding 20 to be the normal number of chromosomes, and in supposing the allosomes of the growth period to be a pair of diplosomes. Also I did not describe the second maturation mitosis.

37. Limnotrechus marginatus Say.

The spermatogenesis is on the whole very similar to that of the preceding species. There were no spermatogonic divisions on my slides.

Growth Period. — There is a monosome, which in the rest stage (*Mo*, Fig. 269, Plate XIII) is longitudinally split: it may be nearly spherical, but more usually is elongate with the split along its length; further, it is usually separated from the plasmosome (*Pl*). These constitute the main differences from *Hygrotrechus.*

First Maturation Division. — There are 10 large tetrads, the autosomes, and 1 small dyad, the monosome (*Mo*, Figs. 271, 272). All of them divide, the monosome equationally.

Second Maturation Division. — There are also 10 autosomes and the half of the monosome (Fig. 274), the latter recognizable upon pole view by its lesser depth. All the autosomes divide, but the monosome (*Mo*, Fig. 273) remains rounded, is placed usually a little nearer one spindle pole than the other, and therefore probably passes undivided into one of the spermatids.

Literature. — My preceding account (1901*b*) was very brief, and I supposed a pair of diplosomes to be present.

CAPSIDÆ.

38. Calocoris rapidus Say.

Spermatogonic Division. — There was only one clear pole view (Plate XIII, Fig. 275), and that showed exactly 30 elements.

Growth Period. — Throughout this period there is a deep-staining, rod-like body close against the nuclear membrane, which on profile gives the effect of a crescent. In the synapsis (Fig. 276, *Mo. 1*) it is more or less ovoid, but it later assumes the form of a bent rod (*Mo. 1*, Fig. 277) and during all the stages except the earliest shows a well-marked longitudinal split. In the later stages this body has usually the form of two bent rods, which may be parallel, or slightly divergent when the space between them is the longitudinal split. This is the larger monosome of the spermatocytes, as will be demonstrated by its later history. Though always prominent in the nucleus by reason of its large size and deep stain, it does not remain completely compact and dense, but sometimes shows a loosening of its texture. Besides this there is a second and much smaller monosome (*Mo. 2*, Figs. 276, 277), usually rod-shaped in the synapsis and more spherical later, generally separated from the nuclear membrane; it shows no signs of a longitudinal split. Both of these monosomes increase considerably in volume, then decrease again during the following prophases. Plasmosomes seem to be absent, and there is no complete rest stage.

First Maturation Division. — In the prophases (Fig. 278) the smaller monosome (*Mo. 2*) can be recognized by its unipartite aspect, the larger one (*Mo. 1*) by its form of two more or less parallel rods. All the other elements are quadripartite autosomes except the two smallest; one of the latter has the shape of two apposed spherules (*Di. 1*, Fig. 278), while the other (*Di. 2*) eventually assumes this form but is the latest of all the chromosomes to become dense in structure; these two smallest elements are probably bivalent diplosomes, because though they are not distinguishable during the growth period they differ from the monosomes by much smaller volume and different form; and I judge that each is bivalent on account of its behavior in the two maturation mitoses.

In the spindle there are always 16 elements, all placed in one plane except one (*Mo. 2*, Figs. 279–283) that lies invariably nearer one spindle pole than the other. This is the only one that seems unipartite, and is the smallest of all; it is undoubtedly the smaller monosome, and has decreased in volume since the prophases. Of the remaining elements one is the larger monosome and it can be recognized on side view only, and then because its long axis lies in the plane of the equator (*Mo. 1*, Fig. 283). Then there are 2 diplosomes (*Di. 1*, *di. 2*) which are very small and next larger than the smaller monosome. The 12 remaining elements are 12 bivalent autosomes, each quadripartite; one of them, that marked *t* in the Figs. 279–281, is unusually large, and for this reason I had originally (1901*b*) supposed it to be quadrivalent; but since there are 30 elements in the spermatogonium this one cannot be more than bivalent.

The 12 bivalent autosomes divide transversely to their lengths, therefore probably reductionally. The two diplosomes also divide, but in what way I have no means of determining. The larger monosome divides and equationally. But the smaller monosome, which always lies a little out of the plane of the other elements, never divides but passes wholly over into that spermatocyte of the second order to which it is nearest. Half the second spermatocytes receive, accordingly, 16 chromosomes, and half of them 15, the one that may be lacking being the smaller monosome.

Second Maturation Division. — Pole views of the second spindle are shown in Figs. 285, 286. One of them is a cell containing the smaller monosome (*Mo. 2*, Fig.

285), while the other is a cell that lacks this body. There are always two diplosomes that can be recognized by their small size, but slightly larger than the smaller monosome. As in the preceding mitosis the smaller monosome always lies a little outside of the plane of the other chromosomes, so in this second mitosis the larger one always lies somewhat to one side of the equatorial plane (*Mo. 1*, Fig. 284); and by virtue of this position it may be recognized even upon pole view (*Mo. 1*, Fig. 285). Fig. 284 shows the 3 smallest elements, which we have found to be the smaller monosome (*Mo. 2*), and the two diplosomes (*Di. 1*, *Di. 2*), all three of them showing a division constriction. This demonstrates that the smaller monosome divides, that the diplosomes also do, and because the 12 autosomes are equally constricted they too must divide. But the larger monosome (*Mo. 1*, Fig. 284) lies nearer one spindle pole than the other, is never constricted, and in the anaphases (Fig. 287) passes without dividing into one of the spermatids.

Accordingly there are in this complicated case: 12 autosomes that divide in both mitoses, 2 diplosomes that do likewise (therefore are probably also bivalent), a smaller monosome that does not divide in the first but does divide in the second mitosis, and a larger monosome that divides in the first but not in the second mitosis. Therefore, each spermatid receives 12 autosomes and 2 diplosomes, while only half of them receive the larger, and only half of them the smaller diplosome; whether any spermatid ever receives both monosomes, or whether any one ever lacks both monosomes, I could not decide, because the chromosomes are closely crowded in the spermatids.

From the relations of the chromosomes in the spermatocytes the elements in the spermatogonium should be as follows: 24 autosomes, 1 larger and 1 smaller monosome and 4 diplosomes, a total of 30 elements which was the number constated to be present there.

Literature. — In my earlier observations (1901*b*) I mistook the larger monosome of the growth period for a plasmosome, because I supposed a plasmosome must be present; what I then called the "univalent chromatin nucleolus" corresponds to what I now denominate the smaller monosome; and I correctly showed that this does not divide in the first maturation mitosis. The following mitosis was not described. Otherwise the complex phenomena were correctly ascertained.

39. Poecilocapsus goniphorus Say.

Growth Period. — This is terminated by a complete rest stage. Attached to the plasmosomes (*Pl*, Fig. 288, Plate XIII), though occasionally separated from them, are a number of safraninophilous dense allosomes. The largest of these (*di. 1*) is always in the form of a pair of short parallel rods, and, therefore, is to be regarded as probably a longitudinally split, univalent element. Three other pairs of different sizes are always to be seen (*Di. 1, Di. 2, Di. 3*) and sometimes a fourth (*Di. 4*). The components of each pair are equal in volume, but whether each pair is to be considered as two diplosomes, or as the division products of a single one, I could not determine since the number of chromosomes in the spermatogonia is unknown.

First Maturation Division.—There are always 18 elements (Fig. 289), 17 large and 1 (*Di. 1*) much smaller. The latter is always bipartite (Fig. 290), never quadripartite, and as will be evident from its later history is an univalent diplosome, and from its size perhaps correspondent to the two bodies marked *Di. 1* in the growth period (Fig. 288). Of the 17 larger elements 1 must be the largest diplosome of the preceding growth period (*di. 1*, Fig. 288), but at this stage it cannot be distinguished with certainty from the other larger elements. In this mitosis the other small diplosomes of the growth period (*Di. 2, Di. 3, Di. 4*) are to be found neither in the spindle nor in the cytoplasm. All 18 elements divide, and this is an equation division of the large and small diplosome, but probably a reduction division of the 16 bivalent autosomes.

Second Maturation Division.—There are 17 larger elements seen on pole views (Fig. 291), 1 less than in the preceding spindle. This is because the large and small diplosome have conjugated end to end, as one may ascertain by careful focussing (*Di. 1, di. 1*). Lateral views (Fig. 292) show that this bivalent element lies always slightly out of the plane of the other chromosomes, and that each component of it is unconstricted. Each of the 16 autosomes divides, but the components of the bivalent diplosome pass without division into opposite spermatids. Two daughter plates of the anaphase are reproduced, as drawn from the same cell at two levels; one exhibits the smaller diplosome (*Di. 1*, Fig. 293), while the other lacks this but shows the larger diplosome (*di. 1*, Fig. 294).

From the number of chromosomes in the maturation mitoses it may be concluded that there are present in the spermatogonia 32 autosomes and 2 diplosomes.

Literature.—My previous account (1901*b*) confused the two maturation mitoses, and did not describe the second one.

40. Lygus pratensis Linn.

Spermatogonic Division.—There were only 2 pole views, on the one I counted 33, on the other 34 elements. The correct number is probably 35 as we shall find.

Growth Period.—One large, longitudinally-split allosome can be distinguished in the spermatocytes; whether there are others could not be determined.

First Maturation Division. — In the spindle there are 19 chromosomes (Plate XIII, Figs. 295, 296). The smallest of them (*Mo*, Fig. 296) is never in the equatorial plane but always nearer one of the spindle poles; it does not divide but passes bodily into one of the spermatocytes of the second order. This minute element would appear to be a monosome, comparable to the smaller monosome of *Calocoris*. There is no sign of it in the chromosomal plate of the following mitosis. Of the 18 elements that lie in the equator (Fig. 295) all divide in this mitosis. Two of them (*Di. 1* and *Di. 2*, *di. 2*) are much smaller than the others; the smaller of the two (*Di. 1*) is a univalent diplosome as its later behavior shows, while the larger is a bivalent element and it may be a pair of diplosomes (though its small size is the only reason to consider it a diplosome). Of the 16 large elements one of the largest, if not the very largest, must be another univalent diplosome, which with the small element *Di. 1* are unequal components of a diplosome pair.

Second Maturation Division. — There are always exactly 17 elements to be seen on pole views of the spindle (Fig. 297), 2 less than in the preceding spindle: this number was found in numerous cases. All are larger than the small monosome of the antecedent mitosis, and this monosome is not to be found in the chromosomal plate; one would expect to find it in the equator of half of the second spermatocytes, as is the case with the correspondent element in *Calocoris*; but it is always absent, and therefore probably lies out in the cytoplasm where it is indistinguishable from small yolk spherules. Further, in the equator there is only one separate small element (Fig. 297, *Di. 2*), and not 2 separate elements (as in the preceding spindle, Fig. 295, *Di. 1*, *Di. 2*). Careful study shows that one of the chromosomes is bivalent, composed of a small one (*Di. 1*, Fig. 298) placed at the end of a much larger one (*di. 1*), the larger one lying invariably a little above or below the equator which enables one to recognize it upon pole view (*di. 1*, Fig. 297). This bivalent chromosome is composed of the division products of the largest and smallest diplosomes of the first spermatocytes, which had divided separately but are now in conjugation. The single separate small element (*Di. 2*, Figs. 297, 298) again divides by itself; it is a little larger than the smaller element of the bivalent pair and therefore represents a half of the bivalent element *Di. 2*, *di. 2* of the former mitosis. The 15 autosomes also divide, and the bivalent diplosome divides reductionally, its smaller component going into one spermatid and its larger one into the other; for this becomes evident from their position within the spindle (Fig. 298, *Di. 1*, *di. 1*), while in the anaphases the larger component (Fig. 299, *di. 1*) comes to lie wholly in one of the daughter chromosomal plates.

There are accordingly in the maturation mitoses: one very small monosome that does not divide in the first spermatocyte, and is not present in the chromosomal plate of the second; a large and small diplosome (*di. 1, Di. 1*) that divide separately and therefore equationally in the first mitosis, but conjugate in the second spermatocytes and undergo a reductional separation there; and a small bivalent element, *Di. 2, di. 2*, that may be another diplosome, which divides in both mitoses as do the 15 autosomes. Consequently each spermatid must receive halves of the 15 autosomes and of the element *di. 2, di. 2*, half of them receive *Di. 1* and the other half receive *di. 1*, and half of them get the monosome.

From these relations we may conclude for the spermatogonium: 30 autosomes, one monosome, one large and one small diplosome (*di. 1, Di. 1*), and a pair of small diplosomes (*Di. 2, di. 2*), a total of 35 elements.

Literature. — In my earlier account I overlooked the small monosome, and did not describe the second maturation division.

II. General Considerations.

1. Behavior and Significance of the Allosomes.

In the Hemiptera heteroptera the allosomes present the following relations in the spermatogenesis:

A. *Only Diplosomes Present*, and these exhibiting the following differences:

A1. The diplosomes conjugate early in the growth period, divide reductionally in the first maturation mitosis, and equationally in the second. This is the case in *Tingis*, where there is a single pair with components of very unequal volume; and in *Acholla* (4 pairs) and *Sinea* (3 pairs), where the diplosomes are very small and the components of a pair of about equal volume. In *Sinea* and *Acholla* they remain dense during the growth period; in *Tingis* it was not determined how they behave during this stage.

A2. One pair of diplosomes which divide separately and equationally in the first maturation mitosis, but in the second spermatocytes conjugate and then divide reductionally. This modus was first discovered by Wilson; I had shown (1901*b*) that in certain species (*Euschistus tristigmus, Oncopeltus, Zaitha*) the diplosomes divide separately in the first maturation mitosis, but I failed to note, because in these species I omitted to describe the second mitosis, that their daughter products unite in the second spermatocytes and there undergo a reductional division. Diplosomes of this behavior Wilson called the "idiochromosomes," and he correctly noted that they are unequal in volume; in *Nezara* alone he states that they are equal, but even here I find that there is always a slight voluminal difference. They always remain more or less dense and compact during the growth period; and in most cases they conjugate early in the growth period as I had previously described, but, as Wilson first demonstrated in detail, separate from each other before taking position in the first maturation spindle. Wilson has described these for *Lygaeus, Coenus, Nezara, Euschistus, Brachymena, Podisus, Trichopepla*; and they are described in the present paper for *Euschistus, Podisus, Mormidea, Cosmopepla, Nezara, Brachymena, Perillus, Coenus, Trichopepla, Eurygaster, Peribalus, Oncopeltus, Zaitha*, and *Poecilocapsus*. In the last named species and in *Trichopepla* much more minute allosomes are found in the growth period, but cannot be distinguished with certainty during the maturation mitoses.

A3. Two or more pairs of diplosomes of diverse behavior. In *Nabis* there are in the spermatocytes two bivalent diplosomes that remain compact during the growth period, divide reductionally in the first maturation division and equationally in the second, and the components of a pair are equal in size; and then another pair of diplosomes that are of very unequal size, which are also distinct during the growth period, but which divide separately and equationally in the first maturation mitosis and in the next mitosis (without conjugation in the equatorial plate) divide reductionally. In *Peliopelta, Ischnodemus* and probably *Cymus* there is a smaller pair, which do not remain compact during the growth period and do not conjugate until late, and these divide reductionally in the first maturation mitosis and equationally in the second; and besides these there is a larger pair of very unequal components which remain apart from one another during the growth period and then retain their dense structure, which divide separately and equationally in the first maturation mitosis, and in the second spermatocytes conjugate in the equatorial plane and then divide reductionally. Then in *Syromastes* Gross has described two pairs of diplosomes: the larger conjugate very early in the growth period, remain dense, divide in the first maturation mitosis reductionally and in the second equationally; while the smaller pair, adequal in volume, undergo changes like the autosomes during the growth period, do not conjugate until after it, and compose a tetrad which divides in the first maturation mitosis but not in the second. Accordingly, this third type of diplosome relations may be said to be a combination of the previous two.

B. *Only Monosomes Present.*—This would appear to be the most unusual condition present in the Hemiptera, and is here described for *Hygotrechus* and *Limnotrechus*, while Henking found it for *Pyrrhocoris*; in these cases the monosome remains compact during the growth period, divides equationally in the first maturation mitosis and does not divide in the second.

C. *Both Diplosomes and Monosomes Present*, showing the following diversities:

C1. One pair of diplosomes of small and adequal volume that usually conjugate in the early growth period and during it may either remain compact or may undergo changes much like those of the autosomes (*Alydus, Metapodius*), divide in the first maturation mitosis reductionally and in the second equationally; and one monosome, much larger than the bivalent diplosome, always compact in the growth period (except in *Œdancala*, and in *Harmostes* it may become more or less reticular), which divides equationally in the first maturation mitosis, but does not divide in the second. This condition was first described by me for *Protenor* and *Œdancala*, then found by Wilson for *Anasa*, *Alydus* and *Harmostes*, and in the present paper it is described for these genera as well as for *Corizus*, *Chariesterus* and *Metapodius*. Accordingly, *Syromastes* would appear to be the only Coreid thus far described which does not conform to this type.

C2. In *Calocoris* there are two bivalent diplosomes that divide in the maturation mitoses first reductionally and then equationally; a smaller monosome that does not divide in the first maturation mitosis, but does divide in the second; and a larger monosome that divides in the reverse order of this. The monosomes remain compact during the growth period, but the diplosomes do not.

C3. In *Lygus* there is a single, very small monosome that does not divide in either maturation mitosis. And one pair of diplosomes of very unequal volume, which divide separately and equationally in the first maturation mitosis, conjugate in the second spermatocytes and divide reductionally. Another bivalent element, the smallest, which divides like the autosomes, may be another diplosome pair, but this could not be distinctly determined by me.

C4. In *Archimerus* Wilson (1905c) finds that the monosome does not divide in the first maturation mitosis, but in the second divides equationally; while a bivalent diplosome with small components of equal volume divides first reductionally and second equationally.

C4. And in *Banasa* Wilson (1905c) describes a monosome that behaves like that of *Archimerus*, together with a pair of very unequal diplosomes that divide in the first maturation mitosis separately and equationally, conjugate in the second spermatocytes, and then divide reductionally.

The other groups where allosomes are known to occur are the following. In the spermatogenesis of the Orthoptera according to the researches of Wilcox (1895), McClung (1899–1905), Sutton (1900, 1902*b*), de Sinéty (1901), and Baumgartner (1904) there is a single monosome said not to divide in the first maturation mitosis but to divide equationally in the second. The only exceptions among the Orthoptera are *Syrbula*, where I showed (1905) there to be a pair of diplosomes which conjugate early in the growth period, and divide first reductionally and then equationally in the maturation mitoses; *Hippiscus* as described by McClung (1900), where a single monosome is stated to divide in both maturation divisions; *Stenopelmatus*, where Miss Stevens

(1905*b*) finds the monosome to disintegrate in the second spermatocyte but to probably reappear in the spermatids; and in *Periplaneta* where Moore and Robinson (1905) conclude there is no allosome, but reinvestigation of this species is needed because Miss Stevens has described a monosome in the closely related *Blattella*. McGill (1904) has described for *Anax*, an Odonate, an allosome that divides in the first maturation mitosis and not in the second; but this author identifies this single element with a pair of chromosomes of the spermatogonium, which makes the phenomena somewhat difficult to interpret. The account of the spermatogenesis of the coleopteron *Cybister*, given by Voinov (1903), I have not seen. Miss Stevens (1905*b*) finds them to be absent in aphids and *Termopsis* (a termite); in the coleopteron *Tenebrio* she describes a pair of very unequal diplosomes that divide in the maturation mitoses first reductionally and then equationally; and in *Sagitta* she describes an allosome that divides in both maturation divisions. In *Agalena* Miss Wallace (1905) finds a pair of diplosomes that do not divide in either maturation mitosis, which is quite different from my own results upon *Lycosa* (1905), to the effect that the pair of diplosomes divide reductionally and then equationally. The spermatogenesis of the Chilopods (*Scolopendra*), as described by Blackman (1905*a*, *b*), is peculiar in that the monosome during the growth period comes to contain all the autosomes, so to form a "karyosphere"; they pass out of it before the first maturation mitosis, where it does not divide, but it divides equationally in the second mitosis; essentially similar results were obtained by Miss Medes (1905) for *Scutigera*. Some of the most interesting and complex relations of monosomes have recently been found by McClung (1905) in various acridiids, consisting in the adhesion of the monosome to one or more autosomes whereby plurivalent elements may be formed not only in the spermatocytes but even in the spermatogonia.

We may now attempt to decide what decisions the diversity of behavior of the allosomes, particularly in the Hemiptera, may give in regard to their genesis and mutual relations.

Since Henking's first discovery of them in *Pyrrhocoris* all observers have been in agreement that they are modified chromosomes. And on the observational basis that we have to-day we are in position to conclude what this genesis may have been. In the first place the ordinary chromosomes, the autosomes, of the Hemiptera are proven to divide in the maturation mitoses first reductionally, and second equationally. The results of Henking, Paulmier, Stevens and myself are in agreement on this issue, and only Gross assumes a reversed order of division; Gross's position is not borne out by his own observations, as I pointed out in another place (1905) and there reasoned, and Grégoire (1905) has strongly seconded me in this, that probably in all Metazoa the first maturation division is reductional and the second equational. On account of the great mass of evidence upon this question, which has been fully discussed in earlier papers of mine, we shall assume it as proven that in the Hemiptera the autosomes divide in this sequence. Therefore, the allosomes being modified chromosomes, those allosomes that divide in the same way as the autosomes do would be genetically closest to the autosomes. Such are the diplosomes of the Coreidæ (except the smaller pair of *Syromastes*), of the Reduviidæ and *Tingis*, *Calocoris*, the smaller diplosomes of *Nabis*, and one of the diplosome pairs of *Peliopelta* and *Ichnodemus*. These diplosomes correspond to the "M-chromosomes" of Wilson. They are in most cases the smallest of all the chromosomes, sometimes very minute, and, except in *Tingis*, are only very slightly different in size. Probably those of them that do not remain dense but become reticular in the growth period, as is the case in *Alydus*, *Metapodius*, *Œdancala* and *Calocoris*, are the least modified, because the most similar in behavior to the autosomes. The other kind of diplosomes correspond to what Wilson has called the "idiochromosomes," and he first distinguished between these and the preceding kind. These usually do, sometimes do not, conjugate in the early growth period, enter the chromosomal plate of the first maturation mitosis separately, and divide there equationally, then in the second spermatocytes (usually but not always after a conjugation in the center of the chromosomal plate) divide reductionally; they always remain more or less dense and compact during the growth period, and are usually very different in volume, though Wilson has shown that in *Nezara* they are nearly equal. Both kinds of diplosomes may occur in the same cell.

We do not know intermediates between these two kinds of diplosomes, though there can well be no doubt that the second is a further modification of the first; because sometimes in the first type the diplosomes may be unequal, and in the second type sometimes almost equal in size, size difference cannot be taken as a criterion of them, and for this reason it seemed to me inadvisable to consider them as quite different allosomes as Wilson has done. The most striking difference between the two types is the discord with regard to the reduction division; in the first type it occurs in the first maturation mitosis, in the second type in the succeeding mitosis. This certainly stands in some relation with the time of conjugation of the elements of the pair, which in the first type is always early in the growth period, while in the second type it may occur then, but frequently does not take place until the stage of the second spermatocyte or may not occur even at that stage. From the series of facts now at hand, we might conclude that the genesis of the diplosomes is as follows. First a pair of autosomes became modified so as to retain their compact nature during the growth period, still maintaining their approximate equivalence in volume. Because such allosomes are usually very small, we might conclude also that they arose from the smallest pair of autosomes. In the next change would appear a growing disparity in size, which, if our last assumption be correct, would be due not to one becoming smaller and to the other becoming larger, but rather to one retaining its original volume and to the other becoming much larger. This second step would then be one of differentiation of the two, a becoming-different, probably implying also difference of metabolic activites. This would account for the lessening affinity of the two as exhibited by the protraction of the time of conjugation. Then would be attained the stage of the second type of diplosomes, no longer united but separate in the first maturation spindle. And the last step would be that, instead of a reduction division of them in this spindle, there would take place there an equational division of each.

In this interpretation, which serves at least to unify the diverse phenomena and is in accord with them, we learn that the two kinds of diplosomes are not really radically different structures, but are rather extremes of a series of modifications.

We may now pass to the question of the genesis of the monosomes. In most cases these are larger than the diplosomes, sometimes the largest of all the chromosomes, more rarely are they very minute, as in *Calocoris* and *Lygus*. Usually the monosome remains dense and compact during the growth period, but in *Œdancala* it becomes reticular and is then practically indistinguishable from the autosomes; in *Harmostes* it becomes reticular to a much less degree. A monosome like that of *Œdancala* is clearly a less modified chromosome than are the monosomes of the other Hemiptera. Then monosomes may divide in the first maturation mitosis but not in the second (*Hygrotrechus, Limnotrechus, Pyrrhocoris,* all the Coreidae except *Syromastes, Œdancala,* and the larger monosome of *Calocoris*); my recent observations show that it is always an equation division, along the line in which the monosome splits in the growth period. But in *Archimerus* and *Banasa*, according to Wilson, the monosome does not divide in the first maturation mitosis but does in the second; I find the smaller monosome of *Calocoris* behaves in the same way, and that in *Lygus* the minute monosome does not divide in either mitosis. Thus with regard to the sequence of division, three kinds of monosomes occur in the Hemiptera, of which the kind that divides reductionally in the first maturation mitosis must be considered the least modified because the one that behaves most like the autosomes.

In an earlier paper (1901*b*) I discussed the question of the genesis of the monosomes; showed that a monosome might be produced by the hybridization of species with different chromosomal numbers, but concluded this to be improbable; and inclined to the view that monosomes arose by some abnormality in mitosis, as by failure of two spermatogonial chromosomes to separate, which led to my assumption that the larger monosomes are bivalent elements. This idea of the bivalence of the monosomes I carried out further in my last paper (1905). This seemed to me to best explain the usually relatively large size of the monosomes. Since then McClung (1905) has demonstrated the occurrence of undoubted bivalent chromosomes in the spermatogonia of certain Orthoptera, which may be a union of two or more autosomes or of a monosome with an autosome.

But Miss Stevens (1905*b*) showed for *Tenebrio* that while in the spermatogenesis there is a pair of diplosomes of very unequal volume, this pair is represented in the ovogenesis by two of equal volume. Then Wilson (1906*b*) compared the ovogenesis and spermatogenesis in a series of Hemiptera, confirming Miss Stevens' conclusion and elaborating it: Wilson's results may be briefly summarized as follows. Where there is a single monosome in the spermatogenesis (as in *Protenor, Harmostes, Anasa* and *Alydus*) there are two in the ovogenesis so that the ovogonia possess always an equal number of chromosomes. And where in the spermatogenesis there is a pair of diplosomes of unequal volume, there is in the ovogenesis a pair with components equal in volume to the larger diplosome of the spermatogenesis. Thus while half the spermatids lack the monosome, and half of them lack the larger diplosome, each ovotid would contain a monosome and each a larger diplosome. And from this phenomenon Wilson concludes, as did Miss Stevens before him, that a spermatozoön containing a monosome or the larger diplosome on fertilizing an egg produces a female individual; but that a spermatozoön lacking either of these gives rise to a male individual.

The point in this important discovery of Wilson's that immediately concerns us is that the modification of autosomes into allosomes has taken place in the spermatogenesis; and that a monosome of the spermatogenesis has originated by the continuance of the larger element of a diplosome pair in the sperm cells, and the loss of the smaller element there. This is a very plausible conclusion, but there are in particular two phenomena that must be explained before it can be accepted. One is, how an allosome becomes lost in the spermatogenesis; and the other is, how the allosomes introduced by the spermatozoön into the ovum behave during the ovogenetic cycle; on both of these questions we know as yet practically nothing. I showed in 1904 for *Anasa* that the pair of minute diplosomes of the spermatogonium are represented in the ovogonium by a pair equivalent in size and appearance. Such equivalent diplosomes we have just found to be probably the least modified kind of allosomes. The commencement of the allosomes may have had then a parallel course in the two sexes. And the point that now needs to be determined is the behavior of the ovogenetic allosomes in the growth period and the maturation divisions.

So we have reached the conclusion that the allosomes are to be considered modified chromosomes, of which the most primitive condition would be pairs of like volume conjugating and dividing in the same way as the autosomes do. One component of each pair must be paternal and one maternal, as I proved some years ago (1901*b*). Therefore, corresponding elements must have become modified in the germ cells of both sexes. A more modified condition would be pairs composed of components of dissimilar volume, not conjugating until the second spermatocyte, and dividing in the maturation mitoses in reverse order from that of the autosomes. Wilson's observations would indicate that this further specialization has taken place in the spermatogenesis alone, but it is by no means proven that such need to have been the case in all species. Finally, as to the monosomes, they may be single surviving components of diplosome pairs of which one has been lost in the spermatogenesis as Wilson concludes; or it is possible that they may have originated by the permanent coalescence of two chromosomes, either autosomes or diplosomes, as I have argued. I wish simply to indicate how diverse the possibilities are, and to point out that we cannot be sure of these conclusions until more is known of the phenomena in the ovogenesis.

As to the function of the allosomes, Paulmier (1899) concluded them to be degenerating chromatin masses: "I would make the suggestion . . . that these small chromosomes, or idants (to adopt for the moment Weismann's terminology) contain "ids" which represent somatic characters which belonged to the species in former times, but which characters are disappearing." Then I argued (1901*b*): "The chromatin nucleoli [allosomes] are in that sense degenerate, that they no longer behave like the other chromosomes in the rest stages; but they would appear to be specialized for a metabolic function. Thus it might be that in the insects the chromatin nucleoli are those chromosomes which exert a greater metabolic activity than the other chromosomes, or which carry out some special kind of metabolism; and from this point of view they would certainly seem to be much more than degenerate organs." Then I pointed out that not infrequently they are attached regularly to plasmosomes; and now I would call attention to the fact that they are still more frequently in contact with the nuclear membrane. Undoubtedly their function must be very different from that of the autosomes, because they appear and behave so different from them. The retention of the compact form and safraninophilous stain, so characteristic of many of them, throughout the growth period and in the rest stage of the spermatogonia, indicates that their nucleinic acid constituent changes less than in the autosomes. The sex determination by them, reasoned by McClung, Miss Stevens (1905*b*) and Wilson (1906), is a secondary function; if they do exercise a differentiation of sex this would be not their primal function but rather an indirect result of their metabolic peculiarities. From their position within the cell there can be little question that they fulfill an important part in the interplay of nuclear and cytoplasmic activity, an influence perhaps in proportion to their size. Yet this influence can hardly be one of the nature of an assimilation process, else the chemical nature of the two allosomes could not remain so constant during the growth period.

2. The Nuclear Element and Chromosomal Difference.

More than twenty years ago Carnoy (1885) spoke of the Metazoan nucleus as containing an "élément nucléinien," by which he meant a continuous complex of linin and chromatin. We now know that his idea of nuclear structure was not exact, that, for instance, in the majority of nuclei there is no well marked chromatin spirem through the rest stage of the cell as he conceived it. Yet Carnoy had probably the right general idea. In my analysis of the spermatogenesis of Peripatus (1900), which was quite largely an examination of the changes of the linin threads, I went into considerable detail into the connection of the chromatin and the linin, and developed the thought very similar to that of Carnoy, that as the nuclear element of the first order should be considered the totality of the linin and chromatin. I conceived of this as a continuous and persisting linin band with which the chromatin masses are always in contact. The unity of this element is best seen in the prophases of cell division, where there is a continuous linin spirem with chromatin masses segregated upon it. But though the linin band becomes very much branched in the rest stage, and the chromatin particles become finely distributed along these branches, yet there is considerable evidence that it always maintains its continuity as a single band. In all spermatogonic divisions the whole band, not only the chromatin masses, probably divides along its entire length, so that each daughter nucleus would receive one half of the original nuclear element; but in the reduction division this band would become transversely divided, therefore broken into as many portions as there are chromosomes. And I showed (1900, 1901*b*) that just after the reduction division, and in the earliest cleavages of the fertilized egg, the chromosomes are most distinct, presenting the appearance of small, independent vesicles. Therefore the reduction division causes the segmentation of the nuclear element, and accordingly it must become reconstituted before the spermatocyte and ovocyte stages of the next generation. All this is in accord with the phenomenon of the paternal and maternal chromosomes forming separate groups in the spindle in only the earlier embryonic cleavages, and not, as Häcker has argued, through the whole germinal cycle.

This was all elaborated at length in the earlier papers of mine referred to, and there shown to explain the mechanics of very diverse cellular changes. To that I would now add another thought. When the nuclear element becomes segmented by the reduction division, which is a division breaking the linin connections between conjugated chromosomes, its later reconstitution, *i. e.*, the restoration of a nuclear continuous nuclear element in the next generation, must take place by the maternal and paternal chromosomes arranging themselves in a continuous chain in such a way that every two correspondent paternal and maternal chromosomes lie together. For this alone would explain why chromosomes of corresponding appearance are placed together in the prophases of division, and how in the synapsis stage of the growth period corresponding chromosomes conjugate unerringly.

The main results of these observations and interpretations amount to this, that the important nuclear element of the first order is a continuous band of linin with which chromatin is always locally connected. Beyond this there is in the nucleus nothing but the karyolymph, the nucleoli (plasmosomes), and minute floating granules (œdematin or lanthanin). With considerable justification we may assign to this nuclear element the main activities of heredity and differentiation, because it is the most constant structure.

Therefore we are to conceive of chromosomes not as separated nuclear masses, but as bodies in continuous physical connection. And each chromosome is a mass not of chromatin alone, but of chromatin always combined with linin, whether the chromatin be condensed as in mitosis, or whether it be finely distributed along delicate linin fibrils as in the rest stage. These two substances must be considered conjointly in any concept of the "hereditable substance," and not, as so many seem inclined to do, only the chromatin.

As elements of a second, lower grade we find the chromosomes. And we may define chromosome as a particular portion of the nuclear element on which the chromatin becomes massed during cell division. We can imagine the relation most simply in this way; there is a continuous linin band, on which chromatin is always suspended, more or less sparsely and irregularly when the cell is not in division, but in compact masses during division; each portion of a linin band on which chromatin is so massed in division is a chromosome. Whether the movement of the chromatin particles on this band is automatic, or whether it is produced by local contractions of the linin, we have no means of deciding; but certainly it is independent of extranuclear energies.

This idea of mine of the chromosomes as mere portions of a continuous nuclear element by no means implies that the chromosomes are not to be considered individuals, *i. e.*, structures that reappear in the same form and number in cell generation after generation. Indeed there is as much evidence that each chromosome is the product of a preceding one and not a new formation, as that a cell is always the division product of a preceding cell. And in all my work I have consistently argued for the chromosomes as persisting structures, in substantiation of the idea of the individuality of the chromosomes founded by Van Beneden, and supported by a great number of students.

Now in any consideration of the chromosomes the question presses on one: Are the several chromosomes of a given nucleus alike in their energies, or are they different? Are they actively or potentially equivalent, or are they not? Weismann and Roux were perhaps the first to take up this question, and Weismann has reasoned on the basis of his determinant hypothesis, that in any cell where the chromosomes are neither very small nor very numerous, each single chromosome is the bearer of all the hereditable qualities of a whole individual of the species. Against such a valence of the chromosome there is much evidence of serious weight, and it has been nowhere more succinctly summed up than in the recent review by Boveri (1904). To this matter of the potentiality of the chromosomes we will now turn.

Boveri has argued very strongly (1904) that particular chromosomes have particular energies, that one chromosome represents certain activities not evinced by another. His own important empirical contribution (1902) to this idea was the analysis of the abnormal development of eggs fertilized by one spermatozoön. And he concluded: "that not a fixed number but a fixed combination of chromosomes is necessary for normal development, and this means nothing else than that the particular chromosomes must possess different qualities."

Another line of evidence is that afforded by the differences in behavior of the chromosomes, when the cell is not molested by experiment. Such are the allosomes, of which we treated in the preceding section. They may behave differently from the autosomes, as we have seen, either by preserving their density in the rest period of the spermatogonia and the growth period of the spermatocytes, or by dividing in the maturation mitoses in a different sequence from the autosomes. Therefore in nuclei containing allosomes there are at least two kinds of chromosomes: the unmodified autosomes, and the modified allosomes; and there can be no doubt that these have different activities.

But we may go further than this. Are we to regard the possession of chromosomes of different kinds, particularly the possession of the highly modified allosomes, as simply a taxonomic peculiarity of certain forms, such as the insects, araneids, chilopods and *Sagitta?* I think not, for if there are such great differences in the chromosomes of these forms, is it not probable that there would be also chromosomal differences in other forms, even if less readily demonstrable?

For leaving the allosomes out of consideration comparative studies are proving dissimilarities of form and size in the unmodified chromosomes, the autosomes. I showed (1901*b*) that in a number of species of Hemiptera there are spermatogonic chromosome pairs marked by peculiarities in size; and that when this is the case there are corresponding bivalent elements in the first spermatocytes, *i. e.*, that these size differences are constant during succeeding cell generations. I also showed in the same memoir that chromosomes of like size conjugate in the synapsis stage, and proved that of the two chromosomes that so conjugate the one is paternal and the other maternal, consequently that the synapsis is to be interpreted as the last stage in fertilization, the conjugation of correspondent chromosomes of opposite nativity. In the next year Sutton (1902) showed that in *Brachystola* all the autosomes compose pairs. And then (1904*a*) I demonstrated that in the spermatogonia of Urodelous Amphibia the twenty-four autosomes can be without difficulty resolved into twelve pairs, the components of a pair being distinguishable not only by size relations but also by peculiarities in form; and I showed this to be true of *Ascaris* also, where the ovotid contains one small and one large chromosome and the spermatozoön introduces one small and one large one. Wilson (1905) has recently found this to be the case for a number of Hemiptera, adding materially to my former observations; and in the present paper this constancy of pairs in the spermatogenesis is detailed for a still greater number of species. We can say that whenever the chromosomes are not too small or too numerous, they can be seen to present certain size relations that remain constant during succeeding cell generations, united sometimes with certain form relations as Baumgartner (1904) also has shown. McClung has likewise found this to hold true for certain of the Orthoptera.

So we are justified in saying that each spermatogonium and ovogonium has a double series of chromosomes, a paternal and a maternal set, which go to make up a series of pairs, the pairs being of gradated sizes or forms, and each pair composed of a paternal and maternal element of approximately equal size and form. The two elements of a pair probably lie close together in the spirem stage of the spermatogonium as I showed elsewhere (1904*a*); and even in the equatorial plate they frequently lie close together. The two elements of such a pair are the ones that conjugate in the synapsis stage, and that separate from each other in the first maturation division.

Accordingly, even where there are no such great differences present as between autosomes and allosomes, distinct pairs can frequently be distinguished, and thereby morphological differences of size and form be made out. It is obvious that chromosomes of different sizes cannot have the same physiological value; they must have activities differing at least in amount. But we may decide that their activities differ also in kind, else a particular chromosome would not always conjugate only with its correspondent in form and size but should be expected to conjugate with any other chromosome. That is to say, there is marked affinity or attraction only between the elements of such a pair, an attraction exhibited by the conjugation process. There is then something correspondent between the elements of a pair, not shared by them with the elements of any other pair, and this can be only a functional peculiarity, one based perhaps upon different metabolic energies. Therefore, as Sutton (1903) has reasoned, a chromosome must be the seat of particular qualities of the individual, not the center of the sum total of the individual's activities. Different chromosomes, that is to say, must have different physiological energies, and the sum of them, that is the whole nuclear element, present the energies of the individual.

Thus the experimental studies and the morphological ones are in accord in this matter, as Boveri (1904) has shown, and more recently Heider (1906). And these constant size and formal differences enable us to analyze the cell constituents much more fully than we could do a few years ago.

Another result I would mention here. When I first discovered the constancy of such chromosome pairs, I concluded that the two components of each pair were exactly equal in form and volume, and so have the others who followed me. In the present paper I have given especial attention to this point, and now find good evidence that the components of each pair are probably constantly slightly different from each other in volume. This is a difficult point to make sure of because it is hard to estimate voluminal mass in such small objects where there is much chance of optical illusion. But in most of those cases of pairs of small diplosomes of approximately equal volume, as those of the coreids, I find that they are always slightly different in volume in the first maturation mitosis, then always different in this respect in the spermatogonium; and here one can be fairly certain of his conclusion, because these bodies are nearly spherical and so relatively easy to compare. Again, in *Corizus alternatus* of the five pairs of autosomes of the spermatogonium, the largest pair (*A*, *a*, Fig. 107) is regularly composed of two relatively enormous elements, one slightly more voluminous and nearly straight, the other slightly smaller and horseshoe shaped. And in *Harmostes*, where I have studied many spermatogonic divisions, all the autosome pairs are unusually distinct, and in each the two components appear constantly very slightly different in volume. This is clearly the case in *Anasa* also. Now in this connection let us recall the discovery of Miss Stevens (1905*b*) and Wilson (1905*a*) that when there is a pair of diplosomes of markedly dissimilar volume, as in *Tenebrio* or *Euschistus*, the smaller must be the paternal element and the larger the maternal. If this is so for these diplosomes, is it not also probable that in any chromosome pair the slightly smaller element may be paternal and the larger one maternal? There would certainly seem to be a probability of this, and if it can be shown to be a constant relation it will give us the means of recognizing, after the determination of the chromosomal pairs, the maternal and paternal chromosomes of each nucleus, and thereby advance our means of analysis still another step.

And a word may be added here to those who may be sceptical as to the possibility of distinguishing particular chromosome pairs. Any one who looks over the plates given in this paper, and notes the chromosome pairs distinguished by corresponding letters, may say that the imagination plays too large a part in such distinctions. But he should recall that we can draw no conclusions without the help of the imagination, and that what we see we must also imagine. But more than this, he should recall that the printed figure can in no way be as clear as the preparation under the focussing microscope since it can reproduce only the profile, whereas the eye sees this and also the depth of the structure. One has only to draw the chromosomes carefully with the camera lucida, then search for correspondent ones upon such drawings, to be convinced of the actual presence of such pairs. And above all, no one has any right to express doubt of these relations who has not made broad comparative observations of his own.

This constant difference of the chromosome pairs, and the probable constant though much slighter differences of the elements of each pair, which are the expression of both morphological and physiological distinction, I would denote by the term "chromosome difference" which expresses the phenomena perhaps a little more precisely than Boveri's term "nuclear constitution."

3. The Number of Chromosomes and Taxonomy.

One incentive to me to make comparative studies of the chromosomes in the Hemiptera was to determine how far the number of chromosomes is constant in a particular group of animals; and certain conclusions were presented in two preceding papers (1901*a*, 1901*b*). From the observations on the Hemiptera then made it appeared that the chromosomal numbers were not constant, so that the determination of the factors governing the number seemed as unexplained as ever before. And in now touching on the question again I find that the problems are as difficult of solution as ever.

Yet it seemed worth while to reëxamine the matter from a taxonomic standpoint, to test the value of chromosome numbers as criteria of racial affinity. And since no one has tabulated the number of chromosomes known in animal species, not since the brief list of cases summarized by Wilson (1900, pp. 206, 207), I have compiled these statistics for the germ cells only of the greater number of described species; there are a number of omissions because some of the literature was inaccessible, but the list is very nearly complete. Data on hybrids are omitted; and data from certain older papers, as that of Carnoy (1885), where no particular pains were given to determining the numbers accurately, are left out. In the first vertical column of each table is given the name of the group, subgroup and species; in the second column the germinal cycle is indicated by the abbreviation "Ov" for ovogenesis, and "Sp" for spermatogenesis, in the third column are the names of the describers; and in the remaining columns the headings "Gonium," "Cyte I," "Cyte II," and "Tid" stand respectively for ovogonium (or spermatogonium), first ovocyte (or spermatocyte), second ovocyte (or spermatocyte), and ovotid (or spermatid). In these tables allosomes are not distinguished from autosomes since the intention is to present the entire chromosomal numbers. When a number is given as, *e. g.*, "10–11" it means that it was not determined whether 10 or 11 is present; but when it is stated "10, 11," it signifies that either 10 or 11 may be present, which of course would be a cycle complicated by the presence of a monosome. For the Hemiptera when my name is given as an authority, reference is made to the observations of the present paper.

Group and Species.	Cycle.	Authority.	Gonium	Cyte I	Cyte II	Tid.
VERTEBRATA.						
1. *Mammalia.*						
Bos taurus	Sp.	Schoenfeld, 1901.		12		
Lepus cuniculus	Ov.	Winiwarter, 1900.	ca. 42			
Mus rattus	Sp.	Lenhossek, 1898.		12	12	12
Mus rattus	"	Moore, 1894.	16	8	8	
Cavia cobaya	"	" 1906.	32	16	16	16
2. *Aves.*						
Columba livia.	Ov.	Harper, 1904.		8	8	8
3. *Amphibia.*						
Triton alpestris } Triton cristatus } Triton punctatus }	Sp.	Janssens, 1901.	24	12	12	12
Salamandra maculosa	"	Meves, 1896; Janssens, 1901.	24	12	12	12
Batrachoseps attenuatus	"	Eisen, 1900; Janssens, 1903.	24	12	12	12
Desmognathus fusca.	"	Kingsbury, 1902; Montg.	24	12	12	12
Plethodon cinereus	"	Montg., 1904; Janssens, 1903.	24	12	12	12
Diemyctilus torosus	Ov.	Lebrun, 1901*b*.		12	12	12
Amphiuma means	Sp.	McGregor, 1899.		12	12	12
Bufo lentiginosus	Ov.	King, 1901, 1905.	24	12	12	12
Rana temporaria	"	Lebrun, 1901*a*.		10	10	
4. *Pisces.*						
Myxine glutinosa	Sp.	Schreiner, 1905.	52	26	26	26
Salmo fario	Ov.	Böhm, 1892.		12	12	12
Scyllium canicula } Pristiurus } Torpedo } Raja }	Sp.	Moore, 1895.	24	12	12	12

Group and Species.	Cycle.	Authority.	Gonium	Cyte I	Cyte II	Tid.
TUNICATA.						
Styelopsis grossularia..........	Ov.	Julin, 1893.	4	8	1	2
Styelopsis grossularia..........	Sp.	" "	4	4	2	1
Phallusia mammillata.........	Ov.	Hill, 1896.		8	8	? 8
Ascidia..........................	"	Boveri, 1890.		9		
ARACHNIDA.						
Agalena naevia	Sp.	L. B. Wallace, 1905.	40	20	19, 21	19, 21
Lycosa insopita	"	Montgomery, 1905.	26	13	13	
CHILOPODA.						
Scolopendra heros	"	Blackman, 1905.	33	17	16, 17	16, 17
Scutigera forceps		Medes, 1905.	37	19	18, 19	
INSECTA.						
1. *Coleoptera.*						
Dytiscus..........................	Ov.	Giardina, 1901.	ca. 40		10	10
Oryctes nasicornis	Sp.	Prowazek, 1901.	12	6	16	8
Tenebrio molitor	"	Stevens, 1905*b*.	20	10		
Hydrophilus	"	Vom Rath, 1892.	16	32	16	16
Cybister roselii..................	"	Voinov, 1903.	ca. 22	13	12	12
Silpha carinata	"	Holmgren, 1902.	32	16	17	17
Agelastica alni	Ov.	Henking, 1892.		12		
Agelastica alni	Sp.	" "	ca. 24	16–17	6–8	6–8
Donacia..........................	Ov.	" "		15	8	
Lampyris splendidula.........	"	" "		6–8		
Crioceris asparagi	"	" "				
2. *Odonata.*						
Anax junius	Sp.	McGill, 1904.	28	14	14	13, 14
3. *Hymenoptera.*						
Apis mellifica....................	Ov.	Petrunkewitsch, 1901.		16	16	8
Lasius niger	"	Henking, 1892.		10	10	
Rhodites rosæ	"	" "		ca. 9		
4. *Isoptera.*						
Termopsis angusticollis	Sp.	Stevens, 1905*b*.	52	26	26	26
5. *Lepidoptera.*						
Bombyx mori	"	Toyama, 1894.	26–28	26–28	28	14
Pieris brassicæ	Ov.	Henking, 1890*a*.		14	14	14
Pieris brassicæ	Sp.	" 1891.	30	14–15	14–15	14–15
Pieris napi.......................	Ov.	" 1890*b*.	50	25		
6. *Orthoptera.*						
(Gryllidæ.)						
Gryllus assimilis................	Sp.	Baumgartner, 1904.	29	15	14, 15	14, 15
Gryllus domesticus............	"	" "	21	11	10, 11	10, 11
Gryllotalpa vulgaris...........	"	Vom Rath, 1892.	12	24	12	6
(Mantidæ.)						
Mantis religiosa	Sp. Ov.	Giardina, 1898.	14	14	14	7
(Blattidæ.)						
Periplaneta americana.........	Sp.	Moore and Robinson, 1905.	ca. 32	16	16	16
Blattella germanica............	"	Stevens, 1905*b*.	23	12	11, 12	11, 12
(Locustidæ.)						
Orchesticus........................	"	McClung, 1902.	ca. 33	17	16, 17	16, 17
Orphania denticauda..........	"	de Sinéty, 1901.	31	16	15, 16	
Stenopelmatus..................	"	Stevens, 1905*b*.	46	24	23	24

Group and Species.	Cycle.	Authority.	Gonium	Cyte I	Cyte II	Tid.
INSECTA (continued).						
7. *Hemiptera* (continued).						
(Phasmidæ.)						
Leptynia attenuata		de Sinéty, 1901.	36	19	18, 19	
(Forficulidæ.)						
Forficula auricularis	"	"	24	12		
Labidura riparia	"	"		6		
(Acrididæ.)						
Brachystola magna............	"	Sutton, 1902.	23	12	11, 12	11, 12
Caloptenus femur-rubrum. ...	"	Wilcox, 1895.	12	24	12	6
Hesperotettix speciosa.........	"	McClung, 1905.	23	11	11, 12	11, 12
Mermiria..	"	" "	23	10	10	10, 11
Syrbula acuticornis	"	Montgomery, 1905.	20	10	10	10
7. *Hemiptera.*						
(Aphididæ.)						
Aphis rosæ.	Ov. Sp.	Stevens, 1905.	10	10	10	5
Aphis œnotheræ.	"	" "	10	5	5	5
(Pentatomidæ.)						
Euschistus tristigmus	Sp.	Montgomery, Wilson, 1906.	14	8	7	7
Euschistus tristigmus	Ov.	Wilson, 1906.	14			
Euschistus variolarius.	Sp.	Montgomery, Wilson, 1906.	14	8	7	7
Euschistus variolarius.	Ov.	Wilson, 1906.	14	8		
Euschistus servus.	Sp.	" "	14		7	7
Euschistus servus.	Ov.	Wilson, 1906.	14		7	
Euschistus ictericus.	Sp. Ov.	" "	14		7	
Euschistus fissilis......	Ov.	" "	14		8	
Euschistus fissilis.	Sp.	" 1905a.	14	8		
Mineus bioculatus.	"	" 1906.			7	7
Podisus spinosus..............	"	Montgomery, Wilson, 1905a.	16	9	8	8
Podisus spinosus................	Ov.	Wilson, 1906.	16			
Mormidea lugens...............	Sp.	Montgomery.	14	8	7	
Cosmopepla carnifex.	"	"	16	9	8	8
Nezara hilaris.	"	" Wilson, 1905a.	14	8	7	7
Nezara hilaris..................	Ov.	Wilson, 1906.	14			
Brochymena.....................	Sp.	Montgomery, Wilson, 1905a.	14	8	7	7
Perillus confluens.............	"	"	14	8	7	7
Cœnus delius....................	"	" Wilson, 1905a.	14	8	7	7
Cœnus delius....................	Ov.	Wilson, 1906.	14			
Trichopepla semivittata	Sp.	" 1905a.	14	8	7	7
Trichopepla semivittata	"	Montgomery.	16	8	7	7
Eurygaster alternatus....... .	"	"		7	6	6
Peribalus limbolaris	"	"	14	8	7	7
Banasa calva...	"	Wilson, 1905c.		15	13, 14	13, 14
(Nabidæ.)						
Nabis annulatus.	"	Montgomery.		10	10	9
(Coreidæ.)						
Archimerus calcarator.	"	Wilson, 1905c.	15	8	7, 8	
Anasa tristis......................	"	" 1905c, Montgomery.	21	11	11	10, 11
Anasa tristis......................	Ov.	" 1906.	22			
Anasa armigera.	Sp.	Montgomery.	21	11	11	
Anasa sp.	"	"	21	11		
Anasa sp.	Ov.	"	22			

Group and Species.	Cycle.	Authority.	Gonium	Cyte I	Cyte II	Tid.
INSECTA (continued).						
7. *Hemiptera* (continued).						
Harmostes reflexulus	Sp.	Montgomery. Wilson, 1906.	13		7	6, 7
Harmostes reflexulus	Ov.	Wilson, 1906.	14			
Corizus alternatus............	Sp.	Montgomery.	13	7	7	6, 7
Corizus lateralis	"	"		7	7	6, 7
Chariesterus antennator......	"	"		13	13	12, 13
Protenor belfragei	"	" Wilson, 1906.	13	7	7	6, 7
Protenor belfragei	Ov.	Wilson, 1906.	14			
Alydus pilosulus	Sp.	Montgomery, Wilson, 1905c.	13	7	7	6, 7
Alydus pilosulus	Ov.	Wilson. 1906.	14			
Alydus eurinus	Sp.	Montgomery.	13	7	7	6, 7
Metapodius terminalis	"	"	21	11	11	10, 11
Syromastes marginatus	"	Gross.	22	11	11	10, 11
(Lygæidæ.)						
Pyrrhocoris apterus......	"	Henking, 1891.	24	12	12	11, 12
	Ov.	" 1892.	ca. 24	12	12	
Lygæus turcicus	Sp.	Wilson, 1905a.	14	8	7	7
Lygæus turcicus	Ov.	" 1906.	14			
Œdancala dorsalis	Sp.	Montgomery.	13	7	7	6, 7
Oncopeltus fasciatus	"	"	16	9	8	8
Peliopelta abbreviata	"	"	14	8, 9	7	7
Ichnodemus falicus	"	"	16	9	8	8
Cymus angustatus	"	"			14	? 14
(Tingitidæ.)						
Tingis clavata	Sp.	Montgomery.		7	7	7
(Phymatidæ.)						
Phymata		"	? 29			
(Reduviidæ.)						
Acholla multispinosa	"	"	32	16	16	
Sinea diadema	"	"		16		
Prionidus cristatus	"	"	26			
(Belostomatidæ.)						
Zaitha........	"	"	24	13	12	12
(Hydrobatidæ.)						
Hygotrechus	"	"	21	11	11	10, 11
Limnotrechus marginatus....	"	"		11	11	10, 11
(Capsidæ.)						
Calocoris rapidus..............	"	"	30	16	15, 16	
Pœcilocapsus goniphorus	"	"		18	17	17
Lygus pratensis.	"	"	? 35	19	17, 18	17, 18
ONYCHOPHORA.						
Peripatus balfouri.	"	" 1900.	ca. 28	14	14	14
CRUSTACEA.						
1. *Branchiopoda.*						
Artemia salina..................	Ov.	Brauer, 1893.	168	84	84	84, 168
Branchipus.	Sp.	Moore, 1894.		10	10	ca. 5
Branchipus grubei.	Ov.	Brauer, 1892.		12	12	12
2. *Copepoda.*						
Cyclops brevicornis	"	Häcker, 1902, 1904.	12	12	6	6
Cyclops strenuus.	"	Rückert, 1894.		11	11	11

Group and Species.	Cycle.	Authority.	Gonium	Cyte I	Cyte II	Tid.
CRUSTACEA (continued).						
2. *Copepoda* (continued).						
Heterocope robusta	"	" "		16		
Diaptomus gracilis...........	"	" "		16		
Diaptomus	Ov.Sp.	Ishikawa, 1891.	8	8	8	4
3. *Isopoda.*						
Oniscus asellus.................	Sp.	Nichols, 1902.		16	16	16
4. *Ostracoda.*						
Cypris reptans........	Ov.	Woltereck, 1890.		12		
5. *Decapoda.*						
Astacus.	Sp.	Prowazek, 1902.		58		
BRACHIOPODA.						
Lingula anatina................	Ov.	Yatsu, 1902.		8		
ENDOPROCTA.						
Pedicellina americana.........	Ov.Sp.	Dublin, 1905.	ca. 22	11	11	11
ECHINODERMATA.						
Strongylocentrotus............	Ov.	Stevens, 1902.	36	18	18	18
Echinus esculentus...........	"	Bryce, 1903.		16	16	16
Echinus microtuberculatus...	"	Boveri, 1905.	{ 18	9	9	9
			{ 36	18	18	18
Toxopneustes....................	"	Wilson, 1900.		18	18	18
PROSOPYGII.						
Phascalosoma....................	Ov.	Gerould, 1903.		10	10	
ANNELIDA.						
Thalassema mellita	"	Griffin, 1900.	24	12	12	12
Myzostoma glabrum............	"	Wheeler, 1897.		12	12	12
Allolobophora fœtida.........	"	Foot, 1898.	22	11	11	11
Hyodrilus coccineus............	"	Vejdovský and Mrazek, 1903.		16		
Rhynchelmis.....................	"	" "		32		
Ophryotrocha puerilis........	"	Korschelt, 1895.	4	4	2	2
Lumbricus	Sp.	Calkins, 1895.	32	16	16	16
Chætopterus pergamentaceus	Ov.	Mead, 1898.		9	9	9
Tomopteris.	"	W. Wallace, 1904.		4		
MOLLUSCA.						
1. *Gastropoda.*						
Enteroxenos östergreni.	"	Bonnevie, 1905.	34	17	17	17
(Prosobranchia.)						
Crepidula plana	"	Conklin, 1902.		30	30	30
Paludina vivipara.	Sp.	Meves, 1902.	14	7	7	7
Pterotrachea	Ov.	Boveri, 1890.		16	16	16
Carinaria.	"	" "		16	16	16
(Pulmonata.)						
Helix pomatia..................	Sp.	Ancel, 1903.	48	24	24	24
Helix pomatia............	"	Prowazek, 1901*b*; v. Rath, 1896.	24	12	12	12
Helix pomatia..................	"	Lee, 1897.	24	24	24	24
Limax maximus.	Ov.	Linville, 1900.		? 16		
Limax cinereo-niger.	Sp.	Vom Rath, 1892.	16	32	16	8
Limnæa elodes	Ov.	Linville, 1900.		16	16	

Group and Species.	Cycle.	Authority.	Gonium	Cyte I	Cyte II	Tel.
MOLLUSCA (continued).						
1. *Gastropoda* (continued).						
(Opisthobranchia.)						
Aplysia punctata	"	Janssens and Elrington, 1904		16	16	16
Aplysia depilans	"	Bochenek, 1899.		16		
Haminea solitaria.	"	Smallwood, 1904.		16	16	
Phyllirhoe..................	"	Boveri, 1890.		16	16	16
Cymbulia peronii..............	"	Nekrassoff, 1903.		16	16	16
2. *Pelecypoda.*						
Mactra.	"	Kostanecki, 1904.		16	16	16
CHAETOGNATHA.						
Sagitta elegans .... } Sagitta bipunctata. ... }	Ov.Sp.	Stevens, 1903, 1905e.	18	9	9	9
GORDIACEA.						
Paragordius varius...........	Ov.	Montgomery, 1904*b*.		7	7	7
Gordius.	"	Camerano, 1899.		ca. 8		
ACANTHOCEPHALA.						
Echinorhynchus gigas.........	Sp.	Kaiser, 1893.	4	4	4	2
NEMATODA.						
Ascaris megalocephala bivalens.	Ov.Sp.	Van Beneden, 1883; Hertwig, 1890; Boveri, 1887; Brauer, 1893.	4	2	2	2
Ascaris megalocephala univalens	"	Carnoy, 1886; Brauer, 1893; Boveri, 1887.	2	1	1	1
Ascaris sp. (from Canis)	Ov.	Lukjanow, 1889.		16	8	4
Ascaris sp. (from Canis)......	Ov.	Carnoy, 1886.		8	4	
Ascaris lumbricoides.	"	Boveri, 1887.	24, 48			
Ascaris clavata.................	"	Carnoy, 1887.		24	24	24
Spiroptera strumosa	"	Carnoy, 1886.		8	4	2
Filaroides mustelarum	"	" "		8	4	4
Ophiostomum mucronatum .	"	" "		6	6	6
Strongylus tetracanthus	"	Meyer, 1895.		6		
NEMERTINI.						
Cerebratulus marginatus	"	Coe, 1899; Kostanecki, 1902.		16		
Tetrastemma vermiculum ...	"	Lebedinsky, 1897.		4	4	2
TURBELLARIA.						
1. *Polycladidea.*						
Prosthiostomum siphunculus	"	Francotte, 1898.		8	8	8
Leptoplana tremellaris	"	" 1897.		8	8	8
Oligocladus auritus	"	" "		8	8	8
Cycloporus papillosus	"	" "		8	8	8
Prostheceraeus vittatus	"	Francotte, 1897; Gérard, 1901; Klinckowström, 1896.		6	6	6
Thysanozoön brocchi..........	"	Schockaert, 1902; Van der Stricht, 1898.	18	9	9	9
Eustylochus ellipticus	"	Van Name, 1899.		10	10	10
Planocera nebulosa.............	"	Van Name, 1899.		10	10	10
2. *Rhabdocoela.*						
Mesostomum ehrenbergi......	"	Bresslau, 1904.		10	5	5

Group and Species.	Cycle.	Authority.	Gonium	Cyte I	Cyte II	Tid.
TURBELLARIA (continued).						
3. *Tricladidea.*						
Planaria simplicissima	"	Stevens, 1904.			3	3
Planaria simplicissima	Sp.	" "		8	4	4
"Freshwater forms"	Ov.	Mattiesen, 1903.		8	4	4
TREMATODA.						
Polystomum integerrimum...	"	Goldschmidt, 1902.		8	8	4
Zoögonus mirus	"	" 1905.	10	10	10	5
Gyrodactylus elegans.	"	Kathariner, 1904.		8	8	4
CNIDARIA.						
Hydra..............................	Sp.	Downing, 1905.	ca. 18	24	24	24
Æquorea forskalea	Ov.	Häcker, 1892.			6	6
Tiara................................	"	Boveri, 1890.		14		
Gonothyrea lovenii	"	Wulfert, 1902.		8		
Clava squamata................	"	Harm, 1902.		ca. 16		

For purposes of comparison the chromosomal numbers of the spermatogonia (and ovogonia), or those of the ovotids (and spermatids), are the safest to consider, because in cells of these generations in almost all cases the chromosomes are univalent, while different observers have varied greatly in their estimates of the valence of chromosomes of the ovocytes and spermatocytes. It is probable that the spermatogonic (or ovogonic) number of chromosomes is always double that of the number in the spermatid (or ovotid), so that the one can be readily calculated from the other; the only exception is in cases of spermatogenesis with a monosome, where the spermatid may contain one more chromosome or one less than half the number in the spermatogonium. And for purposes of comparison the full (not reduced) number of chromosomes is preferable, because in any species all the spermatogonia have the same number of chromosomes, while the spermatids may have different numbers.

Wilson's discovery that when there is an uneven spermatogonic number of chromosomes in the spermatogenesis there is an even number in the ovogenesis introduces a complexity in the comparisons. But this is easily obviated; for so far as known when the spermatogenesis has an uneven number it contains always one chromosome less than the ovogenesis. therefore, *e. g.*, a spermatogonium having 13 chromosomes we can calculate the ovogonium to have 14. In such cases we will use for comparison only the number of the ovogenesis, whether directly ascertained or whether derived by adding one to the spermatogonic number when the latter is an odd one.

When we look over the statistics presented in these tables we find that the number of chromosomes of the ovogonium or spermatogonium (translating odd spermatogonic numbers into even ovogonic ones) may be arranged in their order of frequency as follows:

24 chromosomes is the unreduced number in 30 species, about one-sixth of the whole list; the numbers 32 and 14 occur each in 24 species; the number 16 in 20 species; the numbers 12 and 22 each in 9 species; the numbers 18 and 20 each in 7 species; the numbers 4, 8, 30 each in 6 species; the numbers 28 and 36 each in 5 species; the numbers 10, 34, 48 each in 4 species; the numbers 26, 40, 52 each in 2 species; and the numbers 2, 38, 42, 46, 50, 60, 64, 116, 168, each in only one species.

Thus the full number of chromosomes is below 31 in the greater number of species so far studied.

Certain of these animals show the rare peculiarity of having two normal numbers, one twice that of the other; thus *Ascaris megalocephala* has either 2 or 4, *Ascaris lumbricoides*, 24 or 48, *Helix pomatia*, 24 or 48, and *Echinus microtuberculatus*, either 18 or 36. In each of these species we might distinguish then a variety "univalens" from one "bivalens," as O. Hertwig (1890) has done for *Ascaris megalocephala*. In the last form Meyer (1895) was able to distinguish no anatomical differences between the two varieties, and Herla (1893) has proven that there is frequently crossing between them. But such hybrids contain three chromosomes, not twice the lower normal number. And evidently variation in the normal number, such as that of the four species mentioned, cannot have originated by polyspermy, for three spermatozoa would have to fertilize an ovum to produce double the usual normal number of chromosomes; and Boveri (1902) has shown that such polyspermy results in abnormal development.

Further, two cases are known where the spermatid has a different number of chromosomes from that of the ovotid, *Planaria* and *Syclopsis*, these being cases not due to the presence of a monosome in the spermatogenesis.

Finally, let us examine the constancy of the chromosomal numbers within certain circumscribed groups of animals. In some a certain constancy is to be found: the normal number is 24 in all the urodelous Amphibia; McClung (1905) states there are always 23 in the spermatogenesis of the Acridiidæ among the Orthoptera (but *Syrbula* and *Caloptenus* are exceptions to this); among the Pentatomidæ (Hemiptera) either 14 or 16 is the number (17 species examined), but *Banasa* has probably about 28; in the Coreidæ the numbers are 22 or 14 (one with 16); in all the opisthobranch molluscs examined it is 32; and in the Turbellaria, 12, 16 (most usual), 18 or 20. In most of the other groups of equivalent scope the variation in number is so great that there seems to be no constancy; thus in the hemipteran family Lygæidæ there may be 24, 14, 16 or 28. And in the spermatogenesis of two closely related species of *Gryllus* Baumgartner (1904) finds the numbers to be 21 and 29.

We can decide this much about numerical relations of the chromosomes, that correspondence in number by no means implies community of race; one has simply to list the different animals with the number 24 to be sure of this. On the other hand there is often constancy through smaller groups such as genera or species. The question is then: when we find a genus like *Ascaris*, with chromosomal number ranging from 2 to 48, are we to judge from this variation that chromosomal number has no taxonomic significance, or are we to decide that the forms combined in the genus *Ascaris* are really not generically related?

This is an exceedingly difficult question to decide. If our present relegation of the species of *Ascaris* be justified, then clearly chromosomal numbers have not even generic worth. But our whole classification of somatic individuals is at present merely tentative, and the grouping of the various species of the Nematodes in particular seems to be very artificial. There is uncertainty at both ends of the argument. We must commence with the premise, that seems to me fully justified, that the species is one and the same from the egg up to the adult condition. Therefore it is permissible to classify germ cells as well as adults, and, *e. g.*, to compare chromosomal relations through a series of germ cells as we would conditions of the nervous system through a series of somatic individuals. The chromosomes as portions of the very conservative nuclear element should surely offer as good a basis for genetic comparisons as any set of somatic structures. That is to say, an entirely rational phylogeny of organisms might be founded in part upon relations of the germ cells; therefore nuclear constituents be used as characters quite as much as any other sets of structures. The only reason to prefer comparisons of adult individuals is because they exhibit differentiation more than germ cells do, and not because they are really more differentiated.

Therefore when germ cells show differences in chromosomal numbers, these can signify only differences of the individuals that contain them. And while numerical differences are among the least important of the anatomical characters, yet when they are differences of so important an organ as the nuclear element they should be granted some degree of importance in a rational taxonomy. Consequently, it would be incorrect to place different species, some with 4 and others with 48 chromosomes, in the same genus, for such differences of the chromosomal number must constitute at least genetic and much more than specific difference. Were this not so, we could not explain why in so many cases there is constancy of chromosomal number in groups much higher than genera. Therefore chromosomal number is a character that should be considered in taxonomy.

At the same time number is only one of the properties of chromosomes, they have also other characters of form, arrangement, and process change, some of which will undoubtedly be found to be of greater value than number in the analysis of descent. McClung (1905) was the first to draw attention to arrangement of the chromosomes as a high taxonomic character, thus seconding my idea (1901*a*, *b*) that there should be a comparative phylogenetic study of the germ cells as a check and supplement to the analysis of the phylogeny based upon somatic structures. The foundation of a rational phylogenetic system upon cellular differences is as yet little more than suggested, because the comparative basis is so small and the phenomena so complex. Yet I believe it should be attempted, and that it will be found to be entirely possible.

Perhaps the best way of attacking the problem of the influences determining chromosomal number, is by the analysis of the phenomena in those species where there are two normal numbers.

In conclusion the position of the chromosomes in the equatorial plates of the maturation mitoses of the Hemiptera may be summarized.

Those diplosomes that divide equationally in the first mitosis and reductionally in the second are not central in the first spindle (except in *Oncopeltus*), but are central in the second spindle.

Those diplosomes that divide first reductionally and second equationally are always central in the first maturation spindle (except in the Reduviidae), and more or less excentric in the second spindle (but central in the Reduviidae).

It is therefore the rule that the positions of the diplosomes are reversed in the two maturation spindles; and that they are in the center of the chromosomal plate when they are bivalent (except in the Reduviidae). Consequently the position of the diplosomes is rather a criterion of their valence than a character of any taxonomic importance.

There is a tendency in most of the Hemiptera, when the autosomes are not very numerous, for those of the first maturation spindle to be disposed in a circle around a central one, while there is generally less regularity in the second maturation spindle. Such positions would seem to be dependent upon the interaction of the number of chromosomes and the mechanics of the cell division, and therefore to be of no particular taxonomic importance.

LITERATURE LIST.

ANCEL, P., 1903. Réduction numérique des chromosomes dans la spermatogénèse d'Helix pomatia. Bibliogr. anat., 11.

BAUMGARTNER, W. J., 1904. Some new evidences for the individuality of the chromosomes. Biol. Bull., 8.

BLACKMAN, M. W., 1903. The spermatogenesis of the Myriapods. 2. On the chromatin in the spermatocytes of Scolopendra heros. Ibid., 5.

1905. Idem., 3. The spermatogenesis of Scolopendra heros. Bull. Mus. Comp. Zool. Harvard, 48.

BOCHENEK, A., 1899. Die Reifung und Befruchtung des Eies von Aplysia depilans. Bull. Acad. Cracovie.

BÖHM, 1892. Die Befruchtung des Forelleneies. Sitzber. Ges. Morph. Physiol. München, 7.

BONNEVIE, K., 1905. Das Verhalten des Chromatins in den Keimzellen von Enteroxenos östergreni. Anat. Anz., 26.

BOVERI, T., 1887. Zellen-Studien. 1. Die Bildung der Richtungskörper bei Ascaris megalocephala und Ascaris lumbricoides. Jena.

1890. Zellen-Studien. 3. Ueber das Verhalten der chromatischen Kernsubstanz bei der Bildung der Richtungskörper und bei der Befruchtung. Jena. Zeitsch. Naturw., 24.

1902. Ueber mehrpolige Mitosen als Mittel zur Analyse des Zellkerns. Verh. phys.-med. Ges. Würzburg, N. F., 35.

1904. Ergebnisse über die Konstitution der chromatischen Substanz des Zellkerns. Jena.

1905. Zellen-Studien. 5. Ueber die Abhängigkeit der Kerngrösse und Zellenzahl der Seeigel-Larven von der Chromosomenzahl der Ausgangszellen. Jena.

BRAEM, F., 1897. Die geschlechtliche Entwickelung von Plumatella fungosa. Zoologica, Stuttgart, 23.

BRAUER, A., 1892. Das Ei von Branchipus Grubii von der Bildung bis zur Ablage. Abh. preuss. Akad. Wiss.

1893a. Zur Kenntniss der Reifung des sich parthenogenetisch entwickelnden Eies von Artemia salina. Arch. mikr. Anat., 43.

1893b. Zur Kenntniss der Spermatogenese von Ascaris megalocephala. Ibid., 42.

BRESSLAU, E., 1904. Beiträge zur Entwickelungsgeschichte der Turbellarien. 1. Die Entwickelung der Rhabdocoelen und Alloiocoelen. Zeit. wiss. Zool., 76.

BRYCE, T. H., 1903. Maturation of the ovum in Echinus esculentus. Quart. Journ. Micr. Sci. (N. S.), 46.

CALKINS, G. N., 1895. The spermatogenesis of Lumbricus. Journ. Morph., 11.

CARNOY, J. B., 1885. La cytodiérèse chez les Arthropodes. La Cellule, 1.

1886. La cytodiérèse de l'oeuf. Ibid., 2, 3.

1887. Les globules polaires de l'Ascaris clavata. Ibid., 3.

COE, W. R., 1899. The maturation and fertilization of the egg of Cerebratulus. Zool. Jahrb., 12.

CONKLIN, E. G., 1902. Karyokinesis and cytokinesis in the maturation, fertilization and cleavage of Crepidula and other Gasteropoda. Journ. Acad. Nat. Sci. Philadelphia (2), 12.

DOWNING, E. R., 1905. The spermatogenesis of Hydra. Zool. Jahrb., 21.

DUBLIN, L. I., 1905. The history of the germ cells in Pedicellina americana. Ann. New York Acad. Sci., 16.

EBNER, V. v., 1900. Ueber die Theilung der Spermatocyten bei den Säugethieren. Sitzb. Akad. Wiss. Wien, 108.

EISEN, G., 1900. Spermatogenesis of Batrachoseps. Journ. Morph., 17.

FARMER, J. B., AND MOORE, J. E. S., 1905. On the maiotic phase (reduction divisions) in animals and plants. Quart. Journ. Micr. Sci. (N. S.), 48.

FOOT, K., 1898. The cocoons and eggs of Allolobophora foetida. Journ. Morph., 14.

FRANCOTTE, P., 1897. Recherches sur la maturation, la fécondation et la segmentation chez les Polyclades. Mém. couronnés Acad. roy. sci. Belg.

1898. Idem. — Arch. zool. expér. génér.

GÉRARD, O., 1904. L'ovocyte de premier ordre du Prostheceraeus vittatus avec quelques observations relatives à la maturation chez trois autres Polyclades. La Cellule, 18.

GEROULD, J. H., 1903. The development of Phascolosoma. Arch. zool. expér. génér. (4), 2.

GIARDINA, A., 1898. Primi stadi embrionali della "Mantis religiosa." Monitore Zool. Italiano, 8.

1901. Origine dell' oocite e delle cellule nutrici nel Dytiscus. Internat. Monatsch. Anat. Phys., 18.

GOLDSCHMIDT, R., 1902. Untersuchungen über die Eireifung, Befruchtung und Zelltheilung bei Polystomum integerrimum Rud. Zeit. wiss. Zool., 71.

1905. Eireifung, Befruchtung und Embryonalentwicklung des Zoogonus mirus Lss. Zool. Jahrb., 21.

GRÉGOIRE, V., 1905. Les résultats acquis sur les cinèses de maturation dans les deux règnes. I. La Cellule, 22.

GRIFFIN, L. E., 1899. Studies on the maturation, fertilization, and cleavage of Thalassema and Zirphaea. Journ. Morph., 15.

GROSS, J., 1904. Die Spermatogenese von Syromastes marginatus L. Zool. Jahrb., 20.

GUYER, M. F., 1900. Spermatogenesis of normal and of hybrid pigeons. Chicago.

HÄCKER, V., 1892. Die Furchung des Eies von Aequorea Forskalia. Arch. mikr. Anat., 40.

1902. Ueber das Schicksal der elterlichen und grosselterlichen Kernanteile. Jena. Zeit. Naturwiss., 37.

1904. Bastardirung und Geschlechtszellenbildung. Zool. Jahrb. Supplement, 7.

HARM, K., 1902. Die Entwickelungsgeschichte von Clava squamata. Zeit. wiss. Zool., 73.

HARPER, E. H., 1904. The fertilization and early development of the pigeon's egg. Amer. Journ. Anat., 3.

HEIDER, K., 1906. Vererbung und Chromosomen. Jena.

HENKING, H., 1890a. Das Ei von Pieris brassicae L., nebst Bemerkungen über Samen und Samenbildung. Zeit. wiss. Zool., 49.

1890b. Ueber Reductionstheilung der Chromosomen in den Samenzellen von Insekten. Internat. Monatschr. Anat. Phys., 7.

1891. Ueber Spermatogenese und deren Beziehung zur Eientwicklung bei Pyrrhocoris apterus M. Zeit. wiss. Zool., 51.

1892. Untersuchungen über die ersten Entwicklungsvorgänge in den Eiern der Insekten. 3. Specielles und Allgemeines. Ibid., 54.

HERLA, V., 1893. Étude des variations de la mitose chez l'Ascaride mégalocéphale. Arch. de Biol., 13.

HERTWIG, O., 1890. Vergleich der Ei- und Samenbildung bei Nematoden. Arch. mikr. Anat., 36.

HILL, M. D., 1896. Notes on the fecundation of the egg of Sphaerechinus granularis, and on the maturation and fertilization of the egg of Phallusia mammillata. Quart. Journ. Micr. Sci. (N. S.), 38.

HOLMGREN, N., 1902. Ueber den Bau der Hoden und die Spermatogenese von Silpha carinata. Vorläufige Mittheilung. Anat. Anz., 22.

ISHIKAWA, 1891. Spermatogenesis, ovogenesis and fertilization in Diaptomus sp. Journ. Coll. Sci. Imper. Univ. Japan, 5.

JANSSENS, F. A., 1901. La spermatogénèse chez les Tritons. La Cellule, 19.

JANSSENS, F. A., AND DUMEZ, R., 1903. L'élément nucléinien pendant les cinèses de maturation des spermatocytes chez Batrachoseps attenuatus et Pletodon cinereus. Ibid., 20.

JANSSENS, F. A., AND ELRINGTON, G. A., 1904. L'élément nucléinien pendant les divisions de maturation dans l'oeuf de l'Aplysia punctata. Ibid., 21.

JULIN, C., 1893. Structure et développement des glandes sexuelles; ovogénèse, spermatogénèse et fécondation chez Styelopsis grossularia. Bull. Sci. France et Belgique, 25.

KAISER, J. E., 1893. Die Acanthocephalen und ihre Entwickelung. Bibliotheca zoologica, 7.

KATHARINER, L., 1904. Ueber die Entwicklung von Gyrodactylus elegans v. Nrdm. Zool. Jahrb. Supplement, 7.

KING, H. D., 1901. The maturation and fertilization of the egg of Bufo lentiginosus. Journ. Morph., 17.

1905. The formation of the first polar spindle in the egg of Bufo lentiginosus. Biol. Bull., 9.

KINGSBURY, B. F., 1902. The spermatogenesis of Desmognathus fusca. Amer. Journ. Anat., 1.

KLINCKOWSTRÖM, A. v., 1896. Beiträge zur Kenntnis der Eireifung und Befruchtung bei Prostheceraeus vittatus. Arch. mikr. Anat., 48.

KORSCHELT, E., 1895. Ueber Kerntheilung, Eireifung und Befruchtung bei Ophryotrocha puerilis. Zeit. wiss. Zool., 60.

KOSTANECKI, A., 1902. Ueber die Reifung und Befruchtung des Eies von Cerebratulus marginatus. Bull. Acad. Sci. Cracovie.

1904. Cytologische Studien an künstlich parthenogenetisch sich entwickelnden Eiern von Mactra. Arch. mikr. Anat., 64.

LEBEDINSKY, J., 1897. Zur Entwickelungsgeschichte der Nemertinen. Biol. Centralbl., 17.

LEBRUN, H., 1901a. La vésicule germinative et les globules polaires chez les Anoures. La Cellule, 19.

1902b. Les cinèses sexuelles chez Diemyctilus torosus. Ibid., 20.

LÉCAILLON, A., 1901. Recherches sur l'ovaire des Collemboles. Arch. Anat. Micr. Paris, 4.

LEE, A. B., 1897. Les cinèses spermatogénétiques. La Cellule, 13.

LENHOSSÉK, M. v., 1898. Untersuchungen über Spermatogenese. Arch. mikr. Anat., 51.

LINVILLE, H. R., 1900. Maturation and fertilization in Pulmonate Gasteropods. Bull. Mus. Com. Zool. Harvard.

LUKJANOW, S. M., 1889. Einige Bemerkungen über sexuelle Elemente beim Spulwurm des Hundes. Arch. mikr. Anat., 34.

McCLUNG, C. E., 1902. The spermatocyte divisions of the Locustidae. Kansas Univ. Sci. Bull., 1.

1905. The Chromosome complex of Orthopteran spermatocytes. Biol. Bull., 9.

McGILL, C., 1904. The Spermatogenesis of Anax junius. Univ. Missouri Studies, 2.

McGREGOR, J. H., 1899. The Spermatogenesis of Amphiuma. Journ. Morph.

MATTHIESEN, E., 1903. Die Eireifung und Befruchtung der Süsswasserdendrocoelen. Zool. Anz., 27.

MEAD, A. D., 1898. The origin and behavior of the centrosomes in the Annelid egg. Journ. Morph., 14.

MEDES, G., 1905. The Spermatogenesis of Scutigera forceps. Biol. Bull., 9.

MEVES, F., 1896. Ueber die Entwickelung der männlichen Geschlechtszellen von Salamandra maculosa. Arch. mikr. Anat., 48.

1902. Ueber oligopyrene und apyrene Spermien und über ihre Entstehung, nach Beobachtungen an Paludina und Pygaera. Ibid. 61.

MEYER, O., 1895. Celluläre Untersuchungen an Nematoden-Eiern. Jena. Zeitsch. Naturw., 29.

MOENKHAUS, W. J., 1904. The development of the hybrids between Fundulus heteroclitus and Menidia notata. Amer. Jour. Anat., 3.

MONTGOMERY, T. H., JR., 1898. The spermatogenesis in Pentatoma up to the formation of the spermatid. Zool. Jahrb., 12.

1900. The spermatogenesis of Peripatus (Peripatopsis) balfouri up to the formation of the spermatid. Ibid., 14.

1901a. Further studies on the chromosomes of the Hemiptera heteroptera. Proc. Acad. Nat. Sci. Philadelphia.

1901b. A study of the chromosomes of the germ cells of Metazoa. Trans. Amer. Phil. Soc., 20.

1904a. Some observations and considerations upon the maturation phenomena of the germ cells. Biol. Bull., 6.

1904b. The development and structure of the larva of Paragordius. Proc. Acad. Nat. Sci. Philadelphia.

1905. The spermatogenesis of Syrbula and Lycosa, with general considerations upon chromosome reduction and the heterochromosomes. Ibid.

1906. The terminology of aberrant chromosomes and their behavior in certain Hemiptera. Science (N. S.), 23.

MOORE, J. E. S., 1894. Some points in the spermatogenesis of Mammals. Internat. Monatschr. Anat. Phys., 11.

1894b. Some points in the origin of the reproductive elements in Apus and Branchipus. Quart. Journ. Micr. Sci. (N. S.), 35.

1895. On the structural changes in the reproductive cells during the spermatogenesis of Elasmobranchs. Ibid., 38.

MOORE, J. E. S., AND ROBINSON, L. E., 1905. On the behavior of the nucleolus in the spermatogenesis of Periplaneta americana. Ibid., 48.

MOORE, J. E. S. AND WALKER, C. E., 1906. The meiotic process in Mammalia. University Press of Liverpool.

NAME, W. G. VAN, 1899. The maturation, fertilization and early development of the Planarians. Trans. Conn. Acad. Sci., 10.

NEKRASSOFF, A., 1903. Untersuchungen über die Reifung und Befruchtung des Eies von Cymbulia peronii. Anat. Anz., 21.

NICHOLS, M. L., 1902. The spermatogenesis of Oniscus asellius Linn. Proc. Amer. Phil. Soc., 41.

PETRUNKEWITSCH, A., 1901. Die Richtungskörper und ihr Shicksal im befruchteten und unbefruchteten Bienenei. Zool. Jahrb., 14.

PROWAZEK, S., 1901a. Spermatogenese des Nashornkäfers (Oryctes nasicornis L.). Arbeit. zool. Inst. Wien., 13.

1901b. Spermatogenese der Weinbergschnecke (Helix pomatia L.). Ibid.

1902. Ein Beitrag zur Krebsspermatogenese. Zeit. wiss. Zool., 71.

RATH, O. VOM, 1892. Zur Kenntniss der Spermatogenese von Gryllotalpa vulgaris. Arch. mikr. Anat., 40.

1895. Neue Beiträge zur Frage der Chromatinreduction in der Samen- und Eireife. Ibid., 46.

RÜCKERT, J., 1894. Zur Eireifung bei Copepoden. Anat. Hefte.

SCHOCKAERT, R., 1902. L'ovogénèse chez le Thysanozoon brocchi. La Cellule, 20.

SCHOENFELD, H., 1901. La spermatogénèse chez le taureau et chez les mammifères en général. Arch. de Biol., 18.

SCHREINER, A., AND K. E., 1905. Ueber die Entwickelung der männlichen Geschlechtszellen von Myxine glutinosa (L.). Ibid., 21.

SINÉTY, R. DE, 1901. Recherches sur la biologie et l'anatomie des Phasmes. La Cellule.

SMALLWOOD, W. M., 1904. The maturation, fertilization and early cleavage of Haminea solitaria (Say). Bull. Mus. Comp. Zool. Harvard, 45.

STEVENS, N. M., 1902. Experimental studies on eggs of Echinus microtuberculatus. Arch. Entwicklungsmech., 15.

1903. On the ovogenesis and spermatogenesis of Sagitta bipunctata. Zool. Jahrb., 18.

1904. On the germ cells and the embryology of Planaria simplicissima. Proc. Acad. Nat. Sci. Philadelphia.

1905a. A study of the germ cells of Aphis rosae and Aphis oenotherae. Journ. Exper. Zool., 2.

1905b. Studies in spermatogenesis with especial reference to the "accessory chromosome." Carnegie Institute Publ.

1905c. Further studies on the ovogenesis of Sagitta. Zool. Jahrb., 21.

STRICHT, O. VAN DER, 1898. La formation des deux globules polaires et l' apparition des spermocentres dans l'oeuf de Thysanozoon Brocchi. Arch. de Biol., 15.

SUTTON, W. S., 1902. On the morphology of the chromosome group in Brachystola magna. Biol. Bull., 4.

1903. The chromosomes in heredity. Ibid.

TOYAMA, K., 1894. On the spermatogenesis of the Silk Worm. Bull. Coll. Agric. Imper. Univ. Japan, 2.

VEJDOVSKÝ, F., UND MRÁZEK, A., 1903. Umbildung des Cytoplasma während der Befruchtung und Zellteilung. Arch. mikr. Anat., 62.

VOINOV, D., 1903. La spermatogénèse d'été chez le Cybister Roeselii. Arch. zool. expér. génér. (4), 1.

WALDEYER, W., 1888. Ueber Karyokinese und ihre Beziehungen zu den Befruchtungsvorgängen. Arch. mikr. Anat., 32.

WALLACE, L. B., 1905. The spermatogenesis of the Spider. Biol. Bull., 8.

WALLACE, W., 1904. The oocyte of Tomopteris. Report 73 Meet. Brit. Assoc. Adv. Sci.

WHEELER, W. M., 1897. The maturation, fecundation and early cleavage of Myzostoma glabrum Leuckart. Arch. de Biol., 15.

WILCOX, E. V., 1895. Spermatogenesis of Caloptenus femur-rubrum and Cicada tibicen. Bull. Mus. Comp. Zool. Harvard, 27.

WILSON, E. B., 1900. The cell in development and inheritance. 2d ed. New York.

1905a. Studies on Chromosomes. 1. The Behavior of the idiochromosomes in Hemiptera. Journ. Exper. Zool., 2.

1905b. The chromosomes in relation to the determination of sex in Insects. Science (N. S.), 22.

1905c. Studies on chromosomes. 2. The paired microchromosomes, idiochromosomes and heterotropic chromosomes in Hemiptera. Journ. Exper. Zool., 2.

1906. Idem. 3. The sexual differences of the chromosome-groups in Hemiptera, with some considerations of the determination and inheritance of sex. Ibid., 3.

WINIWARTER, H. V., 1900. Recherches sur l'ovogénèse et l'organogénèse de l'ovaire des Mammifères (Lapin et Homme). Arch. de Biol., 17.

WOLTERECK, R., 1898. Zur Bildung und Entwickelung des Ostracoden-Eies. Zeit. Wiss. Zool., 64.

WULFERT, J., 1902. Die Embryonalentwickelung von Gonothyraea loveni Allm. Ibid., 71.

YATSU, N., 1902. On the development of Lingula anatina. Journ. Coll. Sci. Japan, 17.

UNIVERSITY OF TEXAS, March 26, 1906.

EXPLANATION OF THE PLATES.

All the figures have been drawn by the author with the camera lucida at the level of the base of the microscope, and the reproductions are the size of the originals. Figs. 1-68, 91-106 and 120-133 are drawn at a magnification of about 2,000 diameters, all the others at a magnification of about 2,180 diameters. Lateral views of the first maturation spindles are placed the length of the plate, of the second maturation spindle the width of the plate, which enables one to distinguish them at a glance. The following abbreviations have been employed:

Di, diplosome.

Mo, monosome.

Pl, plasmosome (true nucleolus).

The diplosomes are paired elements, and when their separate components can be distinguished, they are lettered *Di* and *di* respectively; in case there is more than one pair of them to a cell a number is placed after letters, viz., *Di. 1*, *di. 1* would be one pair and *Di. 2*, *di. 2* a second pair; the capital letter is used for the small component of a pair and the small letter for the larger one in those cases where they differ in size. If there is a single monosome present it is lettered simply *Mo*, but if two they are lettered *Mo. 1* and *Mo. 2*. Single letters denote autosomes, a capital and a lower case letter of the same kind (as *A* and *a*) marking the components of a pair; if the capital and the small letter are separated by a comma, as "*A*, *a*," a pair of correspondent ones is denoted; but if a capital is followed by a small letter enclosed in parentheses, as "*A* (*a*)," it is indicated that but one of the elements is present, *i. e.*, either *A* or *a*.

Some of the figures are redrawings of cells previously figured by me, and in such cases this is noted by the date of the paper where the particular cell was first illustrated followed by the number of the original figure, all this being enclosed in parentheses, as "(v. 1901b, Fig. 2)."

PLATE IX.

Figs. 1-14, *Euschistus variolarius*.

Figs. 1-4, spermatogonic monasters (with Fig. 1, v. 1901b, Fig. 2).

Fig. 5, nucleus in synapsis stage.

Figs. 6-9, successive prophases of the maturation mitosis, the last two showing all the chromosomes.

Fig. 10, first maturation monaster.

Figs. 11, 12, second maturation monasters.

Figs. 13, 14, chromosomes of two spermatids.

Figs. 15-22, *Euschistus tristigmus*.

Fig. 15, spermatogonic monaster.

Fig. 16, nucleus of synapsis stage.

Fig. 17, pole view of first maturation spindle.

Fig. 18, lateral view of the same.

Fig. 19, pole view of a plate of daughter elements before their arrangement in the spindle.

Fig. 20, second maturation spindle.

Figs. 21, 22, chromosomes of two spermatids.

Figs. 23-27, *Podisus spinosus*.

Fig. 23, spermatogonic monaster (v. 1901b, Fig. 27).

Fig. 24, nucleus of late synapsis stage.

Fig. 25, oblique lateral view of first maturation spindle.

Fig. 26, pole view, second maturation spindle.

Fig. 27, lateral view of the same stage.

Figs. 28-30, *Mormidea lugens*.

Fig. 28, spermatogonic monaster (v. 1901*b*, Fig. 31); the autosomes *C* and *c* are seen from their ends, and it could not be decided whether *E*, *e* is one or two elements.

Fig. 29, pole view of first maturation spindle.

Fig. 30, pole view of second maturation spindle.

Figs. 31-37, *Cosmopepla carnifex*.

Fig. 31, spermatogonic monaster.

Fig. 32, late prophase of first maturation division.

Fig. 33, pole view, first maturation spindle (v. 1901*b*, Fig. 41).

Fig. 34, lateral view, first maturation spindle (v. 1901*b*, Fig. 40).

Figs. 35, 36, pole views, second maturation spindle.

Fig. 37, chromosomes of a spermatid.

Figs. 38, 39, *Nezara hilaris*.

Fig. 38, spermatogonic monaster (v. 1901*b*, Fig. 11).

Fig. 39, nucleus of postsynapsis stage.

Figs. 40-45, *Brochymena* sp.

Figs. 40, 41, spermatogonic monasters (with 41 v. 1901*b*, Fig. 17).

Fig. 42, oblique lateral view, first maturation spindle.

Fig. 43, pole view, first maturation spindle.

Fig. 44, second maturation spindle.

Fig. 45, pole view of the same stage.

Figs. 46-52, *Perillus confluens*.

Fig. 46, spermatogonic monaster.

Fig. 47, plasmosome and diplosomes of the early prophase of the first maturation division.

Fig. 48, pole view, first maturation spindle.

Fig. 49, pole view of a daughter plate of the first maturation mitosis.

Fig. 50, pole view, second maturation spindle.

Fig. 51, lateral view of the same stage (one of the elements not shown).

Fig. 52, chromosomes of a spermatid.

Figs. 53-58, *Coenus delius*.

Figs. 53, 54, spermatogonic monasters.

Fig. 55, daughter plate of spermatogonic division.

Fig. 56, daughter plate, first maturation division.

Fig. 57, pole view, second maturation spindle.

Fig. 58, lateral view of the same stage.

Figs. 59-65, *Trichopepla semivittata*.

Fig. 59, spermatogonic monaster (v. 1901*b*, Fig. 65).

Figs. 60, 61, spermatocytic nuclei, late growth period.

Fig. 62, spermatocytic nucleus, rest stage.

Fig. 63, idem, early prophase of first maturation division.

Figs. 64, 65, first maturation spindles.

PLATE X.

Figs. 66-68, *Trichopepla semivittata*.

Fig. 66, second maturation spindle.

Fig. 67, pole view of the same stage.

Fig. 68, chromosomes of a spermatid.

Figs. 69–73, *Eurygaster alternatus*.

Fig. 69, spermatocyte nucleus, late postsynapsis.

Fig. 70, first maturation spindle, the chromosomes not in definite arrangement.

Fig. 71, pole view of the same stage.

Fig. 72, pole view, second maturation spindle.

Fig. 73, idem, lateral view.

Figs. 74–80, *Peribalus limbolarius*.

Fig. 74, spermatogonic monaster.

Fig. 75, spermatocyte nucleus, near end of growth period.

Fig. 76, pole view, first maturation spindle (v. 1901*b*, Fig. 37).

Fig. 77, oblique lateral view of the same stage.

Fig. 78, pole view, second maturation spindle.

Fig. 79, daughter plate, first maturation division.

Fig. 80, oblique lateral view, second maturation spindle.

Figs. 81–93, *Nabis annulatus*.

Figs. 81–85, successive prophases, first maturation division.

Fig. 86, pole view, first maturation spindle (v. 1901*a*, Fig. 14).

Figs. 87, 88, lateral views, first maturation spindle.

Fig. 89, pole view of early daughter plate of preceding division.

Figs. 90, 91, second maturation spindles.

Figs. 92, 93, chromosome plates of spermatids.

Figs. 94–106, *Harmostes reflexulus*.

Figs. 94, 95, spermatogonic monasters.

Fig. 96, spermatocyte nucleus, synapsis.

Fig. 97, idem, postsynapsis.

Fig. 98, idem, later postsynapsis.

Fig. 99, idem, rest stage.

Figs. 100, 101, idem, early prophases of first maturation division.

Figs. 102, 103, first maturation spindles (v. 1901*b*, Figs. 113, 116).

Fig. 104, second maturation spindle.

Figs. 105, 106, chromosome plates of spermatids.

Figs. 107–116, *Corizus alternatus*.

Fig. 107, spermatogonic monaster (v. 1901*a*, Fig. 18).

Fig. 108, spermatocyte nucleus, late synapsis.

Figs. 109, 110, idem, postsynapsis.

Fig. 111, idem, rest stage.

Figs. 112, 113, the autosome *A*, *a*, prophase of first maturation division.

Figs. 114–116, successive prophases, first maturation division.

PLATE XI.

Figs. 117–122, *Corizus alternatus*.

Fig. 117, pole view, first maturation spindle.

Fig. 118, lateral view of the same stage.

Fig. 119, daughter chromosomal plate of preceding stage.

Fig. 120, pole view, second maturation spindle.

Figs. 121, 122, second maturation spindles.

Figs. 123–125, *Corizus lateralis.*

Fig. 123, first maturation spindle.

Fig. 124, second maturation spindle.

Fig. 125, late anaphase of second maturation.

Figs. 126–133, *Chariesterus antennator.*

Fig. 126, spermatocyte nucleus, postsynapsis.

Figs. 127, 128, pole views, first maturation spindle.

Fig. 129, lateral view of the same stage.

Fig. 130, pole view, second maturation spindle.

Figs. 131, 132, corresponding daughter plates of second maturation division

Fig. 133, anaphase, second maturation division.

Figs. 134, 135, *Protenor belfragei.*

Fig. 134, spermatogonic monaster (v. 1904b, Fig. 119).

Fig. 135, spermatocyte nucleus, late growth period.

Figs. 136–143, *Alydus pilosulus.*

Fig. 136, spermatogonic monaster.

Fig. 137, spermatocyte nucleus, early synapsis.

Fig. 138, idem, late synapsis.

Fig. 139, late prophase of first maturation division.

Fig. 140, first maturation spindle.

Figs. 141–143, successive second maturation spindles.

Figs. 144–150, *Alydus eurinus.*

Fig. 144, spermatogonic monaster (v. 1901b, Fig. 96).

Fig. 145, spermatocyte nucleus, late synapsis.

Fig. 146, pole view, first maturation spindle.

Fig. 147, lateral view of first maturation spindle.

Fig. 148, daughter plate, early anaphase, first maturation division.

Fig. 149, pole view, second maturation spindle.

Fig. 150, lateral view, second maturation spindle.

Figs. 151–161, *Anasa tristis.*

Fig. 151, spermatogonic monaster.

Figs. 152, 153, spermatocyte nuclei, synapsis stage

Figs. 154, 155, idem, later growth period.

Fig. 156, pole view, first maturation spindle.

Figs. 157, 158, first maturation spindles.

Fig. 159, pole view, second maturation spindle.

Figs. 160, 161, second maturation spindles.

Figs. 162–166, *Anasa* sp.

Figs. 162, 163, oogonic monasters.

Fig. 164, spermatogonic monaster.

Figs. 165, 166, pole and lateral views, first maturation spindle.

Figs. 167, 168, *Anasa armigera.*

Fig. 167, spermatogonic monaster.

Fig. 168, first maturation spindle.

Figs. 169, 170, *Metapodius terminalis.*

Figs. 169, 170, spermatogonic monasters (with 169 v. 1901*d*, Fig. 85).

Plate XII.

Figs. 171-182, *Metapodius terminalis.*

Fig. 171, spermatocyte nucleus, synapsis.
Fig. 172, idem, postsynapsis.
Fig. 173, idem, rest stage.
Fig. 174, late prophase of first maturation division.
Fig. 175, first maturation spindle.
Figs. 176, 177, pole views of the same spindle.
Fig. 178, anaphase of the first maturation division.
Fig. 179, daughter plate, early anaphase, first maturation division.
Fig. 180, pole view, second maturation division.
Figs. 181, 182, second maturation spindles.

Figs. 183-195, *Oedancala dorsalis.*

Fig. 183, spermatogonic monaster (v. 1901*b*, Fig. 154).
Fig. 184, spermatocyte nucleus just before rest period
Fig. 185, idem, rest stage.
Figs. 186-188, successive prophases of first maturation division.
Fig. 189, pole view, first maturation spindle.
Figs. 190, 191, first maturation spindles (with 191 v. Fig. 158, 1901*b*).
Fig. 192, pole view, second maturation spindle.
Fig. 193, second maturation spindle (v. 1901*b*, Fig. 157).
Fig. 194, second maturation anaphase.
Fig. 195, pole view of chromosomes of a spermatid.

Figs. 196-199, *Oncopeltus fasciatus.*

Fig. 196, daughter plate, early anaphase of first maturation division (v. 1901*b*, Fig. 171).
Figs. 197, 198, pole and lateral view, second maturation spindle.
Fig. 199, chromosome plate of a spermatid.

Figs. 200-210, *Peliopelta abbreviata.*

Fig. 200, spermatogonic monaster.
Fig. 201, idem (v. 1901*b*, Fig. 149).
Fig. 202, spermatocyte nucleus, synapsis.
Fig. 203, idem, postsynapsis.
Figs. 204, 205, late prophases, first maturation division.
Fig. 206, pole view, first maturation spindle.
Fig. 207, oblique lateral view of chromosomes of the same division.
Fig. 208, first maturation spindle.
Fig. 209, pole view, second maturation spindle.
Fig. 210, second maturation spindle.

Figs. 211-225, *Ischnodemus falicus.*

Fig. 211, spermatogonic monaster (v. 1901*b*, Fig. 145).
Figs. 212, 213, spermatocyte nuclei, postsynapsis.
Fig. 214, idem, end of growth period.
Figs. 215-219, successive prophases, first maturation division.
Fig. 220, first maturation spindle.
Figs. 221, 222, pole views of first maturation spindles (v. 1901*b*, Figs. 147, 148).
Fig. 223, second maturation spindle.
Fig. 224, pole view, second maturation spindle.
Fig. 225, chromosomes of a spermatid.

Figs. 226–228, *Cymus angustatus*.

Fig. 226, pole view, second maturation spindle (v. 1901b, Fig. 141).
Figs. 227, 228, second maturation spindles.

PLATE XIII.

Figs. 229–236, *Tingis clavata*.

Fig. 229, pole view, first maturation spindle.
Fig. 230, oblique lateral view of the same stage.
Fig. 231, pole view, first maturation spindle.
Figs. 232–234, pole views, second maturation spindles.
Figs. 235, 236, chromosome plates of spermatids.

Fig. 237, *Phymata sp.*

Fig. 237, spermatogonic monaster (v. 1901b, Fig. 200).

Figs. 238–244, *Acholla multispinosa*.

Fig. 238, spermatogonic monaster (v. 1901b, Fig. 207).
Fig. 239, spermatocyte nucleus, rest stage.
Fig. 240, first maturation spindle.
Figs. 241, 242, pole views, first maturation spindle.
Figs. 243, 244, pole views, second maturation spindles (with 243 v. 1901b, Fig. 211).

Figs. 245–250, *Sinea diadema*.

Fig. 245, spermatocyte nucleus, rest stage.
Fig. 246, pole view, first maturation spindle.
Fig. 247, oblique lateral view of chromosomes, first maturation spindle.
Figs. 248–250, first maturation spindles (v. 1901b, Figs. 217, 218).

Figs. 251, 252, *Prionidus cristatus*.

Fig. 251, spermatogonic monaster (v. 1901b, Fig. 224).
Fig. 252, spermatocyte nucleus, rest stage.

Figs. 253–258, *Zaitha sp.*

Fig. 253, spermatogonic monaster.
Fig. 254, spermatocyte, rest stage.
Fig. 255, first maturation spindle.
Fig. 256, pole view, first maturation spindle.
Figs. 257, 258, lateral and pole views, second maturation spindle.

Figs. 259–268, *Hygotrechus sp.*

Fig. 259, spermatogonic monaster (v. 1901b, Fig. 229).
Fig. 260, spermatocyte nucleus, rest stage.
Fig. 261, late prophase, first maturation division.
Figs. 262–264, lateral and pole views, first maturation spindle (with 264 v. 1901b, Fig. 231).
Figs. 265–267, lateral and pole views, second maturation spindle.
Fig. 268, chromosome plate of a spermatid.

Figs. 269–274, *Limnotrechus marginatus*.

Fig. 269, spermatocyte, nucleus, rest stage.
Fig. 270, monosome and plasmosome, early prophase of first maturation division.
Figs. 271, 272, pole and lateral view, first maturation spindle (v. 1901b, Fig. 233).
Figs. 273, 274, lateral and pole view, second maturation spindle.

Figs. 275–287, *Calocoris rapidus*.

Fig. 275, spermatogonic monaster (v. 1906b, Fig. 177).

Fig. 276, spermatocyte nucleus, synapsis.

Fig. 277, idem, end of growth period.

Fig. 278, late prophase, first maturation division.

Figs. 279, 280, pole views, first maturation spindle (with 279 v. 1906b, Fig. 185).

Figs. 281–283, first maturation spindles (with 281 v. 1906b, Fig. 182).

Fig. 284, second maturation spindle.

Figs. 285, 286, pole views of second maturation spindles.

Fig. 287, second maturation anaphase.

Figs. 288–294, *Poecilocapsus goniphorus*.

Fig. 288, spermatocyte nucleus, rest stage.

Fig. 289, pole view, first maturation spindle (v. 1906b, Fig. 196).

Fig. 290, first maturation spindle.

Fig. 291, pole view, second maturation spindle (v. 1906b, Fig. 197).

Fig. 292, second maturation spindle.

Figs. 293, 294, corresponding daughter plates, early anaphase of second maturation division.

Figs. 295–299, *Lygus pratensis*.

Figs. 295, 296, pole and lateral views, first maturation spindle.

Figs. 297, 298, pole and lateral views, second maturation division.

Figs. 299, anaphase of second maturation division.

NOTICE

Preceding volumes of the New Series can be obtained at the Hall of the Society Price, five dollars each.

A few complete sets of the Transactions, New Series, Vols. I—XX are on sale. Price, one hundred dollars.

TRANSACTIONS

OF THE

AMERICAN PHILOSOPHICAL SOCIETY

HELD AT PHILADELPHIA

FOR PROMOTING USEFUL KNOWLEDGE

VOLUME XXI—NEW SERIES

PART IV

ARTICLE IV—*A Study of the Brains of Six Eminent Scientists and Scholars Belonging to the American Anthropometric Society, together with a Description of the Skull of Professor E. D. Cope*

Philadelphia:
THE AMERICAN PHILOSOPHICAL SOCIETY
104 SOUTH FIFTH STREET
1907

ARTICLE IV.

A STUDY OF THE BRAINS OF SIX EMINENT SCIENTISTS AND SCHOLARS BELONGING TO THE AMERICAN ANTHROPOMETRIC SOCIETY, TOGETHER WITH A DESCRIPTION OF THE SKULL OF PROFESSOR E. D. COPE.

BY EDW. ANTHONY SPITZKA, M.D.,

PROFESSOR OF GENERAL ANATOMY, JEFFERSON MEDICAL COLLEGE, LATE FELLOW AND DEMONSTRATOR OF ANATOMY, COLUMBIA UNIVERSITY.

(Read March 16, 1906.)

"Den Körper lasst öffnen; es gewährt diess vielleicht einigen Nutzen. Findet sich ein Theil, der den Aerzten Belehrung gewähren kann, so nehme man ihn in eine anatomische Sammlung auf."

— From Tiedemann's will (1861).

It is owing to the courage and wise forethought of certain advanced thinkers and fruitful contributors to science that the brains of members of the American Anthropometric Society have become available for scientific study. Occasionally an individual has directed his nearest of kin to arrange for the preservation of his brain; such men were Tiedemann, Grote and the two Seguins. But not until the Mutual Autopsy Society of Paris was founded in 1881 was this most legitimate claim of science met by the establishment of an association formed for the express purpose of securing élite brains for scientific study. On this side of the Atlantic, the American Anthropometric Society was the pioneer association founded on similar lines, followed by the Cornell Brain Association under the leadership of Prof. Burt G. Wilder. Not many years after the celebrated Retzius, of Stockholm, in view of the rather negative results of older investigators in the field of cerebral morphology, and with the wish of satisfying himself whether the brains of persons of superior intellectual capacity were or were not to be distinguished from ordinary brains by special anatomical characters, proposed, in conjunction with the physiologist Tigerstedt, that his colleagues bequeath their brains for scientific purposes. The forms of bequest received the signatures of just two men: Retzius and Tigerstedt. Better results had been obtained by the Mutual Autopsy Society of Paris which now possesses ten brains or more, among them those of Gambetta, Bertillon, Véron and de Mortillet. The Cornell Brain Association has bequeathed to it about seventy brains of educated, orderly persons, of which thirteen are already preserved in the Neurological Laboratory at Cornell. There is a large collection at Munich and a smaller one at Göttingen which does not seem to have received any additional brains since Wagner's cessation of work on cerebral morphology.

The American Anthropometric Society was established in 1889 at a meeting which took place at the residence of ———. The founders were: Harrison Allen, Francis Xavier Dercum, Joseph Leidy, William Pepper, and Edward Charles Spitzka. The chief object of the society was the preservation of the brains of its members. Three of the founders of the society have since died and their brains were duly removed and preserved as were those of members who subsequently joined the society and are now deceased. In the order of acquisition, the list of brains in the collection included the following:

1. Joseph Leidy.
2. Philip Leidy.
3. J. W. White, Sr.
4. Andrew J. Parker.
5. Walt Whitman.
6. Harrison Allen.
7. Edward D. Cope.
8. William Pepper.

The brain of Walt Whitman, together with the jar in which it had been placed, was said to have been dropped on the floor by a careless assistant. Unfortunately, not even the pieces were saved. The brain of Dr. White is not in good condition. The brain of Dr. Parker had been allowed to remain in Müller's fluid ever since 1892 and when found was badly broken. Fortunately, there exists an excellent cast of the undissected brain which had been made soon after hardening under the supervision of Dr. Dercum. With the utmost care I was able to restore some of the parts so as to delineate considerable portions of the mesal surfaces as well as to expose and make casts of the insulæ. It is to be regretted that like opportunities were not afforded in the case of Walt Whitman's brain. The brains of Joseph Leidy, Philip Leidy and E. D. Cope are in excellent condition. Of Philip Leidy's brain there also exist casts of the cerebral halves and of the cerebellum and isthmus in one piece. The brain of Harrison Allen had become flattened, while that of William Pepper had been both flattened and distorted.

These brains were first placed at my disposal in the winter of 1902–03 and the objective study of the specimens was completed in time to render a brief report at the meeting of the Association of American Anatomists at Philadelphia in December, 1904. These studies were also briefly referred to in an address before the American Anthropological Association at about the same time. The work bestowed upon these brains was amplified by studies that were conducted throughout the same period upon the brains of other notable persons as well as exceptional brains of various races and of normal, ordinary persons executed in New York State for murder — available for removal and preservation immediately after death and therefore affording for comparison a series of as nearly fresh and perfectly preserved brains as can be. The work was conducted in a systematic manner with the view of utilizing new criteria of brain-measurement and fissural pattern to serve as a basis for the formulation of standards of which we stand so urgently in need. For, in the comparison of human brains one of the chief difficulties to contend with lies in the inadequacy of former attempts to express morphological differences in exact terms, and however irksome and tedious a row of statistical figures may be to the anatomical investigator I could not help but feel how necessary it had become to resort to exact expressions of size and form. Therefore, in addition to my general observations on the surface morphology of these brains, I have ventured to obtain additional facts from a study of measurements in comparative tabulation of the brains of the two Doctors Seguin, Major John W. Powell, George Francis Train and Major J. B. Pond, together with those of ten — for all present intents and purposes — normal brains of men executed by electricity.

I.

A brief review of what has been done with the brains of notable individuals may prove interesting and the writer ventures to interpolate a fairly complete series of references, nearly all in chronological order, to the brains of 130 notable men and four women.

1. Beethoven (1770–1827). German composer. Dr. Johann Wagner, who was present at the autopsy of Beethoven, is quoted by J. von Seyfried as having said that "the convolutions appeared twice as numerous and the fissures twice as deep as in ordinary brains." J. von Seyfried: "Ludwig von Beethoven' Studien." Schaaffhausen: 16. Versamml. d. deutsch. Anthropolog. Gesellsch.; Correspondenzbl. in Vol. XVI of *Arch. f Anthr.*, 1885.

2. Gall, F. Jos (1758–1828), German Anatomist and Phrenologist. In the report of the last illness and post-mortem examination of Dr. Gall there is the following statement: "At the base of the skull four or five ounces of fluid were found. The brain which was not dissected weighed two pounds, ten ounces and a quarter. The right side of the cerebellum was rather larger than the left, and contained a small fibro-cellular tumor, which internally was of a bony structure." According to Topinard the cranial capacity was 1692 cubic centimeters. (Brain-weight = 1198 grams.)

London Medical Gazette, Sept. 13, 1828, page 478. Topinard, Elements d'Anthropologie générale, 1885, p. 628.

3. CUVIER, GEORGE LEOPOLD CHRETIEN FREDERIC DAGOBERT (1769–1832), Naturalist (of German descent), was really a native of Wuerttemberg and his parents belonged to the Germanic, not the Celtic race. The autopsy took place on May 15, 1832, and the following physicians were present: Orfila, Dumesnil, Dupuytren, Allard, Biett, Valenciennes, Lautrillard, Rousseau, Andralueven and Bérard. Two reports were published; one by Bérard and one by Rousseau. Unfortunately there is a discrepancy between these reports relative to the brain-weight, Rousseau's figure being one ounce higher than Bérard's, which, in the metric system, is equivalent to 1830 grams. The cerebellum weighed 191.1 grams. Rousseau gives certain measurements of the head which are worth while recording here.

Max. circumference of head.	60.45 ctm.
Arc from glabella to inion	39.09
Arc over vertex from ear to ear (meatus audit.) .	40.60

The post-mortem report makes no mention of the finding of evidences of hydrocephalus and Bérard says that he never before saw a brain so complexly convolute and with so many deep fissures. Bérard: *Gazette medicale*, May 19, 1832. E. Rousseau: *Lancette française*, May 26, 1832. Topinard: *Memoires de la société d'anthropologie de Paris*, 1883, p. 15. G. Hervé: Le cerveau de Cuvier. *Bull. de la société d'anthropologie de Paris*, 1883, pp. 738–748. Karl E. von Baer: "Lebensgeschichte Cuvier's." *Arch. f. Anthrop.*, XXIV, 1896, pp. 227–275.

4. DUPUYTREN (1777–1835), French surgeon and anatomist. The autopsy was performed on February 9, 1835, thirty-two hours after death. The official report is signed by Doctors Broussais, Cruveilhier, Husson and Bouillaud. The brain-weight (French system) was 2 livres, 14 ounces (1,437 grams). The brain was normal. *Gazette des Hôpitaux*, civils et militaires; 1835, IX, No. 20, p. 77. R. Wagner: "Vorstudien, etc.," I, 1860, p. 96.

5. DÖLLINGER, IGNAZ (1770–1841), German anatomist and physiologist (Munich collection). The fresh weight was not recorded, but Bischoff estimates the loss in weight during immersion in alcohol to have been 41 per cent. The subfrontal gyre was well developed and the parieto-occipital region was largely expanded and complex. Estimated brain-weight 1,207 grams. Bischoff: Das Hirngewicht des Menschen, p. 137. Rüdinger: *Beitr. z. Anatomie des Sprachcentrums* (1882). Rüdinger: *Beitr. z. Anatomie der Affenspalte*, 1882.

6. ABERCROMBIE, JOHN (1780–1844), Scottish physician. The autopsy was con-

ducted by Goodsir in the presence of Doctors Adam Hunter, Alison, Renton, Gillespie, Begbie, Cumming and J. A. Hunter. Except for atheromatous changes in the arteries the brain was normal. Its weight was reported to have been 63 ounces (1,786 grams). *Edinburgh Med. Jour.*, 1845, LXVIII, 231.

7. Chalmers, Thomas (1780–1847). English theologian. The autopsy was conducted by Dr. Hughes Bennett and reported by Dr. Begbie. "The brain weighed 53 ounces avoirdupois and was healthy." (1502.5 grams.) James Begbie: *Edinburgh Monthly Med. Jour.*, XII, 1851, March, p. 205.

8. Donnizetti, Gaetano (1798–1848). Italian composer, died in Bergamo in 1848 of paralytic dementia. The brain weighed 1391 grams. Cappelli: *Arch. ital. per le malatie nervosi*, 1887, XXIV, p. 135. *Neurolog. Centralbl.*, 1887, p. 216.

9. Jeffrey, Lord Francis (1773–1850). Scottish justice and writer. Calderwood quotes the following: "Sir Robert Christison, who, along with Prof. Miller, carefully weighed Lord Jeffrey's brain, favored me with the following extract from his letter to Sir B. Brodie and Dr. Bright: . . . 'The brain was much congested, the archnoid membrane contained much gelatiniform effusion. The encephalon weighed 51[illegible] ounces, the cerebellum 6[illegible] ounces.' . . . Lord Jeffrey was of rather small stature." (Brain-weight, 1471 grams.) Calderwood: The Relations of the Mind and Brain, 1884, p. 23.

10. Webster, Daniel (1782–1852). American statesman (English descent). The autopsy was reported by Dr. Jeffries. The brain was examined by Dr. Jeffries Wyman. The brain-weight was recorded as 3 pounds, 5 ounces, 8 drachms and 17[illegible] grains (avoirdupois). (1518 grams.) The cerebrum alone weighed 2 pounds, 14 ounces and 7 drachms. (1317 grams.) The intracranial capacity is stated to have been 122 cubic inches (1999.5 cubic centimeters). The circumference of the head was 23¾ inches (60.3 ctm.). Jeffries concludes that the brain probably weighed as much as 63¾ ounces (1807 grams) at maturity. Jeffries: *Amer. Jour. Med. Sciences*, 1853, pp. 110–120.

11. Czelakovsky, Franz Ladislaw (1799–1852). Bohemian writer. The brain was removed and examined by Dr. V. D. Lambl in the presence of Purkinjé. The skull is described as being of large size and ovoid shape while the brain was richly convoluted. V. Stanek (and V. D. Lambl): Poslední nemoc F. L. Czelakovského a její predchůdceové. *Czas. Czes. Lék.*, 1864, III, p. 300, 307. Matiegka: Ueber das Hirngewicht des Menschen, *Sitzber. d. k. böhm. Gesellsch. d. Wiss.*, 1902, p. 37.

12. Atherton, Charles G., American politician (U. S. Senator). "The brain weighed 56½ ounces." Brain-weight = 1602 grams. *Boston Med. and Surg. Jour.*, January 18, 1854, p. 512.

13. GAUSS, KARL FRIEDRICH (1777–1855), German Mathematician and Physicist (Göttingen collection). The brain is in many respects the most notable of any in this series. It was preserved in alcohol and the illustrations in Wagner's memoirs were made from the somewhat shrunken specimen. The intracranial diameters were 18 and 15 ctm. (in Vol. II (1862) Wagner gives the diameters of an endocranial cast of Gauss as 18.5 and 14.4 ctm.) while the hardened brain was 17 cm. in length and 12 ctm. in breadth. The fresh brain-weight was 1492 grams; after hardening it weighed 1031 grams. The surface configurations of the cerebrum are remarkable for the multiplicity of fissures and the great complexity of the convolutions. The richness of fissuration is particularly notable in the frontal region while the subparietal regions, especially the marginal and angular gyres, exhibit a relatively enormous expansion. The very thorough morphological studies of this brain are published in Wagner's two memoirs. R. Wagner: "Vorstudien zu einer wissenschaftlichen Morphologie und Physiologie des menschlichen Gehirns als Seelenorgan." (Göttingen) I (1860); II (1862).

14. FUCHS, KONRAD HEINRICH (1803–1855), German Pathologist and Physician (Göttingen collection). Fuchs was a man of medium stature. Death was caused by fatty degeneration of the heart. The fresh brain-weight was 1499 grams. After preservation in alcohol each hemicerebrum weighed 489 grams: the ratio of cerebrum to cerebellum was 88.1 : 11.9. Wagner observes that the central fissures of both sides are interrupted by bridging gyres. The frontal lobes are more massive and more complexly marked than in average brains. The tortuosity of the fissures is especially marked in the left frontal lobe. The asymmetry of the surface-markings on the two sides is more marked than usual. The paroccipital gyres are depressed so that the occipital fissure extends laterad for quite a distance. R. Wagner: "Vorstudien, etc.," II, 1862, pp. 14, 15, 17 and 91.

15. HERMANN, CARL FRIEDRICH (1804–1855), German philologist and archæologist (Göttingen collection). Compared with the brains of Dirichlet and Gauss, Wagner finds this brain to present rather simpler contours. Hermann's stature was about 170 ctm. The fresh brain-weight was 1358 grams. In the hardened specimen, preserved in alcohol, the left hemicerebrum weighed 447 grams, the right, 443 grams. R. Wagner: "Vorstudien, etc.," I and II.

16. SCHUMANN, ROBERT (1810–1856), German composer, when about 44 years of age, became melancholy and attempted suicide. In a communication to v. Wasilewski, by Dr. Richarz of Endenich (near Bonn) concerning the illness and death of Schumann, is the following account of the examination of the brain: "It may be interesting to known that the transverse (acoustic) stria marking the fourth ventricle of the brain

were numerous and finely fashioned. The following abnormalities were revealed: Distended bloodvessels, especially at the base of the brain; ossification at the base of the brain and abnormal development of normal projections, as a new formation of irregular masses of bone, which partially pierced the external covering (dura) of the brain with their sharp points; concretion and degeneration of the two inner coverings (pia-arachnoid) of the brain and unnatural growth of the innermost covering (pia) and the posterior portion of the cerebrum; a considerable atrophy of the whole brain, which weighed 7 ounces (Prussian troy weight) less than is usual in a man of Schumann's age." If we assume 1380 grams to be the average weight for one of Schumann's age, an interpretation of the above statement as to the lesser weight of his brain would give about 1100–1140 grams. Schaafhausen found the cranial capacity to the 1510 cubic centimeters and cites Richarz as giving the actual weight of the brain "2 Pfund, 28½ Loth," or 1475 grams. v. Wasilewski: "Life of Robert Schumann" Transl. by A. L. Alger. Boston, 1871, p. 258. Schaafhausen: *Archiv f. Anthrop.*, XVI, *Correspondenzbl.*, p. 149.

17. Dirichlet, Peter Gustave Lejeune (1805–1859), French mathematician (Göttingen collection). This brain approaches that of Gauss in superiority of development. The frontal lobes are remarkably massive and intricately convoluted. The superfrontal gyre is large and intricately fissured. The fresh brain-weight was 1520 grams. The left hemicerebrum weighed 478 grams, the right 479 grams (after hardening). Wagner only gives a dorsal view of the brain. It would be interesting to compare the development of the sub-parietal regions with those in the brains of other mathematicians such as Gyldén, Kovalevsky, Gauss, Oliver and Siljeström. R. Wagner: "Vorstudien, etc.," I and II.

18. Hausmann, Joh. Friedr. Ludw. (1782–1859), German naturalist (mineralogist) (Göttingen collection). Hausmann's brain is described by Wagner as the smallest and most simply convoluted in his series. There is a nearer approach to symmetry in the arrangement of the surface-markings and Wagner goes so far as to regard this as an expression of arrest in development. Hausmann was a tall man; stature 180 ctm. The brain weighed 1226 grams: after hardening, the left hemicerebrum weighed 360 grams; the right 356 grams. R. Wagner: "Nachrichten," Göttingen, February 26, 1860. R. Wagner: "Vorstudien, etc.," I and II.

19. Walther, German surgeon. There is an allusion to this brain in Wagner's memoir, but no particulars are given. Wagner: "Vorstudien, etc.," I, p. 5.

20. Campbell, Lord John (1779–1861) English Lord Chancellor. Acton, in his report on the post-mortem examination states that the brain, which was examined thirty hours after death, was found to be healthy and weighed 53½ ounces (1517 grams). Acton: *Lancet* (London), August, 1861, II, p. 193.

21. FALLMERAYER, JAKOB PHILIP (1790–1861), German historian (Munich collection), died of an aneurism of the aorta. His stature was 165 ctm. The brain weighed 1,349 grams. The left subfrontal gyre was well developed, but on the whole is smaller than the corresponding region in the brains of Melchior Meyr and Lichtenstein with which Rüdinger compared it. Bischoff: "Das Hirngewicht des Menschen," 1880, p. 136. Rüdinger: *Beitr. z. Anatomie des Sprachcentrums*, 1882.

22. TIEDEMANN, FRIEDRICH (1781–1861), German anatomist (Munich collection), died of pneumonia and cerebral œdema. The autopsy was performed by Buhl and Rüdinger. His stature was 172 ctm. The brain weighed 1,254 grams. It was quite œdematous and the atrophy of the convolutions was marked. The circumference of the head was 54.5 ctm.; of the cranium, 53.1 ctm.; the scalp was very thin. Bischoff estimates that age-atrophy reduced the brain-weight from about 1,422 grams at maturity. Rüdinger states that the subfrontal gyre is particularly well developed on the right side, though large on the left as well. Bischoff: *Sitzungsber. d. k. bayer. Akad. d. Wissensch.*, 1864, I. p. 39, 51–53. Bischoff: "Das Hirngewicht des Menschen," 1880, pp. 136 and 139. Rüdinger: *Beitrag. z. Anatomie des Sprachcentrums*, 1882, p. 44.

23. VON SIEBOLD, EDUARD KASPAR JAKOB (1801–1861), German gynecologist. Wagner examined the brain at the autopsy and states that it was richly fissured and convoluted. A fissure divided the subfrontal gyre into two tiers; it is not stated whether the right or the left side is meant, or both. The preservation of the brain was not permitted. R. Wagner: "Vorstudien, etc.," II. 1862, pp. 14 and 16.

24. LOEDEL. Wagner also had the opportunity of examining the brain of the talented etcher, whose fine engravings illustrate Wagner's first memoir of 1860. The post-parietal region is described as particularly extensive, complex and prominent. R. Wagner: "Vorstudien, etc.," II, 1862 (footnote, p. 32).

25. HARLESS, EMIL (1820–1862), physiologist (Munich collection). The fresh weight of this brain was not recorded. Bischoff, by adding 41 per cent. to the weight of the specimen after preservation in alcohol for a number of years, estimates the original weight at 1238 grams. According to Rüdinger the subfrontal gyre is best developed on the left side. Bischoff: "Das Hirngewicht des Menschen," 1880, p. 137. Rüdinger: *Beitr. z. Anat. d. Sprachcen*, 1882, p. 44.

26. THACKERAY, WILLIAM MAKEPEACE (1811–1863), English humorist. The autopsy was probably performed by Dr. Elliotson. A contemporary newspaper report states that the brain weighed 58½ ounces. "His medical attendants . . . add that he had a very large brain, weighing no less than 58½ ounces." *London Times*, December 25, 1863. Marshall: *Journ. of Anat. and Physiol.*, 1892, Vol. XXVI, p. 445.

27. Lincoln, Abraham (1809–1865), American statesman (U. S. President). The autopsy was performed at noon on April 15, 1865, at the White House. The physicians present were the Surgeon-General Joseph K. Barnes, U. S. A., Assistant Surgeon-General Charles H. Crane, U. S. A., Dr. Robert K. Stone, of Washington, Assistant-Surgeon J. J. Woodward, U. S. A., Assistant-Surgeon W. M. Notson, U. S. A., and Assistant-Surgeon Edward Curtis. Drs. Woodward and Curtis opened the head with the view of finding the track taken by the bullet in order to establish officially the facts of death by homicide. Dr. Curtis writes that owing to the absence of suitable scales he could not weigh the entire brain, but did so piecemeal. "The weighing of the brain gave approximate results only since there had been some loss of brain substance in consequence of the wound during life after the shooting." No official record was made of the weight and to a recent inquiry addressed to Dr. Curtis he states that he has utterly forgotten what the figure was. In a letter written a week after the autopsy Dr. Curtis states that "the figures, such as they were, seemed to show that the brain-weight was not above the ordinary for a man of Lincoln's size."

28. De Morny, Charles Auguste Louis Joseph (1811–1865), French statesman. The brain-weight is stated as 53.6 ounces by Thurnam as being reported in the newspapers "and confirmed by a distinguished anthropologist of Paris." (Brain-weight, 1520 grams.) Thurnam: *Jour. of Mental Science*, 1866.

29. Whewell, William (1794–1866), English philosopher. Whewell died as the result of an accident while riding a horse. "The brain weighed 49 ounces. It was shrunken, the convolutions standing apart instead of being close together." (Brain-weight, 1389 grams.) G. M. Humphrey: *Lancet* (London), March 17, 1866, II, p. 279.

30. Goodsir, John (1814–1867). The autopsy was conducted by Drs. Chiene and Stirling. The brain weighed 57½ ounces (1629 grams). Goodsir's Anatomical Memoirs, 1868, Vol. I. p. 195.

31. Hermann, Friedrich Benedickt Wilhelm von (1795–1868), economist, geometrician, statistician (Munich collection), is said to have been very tall. The brain weighed 1590 grams. The left subfrontal gyre was superiorly developed, according to Rüdinger. Bischoff: Das Hirngewicht des Menschen, 1880, p. 136. Rüdinger: *Beitrag. z. Anat. des Sprachcentrums*, 1882, p. 44.

32. Pfeufer, Karl von (1806–1869), German physician (Munich collection), died of apoplexy. His stature was 170 ctm. The brain weighed 1488 grams. Rüdinger emphasizes the large development of the left subfrontal gyre as compared with the right. The convolutions in general are rather broad and simple. Bischoff: Das Hirngewicht des Menschen, 1880. Rüdinger: *Beitrag. z. Anat. des Sprachcentrums*, 1882, p. 44.

33. SIMPSON, SIR JAMES YOUNG (1811–1870), English physician and archaeologist. The autopsy was performed by Drs. J. B. Pettigrew and John Chiene in the presence of Drs. A. Wood, W. Begbie and J. Noir Munro. "The brain was healthy, the sulci were deep, the convolutions numerous and the substance natural." The brain-weight was 54 ounces (1531 grams). *Lancet* (London), 1870, May 14, p. 717.

34. MEYR, MELCHIOR (1810–1871), German poet and philosophical writer, died of cancer of the stomach. His stature was 170 ctm. His brain weighed 1415 grams. Bischoff states that Meyr's and Fallmerayer's brains had the simplest convolutions in the collection (*i. e.*, up to 1880). Bischoff: "Das Hirngewicht des Menschen," 1880, p. 136. Rüdinger: *Beitrag. z. Anat. d. Sprachcentrums*, 1882, p. 43.

35. BABBAGE, C. (1792–1871), mathematician and inventor (London collection). The brain is preserved in the Museum of the Royal College of Surgeons of England (D. 685). Its weight immediately after removal was 49½ ounces (1403 grams). G. Elliot Smith, in a letter (October 6, 1903), says that Prof. Duckworth, who has looked the brain over, emphasizes the "presence of a well-developed sulcus frontalis medialis of Cunningham and a special richness of sulci of the anterior part of the inferior frontal convolution." Marshall: *Jour. of Anat. and Physiol.*, XXVII, 1892, p. 30. Catalogue of the Physiological Series of Comparative Anatomy in the Museum of the Royal College of Surgeons of England, II, 1902, p. 164.

36. GROTE, GEORGE (1796–1871), English historian. This distinguished writer of Greek history died in June, 1871. Eight years before his death he wrote the following wish:

> "I desire that after my decease my cranium shall be opened by the Professor of Anatomy in University College, London, or by some other competent Anatomist.
>
> "I desire that my brain shall be carefully weighed and examined, and that the weight thereof shall be communicated to Professor Bain, together with any other peculiarities which may be found, especially whether the cerebellum is deficient as compared with the cerebrum."

Prof. John Marshall removed and studied the brain. Its weight, after drainage, was 49¾ ounces (1410 grams); about 12 drachms (45 c.c.) of fluid were collected. "The skull," remarks Marshall, "was unusually thick. The cerebrum and cerebellum, still invested by their membranes were soft and flaccid and easily fell out of shape; and the cerebral convolutions, so far as they could be observed, appeared to be very broad." This breadth of the convolutions became still more obvious after the membranes were removed. Mr. Grote died at the age of 76, and Marshall expresses it as his belief that both age and disease caused a wasting of brain-tissue amounting to perhaps three ounces or more (90–100 grams). That wasting must have taken place is certainly indicated by the accumulation of more than 45 c.c. of fluid in the cranial cavity. Compared with the cerebro-cerebellar ratio in average brains, Grote's cerebellum was relatively small.

The general form of the cranium was brachycephalic but it was decidedly higher than usual. The cerebrum itself was, in accordance with the shape of the cranium, short, broad and deep. The frontal lobes appeared to be very long on their upper surface, very wide in front of the sylvian fissure and both long and broad on their under surface. The parietal lobes were short and wide. The temporal lobes were also wide though short. The occipital lobes were small and shallow. The cerebral convolutions were very massive, being not only broad and deep, but well folded and marked with secondary sulci, especially in the frontal and parietal regions. Marshall states that the callosum was so long that its sectional area was unusually great; and he concludes from the size of the convolutions, the sufficiency of gray matter and from the remarkable number of the white fibers, especially of the transverse commissural ones, that the brain of Grote must be pronounced to have been of very perfect and high organization. Grote's stature was 179 ctm. By descent he was half English, one quarter German and one quarter French. John Marshall: "The Brain of the late George Grote, with Comments and Observations on the Human Brain and its Parts generally." *Jour. of Anat. and Physiol.*, October, 1892.

37. De Morgan (1798–1871), English mathematician (London collection?). The brain was examined by Dr. H. C. Bastian and Dr. Wilson Fox on the third day after death. The brain-weight was 52¾ ounces (1,494 grams). Professor De Morgan had an exceptionally large head. Bastian's measurements are as follows:

	Inches.	Centimeters.
Head circumference	24¾	63
Arc, root of nose to occipital protuberance .	15⅜	39
Ear to ear over vertex .	15½	39.3

"As a consequence apparently of a blindness of the right eye, dating from a few days after birth, the left cerebral hemisphere of De Morgan's brain was smaller than the right. . . . Except for a degenerated condition of the right optic nerve and the corresponding left optic tract there is nothing to be discovered which can possibly account for the smaller size and stunted development of the left hemisphere." Certain measurements of the hardened specimen are given. C. Bastian: "The Brain as an Organ of the Mind," 1880, pp. 391–393.

38. Agassiz, Louis (1817–1873), American naturalist (French descent). The autopsy was reported by Dr. Morrill Wyman. "The weight of the brain was 53.4 ounces" (1,514 grams). Drs. J. J. Putnam and R. H. Fitz were present. The antero-

posterior diameter of the head was 19.7 ctm.; the lateral diameter, 16.3 ctm. The skull is said to have been thick. M. Wyman: *Medical and Surgical Reporter* (Philadelphia). 1874. XXX. p. 131.

39. LIEBIG, JUSTUS VON (1803–1873), German chemist (Munich collection). Bischoff states that the specimen shows advanced age-atrophy and it lost weight very rapidly when placed in alcohol; 34 per cent. in four weeks and nearly 50 per cent. in about seven years. The endocranial cast shows the cranial capacity to have been 1,550 ctm. The cranial circumference was 54.6 ctm. Bischoff estimates the weight of the brain at maturity to have been at least 1,450 grams. The actual weight was 1,352 grams. Liebig's stature was 170 ctm. Bischoff observes further that the cerebral convolutions are more complex than in any other brain in the collection. Rüdinger compares the subfrontal gyres of the two sides and gives a figure which shows enormous development of the parietal-paroccipital region. Bischoff: "Das Hirngewicht des Menschen," 1880, p. 139. Rüdinger: *Beitrag. z. Anat. des Sprachcentrums*, 1882. Rüdinger: *Beitrag. z. Anat. d. Affenspalte*. 1882.

40. NAPOLEON III (1808–1873), French sovereign. The brain-weight only is recorded in Ammon's list. Brain-weight, 1500 grams. Ammon: Die Natürliche Auslese bein Menschen, p. 255.

41. BENNETT, JOHN HUGHES (1812–1875), English physician. The autopsy was performed by Dr. Cadge, assisted by Professor Sanders. The brain weighed 47 ounces (1332 grams). W. Cadge: "On the case of the late Professor Hughes Bennett." *Brit. Med. Jour.*, 1875 (October 9), p. 451.

42. ASSÉZAT, JULES (1832–1876), French political writer and journalist (Paris collection). The brain was very oedematous. The weight, which was not taken until two hours after removal, was 1403 grams. The gyres are complex and the fissures tortuous, especially in the frontal region. The parietal-paroccipital fissure is of great depth, uninterrupted, and is directly confluent with the postcentral fissure. The frontal fissures are frequently interrupted by annectants so that the superfrontal and medifrontal gyres are hardly demarcated from each other. Duval, Chudzinski and Hervé: *Bull. de la société d'Anthropol. de Paris*, 1883, p. 331.

43. PALACKÝ, FRANZ (1798–1876), Bohemian historian. This brain still awaits description in the Royal Bohemian Museum. The postmortem examination took place on the fourth day after death, the body having received an injection of sublimate. Palacký's head was very large, as the following measurements indicate:

Circumference .	60 ctm.
Head length .	. 20
Head width .	17 ctm.

The brain was normal, the cerebral convolutions small and compact, the fissures deep. V. Steflil: Výsledek czastečného pitváni mrtvoly Frant. Palackého. Czas lék. czes. XVI, 1877, p. 169.

44. WRIGHT, CHAUNCEY (1830–1875), American philosophical writer (Cornell collection). This brain was first described by Thomas Dwight. Mr. Wright is said to have been a man of very varied acquirements, a proficient in physics and mathematics, and what may be called a general critic. He was considered an instance of very exceptional mental power. He was of rather large frame, with a large head and a high forehead. Mention is made by Professor Wilder, to whom the brain was subsequently loaned for further examination, of Wright's mental and physical deliberateness. The brain is remarkable in many ways. In the first place, "the simplicity of the fissures and the width and flatness of the gyres are paralleled in the Cornell collection only in the much smaller brain of an unknown mulatto" (Wilder). Secondly, the central fissures (both sides) are interrupted by isthmuses at about the junction of the middle and dorsal thirds. The brain weighed 53½ ounces (1516 grams). T. Dwight: *Amer. Acad. of Arts and Sciences; Proceedings*, XIII, 1877, pp. 210–215. B. G. Wilder: *Jour. Nerv. and Mental Diseases*, XVII, pp. 753–754. B. G. Wilder: *Amer. Neurol. Assoc. Trans.*, 1890. B. G. Wilder: Ref. Handbook of the Med. Sci. (Buck's), 1890. VIII, p. 158; IX, p. 108. B. G. Wilder: *Proc. Assoc. Amer. Anat.*, 1896. B. G. Wilder: Ref. Handbook of the Med. Sci., 1901, II.

45. ASSELINE, LOUIS (1829–1878), French jurist and journalist (Paris collection). The brain-weight is reported by Thulié as 1468 grams, immediately after removal. The paroccipital gyres are depressed, notably on the right side, so that the occipital fissure is confluent with the paroccipital at considerable depth. In general, the cerebrum is fairly well convoluted, but the frontal lobes, though massive, are less fissured than usual. Broca said of it: "Ce n'est pas un cerveau fin; les circonvolutions sont epaissés, presque grossières." The subfrontal gyres are of medium size. The description of this brain drew forth a rabid denunciation of the aims and purposes of the "société mutuelle d'autopsie" by a certain M. Foley. Messrs. Dally and Topinard made vigorous reply. Thulié: *Bull. de la soc. d'anthrop. de Paris*, 1878, p. 161; *ibid.*, 1880, p. 239. Duval, Chudzinski and Hervé: *ibid.*, 1883, pp. 260–274. Broca: *ibid.*, 1883, p. 26. Foley, Dally, Topinard (discussion): *ibid.*, 1883, p. 274.

46. AYLETT, PHILIP A. American physician, a well-known blind physician whose remarkable memory served to make him a celebrated quiz-master for medical students. He died in the Presbyterian Hospital of New York, at the age of 58, on October 5, 1878. His brain weighed 52 ounces (1474 grams).

47. HUBER, JOHANNES (1830–1879), German Philosopher (Munich collection).

The weight of the brain was 1400 grams. The left subfrontal gyre is better developed and more massive as shown by the endocranial cast. Rüdinger gives a figure of the subfrontal region on both sides. Bischoff: "Das Hirngewicht des Menschen," 1880, p. 136. Rüdinger: *Beitr. z. Anat. d. Sprachcentrums*, 1882, pp. 35 and 39.

48. SCHMID, HERMANN THEODORE VON (1815–1880), German jurist and writer (Munich collection), is said to have been a talented linguist and orator and in correlation with this Rüdinger found the left subfrontal region to be the better developed. The brain weighed 1374 grams. Rüdinger: *Beitr. z. Anat. d. Sprachcentrums*, 1882. Rüdinger: *Beitr. z. Anat. d. Affenspalte*, 1882. Ammon: "Die Natürliche Auslese bei den Menschen."

49. BISCHOFF, C. H. E. (1785–1864), German physician. C. H. E. Bischoff's brain-weight is reported in his son's memoir as being 1452 grams. His stature was 172 ctm. The left subfrontal gyre showed a superior degree of development. Bischoff: "Das Hirngewicht des Menschen," 1880, p. 136. Rüdinger: *Beitr. z. Anat. d. Sprachcentrums*, 1882, p. 44.

50. BROCA, PAUL (1824–1880), French Anthropologist (Paris collection). The brain was weighed by M. Kuhff. The brain-weight was 1484 grams. No further records seem to have been made of this brain. Topinard: "Elements d'Anthropologie Générale. 1885, p. 553.

51. SEGUIN, EDOUARD (1812–1880), French-American physician (psychiatrist) (author's collection). The elder Seguin was born at Clamecy, Department of Nièvre, in France. His ancestors for several generations were eminent as physicians, architects, etc. Dr. Seguin received a very thorough education at the colleges of Auxerre and St. Louis and commenced the study of medicine with the celebrated Itard as preceptor. He was subsequently associated with the distinguished alienist and psychologist, Esquirol, in his investigations. The study of what is now known as arrested mental development began with Seguin's devotion to the welfare of the idiot children at the Hôspice de Bicètre and for over forty years he remained devoted to the cause he had made his own. Edouard Seguin was the pioneer in advocating the introduction of the metric system in this country and he is equally noted for his contributions to the subject of medical thermometry. He came to New York in 1850. His brain was removed within twenty-four hours after death by Dr. E. C. Spitzka, assisted by Dr. R. W. Amidon. The brain was normal and weighed "2 pounds, 12 ounces, 54 drams" (44.344 ounces or 1257 grams). At the present time, after over twenty-five years' immersion in alcohol, this weight is reduced to 880 grams, having lost 30 per cent. of its original weight. I have described this brain together with that of the younger Seguin as indicated in the references below. Spitzka, Edw. Anthony: *Proc.*

Assoc. of Amer. Anatomists, XIVth Session (Baltimore, December, 1900). Spitzka, Edw. Anthony: "A preliminary communication of a study of the brains of two distinguished physicians, father and son." *Phila. Med. Jour.*, April 6, 1901. Spitzka, Edw. Anthony: "The redundancy of the preinsula in the brains of distinguished educated men." *Med. Record*, June 15, 1901.

52. VON LASAULX, philologist (Munich collection). The brain weighed 1,250 grams. His stature was about 170 ctm.; death was caused by heart disease. Rüdinger gives a figure showing the complex and expanded development of the parieto-paroccipital region. Bischoff: "Das Hirngewicht des Menschen. 1880, p. 127. Rüdinger: *Beitr. z. Anat. d. Affenspalte*, 1882.

53. BUHL LUDWIG (1816–1880), German anatomist (Munich collection). The brain weighed 1,229 grams. Rüdinger calls attention to the better development of the right subfrontal gyre as compared with that of the left. Bischoff: "Das Hirngewicht d. Menschen." Rüdinger: *Beitr. z. Anat. d. Sprachcentrums*, 1882.

54. VON POEZL, German jurist (Munich collection). Rüdinger mentions the superior development of the left subfrontal region. The weight of the brain has not been published. Rüdinger: *Beitr. z. Anat. d. Sprachcentrums*, p. 14.

55. SCHLEICH, MARTIN (1827–1881), German humorist, writer and orator (Munich collection). Rüdinger states that although the subfrontal regions of both sides are well developed, the left one preponderates. The endocranial cast shows a greater prominence on the left side in the speech-area. The brain weighed 1,503 grams. Rüdinger: *Beitr. z. Anat. d. Sprachzentrums*, p. 43.

56. KOBELL, FRANZ RITTER VON (1803–1882), German geologist and poet. Brain-weight, 1445 grams. Ammon: "Die natürliche Auslese bei den Menschen."

57. MEYER, LUDWIG, German surgeon (Munich collection). The brain is mentioned in Rüdinger's two memoirs, but no brain-weight or other details are recorded. Rüdinger: *Beitr. z. Anat. d. Sprachcentrums*, 1882, p. 44. Rüdinger: *Beitr. z. Anat. d. Affenspalte*, 1882, p. 9.

58. SKOBELEFF, MICHAEL DMITRIEWITCH (1843–1882), Russian general (Moscow collection?), died in Paris of heart paralysis. The autopsy was conducted by Dr. Neiding, assisted by Dr. Béline. Skobeleff's stature was 173 cm.; circumference of the head, 57 ctm.; circumference of the cranium, 54 ctm. The brain weighed 1451 grams. It has probably been preserved in alcohol, for a morphological description by Prof. Zernoff, of Moscow, appeared later. The cerebrum is large and well developed. There is a decided redundancy of the association-areas as compared with the somaesthetic (sensori-motor) zones. The frontal lobes are especially well-developed and the cerebral shape merits the adjective—"bombifrons." "Poids du cerveau de

General Skobeleff." *Bull. de la soc. d'antrop, de Paris*, 1882, p. 539. D. N. Sernoff: "Concerning the anatomical peculiarities in the brains of intellectual men." Proc. II, Session of Russian Physicians at Moscow, Vol. I, pp. 14–33, with 3 figs. (in Russian), Moscow, 1887.

59. Gambetta, Léon (1838–1882). French statesman (Paris collection), died December 31, 1882, but the autopsy was not performed until January 25, 1883. The body was preserved by an injection of zinc chloride. On opening the skull it was observed by Duval that considerable fluid had exuded and that the brain had shrunken. Its weight on removal was 1160 grams. By utilizing the endocranial cast as well as by other methods, Duval estimates the true weight to have been, severally, 1294, 1204 and 1241 grams; average, 1246. Rüdinger's estimate confirms Duval's figures. Krause's estimate brings the figure up to 1314 grams. The cerebrum shows a fair degree of development though no such phenomenal redundancy of the left subfrontal gyre as was originally reported. Chudzinski and Duval: *Bull. de la soc. d'anthrop. de Paris*, 1886, pp. 130, 399. Duval: *Progres medicale*, 1886, No. 30. Rüdinger: *Sitzber. d. k. bayer. Akad. d. Wissensch.*, 1887, p. 69. W. Krause: "Ueber Gehirngewichte," *Allg. Wien. Med. Ztschr.*, 1888, and *Internat. Monatschr. f. Anat. u. Phys.*, V, 1888.

60. Bischoff, Theodor Ludwig Wilhelm (1807–1882), German anatomist (Munich collection), the son of C. H. E. Bischoff (No. 49 of this series). The brain showed signs of senile atrophy and a spot of softening in the occipital lobe. It weighed 1370 grams. Ammon: "Die natürliche Auslese bei den Menschen," p. 255. F. Daffner: "Das Wachsthum des Menschen," p. 274.

61. Kraus, Franz Xavier (1840–1882) (?). German theologian. Jul. Waldschmidt, in his article on cerebral speech-areas, describes the insulæ in the brains of two congenital deaf-mutes, of a laborer, and those of the brains of two highly intellectual members of the faculty of the University of Freiburg, one a theologian, the other a prominent jurist. In reply to a recent injury, Dr. Waldschmidt states that the brain of the jurist was apparently not weighed, while that of the theologian weighed 1800 grams. The names of both were not revealed, but as Franz Xavier Kraus was professor of theology at Freiburg 1878–1882, and as Waldschmidt gives the "theologian's" age as 42, there is little doubt as to whose brain this is. The weight of the brain was obtained by Waldschmidt from Professor Wiedersheim. Jul. Waldschmidt: "Beiträge zur Anatomie des Taubstummengehirns." *Allg. Zeitschr. f. Psych.*, 1887, pp. 371–379. Edw. Anthony Spitzka: "The redundancy of the preinsula in the brains of distinguished educated men." *Medical Record*, June 15, 1901.

62. Lichtenstein, Sigmund, German novelist (Munich collection). Rüdinger

gives a figure showing the broad and complex configuration of the parieto-paroccipital regions and mentions the superior degree of development of the subfrontal gyre on the left side. Rüdinger: *Beitr. z. Anat. d. Sprachcentrums*, 1882, p. 43.

63. WUELFERT, German jurist (Munich collection). Rüdinger gives figures showing superior development of the left subfrontal gyre and of the left insula as compared with the corresponding regions on the right side. The length of the left subfrontal gyre is 23 mm.; of the right, only 16 mm. The brain weighed 1485 grams. Rüdinger: *Beitr. z. Anat. d. Sprachcentrums*, 1882, pp. 38 and 41.

64. HARTER, German jurist (Munich collection). Rüdinger briefly mentions the good development of the subfrontal region. The brain-weight is not recorded. Rüdinger: *Beitr. z. Anat. d. Sprachcentrums*, 1882, p. 44.

65. SCHLAGINTWEIT, German naturalist and explorer. As no initials are given in Ammon's list, it is not clear whether Hermann von Schlagintweit (1826–1882) or his brother Robert (1833–1885) is meant, as both were naturalists. In Ammon's list the age is given as 51 years; but as Hermann was 56 and Robert 53, this does not help us. The brain-weight is given as 1352 grams. O. Ammon: "Die natürliche Auslese bei den Menchen," p. 255.

66. BERTILLON, ADOLPHE (1821–1883), French anthropologist (Paris collection), best known as a productive writer on anthropological topics. His chief faults were said to be his difficulty in speaking, his wretched orthography and his inability to distinguish one melody from another. In these respects Bertillon could almost have been called an aphasic; his attempts to speak in public met with scant approbation and yet, deep in his mind, according to his intimate friends, he could appreciate simile, metaphor and poesy. He has been called a "psychic orator," hampered by a faulty emissary mechanism. These facts are interesting in the light of the post-mortem findings in the examination of his brain.

Bertillon's brain, immediately after removal, weighed 1398 grams. A plaster endocranial cast was also made. The skull also seems to have been preserved. Bertillon's stature was only 156 ctm. After immersion in alcohol for four and a half years the parts of the brain weighed as follows:

Right hemicerebrum .	406 grams
Left hemicerebrum.	434 grams
Cerebellum, pons and oblongata .	117 grams
	957 grams

indicating a loss of 441 grams, or 31½ per cent.

The cerebral fissures are quite tortuous and ramified. The preoperculum

("Broca's cap") is small. The right paracentral gyre is small on the right side. The precentral gyre is relatively small. The ventral part of the left post-central gyre is complex. Chudzinski and Manouvrier consider the callosum small though this does not seem justified by the figures accompanying the report. The frontal lobes show large development while the temporal lobe and the cerebellum are relatively small. The right supertemporal gyre is comparatively smaller than on the left side.

Bertillon was congenitally left-handed and doubtlessly his emissary (motor) speech center lay in the subfrontal gyre of the right hemicerebrum. In fact, this region is correspondingly better developed on the right side. At about the age of ten years, Bertillon became deaf in the left ear. Corresponding to this defect the right supertemporal gyre is narrow, straight and simple, while the left supertemporal gyre is broad, long and sinuous and of much more complex configuration. His partial deafness undoubtedly forced him to depend more upon his visual sense. Whether the better development of the angular gyre on the left side may be correlated with this fact is still a matter of speculation. Chudzinski and Manouvrier: "Étude sur le Cerveau de Bertillon." *Bull. de la soc. d'anthrop. de Paris*, 1887, pp. 558–591. Manouvrier: Les premières circonvolutions temporales droite et gauche chez un sourd de l'oreille gauche (Bertillon). *Bull. de la soc. d'anthrop.*, 1888.

67. Knight, E. H. (1824–1883), American mechanician, author of the "Mechanical Dictionary." He was employed in the U. S. Patent Office and was one of the American Commissioners to the French Exposition of 1880. He is said to have possessed a phenomenal memory. "His brain is reported as having weighed sixty-four ounces, but we are ignorant of the appearances presented by the convolutions." *Boston Med. and Surg. Jour.* (Editorial), February 15, 1883, p. 184.

68. Turgenev, Ivan Sergejewitch (1818–1883), Russian novelist and poet, died in Paris of cancer (myxosarcoma). The autopsy was conducted by Dr. Brouardel in the presence of Drs. Descoust, Segond and Magnin. The examination of the head is reported as follows: (Transl.) "The bones of the skull are thin. The membranes are healthy (normal) and are easily removed from the cortex. The arteries at the base of the brain are dilated and notably atheromatous. The brain is very large and weighs 2012 grams. Neither a tumor, tubercles, or serous or sanguineous exudation was revealed on section. There is no lesion of any kind in the fourth ventricle." Topinard states that the brain was notable for the symmetry of its convolutions. "Procès verbal de l'Autopsie de Monsieur Yvan Tourguéneff, faite le 5. Septembre, 1883, par Monsieur le Docteur Brouardel, Professeur de Médecine légale à la Faculté de Médecine de Paris, en présence du Docteur Descoust, Chef de Travaux de Médecine légale Pratique à la Faculté de Médecine de Paris, du Docteur Paul Segond, Professeur agrégé

de la Faculté de Médecine et Chirurgien des Hôpitaux de Paris et du Docteur Magnin de Bougival (Septembre, 1883). Paris, pp. 21. 5 figs. Topinard: "Elements d'Anthropologie Générale."

69. COUDEREAU, AUGUSTE (1832–1882), French physician (Paris collection). The autopsy was conducted by Prof. Laborde, assisted by Drs. Duval, Chudzinski and Hervé. Just after removal the brain weighed 1390 grams. Half an hour later it weighed 1378 grams. The cerebrum weighed 1183 grams, the cerebellum, 195 (?) grams. The cranium was plagiocephalic. The most notable feature in the cerebrum is the peculiar ramification of the occipital fissure on the meson of the left hemicerebrum. The arrangement is apparently due to the confluence of both the cuneal and adoccipital fissures with the occipital. Duval, Chudzinski and Hervé: *Bull. de la soc. d'anthrop. de Paris*, 1883, p. 377.

70. SIEMENS, WERNER VON (1816–1884), German physicist. The brain is said to have been very oedematous and is cited by Hansemann as having weighed 1600 grams. D. Hansemann: *Ztschr. f. Psych. u. Physiol. d. Sinnesorgane*, 1899, I.

71. SMETANA, FRIEDRICH (1824–1884), Bohemian composer, was a man of small, delicate frame. His death occurred in the course of a paralytic dementia which set in late in life. Owing to this disease the brain showed numerous lesions; atrophy of the convolutions, dilatation of the ventricles, atrophy of the auditory nerves (Smetana became deaf in his latter years), and other pathological signs. The brain weighed only 1250 grams; but, as Hlava remarks, this figure is comparatively high when the marked degree of atrophy is considered. The skull-length was 17 cm., skull-width, 14 cm.; thickness about 1.5 cm. J. Hlava: "Zpráva o pitve mistra Bedřicha Smetany," *Čas. lék. čes.*, XXIII, 1884, p. 323. Matiegka: "Ueber das Hirngewicht des Menschen," 1902, p. 38.

72. LASKER, EDUARD F. (1829–1884), German jurist and politician, died in New York on January 5, 1884. Drs. A. Jacobi and W. H. Welch conducted the autopsy. The brain was found to show spots of softening and general arterio-sclerosis. A note concerning the weight of the brain was subsequently destroyed by fire, but it is cited by Lombroso as being 1300 grams. Lombroso's authority for this figure is incorrectly quoted and cannot be verified.

73. SENZEL (or Seizel ?), French sculptor. The autopsy on Senzel was performed by Chudzinski and Hervé. The brain weighed 1312 grams. Senzel was a talented artist but not particularly eminent intellectually. Manouvrier: "La Quantité dans l'Encephale," p. 280. Manouvrier: In Richet's "Dictionnaire de Physiologie," 1897–1898, p. 688.

74. LUDWIG II (of Bavaria) (1845–1886), German (Bavarian) Sovereign. Ludwig

II, the "mad king," committed suicide on June 13, 1886. The autopsy was performed in Munich on June 15 by Rüdinger, in the presence of Prof. Grashey and Drs. Kerschensteiner, Halm, Hubrich and Rückert. His stature was 191 cm. The brain weighed 1349 grams. W. W. Ireland: *Jour. of Mental Science*, October, 1886, p. 345.

75. Olney, Edward (1827–1887), American mathematician. Professor of mathematics at the University of Michigan, 1863–1887. His stature was about 5 feet, 8 inches; his body-weight about 180 pounds. His brain was removed by Prof. W. J. Herdman, of the same university, and weighed 1,701 grams. Cf. *Phila. Med. Register*, April 27, 1887, p. 337.

76. Riebeck. In Ammon's list is merely given the name "Riebeck" described as "Industr." Possibly Joh. Karl. Otto Ribbeck, a German philologist and critic (1827–1888) is meant. The brain-weight is given as 1,580 grams. Ammon: "Die natürliche Auslese bei den Menschen," 1893.

77. Véron Eugene (1825–1889), French philosophical writer, critic and journalist (Paris collection). Véron's brain belongs to the class of superiorly developed ones. The weight of the brain was unfortunately not ascertained; nor is the cranial capacity known, since the skull was not preserved. By means of a stiff hat worn by Véron, Manouvrier found the antero-posterior diameter to be 194 mm., the transverse diameter, 162 mm. (cephalic index, 83). These figures are well above the average as comparisons with 71 physicians and with 280 soldiers of about the same age show. Manouvrier gives exhaustive measurements of the preserved brain. The right superfrontal gyre is doubled for a large part of its extent. The left subfrontal gyre is well developed. Some of the peculiarities in the fissural pattern which Manouvrier emphasizes are: The left postcentral communicates with the sylvian cleft deeply; also with the parietal and by means of this with the occipital. Finally the calcarine fissure is prolonged to the "fente de Bichât" (hippocampal fissure). On the right side the postcentral also communicates with the sylvian cleft, but the parietal does not run into the occipital. On both sides the paroccipital gyres are deeply situated. There is an odd "fronto-limbic" formation. Manouvrier: Étude sur le cerveau d'Eugene Véron. *Bull. de la soc. d'anthrop. de Paris*, 1892, pp. 238–279. Manouvrier: *ibid.*, pp. 505–529.

78. Rice, A. Thorndyke (1853–1889), American diplomat and journalist. Editor of the *North American Review* and Minister Plenipotentiary to Russia. The autopsy was performed on May 17, 1889, by Drs. E. L. Keyes, E. G. Janeway, E. E. Dunham, H. Goldthwaite, E. Fuller and C. H. Chetwood. Mr. Rice died at the age of 35. The brain weighed fifty ounces (1418 grams). N. Y. *World*, May 18, 1889, p. 4.

79. Nussbaum (1829–1890), German surgeon. Brain-weight, 1410 grams. Daffner: "Das Wachsthum des Menschen," 1902, p. 275.

80. Ferris, B. G. (1802–1891). American jurist (Cornell collection). A prominent lawyer, district attorney, president of the public library and Secretary for the Territory of Utah. Author of "Utah and the Mormons" (1854), and "A New Theory of the Origin of Species." The brain is in the collection of Cornell University (No. 2870) and weighed 1225 grams.

81. Buchner, Hans (1850–1892). "Das stark oedematose Gehirn des Hygienikers Hans Büchner" weighed 1560 grams. Daffner: "Das Wachsthum des Menschen," 1902, p. 275.

82. Grant, R. E., English mathematician. Brain-weight, 45½ ounces (1290 grams). Marshall: *Jour. of Anat. and Physiol.*, XXVIII, 1892, p. 30.

83. Brown, George, Canadian editor. Editor of the *Toronto Globe*. He was over six feet tall. His brain is said to have weighed 56.3 ounces (1596 grams). "The Lost Atlantis and other Ethnographic Studies" (Edinburgh), 1892, p. 376.

84. Harrison, R. A., Canadian jurist, Chief Justice of Canada. His brain weighed 56 ounces (1590 grams). "The Lost Atlantis and other ethnographic Studies" (Edinburgh), 1892, p. 376.

85. Butler, Benjamin F. (1818–1892). American soldier, lawyer and statesman. "The brain is said to have weighed sixty-two ounces" (1758 grams). *Medical Record*, Feb. 11, 1893, p. 186.

86. Curtice, Hosea (1825–1893). American mathematician and educator (Cornell collection). Professor Wilder reports its weight to have been 1612 grams. The cerebrum is large and richly fissured.

87. Whitman, Walt, American poet. The weight of Walt Whitman's brain is variously given as 45.2 ounces (1282 grams) and 43.3 ounces (1228 grams). His stature was 6 feet and in health he weighed about 200 pounds. The brain had been preserved but some careless attendant in the laboratory let the jar fall to the ground; it is not stated whether the brain was totally destroyed by the fall, but it is a great pity that not even the fragments of the brain were rescued. "*In re* Walt Whitman" (Philadelphia), 1893. C. K. Mills: Textbook of Nervous and Mental Diseases."

88. Mallery, Garrick (1831–1894), American ethnologist and soldier. Graduate of Yale University, served in the Civil War with distinction, was admitted to the Bar and later became celebrated for his studies in ethnology. His brain was removed and weighed by Dr. D. S. Lamb. Brain weight, 53 ounces (1503 grams).

89. Oliver, James Edward (1830-1895), American mathematician (Cornell collection), professor of mathematics at Cornell University. He was a philosophic thinker, in not only the higher mathematics, but other sciences and ethics. He was left-handed and absent-minded, but rapid in thought and action. For an account of

his life and writings see Hill's memoir. The brain weighed 1446 grams and has been well preserved. The cerebrum is richly fissured and shows a superior degree of development in many respects. B. G. Wilder: *Jour. of Comp. Anat.*, Vol. V, July, 1895. Wilder: "Buck's Reference Handbook of the Medical Sciences," Vol. II, 1901. G. W. Hill: *Science*, April, 1895.

90. Hovelacque, Alexandre A. (1843–1895), French anthropologist, philosophical writer and deputy (Paris collection). Brain-weight, communicated by Georges Hervé, 1373 grams.

91. Rüdinger, Nicolaus (1832–1896), German anatomist (Munich collection). Brain-weight, 1380 grams. Daffner: "Das Wachsthum des Menschen," 1902, p. 275.

92. Gyldén, Hugo (1841–1896), Swedish mathematician and astronomer (Stockholm collection). One of the most illustrious of Europe's astronomers. His astronomical work was of the mathematical-physical rather than of the observational kind. He was inclined to be speculatively philosophical. He was a clear, logical speaker, a talented musician; of strong constitution, medium height. He was deaf upon the left ear, the result of an ear-trouble in infancy. The brain was removed on the third day after death and was very soft and flaccid. With much care, Retzius was able to preserve the specimen in good shape. The brain weighed 1452 grams. In general the cerebral convolutions are well formed, regular and not notably complex. The prefrontal region is traversed by numerous secondary fissures. The subfrontal gyre is strongly developed on the right side in the *operculum intermedium*; on the left it is peculiar in form; the *pars basilaris* is poorly developed on both sides, being depressed in the depths of the diagonal and precentral fissures. The most notable features in Gyldén's brain are presented in the region around the up-turned end of the sylvian (episylvian ramus). On the right side, the caudal arm of the marginal gyre constitutes a largely developed "operculum parietale posterius" so as to encroach upon and push up (dorsad) the caudal end of the sylvian cleft. In other words, the struggle for cortical expansion has, in this brain, manifested itself in an unusual breadth of the marginal gyre, so broad in fact, as to constitute a veritable operculum. On the left side, the arrangement is somewhat different, but the development is equally pronounced. The episylvian ramus is small and with it the true marginal gyre is small; but dorsad of this there lie three well-developed gyres which necessarily must be considered part of the marginal territory. The interest in this region lies in the fact that it borders upon, and possibly includes, on the one side the central organ of audition, on the other side, the great parietal association area and it is quite likely that it is the special area for the mathematical faculties. G. Retzius: Das Gehirn des Astronomen Hugo Gyldén's. *Biol. Untersuch.*, N. F., VIII, 1, Stockholm, 1898.

93. KOLÁR, JOSEF GEORG (1812–1896), Bohemian dramatist and poet. The autopsy was performed by Prof. Hlava, of Prague. The brain weighed 1300 grams: there was marked age-atrophy. The convolutions are quite sinuous. The subfrontal gyre shows six bends on the left and 5 such on the right side. The skull was later exhumed and studied by Matiegka. Matiegka: Ueber das Hirngewicht des Menschen. *Sitzber. d. k. böhm. Ges. d. Wiss.*, 1902, pp. 38–39. Matiegka: Tělesné ostatky Jana Kollára. *17stnik král. ces. spol. nauk.*, 1904.

94. CHEVE. (?–1896) (Paris collection). A member of the "*société mutuelle d'autopsie*." The brain-weight, communicated by G. Hervé was 1365 grams.

95. GUARDIA, JOSÉ-MARIA (1830–1897) (Paris collection). A member of the "*société mutuelle d'autopsie*." The brain-weight, communicated by G. Hervé, was 1272 grams. Guardia's age was 67 years.

96. MCKNIGHT, GEORGE (1840–1897). American physician (Cornell collection), an eminent physician and writer of sonnets. According to his son some of his sonnets were highly praised by Oliver Wendell Holmes, and Sargent included some of them in the "Cyclopedia of British and American Poetry" (Harper's). The brain is in the Cornell collection (No. 3531). Prof. Wilder states that it weighed 1545 grams.

97. DE MORTILLET, GABRIEL (1821–1898). French anthropologist and ethnologist (Paris collection). The brain-weight, communicated by G. Hervé, was 1480 grams.

98. SEGUIN, EDWARD CHARLES (1843–1898). American physician (neurologist) of French descent (author's collection). Son of Edouard Seguin (No. 51 of this series). The autopsy took place on February 21, 1898, and was made by Dr. J. S. Thacher assisted by Drs. J. Arthur Booth and E. C. Spitzka. Drs. Hallock and Pooley were present. The brain was removed about 30 hours after death, and was found to be normal. It was divided into its principal parts and each weighed separately as follows:

Right hemicerebrum	642 grams.
Left hemicerebrum	653 "
Cerebellum	140 "
Isthmus	67 "
Total weight after dissection and drainage	1,502 "

After nearly three years immersion in a mixture of alcohol and formalin the brain had lost 13 per cent. of its original weight. The brain was studied and a morphological description published by the author. Edw. Anthony Spitzka: "A preliminary communication of a study of the brains of two distinguished physicians, father and son." *Proc. Assoc. Amer. Anat.*, 1900; *Philadelphia Med. Jour.*, April 6, 1901.

99. Konstantinoff, A., Bulgarian litterateur. Though only 25 years old when he died, had already achieved considerable fame as a writer. Matiegka and Watjoff cite the brain-weight as having been 1,595 grams. Matiegka: "Ueber das Hirngewicht des Menschen." 1902, p. 36. Watjoff: *Arch. f. Anthrop.*, XXVI, p. 1,080.

100. Helmholtz, Hermann Ludwig Friedrich (1821–1894), German anatomist, physiologist and physicist. Died of cerebral hemorrhage. The autopsy was performed by Hansemann in the presence of Drs. Renvers, Kirchhoff and Bein. Helmholtz's stature was 169.5 ctm. Head circumference, 59 ctm. Cranial circumference, 55 ctm. Cranial length, 18.3 ctm.; cranial width, 15.5 ctm. (Cranial index, 85.25.) The skull was symmetrical. The weight of the brain together with the included clots of blood was at first 1,700 grams. It was possible to remove about 160 grams of clotted blood, but much more yet remained in the cerebral tissues. The right hemisphere was badly torn by the extensive hemorrhage and it was decided to attempt to make a plaster cast of the left, undamaged hemicerebrum. Hansemann furnishes photographs of this cast, showing the lateral and mesal surfaces. D. Hansemann: "Ueber das Gehirn von Hermann v. Helmholtz. *Ztschr. f. Psychol. u. Physiol. d. Sinnesorgane*, XX, 1899, 1, pp. 13–26, 2 plates.

101. Pettenkofer, Max v. (1818–1900). German pathologist (Munich collection). Bollinger, of Munich, writes: "The brain of Pettenkofer weighed 1320 grams, and in spite of his old age, the cerebrum showed only a moderate beginning atrophy." Daffner states that the cerebrum was richly fissured. Pettenkofer's head had a horizontal circumference of 57.5 cm. It was brachycephalic. Daffner quotes the brain-weight as 1312 grams. Daffner: "Das Wachsthum des Menschen." 1902.

102. Altmann, Richard (1852–1900), German anatomist. An assistant of Professor W. His, in Leipzig and is best known as the discoverer of the "Granula-Theorie." He died in the asylum at Hubertusburg and the author is indebted to the director, Dr. P. Näcke, for several photographs of the hardened brain. The brain-weight was 1460. Altmann's stature was 178 cm.

103. Cory, Robert (1845–1900), English physician. A celebrated authority upon small-pox and vaccination. The autopsy was performed 16½ hours after death. The brain weighed 45 ounces (1276 grams). *St. Thomas Hospital Reports*, XXIX, 1902. *Lancet* (London), March 31, 1900.

104. Steinitz (1836-1900), chess player. Famous champion chess player, died in the Manhattan State Hospital (East) in 1900 after suffering from acute melancholia for about nine months. The immediate cause of death was mitral stenosis. The following is quoted from the autopsy report by Dr. L. C. Pettit: "With a dwarfed appearance (height four feet eleven inches) due to arrested development of the lower

extremities, was found an almost entire occlusion of the common iliac arteries; . . . the aorta . . . was a mere calcareous shell. The brain was almost phenomenal in the development of the orbital and frontal convolutions as shown by their increased number and diminished size. The orbital plates presented deep indentures conforming to the convolutions which were in prominent relief. The entire brain weighed 1462 grams; its relative weight to the body was as one to twenty-eight. The intellect displayed during life, coupled with the degenerative and morbid conditions found after death, seem clearly to place the case under the heading of pseudogenius or mattoid. It is probable that the beginning of a bad end was made, when after defeat he left the chess board and began the study of problems of social reform, anticipating to gain a fortune thereby from his writings. The development of his insanity from that time was gradual; first came annoyances from telepathic influences, then electric shocks; he was able to send messages without instruments; he spent much time gazing into space 'trying to hypnotize Bab the Persian God.' From a partially systematized insanity he soon became overwhelmed with delusions of persecutions and hallucinations." L. C. Pettit: "The Pathology of Insanity." *Proc. Amer. Med.-Psych. Assoc.*, 1901.

105. Giacomini, Carlo (1840–1898), Italian anatomist (Turin collection). About a fortnight prior to his death Giacomini wrote in his will that it was his wish that his bones and his brain be preserved. Sperino published a description of the brain. The weight of the several parts of the brain was as follows:

Right hemicerebrum . .	695 grams.
Left hemicerebrum . . .	614 "
Cerebellum, pons and oblongata .	186 "
Total weight .	. 1495 "

In general the cerebrum is of only moderately complex configuration. Sperino believes that there exist two central fissures on the right side of Giacomini's brain. The author is convinced that Sperino's interpretation of the regions in question is erroneous (see my article, ref. below). Sperino: L'Encefalo dell'Anatomico Carlo Giacomini," *Giornale della R. accad. di Torino.*, Aug., 1900, pp. 737–808. Edw. Anthony Spitzka: "Is the Central Fissure Duplicated in the Brain of Carlo Giacomini, Anatomist?" *Phila. Med. Jour.*, Aug. 24, 1901.

106. Collier, Frank (1856–1901), American lawyer (English-born). A successful attorney and took an active part in politics and social life, enjoying much popularity. His activity is illustrated by the fact, stated by his sister, that at 5 years of age he had read Scott's "Ivanhoe" five times through. During a political campaign

in Chicago (1889) his head was injured. Insanity developed subsequently. The autopsy was performed by Dr. E. P. Noel. The brain was described by Dr. Thor Rothstein. The weight of the brain was 1720 grams. In general the gyres are broad. The right occipital fissure anastomoses with the paroccipital and exoccipital fissures. The callosum, judging from the drawings, seems of large size. R. Dewey: "A case of Circular Insanity." *Jour. Amer. Med. Assoc.*, April 30 and May 7, 1904.

107. Lenz, Rudolf, Hungarian violinist. A pupil of Joachim, was a highly talented violin-virtuoso and professor of music. His brain, immediately after removal, was found to be somewhat softened and weighed 1636 grams. The most notable feature in the cerebrum is the great expansion of the sub-parietal regions, particularly of the right side. J. Ginszman: *Anat. Anz.*, April 12, 1901, XIX, pp. 239–249.

108. Szilagyi, Desider, Hungarian statesman and orator. To judge from the half-tone reproduction accompanying M. Sugar's description of Szilagyi's brain it appears to have been poorly preserved. The weight of the brain was 1380 grams. The article lacks much in the way of precise anatomical observations and betrays but an indifferent familiarity with even general details of macroscopical cerebral morphology. (See the author's more extended criticisms referred to below.) M. Sugar: *Orvosi Hetilap.*, 1902, Nos. 1 and 2. M. Sugar: *Klin. Therap. Wochensch.*, 1902, Nos. 24–25. Edw. Anthony Spitzka: *Medical Critic*, September, 1902, p. 572.

109. Siljeström, Per Adam (1815–1892). Swedish physicist and pedagog (Stockholm collection). An eminent physicist and pedagog; he was connected with the Paul Gaimard Polar Explorations, and is best known for his valuable researches on Mariotte's law and for his efforts in behalf of the school systems of Europe. Most of his work in this line was done subsequent to his visit to the United States in 1849–'50, where he studied the various school systems and published his views. His intellectual abilities are spoken of as having been of the highest order. Siljeström's brain weighed 1,422 grams and is splendidly developed. Its convolutions are particularly rich in the frontal and parietal association areas and it appears in most respects more complex than do those of Gyldén and Kovalewski. The brain shows special order of normal asymmetry so typical of the higher brains. As in Gyldén's and Kovalewski's the right sylvian fissure is shorter (47 mm.) than the left (58 mm.), and the marginal gyre shows a similar complexity; these features are of interest in their possible relation to the mathematical abilities of these persons. G. Retzius: *Biol. Untersuch.*, N. F., X, 1902.

110. Wilson, Henry (1812–1902), American statesman. The name "Henry Wilson" is said to be an assumed name used by Jeremiah Jones Colbraith. He changed the original name when he came of age. He was Vice-President of the

United States with President U. S. Grant. The brain, which was removed by Dr. D. S. Lamb, weighed 49 ounces (1389 grams.)

111. Goltz, (1834–1902), German physiologist. In a communication from Professor Ewald to Professor Schwalbe (the latter informed the writer) the brain of Goltz is reported to have weighed 1395 grams. After the removal of the pia and drainage it weighed 1324 grams.

112. Bouny, Joseph. French jurist and notary (Paris collection). A half-brother of the celebrated geographer E. Réclus and the surgeon Paul Réclus. Bouny's stature was 175 cm. He was very intelligent and his memory is said to have been a remarkable one. The brain, which was fully described by Manouvrier is well developed and 1935 grams. The callosum is unusually small. Manouvrier: Considérations sur l'hypermégalie cérébrale et description d'un éncephale de 1935 grammes, *Rev. Anthrop.*, XII, 1902, December.

113. Mihalkovicz, Hungarian biologist. The brain-weight is quoted as being 1440 grams in Sugar's list. M. Sugar: "Orvosi Hetilap," 1902, p. 8.

114. Powell, John Wesley (1834–1902), American geologist, ethnologist and soldier. On the death of Major Powell in Maine, his remains were embalmed and brought to Washington. Dr. D. S. Lamb performed the autopsy about 60 hours after death. The brain, which weighed 1488 grams, was preserved in formalin and placed at the writer's disposal for morphological study. The most notable feature in this brain was the great redundancy of the sub-parietal regions on the right side, encroaching considerably upon the sylvian cleft. A full description is given in the memoir cited below. Edw. Anthony Spitzka: A Study of the Brain of the Late Major J. W. Powell, *Amer. Anthropologist*, V, 4, October to December, 1903.

115. Letourneau, Charles (1831–1902), French anthropologist (Paris collection). The weight of the brain was 1490 grams, without the cerebellum (?) 1318 grams. *Jour. of Mental Pathology*, June, 1902, p. 269.

116. Levi Hermann, German composer and director. Brain weight, 1690 grams. Daffner: "Das Wachsthum des Menschen," 1902, p. 275.

117. Kupffer, Carl von, German anatomist (Munich collection). Professor Bollinger, of Munich, states that the brain of v. Kupffer weighed 1400 grams.

118. Laborde, Jean Vincent (1830–1903), French physiologist and anthropologist (Paris collection). The brain-weight was low, 1234 grams, largely due, probably, to age atrophy. Dr. Laborde's notable powers of speech led Papillault to examine the subfrontal gyres of the two sides with special care, and he found the left one to be larger and more differentiated. In general, the cerebral convolutions show an average degree of development and complexity. Papillault: "Premières observations

necrologiques sur le Dr. Laborde," *Rev. de l'Ecole d'Anthropologie de Paris*, 1903, XIII, 142.

119. POND, JAMES B. (1838–1903). American soldier and lecture-manager (author's collection). The brain was kindly placed at my disposal by Dr. J. H. Larkin, instructor in pathology at the College of Physicians and Surgeons, Columbia University, to whom the brain had been submitted by the physicians who last attended Major Pond: Drs. McPhee and Pritchard. The brain-weight, after one day in 50 per cent. alcohol and two days in 10 per cent. formalin, was 1407 grams. The cerebrum is somewhat altered in shape, not having been placed immediately after removal in a suitable vessel. When I first saw the brain something in its general physiognomy suggested that this was the brain of a left-handed man. Subsequent inquiry elicited the fact that although Major Pond wrote with his right hand, having probably been taught to do so in school, he used left-handed shears and tied his cravat left-handedly. The cerebrum is very well developed in the association areas.

120. LAVOLLAY, French merchant and publicist (Paris collection). "A member of the societe mutuelle d'autopsie." The brain weighed 1550 grams. (Communicated by Dr. G. Hervé.)

121. TRAIN, GEORGE FRANCIS (1829–1904). American merchant, promoter and traveller (author's collection). The postmortem examination was conducted by the writer, at the request of Mr. Train's physician, Dr. Carleton Simon, about 19 hours after death. The examination was limited to the head, including the removal of the brain, and a ventral hernia was dissected out to ascertain its nature. A death-mask was also made. The principal measurements of the head were:

Circumference .	58.1 cm.
Head length	19.8 cm.
Head width	16.1 cm.

The cranium measured:

Cranial length .	19.2 cm.
Cranial width .	15.5 cm.
Cranial index .	80.7 cm.

The weight of the brain was 1525 grams. Judging from the cranial and cerebral measurements it may be supposed that in middle age Mr. Train's brain weighed about 1600 grams. The cerebrum shows a superior degree of complexity in its surface morphology. Notable features are the intricate fissuration of the frontal lobes, the relative broadness and shortness of these lobes, the great bulk of the parietal and occipital regions, and the notable projection of the cerebrum over the cerebellum (the "aftoverhang," so to speak). The postorbital limbus is well marked on both sides. Edw. Anthony Spitzka: "Postmortem examination of the late George Francis Train," *The Daily Medical* (New York), Feb. 15, 1904.

122. WINCHELL, ALEXANDER. American geologist and educator. The brain was weighed by Dr. W. J. Herdman, Ann Arbor, who states that very accurate scales were not at hand at the time the autopsy was made. The weight was recorded as 58¾ ounces (1666 grams). Dr. Mills publishes some photographs and comments on the morphology of the cerebrum. The subparietal regions are especially complex, particularly on the right side. C. K. Mills: "The Concrete Concept Area," *Medical News*, November 5, 1904, pp. 868–869.

123. (Swedish statesman; not named) (Stockholm collection). The identity of the statesman whose brain is described by Retzius is not revealed in the published account, owing to the refusal of the sons of the deceased to accord permission to divulge the name. Retzius had, however, known him well since his youth and he presents a few general remarks concerning the subject's intellectual capacity. The man showed great aptitude for learning early in life, was very successful in his studies at school and under the faculty of law. He rapidly advanced to the position of minister of finance (age 37), and three years after to that of prime minister. He was a provincial governor up to the time of his death at the age of 53. He is described as a highly gifted jurist, statesman, thinker, orator and philanthropist. Of large stature, dolichocephalic and of blond complexion, he belonged to the genuine Swedish type. His brain, removed on the second day after death by Dr. Curt Wallis, weighed 1489 grams. It was preserved in a mixture of 3 per cent. potassium bichromate and 2 per cent. formal, suspended in the fluid by a string tied to the basilar artery. The form of the brain was thus well preserved. The cerebrum is well formed and richly convoluted. The association areas exhibit a richness and complexity of fissuration, but there is hardly any noteworthy characteristic or redundancy of development in any particular territory. Nor were such findings to be expected. In life the man showed a well-balanced intellect; his aptitudes were good in all directions, not in any special direction alone. Endowed with an excellent memory and good reasoning powers, he showed great skill and clearness of thought in parliamentary debate, without necessarily availing himself of purely rhetorical art. While not naturally devoted to any particular branch of the sciences, creative arts or human action, he could familiarize himself with all of these in the way of facile general understanding. This harmonious construction of the mental abilities is in no small measure correlative with that species of symmetry which this brain exhibited, and which is certainly exceptional in

the richly convoluted brains of persons of highly developed but rather one-sided mental superiority. The left subfrontal gyre was somewhat favored in its development as compared with the same region on the right side. Retzius: *Biol. Untersuch.*, N. F., XI, 1904.

124. TAGUCHI, KAZUYOSHI (1838–1904), Japanese anatomist. The brain of Professor Taguchi was removed on February 5, 1904, by Dr. Yamagawa, President of the Imperial University of Tokio. The body-weight was 49 kilos. The brain weighed 1520 grams.

125. LOVÉN, OTTO C. (1861–1904), Swedish histologist and physiologist (Stockholm collection). Professor Lovén, the Swedish investigator who will be best remembered for his discoveries of the taste-fibers in the papillæ of the tongue of mammals, as well as of vasodilator nerves, had expressed it as his wish that his brain be preserved after death and studied by his friend and associate Gustav Retzius. The brain exhibits a richness of fissures and these are marked by a superior degree of tortuousness and ramification. The subparietal region is very complex in its surface configuration while the central (sensori-motor) regions are only moderately developed. The cortical centers for speech and language are notably large and Retzius brings this into relation with Professor Lovén's notable powers of clear, exact and logical expressions of thought in words; less so in the way of oratorical finesse as in the talented use of the best and most adequate expressions. The weight of the brain is not mentioned, though its size is said by Retzius to have been well above the average. G. Retzius: *Biol. Untersuch*, N. F., XII, 1905.

126. ZEYER, JOHANN, Austrian architect. A brother of the poet, Julius Zeyer. Johann Z. died of chronic nephritis and the brain was quite œdematous. The low weight, 1310 grams, was due to loss of serum. Stature, 174 ctm. The autopsy was performed by Professor Hlava (Prague). The brain was weighed after being dissected and fully 15 minutes after removal from the skull. (Communication from Dr. Matiegka.)

127, BITTNER, GEORG, German-Austrian dramatist and actor. A successful playwright and a member of the celebrated "Meininger Schauspieltruppe." His stature was 173 cm. The autopsy revealed general arteriosclerosis. The brain weighed 1556 grams. The autopsy was performed by Professor Hlava. (Communication from Dr. Matiegka.)

128. GROSS, SAMUEL D., American physician and surgeon. Brain-weight 1361 grams. Cited in Gray's Anatomy (DaCosta's edition), 1905.

129. DE RIALLE, GIRARD, French ethnologist and folklorist, bequeathed his brain and skull to the Anthropological Society of Paris. Bull. de la soc. d'anthrop. de Paris, 1905, pp. 149–150.

130. WISTAR, ISAAC JONES (1827–1905), soldier, scientist and philanthropist (Wistar collection). General Wistar, the founder of the Wistar Institute of Anatomy and Biology at Philadelphia, made the following bequest: "I bequeath to the Wistar Institute of Anatomy and Biology my right arm, said to be a desirable specimen of gunshot anchylosis, and also my brain, to be removed by said institute promptly after my death." General Wistar's brain weighed 49 ounces (avoir.) or 1389 grams.

131. KONING, NARET, musical composer. A director at the opera at Frankfurt a/M. The brain was described by S. Auerbach, who finds in the considerable breadth and configuration of the (supra)marginal gyre, as well as the adjacent portion of the supertemporal, an expression of the greater aptitude for the multitudinous associations in the auditory sphere which distinguished from others less musical. S. Auerbach: Beitrag zur Lokalisation des musikalischen Talentes im Gehirn und am Schadel, *Archiv fur Anatomie und Physiologie, Anatomische Abteilung*, 1906, pp. 197–230, Plates XII–XVII.

132. BÜLOW, HANS VON, Musical composer. This brain is referred to by Auerbach (cited above) as being in the possession of Prof. L. Edinger and his article contains drawings of this brain. The morphologic configuration is characterized by a similar redundancy of development in the auditory association area.

133. MENDELÉEFF, DMITRI (1834–1907), Russian chemist. Professor Bechterew has examined the brain of the late Professor Mendeléeff. It is said to weigh more than 1200 grams, and to be remarkable for the number of its convolutions. *Science*, Vol. XXV, No. 638, March 22, 1907, p. 479.

134. KOVALEVSKY, SONYA (1850–1891), Russian mathematician (Stockholm collection). Mme. Sonya Kovalevsky (neé Sophie Corvin-Kronkovsky) was a pupil of Kirchhoff, Königsberger, Helmholtz and DuBois-Reymond. She wrote theses on mathematical subjects in French and German, spending much of her time in Heidelberg, Berlin, Paris and Stockholm. She was appointed to a chair in the University of Stockholm and here added the Swedish language to the others which she had already mastered. Her brain is a well developed one of the feminine, eury-gyrencephalic type; *i. e.*, it is smaller and less complexly marked than the usual male brain. The marginal gyre, especially upon the right side, is of particular interest, for in its development it resembles the brain of the mathematician Gyldén, also studied by Retzius. The brain was not weighed when removed from the skull. After a period of four years in alcohol its weight was 1108 grams. Retzius estimates the original weight to have been about 1385 grams. G. Retzius: *Biol. Untersuch.*, N. F., IX, 1900, pp. 1–16.

135. WINSLOW, CAROLINE B. (?–1896), American physician (Cornell collection).

The autopsy was performed by Dr. D. S. Lamb and the brain was sent to Prof. Wilder. at Cornell University, immersed in a formalin mixture. Dr. Wilder weighed the brain on March 30, 1897, and found it to weigh 1266 grams. Dr. Winslow was a well-known physician and sociologist.

136. Bittner, Marie (1851–1898), Austrian actress. Death was caused by eclampsia (nephritis gravidarum). The autopsy was performed by Prof. Hlava. The head-length was 17.5 cm., head-width, 15.5 cm. The brain weighed 1250 grams (about 50 grams above the average).

137. Leblais (Madame), French educator (Paris collection). A celebrated educator and orator. Brain-weight, 1260 grams. (Communication from G. Hervé.)

Doubtful Reports of Brains of Eminent Men.

From various sources I have culled the following references to brains of notable men which either lack authority or else seem mythical and exaggerated. I have deemed it best to place them in a separate category pending verification. Vague references have been made to the brains of Voltaire and Rousseau, but I cannot find anything definite about them.

Cromwell, Oliver. The weight of Cromwell's brain is variously given as 2330 and 2233 grams. The earliest reference to any autopsy report that Schuchardt could find was in *Anabaptisticum et enthusiasticum Pantheon und Geistliches Rüst-Haus wider die Alten Quaker und neuen Frey-Geister, etc. Im Jahre Christi 1702 fol.*, p. 12. The following is a translated extract: "Hereupon the body of Cromwell was opened; the intestines were healthy, but the liver was affected and the brain weighed 6¼ pounds." It must be recalled that the above was published forty-four years after Cromwell's death. The body of Cromwell has been disposed of in so many ways by as many writers on the subject that one cannot attach any value to any of the accounts. Cromwell must have had at least three heads, as one skull is preserved in the Ashmolean Museum at Oxford, there is another in the possession of a private individual at Beckenham, while still a third was for a while placed on public exhibition in London. An interesting collection of these stories, together with a photograph of the death-mask, may be found in Laurence Hutton's "A Collection of Death-masks" (Harper's). Schuchardt: Letter to R. Wagner in "Vorstudien, etc.," I, 1860, p. 93.

Lord Byron, George Noël Gordon (1788–1824). An inordinately large figure is usually given for the weight of Lord Byron's brain, viz: 2238 grams. As is well known, Lord Byron died in Missolonghi, in April, 1824. The body was brought to Zante and later to England. Schuchardt, writing to Wagner concerning his efforts to ascertain the facts, says that he was unable to find out when and where the autopsy was performed. The postmortem examination report is printed in the *Gazette de Santé* (August 25, 1825) by the editor, Antoine Miquel; it was reprinted in the *Medico-Chirurgical Review*, N. S., II. 1825, p. 161. From contemporary newspaper reports a similar account was given in *Froriep's Notizen*, IX, p. 143. The weight of the brain is said to have been "6 medicinal pounds." If the autopsy was performed at Missolonghi, the Neapolitan or the Venetian system of weights was probably used; if Neapolitan, the weight would be equivalent to 1924 grams; if Venetian, 1807 grams. If English weights were at hand, which is very unlikely, the weight would be 2238 grams. Even if the Venetian system had been used, the figure (1807 grams) is very high. The original report states that the brain was exceedingly congested and two ounces of blood are said to have been found in the cerebral ventricles. It is very improbable that the brain, if weighed at all, was so with any attempt at accuracy. The crude statement of the weight in a round figure indicates this. Schuchardt: Letter to Wagner in "Vorstudien," I, 1860, p. 93.

LAPLACE (1749–1827). The brain of LaPlace is said to have been in the possession of the anatomist Magendie. Wagner: "Vorstudien," 1860, p. 24.

SCHUBERT, FRANZ (1797–1828). Hansemann and Sperino mention the brain-weight of Schubert (1420 grams) but give no authority for the figure. I cannot find evidence of Schubert's brain having been removed and weighed.

SPURZHEIM, KASPAR (1776–1832). The anatomist and phrenologist Spurzheim was born in Longwich near Trier and died in Boston. It is doubtful whether his brain was actually removed and weighed. The figure for the brain-weight which is commonly quoted (1559 grams) was probably estimated from the cranial capacity (1950 cu. cm.) N. B. Shurtleff: "Anatomical Report on the Skull of Spurzheim." Read April 2, 1835, before the Boston Phrenological Society. *Annals of Phrenology* (Boston), II. 1835, p. 72. Topinard: "Elements d'Anthropologie Générale," p. 628. Manouvrier: La Quantité de l'Encephale." 1855, p. 280.

LAMARQUE (General) (1770–1832). The brain-weight, 1449 grams, was probably estimated from the cranial capacity. Manouvrier: "La Quantité de l'Encephale," 1885, p. 280.

PASCAL (1623–1662). The physicians in attendance at the post-mortem examination are cited as having observed the brain to be very large. Broca, in a later comment, attributes its very large volume to the retarded closure of the anterior fontanelle which is said to have occurred in Pascal's case. Charpentier: "Vie de Pascal," 1854, p. 74. Broca: *Bull. de la soc. d'anthrop. de Paris*, 1861, p. 162.

WILLIAM III. There is an account of the post-mortem examination performed upon William III of England by the "Physitians and Surgeons, comanded to assist at the dissection of the body of the late King" in the *Lancet* of 1702. The following is an extract therefrom: "The Brain was perfectly sound and without any signe of distemper."

The Brain-weight of Notable Men.

In former contributions on the subject of brain-weight the writer has tabulated over 100 brain-weights of notable men. The following list contains, in separate tables, the brain-weights of 115 men of note together with 12 such which are either not well authenticated or were not observed under proper conditions. In the case of Helmholtz, for example, we may only guess at the true figure owing to the extensive cerebral hemorrhage which caused death. An error in transcribing the brain-weight figure for Joseph Leidy probably made the original figure 45½ ounces instead of 54½ ounces; as will be seen in the writer's description of Leidy's brain, the higher figure is more likely to approach the true weight. The brains of Harless, Dollinger and Gambetta were not weighed until after preservatives had been used.

Of the 115 men here tabulated, 7 died insane. Their brain-weights are placed in a separate list and are not included in the recapitulations.

The actual weight of the brains of each of the individuals in the table has doubtless been influenced to a varying extent by the conditions and causes of death. These variations must, however, be disregarded here, except to mention that, as a general rule, the figures are rather lower than they should be by reason of atrophy from old age, or from wasting diseases, or both. In a few cases there is ample proof of this diminution of weight, as for example, in that of the phrenologist and anatomist Gall, who died at the age of 70, after a most active career, and whose brain had shrunken considerably, weighing only 1198 grams. The report of the autopsy mentions this atrophy as well as the existence of "four or five ounces of fluid." The skull of Gall had an internal capacity of 1692 cubic centimeters, from which we may fairly infer that the brain must have weighed fully 1500 grams at maturity. Bischoff for a like reason would raise Tiedemann's 1254 grams to 1422 grams, and von Liebig's 1352 to 1450 grams at the least. At the autopsy on von Liebig there was found "considerable fluid under the arachnoid" and that "the brain had already lost much in its nutrition during the last days of life" may be deduced from the fact that it lost in weight very rapidly after immersion in alcohol, namely, 34 per cent. in the first month and 50 per cent. after about six years. Daniel Webster, with a cranial capacity of 1995 c.c., probably had a brain weighing 1735 grams, whereas after death it weighed over 200 grams less. Spurzheim, with a skull capacity of 1950 c.c., which would indicate a brain-weight of 1695 grams, had an actual weight of only 1559 grams. The brain of von Pettenkofer, who died at the age of 82, showed, Dr. Bollinger writes, a mild degree of beginning atrophy. The brain of the ethnologist and geologist J. W. Powell showed distinct signs of atrophy, and those of Whewell, C. Bischoff, and Fallmerayer are similar examples. That of the Hon. B. G. Ferris, an active lawyer and politician who lived to be 89 years old, is doubtless another instance of such senile atrophy.

Aside from these atrophic changes there occur the inevitable errors due to variations in the amount of fluid and blood contained in the cavities and the brain substance itself, and in the thickness of the pia-arachnoid. These recur so frequently in brain-weighings that in the absence of special data they may be neglected, since relativity of the weights is not much impaired. So far as the writer knows, all of the brains here tabulated were weighed with the pia-arachnoid. As those of Bischoff's and Marchand's tables, used here for comparison, were weighed under like conditions, no further allowance need be made.

Other factors known to affect brain-weight, such as stature, nationality, body-weight and build, etc., cannot well be considered in these cases; the necessary data are insufficient for the purposes of a critical estimate of these influences. Marshall has essayed to do this with the brain-weights of Thackeray, Grote, Grant, Babbage and DeMorgan.

In my table no attempt at correction for the various deteriorating influences above mentioned has been made, and all further discussion is based upon these figures exclusively.

TABLE I.

Name.	Age.	Occupation.	Nationality.	Brain-weight.
Turgenev.	65	Poet and novelist.	Russian.	2012
Bonny.		Jurist.	French.	1935
Cuvier.	63	Naturalist.	German descent.	1830
Knight, E. H.	59	Mechanician.	American.	1814
(Kraus, F. X.).	42	Theologian.	German.	1800
Abercrombie.	64	Physician.	English.	1786
Butler, Benj. F.	74	Statesman.	American.	1758
Olney, Edward.	59	Mathematician.	American.	1701
Levi, Herman.	60	Composer.	German.	1690
Winchell, A.	67	Geologist.	American.	1666
Thackeray.	52	Humorist.	English.	1658
Lenz, Rudolf.		Composer.	German. ?	1636
Goodsir.	53	Anatomist.	English.	1629
Curtice.	68	Mathematician.	American.	1612
Atherton.	49	U. S. Senator.	American.	1602
Siemens.	68	Physicist.	German.	1600
Brown, George.	61	Journalist.	Canadian.	1596
Konstantinoff.	25	Author.	Bulgarian.	1595
Pepper, William.		Physician.	American.	1593
Harrison, R. A.	45	Jurist.	Canadian.	1590
Hermann, F. B. W.	73	Economist.	German.	1590
Riebeck.	61	?	German.	1580
Büchner.	51	Hygienist.	German.	1560
Bittner.	57	Playwright.	German.	1556
Lavollay.		Merchant and publicist.	French.	1550
Cope.	57	Paleontologist.	American.	1545
McKnight.	57	Physician.	American.	1545
Allen, Harrison.	56	Anatomist.	American.	1531
Simpson.	59	Physician.	English.	1531
Train, G. F.	75	Promoter.	American.	1525
Taguchi.	66	Anatomist.	Japanese.	1520
Dirichlet.	54	Mathematician.	French.	1520
De Morny.	54	Statesman.	French.	1520
Webster.	70	Statesman.	American.	1518
Lord Campbell.	82	Statesman.	English.	1517
Wright, C.	45	Philosopher.	American.	1516
Schleich.	55	Author.	German.	1503
Chalmers.	67	Theologian.	English.	1503
Mallery.	63	Ethnologist.	American.	1503
Seguin, E. C.	55	Neurologist.	French descent.	1505
Napoleon III.	65	Sovereign.	French.	1500
Fuchs.	52	Pathologist.	German.	1499
Agassiz.	66	Naturalist.	French descent.	1495
Giacomini.	58	Anatomist.	Italian.	1495
De Morgan.	73	Mathematician.	English.	1494
Gauss.	78	Mathematician.	German.	1492
Letourneau.	71	Anthropologist.	French.	1492
(————.)	53	Statesman.	Swedish.	1489
Powell.	68	Anthropologist.	American.	1488
Pfeufer.	63	Physician.	German.	1488
Wuelfert.	63	Jurist.	German.	1485
Broca.	56	Anthropologist.	French.	1484
Mortillet.	77	Anthropologist.	French.	1480
Aylett.	58	Physician.	American.	1474

TABLE I.—*Continued.*

Name.	Age.	Occupation.	Nationality.	Brain-weight.
Lord Jeffrey.	76	Jurist.	English.	1471
Asseline.	49	Journalist.	French.	1468
Skobeleff.	39	General.	Russian.	1457
Bischoff, C. H. E.	79	Physician.	German.	1452
Gylden.	55	Astronomer.	Swedish.	1452
Kobell.	79	Geologist.	German.	1445
Mihalkovicz.	55	Biologist.	Hungarian.	1440
Dupuytren.	58	Surgeon.	French.	1437
Siljeström.	76	Physicist.	Swedish.	1422
Rice, A. T.	35	Diplomat and editor.	American.	1418
Oliver.	65	Mathematician.	American.	1418
Meyr, M.	61	Philosopher.	German.	1415
Leidy, Philip.	53	Physician.	American.	1415
Nussbaum.	64	Surgeon.	German.	1410
Grote.	75	Historian.	English.	1410
Huber.	49	Author.	German.	1409
Pond, J. B.	65	Soldier and lecture-manager.	American.	1407
Babbage.	79	Mathematician.	English.	1403
Assézat.	45	Journalist.	French.	1403
Kupffer.	73	Anatomist.	German.	1400
Bertillon.	62	Anthropologist.	French.	1398
Goltz.	68	Physiologist.	German.	1395
Coudereau.	50	Physician.	French.	1390
Whewell.	72	Philosopher.	English.	1389
Wistar, Isaac J.	78	General.	American.	1389
Wilson.	61	U. S. Vice-president.	American.	1389
Szilagyi.	61	Statesman.	Hungarian.	1380
Rüdinger.	64	Anatomist.	German.	1380
Schmid.	65	Author.	German.	1374
Hovelacque.	52	Statesman.	French.	1373
Bischoff, T. L. W.	76	Anatomist.	German.	1370
Cheve.		?	French.	1365
Gross, S. D.		Physician.	American.	1361
Hermann, C. F.	51	Philologist.	German.	1358
Liebig.	70	Chemist.	German.	1352
Schlagintweit.	51 ?	Naturalist.	German.	1352
Fallmerayer.	71	Historian.	German.	1349
Bennett.	63	Physician.	English.	1332
Pettenkofer.	82	Pathologist.	German.	1320
Senzel.	50	Sculptor.	French.	1312
Zeyer.	56	Architect.	German.	1320
Kolar.	84	Dramatist.	Bohemian.	1300
Grant, R. E.	80	Astronomer.	English.	1290
Whitman.	72	Poet.	American.	1282 ?
Cory.	55	Physician.	English.	1276
Guardia.	67	?	Spanish.	1272
Seguin, Edouard.	68	Psychiatrist.	French.	1257
Tiedemann.	79	Anatomist.	German.	1254
Lasaulx.	57	Philologist.	German.	1250
Laborde.	73	Physiologist.	French.	1234
Buhl.	64	Anatomist.	German.	1229
Hausmann.	71	Naturalist.	German.	1226
Ferris.	89	Jurist.	American.	1225
Gall.	70	Phrenologist and anatomist.	German.	1198

TABLE I.—*Continued.*

DIED INSANE.

Name.	Age.	Occupation.	Nationality.	Brain-weight.
Collier.	45	Attorney and politician.	English descent.	1720
Steinitz.	64	Chess-player.	German descent.	1462
Altmann.	48	Anatomist.	German.	1460
Donizetti.	47	Composer.	Italian.	1391
Schumann.	46	Composer.	German.	1352
Ludwig II.	41	Sovereign.	German.	1349
Smetana.	60	Composer.	Bohemian.	1250

DOUBTFUL; Could not be verified or were not weighed fresh.

Name.	Age.	Occupation.	Nationality.	Brain-weight.
Helmholtz.	73	Physicist and physiologist.	German.	1700 1508 1440
Combe, Andrew.	49	Phrenologist.	English.	1616
Spurzheim.	56	Anatomist and phrenologist.	German. ?	1559
Leidy, Joseph.	67	Naturalist.	American.	1415 1545
Vajda, Janos.		Poet.	Hungarian.	1500
Lamarque, Gen.	63	General.	French.	1449
(Doctor philos.)	78	?	Swedish.	14 9
Schubert.	70	Composer.	German.	1420
Lasker.		Jurist and politician.	German.	1300
Harless.	42	Physiologist.	German.	1238
Doellinger.	71	Anatomist and physiologist.	German.	1207
Gambetta.	44	Statesman.	French.	1160

Germans and Austrians	38
Americans (incl. Canada)	27
Frenchmen	20
British	14
Swedes	3
Russians	2
Italian	1
Spanish	1
Bulgarian	1
Japanese	1
	108

	Cases.	Average Brain-weight.
Americans (incl. Canadians)	27	1519
British (incl. Scots)	14	1481
Frenchmen	20	1456
Germans and Austrians	38	1439

The average (arithmetical) brain-weight of the 108 individuals is 1473 grams, exceeding the various averages given for the European brain by 75 to 100 grams, and this without allowing for the advanced age of the men in this series.

A better appreciation of the greater average brain-weight of these notable persons can be formed from a glance at the chart (Fig. 1) showing the distribution of "ordinary" and "eminent" brain-weights.

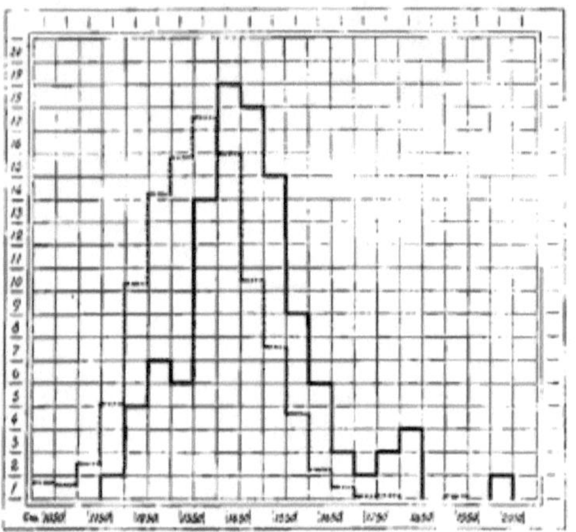

Fig. 1. Chart showing the relatively greater number of heavier brains among the (100) "eminent men" (see solid line) as compared with the distribution of the ordinary brain-weights of the combined series (1334 cases) of Bischoff, Marchand and Topinard — tabulated for convenience in comparison on the bases of 100 cases.*

It shows a relatively greater number of heavier brains among the noted individuals, and the chart in Fig. 2 shows the same relation in another manner. It is further shown that the period of decrease with age is deferred for fully a decade among the more intellectual persons, a point already alluded to by Donaldson and significant in connection with the longevity of healthy persons endowed with high intelligence.

In proceeding to a further analysis it seems best to distribute these men of eminence among the three categories of science, creative arts and "action." In submitting these lists, the writer feels constrained to repudiate any intention of maintaining

* Figures 1, 2, 7, 8, 9, 10, 14 and 21 are reproduced here through the courtesy of the editor of the *American Anthropologist*. They served to illustrate a similar but less detailed discussion on brain-weight and brain-size in connection with the author's studies on the brain of Major J. W. Powell.

the classification above adopted to be one meeting all the requisites involved. The simple division into representatives of science, creative arts and action is necessitated by the smallness of numbers: a proper rubrication would leave more than one important division represented by only one or two individuals. Aside from the failure of three groups to provide for the various branches of mental activity as manifested in various professions—here conventionally adopted—it were doubtful if mature

FIG. 2. Curves of average brain-weights per decade in the series of (97) "eminent men" compared with the Broca-Bischoff-Boyd series. The curves show the eminent men to be higher in the scale, and further that the senile decrease becomes marked a decade later than in the "ordinary" series.

reflection would endorse such classification. The latter is far from a natural one, for it does not regard the intrinsic physiological relations of the professions, arts and sciences. For example, the sharp demarcation of art and science leaves music and mathematics abruptly and remotely separated; yet, whatever justifiable presumption exists as to the relations of cortical fields would assign both to closely situated, nay, in almost identical areas, tracts, and neurones of such. Again, to place, for example, generals in one group, is to throw in a chaos of unrelated units the mathematical genius, the geographical explorer, the expert physicist with the strategic adventurer and opportune gambler of the battlefield chess-board.

With these limitations the following table expresses the results of such classifications in condensed form:

Categories.	No. of Cases.	Average.	Average Brain-weight.
I. *a.* Exact Sciences	9	67.9	1542
I. *b.* Natural Sciences	48	64.0	1453.1
(All Sciences.)	(57)	(64.7)	(1467.1)
II. Fine Arts, Philosophy, etc.	24	57.6	1479.0
III. Men of action (Government, Politics, Law, Military.)	23	61	1516.3
Total averages	107	62.3	1439.3

Of course, every rule has its exceptions, and, with this limitation, the inference that the intellectual status is in some way reflected in the mass and weight of the brain seems generally correct. But further than this our analysis shows that the brains of men devoted to the higher intellectual occupations, such as the mathematical sciences, involving the most complex mechanisms of the mind, those of men who have devised original lines of research (Cuvier) and those of forceful characters, like Ben Butler and Daniel Webster, are generally heavier still. The results are fully in accord with biological truths.

The Cranial Capacity of Eminent Men.

The following list shows the capacity of the skulls of 64 notable men. Not all of these have been measured by exactly the same methods and the result is doubtlessly not quite accurate. Nor can we be quite sure that all of these skulls have been identified correctly. The vicissitudes of the bones of even the most eminent deceased quite preclude authenticity in every case. For example, Welcker has been able to show that a skull alleged to be Schiller's could not have been his at all. The identity of the skull of Sir Thomas Browne is still in dispute.

Another report which has been quoted frequently relates to the skull of Bismarck. I am unable to find any authentic account of a post-mortem examination and all references to the brain-weight and cranial capacity seem to be founded upon certain measurements made upon Bismarck's head during life. These measurements were taken during the summer of 1895 by the sculptor Schaph, of Berlin, who made the Bismarck statue at Cologne. The head-length was 21.2 cm., the head-width 17.0 cm. The cranial capacity was estimated at 1965 cu. cm. This led to the estimation of the probable brain-weight as 1867 grams (Welcker's coefficient being used), or 1710 grams (Manouvrier's coefficient). Mies: Tägliche Rundschau," April 17–18, 1895.

The list of cranial capacities which follows has been collected from numerous sources; the majority are taken from the writings of Welcker, Schaaffhausen, Manouvrier, Topinard, Nicolucci and Holl.

Several investigators have attempted to estimate brain-weight approximately from the cranial capacity. The difficulties that are encountered in this procedure are obvious, for the factors of age, cranial form, state of nutrition and the conditions of disease prior to death influence the calculations considerably. Welcker, Bischoff, Weisbach, Manouvrier, Topinard and Bolk have devoted not a little study to the subject.

Name.	Cranial Capacity in Cubic Centimeters.	Name.	Cranial Capacity in Cubic Centimeters.
Thos. Browne.	1955	Père Prosper, theologian.	1680
La Fontaine, poet.	1950	Hett, physician.	1675
Bésard, banker.	1940	Unterberger, père, painter.	1665
Sestini.	1850	"R. P. X.," theologian.	1663
Blumauer, poet.	1846	Jean Kollar, poet.	1655
Voigt, mathematician.	1826	Père Mallet, theologian.	1650
Blanchard, aeronaut.	1793	Laclôture.	1630
St. Ambrosius, theologian.	1792	"Homme de peine."	1620
Kreibig, violinist.	1785	Thouvenin, artistic bookbinder.	1615
Junger, poet.	1773	Choron, musician.	1608
Gauthier, pedagog.	1770	Petrarch, poet.	1602
Arnoldi, orientalist.	1750	Bünger, anatomist and surgeon.	1600
Cassaigne, jurist.	1750	Hamerling, poet.	1583
Duc de Bourgogne.	1750	Kreutzer, musician.	1579
Beethoven, composer.	1750	Sallaba, physician.	1575
Volta, physicist.	1745	Juvenal des Ursins, historian.	1530
Kant, philosopher.	1740	von Mosheim.	1530
Safarjik.	1738	Gen. Wurmser.	1530
Frère David, mathematician.	1736	Cerachi, sculptor.	1520
Jourdan, Marshall of France.	1729	Alxinger, poet.	1507
De Zach, astronomer.	1715	Fusinieri, physicist.	1502
von Rheinwald, scholar.	1710	Heinse, poet.	1500
Chenovix, chemist.	1709	Haydn, poet.	1500
Carême, cuisinier.	1708	Dante, poet.	1493
Descartes, philosopher.	1706	Bach, composer.	1480
Brunacci.	1701	Scarpa, surgeon.	1455
Gall, phrenologist.	1700	Foscolo, poet.	1426
Unterberger, fils.	1692	Leibnitz, philosopher.	1422
Boileau, poet.	1690	Raphael, painter.	1420
Robert Bruce.	1689	d'Arles, antiquary.	1420
Bigonnet.	1685	de Bassuejole, bishop.	1372
Bordoni.	1681	Philip Meckel.	1320
		Average	1650

Welcker found that the coefficient which expresses the ratio between cranial capacity and brain-weight is not uniform for both large and small skulls. His findings may be summarized in the following table (after Welcker):

Cranial Capacity in Cubic Centimeters.	Coefficient.	
1200–1300	.91	Average .935
1300–1400	.92	
1400–1500	.93	
1500–1600	.94	
1600–1700	.95	

Name.	Age.	Cranial Capacity.	Actual Brain-weight.	Coefficient.
Cope	57	1645	1545	.94
Webster	70	1999.5	1518	.76
Bertillon	62	1553	1398	.89
(Schumann	46	1510	1352	.89)
Liebig	70	1550	1352	.875
Gall	70	1692	1198	.71
(Gambetta	44	1382	1160?	.84?)

Rather in the nature of an experiment than as a final tabulation of estimated brain-weights of eminent men I here employ both Welcker's and Manouvrier's coefficients, the resulting figures being tabulated in parallel:

Name.	Welcker's Method in Grams.	Manouvrier's Method in Grams.	Name.	Manouvrier's Method in Grams.	Welcker's Method in Grams.
Thos. Browne.	1857	1701	Père Prosper.	1597	1462
La Fontaine.	1852	1696	Hett.	1592	1457
Bésard.	1843	1688	Unterberger, père	1578	1449
Sestini.	1757	1609	"R. P. X."	1575	1447
Blumauer.	1752	1606	Jean Kollar.	1567	1440
Voigt.	1733	1589	Père Mallet.	1561	1435
Blanchard.	1702	1560	Laclôture.	1545	1418
St. Ambrosius.	1701	1559	"Homme de peine."	1537	1409
Kreibig.	1695	1553	Thouvenin.	1533	1405
Junger.	1682	1543	Choron.	1528	1399
Gauthier.	1680	1540	Petrarch.	1522	1394
Arnoldi.	1662	1522	Bänger.	1520	1392
Cassaigne.	1662	1522	Hamerling.	1488	1377
Duc de Bourgogne.	1662	1522	Kreutzer.	1485	1374
Beethoven.	1662	1522	Sallaba.	1480	1370
Volta.	1660	1521	Juvenal des Ursins.	1438	1331
Kant.	1653	1514	von Mosheim.	1438	1331
Safarjik.	1650	1512	Gen. Wurmser.	1430	1323
Frère David.	1648	1510	Cerachi.	1429	1322
Jourdan.	1642	1504	Alxinger.	1416	1311
De Zach.	1626	1492	Fusinieri.	1412	1307
von Rheinwald.	1621	1488	Heinse.	1410	1305
Chenovix.	1619	1487	Haydn.	1410	1305
Carême.	1617	1486	Dante.	1388	1299
Descartes.	1615	1484	Bach.	1376	1288
Brunacci.	1610	1480	Scarpa.	1355	1266
Gall.	1609	1479	Foscolo.	1330	1241
Unterberger, fils.	1607	1472	Leibnitz.	1322	1235
Boileau.	1605	1470	Raphael.	1320	1235
Robert Bruce.	1605	1470	D'Arles.	1320	1235
Bigonnet.	160	1466	De Brussnejole.	1262	1193
Bordoni.	1597	1462	Philip Meckel.	1215	1148
			Averages.	1561	1436

Bolk's figures are based upon examinations of 90 male and 50 female brains and skulls. Prior to the 50th year the cranio-encephalic coefficient is .93. This becomes reduced in the succeeding decades until, in the ninth decade the coefficient sinks to .86.

Manouvrier has adopted as a good working coefficient: .87, while Nicolucci's is .885.

Among the notable men discussed in this memoir there are 7 in whom both brain-weight and cranial capacity have been recorded. The resultant coefficients are added in the list. Schumann belongs to the list of the insane, while Gambetta's brain was undoubtedly influenced by the zinc chloride mixture with which the body had been preserved before the autopsy.

III.

Before proceeding to a discussion of the results of anatomical examinations of the brains of the notable persons considered in this memoir the writer ventures to devote this chapter to a general exposition of modern views concerning the inter-relations of the brain and the mind, and to lead up to a consideration of the more complex morphology of the human brain by briefly tracing the stages of its evolution. In this connection it is necessary to give greater prominence to the post-Darwinian conceptions of the fundamental importance of morphological investigations of the relations which the human organism bears to other animal forms, more especially the Primates. The demands of evolution have found favorable response in the primate ancestor of man and the general laws of natural selection must be taken into consideration in this connection quite as much as in any other morphological question. Evolution may be said to consist chiefly in the development of means whereby an animal is best adapted to the environment and successfully meets changed conditions by new adaptations — and man is doing much in directing the steps of his own evolution. The cause and effect of human evolutionary progress are both to be found in the story of man's brain-development. Man's competence to deal intelligently with the problem of his existence determines his superiority to all other types. Man is self-conscious to a remarkable degree and capable of selecting and adopting methods for the preservation of his species in a way which no other animal form has yet attained.

The central nervous system of man and the other vertebrates consists of a symmetrical apparatus called the cerebro-spinal axis, of which the cephalic extremity in early embryonic life exhibits an intense growth-energy that is indicative of the higher functional potentiality of what is to develop into the brain. The spinal cord with its centrifugal nerves for movements and centripetal nerves for impressions, passes into the skull, becoming slightly enlarged to form the oblongata with its life-centers and cranial nerve roots. At the upper edge of the oblongata a thick band of transverse fibers unites the two lobes of the cerebellum: this structure is known as the pons.

Above this the axial fibers divide into two bundles called the cerebral crura, one to the left and the other to the right; and spreading forwards and outwards go to form (in part) the cerebral hemispheres, on the surface of which is a layer of gray substance, the cerebral cortex. The white portion is made up of conducting nerve-fibers, the gray is the sentient and reacting mass containing numerous nerve-cells from which the fibers arise. Many fibers pass to other regions of the gray matter within the hemicerebrum on one side, and also, by means of commissures, to the hemicerebrum of the other side. Of these commissures the callosum is the largest and most important; it is a bundle of white fibers which is largest in the brain of man, smallest (or only just beginning to develop) in the Marsupial and entirely absent in the lower animals.

In the embryo the cerebro-spinal axis begins as a simple tube of nervous tissue, but in the course of development and growth, especially among the higher vertebrates, various segments undergo thickening, expansion, elongation and flexion. It is the enlargement of the brain which causes the formation of the headbend together with the marked modifications in the skull. Some of the encephalic segments are but slightly modified, others become metamorphosed into complex and important structures, while the cavity of the neural tube is represented by the ventricles of the brain and the narrow spinal canal. The most striking specialization in the Primate brain is seen in the cerebral parts. No contrast could be greater than is to be seen in the comparison of the tiny cerebral appendage of the "olfactory brain" of the earliest vertebrates with the huge cerebral mantle and dwindled olfactory apparatus in the Anthropomorpha. This remarkable expansion of the cerebral hemispheres with which man does his thinking is the latest development in the evolution of the brain. If we study brains arranged in phyletic series, say from the fishes through the reptiles and birds to the mammals of low and high order, we see the other segments of the brain progressively overlapped by the cerebral hemispheres until we find in the brain of man that supremacy in size and complexity of thought-apparatus which so distinguishes him from other species. The amplified development of the special senses and of the locomotive organization has involved the augmentation of coordinating systems. Thus the synchronous development of the hand and the intellectual faculties has been one of the most important factors in the forming of the massive brain which places man at the head of animal creation.

Perhaps no theme in all the natural sciences interests us so much as our kinship with the ape. Proofs of the blood-relationship uniting man and monkey abound on all sides and a general agreement as to man's place in the zoological system seems permanently fixed. But in the mental powers of the Anthropomorpha (true apes) in particular we see their kinship with man shown quite as much as in their physical likeness to our species. Their use of the hands and arms and their facial expressions are quite human. In their intellectual recognition of things they are far superior to the lower animals and as they most closely approach man in their mental characteristics we are naturally interested in the architecture of their brain and the mechanism of their mind.

Whatever series of organs is studied and compared, complete justification is found for the claim that the Primates — the highest order of mammals so named by Linnaeus 170 years ago — form a natural monophyletic group. I will not attempt here to discuss the inter-relations of the subgroups or recite the prevailing inferences as to the genealogical tree of man. Suffice it to say that these inferences are yearly amplified and strengthened by new finds in morphological and paleontological lines of research. At all events the tailless apes show in their development the immediate transition to the human form. One species may be nearest to man in the number of ribs as the orang, or in the character of the cranium, dentition and proportional size of the arms, as the chimpanzee. The gorilla is nearest to man in the proportions of the leg to the body and of the foot to the hand, in the curvature of the spine, form of the pelvis and absolute cranial capacity. The gibbon of all the Anthropomorpha is most remote from man, but its erect attitude, its femur and other skeletal parts are more human than in any other genera. Then there are several fossil forms apparently belonging to this group, from *Dryopithecus* (Middle Miocene) to the *Pithecanthropus* in which human characters preponderate. But while fossil specimens of bones and teeth are rare enough, the perishability of the brain renders its natural preservation practically impossible and we are compelled to draw our own inferences concerning the morphology of this organ from a comparison of the brains of modern living forms, assisted by studies of the cranial configuration of extinct types.

Embryological studies are of the greatest aid in elucidating many otherwise obscure stages in development. Thus it is seen that the human and anthropoid cranial form is the universal embryonic norm from which the skulls of all mammals develop. Every skull at or near the time of birth is orthognathic, that is, the facial angle approximates a right angle, and each has a tendency to become more and more prognathic, a type of skull in which the jaws are larger and more prominent. In the gorilla and orang, less so in the chimpanzee, it becomes very prognathic, but in man it is checked by anatomical correlations. The development of the jaw is more or less closely associated with the size of the teeth and consequently with the nature of the diet; the bulk of the masticatory muscles and the temporal area is greater in the more prognathic, heavy-jawed skulls, for the temporal muscle must be larger to overcome the mechanical disadvantages of the longer lever. This muscular influence from without was one of the factors which determined the dolichocephalic type of the older stock. Prognathism becomes more and more checked the higher we go in the scale, and the superior, brainier individuals of the higher races therefore exhibit less prognathism and greater breadth of skull.

We find corroboration of these general statements in the comparative study of the brains and skulls of men of notable intelligence with those of the ordinary population, or of the highly civilized with savage tribes. Many writers have laid stress upon the apparent relation between stature and the intellectual differences of the races of man, their hasty conclusion being that stature had everything and brain-size nothing to do with mental capacity. Though it be granted that the taller Anglo-Saxons have heavier brains than the shorter Hindoos or Bushmen, a further analysis shows this rule to be untenable in the case of other races, notably the Mongolians and their kin, the Eskimos. Brain-weight is influenced by many factors, including age, sex, race, stature, cranial capacity and form, body-build, state of nutrition and mode of death. Brain-weight statistics therefore must be judged with care. It is difficult to give an exact expression of the inter-relation between brain-size and mental capacity. Professor Manouvrier, in 1882, attempted to estimate numerically the two factors in the bulk of the brain, *i. e.*, size of the body and the degree of the intelligence; his formula gave concordant results as a rule, but broke down when applied to extremes. Professor Dubois, in 1897, proposed a different method. He started with the assumption that the brain consists entirely of central parts of the reflex arcs, the function of which is to bring sensory and motor nerves into relation with each other and he concluded that in animals presenting the same degree of physical development the number and weight of these reflex arcs would be proportional, approximately, to the number of sensory nerve-fibers. In two animals in very different stages of psychical evolution but of the same bulk, and having therefore approximately the same number of sensory fibers, the animal in whom the central parts of the reflex arcs attain the greater degree of complexity will have the heavier brain. It appears from the researches of Dubois that the cube root of the square of the weight of the animal multiplied by a constant which varies with each species expresses with fair accuracy the relative size of the surface of the body. If S and s be the weight of the body of two animals their surfaces will be

$$\sqrt[3]{S^2} \text{ and } \sqrt[3]{s^2} \qquad \text{or} \qquad S^{0.66} \text{ and } s^{0.66}.$$

In practice the factor is not exactly 0.6 but 0.56, the extremes being 0.54 and 0.58; thus

$$W = cS^{0.56},$$

in which W = brain-weight, S = weight of the body and c = the factor of cephalization indicating the degree of intelligence. Thus the factor of cephalization is in

Man .	. 2.8186
Monkey .	. 0.7607 to 0.4636
Donkey .	. 0.4390
Horse	. 0.4380
Cat	. 0.3284
Dog	. 0.3586

Among the birds we find the parrot at the head of the list; then come crows, magpies and jays, while the stupid barn-door fowl stands lowest.

Within the range of our own species sufficient material has been collected to permit of general conclusions. Microcephalic idiots have brains far under the size necessary for mental integrity; these unfortunates may live, eat and sleep, but their small

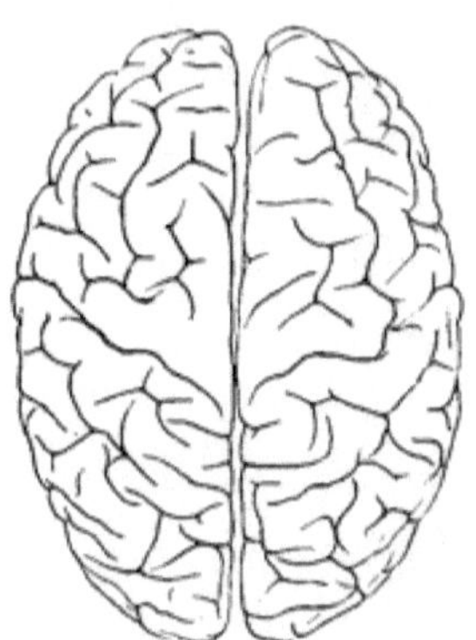

FIG. 5. Dorsal view of a Papuan brain. (In the anatomical laboratory of Columbia University.)

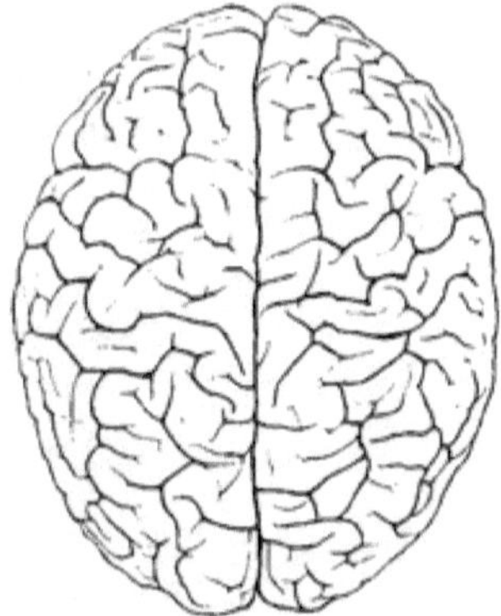

FIG. 6. Dorsal view of the brain of Gauss. (In the Göttingen collection.)

brains are incompatible with even passable intelligence. In most cases they cannot command even the rudiments of a language and communication with others is limited to simple signs and gestures. That a certain class of idiots should possess brains of normal size, or even unusually large brains has been quite disconcerting to casual students of the subject. The heaviest brain on record weighed over 100 ounces, or twice as much as the average normal male brain. In the case of this overburdened youth, however, there was an abnormal increase of useless tissue with a profound diminution in the number of the functional elements. Structural defects of some such kind underlie all similar cases.

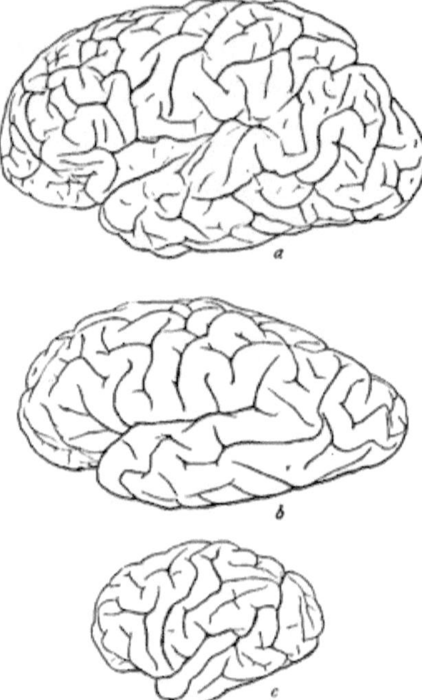

FIG. 7. *a.* Brain of Helmholtz (after Hansemann). *b.* Brain of a Papuan (drawn by the author from a specimen in the Anatomical Museum, Columbia University). *c.* Brain of chimpanzee.

The fruitful investigations of many anatomists and anthropologists have resulted in the tabulation of thousands of brain-weights drawn from all the social and intellectual classes, among which more than one hundred (considered in Table I) are of men of intellectual eminence. Men of the kind who never remain steadily employed and who usually fail to learn even a trade stand lowest in the scale. Above them come the mechanics and trade-workers, the clerks, the ordinary business men and common-school teachers. Highest of all we find the men of decided mental abilities; the geniuses of the pencil, brush and sculptor's chisel, the mathematicians, scholars

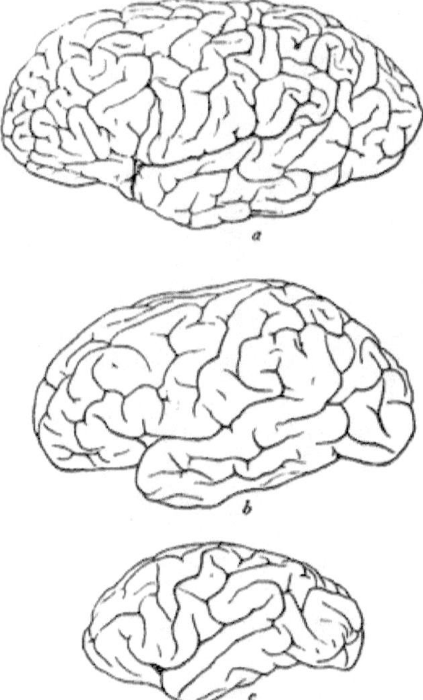

Fig. 8. *a*. Brain of Gauss, mathematician (after Wagner). *b*. Brain of a Bushwoman (after Marshall). *c*. Brain of gorilla (D. 658, Mus. Roy. Coll., Surgeons of England).

and statesmen. Vigorous minds depend not only upon the acquisition of knowledge, but also upon the initiative power of utilizing knowledge to the best advantage; to do this the individual must possess a brain of superior organization. Not only must it be large enough: its elements must consist of the best material and the plan of construction must be one of the most elaborate and efficient kind possible. A Swiss watch of fine construction is a more reliable timepiece than a cheap and hastily manufactured alarm-clock. In like manner the expert anatomist discerns the differences

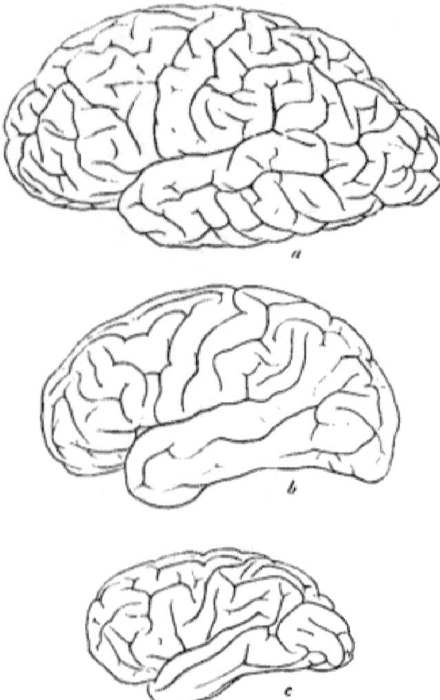

FIG. 9. *a*. Brain of Siljeström, physicist and pedagog, also mathematician (after Retzius). *b*. Brain of "Sartjee" or "Hottentot Venus" (after Gratiolet and Bischoff. *c*. Brain of orang-outang "Rajah" (drawn by the author from specimen received from Dr. Harlow Brooks).

between the simply constructed brains of lower forms and the complex thought-apparatus of man, and even within our own species demonstrable differences in the elaboration of cerebral architecture have been determined. For example, the more numerous, sinuous and ramified the cerebral fissures are, the greater is the degree of expansion of the cerebral cortex, the number of nerve-elements is proportionately increased and the possibilities of coordination of the separate units of thought and action are augmented in a corresponding degree. And where the different parts of the cortex with different functional relations possess still greater potential growth-

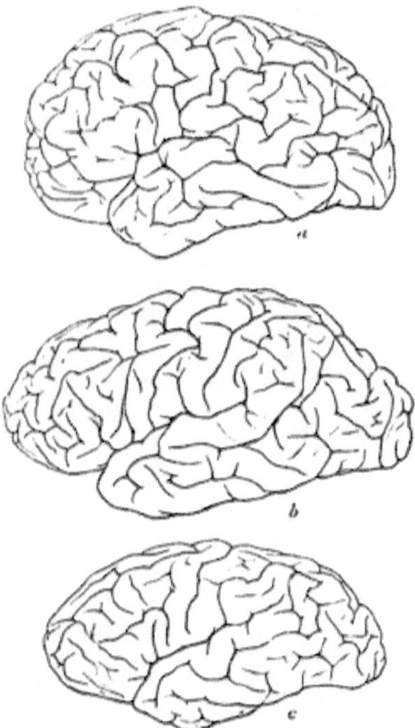

FIG. 10. *a.* Brain of General Skobeleff (after Sernoff). *b.* Brain of Professor Altmann, anatomist (from photograph kindly sent by Dr. P. Näcke, of Hubertusburg). *c.* Brain of Gambetta (after Duval).

energy, the number of infoldings will be greater and the fissuration more accentuated and compact. This is at least true of brains within the primate order of animals. The brain of a first-class genius like Friedrich Gauss is as far removed from that of the savage Bushman as that of the latter is removed from the brain of the nearest related ape. We find expression for these differences not only in the degree of fissural and gyral development of the cerebrum, but also in the actual weight of the brain. The range of brain-weight within the human species is a very wide one, from a Turgeneff's brain weighing 2012 grams or a Cuvier's weighing 1830 grams to that of a Zulu weighing only 1050 grams. There is a distinct gap between the lowest brain-weight of a normal human being and the highest figure recorded for an anthropoid (425 grams in a gorilla), but more finds of a pithecanthropoid character like that found in the Trinil bed in Java will speedily serve to supply the deficiency.

The pattern of the fissures and convolutions in the brains of the higher anthropoids and man presents the same general features in all these types. As we trace the stages of the development of man's great brain through the lower forms we observe how, in a number of ways, in consequence of the demands of evolution, certain regions of the cerebrum assume a greater energy of growth and expand in proportion to the rise in functional dignity of these areas. These regions of "unstable equilibrium" present numerous details of fissural and gyral arrangement which differ not only in different individuals but also in the cerebral halves of the same individual. The careful study of these regional redundancies has resulted in the formulation of a most important statement in the physiology of the central nervous system. Man and the higher anthropoids possess many points in common with reference to their anatomic structure, their habits and their mode of life; but over and above these traits man possesses an associative memory or ability to register and compare sensations far greater than that of the highest ape. Small wonder, then, that this supremacy of the intellect should find somatic expression in the greater size and complexity of structure of the human brain. That is why the association areas constitute the greater portion of the cerebral cortex of man's brain. This relative increase of association-cortex demands a still more intricate inter-connection of the many nerve cells by a multitude of association fibers; hence the great preponderance of white matter in the brain of man as compared with that of any inferior species. These coordinating fibers never project outward from the brain to the periphery. They are as truly representative of the complexity of man's thought-apparatus as the number of inter-connecting wires within a telephone "central" station is indicative of the amplitude of connections possible in that system. A brain made up of gray matter only would be as useless as a telephone system with all its inter-connecting wires destroyed.

With the aid of the microscope the maturing of the brain-elements can be followed from the earliest stages of embryonic life to the period of senescence. One of the important stages in the growth of each nerve-element within the brain is the acquisition of a medullary sheath which surrounds the axis-cylinder process (axone) along which impulses are carried. The curious fact to be remembered in this connection is that the function of nerve-fibers within the brain is only established when the medullary sheath has developed. But this development of mature nerve-fibers does not occur simultaneously throughout the brain, but step by step in a definite order of succession; equally important bundles of fibers are developed (medullated) simultaneously, but those of dissimilar importance develop one after another in accordance with a biological law recently formulated by Professor Flechsig. This successive medullation of bundles of fibers going to the various areas of the cortex closely corresponds to the successive awakenings of mental activities and faculties in the growing child. Now whether a given child shall be normal, backward or precocious depends largely, if not wholly, upon this progressive ripening of the numerous nerve-elements of the brain. When the maturing process is a slow one and the stimulating training of ordinary educational methods finds only slight response, the child remains backward and may ever be feeble-minded. Contrariwise, the rapid and early development of a brain that is generously planned to begin with often results in a mental superiority that is only found in the precocious genius. Why some brains develop slowly and others rapidly is another question to be relegated to the consideration of the "inequality of man." In the precocious genius it must for the present be assumed that the ripening of the nerve-fibers is perhaps stimulated by some obscure bio-chemical conditions which are less marked or less effectual in the ordinary child. It is fair to assume some such chemical factor, for the absence or impairment of function of the thyroid gland, which is invariably associated with mental failure and retention of the infantile state so characteristic of sporadic cretinism, cannot be disregarded in this connection. We need not assume that the secretions of the thyroid gland alone are essential; many other substances, as yet undiscovered, may be as necessary. Who knows whether there may not be some substance which stimulates brain-development just as the adrenal secretion stimulates the unstriped muscle cells of the arterial system to contract. Indeed, the early ripening of the brain sometimes seems to be an expression of over-stimulation by some substance either in itself toxic or produced in abnormal quantity or strength. It is suggestive that some infant prodigies fail to uphold themselves beyond the age of puberty and usually fall prey to the ravages of tuberculosis or other constitutional diseases.

The history of the latest epoch of animal life upon this planet is the history of the development of man's progressive brain. The attainment of the erect attitude by *Pithecanthropus*, our direct ancestor, the gradual acquisition of reasoning and ideation as well as manual skill were the chief factors in bringing about the superior structure of the human brain. Perhaps the most important stimulus to brain-development was afforded by the acquisition of the faculty of speech — "the most human manifestation of humanity," as Huxley termed it — and the successful localization of this faculty in certain regions of the cerebrum was the first of a series which resulted in the delineation of a good working-map of the somesthetic* sense- and association-areas of the brain. As a doctrine slowly evolved out of the primitive ideas of the phrenologist Gall, cerebral localization remains firmly established and now renders surgical intervention possible in cases heretofore considered beyond aid. In some quarters there is a tendency to revert to phrenology and phrenological methods in localizing the passions and emotions — the moral qualities as distinguished from the intellect. It is a fascinating topic and much has been thought and said upon it. In a crude way every one is a phrenologist and a physiognomist, for it is common to hear it said of this or that individual: "He has a brutal head; a brutal face"; "A noble head, a fine face" — without exactly knowing why we say so. It would be a great benefit to the community if the subtle moral qualities could be gauged and expressed in exact terms. The most recent attempt to do this was made by Dr. Bernard Hollânder in his book: "The Mental Functions of the Brain." His claims are very pretentious and he departs but little from the old theories of phrenology throughout his argument. The work contains many errors and the data are handled so loosely that one is easily prejudiced against the author's views and one may rightly question the soundness of his judgment. On the whole the work has added little to the conclusions previously arrived at in clinical neurology.

As for the correlation of cranial development with the mental and moral attributes of an individual, phrenology has signally failed to afford a satisfactory means for investigation. To some degree the characters of skull-form indicate relatively greater development of this or that division of the brain, but always in corroboration of our present-day knowledge concerning the localization of the mental functions only. Thus in composers like Bach and Beethoven the skull indicated an enormous development of the posterior association areas. In the skull of the philosopher Leibnitz there was a great development of the right parietal and left subfrontal regions. The same was true of the skull of Immanuel Kant.

When we come to consider cerebral localization in the light of brain-evolution, it will be seen that the acquisition of such mental functions as language, abstract thought, ideation and reasoning have been the chief factors in bringing about the superior structure of the human brain, and, and we have just learned, any given region of the cortex gains in functional dignity with the increase of its association. When we remem-

* By somesthetic areas I mean those which are devoted to the registration of cutaneous impressions, impressions from the muscles, tendons and joints; in short, the sense of movement.

ber that the cortex of the human brain contains, in round numbers, 9,000,000,000 functional nerve-cells, we need not wonder at man's capacity for the manifold registration of sensations and the numerous transformations that characterize his mental processes.

Considering now the chief mental faculties, we find that in man's sensory apperception of things vision and audition play the most important rôles in the development of intelligent thought. As Jastrow has entertainingly written in his paper: "Eye-mindedness and Ear-mindedness" . . . "Man is a visual animal; as a race we are eye-minded. We regard "seeing" as believing; and we say "we see" when we comprehend."

But not all men are endowed with the same visual and visualizing powers, and such variations form a basis for interesting studies. Among scientists, for example, some will be found to be good visualizers, observers of concrete things with good powers of memorizing and recalling their visual impressions. Others are poor visualizers, owing, perhaps, as Galton remarks, "to their busying themselves with abstractions and generalizations, in which such a faculty would be inconvenient and thus fail to be cultivated." In the brains of Joseph Leidy and Cope, hereinafter described, this difference between the thinker in the abstract and the observer of the concrete appears to be expressed in the relative redundancy of the frontal sphere of abstract thought in the one brain, and of the posterior association areas in the other.

Next to sight, the sense of hearing is the most valuable intellectual instrument. This faculty, too, varies with individuals and the "auditory type" is rarer than the visual type. Beethoven and Mozart are examples of its highest development. The fact that Beethoven was deaf does not invalidate the theory that his central auditory associations were superiorly developed.

The tactile and muscular sensations and the faculties of taste and smell also enter into our psychic life in different degrees. Artists and others skilled in the use of their hands use the tactile and muscular sense considerably in association with the visual and auditory faculties. When, however, a person is deprived of sight and hearing, the tactile sense may be developed to such an unusual extent as to practically recompense the individual. We see a "tactile memory" remarkably developed in the cases of Laura Bridgman, Helen Keller and others. Miss Sullivan, the teacher of Miss Keller, writes that both she and Miss Keller "remember in their fingers" what they have said. For Miss Keller to spell a sentence in the manual alphabet impresses it on her mind just as we learn a thing from having heard, seen or uttered it many times and can call back the memory of its sound or appearances.

Thus we see how the senses help our minds to become cognizant of our environment and form the basis of imagination, memory, thought and reasoning; and now we see how this very combination of sight, hearing and muscular movement leads us to recognize at once the importance of the relation of these powers to that great corti-

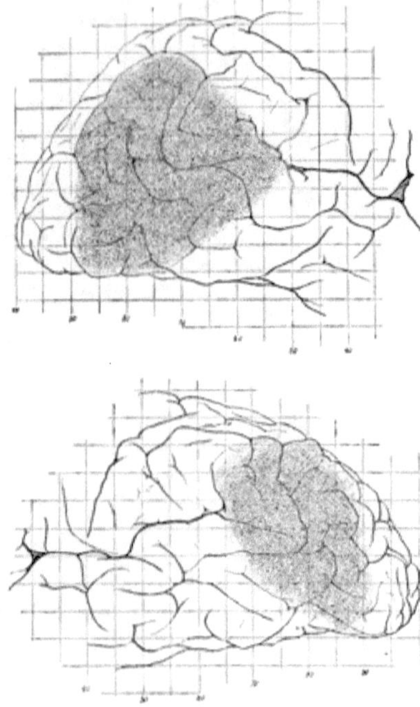

FIG. 14. Views of right (upper figure) and left (lower figure) parieto-occipito-temporal regions in the brain of Maj. J. W. Powell; corresponding parts shaded. The squares mark off areas in centesimals of the cerebral length. Note the preponderance of the right side over the left.

cal area which we know to be concerned in their association. It is this region which we observe to be remarkably expanded in the human brain as compared with that of the anthropoids. There are evidences presented by the brains of highly intellectual persons which show this region to be especially redundant, not only as compared with other brains, but particularly of the right (or preponderatingly sensory) half as compared with the left.

In the mental life of man the power of speech plays so important a part that I will briefly refer here to its chief anatomic relations. The evolution of the faculty of speech has been admirably epitomized by Cunningham in the following words: "Some cerebral variation, probably trifling and insignificant at the start, and yet pregnant with the most far-reaching possibilities, has in the stem-form of man contributed to that condition which rendered speech possible. This variation, strengthened and fostered by natural selection, has in the end led to the great double result of a large brain with wide and extensive association-areas and articulate speech; the two results being brought about by the mutual reaction of the one process upon the other."

Let us examine briefly the evidences of cerebral research which bear upon the brain-centers directly concerned in the speech-faculty. In the first place, the center for articulate speech, meaning thereby the center for the control of the tongue and other muscles employed in articulation, has been localized in the subfrontal gyre and adjacent portion of the precentral, in the left hemicerebrum in right-handed persons and in the right half in left-handed persons. Nearly all observations upon this region agree in ascribing a superior development with reference to size and differentiation in the brains of intellectual persons. Further than this, Rüdinger, Schwalbe, Kupffer and others have found the corresponding region in the skulls of eminent men gifted with a superior command of language (Wülfert, Huber, Kant) to bulge more on the left than on the right side.

A region which I believe, however, to be of not a little importance with reference to the intellectual powers, particularly that of speech, is the insula. This is the purest association center in the brain and its surface-configuration is somewhat of an index of the degree of development of the general cerebral surfaces, particularly of those parts which are more or less in juxtaposition with it and more or less intimately connected with it functionally. Not only is the insular cortex the thickest in the cerebral mantle, but the abundance of the fusiform cells in the deepest layer has given origin to the claustrum and the arcuate association fibers connected with these cells are so numerous as to give origin to the paraclaustral lamina or capsula extrema. This massive system of association neurones and tracts connecting the receptive sense-areas (chiefly the auditory and visual) related to the understanding of the written and spoken word with the emissary centers for articulate speech is most highly developed in the brain of man and one is justified in assuming that in this region language is organized into propositions and arranged for outward projection: it may be termed a language-arrangement center. As a rule, in the brains of intellectual persons, not only is the left insula the larger and more differentiated, but more than this, the preinsula, which is in close juxtaposition with the cerebral centers for articulate speech, is most redundant. The significance of this redundancy of the pre- or postinsula, as the case may be, in its relation to the greater or lesser development of neighboring somesthetic and sense-areas, seems strongly emphasized in the form of the insulæ of the cetacea and proboscidea. In these animals the postinsular region is broader, more massive and more convoluted, a feature which, in the cetacea at least, is concomitant with the amplitude of the cortical field of the eighth pair of cranial nerves, the functions transmitted by which—both equilibrium and audition—are highly developed in the cetacea. Here we again see how the insula, in its several parts, shares in its development that of the adjacent sense-center, as in the cetacean brain just alluded to; and in man, with that of the center for articulate speech. Thus it is that the development of the preinsular region is actually an intense expression of that feature by which the human brain excels that of any other animal. And the more a man be a gifted dialectician, the more demonstrable does this redundancy seem to be. Heredity is a potent factor in this connection. As defects in speech are so likely to be repeated in a family line, it seem that its skilled employment by the ancestor is similarly reflected in the way of facile acquirability on the part of the descendant. The speech-faculty in its intimate relations to thought expression, to memory, in its reading-form to sight, in writing to manual muscular innervation, exquisitely hereditary as it is in life, and accurately localizable in the ravages of disease, as shown after death, makes the study of the insula and adjacent regions highly interesting.

We have seen that men are as variously endowed with intellectual powers as they are with any other traits. It is our business to endeavor to ascertain why and how some are more, some less gifted than others. It is not enough merely to admire the genius of an Archimedes, a Newton, a Michel Angelo or a Bacon; we wish to know how such men of "brains" were capable of their great efforts of the intellect and what gave them the capacity for doing great things, as it were, "without taking pains." When we remember that in the human species the brain has attained the highest degree of perfection, and experience teaches that the manifestations of brain-action differ considerably in the races and social classes; when we remember that all that has ever been said or written, carved or painted, discovered or invented, has been the aggregate product of multifarious brain activity, it seems but reasonable to seek for the somatic bases for these powers and their differences in different individuals. That the brains of men intellectually eminent should come to the hands of anatomists for the purposes of correlating, if possible, the encephalic weight, form and fissural pattern with their mental abilities in life, is but a sign of scientific progress and the subject should form no unimportant branch of anthropometric research. We know the mind of man to differ most from that of the brute in the unusual development of the associations of recepts and concepts, *i. e.*, the powers of reasoning. But if in the brain of the average man there be a hundred, or two hundred, or five hundred connections for every fact that he remembers, their number is many times greater in that of the intellectually superior genius. An elaboration of brain-structure must therefore accompany the higher intelligence and it is in this direction that our researches must be pursued.

I have endeavored to point out in the preceding lines some of the methods of study that give most promise of success in our inquiry. Some of the problems which have been receiving the most attention up to the present time are based upon the microscopic study of the unit of the nervous system, the neurone or nerve-cell and its axone with the numberless dendrites, and upon the intricate grouping and chaining of these millions of neurons within the central nervous system. Not less important are the studies of the morphologic appearances of the cortical surface, the comparative extent of certain cortical areas, upon the weight of the brain and its component parts as well as in comparison with that of the spinal cord; of the ratio between the collective cross-section area of the cranial nerves and of the spinal cord; of the number of fibers in different tracts, be they efferent, afferent or associative (such as the callosum); on the relative bulk of gray and white matter; on the progressive myelinization of different nerve-fiber tracts, and so on almost without end.

IV.

Turning now to the objective studies which it is the chief purpose of this memoir to present, I now proceed to the detailed description of the brain of the six eminent American scientists and scholars who were members of the American Anthropometric Society.

Professor Cope stood forth as a great paleontologist. Professor Joseph Leidy was a recognized leader of natural science who, while he developed many new facts and deduced new laws, yet had that rare faculty of conveying to others—in simplified and systematized form—those fundamental principles of biology so difficult for the ordinary student to grasp. Dr. Philip Leidy was a celebrated physician and surgeon who served with distinction through the Civil War and who later attained high position in various spheres of human activity by dint of strong and inherent executive ability. Dr. Pepper stood in the first rank among clinicians and men of affairs. Professor Harrison Allen exhibited not a little aptitude in the direction of comparative anatomy and zoology and would doubtlessly have achieved much more for science had not his conscientious devotion to an active medical practice interfered therewith. An untimely death prevented the name of Dr. A. J. Parker from becoming as famous among cerebral morphologists as was indicated by his valuable and original contributions to the science of brain morphology.

It is with the assurance that I have endeavored to conduct the studies of these notable specimens in an impartial, unprejudiced frame of mind, though ever heedful of the fact that I was dealing with the brains of men belonging to a most brilliant coterie of intellectual masters and leaders, that I now submit my observations in published form.

At the risk of being thought repetitious I wish to add another word as to the legitimacy of the demands of science for more such brains. Investigations of this kind are chiefly prevented by the objections of the relatives of the deceased. The very suggestion of an autopsy with this object in view is looked upon with horror. I think, however, that in time people will learn that an anatomic examination of this kind, conducted with expert hands, no more violates respect for the body of the deceased than does the embalming process. To me the thought of an autopsy is certainly less repugnant than I imagine the process of cadaveric decomposition in the grave to be.

The methods pursued in the course of my studies on these six brains has been to note: (*a*) observations on the present weight of the encephalic parts and the relations which these bear to each other; (*b*) a systematic description of the fissural and gyral pattern; (*c*) stereographic drawings of the cerebral halves from the dorsal, ventral, mesal and lateral aspects; (*d*) direct measurements; (*e*) projection measurements based upon the stereographic drawings and carried out according to a scheme devised and adopted by the author some time ago. Although a number of systems of measurement have been proposed, not all have stood the test of time and critics. I find those measurements best which can be reduced from absolute to relative values wherein some unit of length, preferably the maximum cerebral length, is used as a basis of expression rather than so many inches or centimeters. Hence I prefer to use centesimals of the length of the cerebrum in order that such records may be found useful by other workers in the same field. Of course any method of measurement cannot be well employed except on brains which have not suffered undue distortion during the process of hardening. The system formulated here may not be, in its several parts original with the author, for many items have in fact been chosen from the writings of Cunningham, Broca, Chiarugi, Marshall, Huschke, Hrdlicka, Eberstaller and others, but as a newly combined system it appears to cover the salient points in the matter of cerebral measurement. The measurements of the cerebrum, cerebellum and pons are recorded separately.

First, and most important, those of the cerebrum comprise its principal diameters and circumferences, the arc measurements along the dorsi-mesal border and a series of horizontal distances to be described below.

The principal measurements of the cerebrum are given directly in centimeters; they are as follows:

Maximum length, left hemicerebrum.
Maximum length, right hemicerebrum.
Maximum width of cerebrum.
Cerebral Index $\left\{\frac{\text{Breadth} \times 100}{\text{Length}}\right\}$.

Horizontal circumference:

Maximum width, left hemicerebrum.
Maximum width, right hemicerebrum.
Left occipito-temporal length.
Right occipito-temporal length.
Length of callosum.
Left centro-temporal height.
Right centro-temporal height.
Left centro-olfactory height.
Right centro-olfactory height.

The arc measurements are made according to Cunningham's method, consisting essentially in the measurement by means of a tape (I employed one 6 mm. wide) along the dorsi-mesal margin from a point corresponding to the level of the lateral part of the orbitofrontal border, to the most caudal point on the occipital pole. From the cephalic point measurements to the dorsal end of the central fissure (or its transit across the dorsi-mesal border) and thence to the dorsal intersection of the occipital fissure are recorded and converted into centesimals of the total fronto-occipital marginal arc. The component segments of the total arc represent relative values to which the terms frontal index, parietal index and occipital index are given and they afford the best means possible for determining the relative marginal extent of these cerebral lobes. Thus the importance of measuring the occipital index was recognized by even so early an observer as Gratiolet, and later observations would seem to suggest that, other things being equal, relative smallness of the occipital arc signified superiority of cerebral development. Cunningham has ascertained the occipital index in several of the primates:

Homo (male)	20.8	Cynocephalus	29.7
Homo (female)	21.7	Mangaby	30.5
Orang . .	23.2	Macaque .	31.0
Chimpanzee	24.2	Cercopithecus	32.9
Hamadryas .	29.5	Cebus	33.1

The third method of measurement, and one which readily affords a means of understanding the relative expanse — be it preponderance or a reduction — of the lobes or special cortical areas of one side as compared with the other, and of one brain as com-

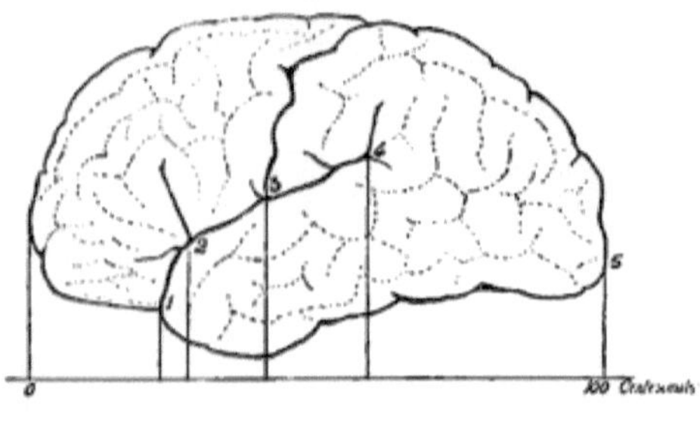

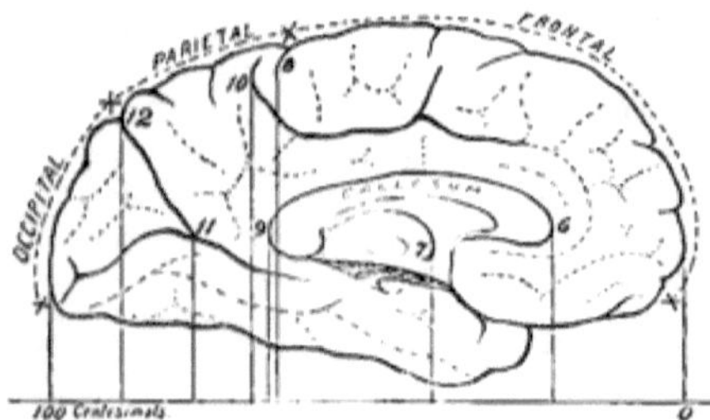

Fig. 21. Showing some useful methods of brain-measurement and indicating the important points employed in the author's system.

pared with others, is one which was used to some extent by Hrdlicka and which the writer has ventured to amplify. The method of procedure is as follows: A horizontal plane passing through the ventral border of the frontal and occipital poles at the mesal border, as shown by the line *AB* in Fig. 21. This horizontal plane has the additional advantage of being parallel to Chipault's plane referred to the skull. A plane vertical to this assumed horizontal plane passes through the most cephalic point of the cerebrum. From this cephalic plane horizontal distances are measured to various points and are converted into centesimals of the cerebral length. Various mechanical aids may be employed to determine these distances with accuracy. With the aid of a stereograph, ordinates were drawn from the selected points to the horizontal line and the abscissæ thus obtained were directly measured. These values were verified by further measurements upon the specimen itself with sliding compasses, the hemicerebrum being placed on a graduated plane similar to Mathieu's instrument. The subsequent conversion of these figures into centesimals of the hemicerebral length allows of comparison with other brains, no matter what their size or what the degree of shrinkage may be so long as there is no actual distortion.

The horizontal distances which have been recorded in the brains here studied are as follows:

LATERAL SURFACE.

From the cephalic point to

1. Tip of temporal lobe.
2. Junction of sylvian and presylvian fissures.
3. Ventral end of central fissure.
4. Junction of sylvian and episylvian fissures.
5. Caudal point.

MESAL SURFACE.

From the cephalic point to

6. Cephalic edge of callosum.
7. Porta (Foramen of Monro).
8. Dorsal end of central fissure.
9. Dorsal intersection of paracentral fissure.
10. Caudal edge of callosum.
11. Occipito-calcarine junction.
12. Dorsal intersection of occipital fissure.

The measurements of the cerebellum and pons are practically restricted to the principal diameters.

Unless otherwise mentioned, the length of a fissure was obtained by laying a wet string along its course. The fissural depths were determined by means of a flat sound with smooth rounded end and graduated in millimeters.

In the description of the fissures and gyres the author enployed the following schema in order to secure an orderly manner of treatment for all the brains:
The interlobar fissures:

The sylvian fissure and its rami (comprising the basisylvian, sylvian, presylvian, subsylvian, episylvian and hyposylvian).
The central fissure.
The occipital fissure.
The calcarine fissure.

Fissures of the frontal lobe :
(Lateral surface.)
Precentral fissural complex (comprising the supercentral, precentral and transprecentral).
Diagonal.
Superfrontal.
Paramesial.
Medifrontal.
Subfrontal.
Orbitofrontal.
Radiate.
(Mesal surface.)
Callosal.
Supercallosal.
Medicallosal.
Paracentral (and inflected).
Frontomarginal.
Rostral.
Subrostral.
Transrostral.

Orbital surface :
Orbital (and transorbital).
Olfactory.

Gyres of the frontal lobe :
(Lateral surface.)
Precentral.
Superfrontal.
(Inflected.)
Medifrontal.
Subfrontal.
(Mesal surface.)
Superfrontal.

Paracentral.
Callosal (in part).

Orbital surface:
Mesorbital.
Orbital gyres (various forms).
(Postorbital limbus.)

Fissures of the parietal and occipital lobes:
(Lateral surface.)
The postcentral fissural complex (comprising the postcentral, subcentral and transpostcentral).
Parietal.
Transparietal.
Paroccipital.
The exoccipital fissural complex.
Adoccipital.
Preparoccipital.
Postparoccipital.
Preoccipital (?).
Suboccipital (?).
Pomatic (?).
Lambdoidal (?).
Terminations of the supertemporal, episylvian and meditemporal fissures.
(Mesal surface.)
Precuneal.
Intraprecuneal.
Cuneal.
Postcuneal.

Gyres of the parietal and occipital lobes:
(Lateral surface.)
Postcentral.
Parietal.
Paroccipital.
Marginal.
Angular.
Postparietal.
(Mesal surface.)
Cuneus.

Precuneus.
Callosal (in part).
Fissures of the temporal lobe:
(Ventro-lateral surface.)
Supertemporal.
Meditemporal.
Subtemporal.
Collateral.
Postrhinal (or amygdaline).
Hippocampal.
(Dorsal or sylvian surface.)
Transtemporals.
Gyres of the temporal lobe:
Supertemporal.
Meditemporal.
Subtemporal.
Subcollateral.
Subcalcarine.
Transtemporals.
The insula:
Preinsula.
Postinsula.
Circuminsular fissure.
Transinsular fissure.
Insular fissures.

JOSEPH LEIDY.

Born in Philadelphia, September 9, 1823, son of Philip Leidy and Catherine Mellick. Joseph Leidy was the third of four children by this marriage. When but a year and a half old he experienced in the death of his mother a loss that would be usually regarded as irreparable. His father, however, in marrying shortly afterwards Christiana, the sister of his first wife, gave to Joseph one of whom he said upon one occasion, "I knew no other mother; to her I owe every advancement in life."

Joseph Leidy's early education was obtained at private schools. From his earliest days he was a great lover of nature and many authentic stories are told of days and months spent in the open air in the study of animal life in all its forms. At the age of nineteen he began the study of medicine at the University of Pennsylvania, gradnating in 1844, and practising thereafter for about two years. Leidy was not long, however, in recognizing that his true vocation lay in the untrodden domains of biology. During a long and active career he not only developed many new facts in zoology and comparative anatomy but he described many new forms of life, correlated the existing facts, deduced new laws therefrom and, in short, did the chief pioneer work in formulating the laws and fundamental principles of a systematic science of biology. While yet a student Dr. Leidy, by his skill in dissecting, had impressed Professor Hornor most favorably and he was, therefore, shortly after his graduation, appointed to the position of prosector to the chair of anatomy. In the summer of 1845 Dr. Leidy was elected a member of the Boston Society of Natural History, a great compliment for so young a man, and a few weeks later he was elected to the Academy of Natural Sciences of Philadelphia, with which institution his name was inseparably connected until the day of his death. Through the opportunities for advancement liberally afforded by this society, he was enabled to accomplish the scientific work of his life. He was chairman of its board of curators during the last forty-four years of his life. In 1848 and 1849 Dr. Leidy accompanied Dr. Hornor and Dr. George B. Wood on visits to Europe, affording him not only the opportunities of seeing the great museums of Europe under most pleasant auspices, but also of making the acquaintance and acquiring the friendship of such distinguished anatomists and physiologists as Owen, Majendie, Milne-Edwards, Hyrtl, Johannes Müller, and many others.

At the age of thirty he succeeded Dr. Hornor as professor of anatomy in the University of Pennsylvania. This position he held with the most distinguished success till his death, a period of nearly forty years. As a teacher of anatomy, and as director of the Biological Department of the University since its establishment in 1884, Joseph Leidy attained his undisputed preëminence because his knowledge of human anatomy was supplemented by familiarity in detail with the anatomy of every phase of animal life from the amoeba to the higher mammalia. He possessed a masterly ability to so present anatomic facts that this ordinarily dry and difficult subject became comparatively easy to master, chiefly because Leidy knew how to simplify his subject matter and convey it to others. His writings, comprising nearly 600 treatises, are equally notable for lucid expression, simplicity of presentation and accuracy of observation, and his book on Human Anatomy became the standard treatise in most medical schools.

Joseph Leidy's scientific work embraced many fields: Biology in all its branches, geology, mineralogy and botany, — in short the natural sciences as a whole. For an explicit description of these achievements the reader is referred to the more thorough review in Dr. Henry C. Chapman's memoir in the *Proceedings* of the Academy of Natural Sciences of Philadelphia of 1891.

It is indeed doubtful if any great character of history was so simple, so absolutely uninfluenced by honors, so unconceited, so just or so kindly as was Joseph Leidy. He was not only modest, but noticeably unobtrusive, though far from being a recluse. From the ordinary standpoint Dr. Leidy's life might be regarded as uneventful, probably because of his steadfast and unselfish devotion to the study of nature. He was never dogmatic or assertive even in those things that were indisputable. He sunk his personality in his science; a retrospect of his life reveals a long vista of achievements in which not a trace of self is perceptible; a long and useful career unsullied by a stain and characterized as much by its sweetness, simplicity and goodness as by its great mental achievements. Not only was he universally honored, respected and loved in life, but his fame as America's greatest naturalist will long endure after his death.

". . . The points of pathological interest were the presence of a hemorrhagic pachymeningitis on the right side and an unusual hardness (atheroma) of the blood-vessels at the base. . . ."

(From Jos. Leidy, Jr.)

The following note in the handwriting of J. A. Ryder, the preparator, accompanied the specimen:

"Brain of Professor Joseph Leidy, M.D. Removed May 1, 1891. Placed in refrigerator in Müller's fluid May 1, 1891. Ice kept in refrigerator till May 22. Kept in Müller's fluid at ordinary temperature from May 22 to June 10, 1891. Washed in water, June 10, to remove excess of Müller's and washings repeated till the 15th of June. Placed in 70 per cent. alcohol, June 15, 1891.

J. A. Ryder,
Custodian.

The weight of the fresh encephalon was reported to have been 45.5 oz. (Troy) by Professor Harrison Allen, who removed and weighed the brain. The brain of Dr. Philip Leidy, who died within 24 hours of Joseph, was also reported to have weighed 45.5 oz. (Troy) by Dr. Dercum who used the same scales and weights. The writer feels confident that the figure for Dr. Philip Leidy's brain-weight is correct, but is inclined to wholly reject the figure as given by Dr. Allen for the brain-weight of Joseph Leidy. Dr. Allen was much attached to Dr. Joseph Leidy and during the autopsy is said to have been very much affected and noticeably nervous. Dr. Dercum, who was present at the time, also thinks that Dr. Allen made an error in recording the brain-weight as cited.

I have attempted to justify my belief by calculations based on a comparison of the present weights and dimensions of the two Leidy brains, assuming that, inasmuch as the two men died practically together and the brains were subjected to very similar conditions of preservation and have lain immersed in like fluids for equal periods of time, any errors involved and allowances called for must be really very trifling.

I.

The present weights of the encephalic parts of the two Leidys are as follows:

	Joseph Leidy.	Philip Leidy.
Left hemicerebrum	565	525
Right hemicerebrum	595	522
Cerebellum	128 } 165	162
Pons and oblongata	37 }	
	1325	1209

A glance will show that while the weight of the isthmus and cerebellum is almost alike in the two brains, there is a material difference between the weights of the cerebral parts.

II.

Now assuming Philip Leidy's original brain-weight (1415 grams) to have been correct, we have:

$$1209 : 1415 :: 1325 : x.$$

The value of x is, therefore, 1550.

Again, multiplying the present figures of the weight of Philip Leidy's hardened brain by (approximately) 1.16 in order to obtain the original weights, we have:

Left hemicerebrum	615 }	Cerebrum 1225
Right hemicerebrum	610 }	
Cerebellum, pons and oblongata	190	
	1415 grams	

Endeavoring now to arrive at the weight of Joseph's cerebrum, we have:

$$1047 : 2125 :: 1160 : x.$$

The value of x is, therefore, 1356.

This leads us to assume that Joseph Leidy's brain must have weighed:

Left hemicerebrum	660
Right hemicerebrum	690 or more
Cerebellum, pons and oblongata	195
Approximately	1550 grams

III.

Next let us look at the relative dimensions of the two brains:

	Joseph Leidy.	Philip Leidy.
Max. length, left hemicerebrum .	17.9	15.6
Max. length, right hemicerebrum .	18.2	15.9
Max. width .	13.4	12.4
Circumference	51.0	46.2
Left centro-temporal height .	11.2	10.4
Right centro-temporal height	11.6	10.5
Left centro-olfactory height .	10.1	8.8
Right centro-olfactory height . .	10.2	8.8

Joseph Leidy's brain is even larger than that of Cope, which weighed 1545 grams.

IV.

In view of all this I am led to assume that the error must have arisen during the recording of the weight while in haste as well as under the stress of performing a necroscopy upon the body of a dear friend and associate.

THE CEREBRUM.

In all its parts the cerebrum shows a high degree of complexity, particularly in the parietal and occipital regions. Viewed dorsally, the cerebrum appears elliptical in shape, the left parieto-temporal region being the most prominent. The left frontal lobe, owing to some flattening while hardening appears less massive than the right, but is not so actually. Although fissural complexity prevails generally, the parieto-occipital regions show the highest degree of differentiation. The left frontal is more complex than the right but it is difficult to decide in which half the caudal regions preponderate in this respect. Generally speaking the right parieto-occipital areas seem more extensive than the left. Viewed laterally, and comparing the two sides, the left preoperculum is the better developed, and the right parieto-occipital and parieto-temporal transitions preponderate over the corresponding regions of the left side. Viewed ventrally, the right temporal lobe is broader, more massive and more richly fissured, and the same may be said for the orbital surface of the right frontal lobe. The right occipital pole, as is usual, is slightly deflected laterad, but appears to be, nevertheless, more massive than the left. Taking the brain as a whole, the right side seems to preponderate in not a few respects. Its greater weight, together with the more complex degree of fissuration and the greater extent of the caudal parts quite over-balances the high degree of development of the left frontal region. In measuring the horizontal semi-circumferences no appreciable difference can be found between the two sides.

The unusual dimensions of the callosum call for comment. The writer cannot recall having ever before seen this structure of such great size as in the brain of PROFESSOR J. LEIDY. Its cross-section area is 10.606 sq. cm., nearly twice the average size. Its great length, 8.5 cm., or 46.7 per cent. of the total hemicerebral length, is striking. At the genu its thickness is 11 mm., the average thickness of the body is 9 mm., while the maximum thickness of the splenium is 16.5 mm. It is the caudal part of the callosum which is particularly massive, and that portion of the splenium which "rolls under" (the "cauda corporis callosi" of Retzius and the *splenium propre* of BEEVOR) is certainly of unusual size. In the chapter on the comparison of the brains of PROFESSOR COPE and J. LEIDY, these features will be discussed in detail.

LEFT HEMICEREBRUM. THE INTERLOBAR FISSURES. *The Sylvian Fissure and its Rami.* — The length of the sylvian from its presylvian junction to the episylvian is 6.3 cm. Its course is moderately sinuous and its walls are in close apposition. Its angle with the plane passing through the ventral margins of the frontal and occipital poles is 29°. Its depth at the presylvian point is 13 mm.; medisylvian 18 mm.; postsylvian, 27 mm. The presylvian ramus is 1.1 cm. in length and springs from the sylvian much further caudad than on the right side, and more so than in most brains. The subsylvian ramus is short but well marked, and anastomoses cephalad with an independent segment (possibly of the orbito-frontal).

The basisylvian, measured from the tip of the temporal lobe is 20–21 mm. in depth. Caudad the sylvian terminates in a short (7 mm.) episylvian ramus. There is no hyposylvian.

The Central Fissure. — The length of the central on this side is 10.3 cm., a trifle longer than that of the right, as well as much more sinuous and more ramified. It anastomoses cephalad with the supercentral and caudad with the subcentral. The general direction of the fissure makes an angle of about 60° with the intercerebral cleft.

The Occipital Fissure. — The length on the meson is 3.5 cm.; on the convex surface 1.3 cm. At a point 1.3 cm. distant from the occipito-calcarine junction, the fissure is joined by an unusually long and well-marked adoccipital, giving rise to an apparent bifurcation of the occipital, not infrequently noted in some other brains.* The fissure makes an angle of about 50° with the (arbitrary) horizontal plane chosen in these studies, an extreme opposite to the very much greater angle described by this fissure in the brain of PROFESSOR COPE. In Leidy's case this caudal deviation of the fissure is due to the interpolation of a well-marked *cuneolus, i. e.*, the wedge-shaped piece marked off by the adoccipital.

* In the brain of DR. COUDEREAU there was an apparent trifurcation of the occipital.

The Calcarine Fissure.—The calcarine and postcalcarine parts join to form a simple uninterrupted fissure of quite sinuous course. Its total length is 6.2 cm.

The occipital and calcarine fissures meet at considerable depth and continue as the occipito-calcarine stem, passing cephalad for 3 cm. to within 1 cm. of the hippocampal fissure.

FISSURES OF THE FRONTAL LOBE (LATERAL SURFACE). *The Precentral Fissural Complex.*—The supercentral fissure is of the usual zygal shape, anastomosing cephalad directly with the superfrontal and caudad with the central. Both the dorsal and ventral limbs are long, so that the entire lateral extent of the fissure reaches 6.5 cm. Separated from the supercentral by an isthmus is the tortuous and well-marked precentral fissure. The precentral dips into the sylvian cleft, while its cephalodorsal ramus (Quain's "anterior precentral ramus") anastomoses with the medifrontal. There is no transprecentral and no diagonal fissure on this half.

The superfrontal fissure is well-marked, extensive, and though quite ramified, does not pursue a very tortuous course. It is 8.8 cm. in length, and runs fairly parallel to the intercerebral cleft. Three paramesial segments mark the superfrontal gyre, imperfectly dividing the convolution into two longitudinal tiers. In the prefrontal region there is a marked tendency to transverse fissuration.

The medifrontal fissure, from its origin at the precentral ramus, passes cephalad for 3 cm. to end in a Y-shaped manner. The fissure is a good example of the compound zygal forms, the two zygons joining by a ramus and stipe respectively.

Rather unusual appearances are presented by the subfrontal. The main (longitudinal) portion is extremely short, terminating cephalad in an irregular radiate fissure, while caudad it sends a long ramus toward the Sylvian, parallel with the radiate. Dorsad it gives off three short rami. The orbitofrontal may be traced as an irregular, but fairly extensive fissure, in a part of its course resembling an additional medifrontal segment.

MESIAL SURFACE.—The supercallosal sweeps cephalad uninterruptedly from its junction with the paracentral for 12.5 cm., terminating just ventrad of the rostrum. The paracentral is rather short and irregular; its caudal limb is tortuous and anastomoses superficially with the central fissure: the cephalic limb is straight. There is also an intraparacentral ramus. There is no inflected fissure. The frontomarginal fissure is particularly well marked in this case; except for a slight interruption just cephalad of the genu, it attains a length of 11 cm., joining the rostral fissure cephalad. The rostral fissure is 4.5 cm. in length; a short subrostral is also present, anastomosing with the olfactory fissure. The terminal hook of the supercallosal bears some resemblance to the *transrostral* of RETZIUS.

Orbital Surface.—Two fissural segments mark the orbital surface, each of zygal shape. The larger caudal one has a transverse zygon or stem, with two long cephalic rami embracing the smaller segment. The olfactory fissure is about 4 cm. in length and anastomoses with the subrostral, as described above.

Gyres of the Frontal Lobe (Lateral Surface).—The precentral gyre is massive and complex. The superfrontal is of usual size, but tends to partial subdivision in a longitudinal manner, owing to the paramesial fissural segments. The medifrontal gyre is notably extensive, and intricately fissured, particularly by transverse pieces. The subfrontal area is not of the common form, but seems rather made up of three convolutions separated by transverse fissures (one of these being the radiate). These fissures are very deep, and the cortical expanse in this area is doubtlessly greater than in average brains.

Mesal Surface.—The marked fissuration of the superfrontal gyre on the mesal surface by means of the long, tortuous and much-ramified frontomarginal fissure gives it a complex appearance. The paracentral gyre is rather small. The frontal portion of the callosal gyre is simple.

Orbital Surface.—The mesorbital gyre is narrow. The remainder of this surface may be said to be divided into a preorbital and a postorbital region by the larger of the two zygal orbital fissures. The preorbital region consists of a V-shaped gyre embracing a quadrate area within the cephalic arms of the smaller orbital fissures. The postorbital region is of a simple conformation, indented by an orbital limb of the basisylvian cleft. Mesad and laterad of the larger orbital fissure there are gyral portions of fair size.

Fissures of the Parietal and Occipital Lobes (Lateral Surface). *The Postcentral Fissural Complex.*—The dorsal postcentral segment is readily identified. It is 4 cm. in length, anastomoses superficially with the caudal limb of the paracentral but is otherwise independent. In seeking out the representation of the subcentral we meet with such exceedingly intricate foldings in the region comprising the ventral portion of the postcentral gyre and the marginal gyre that it is difficult to determine the exact interpretation of all the features presented here. The irregular tri-radiate fissure, whose limbs anastomose, cephalad with the central and caudad with the parietal, while doubtlessly the subcentral is certainly of unusual appearance. Between its ventral ramus and the end of the central lies the Y-shaped transpostcentral, dipping into the sylvian cleft.

The fissure lying dorsad of the subcentral and for the greater part of its course running parallel with the dorsal limbs of the subcentral is the parietal. The peculiar arrangement of the fissures in this region requires particular attention. At a point directly dorsad of the episylvian ramus there occurs an anastomosis of three fissures, viz.: the subcentral, parietal, and intermedial. The gyre between the parietal and subcentral dips below the general surface as it passes caudad, and by means of the indenting ramus near its end has the appearance of a dimple, or cortical islet, from which radiate a number of fissural rami. The appearance is a very unusual one, and is best seen in Fig. 24.

The paroccipital is notable for the length and direction of its zygon or stem. This is 3.5 cm. in length, and converges towards the median line cephalad, instead of being parallel to or converging toward this plane caudally, as is seen in ordinary brains. RÜDINGER describes a similar feature in the brain of JUSTUS V. LIEBIG, where the redundancy of the paroccipital gyre is apparently so great as to push the corresponding fissure far laterad. In LEIDY's case it is the caudal arm of the paroccipital gyre which is immensely developed, and hence the caudo-lateral deviation of the main course of the fissure. The cephalic paroccipital stipe is short and passes near the occipital; the cephalic ramus bifurcates to embrace the parietal, and the mesial limb anastomoses with a transparietal piece. The caudal ramus and stipe together form a T-shaped ending* passing parallel with the ventro-lateral border of the hemicerebrum, instead of approximately vertical to it, as is the rule.

Between the episylvian and the terminal portion of the supertemporal lies an intermedial fissure of more complex arrangement than is common. It is irregularly zygal in shape and one of its rami anastomoses deeply at the site of the subcentral-parietal junction.

The fissuration in the occipito-temporal transition is so intricate in this case that in the present state of our knowledge concerning the interpretation of these fissures no definite statements can be made. It is to be hoped that further studies may help to elucidate some of the problems presented here.

MESIAL SURFACE. — The precuneal fissure is of the usual zygal shape with a short stem or zygon running parallel with the callosal fissure. The cephalic rami are both long; the dorsal one reaching the dorsi-mesal margin. A short intraprecuneal lies dorsad.

The adoccipital fissure, marking off a *cuneolus* has been described on page 246. The cuneus is quite intricately marked by three fissural segments, one of which passes well onto the convex surface in the redundant arm of the paroccipital gyre.

GYRES OF THE PARIETAL AND OCCIPITAL LOBES (LATERAL SURFACE). — The postcentral gyre is unusually massive, particularly in its middle and ventral portions. It

* Called by ECKER the "transverse occipital," and supposed by him to represent a part of the "Affenspalte"; see, however, the writer's paper, "The Fissural Integrality of the Paroccipital," 1900.

is interrupted by the junction of the subcentral with the central and the other neighboring fissures and their rami help to make the gyre quite a tortuous one. The parietal gyre is of complex appearance but not particularly large. The unusual shape of the paroccipital has been alluded to above. It should here be noted however that the most striking feature is that the caudal arm (*i. e.*, the postoccipital portion) of the paroccipital gyre is tenfold greater in area than the cephalic area. Its great width has caused the marked lateral deviation of the paroccipital fissure as it passes caudad,

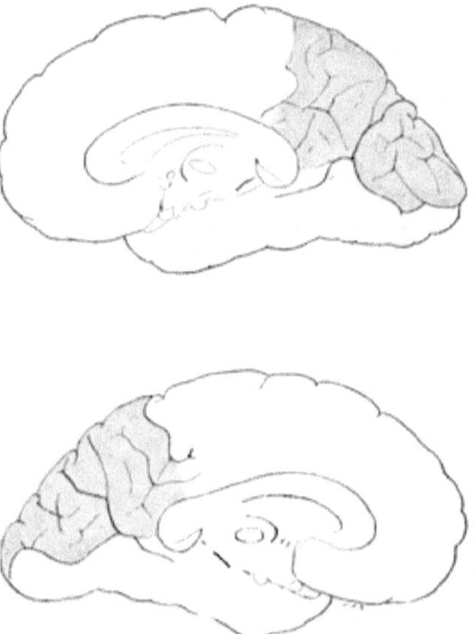

FIG. 22. Mesal aspects of the cerebral halves of Joseph Leidy. The cuneus and precuneus are shaded. The upper figure shows the mesal aspect of the right half; the lower figure shows the left half.

and this feature is perhaps of not a little significance in relation to LEIDY's observational powers. Whatever psycho-physical interpretation may attach to the redundancy of this part of the paroccipital, it cannot be denied that it is an expression of the highest development of the *première pli de passage externe* of the anthropoids.

The marginal and angular gyral districts present very interesting features. The marginal in particular is of most complex configuration and seems to portray the wonderful powers of associational and dissociational observation which PROFESSOR LEIDY possessed in life; the somatical-psychological aspect of this proposition will be discussed in the sequel.

The cuneus and precuneus together with the interpolated cuneolus present a wide expanse in sharp contrast with the reduced corresponding areas in the brain of PROFESSOR COPE.

FISSURES OF THE TEMPORAL LOBE (LATERO-VENTRAL SURFACE). — The supertemporal fissure pursues a very tortuous course. Its length, measured with a moist string, is 15 cm. At its middle third it makes several sharp turns, and throughout its course it gives off a number (6–7) of rami. One long ramus traverses the meditemporal gyre and reaches to the ventro-lateral border of the hemicerebrum. The caudal termination of the fissure in the gyre embraced by the paroccipital and its cephalic ramus is simple. Near the cephalic terminus of the fissure, at what appears like a zygal segment, there is a small sunken area or "islet," due to a peculiar rolling over, or opercular formation of the adjacent meditemporal gyre.

The course of the meditemporal fissure can be traced along two segments. The subtemporal pursues an unusual course. Cephalad it anastomoses with the collateral; it then passes caudo-laterad in a tortuous manner, reaches the ventro-lateral border, and passes onto the convex surface to anastomose with a meditemporal segment. Another piece lies further caudad, but this also anastomoses with the collateral near its middle. The arrangement of the collateral and subtemporal fissures is that of a stem with two branches on one side of it.

The collateral fissure, aside from the two anastomoses above mentioned presents nothing unusual. Its length is 10 cm. The post-rhinal (or amygdaline) fissure is only indicated by a shallow groove.

GYRES OF THE TEMPORAL LOBE. — All the gyres of the temporal lobe are notable for their massiveness, breadth and complexity. The supertemporal gyre is quite tortuous, the subtemporal quite massive. The subcollateral makes up in breadth what it loses in length by the peculiar anastomosis of the subtemporal with the collateral. The subcalcarine and hippocampal gyres are clean-cut and well-shaped.

THE INSULA. — The insula shows a good development. The gyres are full and the intervening fissures quite deep. There are five preinsular gyres, while the postinsular gyre is subdivided into two caudal portions, giving seven peri-insular digitations. Compared with the right insula it exhibits a superior degree of differentiation.

RIGHT HEMICEREBRUM. THE INTERLOBAR FISSURES. *The Sylvian Fissure and its Rami.* — The sylvian fissure is slightly sinuous, its walls are in close apposition, and its caudal termination is simple, there being no sharp turn in passing into the episylvian. There is a short hyposylvian. The length of the sylvian proper, between the presylvian and its junction with the epi- and hyposylvian rami is 4.2 cm. The presylvian is simple, 1.8 cm. in length; the subsylvian, 2 cm. in length, anastomoses with the radiate. The episylvian appears as the direct continuation of the sylvian, though an examination of its depths shows it to spring from the caudal angle of the circuminsular fissure. Its length is 2.6 cm. The hyposylvian ramus is a trifle over 1 cm. in length.

The Central Fissure.—The central fissure, 10 cm. in length, pursues a much straighter course than on the left side. It anastomoses with the supercentral. In its general direction it makes an angle of 62° with the intercerebral cleft.

The Occipital Fissure.—Its length on the meson is 2.8 cm., on the dorsum 2 cm. At a point 1.7 cm. from the occipito-calcarine junction, the fissure is joined by an adoccipital of lesser extent than on the left half, but giving a similar appearance of "bifurcation" of the occipital. The fissure makes an angle of about 52° with our horizontal plane.

The Calcarine Fissure.—The calcarine fissure springs from its junction with the occipital almost as if a continuation of the latter, so that the angle of the cuneus is exceedingly obtuse (150°). The fissure then sweeps caudad in a sinuous manner for 5.7 cm., terminating at the occipital pole. A cuneal fissure joins it in its caudal third. The occipito-calcarine stem is 3.8 cm. in length.

Fissures of the Frontal Lobe (Lateral Surface). *The Precentral Fissural Complex.*—The supercentral is a tri-radiate fissure whose cephalic arm is continuous with the superfrontal. The ventral ramus joins the central. The precentral is of zygal shape, the dorso-cephalic ramus being continuous with the medifrontal. The transprecentral, springing from the sylvian cleft, but otherwise independent, is 1.5 cm. in length.

The diagonal, 3.5 cm. in length, lies just cephalad of the precentral, is superficially confluent with the sylvian and anastomoses cephalad with the subfrontal. The superfrontal is a tortuous fissure, passing well cephalad without interruption with a length 9 cm. The medifrontal is exceedingly well marked. Springing from the precentral it pursues a very tortuous course, sending off a number of rami, and terminating in a bifurcation, the lateral limb anastomosing with the orbitofrontal. Its total length is 7 cm. The subfrontal is a more extensive fissure than that of the left side. It anastomoses with both the diagonal and the orbitofrontal.

The orbitofrontal is a very tortuous combination of segments. It anastomoses with the subfrontal and medifrontal fissures, and reaches to the mesial border. Its length, measured with a wet string, is 7.5 cm. The radiate, 3.5 cm. in length, anastomoses with the subsylvian, the subfrontal, and superficially with the orbitofrontal.

MESIAL SURFACE. — The supercallosal, measured from its junction with the paracentral, is 12.5 cm. in length. It sends off a number of rami, several of which join frontomarginal segments in the superfrontal gyre. The paracentral is a moderately sinuous fissure; its caudal limb passes vertically, while the cephalic limb is barely indicated by a slight notch. There is an intraparacentral piece of zygal shape whose course is parallel to the main fissure, and whose cephalic rami lie in the ideal prolongation of the cephalic limb bounding the paracentral gyre. Dorsad of this, across the dorsi-mesal margin lies a tri-radiate piece which may represent the inflected (not unlike that seen in the brain of the Eskimo "NOOKTAH," right hemicerebrum; see the writer's paper, 1902).

There are two medicallosal segments in the callosal gyre; a long one (1.5 cm.) lying dorsad of the callosum, a shorter one cephalad of the genu.

The rostral fissure is 5 cm. in length, while an irregular subrostral passes over the margin to lie cephalad of the olfactory fissure.

ORBITAL SURFACE. — The arrangement of the orbital fissures resembles that of the left half, but the transorbital segment is better marked. On the whole, the orbital surface of this side is of a more complex appearance. The olfactory fissure is 4.2 cm. in length.

GYRES OF THE FRONTAL LOBE (LATERAL SURFACE). — The precentral gyre is of uniform breadth and of a good size. It is traversed by the central-supercentral anastomosis and indented by short rami of the central and precentral. The superfrontal is quite broad and distinctly demarcated. Six fissural segments, generally of transverse direction mark its surface. The medifrontal is notable for its great breadth and for its distinct division into two tiers. The transverse breadth of the medifrontal district averages about 4 cm., a large dimension as compared with ordinary brains. The subfrontal gyre is correspondingly reduced to a width of about 2.5 cm., and is in every way smaller than its fellow on the left side. All the frontal gyres may be described as well-developed and as particularly complex in the prefrontal region.

MESIAL SURFACE. — On the mesial surface the superfrontal gyre is of good uniform width, marked by several rami of the supercallosal and by a number of frontomarginal segments. The paracentral gyre is of rectangular shape, and taking the cephalic limbs of the intraparacentral as representing the ideal continuation of the abbreviated cephalic limb of the paracentral proper, the gyre has a length of 4 cm.; somewhat greater than on the left side. The frontal portion of the callosal gyre exhibits a tendency to subdivision by two medicallosal segments.

ORBITAL SURFACE. — This surface is rather more complex in appearance than that of the left half, due to the greater number of fissures and to their increased ramification. It should be mentioned here that the mesorbital gyre is very narrow.

FISSURES OF THE PARIETAL AND OCCIPITAL LOBES (LATERAL SURFACE). *The Postcentral Fissural Complex.* — There is a triradiate postcentral piece whose dorsal rami embrace the extremity of the caudal paracentral limb. The subcentral is the more important element in the postcentral complex. Dorsad it is confluent with a segment of the parietal, ventrad it dips into the episylvian, while its length is 4.5 cm. In its course it sends a ramus well across the postcentral gyre and caudad it joins the curved intermedial. There is also a distinct transpostcentral.

The parietal fissure presents unusual features. An isthmus near its middle breaks up the fissure into two segments; the cephalic one being confluent with the subcentral, while the caudal one is independent and sends off two long rami, dorsi-cephalad and ventro-caudad, respectively. A narrow isthmus separates it from the paroccipital. The paroccipital is of the usual zygal shape and anastomoses caudo-ventrad with one of the exoccipital elements. The cephalic stipe is embraced between the occipital and adoccipital.

Two exoccipital elements can be made out on this half. Both are tri-radiate; the dorsal one is confluent with the paroccipital and with a cuneal fissure; the ventral one is independent. The latter is interesting because there is a decided opercular formation of the part constituting the caudal wall of this fissure. It stands out quite prominently and caps over a part of the fissure and the adjacent (depressed) gyres.

In the subparietal area the fissuration is very intricate. The up-turned end of the supertemporal joins the parietal over a vadum. There is a curved intermedial between the last-mentioned fissure and the episylvian, also joining the parietal.

MESIAL SURFACE. — The precuneal fissure is zygal and anastomoses with the paracentral. Other segments help to make the precuneus of complex appearance. The cuneus is also well supplied with fissures, there being three well-defined elements, one of them joining the calcarine fissure.

GYRES OF THE PARIETAL AND OCCIPITAL LOBES (LATERAL SURFACE). — The postcentral gyre is very broad throughout. The parietal is large and complicated. The paroccipital is of very good extent, and, similar to the same gyre on the left side, is small in its cephalic portion, but broad caudad of the occipital fissure.

In the sub-parietal region, comprising the marginal, angular and post-parietal gyres, we see the great breadth and massiveness as well as the regular complexity of configuration so distinctive of this brain in the "posterior association area." Compared with the left side it is not only more intricately fissured, but because of its somewhat greater mass it encroaches further upon its sylvian cleft, materially shortening it.

Mesial Surface.—The cuneus and precuneus are both of much greater extent and also rather more richly fissured than the corresponding parts of the left half.[3] The markedly obtuse angle of the cuneus at the point of junction of the occipital and calcarine fissures is quite notable. The cuneolus on this side is smaller than on the left.

Fissures of the Temporal Lobe (Ventro-lateral Surface).—The supertemporal fissure is well-developed, quite sinuous and attains the great length of 14 cm. It anastomoses with a meditemporal segment and superficially with the parietal. The meditemporal is represented by four independent segments of which the caudal one is quite complex. Two fissural pieces represent the subtemporal; the cephalic one is tri-radiate and communicates with a meditemporal segment. The collateral is not very long. An independent part of it, cephalad, joins the postrhinal (amygdaline) groove.

Gyres of the Temporal Lobe.—The supertemporal gyre is narrow cephalad but broadens out very much in the region of transition into the subparietal lobule (*i. e.*, marginal gyre). There is a compensatory cephalic widening of the meditemporal gyre, the caudal part being of moderate width. The subtemporal gyre is of the usual dimensions except in its caudal part where it broadens out in the transition into the very redundant expanse of the postparietal region.

The Insula.—The right insula resembles that of the left in most respects but is slightly less massive as shown by the depths of the Sylvian. The preinsular region is not so expansive and the transinsular fissure passes further cephalad than on the left side.

Principal Measurements of the Cerebrum.

(*After Hardening.*)

	Centimeters.
Maximum length, left hemicerebrum	17.9
Maximum length, right hemicerebrum	18.2
Maximum width of cerebrum (cerebral index = 74.9)	13.4
Horizontal circumference	51
Maximum width, left hemicerebrum	6.7
Maximum width, right hemicerebrum	6.7
Left occipito-temporal length	13.2
Right occipito temporal length	13.3
Length of callosum	8.5
or 46.7 per cent. of total cerebral length.	

[3] Pieces of sheet-lead, of uniform thickness and density, as ascertained by a number of control-tests, cut of the same size as the visible surface of the precuneus and cuneus together weighed as follows: Left, 31.8 gms.; right, 35 gms. Ratio of left to right as 100 : 110.

PRINCIPAL MEASUREMENTS OF THE CEREBRUM.

Right centro-temporal height	11.2
or 62.57 centesimals, in terms of total cerebral length.	
Right centro-temporal height	11.6
or 64.26 centesimals.	
Left centro-olfactory height	10.1
Right centro-olfactory height	10.2

ARC MEASURES ALONG THE DORSI-MESAL MARGIN.

(*Cunningham's Method.*)

LEFT HEMICEREBRUM.

	Centimeters.
1. Cephalic point to central fissure	16.
2. Central fissure to occipital fissure	7.2
3. Occipital fissure to occipital pole	5.9

RIGHT HEMICEREBRUM.

1. Cephalic point to central fissure	16.0
2. Central fissure to occipital fissure	6.5
3. Occipital fissure to occipital pole	6.8

CEREBRAL INDICES.

(*Based on Arc Measures given above.*)

	Left.	Right.
Frontal index	54.95	54.60
Parietal index	24.74	22.18
Occipital index	20.27	23.12

HORIZONTAL DISTANCES.

(Expressed in centesimals of the total hemicerebral lengths.)

From the Cephalic Point to	Left.	Right.
1. Tip of temporal lobe	28.8	26.9
2. Sylvian-presylvian junction	33.8	30.2
3. Ventral end of Central f.	40.5	42.3
4. Sylvian-episylvian junction	67.2	51.1
5. Caudal point	100.0	100.0
6. Cephalic edge of callosum	18.8	18.4
7. Porta (Foramen of Monro)	40.2	40.1
8. Dorsal end of central f.	57.5	57.7
9. Dorsal intersection of paracentral f.	70.0	62.9
10. Caudal edge of callosum	66.6	64.7
11. Occipito-calcarine junction	75.5	76.1
12. Dorsal intersection of occipital f.	87.2	86.8

CEREBELLUM—PONS, OBLONGATA.—These parts all show a good degree of development. A notable feature is the great size and massiveness of the pons and parts connected with it. The postgemina are smaller, but stand out higher, while the praegemina are larger, broader and more rounded off.

The cerebellar peduncles, particularly the pre- and medipeduncles are seen, on section, to be of great massiveness.

MEASUREMENTS OF THE CEREBELLUM.

	Centimeters.
Maximum height	5.6
Maximum cephalo-caudal diameter, left hemisphere	6.4
Maximum cephalo-caudal diameter, right hemisphere	6.5
Dorsal length of vermis	3.6
Maximum depth, caudal incisure	1.5
Maximum lateral width	10.1
MEASUREMENTS OF THE PONS.	
Maximum length	2.9
Maximum thickness	3.0

DR. PHILIP LEIDY.

Born in Philadelphia, December 29, 1838, son of Philip Leidy and Christiana Taliana Mellick.* With the exception of his paternal grandmother, Catherine Le Febre, the sister of Francis Joseph Le Febre, Duke of Dantzig, Marshal under Napoleon I, he was of German extraction. The original Carl Ludwig Leidy (Leydig) emigrated to America in 1727 from the Rheinish-Palatinate (Oberstein).

Dr. Leidy's grandfather, Jacob Leidy, served in the American Revolution as Ensign, 1777–1778; subsequently promoted to First Lieutenant in Capt. John Cope's Company, Pennsylvania Line. His great uncle, Dr. John Leidy, was commissioned Surgeon in the American Revolution, in the command of Col. Timothy Green, Pennsylvania Line. His father, Philip Leidy, served in the war of 1812 and Mexican war, 1845.

* Joseph and Philip Leidy were half-brothers whose mothers were half-sisters. The relationship may be shown as follows:

brothers

Peter Mellick × Miss Clingman — Michael Mellick × Miss Christian

Catherine Mellick — Christiana Mellick

John Jacob Leydig × Catherine LeFebre
1st Lieut. American Revolution; Pennsylvania Line. — sister of Francis Joseph LeFebre (Duke of Dantzig)

Philip Leidy 1st × Catherine Mellick
Philip Leidy 1st × Christiana Mellick

Catherine was Joseph's mother while Philip Leidy II. was the son of Christiana.

Dr. Leidy was educated by private tutors and in the public schools of Philadelphia. Matriculated in the Medical Department, University of Pennsylvania, 1857. His student days were spent in the office of his brother and preceptor, Prof. Joseph Leidy. Graduated in medicine 1859. Was immediately appointed Resident Physician, Philadelphia Hospital (Blockley). Entered the United States service, War of Rebellion, as Examiner of Recruits, June 8, 1861. Assigned at the first battle of Bull Run to the 106th Regiment, Pennsylvania Volunteers, as Assistant Surgeon with the rank of First Lieutenant. After the battle of Balls Bluff, established the *first* general field hospital of the war, near Poolesville, Maryland. Was in all the engagements of the army during the Peninsula campaign. His ability for organization attracted the attention of his superior officers, which resulted in his transfer to the 119th Regiment, Pennsylvania Volunteers, as Surgeon with the rank of Major, with a special detail to establish the Wager Hospital, the first general hospital in the Shenandoah at Bolivar Heights, 1862. Shortly after he was appointed Assistant Medical Director of General Sumner's Division, Post Surgeon at Winchester, Virginia, and Director of the Department of the Shenandoah on General Sheridan's Staff. Later, Surgeon-in-Chief 3d Brigade, 1st Division, 6th Army Corps. One of the Chief Operating and Consulting Surgeons of the 6th Army Corps. During 1864–65, Surgeon-in-Chief of the hospitals of the 6th Army Corps during the siege of Richmond and Petersburg. Dr. Leidy served upon special detail duty in every engagement of the Army of the Potomac, and with General Sheridan in the Valley of Virginia. At the close of the war Dr. Leidy was tendered but declined the appointment of Surgeon in the medical department of the Regular Army.

From 1866–1870 he was United States Examining Surgeon at Philadelphia. From 1873–1882 Port Physician of the city of Philadelphia; 1884 Physician-in-Chief of the insane department of the Philadelphia Hospital; 1886 appointed Consulting Physician to the same institution. Dr. Leidy served various charitable institutions in Philadelphia in a consulting capacity. He was the author of various articles upon medical and scientific subjects and of reports to the medical and surgical department of the War of the Rebellion.

President of the Medico-Chirurgical Society of Philadelphia; President Northern Medical Society, Philadelphia; member of the College of Physicians, Board of Education, and of various medical and scientific societies. Died April 30, 1891.

(Above notes computed from the records of the United States War Department, etc.)

Dr. Leidy died of the broncho-pneumonia of grippe. The brain was removed and weighed by Dr. F. X. Dercum. The encephalic blood-vessels presented numerous mustardseed-like patches of atheroma but nothing else unusual. The brain was preserved in Müller's fluid and later transferred to alcohol. Casts of the cerebral halves and of the cerebellum, pons and oblongata (in one piece) were subsequently made under Dr. Dercum's supervision.

The brain was weighed while fresh, by Dr. Dercum, with the same scales which Dr. H. Allen employed in weighing the brain of Joseph Leidy. Troy weights were used. The brain-weight of Philip Leidy, as determined by Dr. Dercum, was 45.5 oz. (Troy) equivalent to 1415 grams. The weights of the encephalic parts on November 2, 1904, were as follows:

Left hemicerebrum . .	525 grams.
Right hemicerebrum .	522 "
Cerebellum, pons and oblongata	162
Total . . .	1209 grams.

The loss in weight through the removal of the pia-arachnoid and through the action of the preservatives during the long period of immersion (1891–1904) amounts to 206 grams or 14.5 per cent. of the original weight.

THE CEREBRUM.

The cerebrum shows a high degree of complexity and richness of fissuration in all its parts. Viewed dorsally the right half appears slightly longer. Except for the more prominent fronto-lateral curve and blunter occipital pole on the left side the cerebrum is quite symmetrical in form. Viewed laterally and comparing the two sides, the left preoperculum is seen to be the better developed and, as in the brain of Joseph Leidy, the right sub-parietal areas are much more extensive. Viewed ventrally the right temporal lobe appears more massive while the left temporal is more richly fissured; the same comment applies to the appearances of the orbital surfaces. The left semi-circumference is 22.8 cm.; the right semi-circumference it 23.4 cm.

Although the callosum in this brain is not as large as that of Joseph Leidy it is of unusual proportions. The callosal length is 8 cm., nearly 1 cm. above the average; and while the average in ordinary brains is equivalent to less than 42 per cent. of the total cerebral length, in this specimen it is equal to 50.6 per cent. Even the large callosum of Joseph Leidy, 8.5 cm. in length, is equivalent to 46.7 per cent. of the cerebral length. The cross-section area of the callosum in the brain of Philip Leidy is 7.01 sq. cm., while the average in ten ordinary brains was found to be 5.63 sq. cm. Other structures, so far as the fragility of the specimen permitted of more or less thorough examination, were of normal and average form and size.

LEFT HEMICEREBRUM. *The Interlobar Fissures. The Sylvian Fissure and its Rami.* — The length of the sylvian fissure from its presylvian junction to the episylvian is 4.8 cm. The sylvian angle is 20°. The depths are as follows: Presylvian, 12 mm.; medi-sylvian, 18 mm.; post-sylvian, 31 mm. The presylvian ramus is 2 cm. in length. There is no subsylvian ramus present. Caudad the sylvian terminates in an episylvian with but slight change in direction and a hyposylvian ramus anastomoses with the supertemporal fissure.

The Central Fissure. — The length of the central fissure is 10.5 cm., or 1 cm. longer than that of the right as well as much more sinuous and more ramified. A slight vadum separates it from the supercentral.

The Occipital Fissure. — The length on the meson is 3.5 cm.; on the convex surface, 1.5 cm. The fissure is quite deep and the interdigitating subgyres are well marked. Near the dorsi-mesal margin it is joined by a small tri-radiate adoccipital. As in the brain of Joseph Leidy the occipital fissure makes an angle of about 50° with our horizontal plane.

The Calcarine Fissure. — The calcarine and postcalcarine elements join to form an uninterrupted fissure of moderately sinuous course. Its total length is 5.2 cm. The occipito-calcarine stem is 2 cm. in length.

Fissures of the Frontal Lobe (Lateral Surface). The Precentral Fissural Complex. — The supercentral fissure is of the usual zygal shape, anastomosing cephalad with the superfrontal. Measuring along the full extent of the dorsal and ventral limbs the fissure has a length of 6.5 cm. The precentral is quite tortuous and ramified. It anastomoses over a vadum with the diagonal and transprecentral elements which in this specimen are so closely crowded as to appear practically merged.

The superfrontal fissure is represented by two well-marked segments. Two paramesial pieces, one quite small, mark the superfrontal gyre. In the prefrontal region transverse fissuration prevails.

The medifrontal fissure is characterized by marked tortuosity and numerous ramifications; its extent is quite considerable. The subfrontal is a rather short but tortuous fissure quite independent of all neighboring fissures. There is one distinct orbitofrontal segment.

Mesal Surface. — The supercallosal sweeps cephalad uninterruptedly from its junction with the paracentral for 7 cm., terminating just cephalad of the genu (callosi). The paracentral is of simple form and average extent. There is an independent intraparacentral piece, but no inflected fissure. The frontomarginal segments are very well marked; there are three distinct pieces of which the cephalic one anastomoses with the rostral fissure. The rostral is 4 cm. in length; there is also a shorter subrostral.

Orbital Surface. — The orbital fissure is quite complexly ramified. The olfactory fissure is 4 cm. in length.

Gyres of the Frontal Lobe (Lateral Surface). — The precentral gyre is sinuous and of lesser width than its fellow on the right. The superfrontal is of moderate width. The medifrontal is quite extensive and complexly marked by the medifrontal fissure with its numerous branches. The perfect continuity of the medifrontal fissure tends to produce the "four-tier type" of frontal lobe in one portion at least. The subfrontal gyre of this side is more distinctly demarcated than its fellow on the right. (Compared with that of Joseph Leidy it is relatively smaller.)

The mesal surface is quite definitely divided into three tiers by the concentric and fairly distinct supercallosal and frontomarginal fissures. The paracentral gyre is of good size and regular shape. The frontal portion of the callosal gyre is quite simple and only slightly marked by a medicallosal groove.

Orbital Surface. — The left mesorbital gyre is broader than that of the right. The rest of this surface is quite complexly marked by the much-ramified orbital fissure. A postorbital limbus is present.

Fissures of the Parietal and Occipital Lobes (Lateral Surface). The Postcentral Fissural Complex. — The dorsal postcentral segment is a wholly independent zygal fissure of limited extent. The subcentral is directly continuous with the parietal fissure and anastomoses with the transpostcentral dipping into the sylvian cleft.

The parietal fissure is 4.5 cm. in length and anastomoses caudad with the paroccipital, ventrad with the supertemporal. There is a T-shaped transparietal communicating at the dorsi-mesal margin with the intraprecuneal. The paroccipital is of the usual zygal shape.

Mesal Surface. — The precuneal fissure is irregularly zygal and anastomoses with the paracentral and intraprecuneal fissures. The adoccipital fissure has been mentioned in the description of the occipital fissure. There are well marked cuneal (triradiate) and postcuneal (quadri-radiate) segments in the cuneus.

Gyres of the Parietal and Occipital Lobes (Lateral Surface). — The postcentral gyre is much wider than the precentral. The parietal gyre is wider than its fellow on the right; the paroccipital is also larger and of simpler appearance. The marginal and angular gyres are all massive and complexly marked.

Mesal Surface. — Both cuneus and precuneus are of good size, especially the latter, and the fissural markings are quite intricate.

Fissures of the Temporal Lobes (Latero-ventral Surface). — The supertemporal fissure presents a markedly tortuous course and seems to be made up rather of connected zygal segments, in this respect very much resembling the brain of Joseph Leidy.

Caudally it anastomoses deeply with the parietal and a meditemporal segment. The meditemporal is represented by two zygal segments. The subtemporal is more clearly defined and of a good length. The collateral fissure is 10 cm. long. The postrhinal is barely indicated.

The gyres of the temporal lobe are notable for their complex and irregularly tortuous conformation. The subcollateral is of considerable width.

The Insula. — It was not practicable to examine the insulæ thoroughly owing to the fragility of the specimen. The depths of the sylvian cleft on both sides are as follows:

	Left.	Right.
Pre-sylvian depth .	12	13
Medi-sylvian depth .	18	23
Post-sylvian depth .	31	31

Right Hemicerebrum. The Interlobar Fissures. The Sylvian Fissure and its Rami. — The length of the sylvian fissure is 4.5 cm. The sylvian angle is 18°. The depths are as follows: Presylvian, 13 mm.; medi-sylvian, 23 mm.; post-sylvian, 31 mm. The presylvian ramus is 2 cm. in length, the subsylvian about the same. The episylvian ramus is more vertical in direction than that of the left side. The hyposylvian is merely indicated by an incisure.

The Central Fissure. — The length of the central fissure is 9.5 cm. and it is less sinuous and less ramified than the left central. It does not anastomose with any of the neighboring fissures.

The Occipital Fissure. — The length on the meson is 3.3 cm.; on the convex surface, 1.5 cm. It is joined by a well-marked cuneal fissure which gives the occipital an appearance of bifurcation. The occipital angle approaches 65°; this is due to the more caudal situation of the occipito-calcarine junction as compared with the left side.

The Calcarine Fissure proper is 4 cm. in length. A slight vadum separates it from the postcalcarine, a triradiate fissure situated well upon the occipital pole. The occipitocalcarine stem is over 3 cm. in length and almost totally traverses the hippocampal gyre.

Fissures of the Frontal Lobe (Lateral Surface). The Precentral Fissural Complex. — The supercentral fissure is of zygal shape and directly continuous cephalad with the superfrontal: a well-marked paramesial with long transverse caudal rami closely approaches the former fissure. The precentral is well marked and sends off a long "anterior precentral" ramus.

The superfrontal runs well cephalad and presents a marked resemblance to the same fissure in the right half of Joseph Leidy's brain. The medifrontal is 7 cm. in length, quite tortuous and likewise of similar conformation to that of Joseph Leidy. The subfrontal is apparently divided into two segments, of which the cephalic one joins the radiate fissure.

Mesal Surface.—The supercallosal proper is shortened by the intervention of an oblique isthmus joining the superfrontal and callosal gyres as is commonly observed in cases of so-called "duplication of the (old) callosomarginal." The paracentral fissure is markedly tortuous and ramified. The rostral fissure anastomoses with the fronto-marginal-supercallosal piece and cuts across the hemicerebral border.

Orbital Surface.—The orbital fissure is a simple zygal fissure. The olfactory is 4 cm. in length.

Gyres of the Frontal Lobe (Lateral Surface).—The precentral gyre is somewhat wider and of simpler configuration than that of the left side. The superfrontal is of good size and very much resembles that of Joseph Leidy's right hemicerebrum. The medifrontal gyre is rather larger, the subfrontal a trifle smaller as compared with those of the left side.

The *mesal surface* is not so clearly divided into three tiers except where the supercallosal fissural segments overlap in parallel. The paracentral gyre is smaller and of irregular shape. The callosal gyre is quite broad just ventrad of the paracentral and is marked by a short medicallosal fissure.

Orbital Surface.—The mesorbital gyre is a trifle less wide and the general surface is less complexly marked than on the left side.

The postorbital limbus is somewhat more marked on this side.

Fissures of the Parietal and Occipital Lobes (Lateral Surface). The Postcentral Fissural Complex.—The postcentral, subcentral, parietal and intermedial (thence supertemporal) fissures anastomose within a small area in a way that is in many respects similar to the confluence of these fissures in the left half of Joseph Leidy's cerebrum. The subcentral is continuous with the transpostcentral dipping into the sylvian cleft on the left side. The tendency to transverse fissuration has abbreviated the parietal fissure considerably and it is separated from the paroccipital by an isthmus. The paroccipital is of irregular zygal shape with numerous rami. The exoccipital complex in this case shows a well-defined "sulcus lunatus" (Elliot Smith) and a prelunate ramus.

Mesal Surface.—The precuneal fissure is of markedly irregular zygal type. Two fissures mark the cuneal surface, one already described as joining the occipital fissure, the other anastomosing with the calcarine.

Gyres of the Parietal and Occipital Lobes (Lateral Surface).—The postcentral gyre is of good width in its dorsal two-thirds but quite narrow ventrad of this. The parietal is rather narrower than that of the left and of more irregular configuration; the paroccipital is also smaller. The angular and postparietal areas are markedly extensive.

Mesal Surface.—The precuneus presents a very complex configuration owing to the numerous ramifications of the precuneal and intraprecuneal fissures. The cuneus is of average size and form.

Fissures of the Temporal Lobe (Latero-ventral Surface).—The supertemporal fissure is less tortuous than that of the left half: the length of the main segment is 9.5 cm.

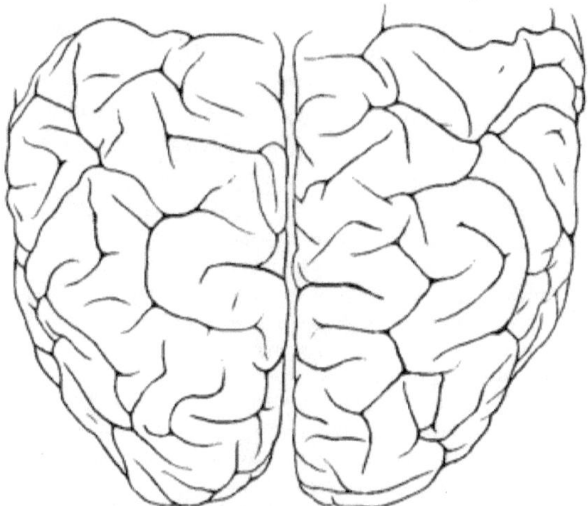

FIG. 35.—Dorsocaudal view of the brain of Philip Leidy.

Caudo-dorsad it anastomoses with the complex intermedial-parietal junction. The meditemporal fissure is represented by several zygal segments. The subtemporal is well marked and long. The collateral fissure is 11 cm. long, while the postrhinal is indicated by a shallow groove.

Gyres of the Temporal Lobe in this half are much more regular in contour than those of the left half. They all tend to preserve a uniformity of width which is in marked contrast to the irregular appearances presented in the left hemicerebrum.

ANDREW JACKSON PARKER, M.D.

Born in Philadelphia, August 17, 1855. He was of New England parentage. He was educated in the public schools and while in the grammar school, he attracted attention because of his unusual brightness and unusual facility in the writing of compositions. While a student at the Central High School, he became greatly interested in scientific subjects. He had the unique distinction of never attaining less than the highest possible mark in either physics, chemistry or mathematics.

He matriculated in the medical department of the University of Pennsylvania in the spring of 1874 and while there enjoyed the great privilege of being the personal student and pupil of Prof. Joseph Leidy. Professor Leidy became greatly interested in Parker as did also Dr. Henry C. Chapman. Parker evinced an especial interest in the purely scientific branches of medicine and concentrated his attention upon general biology and comparative anatomy. Clinical medicine interested him very little. Under the stimulus of Leidy, he studied the protozoa and to a large extent invertebrate forms, while he diligently dissected the great mass of vertebrate material placed in his hands by Professor Chapman. He was especially fortunate in having placed at his disposal a large number of brains of apes and monkeys. With the aid of the coroner, he collected quite a number of negro brains.

At his graduation in 1877, he presented a thesis on "The Morphology of the Cerebral Convolutions with Special Reference to the Order of Primates." This thesis was awarded a prize and later formed the nucleus of a more elaborate paper which was subsequently awarded the Boyleston prize of Harvard University and which was published in the Proceedings of the Journal of the Academy of Natural Sciences, Volume X. At the age of twenty-four, he was appointed professor of comparative anatomy in the University of Pennsylvania, which position he held until he was thirty-one, when ill-health compelled his resignation.

Dr. Parker was five feet, seven inches in height, of rather slight build, though he was muscularly very strong. His features were well defined, the nose being prominent and rather aquiline, while the chin was exceedingly well developed and pronounced. His eyes were large and so prominent as at times to suggest a slight degree of exophthalmus. He was of dark complexion. He was an omnivorous reader; his favorite subjects by far were those which related to scientific matters, but he was thoroughly at home in general literature. He was a devoted disciple of Spencer and Huxley and a great admirer of Tyndall, Darwin and the other great scientists of his day. His scientific papers were characterized by accuracy of statement, clearness of thought and systematic and logical arrangement of the subject matter. They were always original in character. In scientific debate, he was logical, forceful and convincing. He perceived almost as by instinct the important and vital matters of an issue and relegated the secondary and unimportant questions to their proper places. He was always broad and philosophical in his conceptions and brought to bear upon a given biological problem a wealth of physical, chemical and mathematical knowledge.

His command of English was remarkable. He talked with great facility, and, when occasion offered, as in after-dinnar speaking, he became eloquent to a degree. He was always ready to speak, never paused for a word, and had a rich flow of imagery.

He acquired a reading knowledge of both French and German, but never took the trouble to become proficient in either of these tongues. The explanation probably lay in the fact that to him language was merely an instrument of communication and not of itself interesting, and he never for this reason seriously applied himself. All other knowledge he acquired with extreme rapidity and facility and readily coördinated the newly acquired facts with those already in his possession. His method of thought was systematic in the extreme, and his mind was a store-house in which everything was well classified and arranged. In addition he possessed an excellent memory, which in debate or after-dinner speaking served him to good purpose in rendering spontaneous citations.

His perceptions were very acute and his muscular coördinations were very accurate. He was a remarkably good shot and was fond of out-of-door exercise. He was exceedingly fond of music, of which he possessed not only a keen appreciation, but a profound and philosophic comprehension. He not only enjoyed it thoroughly, but he was especially fond of discussing its physics and mathematics. Art in its other forms appealed to him in but an average degree.

He was diffident in manner, and while his acquaintance was large, he had but few intimate friends. His tastes were rather Bohemian and unconventional, and though not devoid of a feeling of reverence, he was an outspoken agnostic.

As regards his scientific work, he was rather indifferent in the matter of publication. When he had satisfied his own mind as to a given question he would only exceptionally publish the results. For this reason the number of his published articles is rather limited, the most important of them being the one on the cerebral convolutions of the primates already mentioned. An important investigation which he never completed was on the interaction of crystalloids and colloids and embraced a large number of experiments of crystallizations in various colloid media. In talking with his friends, he claimed that in the interaction of crystalloids and colloids is to be sought an explanation of much of the mystery underlying organic forms. Unfortunately his dilatory habits interfered with the publication of his experiments, and to this his steadily increasing ill health also contributed. He finally died of an attack of pneumonia at thirty-six. He was unmarried.

His intellectual make-up is well illustrated in his paper on the convolutions of the primates. It is replete with observations which form the basis of a brilliant generalization, and it concludes with a novel and remarkable application of mathematical principles in explanation of the arrangement of the convolutions. His intellectual development was unquestionably precocious; at twenty he had the balance, force and judgment of much older men.[3]

The brain was found to have remained in Müller's fluid ever since 1892. As a natural result the brain-substance had become exceedingly fragile and had suffered badly from subsequent handling. It had been broken into numerous fragments when received by me and it was only with the utmost care that I was successful in delineating the greater part of the mesal aspect of the cerebral halves. Fortunately a cast of the undissected brain had been made under Dr. Dercum's supervision and with the help of this cast and such of the fragments as were still useful, the author was able to reconstruct much of the cerebral contour. The objective study as hereinafter reported is therefore based upon combined observations upon the cast and the brain fragments and is necessarily incomplete in some respects. By means of more extensive dissection than would have been warranted in a better preserved brain it was possible to completely expose the insulæ and make casts of them. This was done with great care and the result was excellent.

Unfortunately the weight of this brain is not on record. Judging from the dimensions of the cast of the brain, it must have weighed about 1500 grams, or somewhere within the range of 1475 to 1525 grams.

The Cerebrum.

This specimen is one of the most richly fissured brains in the series. The frontal and parieto-occipital areas are particularly rich in secondary fissures and ramifications and one is reminded of the brachycephalic type of cerebrum. The left hemicerebrum is the most notable in every respect.

Left Hemicerebrum.

The Interlobar Fissures. The Sylvian Fissure and its Rami.—The sylvian fissure is 6 cm. in length and curves gently dorsad to terminate as the episylvian ramus, 3 cm. in length, there being no hyposylvian ramus. The sylvian angle is 20°. The depths of the sylvian fissure are as follows: Presylvian depth, 13 mm.; medi-sylvian,

[3] The writer is indebted to Dr. F. X. Dercum for this biographical sketch of A. J. Parker.

19 mm.; post-sylvian, 25 mm. The presylvian ramus is 2 cm. in length while the subsylvian is absent.

The Central Fissure is 9.5 cm. in length and slightly more sinuous than that of the right half. Its inclination to the meson is 68°. The central does not anastomose with any of the neighboring fissures.

The occipital fissure is 4.8 cm. in length on the meson, 2.5 cm. on the dorsum. Its course is sinuous throughout and on the dorsum it anastomoses with the cephalic stipe of the paroccipital.

The calcarine fissure could not be examined, owing to the extensive loss of the occipital parts. The occipito-calcarine stem anastomoses with the precuneal and collateral fissures.

Fissures of the Frontal Lobe (Lateral Surface). The Precentral Fissure Complex.— The supercentral fissure is a simple tri-radiate piece whose cephalic ramus is directly continuous with the superfrontal. The ventral and dorsal limbs run parallel with the central fissure, their total length being 5 cm. The precentral fissural element is less extensive itself but sends a long "anterior precentral ramus" well across the medifrontal gyre and by means of the diagonal element it communicates directly with the sylvian cleft. There is a well-marked transprecentral.

The superfrontal fissure is distinct for a length of 6 cm. from its supercentral origin. The fissural markings in the prefrontal region are too intricate to be distinguished by names. There is an orbitofrontal piece from which springs a short medifrontal. The subfrontal fissure is very well marked.

Mesal Surface.—So far as the fragments of this specimen permit of examination the supercallosal fissure appears in two segments separated by an oblique isthmus. There are several frontomarginal segments and a well-marked rostral fissure. The paracentral is extensive and unusually ramified.

The orbital surface is marked by a much-ramified-quadri-radiate orbital fissure together with several smaller independent segments.

Gyres of the Frontal Lobe (Lateral Surface).—The precentral gyre is of average width. The superfrontal gyre is well-developed and marked by a distinct paramesial fissure and several unnamed segments. The medifrontal is of good width and marked by numerous transverse fissures. The subfrontal gyre is larger and better developed than that of the right side.

The mesal surface is incompletely preserved. The three-tier type prevails. The paracentral gyre is large and of a rectangular shape.

Orbital Surface.—The mesorbital gyre is rather narrow. The irregularly zygal orbital fissure makes the configuration of this surface rather intricate as compared with the more regular markings on the right side.

Fissures of the Parietal and Occipital Lobes (Lateral Surface). The Postcentral Fissural Complex is an irregular zygal piece whose dorsal arms embrace the caudal limb of the paracentral fissure. An oblique transparietal anastomoses with it while a caudal ramus joins a parietal fissure, the subcentral anastomosing with both. The whole arrangement is quite unusual and complex. There is a well-marked transpostcentral. The parietal itself is short but sends off long rami dorsad and ventrad. The paroccipital is separated from the parietal by an isthmus but its cephalic stipe joins the occipital. The paroccipital is of the usual zygal form with long curved stipes.

Mesal Surface.—The precuneal fissure is exceedingly complex and anastomoses with both the paracentral and the occipito-calcarine stem. (The cuneal fissures cannot be described owing to the destruction of the part.)

Gyres of the Parietal and Occipital Lobes (Lateral Surface).—The postcentral gyre is of good width and marked by numerous fissural rami and independent pieces. The parietal gyre presents intricate fissure-markings. The marginal and angular gyres are exceedingly well developed but less so than the corresponding areas on the right side.

Mesal Surface.—The intricate markings of the precuneus have already been alluded to. (The cuneus cannot be described owing to destruction of the part.)

Fissures of the Temporal Lobe (Latero-ventral Surface).—The supertemporal fissure is represented by two short cephalic segments while the caudal piece, 9.5 cm. in length, anastomoses with the subcentral-parietal junction over a vadum. The meditemporal is represented by several segments rich in transverse anastomoses. The remaining fissures of the temporal lobe cannot be described owing to the destruction of the parts.

Gyres of the Temporal Lobe.—The supertemporal gyre is well defined, fairly sinuous and traversed by an arm of the second supertemporal fissural segment. The remaining gyres, so far as they can be examined, present a very complex and tortuous configuration.

Right Hemicerebrum.

The Interlobar Fissures. The Sylvian Fissure and its Rami.—The sylvian fissure is 5.9 cm. in length, its course is moderately sinuous and the sylvian angle is 26°. Its depths are as follows: Pre-sylvian, 16 mm.; medi-sylvian, 21 mm.; post-sylvian, 25 mm. The presylvian fissure is short, while the subsylvian attains a length of 2.5 cm. The episylvian ramus joins the subcentral fissure. The hyposylvian is short.

The central fissure is 10 cm. in length and its course is less sinuous than that of the left side.

The occipital and calcarine fissures could not be thoroughly examined, owing to the extensive loss of the occipital portions of the brain.

Fissures of the Frontal Lobe (Lateral Surface). The Precentral Fissural Complex.—The supercentral presents a form similar to its fellow on the left, but is shorter. The precentral is more distinct and does not dip into the sylvian cleft.

The superfrontal can be traced for 4 cm. from its origin but cannot be distinguished in the intricate markings of the prefrontal regions. The orbitofrontal and medifrontal fissures are more distinctly marked on this side. The subfrontal is well-marked and anastomoses with the diagonal fissure.

Mesal Surface.—The supercallosal fissure presents a very tortuous course and gives off several vertical rami. A fairly long frontomarginal in the precallosal region gives a well-marked appearance of the three-tier type. There is a fairly long rostral fissure. The paracentral fissure is curved and sends off several rami.

Orbital Surface.—The arrangement of a transorbital fissure with longitudinal rami gives an appearance of a postorbital gyre with several sagittally-directed pre-orbital gyres. The mesorbital gyre is somewhat broader than its fellow on the left.

Gyres of the Frontal Lobe (Lateral Surface).—The precentral gyre is of regular contour. The superfrontal gyre is quite broad, the medifrontal is complexly marked, while the subfrontal is of smaller extent than that of the left side.

The mesal surface of the superfrontal gyre is marked by numerous rami of the supercallosal fissure. The callosal gyre is marked by numerous independent segments and by several rami of the paracentral.

Fissures of the Parietal and Occipital Lobes (Lateral Surface). The Postcentral Fissural Complex.—It is by no means easy to identify all the segments of this complex. The postcentral is a small zygal segment while the subcentral is a more extensive fissure which anastomoses with the parietal and episylvian fissures. There is a long transpostcentral.

The parietal fissure pursues a very irregular course, anastomoses with the supertemporal but is separated from the paroccipital by a slight vadum. The paroccipital is irregularly zygal. There is a well-marked transparietal.

Mesal Surface.—The precuneal fissure is a quadri-radiate zygal fissure. Numerous independent pieces mark the precuneus, while the cuneal surface could not be examined.

Gyres of the Parietal and Occipital Lobes (Lateral Surface).—The postcentral gyre is of fair width but less intricately marked than that of the left. The parietal gyre is likewise of simpler contour. The marginal and angular gyres, on the other hand, are notable for their extent and rich fissuration.

Fissures of the Temporal Lobe.—The supertemporal fissure pursues a tortuous course and measures, to its junction with the parietal fissure, 14 cm., an unusual length. Several meditemporal segments, each considerably branched, mark this surface. The other fissures could not be thoroughly examined.

Gyres of the Temporal Lobe. — The supertemporal gyre is quite tortuous and well developed. The remaining gyres are of good width and, so far as could be examined, appeared to be richly marked by fissures.

The Insula. — As stated above, it was possible to examine the insulae more closely than in any other brain in this series because the dissection necessary to expose these parts was permissible in a specimen already worthless for other purposes. Casts of the insulae thus exposed were carefully made with a wax-paraffine mixture and from these several positive casts in plaster of Paris were secured for permanent use.

Both insulae show a high degree of development, but with one notable difference, viz.: the preinsula, or that portion nearest the motor speech centers of the cerebral mantle, is larger, better developed and more prominent on the left side than on the right. The dimensions of the insulae are:

	Left	Right.
Cephalo-caudal length .	5.4 cm.	4.9 cm.
Transinsular diagonal width	4.2 "	3.9 "
Dorso-ventral width . . .	3.5 "	3.4 "
Height of the insular from the mesal surface .	4.5 "	4.4 "

These measurements show that the left insula as a whole is also larger than its fellow on the right side.

HARRISON ALLEN.

Born in Philadelphia, April 17, 1841. His parents were Samuel Allen and Elizabeth Justice Thomas. His ancestors accompanied William Penn, and on his father's side he was descended from Nicholas Waln, distinguished in the early history of Philphia. Although he would have preferred pure science, financial considerations led him to study medicine, including dentistry, at the University of Pennsylvania. He was on duty for a time at the Blockley Hospital, and on January 31, 1862, he was appointed Acting Assistant Surgeon U. S. A., and Assistant Surgeon, July 30, 1862, serving in hospitals and in the defences of Washington until the acceptance of his resignation, December 8, 1865. He then ranked as Brevet Major.

Dr. Allen now practised his profession with assiduity and success. His dental education facilitated specialization in respect to the air passages, and in 1880 he was President of the American Laryngological Association. Of his strictly medical and surgical publications (numbering about fifty) most relate more or less directly to his specialty.

But while he earned his living by medicine Dr. Allen devoted much time and thought to science and published many valuable contributions on comparative and human anatomy. In Professor Wilder's biography of Dr. Allen, from which these data are taken, about 200 monographs are listed. His investigations on the bats of

North America, on crania from the Hawaiian Islands and congenital malformations are most notable. He was professor of zoölogy and comparative anatomy in the University of Pennsylvania from 1865 to 1876; professor of physiology from 1878 to 1885; professor of comparative anatomy and zoölogy, 1891–96. Dr. Allen was an active or corresponding member of numerous scientific societies in this and in other countries, and was President of the American Society of Naturalists in 1887 and in 1888. A large part of his work was done at the Academy of Natural Sciences of Philadelphia and published in its proceedings. He was President of the Contemporary Club of Philadelphia; Curator of the Wistar Institute of Anatomy; President of the Anthropometric Society, and succeeded Professor Joseph Leidy as President of the Association of American Anatomists.

Dr. Allen died November 14, 1898. As a member of the Anthropometric Society he directed that his brain should be entrusted to that organization; his body was cremated. The autopsy revealed the cause of his death as heart failure, due to fatty degeneration; he had in his later years also been subject to rheumatism.

(For further details see biography by B. G. Wilder, Proceedings of Association of American Anatomists, December, 1897; also Science, pp. 262–265, 1898.)

THE BRAIN.

The weight of the encephalon, after having been immersed for 15 minutes in a mixture of water, formalin and alcohol, was 54 ounces avoirdupois, or 1531 grams, a weight which closely approaches that of Cope. After having lain immersed for nearly six years and after the removal of the pia from the cerebral halves, the weight of the encephalic parts was as follows:

Left hemicerebrum	525 grams.
Right "	540 "
Cerebellum	155 "
Pons and oblongata	28
	1248 grams.

The loss in weight amounts to 283 grams or 18.4 per cent. of the original weight.

THE CEREBRUM.

The entire brain has unfortunately suffered much distortion. It had rested upon its ventral surface so that the cerebellum pressed up against the caudal parts of the cerebral halves, flattening these considerably and spreading the occipital poles apart. The distortion is such that measurements are of no value except with reference to isolated and unaffected regions and of single fissures. The accompanying drawings represent the actual appearances presented by the cerebral parts as they have hardened in this distorted condition. Owing to this manifest displacement the writer refrains from attempting to describe the general appearances of the cerebrum as a whole; a morphological description of the fissures and gyres must suffice.

The large relative size of the callosum is striking and will be discussed more at length in the sequel. The crura cerebri are also quite large.

LEFT HEMICEREBRUM. *The Interlobar Fissures. The Sylvian Fissure and its Rami.*—The sylvian fissure is extremely short, only 3.9 cm. in length. Its depths are as follows: Presylvian depth, 15 mm.; medi-sylvian, 21 mm.; post-sylvian 28 mm. The presylvian ramus bifurcates and with its larger arm attains a length of 3 cm. The subsylvian is short. The episylvian is 3 cm. in length and there is a short ramifying hyposylvian.

The central fissure pursues a very sinuous course, exhibiting seven alternate curves and attaining a length of 11 cm. It anastomoses with the postcentral and supercentral.

The occipital fissure, on the mesal surface, is 3 cm. in length; on the dorsum it curves cephalad. A postparoccipital segment which dips into the occipital cleft joins it (superficially) with the paroccipital. On the dorsal surface it is characterized by a marked turn cephalad.

The calcarine fissure and postcalcarine fissure together attain a length of 6.5 cm., the terminal part passing well onto the convex surface. The occipito-calcarine stem is nearly 3 cm. in length.

Fissures of the Frontal Lobe (Lateral Surface). The Precentral Fissural Complex.—The supercentral is tri-radiate, its cephalic arm continuing as the superfrontal. The ventral limb anastomoses with the central. The precentral segment is 4 cm. in length and anastomoses with the subfrontal. There is a short trans-precentral but no diagonal fissure.

The superfrontal fissure consists of two segments: the caudal one springs from the supercentral and is 4 cm. in length; the cephalic one is shorter but pursues a more tortuous course and is more ramified. The intricacy of the prefrontal region is such as to make it difficult to trace the fissural integers and the reader must be referred to the figures.

Mesal Surface.—The supercallosal fissure springs from the paracentral, attains a length of 10 cm. and anastomoses with the rostral fissure. The paracentral is rather short (2.6 cm.) and sends off several rami. A number of fronto-marginal segments, mostly of zygal shape, mark the superfrontal gyre on the mesal surface. The rostral fissure joins a transrostral element, forming a U-shaped piece.

Orbital Surface.—The fissuration on this surface is quite complex and difficult to describe in words; the reader is again referred to the illustration.

Gyres of the Frontal Lobe. (Lateral Surface). — The precentral gyre of this half is rather broader than that of the right half and at its middle it is interrupted by the central-supercentral anastomosis. The superfrontal gyre is well defined in its caudal half, its lateral boundary being lost in the complexity of the prefrontal region. The medifrontal gyre is wide and the subfrontal is larger than the corresponding region on the right side. The left frontal lobe throughout is far more complexly fissured and is considerably differentiated from the common type.

FISSURES OF THE PARIETAL AND OCCIPITAL LOBES. *Lateral Surface. The Postcentral Fissural Complex.* — The postcentral fissure, 8 cm. in length, describes an irregular zig-zag course anastomosing ventrad with the subcentral and caudad with the parietal. The T-shaped subcentral is small and anastomoses with both the central and postcentral fissures. The parietal fissure bears an unusual relation to the paroccipital. Instead of joining the latter by a cephalic ramus, the parietal lies for the most part laterad of the paroccipital and then, with an abrupt mesal sweep, the parietal joins the paroccipital opposite the occipital incisure.

A well-marked intermedial fissure which joins the parietal demarcates the extensive marginal gyre from the angular while a second smaller "intermedial" lies between the intermedial proper and the episylvian.

Mesal Surface. — The precuneal is of irregular zygal shape and several smaller fissures mark the surface of the precuneus. A small cuneal fissure running parallel with the calcarine marks the cuneus.

Gyres of the Parietal and Occipital Lobes. Lateral Surface. — The postcentral gyre is very broad in its middle third. The parietal is of good width, but comparatively short, while the paroccipital occupies an odd position owing to the cephalic turn of the dorsal part of the occipital fissure. The marginal is quite wide; at its transition into the supertemporal gyre it is characterized by a distinct operculation. It is to this overlapping that the shortening of the sylvian fissure is chiefly due. The angular gyre is fairly complex and is characterized by its overlapping of the parietal-paroccipital.

Mesal Surface. — The comparative smallness of the cuneus and the larger size of the precuneus are to be noted.

Fissures of the Temporal Lobe. — The supertemporal fissure is represented by two segments, a short cephalic and a longer caudal one; the latter is quite tortuous and ramified. In the medi and subtemporal regions the transverse tendency of the fissures does not permit of a clear determination of the medi and subtemporal fissures as they are commonly seen. The collateral fissure is more clearly marked. The postrhinal is merely indicated by a groove.

The supertemporal gyre is particularly large at its transition into the marginal and angular gyres. The remaining temporal gyres all show a good degree of development.

The insula is well-formed, so far as could be seen, though not large. There are four preinsular and one postinsular gyres. Compared with that of the right side it is better differentiated and the insular pole is more prominent.

RIGHT HEMICEREBRUM. *The Interlobar Fissures. The Sylvian Fissure and its Rami.*—The sylvian fissure is even shorter than that of the left side, being only 3.5 cm. in length. Its depths are as follows: At the presylvian point 15 mm.; medisylvian, 24 mm.; post-sylvian, 28 mm. The presylvian is 3 cm. long; the subsylvian is absent. The epi-sylvian and hyposylvian rami much resemble those of the left half.

The central fissure is somewhat less sinuous than that on the left side and its length is 11.5 cm.

The occipital fissure, on the mesal surface, is 3 cm. in length; its dorsal termination is almost hidden through the close approximation of adjacent parts, together with almost complete submergence of the paroccipital gyre.

The calcarine fissure and postcalcarine together attain a length of 7 cm. The occipito-calcarine stem is 3 cm. in length.

Fissures of the Frontal Lobe (Lateral Surface). The Precentral Fissural Complex.—The supercentral is tri-radiate; from it springs the suprafrontal. The precentral is short but much ramified, from it springs the subfrontal. There is a short transpre-central.

The superfrontal fissure lies in the postfrontal region, joining the medifrontal cephalad. The medifrontal, springing from the orbitofrontal, pursues a very flexuous course. The subfrontal fissure is short. There is well-defined radiate fissure, which seems to be duplicated by a parallel element (*rdl''*) just ventrad of the principal fissure.

Mesal Surface.—The supercallosal is represented by a long cephalic segment, much ramified and anastomosing with the rostral, while a caudal segment joins the paracentral. The paracentral is of the usual type. The rostral fissure is 5 cm. in length: the subrostral is slight.

Orbital Surface.—The fissures include a well-marked transorbital fissure together with a zygal and a tri-radiate piece in the preorbital region.

Gyres of the Frontal Lobe (Lateral Surface).—The precentral gyre is of rather a finer contour and not so wide in its middle part as that of the left side. The superfrontal is of good width and marked by several paramesial segments. The medifrontal is very wide and exceedingly complex in its fissuration. The subfrontal shows nothing notable and is less extensive than that of the left.

The mesal surface of the superfrontal is fairly complex but not as wide throughout as the corresponding gyre on the left side. The paracentral gyre is somewhat larger than that of the left.

Fissures of the Parietal and Occipital Gyres. (Lateral Surface.) The Postcentral Fissural Complex. — It is rather difficult to determine the limits of the segments which

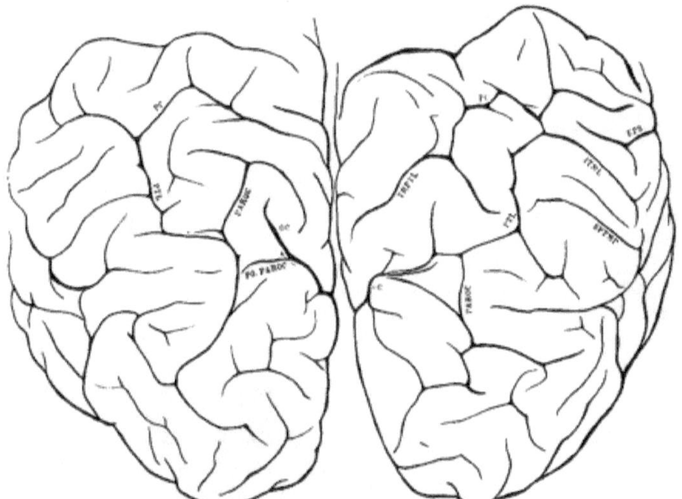

FIG. 50.—Dorso-caudal view of the brain of Harrison Allen.

make up the postcentral fissural complex. On the whole it is an extremely irregular system with numerous modifications. It joins the parietal and the zygal transparietal. The transpostcentral is unusually long.

The parietal fissure joins the paroccipital fissure in the usual manner. The cephalic stipe of the paroccipital dips into the occipital cleft so that on a superficial view the two fissures appear to be confluent. Beside the exoccipital complex and the supertemporal fissure the intermedial may be mentioned, appearing as a branch of the parietal.

Mesal Surface. — The precuneal fissure is of the usual zygal shape with fairly long stem and anastomosing cephalad with the paracentral. The cuneus is marked by an independent cuneal fissure and by a postcuneal fissure.

Gyres of the Parietal and Occipital Lobes. (Lateral Surface.) — The postcentral is of irregular contour and, in general, quite broad. There is not a very distinct demarcation from the parietal gyre. Of the paroccipital gyre its caudal arm only is visible upon the surface.

The marginal gyre is less extensive than that of the left but the angular gyre of this side is larger than its fellow of the left half.

Mesal Surface. — The precuneus is smaller than that of the left and somewhat less complexly marked by fissures. The cuneus does not differ much from its fellow in size or contour.

Fissures of the Temporal Lobe. — The supertemporal is very tortuous and much ramified. Caudally it anastomoses with an exoccipital element. The meditemporal is well marked and attains a length of 9 cm. The subtemporal is represented by only a few small segments. The collateral fissure is 9.5 cm. in length. The postrhinal is a well marked and fairly deep groove.

Gyres of the Temporal Lobe. — The gyral development of the lobe is, on the whole, quite similar to that of the left half. There is not so marked a tendency toward transverse fissuration, however, so that the identification of fissures and gyres is comparatively easy.

The Insula. — As on the other side, the insula is not of any notable size. Furthermore the right insula is of somewhat simpler contour and the preinsular pole is less prominent.

Remembering the distorted condition in which the brain has come to our hands the measurements herewith given are not of great value. In a general way, however, they may convey some idea of the dimensions and permit one to form some judgment as to the allowances that ought to be made for the displacement. The callosum, at least, can be said to have suffered little change during the stages of preservation.

Length of cerebrum . .	16.8
Width of cerebrum	14.1
(Cerebral Index 84.)	
Semi-circumference (each half) .	24.
Length of callosum	8.0
(or 47.6 per cent. of cerebral length.)	

EDWARD DRINKER COPE.

Born in Philadelphia, July 28, 1840, of distinguished American ancestry. In boyhood he showed great independence in character and action, incessant activity in mind and body, and quick and ingenious thought. At the age of nineteen he went to Washington to study and work in the Smithsonian Institution under Spencer F. Baird. In April, 1859, he contributed his first paper to the Academy of Natural Sciences, "on the primary divisions of the Salamandridæ, with a description of two new species." He followed this by a full description, in the same year, of reptiles brought from West Africa by Du Chaillu, naming several new forms; also by a catalogue of the venomous snakes in the museum. In the succeeding three years he made twenty-four communications upon the Reptilia and established himself, at the age of twenty-two, as one of the leading herpetologists of the country. He exhibited a wide range of self-acquired knowledge and keen powers of systematic diagnosis and generalization. He was professor of natural science in Haverford College (1864–1867) and professor of geology and paleontology in the University of Pennsylvania (1886–1897). H. F. Osborn speaks of Cope as the "last and the most distinguished of the old school of comparative anatomists." While connected with the U. S. Geological Survey, under Dr. Hayden, he made explorations in Wyoming and Colorado (1872–73), which resulted in the discovery of many new types of fishes, mosasaurs, chelonians, dinosaurs and other reptiles. He spent his summers in the Bad Lands, rapidly accumulating an enormous collection of fossils and publishing exhaustive memoirs. At his death, in 1897, he left twenty octavo and three great quarto volumes of collected researches. Cope is not to be thought of merely as a specialist in paleontology, but rather as a philosophic anatomist, who, while less logical and less accurate than Huxley, was more creative and constructive and never let an opportunity slip by of at least throwing out an hypothesis as to the phyletic relations of every great type he studied, and many of these random guesses have been confirmed.

Cope worked deliberately, and gave his whole mind to one subject at a time, if he considered it of special importance, this power being aided by his remarkable memory of species and of objects long laid aside for future reference. His field exploration was characterized by great enthusiasm and indefatigable energy. Many friends in this country and abroad have spoken of the invigorating nature of his companionship. In times of relaxation he displayed a large fund of amusing anecdotes of the experiences, mishaps and frailties of scientists, his own as often as those of others. Some of his countrymen have allowed certain of his characteristics to obscure his stronger side, and during his life he received few of the honors such as foreigners are wont to bestow upon their countrymen of note; yet few men have done as much as Cope to push the world's thought along. His face reflected his character. His square and prominent forehead suggested his vigorous intellect and marvelous memory; his brilliant eyes were the media of exceptional keenness of observation; his prominent chin was in traditional harmony with his aggressive spirit.

(Compiled from biography of H. F. Osborn; *Science*, May 7, 1897, and *Century Magazine*, November, 1897.)

The Brain.

The weight of the fresh encephalon, with the pia-arachnoid still attached, was 54.5 ounces, equivalent to 1545 grammes, a weight which exceeds that of the average male brains of whites by about 150 grammes. (See Table I.) After immersion in an alcohol-formal mixture, and after removal of the pia, the weight of the encephalic parts was as follows:

Left hemicerebrum .	475.8
Right hemicerebrum . .	448.9
Cerebellum, pons and oblongata	153.5
Total . .	1078.2

The loss in weight amounts to 467 grammes, or 30 per cent. of the original weight.

The Cerebrum.

In general, the cerebrum presents a fairly complex development, with intricate fissuration and a bold contour of the numerous gyres. Viewed dorsally, its great breadth (cerebral index 81.8) is readily noted, as also the relatively greater fullness of the left hemicerebrum in the region of the fronto-parietal operculum and the adjacent parts. Of the frontal lobes, the left seems the more complexly and deeply fissured, as well as the more massive. Viewed laterally, and comparing the two sides, the preoperculum is better developed and more massive on the left side, as is also the region about the left marginal and angular gyres. The right super-parietal region, however, is more massive than on the left side, though, if we compare this brain with some others of eminent men, Gyldén's for example, this portion of the cerebrum is not particularly large in its development. In the ventral view, the right temporal lobe is slightly longer and of more slender contour than the left, which is considerably broader and thicker. The fissuration is also more marked on the left side. The greater breadth of the orbital surface of the left half is quite apparent. On the whole it may be said that there is a slight preponderance in the size and in the degree of fissuration of the left as compared with the right half. The horizontal semi-circumference on the left side, measuring between the hemicerebral poles, exceeds that of the right side by 1 cm.; these measures are, respectively, 23 and 22 cm.

Left Hemicerebrum. *The Interlobar Fissures. The Sylvian Fissure and its Rami.* — The sylvian fissure attains a length of 5.9 cm., its walls are in close apposition, and its course is quite tortuous. Its angle with a plane passing through the ventral margins of the frontal and occipital poles is 28°. Its depth at the pre-sylvian point is 13 mm.; medi-sylvian depth 19 mm.; post-sylvian depth 25 mm. The presylvian ramus is 2.5 cm. in length and anastomoses caudally with the diagonal. The subsylvian is short. The basisylvian, measured from the tip of the temporal lobe is 20 mm. in depth. Caudad, the sylvian terminates in the episylvian ramus 2.4 cm. in length. The hyposylvian is absent.

The Central Fissure. — Measuring with a wet string, this fissure is 11.8 cm. in length; measured with a pair of compasses, 8.2 cm., quite above the average. It does not anastomose with any other fissure and has only one short caudal ramus near its ventral end. The course of the fissure can be resolved into seven alternate curves, instead of the usual five. Several interlocking subgyres may be seen in its depths but there is no appreciable "central vadum." The ventral end is separated from the sylvian by an isthmus 6 mm. in width; the dorsal end appears on the mesial aspect for 1.5 cm. The general direction of the fissure makes an angle of 53° with the intercerebral cleft.

The Occipital Fissure. — Its length on the meson is 2.8 cm.; on the convex surface 2.3 cm. It sends one ramus into the cuneal surface and terminates on the dorsum in a furcal manner, the cephalic limb communicating with the cephalic stipe of the paroccipital at a depth of 8 mm. over a very narrow submerged isthmus — the reduced cephalic limb of the paroccipital gyre. Notable is the obtuse angle which the fissure makes with the (arbitrary) horizontal plane alluded to above: namely 70°. In most brains this angle approximates 60°. The fissure therefore does not approach the callosum as much as is the rule, and its junction with the calcarine is effected much further caudad than usual.

The Calcarine Fissure. — The calcarine fissure describes an angular course, bending sharply dorsad near its junction with the occipito-calcarine stem. It terminates caudally in a T-shaped bifurcation, the ventral arm of which again bifurcates. Each of these bifurcations embraces an independent fissural segment, of which the ventral one probably corresponds to the postcalcarine, "or sulcus extremus" of Schwalbe.

The occipital and the calcarine meet at considerable depth to pass into the occipito-calcarine fissural stem. This passes cephalad for 3.7 mm. and comes within 1 mm. of anastomosing with the hippocampal fissure.

Fissures of the Frontal Lobe (Lateral Surface). *The Precentral Fissural Complex.* — This consists of three segments: an independent supercentral, and two superficially confluent precentrals. The supercentral is fundamentally of triradiate shape, though it exhibits a tendency to zygal form; its maximum length, parallel with the central, is 4 cm. The dorsal limbs embrace an inflected gyre, as determined by the existence of a short inflected fissure. Of the two precentral segments, the dorsal one (*PRC'*, Figs. 57 and 60) extends well across the medifrontal gyre and anastomoses with the superfrontal over a vadum 5 mm. in depth. Ventrad, over another vadum of about the same depth, it joins the second precentral segment. The latter (*PRC''*, Figs. 57 and 60) joins the diagonal, and by means of this the sylvian fissure. Near the dorsal end of this second precentral segment there arises a long ramus (3.5 cm.) which nearly traverses the entire medifrontal gyre. This corresponds to the "anterior precentral" of the authors, and we thus see two precentral elements which tend to run parallel with each other for a fair distance, including between them not a small portion of the medifrontal.

The transprecentral appears on the convex surface for 1.5 cm., and does not communicate with any other fissure. The diagonal fissure is short, joins the precentral as described above, and anastomoses with the presylvian over a vadum.

The superfrontal fissures does not, as is usual, spring from the supercentral, but beginning in a simple manner it passes cephalad in an extremely tortuous, zig-zag course, sending off several rami, attaining a length of 8 cm. for the principal segment. Further cephalad, the fissure may be traced a part of the distance, but in the highly complex prefrontal region it is difficult to determine. Numerous transverse pieces mark the superfrontal gyre.

The medifrontal fissure is a distinctly marked segment, coursing about midway between and parallel with the super- and subfrontal fissures. It has numerous rami, and far cephalad it anastomoses with the prefrontal part of the superfrontal. As the fissure passes toward the frontal pole, it converges toward the mesial plane, making an angle of about 38° with it.

The subfrontal fissure is practically an independent one; its main part is of zygal form, with an extensive dorso-cephalic ramus which reaches well toward the frontal pole and by its many ramifications helps to make this region so very complex.

The orbitofrontal seems to be represented by at least two well-defined segments; the mesial one traverses the frontal pole to appear on the mesial aspect; the lateral one is tri-radiate. Both segments are independent. There is a long (3.7 cm.) radiate fissure, independent, which marks the rather large preoperculum.

MESIAL SURFACE. — The supercallosal, from its junction with the paracentral to its termination ventrad of the rostrum of the callosum, is an uninterrupted fissure of a length of 9.5 cm., and sends off five distinct rami into the superfrontal gyre. A short parallel fissure, which may be conveniently called the medicallosal, marks the callosal gyre just dorsad of the genu of the callosum.

The paracentral fissure is of the usual form, the stem being 4 cm. in length; the cephalic limb 1.4 cm.; the caudal limb 1.3 cm. on the meson, and 1.7 cm. on the dorsum. There is a short inflected fissure appearing on both the dorsal as well as the mesial aspect, and situated, as is the rule, caudad of the cephalic paracentral limb.

In the superfrontal gyre there is a very short frontomarginal segment confluent with one of the rami of the supercallosal. The rostral fissure is distinct, 4.7 cm. in length and independent; the subrostral is merely indicated by a slight furrow.

Orbital Surface. — There are two orbital fissures separated from each other by a shallow vallum; the mesial one is of zygal shape, the lateral one quadri-radiate, resembling the letter "K." The olfactory fissure is simple and attains a length of 3.8 cm. The cephalic end becomes visible on the mesial aspect.

Gyres of the Frontal Lobe (Lateral Surface). — The precentral gyre of this half is slightly less massive, and of rather less tortuous configuration than its fellow on the right side. The ventral portion is the broader. The superfrontal gyre is of good width throughout and beside the numerous indentations of the exceedingly ramified superfrontal, is richly supplied with smaller fissures, notably in the prefrontal portion, and generally of transverse direction. The medifrontal gyre is broad, particularly in the caudal portion where the well-marked "anterior precentral" has already been noted. The intricate fissuration in the prefrontal region gives this part of the gyre a very complex appearance, and it is difficult to trace the fundamental fissural pattern here. The existence of a fairly long medifrontal fissure divides the gyre into two tiers. The subfrontal gyre is the one to which the massiveness of the left as compared with right frontal lobe is due. The great width of the medifrontal gyre would seem to apparently diminish the area of the subfrontal, but this is more than compensated for by its greater longitudinal expanse. Measurements taken from the ventral end of the central (or any other point of general constancy) to various corresponding points in the subfrontal gyre of the two sides shows that of the left to be considerably larger than the right in practically all its dimensions. The greater massiveness of the left subfrontal is readily appreciated when the two hemicerebra are compared with each other.

Mesial Surface. — The superfrontal, on its mesial surface, appears as a broad, richly-fissured gyre, of a width ranging between 2.9 cm. and 2.1 cm., and giving an impression of redundancy: few brains show quite so much cortical expanse in this region. The paracentral gyre is of good size and bold contour; its length is about 4 cm., its width between 2 and 2.7 cm. Its dorsi-mesal margin is indented by the central and inflected fissures, and its surface is marked by one vertical and one longitudinal intraparacentral segment: the latter is confluent with the caudal paracentral limb over a vadum.

That part of the callosal gyre which is cephalad of the precuneus, aside from the medicallosal fissure described above presents nothing unusual.

ORBITAL SURFACE is slightly concave, fairly well fissured and of rather broader expanse than on the left side. The mesorbital gyre is quite narrow. The remainder of this surface tends more to sagittal than to transverse division.

A certain peculiarity observable on this surface consists in the formation of a prominent eminence in the form of a limbus which is in apposition to the temporal apex as if struggling for the occupation of the middle fossa of the skull. This formation, to which I venture to give, provisionally, the name "postorbital limbus" is demarcated by a distinct incisure in which the wings of the sphenoid bone were received. As a result of this protrusion of the orbital parts into the middle fossa, the basisylvian fissure necessarily falls below the margin of the sphenoidal wings instead of being just at it. This is best seen in Fig. 2.

I find but one description in literature of a similar peculiarity, given by Retzius in "Das Gehirn eines Lappländers."* The limbus is shown in Wagner's plate of Gauss's brain, and the writer has since observed it in a Japanese brain.†

FISSURES OF THE PARIETAL AND OCCIPITAL LOBES (LATERAL SURFACE). *The Postcentral Fissural Complex.*—The postcentral boundaries are quite unusual and atypical. Instead of the usual long postcentral, only a small furcal segment is represented, embracing the caudal limb of the paracentral. The subcentral segment is also short and joins the parietal. Between the postcentral and subcentral lie two unnamed fissures; of these one runs obliquely across the postcentral gyre. The transpostcentral rises deeply from out of the sylvian cleft and divides into two rami.

The parietal fissure is deep and passes without interruption from the subcentral to become confluent with the paroccipital. In its course it sends off several short rami and joins the second (caudal) intermedial (*itml"*, Figs. 1 and 3). A transparietal (Brissaud) 4.5 cm. in length marks the parietal gyre.

The paroccipital is of the usual zygal form (Fig. 7) and is peculiar in that its cephalic stipe joins the occipital. The parietal joins the cephalic ramus, while the other paroccipital branches are free from anastomoses.

It remains to describe the two intermedials. The cephalic one (*itml'*), demarcating the marginal gyre from the angular, is a very small furrow: the caudal one (*itml"*),

* Retzius, *Internat. Beiträge z. Wiss. Med.*, I, p. 41, 1891.

† E. A. Spitzka, *American Journal of Anatomy*, Vol. II, 1903; Philadelphia Medical Journal, April 11, 1903.

demarcating the angular from the postparietal, is deep, ramified, and joins the parietal at considerable depth. The upturned ends of the episylvian, the supertemporal and the meditemporal, around which the three divisions of the subparietal lobule curve, are well marked and extensive.

The Exoccipital and Fissural Complex.—There are two exoccipital segments; the one (*eop'*) of zygal shape, with its longest ramus passing near to the occipital pole, its dorsocephalic ramus joining a segment of the meditemporal: the other (*eop''*) corresponding to the "sulcus occipitalis lateralis" of the authors, being a sinuous and much ramified fissure which also joins the meditemporal segment. Its caudal terminus closely approaches the postcalcarine.

MESIAL SURFACE.—The precuneal fissure may be regarded either as a zygal fissure with two short caudal rami, or, more properly, as a tri-radiate fissure with furcal caudal and dorsal limbs. It is independent. There are two small intraprecuneals.

The cuneus is marked by a large tri-radiate postcuneal, a cuneal ramus of the occipital, and a vertical ramus of the calcarine.

GYRES OF THE PARIETAL AND OCCIPITAL LOBES (LATERAL SURFACE.)—The postcentral gyre is quite flexuous, of irregular contour, and is in general less broad than its fellow on the right half. The parietal is of good width and is marked by the distinct transparietal. Its longitudinal extent is, however, less than most brains exhibit. The paroccipital gyre is of unusual form, due to the anastomosis of the paroccipital fissure with the occipital. The larger caudal portion is marked by two (postparoccipital) fissures.

Of the three divisions of the subparietal region the angular and postparietal gyres are very well developed, but the marginal is rather smaller than common. The significance of this feature will be discussed in the summary.

MESIAL SURFACE.—The precuneus is remarkably small, as is indicated by the small parietal index, 13.1. Its width, measuring between the caudal paracentral limb and the occipital, is only 2.4 cm. This reduction of its size is due to the great extent of the frontal lobe; in average brains we find the caudal paracentral limb to cut the dorsi-mesal margin at a point just dorsad of the edge of the splenium of the callosum; in Cope's brain it reaches further back by fully 1 cm. The cuneus, too, is small, but here the reason is a different one, depending on the closer proximity of the occipito-calcarine junction to the dorsi-mesal margin. In most brains this junction occurs at about 3.5 cm. from the margin; in Cope's brain it is 2.8 cm., bringing the point of the wedge further away from the splenium.

The callosal gyre, in its passage into the hippocampal becomes very narrow, owing to the close approach of the occipito-calcarine fissural stem to the hippocampal fissure.

FISSURES OF THE TEMPORAL LOBE (LATERO-VENTRAL SURFACE). — The supertemporal fissure is unusually tortuous, running in a widely diverging zig-zag path, and attaining the unusual length of 16 cm., measured with a wet string. It sends off numerous rami, one at each change in its direction and twice in its course it anastomoses with meditemporal segments. The latter fissure is represented by at least five pieces, of irregular shape and disposition and anastomosing frequently with neighboring fissures. The most caudal segment, in the postparietal region, anastomoses with both exoccipitals; with the second one of these (*EOP''*) in a very circuitous manner. The subtemporal is well-marked, of a length of 8 cm., and anastomoses with the meditemporal-exoccipital junction as well as the collateral fissure. The collateral fissure is divided into two segments by an isthmus; the cephalic segment is joined by the amygdaline (postrhinal).

GYRES OF THE TEMPORAL LOBE. — The supertemporal gyre is of tortuous irregular contour; its cephalic portion is uniformly narrow, its middle and caudal parts irregularly broad. The medifrontal is of good width, but is not distinctly demarcated from the subtemporal in its caudal part. The remaining temporal gyres present nothing unusual; they are all quite massive and very richly fissured.

THE INSULA. — In order to examine the insula, the opercula were carefully and gradually forced apart by insertion of cotton wads, in increasing quantity on successive days until the insular region was fairly exposed (Fig. 8). The transinsular fissure is long, the shorter insular fissures are all distinct and the entire insula is divided into four short (preinsular) gyres and one long (postinsular) gyre whose caudal part is again divided by a short accessory fissure: making in all six peri-insular digitations. Compared with the right insula it is better developed in every respect; broader, more massive (shown by a comparison of the depths of the sylvian fissures) and better fissured.

RIGHT HEMICEREBRUM. *The Interlobar Fissures. The Sylvian Fissure and its Rami.* — The sylvian fissure is only 4.8 cm. in length. Its course is less tortuous than that of the sylvian on the left side and is in general somewhat deeper. Its pre-sylvian depth is 14 mm.; the medi-sylvian, 21 mm.; the post-sylvian, 25 mm. The presylvian ramus is 1.8 cm. in length and joins an oblique segment in the subfrontal gyre. The subsylvian is hardly represented. Caudally the sylvian passes without much change of direction into its episylvian ramus, 1.5 cm. long. The hyposylvian is absent. The basisylvian is 20 mm. deep.

The central fissure, measured with a wet string, is 12 cm. in length; measured by compass, 8.5 cm., a trifle longer than its fellow on the left side. There are the same seven alternate curves and in general the fissure on this side is more tortuous than the one on the left, as will readily be appreciated by glancing at Figure 3. It sends a well-marked ramus into each of the adjacent gyres. The fissure is of good depth throughout, and independent of neighboring fissures. Its ventral end is separated from the sylvian, and its dorsal end is visible on the mesial aspect for about 1.5 cm.

The occipital fissure, as on the left side, ascends to the dorsi-mesal margin at a more obtuse angle than is common; in this case it is 68° (on the left it is about 70°). Its length on the mesial surface is 2.9 cm., on the dorsum 2 cm. As on the left half there exists a submergence of the cephalic arm of the paroccipital gyre; the cephalic stipe therefore is likewise confluent with the occipital, but in this case at a greater depth.

The calcarine fissure runs a very irregular zig-zag course, with numerous rami, and terminates just at the pole. Somewhat caudad of this terminus there is a short segment which corresponds with the piece on the left half presumed to be the post-calcarine ("sulcus extremus" of Schwalbe).

The calcarine and occipital fissures meet at nearly a right angle to continue as the occipito-calcarine stem for a distance of 3.8 cm., and just as in the left half, almost reaching the hippocampal fissure.

Fissures of the Frontal Lobe (Lateral Surface). *The Precentral Fissural Complex.* — In this case there are two segments, the supercentral and precentral. The former is of zygal form with its dorso-cephalic ramus confluent with the superfrontal. It is separated from the precentral by a superficial isthmus. The precentral is of good length and sends a long ("anterior precentral") ramus nearly across the medifrontal gyre, resembling its fellow on the left in this respect. Further ventrad springs another ramus which joins the "anterior precentral" by an oblique anastomosing fissure; in this way a gyral islet is formed which lies a trifle below the general surface of the cerebrum.

There is a short transprecentral, while the diagonal is absent.

The superfrontal is quite tortuous and as on the left side, is interrupted at about the cephalic third. The cephalic shorter segment is of zygal shape, but includes a depressed gyral "islet" similar to the one mentioned in the description of the precentral. As for the remaining fissures of this surface it is exceedingly difficult to recognize the typical pattern. While there are small scattered segments corresponding to the courses of the medifrontal and subfrontal fissures it is hard to trace them with any degree of certainty. The intricacy of the fissural arrangement here will best be appreciated on studying Fig. 4. One fissure, however, is distinctly marked, namely, the orbitofrontal. It is 3 cm. in length, and is joined by a piece which by its analogy with the fissuration of most brains can safely be named a medifrontal segment.

Mesial Surface. — The supercallosal is duplicated, i. e. represented by two segments which for a part of their course run parallel with each other. The caudal part, from its junction with the paracentral passes to cephalad of the genu, with a length of 6 cm.; the cephalic segment curving around the genu is 7 cm. in length. Both segments send off rami into the superfrontal gyre.

The paracentral fissure is of the same extent as on the left half, and sends off an intraparacentral ramus. Strictly speaking, there is not a true inflected fissure present; for the piece lying in the situation corresponding to the left inflected does not traverse or even reach the dorsi-mesal margin.

There is an independent rostral fissure.

Orbital Surface. — The fissures are three in number, exclusive of the olfactory. The principal one of the orbital fissures is the transorbital of Weisbach 3 cm. in length. The olfactory fissure is simple and 4 cm. in length. Only the extreme end is visible on the mesial aspect.

Gyres of the Frontal Lobe (Lateral Surface). — The precentral gyre is a trifle more tortuous and massive than on the left side. The superfrontal gyre is well demarcated and intricately fissured. The medifrontal and subfrontal together are of complex appearance, and are not clearly bounded from each other by distinct and typical fissures, since there is a tendency toward transverse, rather than longitudinal fissuration.[a]

Mesial Surface of the superfrontal is of similar expanse as on the left and is quite richly fissured. The paracentral gyre is of about the same size as on the left side, and its surface is marked by two intraparacentrals and a ramus of the paracentral. The dorsi-mesal margin is indented by the central and by a small unnamed segment just cephalad of the central.

Through the duplication of the supercallosal and the consequent deviation of the first segment toward the callosum, the callosal gyre is quite narrow in its cephalic part; caudad it is broader and marked by several fissures.

Orbital Surface. — The mesorbital gyre is a trifle narrower than that of the left side; the orbital surface generally is well fissured, but of less extent than that of the left half. The transorbital fissure permits of a division into a postorbital and several preorbital gyres. There is a slight tendency toward the formation of a "limbus" as has been noted on the left side.

Fissures of the Parietal and Occipital Lobes (Lateral Surface). *The Postcentral Fissural Complex.* — This consists of the usual two (postcentral and subcentral)

[a] On the right side of the brain of Czolgosz there is similar tendency shown in the division of the subfrontal fissure into two segments with intervening transverse pieces.

segments. The postcentral is irregularly branched and is separated from the subcentral by a small sub-isthmus. From near the middle of the fissure springs an anastomosing branch which joins the parietal and with the latter marks off a gyral "islet" not unlike that seen in the left half of Joseph Leidy's cerebrum. The subcentral fissure is moderately curved, sends off one ramus into the postcentral gyre and caudad joins both the intermedial and the parietal. As stated before it is only superficially joined by the postcentral. The transpostcentral appears on the lateral aspect as a furcal fissure with its cephalic limb the longer and quite curved.

The short parietal fissure is limited caudad by a paroccipital isthmus, and is joined by the second intermedial (*ITML''*) as well as by a short branch of the postcentral. A well-marked transparietal traverses the parietal gyre and crosses the margin to pass into the precuneus. Its total length is 5.5 cm.

The paroccipital, as was noted on the left half, also joins the occipital fissure by means of its cephalic stipe. The cephalic ramus is separated from the parietal while the caudal ramus joins the exoccipital.

The intermedials are two in number (with a possible third). The first (*itml'*) between the the marginal and angular gyres joins the subcentral; the second (*itml''*) joins the parietal. Another independent fissure, lying parallel to and between the second intermedial and the terminus of the meditemporal might be named the "intermedialis tertius."

The Exoccipital Fissural Complex.—The arrangement of the exoccipital segments is interesting. The "occipitalis anterior" and the "occipitalis lateralis" of the authors (our *eop'* and *eop''* respectively) are fused into one complex, very much ramified fissure which by its conjunction with the paroccipital and its close approach to the postcalcarine caudad, serves to demarcate the lateral boundary of the occipital lobe with fair accuracy.

Mesial Surface.—The precuneal fissure is seen to be of quadri-radiate shape and independent of neighboring fissures. The intraprecuneal piece has been described as confluent with the transparietal on the dorsum. The cuneus is marked by a triradiate postcuneal which is almost the exact counterpart of the same fissure on the left side. Two rami of the calcarine and two vertical independent fissures mark the cuneal surface.

Gyres of the Parietal and Occipital Lobes (Lateral Surface).—The postcentral gyre is a little broader and somewhat more flexuous than the left postcentral. Especially deep are the indentations by the rami of the postcentral fissure. The parietal gyre is a trifle broader than the left, and of more complex appearance, particularly in that region where practically a gyral "islet" is formed. The paroccipital gyre is quite massive and broad in its caudal part; the cephalic part is reduced and cut off by the occipital-paroccipital anastomosis.

The various regions of the subparietal lobule, including the marginal, angular and postparietal gyres, while exhibiting a good degree of development, are of smaller extent than on the left side. Their lesser massiveness has been noted above in the description of the *norma dorsalis*.

Mesial Surface. — The right precuneus is likewise unusually small, attaining a width of only 2.7 cm. (measuring between the caudal limb of the paracentral and the occipital fissure). Its general appearance resembles that of the left very well. The cuneus too is of similar size and shape and the remarks concerning the distance of the "wedge" from the callosum apply to this side as well. The occipito-calcarine junction takes place 2.7 cm. from the dorsi-mesal margin, and 2.1 cm. from the caudal edge of the splenium, practically identical with the distances on the left side. As on the left, the hippocampal gyre becomes extremely narrowed by the close approach of the occipito-calcarine stem to the hippocampal fissure.

Fissures of the Temporal Lobe (Latero-ventral Surface). — The supertemporal fissure is on this side more regular in its course and is shorter, being 13.5 cm. in length. It bifurcates caudally, embracing the second intermedial (*itml"*) between its limbs. It anastomoses with the sylvian as well as with the meditemporal segment. The meditemporal is represented by two irregularly ramifying segments, of which the caudal one anastomoses with the subtemporal. The latter fissure is of rather unusual extent, referring especially to the caudal piece which extends far caudad, and fuses with the lateral arm of the collateral, and combined with the latter almost reaches the calcarine fissure near the occipital pole. The cephalic subtemporal segment is of quadri-radiate type and also anastomoses laterally with the collateral.

The collateral attains a maximum length of 11 cm. It bifurcates caudally, anastomoses with the subtemporal as described above, and also with the occipito-calcarine fissural stem. The amygdaline is merely indicated by a shallow furrow which passes out of the basisylvian.

Gyres of the Temporal Lobe. — Compared with that of the left, the right supertemporal gyre is a trifle wider and of much more uniform shape. The same may be said of the remaining gyres; they are generally less complex than on the left.

The Insula. — The right insula is smaller than the left and presents only five peri-insular digitations, there being one postinsular and four preinsular gyres. (See Fig. 9.)

PRINCIPAL MEASUREMENTS OF THE CEREBRUM.

(After Hardening.)

	Centimeters.
Maximum length, left hemicerebrum	16.5
Maximum length, right hemicerebrum	16.4
Maximum width of cerebrum	13.5

(Cerebral Index, 81.8.)

Horizontal circumference	47.3
Maximum width, left hemicerebrum	6.8
Maximum width, right hemicerebrum	6.6
Left occipito-temporal length	12.8
Right occipito-temporal length	13.0
Length of callosum (or 43.7 per cent. of total cerebral length).	7.2
Left olfactory nerve, length	3.2
Right olfactory nerve, length	3.6

ARC MEASURES ALONG THE DORSI-MESAL MARGIN.

(Cunningham's Method.)

Left Hemicerebrum.

	Centimeters.
1. Cephalic point to central fissure	15.5
2. Central fissure to occipital fissure	3.1
3. Occipital fissure to occipital pole	5.0

Right Hemicerebrum.

1. Cephalic point to central fissure	15.5
2. Central fissure to occipital fissure	3.0
3. Occipital fissure to occipital pole	5.0

Cerebral Indices.

(Based on the arc measures given above.)

	Left.	Right.
Frontal index	65.6	65.9
Parietal index	13.1	12.8
Occipital index	21.2	21.3

HORIZONTAL DISTANCES,

Expressed in Centesimals of the Hemicerebral Lengths.

(For description of the method by which these measurements were made, see the chapter on "Brain measurement" in the introduction of this memoir.)

	From the Cephalic point to—	Left.	Right.
Lateral Aspect.	1. Tip of temporal lobe	23.6	22.5
	2. Sylvian-presylvian junction	29.1	29.9
	3. Ventral end of Central f.	43.6	40.2
	4. Sylvian-episylvian junction	60.6	54.8
	5. Caudal point	100.0	100.0

Mesial Aspect.	6. Cephalic edge of callosum . .	21.7	21.9
	7. Porta (For. of Monro) . . .	40.0	40.2
	8. Dorsal end of Central f. . . .	67.9	68.8
	9. Dorsal intersection of Paracentral f. .	72.7	70.7
	10. Caudal edge of callosum . .	65.4	65.8
	11. Occipito-calcarine junction .	78.7	79.3
	12. Dorsal intersection, occipital f. .	87.2	86.5

CEREBELLUM, PONS, OBLONGATA.—These parts all show good development, and are generally of symmetrical conformation. It might be mentioned that the striæ acusticæ on the floor of the fourth ventricle are only faintly discernible.

MEASUREMENTS OF THE CEREBELLUM.

	Centimeters.
Maximum height	5.9
Maximum cephalo-caudal diameter, left hemisphere .	6.5
Maximum cephalo-caudal diameter, right hemisphere	6.3
Dorsal length of vermis	4.0
Maximum depth, caudal incisure	1.6

MEASUREMENTS OF THE PONS.

Maximum length	2.6
Maximum thickness	2.4

THE BRAIN OF DR. WILLIAM PEPPER.[*]

Died in California on July 28, 1898, and his body was injected with an embalming fluid before its removal to Philadelphia. An examination of the thoracic and abdominal viscera was made by Dr. A. E. Taylor in California. Dr. William G. Spiller of Philadelphia removed the brain in Dr. Pepper's home and found that the injection had not been satisfactory for the brain was soft. The brain was placed in 10 per cent. formalin, supported on cotton. In May, 1904, it was transferred to 95 per cent. alcohol.

Immediately after its removal from the skull the brain weighed 1593 grams (Dr. Spiller). The weight of the hardened encephalic parts in July, 1904, was as follows:

Left hemicerebrum	487 grams.
Right hemicerebrum	488
Cerebellum, pons and oblongata, . .	116
Total	1091

indicating a loss of 502 grams or 32 per cent. of the original weight.

The brain is flattened and somewhat distorted. The cerebral peduncles were nearly torn through and the separation was completed by a knife-cut. The cotton placed at the sides of the cerebrum has pressed the temporal lobes together so as to nearly hide from view all the basal parts of the thalamencephalon. The chief altera-

[*] For a sketch of Dr. Pepper, see his life by F. N. Thorpe, Philadelphia, J. B. Lippincott Co. 1904.

tions of form consist in a flattening and lengthening together with an irregular reduction of the lateral diameters of the cerebrum.

In consistency the brain is only moderately firm and does not admit of much handling. The main cerebral arteries are atheromatous. There are no signs of gyral atrophy.

The callosum shares in the undue lengthening of the cerebrum, being 8.6 cm. long. At the genu its thickness is 10 mm., the average thickness of the body is 5 mm., while the maximum thickness of the splenium is 11 mm.

LEFT HEMICEREBRUM. *The Interlobar Fissures. The Sylvian Fissure and its Rami.* — The length of the sylvian fissure is 5.7 cm. Its course is nearly straight and its walls are in close apposition. The sylvian angle is approximately 20°. Its depths are as follows: Presylvian 9 mm.; medi-sylvian, 15 mm., post-sylvian, 27 mm.[a] The presylvian ramus is furcal. The reason for interpreting the arrangement here as a bifurcated presylvian rather than a conjunction of a subsylvian with the presylvian is that the radiate fissure in the usual arrangement lies within the preoperculum embraced by the sub- and presylvian rami. A subsylvian ramus is not present. The episylvian is 1.5 cm. in length. The hyposylvian is short and superficially confluent with a supertemporal segment.

The central fissure is 10.5 cm. in length, quite sinuous and of a good depth throughout. There is no anastomosis with any neighboring fissure.

The occipital fissure is very deep, shows numerous interdigitating subgyres, is 4 cm. in length on the meson and 2.5 cm. on the dorsum. It meets the calcarine fissure at an obtuse angle owing to the abutment of a spur from the precuneal-hippocampal junction.

The calcarine fissure is quite tortuous and runs uninterruptedly into the tri-radiate postcalcarine. The occipito-calcarine stem is 2.5 cm. in length.

Fissures of the Frontal Lobe (Lateral Surface). The Precentral Fissural Complex. — The supercentral is irregularly zygal and gives off the superfrontal cephalad. The precentral proper anastomoses with the superfrontal, the subfrontal and, via the short transprecentral, the sylvian fissure as well.

The superfrontal attains a length of 8 cm. The medifrontal springs from the orbitofrontal and is 4 cm. in length. The subfrontal is irregularly zygal, its stem being 3 cm. in length. The radiate fissure is independent and 3.5 cm. in length.

Mesal Surface. — The supercallosal fissure is separated from the paracentral, sends off two distinct rami across the superfrontal gyre near the frontal pole and is 10.5 cm. in length. A medicallosal fissure, 3.5 cm. long, marks the callosal gyre. The para-

[a] These depths are practically useless owing to the great distortion suffered by this specimen.

central fissure is of the usual form except that the element of the cephalic limb may be represented in the caudal piece of the supercallosal. There is a well-marked inflected fissure, over 3 cm. in length, and a frontomarginal piece marks the superfrontal gyre. The rostral and subrostral fissures are irregularly represented.

Orbital Surface. — The orbital fissure is H-shaped. The olfactory fissure is simple and 4.5 cm. in length.

Gyres of the Frontal Lobe (Lateral Surface). — The precentral gyre is of good proportions and particularly wide in its ventral third, where the emissary-motor centers for the faculty of speech lie. The remaining frontal gyres, superfrontal, medifrontal and subfrontal, are all well developed, wide and fairly complexly fissured.

The mesal surface of the superfrontal gyre is of good width and in its prefrontal portion exhibits a high degree of complex configuration. The paracentral gyre is of average size and the callosal gyre, as noted above, is for a portion of its extent subdivided into two tiers by a medicallosal fissure.

Fissures of the Parietal and Occipital Lobes (Lateral Surface). The Postcentral Fissural Complex. — The postcentral fissure is 4.5 cm. in length; its dorsal limbs, very obtusely divaricated, embrace the annectent gyre curving around the caudal limb of the paracentral. It sends off several rami and anastomoses with the parietal. The interpretation of the fissural parts in the region usually occupied by the subcentral, so useful in demarcating the postcentral gyre from the marginal is in this case obscured. There is a complexly ramified transpostcentral, together with two elements of a subcentral, of which one continues into the postcentral-subcentral piece. The parietal fissure is 4 cm. in length and joins the zygon of the paroccipital fissure. The paroccipital is of a compound zygal type. There is a well-marked and sinuous transparietal which anastomoses with the postcentral. The fissuration in the parieto-occipital transition is quite complex.

Mesal Surface. — The precuneal fissure is of irregular zygal shape and anastomoses with the paracentral. The intra-precuneal is continuous across the dorsi-mesal border with the transparietal. A cuneal fissure communicates with the occipital. A tri-radiate postcuneal lies at the dorsi-mesal margin of the cuneus.

Gyres of the Parietal and Occipital Lobes (Lateral Surface). — The postcentral gyre is of fair size and usual flexuosity. The parietal gyre is of good breadth, as is the paroccipital. The marginal gyre is particularly extensive.

Mesal Surface. — The precuneus is of good size, but the cuneus is relatively reduced.

Fissures of the Temporal Lobe. — The supertemporal fissure is notably interrupted in two places, presenting three segments, of which the middle one dips into the sylvian cleft. Caudally the fissure anastomoses with several other fissural elements, which render a precise description very difficult. The meditemporal and subtemporal fissures are quite ramified. The collateral fissure is quite long and anastomoses with the postcalcarine fissure.

Gyres of the Temporal Lobe. — The supertemporal gyre is narrowed near the episylvian fissure. The other temporal gyres are broad and complexly fissured. The subcalcarine gyre is especially broad in its caudal portion. The hippocampal gyre is rather narrow.

Owing to the fragility of the specimen the insulæ could not be examined in either hemicerebrum.

RIGHT HEMICEREBRUM. *The Interlobar Fissures. The Sylvian Fissure and its Rami.* — The sylvian fissure is very short (4 cm.) and its presylvian and subsylvian rami are considerably divaricated. The episylvian is 3 cm. in length; the hyposylvian 1 cm. Several fissures dip into the sylvian cleft.

The Central Fissure is fairly sinuous, is 10.5 cm. in length and anastomoses with the postcentral over a very superficial vadum.

The Occipital Fissure. — On the meson measures 3 cm.; on the dorsum, 2 cm. At the dorsi-mesal margin there is a small fossette where the occipital apparently divides into four rami. The vertical piece is the adoccipital.

The Calcarine Fissure. — The combined calcarine-postcalcarine is a simply sinuous fissure of a length of 6 cm., terminating caudally in a T-shaped bifurcation. The occipito-calcarine stem is a complex affair.

Fissures of the Frontal Lobe (Lateral Surface). The Precentral Fissural Complex. — The supercentral and precentral elements are confluent and quite ramified. From the combined fissure springs the superfrontal. The latter is interrupted by a transverse gyre which is demarcated by a very extensive transverse fissure passing from the dorsi-mesal border nearly to the subfrontal fissure. In the prefrontal region there are several other but shorter transverse pieces. The medifrontal springs from a short orbitofrontal and is 4 cm. in length. The subfrontal, together with the diagonal and radiate fissures which anastomose with it, is a very extensive complex.

Mesal Surface. — The arrangement of the fissures on the mesal surface is as follows: The paracentral is continuous cephalad with the frontomarginal (which appears like a duplication of the supercallosal), the supercallosal proper is rather short (6 cm.), the rostral fissure attains a length of 6 cm., while the subrostral is also quite long (3.5 cm.). There is a tri-radiate intraparacentral.

Gyres of the Frontal Lobe (Lateral Surface). — The precentral gyre is of good breadth, the superfrontal is fairly fused with the dorsal tier of the medifrontal by the numerous transverse gyres above mentioned, the ventral tier of the medifrontal is particularly broad while the subfrontal is quite well convoluted.

Mesal Surface.—The superfrontal gyre, on its mesal aspect, is distinctly divided into two tiers by the long and continuous frontomarginal fissure. The paracentral gyre is 4.5 cm. in length. The callosal gyre presents nothing unusual.

Fissures of the Parietal and Occipital Lobes (Lateral Surface). The Postcentral Fissural Complex.—The postcentral and subcentral together form a moderately sinuous fissure from which the parietal fissure arises. Dorsally the postcentral terminates in a T-shaped bifurcation. The total length is 7 cm. The parietal fissure is short, terminating caudad in a bifurcation, each of the furcal arms being again bifurcated. There is a well-marked transparietal. The paroccipital becomes continuous caudo-laterad with several fissures in the parieto-occipital region.

Mesal Surface.—The precuneal fissure is irregularly zygal and is joined by the intraprecuneal extension of the transparietal. A curved cuneal fissure, independent, marks the cuneus. There is a zygal postcuneal fissure.

Gyres of the Parietal and Occipital Lobes.—The postcentral gyre is, in general, a trifle narrower than its fellow on the left side. The parietal gyre is of good width; the paroccipital is quite complexly convoluted. The subparietal district is extremely large as is shown by the great encroachment of this area upon the sylvian fissure.

The precuneus is of good size. The cuneus is relatively small.

Fissures and Gyres of the Temporal Lobe.—The supertemporal fissure is represented by two segments, a short one at the temporal apex, a longer one caudad. Its caudal extension is considerably abbreviated. The meditemporal and subtemporal fissures are represented by several segments difficult to trace clearly. The tendency to transverse anastomoses of the fissures and their frequent interruption by transverse or oblique gyral isthmuses is very marked in the entire temporal lobe.

A BRIEF DESCRIPTION OF THE SKULL OF PROFESSOR E. D. COPE.

The skull is in fairly good condition. The calva has been separated by a saw-cut, and a portion of the parietal bone in the left temporal fossa is missing. The specimen is remarkable on account of the proportionately large size of the cranium as compared with the face, in this respect approaching the notable skull of Kant. The bones are thin but of considerable hardness and density. The alveolar processes of both jaws are absorbed to a considerable degree, serving to accentuate the relative smallness of the facial portion.

The parietal bones are notable for their expanse; the temporal ridges pass considerably ventrad of the middle of the bone; less than one-third of the parietal lies in the temporal fossa. The squama is reduced. The sutures in general show a fine serration. The appended measurements give further details which I will not recount here. The following characters of the skull may, however, be mentioned.

The skull is nearly mesaticephalic; there is facial orthognathism; the mandible is delicate; the nasal spine is pronounced. The nasion depression is quite marked; the malars are not very prominent; the zygomæ are quite delicate. The glabella is moderate; the supraorbital ridges are slight and most marked in their mesal portions, near the glabella. There is no pronounced sagittal elevation.

On the base of the skull may be noted: the styloids as well as the vaginal and spinous processes are well preserved; the styloids are strong and 2.5 cm. in length. The right jugular foramen is larger than that on the left side. The petrous portions are quite sunken within the surrounding parts as viewed ventrally. The basi-occipital and sphenoid are fused.

The internal capacity of the cranium, measured with dry mustard seed, is 1645 c.c. The weight of the skull minus mandible is 670 grams; the weight of the mandible is 72 grams.

MEASUREMENTS.

Internal capacity	1645 c.c.
(Brain-weight)	1545 grams.
(Ratio of cranial capacity to brain-weight)	100 : 94
Weight of cranium	670 grams.
Weight of mandible	72 "

Cranial Measurements.

Maximum antero-posterior diameter (L.)	18.8 cm.
Glabella-inion diameter	18.3
Intertuberal diameter	18.3
Maximum lateral diameter (B.)	14.2
Bi-auricular diameter	12.7
Minimum frontal diameter	9.2
Height, Basion to Bregma (H.)	13.5
L. + B. + H.	465
Modulus of L. B. H.	155
Bi-stephanic diameter	11.5
Height, Opisthion-Bregma	15.2
Auriculo-bregmatic height	12.0
Nasion-basion line	10.2
Basion-alveon line	9.2
Intermastoid line	10.7
Foramen magnum, antero-posterior diameter	3.9
Foramen magnum, lateral diameter	3.0
Pre-auricular projection	9.3
Post-auricular projection	9.5

Horizontal circumference	52.8
Pre-auricular arc (52 per cent.)	27.4
Post-auricular arc (48 per cent.)	25.4
Frontal (sagittal) arc	13.0
Parietal arc	12.7
Occipital arc	12.0
Total sagittal arc	37.7
Sagittal arc + foramen magnum + nasion-basion line	51.8
Nasion-inion arc	33.5
Inion-opisthion arc	4.2
Lambda-inion arc	7.8
Auriculo-calvarial arc	34.0
Auriculo-calvarial arc over bregma	32.0
Bi-auricular diameter + auricular-calvarial arc	47.7

Measurements of Face.

Facial width (between zygomatic-maxillary suture)	12.2 cm.
Bi-zygomatic diameter	12.8
Facial height	——
Nasion-alveon line	5.8
Nasal height	4.8
Nasal width	2.1
Interorbital septum (or 21.5 per cent. of line between orbital ends of malo-frontal sutures)	2.0
Orbital height	3.4
Orbital width	4.0
Orbital depth	4.5
Maximum exterior width of superior alveolar arch	5.7
Between supraorbital foramina	5.6
Between infraorbital foramina	4.5
Palate length	4.0
Palate width	3.9
Between mental foramina	4.6
Facial angle (Cloquet)	80°
Facial angle (Jacquart)	78°

Indices

Cranial index (L. : B.)	77.6
Length : height	71.9
Breadth : height	95.1
Length : nasion-basion line	54.2
Index of occipital projection	50.5
Frontal index	34.5
Parietal index	33.6
Occipital index	31.9
Nasal index	43.7
Orbital index	85.0
Palatine index	97.5

Internal Cranial Measurements.

Maximum internal antero-posterior diameter .	{ left	16.8
	{ right	16.7
Maximum internal lateral diameter		13.7
Occipito-temporal diameter .	{ left	14.1
	{ right	13.9
Internal basion-bregma height		13.0

SUMMARY.

It were unwarranted to propose conclusions of wide significance upon so little material and only brief comments are offered here upon the most notable findings in these brains. In general the cerebral surface shows complex development with intricate fissuration and a bold contour of the numerous gyres. In some brains one or another region preponderates over other regions in the degree of development. The parieto-occipito-temporal area is generally the most redundant. The brains of the two Leidys show a general superficial or physiognomic resemblance but aside from a few points, as for instance in the course of the right superfrontal fissures, there is not so marked a likeness as I was able to demonstrate in the brains of the three Van Wormer brothers. But as in the case of the three brothers, the isthmus and cerebellum are almost identical in size and weight, while the cerebrum of Joseph is immense as compared with Philip's. Philip's callosum seems to have striven to attain the great size of Joseph's and is therefore disproportionately long. Philip's brain does not exhibit the great preponderance of the right parieto-occipital areas which characterize Joseph's cerebrum. This redundancy is remarkable in the right hemicerebrum of Pepper's brain and the distortion suffered by this specimen is particularly deplorable.

A remarkable contrast is shown by a comparison of Joseph Leidy's brain with that of Cope, and it is best expressed by the ratio which the mesal area of the frontal lobe bears to the cuneus precuneus area. This ratio in most brains is

70 : 30

In the brain of Joseph Leidy it is:

66 : 34

In Cope's brain it is:

73 : 27

The difference can be seen in the drawings shown in Figure 75, in which the cuneus-precuneus area is shaded while the mesal area of the frontal lobe is left unshaded. Recalling now the functions of the two great association areas under discussion, the surmise that we have here a true somatic expression of naturally endowed superiority of the powers of conception of the concrete in the one brain, and of remarkable powers of thought in the abstract in the other brain, were one which past experiences in cerebral localization seem to justify. Cope was more creative and constructive, philosophic and formative than Leidy; Leidy was a far keener observer of things, quick at seeing analogies and comparisons, coupling his multitudinous observations into generalizations and systematizations in a superior manner. Leidy was a good visualizer, and

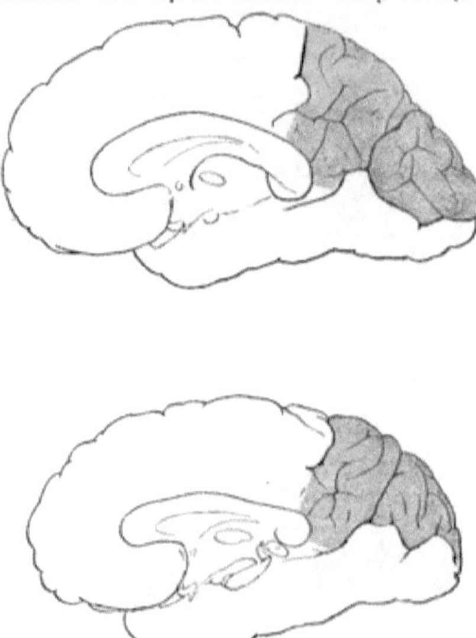

FIG. 75. The upper drawing represents the mesal view of the right hemicerebrum of Professor Leidy; the lower drawing the same view of the brain of Professor Cope. Cuneus and precuneus shaded. In the case of Professor Leidy, the area of the cuneus and precuneus together (shaded) is to that of the frontal lobe (unshaded) as 34 : 66; in Professor Cope's, the ratio is as 27 : 73 (these ratios were determined by weighing pieces of sheet-lead carefully cut of exactly the same size). In other words, there is a relative redundancy of the parieto-occipital areas in Professor Leidy, while in Professor Cope it is the frontal area which preponderates.

possessed good powers of memorizing and recalling visual impressions. He excelled in his abilities as a microscopist, as shown by his monumental work in parasitology, helminthology and upon the rhizopods. But Cope, I take it, busied himself much more with abstract generalizations, though I wish by no means to imply that his observational powers were in any way defective. I merely wish to emphasize in what way these two men were so differently endowed by nature. I had been led to search in this direction by my findings in the brains of Major J. W. Powell, concerning whose mental traits I once knew nothing, but whose great parieto-occipito-temporal association area (particularly in the right or preponderatingly sensory half) led me to venture the presumption that this redundancy probably corresponded to a superior ability to register and compare the impressions in the visual, auditory and tactile spheres (which together form the concept sphere). That Major Powell's intimate friends and co-workers corroborated, in general, these presumptions, was indeed gratifying, and I trust that the similar venture in the case of Cope and Leidy meets with like approval.

Another interesting somatic expression is to be found in a comparative tabulation of the "cerebro-cerebellar ratio." The cerebro-cerebellar ratio of weight is expressed by the weight of the cerebrum as compared with that of the cerebellum, the latter being taken as 1. By "cerebrum" in this connection is really meant a part of the diencephalon as well, the division of the parts being made by the customary cut passing cephalad of the pons and usually between the pre- and postgemina. In the following list are tabulated the cerebro-cerebellar ratios in the brains of eleven eminent and ten ordinary men:

TABLE, CEREBRO-CEREBELLAR RATIO.

E. C. Seguin	1:9.0		
Edouard Seguin	9.0		
Jos. Leidy	9.0	F. Van Wormer	1:9.0
G. F. Train	8.8		
Wm. Pepper	8.7		
J. W. Powell	8.4		
Hosea Curtice	8.4		
Daniel Webster (estimated)	8.2	Koepping	8.2
Philip Leidy	8.1	Tobin	8.1
J. B. Pond	8.0		
		Gaimari	7.7
		W. Van Wormer	7.4
		B. Van Wormer	7.4
		Burness	7.4
		Czolgosz	7.3
		Ennis	7.3
Harrison Allen	7.0	Turkofski	7.0

A glance at the list shows that while in ordinary men the ratios cluster around 1 : 7.5, among eminent men it is fully a unit higher: that is to say, the cerebrum, or essential-thought apparatus, is relatively more massive, while the somatic organ of motor coördination (cerebellum) remains relatively reduced.

Certain special studies on the form and size of the callosum in various brains prompt me to introduce some remarks concerning the prevailing ideas about the relative importance of white and gray matter (or, using more appropriate terms, the alba and cinerea). So much has been said of the gray matter and its constituent nerve-cells that the very notable researches of Flechsig and his co-workers in the field of myelin-development is often overlooked. Were it not for the manifold connection of such cells with each other, as well as with the periphery by means of the millions and

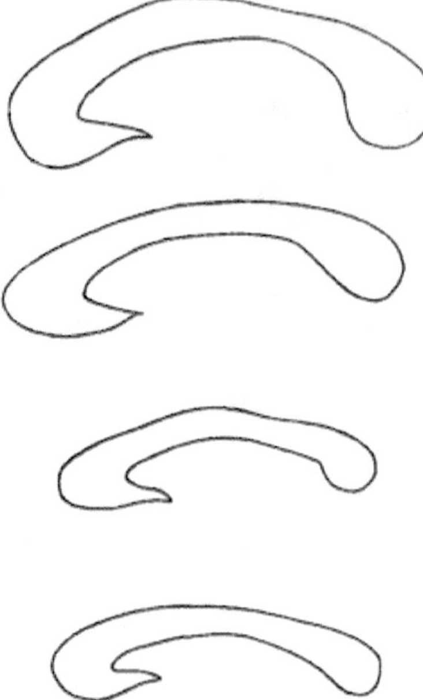

FIG. 76. Outline drawings of the cross-section of the callosum of 1. Professor Joseph Leidy, morphologist; 2. Dr. Edward C. Seguin, neurologist; 3. A laborer, white; 4. A negro.

millions of fibers, such a brain, as already pointed out, would be as useless as a multitude of telephone or telegraph stations with all inter-connecting wires destroyed. The bulk of (normal) white matter in the brain therefore signifies elaborated gray matter and hence the significance of brain-weight in relation to brain-powers; for even though there be, as has been computed, over nine billion cells in the cortex, their weight is probably less than 1 per cent. of the total brain-weight.[3] But if there is still more intricate inter-connection of nerve-cells, out of proportion as it were (by means of untold numbers of association fibers), the mass of white matter must necessarily be greater. So characteristic is this preponderance of white matter in the brain of man, and so needful is such an elaboration and amplification of the cerebral architecture to the workings of the human mind, that it is only necessary to glance at the cross-sections of the brains of lower animals as compared with that of man (Fig. 13), while we pause to think that, after all, it is this enormous coördination of the sep-

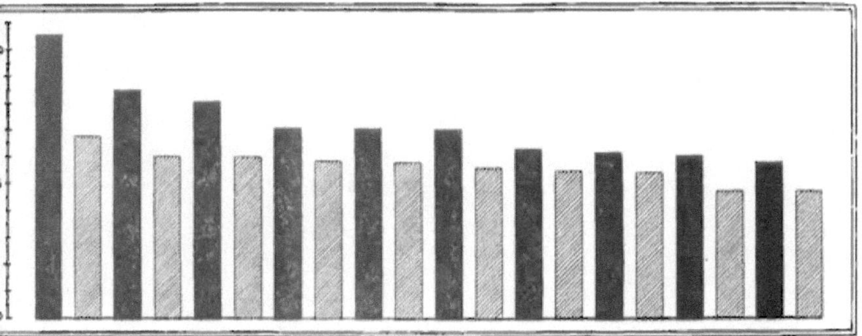

FIG. 77. Chart showing the cross-section areas of the callosum (in square centimeters) in the brains of ten eminent men (see solid black), compared with ten such of ordinary laborers, mechanics, etc. (see shaded figures). The largest callosum (10.6 sq. ctm.) is that of Professor Joseph Leidy, the eminent morphologist; the smallest (4.7 sq. ctm.) is that of a laborer of ordinary intelligence.

arate units of thought and action which constitutes the somatic basis of the highest mental functions. And in the Mammalian series, as we ascend from the small-brained Marsupial with few callosal fibers, intermingled with those of the dorsal or hippocampal commissure to the great neo-pallial commissure which the brain of man exhibits, we may perceive an indication of the elaboration of at least one division of the great complex of association systems: I refer now to the bilateral coördinations exclusively. But beyond the fact that the fibers of the callosum connect like regions in the two hemicerebra little more is expressed, and yet every case of deficiency or disease of this structure is attended by more or less profound weak-mindedness or downright idiocy, not to speak of hemiparetic and other affections. And the examination of the brains of these notable men, possessing large capacity for doing and thinking much

[3] Hammarberg, Thompson and Donaldson.

more than their fellows, shows the converse to be quite as true. Compared with ordinary men, individually and collectively, they have larger callosa (Figs. 76, 77). The callosum of Joseph Leidy exceeds in cross-section area that of any other in this series or recorded in literature. Here again, then, we have an index in somatic terms of how we may distinguish the brain of the genius or talented man from that of persons of only ordinary abilities.

TABLE A.

MEASUREMENTS OF THE BRAINS OF THE SIX SCIENTISTS AND SCHOLARS DESCRIBED IN THIS MEMOIR, TOGETHER WITH THOSE OF THE BRAINS OF MAJOR J. W. POWELL, DR. E. C. SEGUIN, AND GEORGE FRANCIS TRAIN, COMPARED WITH THE AVERAGES OBTAINED IN THE BRAINS OF TEN ORDINARY MEN TABULATED IN TABLE B.

Name	Joseph Leidy	Philip Leidy	A. J. Parker	H. Allen	E. D. Cope	Wm. Pepper	J. W. Powell	E. C. Seguin	G. F. Train	Avs. of 9 Eminent Men	Avs. of 10 Ordinary Men
Age	67	53	36	56	57	......	68	55	75	58	33
Brain weight (grams)	1545*	1415	1475*	1531	1545	1593	1488	1502	1525	1513	1443
Brain length	18.2	15.9	17.3	16.8	16.5	18+	17.4	17.5	16.8	17.2	17.2
Brain width	13.4	12.2	12.6	14.1	13.5	12.3	13.8	12.5	14.7	13.2	13.9
Cerebral index	74.9	77.2	73.6	83.9	81.8	......	79.3	71.4	88.0	78.7	81.0
Horizontal circumference	51.0	46.2	48.0	50(48)	47.3	50.0	50.3	49.0	52.5	49.4	50.2
Width, left hemicerebrum	6.7	6.1	......	7.1	6.8	6.1	7.1	6.3	7.4	6.5	6.93
Width, right hemicerebrum	6.7	6.1	......	7.0	6.6	6.2	6.7	6.2	7.3	6.4	6.98
Left occipito-temporal length	13.2	11.9	13.3	12.0	12.8	13.3	13.6	13.3	13.3	13.1	13.3
Right occipito-temporal length	13.3	12.0	13.7	11.6	13.0	13.7	13.0	13.4	13.3	13.1	13.1
Length of callosum	8.5	8.0	7.15	8.0	7.2	8.6	7.4	7.9	7.3	7.7	7.26
Percentage of callosal length compared with brain-length	46.7	50.6	41.5	47.6	43.7	47.7	42.5	45.1	43.7	45.5	41.3
Left centro-temporal height	11.2	10.4	10.2	9.5	10.5	8.7	10.1	10.7	11.1	10.2	10.8
Right centro-temporal height	11.6	10.5	10.3	9.1	10.5	8.5	10.4	11.2	11.2	10.3	10.9
Left centro-olfactory height	10.1	8.8	9.2	8.7	8.7	6.7	7.7	9.0	9.0	8.6	8.9
Right centro-olfactory height	10.2	8.8	9.2	8.4	8.7	7.0	8.0	9.5	9.1	8.8	9.0
Arc Measures:											
Left — Frontal arc	16.0	14.3	14.0	13.0	15.5	14.5	15.5	16.0	16.0	15.0	15.5
Left — Parietal arc	7.2	5.4	5.5	4.5	3.1	5.5	5.0	6.0	5.5	5.3	5.7
Left — Occipital arc	5.9	5.8	5.5	6.0	5.0	6.0	5.3	7.0	6.5	5.3	5.7
Right — Frontal arc	16.0	14.5	14.0	14.0	15.5	13.6	16.0	16.0	16.0	15.0	15.5
Right — Parietal arc	6.5	5.0	6.0	4.0	3.0	6.8	5.0	8.0	6.0	5.6	5.5
Right — Occipital arc	6.8	6.0	5.0	5.5	5.0	5.6	5.0	5.5	6.0	5.6	5.9
Cerebral Indices:											
Left — Frontal index	54.95	56.1	56.0	55.3	65.6	55.7	60.0	54.2	57.0	57.2	57.7
Left — Parietal index	24.74	21.2	22.0	19.1	13.1	21.1	19.4	20.3	19.8	20.1	21.0
Left — Occipital index	20.27	22.7	22.0	25.6	21.2	23.1	20.5	25.4	23.2	22.7	21.3
Right — Frontal index	54.60	56.8	56.0	59.0	65.9	52.3	61.5	54.2	57.0	57.5	57.7
Right — Parietal index	22.18	19.7	24.0	17.0	12.8	26.1	19.2	27.1	21.5	21.3	20.4
Right — Occipital index	23.12	23.5	20.0	23.5	21.3	21.5	19.2	18.7	21.5	21.4	22.1
Horizontal Distances: (Expressed in centesimals of the hemicerebral length) From the cephalic point to—											
Left Lateral Aspect — 1. Tip of temporal lobe	28.8	25.5	25.9	......	23.6	......	23.0	25.6	22.0	25.7	24.0
Left Lateral Aspect — 2. Sylvian presylvian junction	33.8	28.7	30.5	......	29.1	......	31.0	29.1	29.4	30.2	30.4
Left Lateral Aspect — 3. Ventral end of central fissure	40.5	40.1	42.0	— —	43.6	......	40.0	44.0	42.0	41.7	44.4
Left Lateral Aspect — 4. Sylvian-episylvian junction	67.2	56.0	60.5	......	60.6	......	63.7	60.0	61.2	61.3	60.5
Left Lateral Aspect — 5. Caudal point	100	100	100	......	100	......	100	100	100	100	100
Left Mesal Aspect — 6. Frontal edge of callosum	18.8	16.9	......	......	21.7	......	2.01	20.0	21.0	19.7	22.0
Left Mesal Aspect — 7. Porta (Foramen of Monro)	40.2	37.6	......	......	40.0	......	40.2	42.5	42.1	40.4	41.2
Left Mesal Aspect — 8. Dorsal end of central fissure	57.5	59.2	57.5	......	67.9	......	61.2	65.7	65.0	62.0	63.9
Left Mesal Aspect — 9. Dorsal intersection of paracentral f.	70.0	66.2	65.1	......	72.7	......	64.9	70.3	71.1	68.6	68.2
Left Mesal Aspect — 10. Caudal edge of callosum	66.6	67.5	......	......	65.4	......	63.2	68.6	65.0	66.0	64.2
Left Mesal Aspect — 11. Occipito-calcarine junction	75.5	72.6	......	......	78.7	......	57.3	77.0	74.7	72.6	74.7
Left Mesal Aspect — 12. Dorsal intersection of occipital f.	87.2	88.5	84.1	......	87.2	......	86.7	91.4	95.0	88.6	86.2

* Estimated brain weight.

NOTE.—Blank spaces indicate that the measurement could not be made or, because of distortion while hardening, was not available for the purposes of comparison. The absolute measurements of the brains of the eminent series are often below those determined in the brains of the ordinary series for the reason that most of the former were preserved in alcohol or mixtures containing alcohol, and therefore producing more or less shrinkage, while the latter were all preserved in formaldehyde and underwent little or no shrinkage. The figures expressing relativity (in centesimals or percentage) are the most useful for analysis.

TABLE B.

MEASUREMENTS OF THE BRAINS OF TEN ORDINARY AND NORMAL INDIVIDUALS.

These brains were removed promptly after execution by electricity and placed in a formaldehyde mixture while still firm and fresh, affording an ideal opportunity for securing measurements upon brains which have suffered a minimum of distortion.*

Name	Turkelski	Willis Van Wormer	Burton Van Wormer	Fred Van Wormer	Gaimari	Ennis	Tobin	Koepping	Bergström	Barness	Averages
Age	41	27	23	21	31	30	40	22	55	45	33
Brain-weight	1295	1340	1358	1630	1340	1290	1520	1590	1490	1503	1443
Brain length	16.6	16.8	17.3	18.3	16.0	16.6	17.6	17.9	16.8	18.4	17.2
Brain width	13.7	13.9	14.0	14.7	14.1	13.2	14.3	14.0	14.0	13.4	13.9
Cerebral index	82.5	83.2	80.9	80.3	88.1	79.5	81.2	78.2	83.3	73.2	81.0
Horizontal circumference	48.5	48.5	50.5	53.0	49.2	47.5	51.5	51.7	50.5	51.0	50.2
Width, left hemicerebrum	6.8	7.0	7.0	7.3	7.1	6.4	7.1	7.0	7.0	6.6	6.93
Width, right hemicerebrum	6.9	6.9	7.0	7.4	7.0	6.6	7.2	7.0	7.0	6.8	6.98
Left occipito-temporal length	12.5	12.8	13.3	13.9	12.8	12.8	13.0	13.8	13.2	14.2	13.3
Right occipito-temporal length	12.5	12.6	13.3	13.9	12.7	12.3	13.0	13.7	12.0	13.9	13.1
Length of callosum	6.1	7.2	7.2	7.2	6.6	7.1	7.4	7.8	7.0	8.0	7.26
Percentage of callosal length	36.7	42.2	41.6	39.3	41.2	42.7	42.0	43.6	40.2	43.5	41.3
Left centro-temporal height	10.7	10.0	10.2	11.1	10.7	10.5	11.2	11.6	10.9	11.0	10.8
Right centro-temporal height	10.7	9.9	10.2	11.2	10.6	10.7	11.3	11.4	11.6	11.1	10.9
Left centro-olfactory height	8.4	8.4	8.7	8.9	9.6	8.7	9.3	9.5	9.2	9.2	8.9
Right centro-olfactory height	8.1	8.7	8.7	8.9	9.0	8.9	9.6	9.5	9.3	9.3	9.0
ARC MEASURES:											
Left: Frontal arc	13.5	14.5	16.0	17.0	16.0	14.5	16.5	16.0	15.5	16.0	15.5
Left: Parietal arc	5.5	5.5	5.2	5.7	5.5	5.5	6.5	6.0	6.0	5.0	5.7
Left: Occipital arc	5.5	6.0	6.0	6.8	5.5	5.0	5.0	6.0	5.5	6.0	5.7
Right: Frontal arc	13.5	15.2	16.0	17.2	16.0	14.0	16.5	16.0	15.5	15.0	15.5
Right: Parietal arc	5.5	5.3	5.0	5.3	5.5	5.5	6.2	5.7	4.8	6.0	5.5
Right: Occipital arc	5.5	5.5	6.2	7.0	5.5	5.5	5.3	6.3	6.7	6.0	5.9
CEREBRAL INDICES:											
Left: Frontal index	55.1	55.7	58.8	57.6	59.2	58.0	58.9	57.0	57.4	59.2	57.7
Left: Parietal index	22.4	21.1	19.1	19.3	20.4	22.0	23.2	21.5	22.2	18.5	21.0
Left: Occipital index	22.4	23.1	22.0	23.1	20.4	20.0	17.9	21.5	20.4	22.3	21.3
Right: Frontal index	55.1	58.1	58.8	58.3	59.2	56.0	58.9	57.0	57.4	55.4	57.7
Right: Parietal index	22.4	20.4	18.4	17.9	20.4	22.0	22.2	20.4	17.8	22.3	20.1
Right: Occipital index	22.1	21.1	22.7	23.8	20.4	22.0	18.9	22.6	24.8	22.3	22.1
HORIZONTAL DISTANCES: (Expressed in centesimals of the hemicerebral length) From the cephalic point to—											
Left Lateral Aspect: 1. Tip of temporal lobe	25.4	24.4	23.7	25.6	21.8	24.1	23.6	24.0	25.1	22.1	24.0
Left Lateral Aspect: 2. Sylvian-presylvian junction	30.2	30.9	30.0	28.4	28.1	32.0	30.1	30.8	32.7	30.6	30.4
Left Lateral Aspect: 3. Ventral end of central fissure	40.9	45.8	45.4	44.8	43.4	48.1	45.0	40.9	45.6	42.6	44.4
Left Lateral Aspect: 4. Sylvian-episylvian junction	55.5	66.0	......	66.1	55.0	59.7	58.0	60.0	66.6	57.4	60.5
Left Lateral Aspect: 5. Caudal point	100	100	100	100	100	100	100	100	100	100	100
Left Mesal Aspect: 6. Frontal edge of callosum	24.2	21.7	21.4	22.4	22.5	22.9	22.1	20.1	22.8	20.2	22.0
Left Mesal Aspect: 7. Porta (Foramen of Monro)	42.0	40.4	41.6	40.9	41.2	42.1	40.6	41.3	42.2	39.4	41.2
Left Mesal Aspect: 8. Dorsal end of central fissure	59.7	60.6	65.3	60.1	73.1	66.2	62.5	58.6	70.1	62.0	63.9
Left Mesal Aspect: 9. Dorsal intersection of paracentral f.	62.7	66.6	72.2	65.5	77.5	69.9	68.2	63.7	73.1	62.9	68.2
Left Mesal Aspect: 10. Caudal edge of callosum	61.5	64.9	64.1	62.8	65.0	65.0	64.2	63.9	63.7	66.6	64.2
Left Mesal Aspect: 11. Occipito-calcarine junction	75.7	75.0	76.3	74.3	73.1	79.5	76.1	72.0	73.1	72.1	74.7
Left Mesal Aspect: 12. Dorsal intersection of occipital f.	84.0	85.1	87.2	83.0	91.9	85.5	88.0	85.4	89.4	82.5	86.2
Right Lateral Aspect: 1. Tip of temporal lobe	24.2	24.1	21.9	22.1	21.2	24.2	20.5	22.4	25.3	24.0	23.0
Right Lateral Aspect: 2. Sylvian-presylvian junction	29.0	31.9	28.3	33.3	30.0	31.0	26.3	30.3	31.9	28.2	30.0
Right Lateral Aspect: 3. Ventral end of central fissure	42.6	46.4	41.0	47.0	40.6	42.8	40.0	38.2	42.2	41.3	42.2
Right Lateral Aspect: 4. Sylvian-episylvian junction	60.9	54.8	56.0	56.8	53.7	54.6	54.2	52.2	59.0	57.4	55.9
Right Lateral Aspect: 5. Caudal point	100	100	100	100	100	100	100	100	100	100	100

* In a forthcoming treatise on the brains of criminals these and other brains, secured through the courtesy of Mr. C. V. Collins, superintendent of New York prisons, and Warden Addison Johnson, will be more fully described.

TABLE A.—*Continued.*

EASUREMENTS OF THE BRAINS OF THE SIX SCIENTISTS AND SCHOLARS DESCRIBED IN THIS MEMOIR TOGETHER WITH THOSE OF THE BRAINS OF MAJOR J. W. POWELL, DR. E. C. SEGUIN, AND GEORGE FRANCIS TRAIN, COMPARED WITH THE AVERAGES OBTAINED IN THE BRAINS OF TEN ORDINARY MEN TABULATED IN TABLE B.

Name	Joseph Leidy	Philip Leidy	A. J. Parker	H. Allen	E. D. Cope	Wm. Pepper	J. W. Powell	E. C. Seguin	G. F. Train	Avs. of 9 Eminent Men	Avs. of 10 Ordinary Men
Right Lateral Aspect: 1. Tip of temporal lobe	26.9	26.0	22.9	......	22.5		23.2	23.0	21.4	22.3	23.0
2. Sylvian-presylvian junction	30.2	31.4	27.7	......	29.9		30.4	27.5	30.3	29.6	30.0
3. Ventral end of central fissure	42.3	40.2	40.1	......	40.2		39.1	42.0	41.7	40.8	42.2
4. Sylvian-episylvian junction	51.1	59.4	57.0	......	54.8		51.7	57.5	53.5	55.5	55.9
5. Caudal point	100	100	100	......	100		100	100	100	100—	100
Right Mesal Aspect: 6. Frontal edge of callosum	18.4	16.9	......	......	21.9	......	20.1	20.5	20.9	19.8	22.0
7. Porta (Foramen of Monro)	40.1	......	......	......	40.2	......	40.2	42.5	41.7	40.9	44.0
8. Dorsal end of central fissure	57.7	60.4	58.7	......	68.8	......	64.4	67.2	66.6	63.4	64.3
9. Dorsal intersection of paracentral f.	62.9	66.0	64.7	......	70.7	......	66.6	71.8	70.2	67.5	69.2
10. Caudal edge of callosum	64.7	68.0	......	......	65.8	......	63.2	66.7	64.3	65.4	64.2
11. Occipito-calcarine junction	76.1	76.7	......	......	79.3	......	73.8	84.0	76.8	78.1	75.5
12. Dorsal intersection of occipital f.	86.8	87.4	85.9	......	86.5	......	86.7	96.5	91.0	88.7	87.2
OSS-SECTION AREA OF CALLOSUM	10.61	7.01	7.07	8.04	5.77	7.07	6.12	8.48	6.31	7.39	5.63
EREBRO-CEREBELLAR RATIO: (Weight of *cerebellum* = 1)	9.0	8.1	......	7.0	8.0	8.7	8.4	9.0	8.8	8.4	7.7
EASUREMENTS OF CEREBELLUM: Max. height	5.6	5.5	......	......	5.9	4.6	5.2		5.4	5.4	5.7
Max. cephalo-caudal diam., left	6.4	6.2	6.2	......	6.5	6.7	6.0		6.1	6.3	6.5
Max. cephalo-caudal diam., right	6.5	6.2	6.2	......	6.3	6.7	5.7		6.4	6.2	6.5
Dorsal length of vermis	3.6	3.8	......	......	4.0	4.2	3.4		4.1	3.9	3.9
Max. depth of caudal incisure	1.5	1.4	1.4	......	1.6	1.2	1.1		1.4	1.4	1.5
Max. width	10.1	10.0	9.5	......	......	7.9	10.1		10.3	9.6	10.4
EASUREMENTS OF THE PONS: Max. length	2.9	2.9	2.4	......	2.6	......	2.6	......	2.5	2.6	2.7
Max. thickness	3.0	......	......	......	2.4	......	2.7	......	2.8	2.7	2.5

NOTE.—Blank spaces indicate that the measurement could not be made or, because of distortion while hardening, was not available for e purposes of comparison. The absolute measurements of the brains of the eminent series are often below those determined in the brains the ordinary series for the reason that most of the former were preserved in alcohol or mixtures containing alcohol, and therefore oducing more or less shrinkage, while the latter were all preserved in formaldehyde and underwent little or no shrinkage. The figures pressing relativity (in centesimals or percentage) are the most useful for analysis.

TABLE B.—*Continued.*

MEASUREMENTS OF THE BRAINS OF TEN ORDINARY AND NORMAL INDIVIDUALS.

These brains were removed promptly after execution by electricity and placed in a formaldehyde mixture while still firm and fresh, affording an ideal opportunity for securing measurements upon brains which have suffered a minimum of distortion.*

Name	Turkofski	Willis Van Wormer	Burton Van Wormer	Fred Van Wormer	Gaimari	Ennis	Tobin	Koepping	Bergstrom	Burness	Averages
Right Mesal Aspect: 6. Frontal edge of callosum	24.2	21.7	21.4	22.0	22.5	22.9	22.1	20.2	23.5	19.0	22.0
7. Porta (Foramen of Monro)	42.0	40.3	41.1	41.5	40.6	42.2	40.6	40.0	42.2	39.4	41.0
8. Dorsal end of central fissure	60.3	64.1	62.4	61.7	68.7	67.7	66.3	65.7	67.4	58.9	64.3
9. Dorsal intersection of paracentral f.	64.5	70.5	68.8	68.3	73.1	71.4	69.7	68.5	72.3	62.5	69.2
10. Caudal edge of callosum	61.5	64.5	63.6	63.3	63.1	67.9	64.0	64.6	65.6	65.7	64.2
11. Occipito-calcarine junction	74.0	73.5	73.9	72.1	78.7	77.0	78.2	78.0	77.7	71.7	75.5
12. Dorsal intersection of occipital f.	85.0	89.7	86.7	84.1	91.1	89.4	89.0	85.3	87.3	84.2	87.2
CROSS-SECTION AREA OF CALLOSUM	4.71	5.80	5.41	5.20	4.72	5.49	5.62	6.75	5.98	5.81	5.66
CEREBRO-CEREBELLAR RATIO: (Weight of cerebellum = 1)	7.0	7.1	7.4	9.0	7.7	7.3	8.1	8.2		7.4	7.7
MEASUREMENTS OF CEREBELLUM:											
Max. height	6.1	5.2	5.1	5.1	5.4	5.6	5.9	6.3	6.3	6.0	5.7
Max. cephalo-caudal diam., left	6.1	6.7	6.9	7.0	6.1	6.4	6.5	6.3	6.5	6.5	6.5
Max. cephalo-caudal diam., right	6.1	6.7	6.9	7.0	6.1	6.4	6.5	6.5	6.5	6.5	6.5
Dorsal length of vermis	4.1	4.0	4.0	4.0	3.3	3.6	3.7	3.9	4.0	4.1	3.9
Max. depth of caudal incisure	1.5	1.5	1.5	1.7	1.5	1.5	1.3	1.6	1.7	1.7	1.5
Max. width	10.4	10.6	10.8	11.0	10.5	9.8	10.7	10.6	11.2	10.7	10.4
MEASUREMENTS OF THE PONS:											
Max. length	2.1	2.7	2.7	2.7	2.6	2.7	2.5	3.2	2.9	2.8	2.7
Max. thickness	2.3	......	......	......	......	......	2.8	......	......	2.5	2.5

* In a forthcoming treatise on the brains of criminals these and other brains, secured through the courtesy of Mr. C. V. Collins, superintendent of New York prisons, and Warden Addison Johnson, will be more fully described.

In conclusion the writer desires to acknowledge many courtesies and kindly encouragements proffered him by Doctors F. X. Dercum, Horace Jayne, Judson Daland and Joseph Leidy, Jr., members of the American Anthropometric Society.

ABBREVIATIONS USED IN THE FIGURES OF THE BRAINS.

GYRES.

ANG.G.	Angular.	*PO.ORB.G.*	Postorbital.
CL.G.	Callosal.	*PRC.G.*	Precentral.
HMP.G.	Hippocampal.	*PR.ORB.G.*	Preorbital.
INS.	Insular.	*PTL.G.*	Parietal.
PR.INS.G.	Preinsular.	*SBCLC.G.*	Subcalcarine.
PO.INS.G.	Postinsular.	*SBCLT.G.*	Subcollateral.
MARG.G.	Marginal.	*SBFR.G.*	Subfrontal.
MFR.G.	Medifrontal.	*SBTMP.G.*	Subtemporal.
MORB.G.	Mesorbital.	*SPFR.G.*	Superfrontal.
MTMP.G.	Meditemporal.	*SPTMP.G.*	Supertemporal.
PARC.G.	Paracentral.	*PPTL.G.*	Postparietal.
PAROC.G.	Paroccipital.	*IFL.G.*	Inflected.
PC.G.	Postcentral.		

FISSURES.

ADOC.	Adoccipital.
AMYG.	Amygdaline.
BS.	Basisylvian.
C.	Central.
CL.	Callosal.
CLC.	Calcarine.
CNL.	Cuneal.
DG.	Diagonal.
EOP.	Exoccipital.
EOP'.	
EOP''.	
EPS.	Episylvian.
FMG.	Frontomarginal.
HMP.	Hippocampal.
HPS.	Hyposylvian.
ORBFR.	Orbitofrontal.
ORBFR'.	
PARC.	Paracentral.
CPH.L.	cephalic limb.
CD.L.	caudal limb.
PAROC.	Paroccipital.
PC.	Postcentral.
PC'.	
PCLC.	Postcalcarine.
PML.	Paramedial.
POCN.	Postcuneal.
PRC.	Precentral.
PRC'.	
PRCN.	Precuneal.
PRS.	Presylvian.
PTL.	Parietal.
RDT.	Radiate.
RST.	Rostral.
S.	Sylvian.

IFL.	Inflected.
IPARC.	Intraparacentral.
IPRCN.	Intraprecuneal.
ITML.	Intermedial.
ITML'.	
MCL.	Medicallosal.
MFR.	Medifrontal.
MFR'.	
MTMP.	Meditemporal.
MTMP'.	
MTMP''.	
OC.	Occipital.
OCLC.	Occipito-calcarine stem.
OLF.	Olfactory.
ORB.	Orbital.
SBC.	Subcentral.
SBFR.	Subfrontal.
SBFR'.	
SBRST.	Subrostral.
SBS.	Subsylvian.
SBTMP.	Subtemporal.
SBTMP'.	
SPC.	Supercentral.
SPCL.	Supercallosal.
SPCL'.	
SPFR.	Superfrontal.
SPFR'.	
SPTMP.	Supertemporal.
SPTMP'.	
TRORB.	Transorbital.
TPRC.	Transprecentral.
TRPC.	Transpostcentral.
TRPTL.	Transparietal.
TRINS.	Transinsular.

NOTICE

Preceding volumes of the New Series can be obtained at the Hall of the Society. Price five dollars each.

A few complete sets of the Transactions, New Series, Vols. I—XX, are on sale. Price, one hundred dollars.

TRANSACTIONS

OF THE

AMERICAN PHILOSOPHICAL SOCIETY

HELD AT PHILADELPHIA

FOR PROMOTING USEFUL KNOWLEDGE

VOLUME XXI—NEW SERIES

PART V

ARTICLE V.—*A Search for Fluctuations in the Sun's Thermal Radiation Through Their Influence on Terrestrial Temperature.* *By Simon Newcomb.*

Philadelphia:
THE AMERICAN PHILOSOPHICAL SOCIETY
104 SOUTH FIFTH STREET
1908

ARTICLE V.

A SEARCH FOR FLUCTUATIONS IN THE SUN'S THERMAL RADIATION THROUGH THEIR INFLUENCE ON TERRESTRIAL TEMPERATURE.

By Simon Newcomb.

(Read October 4, 1907.)

PREFATORY NOTE.

The purpose of the following study is two-fold. The subject of periodicity in meteorological phenomena, and its relation to the sun, is prominent in scientific literature; and the author desired to treat it by methods different from the usual ones. He also wishes to submit to the courteous consideration of meteorologists the question whether the methods here developed can not be advantageously used in other branches of their science.

The work has been carried through under the auspices of the Carnegie Institution, the Trustees of which have enabled the author to avail himself of the necessary appliances, facilities, and computing assistance. Acknowledgment is also due to the U. S. Weather Bureau, the Chief of which has placed at the author's disposal, without restriction, the rich body of material contained in its records, as well as the printed collections in its library; and to the Director of the *Deutsche Seewarte* of Hamburg for the courteous transmission of unpublished material.

ANALYTICAL TABLE OF CONTENTS.

Introduction: — Review of the field; — general principle of the methods adopted; — necessity for a criterion for distinguishing between fluctuations of temperature proceeding from local causes and from general causes common to the entire globe. Pp. 311-315.

CHAPTER I.

Methods of Investigating Fluctuating Quantities.

§ 1. *Fluctuations in a fixed period.* The period being supposed known, the amplitude of the departure at any time may be expressed in a Fourier series of which the coefficients can be determined by the method of least squares. Pp. 315-317.

§ 2. *Irregular fluctuations tending toward a definite period; the method of time-correlation.* When the fluctuation, not having a definite period, yet has a periodic tendency, this tendency can be brought out by the method of time-correlation, which is also applicable to the determination of an unknown period. Pp. 317–321.

§ 3. *Treatment of fluctuations without discernible period.* Criterion for deciding whether seemingly irregular fluctuations of temperature in widely separated regions of the globe have any common element: method of determining this element. Pp. 321–325.

§ 4. *Case when different weights are assigned to different regions.* Pp. 325–326.

§ 5. *Method of combining regions in pairs.* Pp. 326–328.

CHAPTER II.

REVIEW OF DATA AND PROCESSES.

§ 6. *Choice and combination of material.* Pp. 328–332.

§ 7. *Arrangement of the work.* P. 332.

CHAPTER III.

DISCUSSION OF ANNUAL DEPARTURES OF TEMPERATURE.

§ 8. *Fluctuation having the period of the sun spots.* Work of Köppen,—hypothesis of a harmonic inequality in temperature corresponding to the sun spot period—method of determining the coefficients of the fluctuation—amount and formulæ of the sun spot fluctuation as determined from all readily available observations. Pp. 332–341.

§ 9. *Irregular fluctuations in the mean annual temperature.* Annual departures on which the results are based—evidence of correlation between annual temperatures in neighboring regions—correlations of stations by pairs—small outstanding systematic residuals showing a quasi-periodic character, the seeming period being about six years. Pp. 341–347.

§ 10. *Time correlations among annual world temperatures.* A six-year periodicity strongly brought out from 1871 to 1900, but not in earlier years from 1820. Pp. 347–350.

CHAPTER IV.

DISCUSSION OF MONTHLY DEPARTURES.

§ 11. *Discussion of Dove's departures.* Comparison of departures of temperature in widely separated regions collected by Dove—a seeming slight correlation is indicated. Pp. 351–355.

§ 12. *General discussion of monthly departures from 1872 to 1900.* A well marked correlation is found, which may be attributed to the fact that some pairs of stations compared were geographically in each other's neighborhood—evidence of correlation in this case—omitting these, some evidence of fluctuations common to the whole earth, of which the mean amplitude is ±0°.18 C.—this result is in part due to the failure to correct the temperatures for the sun spot period, and partly represents the systematic fluctuations of the annual departures already found. Pp. 355–362.

CHAPTER V.

STUDY OF TEN-DAY TERMS.

§ 13. *Stations and material used.* Pp. 363–365.

§ 14. *Tabular exhibit of ten-day departures during the period 1871–1904.* Summation of the squares through annual periods. Result, absence of any correlation whatever. Pp. 365–375.

§ 15. *Search for variations synchronous with the sun's synodic rotation by the method of time correlation.* When a tendency toward a periodic variation can be expected — choice of San Diego as a station — time correlation through a period of 33 years from 1872 to 1904; result, only a suspicion of a periodic tendency, the amplitude being two or three hundredths of a degree — further illustration of the method from the general ten-day departures — tendency toward a persistence of temperature conditions through periods of more than 40 days. Pp. 375–379.

CHAPTER VI.

Discussion of Results.

§ 16. *Summary of conclusions.* Actuality of the sun spot fluctuation — uncertain evidence of fluctuations having a shorter period — limitation within which the conclusions are to be interpreted. Pp. 379–381.

§ 17. *Relation between solar radiation and meteorological processes.* The present study limited to thermal radiation — the question whether other emanations producing auroræ and magnetic storms have any appreciable thermal effect — relation between fluctuations of the solar radiation and the fluctuations of temperature hence arising — possible causes of change in the solar radiation — definitive outcome of the investigation. Pp. 381–384.

§ 18. *Comparison with results of Langley's work of 1884.* Pp. 384–387.

INTRODUCTION.

The view that the rate at which the sun radiates thermal energy is or may be variable finds frequent expression in scientific literature. The inference of such variability may be drawn from two sources: one direct measures with the bolometer, the other, meteorological phenomena, especially variations of temperature at the earth's surface. Many years ago Lockyer pointed out that a cycle corresponding to that of the solar spots was indicated in the agricultural productions of India. A similar cycle has been sought for in the variations of temperature at special places, and in a variety of meteorological phenomena. Brückner has in an elaborate work adduced evidence to show a cycle of about 35 years in meteorological changes generally, those of temperature included. Although the fluctuations here described are not always expressly attributed to the action of the sun, it would be difficult to account for them in any other way than by fluctuations in the sun's radiant energy.

Bigelow's many and long-continued researches on meteorological phenomena, with the view of determining their laws and periods of variations and their relation to the activity of the sun, have also led him to an affirmative conclusion. The best marked period he has sought to establish is one corresponding to the period of the sun's synodic rotation. But the actual conclusions deducible from his work seem to relate to the electric and magnetic effects of the solar activity, rather than to purely thermal effects, which alone are studied in the present work.

Strong evidence on the affirmative side of the question was adduced by Langley, in a discussion of bolometric measures of the sun's radiation in 1902–3, compared with fluctuations in the general terrestrial temperature. During the year 1903 especially, the bolometer showed well-marked periods during which there seemed to be a remarkable diminution of intensity of the sun's radiation. On comparing these fluctuations with those of the temperature in various regions of the globe, derived from the *Dekadenberichte* of the Hamburg Seewarte, a seeming correspondence was shown between the two classes of fluctuations. The relation was exhibited by curves, but was not reduced to the form of an exact numerical relation with a determined probable error.

Notwithstanding the volume of observation and investigation bearing on the subject, and generally supposed to point to the actual existence of fluctuations in the sun's heat, the question cannot be regarded as settled until more precise numerical results than any yet reached are worked out. The drawing of conclusions from any system of direct measures of the sun's radiation, whether made by the bolometer or any other instrument, is subject to the seemingly insurmountable difficulty that the variations in the transparency and temperature of the atmosphere, especially in the higher regions, which may materially affect the measures, cannot be accurately determined. It is equally impossible to determine with precision the varying fraction of the heat which may be intercepted by the atmosphere, and to eliminate the radiation of the matter contained in the atmosphere itself. The uncertainty arising from these ever-varying causes might indeed be reduced indefinitely by comparing simultaneous observations at points so widely separated that no common atmospheric cause could affect the measures at any two stations. But, so far as the writer is aware, no attempt to organize such a series of determinations has yet been made.

On the other hand, when it is proposed to detect fluctuations in the solar radiation by observations of temperature, we meet with the difficulty that the temperature is everywhere subject to fluctuations from local causes, especially the varying aërial circulation, which it is impossible to determine, or to eliminate individually. Hence, in studying the fluctuations of temperature at any one place or in any one region, the problem arises of distinguishing between those due to local causes, and those due to changes in the original source of heat.

The purpose of the present work is to develop and apply the methods best adapted to secure definite results, especially the methods of investigating correlations between irregularly fluctuating quantities. The fundamental principle of this method is the same as that applied by the author long ago in collaboration with E. S. Holden, in discussing the question whether measured variations in the sun's apparent diameter were real: and, more recently, whether there existed any tendency toward unisexuality in families. This method is applicable to fluctuations so irregular that no law, periodic or otherwise, can be detected in their course. Periodicity is to be detected by other methods, involving somewhat different principles, which will also be developed.

In investigating the question it is well to consider in advance the general character of the fluctuations which may be expected. The first question to arise is: assuming that the sun's activity, as determined by terrestrial observations, is subject to a periodic change, what periods are the most likely? The reply to this is that there are only two periods which can be assigned in advance with any plausibility. One is that of the sun-spots; the other that of the sun's synodic rotation. The latter period would arise if one hemisphere of the sun were occasionally at a higher temperature than the other through two or more successive rotations. We must regard this as highly probable if the solar radiation is subject to any change whatever. It is, in fact, rather unlikely that any cause affecting the temperature of the solar envelope would act at one and the same time over the whole of the photosphere. If a difference in the two hemispheres were permanent, or even if it continued through large fractions of a year, there would be no difficulty in detecting it. As a matter of fact, permanence is scarcely to be expected, and it is in consequence difficult to distinguish between irregular fluctuations and those having this origin.

Granting that some region of the photosphere experienced a rise or fall of temperature which continued through an entire rotation, the effect would be seen in a corresponding fluctuation in the general temperature of the earth. From what is known of motions in the photosphere, it is clearly impossible that two different regions of the solar photosphere at the same latitude and the same altitude can be permanently at different temperatures. But even if the difference in question ordinarily continued only through two or three months, there would be no difficulty in detecting the periodic effect as special regions of the photosphere would successively be brought into view by the sun's rotation. On the other hand, if the inequality of temperature did not ordinarily continue through a single rotation, the effect could not be distinguished from that of irregular fluctuations.

The problem of determining whether there is any period in terrestrial temperature corresponding to that of the solar spots is one of such simplicity that it need not be dwelt upon in the present connection. It will be studied in the course of the present paper.

The really difficult problem is that of detecting with certainty irregular fluctuations in the radiation. The difficulty arises from the fact just mentioned that the fluctuations of temperature are everywhere determined by varying and accidental meteorological causes, especially the motion of large bodies of air from one region to another, and the varying presence of water in its various forms in the atmosphere. Leaving out these disturbing causes it is very natural, when the temperature of a wide region is markedly above or below the normal for a considerable period, to attribute the condition to a change in the amount of heat received from the sun. The question of the reality of this cause admits of an obvious test. A change in the sun's radiation will necessarily affect every part of the earth. If therefore a change of temperature in one region has this cause as a factor we may, accidental causes aside, expect a similar change in every other region. The problem is thus reduced to that of detecting a correlation between the fluctuations of several varying quantities.

Since the ordinary fluctuations of temperature are mainly due to local causes, we may expect the average or general temperature of the entire globe to be sensibly constant if the sun's radiation is invariable. To speak more precisely if, on any one day, it is found that the temperature in every part of the earth is in the general average above or below the normal, we might rationally attribute this result to the sun. We thus see that a very obvious way of testing the constancy of the solar radiation is to determine the deviation of the temperature from the normal on any one day over all points of the globe, and form their mean. The fluctuations of this mean would represent those of the sun's radiation.

It being impossible to extend observations over the entire globe we must accept the results of observations made within regions at which observations of temperature are actually available. But even then it would be an error to conclude that variations in the general mean must be due to the sun or any other common cause. It is not to be expected that the accidental deviations in different regions completely neutralize each other. The question must therefore be open, after we have determined the changes of mean temperature from time to time over the whole globe, whether the mean fluctuations outstanding are purely accidental, or are due to changes in the thermal energy received from the sun. A rigorous method of treating this question will also be developed.

It follows that, in order to reach a well-grounded conclusion, some criterion is necessary to determine whether the changes in the general temperature of the globe are due to changes in the solar radiation, or to accidental terrestrial causes. No criterion which will decide this question in any individual case is possible, but there is a criterion by which the average amount of the cosmical fluctuation, if it be appreciable, can be determined. To show the simplest example of its application let the deviation of the temperature from the normal be observed from day to day and from year to year in two regions of the earth so widely separated that no common purely terrestrial cause can affect the two places at the same time. Then, by the law of probabilities, we should find in the long run that there was no permanent correlation between the fluctuations at the one place and at the other. For example, calling the two regions A and B, if we put into one class all the days on which the temperature in region A is markedly above the normal, and in another class all the days in which it is markedly below normal; and if we take the temperatures in the distant region B for the same two classes of days, then, in the absence of any correlation, we should find the mean temperatures at B to be the same in the two classes. If we found that the mean temperature at B was above the normal when it was above the normal in A, and below it in the contrary case, it would show that there was some common cause affecting the two places. Should the mean temperature in B be entirely independent of that in A it would show that there was no common cause affecting the temperature of the two places and therefore that the fluctuations were not due to changes in the sun's radiation.

By this criterion the existence of either periodic or non-periodic changes can be equally well established, provided that a sufficiently long series of observations is made use of. But it does not enable us to determine the law of change, but only the general fact. When the general form of the law is known, especially when the fluctuations are of definite period, other methods may be applied.

CHAPTER I.

METHODS OF INVESTIGATING FLUCTUATING QUANTITIES.

§ 1. *Fluctuations in a Fixed Period.*

The quantities with which we are concerned in the present paper are in the nature of observed departures from normal or mean values. Such departures may be either results of observation, or they may be derived *a priori* from some theory which is to be tested by observation. Those considered in the present paper are of the first class. We shall take up the general problem of studying fluctuations by considering it in the form suggested by the special problem now before us.

At every place and in every region on the surface of the earth there is for every day a certain mean temperature, best determined by reading the thermometer at a number of equi-distant intervals. These means may be extended through periods of any length, thus giving a series of temperatures extending indefinitely year after year. The temperatures thus observed undergo fluctuations in an annual period, which may be represented either by a Fourier series, or by a smoothed curve extending as nearly as may be through all the observed temperatures. A normal mean temperature for each day throughout the year at any one place may thus be determined from the observations of a number of years—the more the better. Subtracting the normal temperature of each day, or through a period of several days, from the mean temperature actually observed through the same period, we have a certain departure from the normal, due to accidental or systematic causes. To fix the ideas I shall designate the period for which the mean of these departures is taken as a *time-term*, or *term* simply. The data then given by observation comprise the mean departures for a long number of terms, each considered as a unit, and forming so far as possible a continuous series.

The most obvious classification of such departures is into periodic and irregular. In the rigorous mathematical sense a periodic departure is one which always returns to the same value at the end of an interval P of time, called the period. This may be either known or assumed in advance, or regarded as unknown. It cannot, however, be determined as an unknown quantity from conditional equations, because it is impracticable so to introduce it as to give the equations a soluble form. If not regarded as known we have to proceed by the method of trial and error. In this form the question will be whether a certain assumed period P is indicated by observed departures. If the fluctuation had no other term than a purely periodic one as thus defined, its existence could be ascertained by simple inspection. Imagining the fluctuations to be expressed by the ordinates of a curve of which the abscissa is the time, we only have to measure on the axis of abscissas from any arbitrary point, the series of distances P, $2P$, $3P$, etc., to the end of the series. We then take a number of intermediate points and erect at each an ordinate expressing the observed departure. If P is the true period the ordinates would have the same value at all the points distant from each other by a multiple of P. Practically, however, we always have to deal with the case in which other fluctuations than those of period P enter. We thus have accidental deviations superposed upon the periodically recurring departures, which may quite mask them. In this case it is necessary to take the mean value of the observed departure at the several moments P, $2P$, etc., after the initial moment. The mean of all these values would be that corresponding to the initial phase. Taking, as an example, the fluctuations represented in Figure (2), we see that the departure is positive at the beginning of a period.

The method of deciding whether a fluctuation of an assumed period P really exists is this. We divide each period into any convenient number of equal parts by the points 1, 2, 3, etc. We then taket he mean of all the ordinates at the several points 1; the mean for the points 2, for the points 3, etc. The several means then show the mean fluctuation during any one period. The absence of any fluctuation in the given period would be shown by these mean values differing from each other only by quantities which might be the result of the accidental deviations.

If the period is unknown, we must discover it tentatively by taking for P the value which gives the best marked mean fluctuation, or the greatest range of value among the mean departures.

In the numerical computation on this principle, after the period is known, or has been discovered, the most general mode of proceeding is that of development in a Fourier series. We take an angle N increasing uniformly with the time at such a rate that it goes through 360° in the period P. Then, if we represent the departure at any time by v, we assume it, considered as a function of the time, to be developable in the form

$$v = x_0 + x_1 \cos N + x_2 \cos 2N + \cdots + y_1 \sin N + y_2 \sin 2N + \cdots$$

Regarding x_0, x_1, x_2, $\cdots y_1$, y_2, as unknown quantities, the coefficients of these quantities at each epoch of observation will be the sines or the cosines in the second number of the equation. Substituting for each moment of observation the values of these sines and cosines, and taking the observed departures for v, we shall have a system of equations for determining the unknowns. The solution of these equations by the method of least squares will give the values of the unknowns which best represent the observations.

This method is sometimes employed in meteorology to determine and express the diurnal and annual fluctuations in the temperature. For reasons not necessary to detail at present, the method of forming the mean values, in the manner first set forth, and then finding the curve which best fits them, is preferable except when, for any reason, all multiples of N above the first are omitted. In this last case the fluctuation will be a purely harmonic one, the coefficients of which can be determined with great facility by equations of condition. An example will be given in investigating the fluctuations in temperature having the sun-spot period.

§ 2. *Irregular Fluctuations Tending Toward a Definite Period. — the Method of Time Correlation.*

There is a class of fluctuations in which the period may be fairly definite, but yet for which the preceding method would give no period whatever. This occurs when we have a superposition of two classes of causes, or two sources of departure, one of which, by itself, would result in a fluctuation in a definite period, while the other is in the nature of perturbations, resulting in disturbances of the phase either continuously or from time to time, and leading to seeming frequent changes in the length of the period. If the preceding or any other method resting on the assumption of unchanging period be applied to this case, the result might be that no period whatever would give a definite fluctuation. In other words a series of departures taken at equi-distant moments would, in the long run, have for their mean either an evanescent value, or a constant value for all phases.

To this class of fluctuations belong the ocean waves. If these are carefully observed we shall generally find in them a tendency in a given state of the weather to follow each other at fairly definite intervals, perhaps at 10, 15 or 20 seconds, according to the distance between the crests. But should we take the mean period, however exact, and record the phase of the wave at any long series of moments separated by exactly this period, we should find no one phase always recurring at the moments thus defined. After a few seemingly regular recurrences of the wave, its height diminishes, perhaps almost to zero, or a fresh series of waves of similar period begins at a different phase from that determined by the preceding waves.

Another case of the same kind is afforded by the swing of a pendulum which is subjected to a continually repeated disturbance, sometimes nearly stopping it, sometimes accelerating it, and sometimes changing the phase of the swing. How frequently soever these disturbances may follow each other, there will always be in the motion of the pendulum a tendency toward its regular period as a function of its length. But it may be impracticable to determine any definite time of oscillation through a long series of observations. In cases like these the perturbations may be so considerable, and follow each other at such short intervals, and the regular mean amplitude of the fluctuation may be so small or variable, that it will be impossible to detect the tendency toward a regular period, except by the application of some special method. To devise a method we must find some criterion for distinguishing between a tendency toward a definite period and complete irregularity.

Any tendency toward a definite period P may be defined in the following way: Let τ be the observed departure at any moment, and τ' the departure at a definite interval P following it. Now if there be really a tendency toward the period P, τ' should differ from τ only by the difference of perturbations, or accidental deviations, which may however be larger than either of the undisturbed departures, and therefore may completely mask the tendency toward equality between τ and τ'. However this may be, the undisturbed departure midway of the period, that is, at the moment $\frac{1}{2}P$, will have the opposite sign τ and τ'. It follows that in the general average, by comparing a large number of departures in triplets, the individual members of which are distant $\frac{1}{2}P$, and calling τ_1 the mean of all the middle departures, the excess of $\tau' - \tau_1$ will in the general average be opposite in sign from τ' itself. If a period be found for which this holds true in the general mean, we have a tendency toward a rhythmical movement in the period P.

The detection of such a period is easy by a method which we may call that of *time-correlation.* The nature of the criterion will be most readily seen by the graphic representations in Figures 1 and 2. Let Figure 1 represent an approximately harmonic fluctuation. If the ordinate at 0 represents the initial variable quantity, there

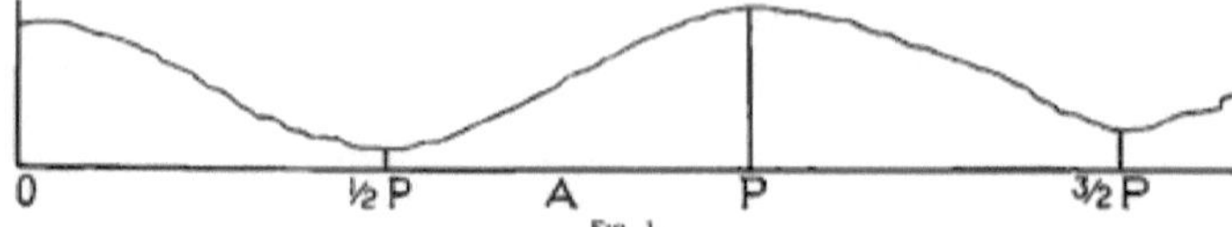

FIG. 1.

will always be a rising phase between the points ½*P* and *P*; say near the point *A* at ¾ of a period from *O*. If our initial departure is near ¾*P*, then we shall have a descending phase between *P* and 3/2*P*, which is ½ of a period further on.

Now, imagine that the regular fluctuations thus represented have superimposed upon them accidental deviations so large as to mask the harmonic character of the fluctuations. Were these accidental deviations superimposed upon a harmonic motion in a continuous succession of periods, they could be detected by continuing one system of observations through a number of periods, because they would then be eliminated from the mean. But we are supposing a case in which the period is itself disturbed.

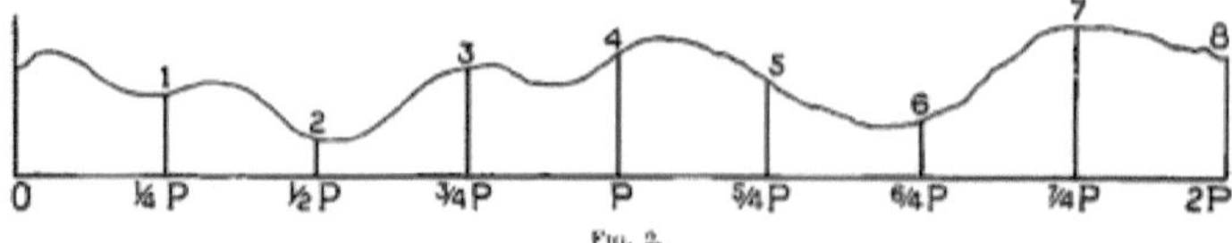

FIG. 2.

What we therefore have to do is to take a number of starting points, numbered 0, 1, 2, etc., and continue the series from each so far as we deem it useful to do so. In these several series the accidental deviations will still be eliminated, ultimately leaving in the general mean a tendency toward the harmonic phase as described.

Such a case is shown in Figure 2. Here there is not evident to the eye any tendency toward an exact period. But a study of the diagram shows that by measuring off equidistant intervals to the points *P*, 2*P*, etc., the departure is, in the general mean positive, while at the middle points of the spaces it is, in the general mean, negative. A criterion is thus offered by which any periodic tendency may be brought out.

We shall now show the method of time-correlation by which not only a period of any length, but any tendency toward a period, may be shown. The period being regarded as entirely unknown, the observed departure from the general mean at any moment may be regarded as due to the periodic term which we seek, with accidental deviations superimposed. Let us put $\mathbf{a}_0$ for the departure at some initial moment; then let us take a series of equi-distant intervals of time, starting from the initial one, and let us put

$$\mathbf{a}_1, \mathbf{a}_2, \mathbf{a}_3, \cdots, \mathbf{a}_n$$

the deviations at the ends of the intervals t, $2t$, $3t$, ... nt. If there is any tendency toward a rhythmical motion in these departures, having a period greater than $2t$ but less than nt, then, in the general average, assuming $\mathbf{a}_0$ to be positive, we should find first a diminution and then an increase in the series of **a**'s; that is, the curve representing the departures would be convex to the axis of abscissas.

Since one departure may be taken for the initial one as well as another, we may repeat this process with a_1, a_2, etc., as the initial departures, carrying the products in each case to the requisite number of terms. We shall thus have a series of products which may be continued as far as the series of observed departures extends. Taking as an example $n = 5$, the arrangement is the following:

	$\mathbf{a}_0^2$	$\mathbf{a}_0\mathbf{a}_1$	$\mathbf{a}_0\mathbf{a}_2$	$\mathbf{a}_0\mathbf{a}_5$
	$\mathbf{a}_1^2$	$\mathbf{a}_1\mathbf{a}_2$	$\mathbf{a}_1\mathbf{a}_3$	$\mathbf{a}_1\mathbf{a}_6$
	$\mathbf{a}_2^2$	$\mathbf{a}_2\mathbf{a}_3$	$\mathbf{a}_2\mathbf{a}_4$	$\mathbf{a}_2\mathbf{a}_7$
	⋮	⋮	⋮	⋮
Sums:	$[\mathbf{aa}]$	$[\mathbf{aa}_1]$	$[\mathbf{aa}_2]$	$[\mathbf{aa}_5]$

This arrangement suggests the solution by least squares of a problem which may be put into the following form. Starting as before with the initial departure a_0, if the fluctuation be a purely harmonic one, the departure at the end of half a period would always be $-a_0$, that at the end of a period $+a_0$, etc. In general the departure at any time t will be of the form $a_0 + x$, x being a periodic function of t. Consequently the actual deviations a_1, a_2, etc., will be of the form

$$a_1 = a_0 x_1 \pm e_1;\ a_2 = a_0 x_2 \pm e_2;\ \text{etc.}$$

e_1, e_2, etc., being the purely accidental parts of the deviations. The problem thus resolves itself into determining a series of factors x_1, x_2, x_3, etc., by means of the conditional equations

$$a_1 = a_0 x_1;\ a_2 = a_0 x_2;\ \text{etc.}$$

These may be combined by the method of least squares. The normal equation is

$$[a_v a_v] z_i = [a_v a_i]$$

from which z_i is at once found. Thus, putting $i = 1, 2, 3$, etc., we shall have a series of quantities

$$z_1, z_2, z_3, \ldots, z_n$$

of which numerical values may be determined from the equations. A tendency toward a rhythmical deviation of the kind we are in search of will be shown by an increasing value of z at the time corresponding most nearly to the completion of the period. If there is no tendency toward any period between the limits $2t$ and nt the series of z's will converge in the general mean toward the value zero.

§ 3. *Treatment of Fluctuations without Discernible Period.*

The method developed in the two preceding sections is applicable to a single series of observations of fluctuating quantities of any kind, and will enable us to determine any periodic tendency in them. We have now to consider the case in which the periodicity is not discernible. In this case results are to be derived by comparisons of different series of observations made simultaneously at different places. Our treatment will be that of the special case of departures in temperature; but the method may of course be applicable in the wider field of fluctuating quantities in general.

We know that deviations of the temperature from the normal are of constant occurrence at every point of the globe. We also know that these are due, in great part at least, to local causes, especially the motion of the air from region to region, and the varying effects of cloud and moisture. But they may also be due in part to changes in the sun's radiation of heat, or other general causes. The question is what evidence can be found to indicate the action of a general cause affecting the whole earth simultaneously. It is plain enough that observations at one place, no matter how long continued, would never enable us to distinguish between fluctuations of temperature due to local causes and to the sun. But by comparing simultaneous observations in regions of the earth so widely separated that the same local causes could not have influenced the temperatures in both regions, it is possible to determine, approximately at least, by a statistical method which we shall now develop, what part the sun or other general cause may play in the fluctuations.

The data for our problems are the simultaneous departures of temperature from the normal, in a number n of regions, through a series of terms of equal length in time, this length being chosen so as to best meet the requirements of the problem. Let us put

$$r_1 \quad r_2 \quad r_3 \qquad r_n$$

the n simultaneous departures of the temperature from the normal in the n regions for any one term.

Considering the problem thus suggested as that of determining the normal departure of a world temperature, produced by any cause affecting the whole earth, such as a change in the sun's radiation, the obvious method of determining this world deviation is to take the mean of all the separate departures r_i, observed in various regions. Let us then put τ, for the apparent mean departure of the world temperature from the general normal. This apparent departure is determined by the equation

$$n\tau = r_1 + r_2 + r_3 + \cdots + r_n = \Sigma_i r_i \tag{1}$$

or

$$\tau = \frac{\Sigma_i r_i}{n} \qquad (i = 1, 2, \cdots, n)$$

Before taking up the question of a cosmical cause affecting the world-temperature, let us consider the problem as that of determining the probable error of the departure of the world-temperature from the normal. To do this we subtract τ from the individual deviations, r_i. We then have a series of residuals, v_1, v_2, etc.

$$v_1 = r_1 - \tau, \quad v_2 = r_2 - \tau, \quad \cdots, \quad v_n = r_n - \tau$$

Following the method of least squares let us form the squares of these residuals

$$v_1^2 = r_1^2 - 2\tau r_1 + \tau^2$$
$$v_2^2 = r_2^2 - 2\tau r_2 + \tau^2$$
$$\cdots\cdots\cdots$$
$$v_n^2 = r_n^2 - 2\tau r_n + \tau^2$$

Putting ϵ for the mean deviation and summing these residuals we shall have by the theory of least squares the probable equation

$$(n-1)\epsilon^2 = \Sigma_i v_i^2 = \Sigma_i r_i^2 - n\tau^2 \tag{2}$$

Conceive now that we determine the deviation of the world-temperature in this way through a number of time-terms, arriving at a series of values of τ, each having its mean error ϵ_i. It is clear that the value of the mean error should not be determined separately for each term from the discordances for that term alone, but from the residuals throughout the whole period. If c be the entire number of time-terms the number of these residuals will be nc. We represent by Σ_j a summation through the c terms, and by $\Sigma_{i,j}$ a summation of all the nc values. Then, by adding the c equations of the form (2) we have the probable equation

$$c(n-1)\epsilon_i^2 = \Sigma_{i,j} r^2 - n\Sigma_j \tau^2 \tag{3}$$

Also, by squaring the equation (1) and adding the r squared equations we find

$$n^2 \Sigma_j \tau^2 = \Sigma^2_{i,j} e^2 + 2\Sigma ee'$$

where $\Sigma ee'$ represents the sum of the $rn(n-1)$ products of each two departures in every term. If these departures e are purely accidental deviations from means the ratio of $\Sigma ee'$ to Σe^2 will tend toward zero as the number of terms is indefinitely increased.

Dropping them we find the condition

$$n^2\Sigma_j \tau^2 = \Sigma_{i,j} e^2$$

Hence, if we put,

$$\Delta = n^2\Sigma_j \tau^2 - \Sigma_{i,j} e^2 \tag{4}$$

the criterion for the independence of each e from the others will be

$$\Delta = 0 \tag{5}$$

If this equation is not satisfied within the probable limits of the accumulated accidental errors, it will show that the hypothesis of the complete independence of the temperatures of the different regions is not established, and that there is some correlation between them. This may arise from any common cause affecting the temperature at two or more of the stations. Let us suppose a varying cosmical cause affecting the entire earth, the result of which is to raise the world-temperature during any one term by an amount τ_0. Each observed departure will then be made up of two parts:—

(1), the common departure τ_0 for the whole world;

(2), an accidental local deviation peculiar to the region. We shall then have, as the value of each individual departure in any region during any one term

$$e_i = \tau_0 + e_i' \tag{6}$$

e' being the purely accidental deviation, whose mean value is ϵ.

Form the sum of the squares of the equations (6) for the n values of the e, for any one term

$$\Sigma_i e_i^2 = n\tau_0^2 + 2\Sigma_i \tau_0 e_i' + \Sigma_i e_i'^2 \tag{7}$$

The mean value of e' being the same as that of ϵ, and each value of e' being independent of τ_0, we have the probable equation

$$\Sigma_i \tau_0 e_i' = 0$$

Summing the equation (7) for the r time-terms and putting ϵ^2 for the mean e'^2 we have

$$\Sigma_{i,j} e^2 = n\Sigma_j \tau_0^2 + nr\epsilon^2 \tag{8}$$

Now let us treat the mean departure τ in the same way. We put ϵ, the mean of the purely accidental part of τ. Then in each time-term,

$$\tau = \tau_0 + \epsilon$$

Squaring and summing the t values of τ we have

$$\Sigma_t \tau^2 = \Sigma_t \tau_0^2 + 2\,\Sigma \epsilon \tau_0 + \Sigma_t \epsilon^2$$

For the same reason as in the individual deviations we have

$$\text{Probable } \Sigma \epsilon \tau_0 = 0$$

$$\text{Probable } \quad \epsilon^2 = \frac{e^2}{n}$$

and thus the equation becomes

$$\Sigma_t \tau^2 = \Sigma_t \tau_0^2 + \frac{te^2}{n}$$

Eliminating e^2 between this equation and (8) we find by using (4)

$$n(n-1)\Sigma_t \tau_0^2 = n^2 \Sigma_t \tau^2 - \Sigma_v v^2 = \Delta \qquad (9)$$

The second member of this equation is computed by summing the squares of all the τ's, which are t in number, and also the squares of all the nt individual departures. Having thus found t values of Δ, the sum of which we shall call Δ simply, the probable mean world-deviation τ_0 is given by the equations

$$nt(n-1)\tau_0^2 = \Delta$$

$$\text{Probable mean } \tau_0^2 = \frac{\Delta}{nt(n-1)} \qquad (10)$$

When several periods, for which the number of regions was unequal, are to be combined, the final equation for τ_0^2 should be put into the form

$$\Sigma tn(n-1)\tau_0^2 = \Sigma\Delta$$

This value of τ_0^2 will be subject to a probable error arising from the probable accumulation of accidental deviations in the sum of all the quantities which form it. Our conclusions as to its value must depend upon how far its actual value exceeds this probable accidental deviation. If within the limits of probable deviation, we must consider that the evidence is against its having any determinable value. The probability of its having a real value increases with its magnitude as compared with the probability of the accidental value.

It may happen that $\Sigma\Delta$ comes out negative. This would signify that, instead of the simultaneous temperatures in the different regions being independent, or affected by a common cosmical cause, one region on the average becomes hotter or colder at the expense of another. In other words the conclusion would be that when the temperature was above the normal in one region, it was more likely than not to be below it in other regions, and *vice versa*. Thus the conclusion as to a positive correlation,—no correlation or a negative correlation—depends upon whether Δ is positive, evanescent or negative.

§ 4. *Case when Different Weights are Assigned to Different Regions.*

For the sake of simplicity we have developed the preceding method on the assumption that in determining the general departure τ the different stations or regions are all entitled to the same weight. But if the accidental deviations are smaller at some stations than at others it is clear that the observations at such stations will be of greater weight for the detection of cosmical causes. We should therefore assign weights to the several stations determined by the usual methods. Let these weights be

$$w_1, w_2, \cdots, w_n \qquad (11)$$

and let us call W their sum. The preceding equations will then be replaced by the following:

Instead of using (1) for determining τ we use the equation

$$W\tau = w_1 r_1 + w_2 r_2 + \cdots + w_n r_n = \Sigma_i w_i r_i \qquad (12)$$

Let us put ϵ_i for the mean accidental deviation of r_i and ϵ_τ for that of τ. The mean deviation of any one product $w_i r_i$ is then $w_i \epsilon_i$ and the squared mean deviation of the sum of all these products for any one term, if uncorrelated, is

$$\Sigma w_i^2 \epsilon_i^2$$

The mean ϵ_τ should in this case satisfy the equation

$$W^2 \epsilon_\tau^2 = w_1^2 \epsilon_1^2 + w_2^2 \epsilon_2^2 + \cdots + w_n^2 \epsilon_n^2 \qquad (13)$$

If the observed deviations r are wholly in the nature of accidental deviations from a mean value, we may take for each ϵ_i^2 the mean of all the r_i^2; and τ being then a purely accidental deviation of the mean, we should have the probable equation

$$\epsilon_\tau^2 = \text{mean } \tau^2$$

The criterion for deciding whether the deviations are purely accidental may therefore be written in the form $\Delta = 0$, where for any one time-term

$$\Delta_j = W'^2\tau^2 - (w_1^2 r_1^2 + w_2^2 r_2^2 + \cdots + w_n^2 r_n^2)$$

There being r time-terms in all, each will give a value of Δ, the sum of which we call Δ simply.

Summing all r of these probable relations the criterion will become

$$\Delta = \Sigma_j W'^2\tau^2 - \Sigma_j \Sigma_i w_i^2 r_i^2 = 0 \qquad (j = 1, 2, \cdots, r) \qquad (16)$$

If the value of Δ comes out too large to be regarded as the accumulated effect of chance deviations, we must, as before, find a mean deviation τ_0, common to all the stations for each separate term of observation, which will reduce the second member to the value Δ. We do this by the same process as that when the weights are taken as equal. We have, as before, the probable equations

$$\Sigma\tau^2 = \Sigma\epsilon_0^2 + \Sigma\tau_0^2$$
$$\Sigma_i r_i^2 = \Sigma_i \epsilon_0^2 + \Sigma\tau_0^2$$

Substituting these values in (16) the terms in ϵ^2 all drop out by virtue of the relation (15), and we have left the probable equation

$$\Sigma_j (W'^2 - \Sigma_i w^2)\tau_0^2 = \Delta \qquad (17)$$

which determines a probable mean value of τ_0^2, and therefore of τ_0 on the same principles as when the weights are equal.

§ 5. *Comparison of Regions when Taken by Pairs.*

When only two regions are compared the process of § 3 may be simplified. Calling r and r' the observed departures when only two regions are considered we shall have

$$2\tau = r + r'$$

for each term of observation. Hence

$$2\tau^2 - \tfrac{1}{2}(r^2 + r'^2) = rr'$$

Summing for all r terms, as before

$$2\Sigma_j \tau^2 - \tfrac{1}{2}\Sigma_j (r^2 + r'^2) = \Sigma_j rr'$$

Thus, putting $n = 2$ in (9) and (10) we find for each time-term the simple expression

$$\text{Mean } \tau_0^2 = \frac{\Sigma rr'}{r} = \text{Mean } rr' \qquad (18)$$

which is much simpler in this case than the formula (10).

We may, if we choose, reduce the results for any number of regions in the same way by taking the regions in pairs. By squaring (1) we have, for any one term of observation,

$$n^2\tau^2 = \Sigma_i r_i^2 + 2\Sigma_{i,k} r_i r_k \tag{19}$$

in which each individual product $r_i r_k$ is formed from each pair of the individual r's for the time-term, so that we have $n(n-1)$ products $r_i r_k$ for each of the t time-terms.

Summing the series for all the time-terms during which n remains the same, we have

$$n^2\Sigma_j \tau^2 = \Sigma_{i,j} r^2 + 2\Sigma_{i,j,k} r_i r_k \tag{20}$$

Combining this with (9) we have

$$n(n-1)\Sigma_j \tau_o^2 = 2\Sigma_{i,j,k} r_i r_k$$

Taking τ_o to represent the mean value of the cosmical fluctuation through t terms, we have

$$\Sigma_j \tau_o^2 = t\tau_o^2 \tag{21}$$

Also,

$$\Delta = 2\Sigma^3 rr'$$

where, for brevity, we put Σ^3 for the triple summation of the products. We are thus enabled, when we so desire, to compute Δ, and hence the value of τ_o^2, for each time-term and each pair of stations taken separately. The final mean of τ_o^2 which we thus derive instead of (10) is

$$\text{Mean } \tau_o^2 = \frac{2\Sigma^3 rr'}{n(n-1)} \tag{22}$$

The number of combinations of n stations being $[n(n-1)]/2$, this is equivalent to

$$\text{Mean } \tau_o^2 = \text{Mean } rr' \tag{23}$$

which may be found by summing (18) for the pairs of stations and all the time-terms. For considerable values of n this equation is more laborious in use than (10) or (17), but it has the advantage of showing whether a correlation among the departures of temperature exists for all the stations, or is confined to a limited number of stations.

The preceding value of τ_o^2 has been derived for the sake of simplicity, as if the weights were all equal. When the pairs of stations are all considered individually, no difference of assigned weights will affect the resulting individual value of τ_0^2. But if we combine the $[n(n-1)]/2$ individual values thus derived, we must assign them their proper weights. These we find by dealing with (16) in the same way that we have dealt with $n^2\tau^2$ when the weights were each 1. By squaring (12) and summing for the t time-terms, we find

$$\Sigma_i\Sigma_j w_i^2 r_i^2 = \Sigma_j W^2\tau^2 - 2\Sigma_{i,k,j} w_i w_k r_i r_k \tag{24}$$

This, substituted in (16), gives

$$\Delta = 2\Sigma_{i,k}\, w_i w_k r_i r_k \qquad (25)$$

With equal weights we have, from any one pair of stations, ($n = 2$)

$$\Delta = 2\Sigma_i\, r r' \qquad (26)$$

It follows that if we put $\Delta_{i,k}$ the special value of Δ found for any pair of stations without regard to weights, the final value for use in (17) when the weights are taken account of is

$$\Delta = \Sigma_{i,k}\, w_i w_k \Delta_{i,k} \qquad (27)$$

and we shall then have

$$\text{Probable mean } \tau_a^2 = \frac{\Sigma_{i,k}\, w_i w_k \Delta_{i,k}}{\Sigma W^2 - \Sigma_{i,j}\, w^2} \qquad (28)$$

CHAPTER II.

Review of Data and Processes.

§ 6. *Choice and Combination of Material.*

From the preceding exposition of the general method applied it will be seen that, since our result is based on systematic or accidental departures alone, and not on absolute temperatures, our main requirement is long series of observations of temperature, at widely separated points of the earth's surface, made and reduced on a plan which should be uniform for each point, but might vary to any extent from one point to another. A single observation of temperature on each day would suffice in the long run, provided it were made at the same hour throughout. Of course a better result is reached from a number of daily observations at given hours: but this is less essential than uniformity of system at each separate station.

In planning the work it was hoped that the much-criticised labor spent in accumulating meteorological observations might be found not so ill-directed as is sometimes thought. Unvaried routine, even if unintelligent, in the method of making and publishing the observations would be an advantage in a case where errors and defects in the instruments and methods are unimportant for the result, so long as they remained unchanged. But, when the actual material was sought out and examined, disappointment was nearly everywhere the result. Outside a few government establishments supported by civilized nations or other permanent organizations, diversity instead of uniformity was found to prevail,—even unintelligent adherence to any routine system of making, reducing, and publishing the observations being rare. The amount of available material was also diminished by the fact that a very important part of the best-planned meteorological observations are made only to determine the climatology of the region, and are abandoned when this requirement is satisfied. The importance of supplying in a satisfactory way this want of uniformity and continuity has given a certain disjointed character to the material used in the present investigation. With this preliminary remark we pass to the selection of the actual material.

Since the effect of any change in the daily amount of energy radiated by the sun will be more strongly felt in those regions most exposed to that radiation, it follows that tropical stations should have the preference over those of high latitudes. At the same time, the longer the period through which a set of observations extends the less the importance of this preference. I have therefore not made use of observations in the northern countries of Europe in comparing and observing monthly and ten-day means; but have utilized a wider range of annual means. No precise limits as to latitude have been set in any one case, the choice necessarily depending on general availability.

Deviations of temperature have less weight the wider the range of accidental variation from day to day. It was therefore deemed advisable to omit regions where the temperature fluctuated rapidly. But this requirement also was relaxed in case of terms of long period, because the purely accidental effects would be more and more diminished as longer periods were taken.

In selecting records to be used we must distinguish the essential from the non-essential features. As the object is not to determine the actual mean temperature in the several regions, but fluctuations only, it is nearly indifferent how the daily means are derived. The mean temperature for the whole twenty-four hours is preferable to a single observation at one and the same hour only because the purely accidental deviation will then be smaller. This actual mean is also preferable to the mean of the maximum and minimum temperatures, but the advantage in this case is not sufficiently well marked to justify a great expenditure of labor to secure it. What is essential is that a uniform system of observed temperatures should extend through a sufficient number of years to enable a table of normal temperatures for each month or each decade of the year to be formed. But it is not necessary that even this table should be one entitled to great weight. In fact without any normal standard, the mean deviations from day to day, or from period to period, would be entitled to some weight. While some pains have been taken to construct a table of normal temperatures for several of the stations, this part of the work has not been regarded as definitive, and is not published in this paper.

From the nature of our method, as developed in the preceding chapter, our first step must be to divide the surface of the earth into regions, within each of which the accidental changes of temperature may be supposed independent of those in every other region. Having done this, we are not confined to a single observing station in each region. In fact the more observing stations used in each, and the more widely they are separated, the greater will be the weight to which the mean result for the region is entitled.

We shall now review the material made use of, and the method of handling it, so far as seems necessary to enable critical investigators to examine and test the processes in detail, and to form a judgment as to the reliability of the result. An entirely systematic statement of the plans and methods is difficult from the fact that they had to be changed in detail from time to time as the work progressed, owing to the unexpected cases of incompleteness and other imperfections which showed themselves here and there as the compilation went on. Lack of uniformity in treatment has also arisen from the discovery from time to time of new material which it was thought advisable to use in the work. Moreover a certain perfection of method originally aimed at, involving a rigorous reduction to a 24-hour mean for every day, was found impracticable, and such means as chanced to be available had very generally to be used. The effect of this drawback upon the results of the work itself is practically quite unimportant; but it prevents the material made use of from having the completeness and certainty that it otherwise might have claimed as a basis for more extended meteorological researches.

It may be added that the conclusions reached in the research can be judged without any reference to the original materials on which the work is based; but, as already intimated, a knowledge of this material will not only facilitate the judgment of any details but will be of assistance to any one desiring to review and extend the work. The following are the sources from which the data were mostly derived.

Records of the United States Weather Bureau.—The original plan was to choose a number of widely separated stations in the United States and, from the manuscript records of the Bureau, to reduce the recorded mean temperature of each day to the rigorous 24-hour mean, and then obtain a daily deviation from the normal during the entire period. But the discussion of the entire 35 years of records on this plan was found to be too laborious, especially as the hours and system of observation had been changed twice during the history of the bureau. It was therefore deemed sufficient to take as the standard temperature for each day the mean of the maximum and minimum temperatures. This was, for the most part, reduced to the 24-hour mean when data for doing so could be readily found.

The Argentine Republic.—The main source for this region has been the publications of the *Officina Meteorologica Argentina.* I am also indebted to Dr. Davis, Director of the Meteorological Office, for the communication of observations additional to those found in the published volumes. The number of stations used in these years was different in different years. Generally six or eight were available.

Havana: Observaciones Magneticas y Meteorologicas del Real Collegio de Belen de la Compania de Jesus en la Habana. Habana, Imprenta del Avisador Commercial Aucargura 30, 1890.

Jamaica: Temperatures in Kingston, Jamaica. Jamaica; Government Printing Office. Doc. No. 275.

Mauritius: Meteorological Observations taken during a number of years, and published annually as a Mauritius blue book.

Bombay: Magnetic and Meteorological Observations at the Government Observatory, Bombay. Bombay, printed at the Government Central Press, 1895.

Batavia: Observations made at the Royal Magnetical and Meteorological Observatory, Batavia, 1900. Here only one station is available and the deviations as will be seen from the table are larger in the mean than in the case of any others that have been included. They received therefore only the weight 1.

Ceylon: Administrative Reports on Meteorology. No general title in detail. These publications contain monthly and annual means of observations at a number of stations on the island. The deviations used here and elsewhere are the means of generally six or more stations in various parts of the island.

Australia: The sources for these observations are the annual publications of the Adelaide Observatory by Sir Charles Todd. The means given are generally those at five or six different stations.

Madras: Results of the meteorological observations made at the Government Observatory at Madras. — 1861–1890. Madras, 1892. Also other volumes partly without title and partly bearing a similar title.

Manila: Census of the Philippine Islands, 1903, Bulletin 2. The Climate of the Philippines by Rev. Jose Algue, Director of the Philippine Weather Bureau, published by the Census Office, Washington, 1904.

Apia: The *Deutsche Ueberseeische Meteorologische Beobachtungen* contains meteorological observations at a number of coast and island stations; but, for the most part, the observations are not pursued continuously through a sufficient period to be well adapted to the present work. The best station for our purpose proved to be Apia where the record is nearly complete since 1890. The unpublished results up to 1904 were courteously communicated by the Director of the *Deutsche Seewarte* at Hamburg.

In equability and uniformity of temperature this station not only leads every other on the list but every region. If therefore internal consistency had been the sole guide in assigning weights, it would be entitled to greater weight than any other two stations. But there is always a possibility at any one station of varying systematic errors from one cause or another. Hence, it has received no greater weight than the best of the remaining stations.

§ 7. *Arrangement of the work.*

Owing to the complexity of the conditions which have determined the final form of the work, the task of studying its processes will be facilitated by a condensed statement of its arrangements. The main features to be borne in mind are the following:

Firstly, as regards geographic distribution; that portion of the earth best available for the purpose is divided into regions within each of which the fluctuations of temperature are *primâ facie* independent of those in other regions. The question whether this independence is real is regarded as open to question and therefore has been investigated in special cases where a correlation is possible.

Then, within each region as many stations of observation as practicable are to be selected in order that the accidental fluctuations of the regions may be reduced. Frequently there is but one station in a region.

Secondly, as to the time; the whole period included in each special branch of the discussion is divided up into time-terms. The time-terms actually used are three, (1) the year; (2) the calendar month; (3) the decade.

Were the work ideally complete in every particular, we should logically begin with the decade, then pass to the month, and then to the yearly terms, because this is the order in which the observations are made and the work has to be done. But, for reasons not necessary to set forth at length, the different series of time-terms are presented in reverse order, beginning with the year.

The material used is different for the three classes of terms. In discussing the ten-day terms it was found that, quite apart from the labor of forming ten-day means, the available material in the form of daily observations was comparatively limited. But monthly and annual means are found in so many publications that the data available for this branch of the research is great. This additional wealth of material has permitted the use of a much greater number of regions than are available for the ten-day means.

CHAPTER III.

Discussion of Annual Deviations of Temperature.

§ 8. *Fluctuations Having the Period of the Sun-spots.*

Proceeding according to the plan mapped out, our first step will be to determine the fluctuations in temperature corresponding to the 11-year inequality in the solar spots. This periodic change in the amount of solar spottedness indicates that a change of some sort is going on in the sun; and if the radiation of the latter is subject to any periodic change, we must expect this to be one of the principal periods. Two methods of investigation are open to us, which would be identical if the variation in the spottedness were a rigorously harmonic fluctuation in a fixed period. One is to take the degree of spottedness from time to time as the term of comparison; the other is to assume a period in the general terrestrial temperature exactly equal to the mean period of the spots, and determine the coefficients of the fluctuation so as to best satisfy the observations. The second method seems preferable because we have some reason to suppose that the degree of spottedness is a secondary rather than a primary phenomenon. The writer showed in his paper on the period of the solar spots that the irregularities in the period of the observed phenomenon tended to compensate themselves, in the course of time returning to an original primordial period. This was especially shown by the fact that about 1760–90 the epochs of maximum and minimum were accelerated for several years, but afterward returned to the original places in the period. That is to say we have in the spots a fairly exact period subject to fluctuations on one side and on the other. Now the change in radiation is as likely to follow the rigorous period as to follow the apparent phenomena of spots.

The irregular and fragmentary character of our data affords another reason for taking as the basis of our work the hypothesis of a period of 11.13 years simply. If we had at our disposal a uniform and homogeneous system of observations in various widely separated regions, extending through a long period, either method could be applied with equal facility. But the fragmentary character of the actual data would render weak a comparison of the temperature during a period of such great bespottedness as that of 1870–71 with that of the year 1900, during which there were very few spots.

The most exhaustive attempt with which I am acquainted to discover the relation between the solar spottedness and the terrestrial temperature is that of Köppen.[*] The material made use of comprises mean fluctuations of temperature in various regions of the globe, from 1767 to 1877. The regions were classified according to their latitude as tropical, sub-tropical, warm, temperate, etc. The general conclusion was that the temperature of the tropical regions was lower by about 0°.73 C. near the time of maximum sun spots than near the time of minimum. It is known that the spots radiate less heat in proportion to their surface than does the photosphere, and the general nature of this result is the same as if the temperature per unit area of the non-spotted photosphere were invariable, so that the total radiation was diminished

[*] *Zeitschrift der Oesterreichen Gesellschaft für Meteorologie*, VIII Band.

by the spots. The fluctuation of terrestrial temperature was shown to be the greatest in the equatorial regions, and to diminish progressively as the latitude increased to north or south. There were also indications of a non-correspondence between the epochs of maximum and minimum temperatures, and the minimum and maximum of spottedness, but the determination of the difference must be considered as weak, in view of the uncertainty of the data and the minuteness of the fluctuation.

The writer proposes to reinvestigate this question, using both Köppen's data and more recent observations, in order to apply the more rigorous method of equations of condition. We assume only that the mean temperature at the earth's surface fluctuates harmonically in a period of 11.13 years. This hypothesis may be represented in the general form

$$\Delta\tau = x \cos \mu t + y \sin \mu t + z \qquad (29)$$

where μ is to be so taken that the angle μt shall go through 360° in the given period. Taking the year as the unit of time this gives

$$\mu = 32°.35$$

The epoch from which t is measured is quite arbitrary, because when, after deriving x and y from observations, we reduce the expression to a monomial

$$\Delta\tau = \rho \sin (\mu t + c)$$

the value of $\mu t + c$ for a given moment of time will be the same, whatever the chosen epoch for $t = 0$.

Putting, for brevity,

$$a = \cos \mu t\,;\quad b = \sin \mu t$$

each observed deviation of temperature, $\Delta\tau = n$, will give the equation of condition

$$ax + by + z = n$$

These conditional equations being treated by the method of least squares we shall have the normal equations

$$\begin{aligned}[aa]x + [ab]y + [ac]z &= [an]\\ [ab]x + [bb]y + [bc]z &= [bn]\\ [ac]x + [bc]y + [cc]z &= [cn]\end{aligned}$$

Having found x and y from these equations we may substitute them in (15), and reduce the trigonometric terms to a monomial by computing ρ and c from

$$\begin{aligned}\rho \cos c &= x\\ \rho \sin c &= -y\end{aligned}$$

The harmonic fluctuations of which we are in search will then be

$$\Delta\tau = \rho \cos (\mu t + c)$$

In the actual investigation I have taken the epoch 1844.6 as that from which t is counted. This epoch corresponds to a sun-spot minimum; but this is unimportant at the present moment. From this starting point the value of the angle of μt was taken for the middle of each year, and its sine and cosine, with their squares and products, were computed with results shown in the following table:

TABLE I.

Coefficients for Detecting Fluctuations Having the Sunspot Period.

Year	a	b	a^2	b^2	ab	Year	a	b	a^2	b^2	ab
1820	+0.5	−0.9	0.25	0.81	−0.4	1865	−0.7	−0.7	0.49	0.49	−0.5
21	−0.9	−0.5	0.81	0.25	−0.4	66	−1.0	−0.2	1.00	0.04	−0.2
22	−1.0	0.0	1.00	0.00	+0.4	67	−0.9	−0.4	0.81	0.16	+0.3
23	−0.8	+0.6	0.64	0.36	+0.5	68	+0.6	+0.8	0.36	0.64	+0.5
24	−0.4	−0.9	0.16	0.81	+0.3	69	+0.1	+1.0	0.01	1.00	+0.1
1825	−0.2	+1.0	0.04	1.00	−0.2	1870	−0.5	−0.9	0.25	0.81	−0.4
26	−0.7	+0.7	0.49	0.49	−0.5	71	−0.9	+0.5	0.81	0.25	−0.4
27	−1.0	+0.3	1.00	0.09	−0.2	72	−1.0	0.0	1.00	0.00	0.0
28	−1.0	−0.3	1.00	0.09	+0.3	73	−0.8	−0.6	0.64	0.36	+0.4
29	−0.6	−0.8	0.36	0.64	−0.5	74	−0.4	−0.9	0.16	0.81	+0.4
1830	−0.2	−1.0	0.04	1.00	+0.1	1875	−0.2	−1.0	0.04	1.00	−0.2
31	+0.4	−0.9	0.16	0.81	−0.4	76	+0.7	−0.7	0.49	0.49	−0.5
32	+0.8	−0.5	0.64	0.25	−0.4	77	+1.0	−0.3	1.00	0.09	−0.3
33	+1.0	0.0	1.00	0.00	0.0	78	+1.0	+0.3	1.00	0.09	+0.3
34	+0.8	+0.5	0.64	0.25	+0.4	79	+0.7	+0.8	0.49	0.64	+0.6
1835	+0.4	+0.9	0.16	0.81	+0.4	1880	+0.1	+1.0	0.01	1.00	+0.1
36	−0.1	+1.0	0.01	1.00	−0.1	81	−0.4	+0.9	0.16	0.81	−0.4
37	−0.6	+0.8	0.36	0.64	−0.5	82	−0.8	+0.6	0.64	0.36	−0.5
38	−1.0	+0.3	1.00	0.09	−0.3	83	−1.0	0.0	1.00	0.00	0.0
39	−1.0	−0.3	1.00	0.09	+0.3	84	−0.9	−0.5	0.81	0.25	0.4
1840	−0.7	−0.7	0.49	0.49	+0.5	1885	−0.4	−0.9	0.16	0.81	+0.4
41	−0.2	−1.0	0.04	1.00	+0.2	86	+0.1	−1.0	0.01	1.00	−0.1
42	+0.4	−0.9	0.16	0.81	−0.3	87	+0.6	−0.8	0.36	0.64	−0.5
43	+0.8	−0.6	0.64	0.36	−0.5	88	+0.9	−0.3	0.81	0.09	−0.3
44	+1.0	0.0	1.00	0.00	−0.1	89	+1.0	+0.2	1.00	0.04	+0.2
1845	+0.9	+0.5	0.81	0.25	+0.4	1890	+0.7	+0.7	0.49	0.49	+0.5
46	+0.5	+0.9	0.25	0.81	+0.4	91	+0.2	+1.0	0.04	1.00	+0.2
47	−0.1	+1.0	0.01	1.00	−0.1	92	−0.3	+0.9	0.09	0.81	−0.3
48	−0.6	+0.8	0.36	0.64	−0.5	93	−0.8	+0.6	0.64	0.36	−0.5
49	−0.9	+0.4	0.81	0.16	−0.3	94	−1.0	+0.1	1.00	0.01	−0.1
1850	−1.0	−0.2	1.00	0.04	+0.2	1895	−0.9	−0.4	0.81	0.16	+0.4
51	−0.7	−0.7	0.49	0.49	+0.5	96	−0.5	−0.9	0.25	0.81	+0.4
52	−0.2	−1.0	0.04	1.00	+0.2	97	0.0	−1.0	0.00	1.00	0.0
53	+0.3	−1.0	0.09	1.00	−0.3	98	+0.5	−0.8	0.25	0.64	−0.4
54	+0.8	−0.6	0.64	0.36	−0.5	1899	+0.9	−0.4	0.81	0.16	−0.4
1855	+1.0	−0.1	1.00	0.01	−0.1	1900	+1.0	+0.1	1.00	0.01	+0.1
56	+0.9	+0.4	0.81	0.16	+0.4	01	+0.8	+0.7	0.64	0.49	+0.6
57	+0.5	+0.8	0.25	0.64	+0.4	02	+0.3	+1.0	0.09	1.00	+0.3
58	0.0	+1.0	0.00	1.00	0.0	03	−0.3	+1.0	0.09	1.00	−0.2
59	−0.5	+0.8	0.25	0.64	−0.4	04	−0.7	+0.7	0.49	0.49	−0.5
1860	−0.9	+0.4	0.81	0.16	−0.4	1905	−1.0	+0.2	1.00	0.04	−0.2
61	−1.0	−0.1	1.00	0.01	+0.1	06	−0.9	−0.4	0.81	0.16	+0.3
62	−0.8	−0.6	0.64	0.36	+0.5	07	−0.6	−0.8	0.36	0.64	+0.5
63	−0.3	−0.9	0.09	0.81	+0.3	08	−0.1	−1.0	0.01	1.00	+0.1
1864	+0.2	−1.0	0.04	1.00	−0.2	1909	0.5	−0.9	0.25	0.81	−0.4

With this table the computation of x and y is so easy a matter that I have for the most part computed all the series of observations I could find which extended through as long a time as a single spot-period. Each station is generally treated separately; but in a few instances I have combined the results of neighboring stations into a single mean. I forego any detailed description of the various methods by which the material, even when accurate, had to be treated in order to obtain the best annual means, presumably referred to a uniform standard. The more important sources are those already cited.

The following table shows the observed annual deviations formed from my own work. But in addition to these I have included observations, often fragmentary, made at British colonial stations, and published in the British meteorological reports:

TABLE II.

Mean Annual Departures of Temperature at Stations or in Regions.

	U. S. Fahr.	Habana C.	Kingston Fahr.	Argentine C.	Bombay Fahr.	Madras Fahr.	Calcutta Fahr.	Ceylon Fahr.	Manila C.	Australia Fahr.	Batavia C.	Ayda C.	Mean C.
1871	+0.8		......	......	+0.5	+0.3	0.0	......			−0.5	......	+0.18
72	−0.1		......	−0.04	−0.7	−0.3	+0.7	......		......	−0.4	......	−0.12
73	+0.3		......	+0.13	−0.7	−0.3	+0.7	......			−0.2	......	−0.03
74	+0.2	−0.1	......	−0.29	−1.3	−0.7	−0.2	......			−0.7	......	−0.28
1875	−0.3	+0.1	......	−0.01	−0.3	+0.1	−0.2	......	......	......	−0.2	......	−0.04
76	+0.2	−0.3	......	0.00	−0.3	+0.2	+1.0	......	......	......	−0.2	......	−0.01
77	+0.4	−0.1	......	+0.60	+0.7	+0.6	+0.1	......	......	......	+0.4	......	+0.25
78	+0.3	+0.1	......	−0.28	+0.5	+1.2	+1.0	......	......	......	+1.2	......	+0.31
79	+0.2	−0.2	......	+0.13	−1.0	−0.2	+0.9	......		......	−0.2	......	−0.08
1880	−0.1	+0.2	......	0.00	−0.1	−0.1	−1.0	......		......	−0.6	......	−0.10
81	+0.6	+0.1	+0.2	+0.22	+0.4	+0.3	−0.5	+0.2		......	+0.2	......	+0.14
82	+0.5	+0.4	0.0	−0.05	−0.5	0.0	0.0	−0.2	......	......	−0.4	......	+0.02
83	+0.6	+0.4	+0.2	+0.24	−0.8	−0.3	−1.0	−0.6	−0.2	−0.4	−0.2	......	−0.07
84	+0.4	0.0	−0.3	+0.25	−0.8	−0.7	−1.3	−0.5	−0.6	−0.1	−0.3		−0.23
1885	0.0	−0.5	+0.6	−0.02	−0.4	−0.2	+0.2	−0.1	−0.1	+0.2	−0.1		−0.08
86	−1.0	−0.2	+0.7	+0.16	−0.1	−0.5	......	0.0	−0.2	+0.1	+0.2	......	−0.08
87	−0.2	0.0	−0.4	+0.38	−0.9	−0.4	......	−0.5	−0.2	0.0	−0.5	......	−0.14
88	−0.5	+0.2	+0.6	+0.64	+0.5	−0.2	......	+0.2	+0.1	+1.2	+0.4	......	+0.20
89	+0.2	+0.2	+0.9	−0.22	0.0	0.0	......	+0.3	+0.6	+0.7	+0.8	......	+0.22
1890	+0.9	+0.1	−0.6	−0.29	−0.3	−0.3	......	−0.2	−0.2	+0.6	−0.4	−0.21	−0.07
91	−0.2	0.0	+0.2	+0.08	−0.1	......		−0.2	0.0	−0.4	+0.5	−0.24	−0.04
92	−0.8	−0.4	−0.7	−0.71	+0.7	......		−0.1	+0.1	−0.5	+0.7	−0.72	−0.23
93	−0.3	+0.2	−0.9	−1.3	−0.7	......		−0.6	−0.2	0.0	−0.5	−0.62	−0.35
94	−0.3	−0.2	−0.8	−0.2	0.0	......		−0.2	−0.2	−0.6	−0.2	−0.24	−0.20
1895	−1.0	−0.1	−0.2	+0.6	0.0	......	......	−0.1	−0.1	−0.1	+0.1	−0.32	−0.09
96	+0.4	0.0	+0.4	+1.1	+1.1	......	......	+0.4	0.0	−0.5	+0.6	−0.31	+0.19
97	+0.1	+0.2	+0.3	−0.2	−0.1	......	......	+0.7	+0.6	+0.1	+1.1	+0.21	+0.22
98	−0.1	−0.2	−0.6	−0.4	+0.7	......	......	+0.3	0.0	+0.5	+0.2	+0.07	0.00
99	−0.4	+0.3	......	......	+0.4	......	......	0.0	−0.2	−0.4	0.0	+0.20	+0.02
1900	+0.5	+0.1	......	......	+0.4	......	......	+1.1	+0.5	−0.7	+0.6	+0.36	+0.27
01	−0.9	−0.4	......	......	+0.2	......	......	+1.7	+0.1	+0.3	......	+0.51	+0.14
02	−0.2	+0.4	......	......	+0.5	......	......	......	−0.1	......	......	+0.50	+0.12
03	−0.7	−0.1	......	......	......	......	......	......	......	......	......	+0.55	0.00
04	−0.6	......	......	......	......	......	......	......	......	......	......	+0.13	−0.08
Σ_v	8.1	5.5	4.6	8.5	8.8	4.1	5.1	4.6	4.3	4.3	12.0	4.8	
Mean v^2	0.24	0.18	0.26	0.32	0.28	0.21	0.34	0.22	0.21	0.23	0.40	0.32	
w	3	4	3	3	3	4	2	1	1	3	1	3	

The following example of the computation of the fluctuation from the annual departures at Kingston, Jamaica, will make the process clear:

Coefficient of Sunspot Fluctuation at Kingston, Jamaica.

Years	Mean Temperature	Deviation	$a\Delta t$	$b\Delta t$
1881	79.0	+0.2	−0.1	+0.2
82	78.8	0.0	0.0	0.0
83	79.0	+0.2	−0.2	0.0
84	78.5	−0.3	+0.3	+0.2
1885	79.1	+0.3	−0.2	−0.5
86	79.5	+0.7	+0.1	−0.7
87	78.4	−0.4	−0.2	+0.3
88	79.4	+0.6	+0.5	−0.2
89	79.7	+0.9	+0.9	−0.2
1890	78.2	−0.6	−0.4	−0.4
91	79.0	+0.2	0.0	+0.2
92	78.1	−0.7	+0.2	−0.6
93	77.9	−0.9	+0.7	−0.5
94	78.0	−0.8	+0.8	−0.1
1895	78.6	−0.2	+0.2	+0.1
96	79.2	+0.4	−0.2	−0.4
97	79.1	+0.3	0.0	−0.3
1898	78.2	−0.6	−0.3	+0.5
Mean	78.8	Σ = −0.1	+2.1	−2.0

Σa	Σb	Σa^2	Σb^2	Σab
−3.4	−0.9	2.78	3.23	−0.6
−3.4	+1.7	2.79	3.07	−0.6
−2.7	2.4	2.95	2.98	+0.3
−3.0	−1.6	8.52	9.28	−0.9

Normal Equations:

$$8.52\,x - 0.9\,y - 3.0\,z = +2.1$$
$$-0.9\,x + 9.28\,y - 1.6\,z = -2.0$$
$$-3.0\,x - 1.6\,y + 18.0\,z = -0.4$$

$$\text{Result}\begin{cases} x & +0.23 \\ y & -0.20 \\ z & 0.02 \end{cases}$$

In addition to the observations collected by myself for this work, I have made use of those of Köppen cited in the paper already referred to. This course was adopted because it did not seem necessary to repeat Köppen's work, even were the means of doing so available, which was not the case for the earlier observations. So far as I could infer from an examination of his work, and its comparison with published records, it is practically complete for all our present purposes. It is possible that there is a slight duplication of some of the observations in the work of Köppen and of myself, arising from the fact that his series and mine in a few cases overlap. But these cases are too few to be important, and only amount to assigning double their proper weight to the few duplicated records.

The results for x and y, with the numbers necessary for their final combination, are shown in Table III. The first column gives the place, or in a few cases the region, in which the observations were made. Down to Barbadoes the temperatures were those worked up by myself. The nine following are the regions within which the deviations were given and discussed by Köppen.

The value of x and y are in all cases expressed in degrees Centigrade, although the original deviations were often expressed in degrees of the Fahrenheit scale.

TABLE III.

Coefficients Expressing Observed Fluctuations of Temperature through the Sunspot Periods at Various Places or in Various Regions in the Form: $\Delta\tau = x \cos c + y \sin c$.

Place	Period of Obs.	x	y	W	Σ^2	w	$\cos c$
Calcutta	1868-85	+0.22	0.06	9	0.48	6	1.0
Ceylon	1881-95	+0.23	+0.02	10	0.32	10	1.0
Bombay	1846-91	+0.09	−0.01	28	0.37	25	1.0
Madras	1861-9	+0.14	−0.08	15	0.28	16	1.0
Manila	1883-02	+0.20	0.00	10	0.08	12	1.0
Scutari	1865-86	−0.11	0.09	11	1.53	3	0.9
Malacca, etc.	1893-03	+0.17	−0.23	5	0.30	5	1.0
Apia	1890-04	+0.20	+0.07	7	......	15	1.0
Mauritius	1885-96	−0.12	−0.11	6	0.22	9	1.0
Natal	1872-86	+0.25	0.08	7	1.90	1	0.9
Batavia	1866-00	+0.27	0.08	17	0.23	20	1.0
Australia	1883-01	+0.17	−0.05	9	0.24	13	0.8
Malta	1865-81	+0.06	−0.02	9	0.26	11	0.8
Gibraltar	1851-82	−0.07	−0.31	12	1.20	3	0.8
Washington	1871-04	+0.14	0.00	17	1.25	1	0.8
Key West	1871-04	−0.21	−0.01	17	0.71	8	0.9
St. Louis	1871-04	+0.28	−0.16	17	1.70	3	0.8
Galveston	1871-04	0.06	+0.07	17	0.73	8	0.9
San Diego	1871-04	+0.17	0.09	17	1.01	5	0.9
Bermuda	1856-79	−0.28	−0.29	7	0.78	2	0.9
Havana	1871-93	0.00	0.06	15	0.07	10	0.9
Kingston	1884-98	−0.13	0.12	9	0.31	10	0.9
Barbados	1865-82	+0.14	−0.13	9	2.07	1	0.9
S. Africa	1842-67	+0.02	0.08	12	0.13	20	0.8
Trop. America	1821-69	−0.16	−0.07	22	0.24	25	1.0
S. E. States	1823-59	−0.01	+0.14	18	0.67	9	0.8
Farthest India	1820-62	+0.29	−0.08	21	0.17	25	1.0
India & Sunda	1840-58	+0.01	−0.20	9	0.14	10	1.0
China Japan	1841-55	+0.29	0.53	8	0.26	10	0.7
Temp. S. Amer.	1843-60	−0.06	0.19	9	0.11	15	0.8
Australia	1841-70	+0.08	0.00	15	0.13	20	0.8
Mediterranean	1820-70	+0.11	−0.02	26	0.20	25	0.7

Column W gives approximately the integral part of the coefficient aa or bb. In the case of observations extending through any integral number of periods these two values would be the same. Practically they are always so nearly the same, approximately half the number of years, that it was unnecessary to make any distinction between them. In other words, the values of x and y may be regarded as always of equal weight.

Were the accidental fluctuations at the several stations equal in amount, W would be the weight to assign to each result. But, as a matter of course, different points and different regions are subject to different mean fluctuations. The mean of the squares of these fluctuations is shown in the column Σ^2. In a rigorous treatment by the method of least squares the value of Σ should be derived from the residuals left when the concluded values of the unknown quantities are substituted in the equation of condition. But, for obvious reasons, we should not find the residuals from each special solution, but by substituting the final values of the unknowns derived from the combination of all the data. Even then the weight might frequently be illusory.

through a purely fortuitous accordance of the observations with the final results. Actually, therefore, I have deemed it best to use for Σ^2 simply the mean square of the actually observed deviations from the normal.

The weights to be assigned will then be proportional to $W \div \Sigma^2$. In order to express them in convenient units I have put approximately for the weight $w = W \div 3\Sigma^2$. This formula has not however been without some modifications as will be seen by the columns W, Σ^2, and w. Owing to the possibility of systematic errors at any one station the stations which by the formulae would be entitled to great weight have their weights slightly diminished, and no station is allowed a greater weight than 25.

It was found by Köppen that the fluctuation was greatest in the tropics, and diminished in either direction as the latitude increased. This is what we should expect. We may therefore plausibly suppose its amount at any place to be proportional to the insolation, or to the cosine of the latitude. The value of this cosine to a single place of decimals is given in the last line of the table.

It now remains from all the numbers of this table to derive the most probable values of x and y for the equatorial regions. The values given are those derived from observation in each region, without correction for latitude. Putting x_0 and y_0 for the values at the equator we form from each given x and y an equation of condition in the form

$$x_0 \cos \phi = x$$
$$y_0 \cos \phi = y$$

The final values are

$$x_0 = \frac{\Sigma w x \cos \phi}{\Sigma w \cos^2 \phi}$$

with a corresponding expression for y.

We find, from the numbers of the table,

$$\Sigma w x \cos \phi = +\ 37.5 \qquad \therefore x_0 = 0.13$$
$$\Sigma w y \cos \phi = -\ 6.2 \qquad y_0 = -0.02$$
$$\Sigma w \cos^2 \phi = 298 \qquad \rho = 0.13$$
$$e = 9^\circ$$

Hence, for the sun-spot fluctuation :

$$\Delta\tau = 0^\circ.13 \cos \mu t - 0^\circ.02 \sin \mu t = 0^\circ.13 \cos (\mu t + 9^\circ)$$

The expression has been derived without any reference to the actual epochs of the solar spottedness. All that we have done is to assume a period of 11.13 years in the temperature, and determine what constants of a harmonic fluctuation in this period will best represent the observations. It now remains to compare the epochs of temperature thus derived with those of the spots. This is done in Table IV. In studying this table it must be noted that the given epochs are not those derived individually from the observations in each case, but are the results of the general formulae which best represent all the observations. Consequently, the difference between the sunspot epochs and the temperature epochs as derived are constant in each of the respective phases of maxima and minima.

TABLE IV.

Comparison of Epochs of Temperature and Sun-spots.

Max. Temp.	Min. Spots	Δ	Min. Temp.	Max. Spots	Δ
y	y	y	y	y	y
1844.3	44.6	−0.3	1849.9	49.3	+0.6
1855.4	55.8	−0.4	1861.0	60.4	+0.6
1866.6	66.9	−0.3	1872.1	71.5	+0.6
1877.7	78.0	−0.3	1883.3	82.6	+0.7
1888.8	89.2	−0.4	1894.5	93.8	+0.7
1900.0	00.3	−0.3	1905.6	04.9	+0.7

It will be seen that, in the general mean of all the epochs, the temperature epoch follows the spot epoch, the comparisons of each phase being

Maximum temperature — minimum sunspots	y − 0.33
Minimum temperature — maximum sunspots	+ 0.65
Mean of all the comparisons	+ 0.16

The difference between the comparisons of the two phases arises from the fact that, by the method adopted, the intervals between the maxima and minima of temperatures necessarily come out equal, while those between the maxima and minima of sunspots are unequal.

The general conclusion is that the fluctuations of temperature follow very closely those of the sunspots, according to the law first clearly brought out by Köppen. The slight lagging of $0^y.16$, or two months, is too small to be regarded as the result of anything but accidental deviations, being less than the probable error of its amount.

Very remarkable is the fact that the actual fluctuation is less than half that found by Köppen. In order to show whether, when treated by the more rigorous method, the deviations of temperature used by him would give a different result from mine, we have only to find the general result of his data taken separately. This we do by deriving the mean values of x and y from his data alone, the individual results of which are found in the last nine lines of the table. These give

$$x = 0^{\circ}.13 \qquad y = -0^{\circ}.05$$

Accidentally, the principal coefficient of the fluctuation is practically the same whether derived from his observations or from the others.

Although the reality of this 11-year fluctuation seems to be placed beyond serious doubt, the amplitude being several times its probable error, its amount is too small to produce any important direct effect upon meteorological phenomena.

§ 9. *Study of Irregular Fluctuations of the Mean Annual Temperature.*

The next question before us is whether, after correcting the annual departures of temperature for the sun-spot inequality, indications can be found of fluctuations in the general temperature other than those arising from accidental deviations. In this study we apply the statistical method developed in Chapter II, § 4, preceding. The data are shown in Table V, which is formed from Table II by reducing to the centi-

TABLE V.

Reduced Annual Deviations of Temperature at Stations or in Regions in Degrees C.

Year	U. S.	Habana	Kingston	Argentina	Bombay	Madras	Calcutta	Ceylon	Manila	Australia	Batavia	Apia	India
	°	°	°	°	°	°	°	°	°	°	°	°	°
1871	+.32	......	......	......	+.42	+.32	+.12	......	......	......	−0.38	......	+.31
72	+.03	......	......	+0.60	−.27	−.07	+.53	......	......	......	−0.27	......	.00
73	+.20	......	......	+0.22	−.31	−.11	+.49	......	......	......	−0.11	......	−.04
74	+.13	−.07	......	−0.26	−.67	−.37	−.07	......	......	......	−0.67	......	−.40
1875	−.24	+.06	......	−0.05	−.24	+.06	−.14	......	......		−0.24		−.08
76	.00	−.40	......	−0.10	−.30	.00	+.50	......	......	......	−0.30		+.01
77	+.07	−.23	......	+0.47	+.27	+.17	−.03	......	......	......	+0.27	......	+.16
78	+.08	−.02	......	−0.40	+.18	+.58	+.48	......	......	......	+1.08	......	+.42
79	+.03	−.27	......	+0.06	−.67	−.17	+.43	......	......	......	−0.27	......	−.20
1880	−.10	+.20	......	0.00	−.10	−.10	−.60	......	......	......	−0.60	......	−.21
81	+.37	+.17	+.17	+0.29	+.27	+.27	−.23	+.17	......	......	+0.27	......	+.16
82	+.42	+.52	+.12	+0.07	−.18	+.12	+.12	+.02	......	......	−0.28	......	+.02
83	+.43	+.53	+.23	+0.37	−.27	−.07	−.47	−.17	−.07	−.07	−0.07	......	−.21
84	+.30	+.10	−.10	+0.35	−.30	−.30	−.60	−.20	−.50	.00	−0.20	......	−.32
1885	+.04	−.46	+.34	+0.02	−.16	−.06	+.14	−.06	−.06	+.14	−0.06	......	−.03
86	−.63	−.23	+.37	+0.13	−.13	−.33	......	−.03	−.23	+.07	+0.17	......	−.17
87	−.19	−.09	−.29	+0.29	−.59	−.29	......	−.39	−.29	−.09	−0.59	......	−.11
88	−.43	+.07	+.17	+0.51	+.17	−.23	......	−.03	−.03	+.57	+0.27	......	−.03
89	−.02	+.08	+.38	−0.34	−.12	−.12	......	+.08	+.48	+.28	+0.68	......	−.03
1890	+.42	+.02	−.38	−0.37	−.28	−.28	......	−.18	−.28	+.22	−0.48	−.29	−.24
91	−.11	−.01	+.09	+0.07	−.11	......	......	−.11	−.01	−.21	+.069	−.25	−.11
92	−.34	−.34	−.34	−0.65	+.26	......	......	−.04	+.16	−.24	+0.16	−.26	+.09
93	−.09	+.31	−.39	−1.19	−.29	......	......	−.19	−.09	+.11	−0.39	−.51	−.23
94	−.07	−.07	−.27	−0.07	+.13	......	......	+.03	−.07	−.17	−0.07	−.11	+.07
1895	−.49	+.01	+.01	+0.71	+.11		......	+.01	+.01	+.01	+0.21	−.21	+.03
96	+.25	+.05	+.25	+1.15	+.65		......	+.25	+.05	−.25	+0.65	−.26	+.42
97	+.08	+.18	+.18	−0.22	−.12		......	+.38	+.58	+.08	+1.08	+.10	+.17
98	−.19	−.29	−.39	−0.49	+.31		......	+.11	−.09	+.21	+0.11	−.02	+.20
99	−.33	+.17	......	......	+.07		......	−.13	−.33	−.33	−0.13	+.07	−.04
1900	+.18	−.02			+.08		......	+.18	−.28	−.52	+0.48	+.24	+.31
01	−.59	−.49			+.01		......	+.81	+.01	+.11	......	+.42	+.47
02	−.12	+.08			+.28		......	......	−.12	......	......	+.48	+.28
03	−.35	−.05			......		......	......	......	......	......	+.60	......
1904	−.19								......	......	......	+.24	......
Wt. *w*	3	4	3	3	3	4	2	4	4	3	1	3	4

grade scale and correcting the departures for the sun-spot fluctuation. They are given in some cases for the individual stations, and in others for entire regions. The column "India" is the weighted mean of the four Indian stations alone, which has been separately formed for a reason which will hereafter be shown.

In combining the departures into a general mean it is advisable to assign different weights to different stations, on account of the diversity of the mean fluctuation, as shown in the several columns. If we could regard each departure as independent of all the others, and free from any source of systematic error, the weights would be proportional to the inverse square of the mean fluctuations, as given in each column. But this course would result in giving too great a relative weight to the stations of small fluctuation. Actually, in the first combination, the weights used are those at the bottom of the several columns.

TABLE VI.

Treatment of Annual Departures.

Year	τ_1'	τ_1	$\Delta\tau$	ϵ'	W''	$W''^2\epsilon'^2$	$\Sigma w'^2 e^2$	ϵ	W'	$W'^2\epsilon^2$	$\Sigma w^2 e^2$
1871	+0.48	+0.19	−0.12	+0.30	13	15.2	5.7	+0.31	8	5.76	4.16
72	−0.12	+0.12	−0.13	+0.01	16	0.0	2.0	+0.01	11	0.01	0.19
73	−0.03	+0.03	−0.09	+0.06	16	0.9	3.2	+0.12	11	1.69	1.35
74	−0.28	−0.21	−0.03	−0.25	20	25.0	7.4	−0.20	15	9.00	3.94
1875	−0.04	−0.04	+0.04	−0.08	20	2.6	1.2	−0.08	15	1.44	0.70
76	−0.01	−0.05	+0.10	−0.11	20	4.8	4.6	−0.15	15	4.84	2.74
77	+0.25	+0.24	+0.13	+0.12	20	5.8	3.8	+0.11	15	2.56	3.26
78	+0.31	+0.24	+0.12	+0.19	20	14.4	8.1	+0.12	15	2.89	5.59
79	−0.08	−0.05	+0.07	−0.15	20	9.0	6.2	−0.12	15	3.64	1.99
1880	−0.10	−0.06	0.00	−0.10	20	4.0	2.7	−0.06	15	0.81	1.73
81	+0.14	+0.16	−0.07	+0.21	27	32.1	4.8	+0.23	18	16.81	3.21
82	+0.02	+0.08	−0.12	+0.14	27	14.3	6.5	+0.20	18	14.44	6.40
83	−0.07	+0.02	−0.13	+0.06	34	4.2	9.8	+0.15	25	14.44	8.58
84	−0.23	−0.16	−0.10	−0.13	34	19.5	9.8	−0.06	25	1.96	8.00
1885	−0.08	−0.07	−0.04	−0.04	34	1.8	5.1	−0.03	25	0.49	4.51
86	−0.08	−0.07	+0.03	−0.11	32	12.4	7.1	−0.10	25	6.25	7.17
87	−0.14	−0.10	+0.09	−0.23	32	54.2	10.1	−0.19	25	22.09	6.59
88	+0.20	+0.24	+0.13	+0.07	32	5.0	7.9	+0.11	25	7.29	7.31
89	+0.22	+0.26	+0.12	+0.10	32	10.2	7.9	+0.14	25	12.25	7.09
1890	−0.07	−0.05	+0.08	−0.15	35	27.6	8.7	−0.13	28	12.96	7.88
91	−0.04	−0.04	+0.01	−0.05	31	2.4	1.6	−0.05	28	1.96	1.48
92	−0.23	−0.26	−0.06	−0.17	31	27.8	10.1	−0.20	28	31.36	9.26
93	−0.35	−0.35	−0.11	−0.24	31	55.4	20.0	−0.24	28	46.24	19.40
94	−0.20	−0.21	−0.13	−0.07	31	4.7	1.2	−0.08	28	5.76	1.34
1895	−0.09	−0.09	−0.11	+0.02	31	0.4	7.2	+0.02	28	0.16	7.10
96	+0.19	+0.17	−0.05	+0.24	31	55.4	10.2	+0.22	28	36.00	17.00
97	+0.22	+0.22	+0.02	+0.20	31	38.1	10.7	+0.20	28	31.36	8.66
98	0.00	−0.03	+0.09	−0.09	31	7.8	7.0	−0.12	28	12.25	6.67
99	+0.02	−0.01	+0.13	−0.11	25	7.6	4.6	−0.14	22	7.29	4.27
1900	+0.27	+0.25	+0.12	+0.15	25	14.1	9.4	+0.13	22	7.29	7.23
01	+0.14	+0.08	+0.09	+0.05	24	1.4	10.3	−0.01	21	0.09	12.63
02	−0.12	+0.13	+0.02	+0.10	17	2.9	3.3	+0.11	18	3.61	3.67
03	0.00	0.09	−0.05	+0.05	10	0.3	4.3	+0.05	10	0.25	4.49
1904	−0.08	−0.08	−0.11	+0.03	6	0.0	0.9	+0.03	6	0.01	0.85

The process of applying the criterion for correlation is shown in Table VI. To illustrate the method as fully as possible, two combinations of the data have been made. In the first the four Indian stations are treated as independent, in the second their mean is used as a single region. The second and third columns show the general mean departures of temperature, uncorrected for the sun spot fluctuations, as formed from the departures in Table II. In the first of these the four Indian stations are treated as if they were independent; in the second their combined mean is used, as found from the last column of Table V.

$\Delta\tau$ is the sun-spot fluctuation. Subtracting it from the two columns of means we have a world-departure of temperature, found in the columns τ' and τ, according to the use of the Indian stations. Following each of these is its weight, which is the sum of the weights of the individual departures.

Fixing our attention on these world-departures we note that their general mean value is about $\pm 0^\circ.13$, and that in only 7 of the 34 years does it rise to $0^\circ.2$. If we could regard these departures as actual means for the entire globe, they would indicate corresponding fluctuations in the sun's radiation. But, before we can draw any conclusion to this effect, we must determine whether the departures exceed in their general mean the values to be expected from the accidental deviations in the separate regions.

As the statistical method has been set forth, the sum of the squares of the general deviations τ are derived from any unbroken series of observations at a number n of stations extending through a number r of years. In substance, the method consists in subtracting from the sum of the squares of the products $H\tau$ the portions of the squares which would be due to the accidental deviations, or $\Sigma w^2 \epsilon^2$. The remainder $\Sigma H^2\tau^2 - \Sigma w^2\epsilon^2$, which we have called Δ, is proportional to the sum of the squares of the deviations for the whole globe, as shown by the equations (16) and (17). We might subtract for each unbroken series, not the squares of the actual regional deviations ϵ, but the product of the mean values of ϵ^2 by r. The final result would obviously be the same in either case.

We now sum the columns $H'^2\tau'^2$ and $w'^2\epsilon'^2$ to find the value of Δ, dividing the time into convenient terms of four or five years as follows:

Term	$H'^2\tau'^2$	$w'^2\epsilon'^2$	Δ	H'^2
1871-74	41.1	18.3	+ 22.8	1081
1875-79	36.6	23.9	+ 12.7	2000
1880-84	74.1	33.6	+ 40.5	4170
1885-89	83.6	38.1	+ 45.5	5252
1890-94	117.9	41.6	+ 76.3	5069
1895-99	119.3	48.7	+ 70.6	4469
1900-04	18.7	37.2	− 18.5	1626
Sum	491.3	241.4	249.9	23667

The weight assigned to each station and region being taken as constant we have

$$\Sigma_{i,j} w^2 = r_1 w_1^2 + r_2 w_2^2 + \cdots + r_n w_n^2$$

r being, in each case, the number of years through which the observations extend.

To find the mean cosmical fluctuation indicated we have, for use in (17)

$$\Sigma W'^2 - \Sigma' w^2 = 20766$$

$$\text{Mean } \tau_o^2 = \frac{\Delta}{\Sigma W'^2 - \Sigma' w^2} = .012$$

$$\therefore \text{mean } \tau_o = \pm 0°.11 \text{ C.}$$

This is the mean general fluctuation of temperature of the earth from year to year which is indicated by the data of observation.

But, before we accept this as really cosmical, we must find whether it affects all the stations, or whether the correlation exists only between stations so situated that they may be subject to like departures of temperature through the great movements of the air from one region to another.

The four Indian stations are especially in close proximity; we shall therefore discuss their departure by themselves, to decide whether they show any well-marked correlation. In doing this it will be unnecessary to make any distinction of weights. We shall therefore put $w = 1$ in each case, which will make W' identical with the number of stations. Of course we must then use for τ the unweighted means, which are slightly different from those of Table V. Starting with 1871, we find these to be $\tau = +0°.29, +0°.06, +0°.02$, etc., instead of $+0°.31, 0°.00, -0°.04$, etc. For use in the equation (9) the values of $n\tau^2$ are .252, .011, .001, etc. These we sum by periods during which the number of stations remains unchanged. Then we sum the individual departures in the same way, and divide each annual sum by n. We have for 1871, $\Sigma r^2 = .12^2 + .32^2 + .12^2 = 0.293$. This gives, for 1871, $\Sigma r^2 \div n = .098$, in using which two decimals are amply sufficient. Carrying through this computation for each year and summing by periods, we find the following results:

Period	n	$n^2\Sigma\tau^2$	Σr^2	Δ
1871–80	3	4.7	1.0	3.7
1881–85	4	3.1	1.2	1.9
1886–90	3	2.4	1.0	1.4
1891–01	2	2.4	1.9	0.5
		12.6		7.5

The positive correlation shown by Δ is so clearly marked as to leave no doubt, a result which accords with what we might anticipate from the geographical proximity of the stations.

We next investigate the result when the four Indian stations are combined into a single mean, which is found in the last column of Table V. The general world-departure then found is shown in column τ of Table VI. and the computation of the two series whose difference shows the correlation is shown in the last two columns of the table. Summing by terms as before, we have the following numbers:

Term	$W'^2\tau^2$	N^2r^2	Δ	W''
1871–74	16.4	9.6	+ 6.8	531
1875–79	15.3	14.3	+ 1.0	1125
1880–84	48.5	27.9	+ 20.6	2123
1885–89	48.4	32.7	+ 15.7	3125
1890–94	97.3	39.3	+ 58.0	3920
1895–99	87.1	43.7	+ 43.4	3620
1900–01	11.2	28.8	− 17.6	1385
Sum	324.2	196.3	127.9	15829

We thus have for the entire period of investigation

$$\Delta = 127.9$$

The value of the general fluctuation is thus reduced to

$$\tau_u = \pm 0^\circ.07$$

a quantity not greater than its probable error.

But we still cannot assume that all the regions are so distant from each other as to be unaffected through an entire year by any common terrestrial cause, especially the winds. Considering first the proximity of the stations, we notice that Havana and Kingston may be regarded as in the same region with each other, and with the United States. Moreover, the Southeastern Asiatic and Australian stations are so linked in a geographical series that we cannot regard each as necessarily independent of that next to it. On the other hand North America, South America, Apia and the Asiatic-Australian series form four sets which we cannot deem to be correlated except through the action of a cosmical cause, presumably fluctuations of the sun's radiation, which would affect all the stations, how widely soever separated. We therefore inquire whether the correlation we have found is or is not quite general for the earth by correlating the stations in pairs by the method shown in § 5. Beginning with the widely separated stations we correlate the three North American regions, United

States, Havana and Kingston with the distant ones, shown in the following table with the result :

Correlation Between North American and Distant Regions, Taken Two by Two.

	U. S.		Havana		Kingston	
	$\frac{1}{2}\Delta$	$ww'e$	$\frac{1}{2}\Delta$	$ww'e$	$\frac{1}{2}\Delta$	$ww'e$
Argentina	+2.6	243	−2.6	300	+11.8	162
Apia	−1.3	135	−2.8	168	+ 3.5	81
Manila	−1.1	240	+0.3	320	+ 5.4	192
India	−0.8	384	−6.0	464	+ 2.3	216
Batavia	−1.6	90	−0.4	108	+ 3.5	54
Australia	−2.1	171	1.0	228	+ 1.2	144
Sum	−4.8	1263	−8.2	1588	+27.7	849

The correlation between Argentina and distant regions is as follows :

Argentina :	Apia	$\frac{1}{2}\Sigma\Delta = + 3.6$	$ww'e =$ 81
"	Manila	" − 1.6	" 192
"	India	" + 1.2	" 324
"	Batavia	" + 2.0	" 81
"	Australia	" − 2.6	" 144
	Sum	+ 2.6	822

We have finally the correlation between Apia and the Indo-Australian regions.

Apia :	Manila	$\frac{1}{2}\Sigma\Delta = + 2.6$	$ww'e =$ 156
"	India	" + 5.8	" 156
"	Batavia	" + 1.0	" 33
"	Australia	" − 0.3	" 108
	Sum	+ 9.1	453

The curious synchronism between the annual departures of Kingston and all the most distant stations, especially Argentina, may well excite notice. But I do not conceive that we can attribute it to anything but chance coincidence.

We next take the pairs between which we should expect correlation on account of their proximity. A detailed exhibit of the results does not seem necessary. The summation of $ww'ee'$ gives :

United States ; Havana–Kingston	3 pairs	$\Delta = + 15.7$
Indo-Australian series	6 pairs	$\Delta = + 20.3$

The complete summation of the values of $\bar{\Delta}$ gives 62°.3, in fair agreement with that derived from the combination of the squares of the deviations.

It seems therefore that, of the 36 pairs of regions, 9 which were in proximity contribute more than half to the making up Δ, the correlation number. Of these 9, the two extremes, India-Australia and Manila-Australia, are so distant from each other that they should be included in the class not subject to any common cause of change of temperature. Their contributions to $\frac{1}{2}\Delta$ are:

India-Australia	$\frac{1}{2}\Delta = -3.0$	$ww'e = 228$
Manila-Australia	" $= -0.7$	" $= 228$
Sum	-3.7	456

We now have the following equations for the mean value of that portion of the fluctuations of mean annual temperature which we may attribute to a general cause affecting the whole earth:

United States and dist. points	6 pairs	$1263\tau_0^2 =$	$-$ 4.8
Havana " " "	6 "	1588	$-$ 8.3
Kingston " " "	6 "	849	+ 27.7
Argentina " " "	5 "	822	+ 2.6
Apia " " "	4 "	453	+ 9.1
Australia " " "	2 "	456	$-$ 3.7
Total	29	$5431\tau_0^2$	+ 22.6

This gives

$$\tau_0^2 = .0042$$

$$\tau_0 = \pm 0.065 \text{ C.}$$

This fluctuation, if regarded as real, is too minute to produce any important meteorological effect. That it may well arise from the accidental deviations is shown by the fact that, had Kingston been omitted, τ_0^2 would have come out negative, indicating a tendency toward an equalization of the general temperature of the globe from year to year. But there is nothing to justify us in rejecting Kingston for this reason, though a careful analysis might show that we have given it greater relative weight than it is entitled to. The same remark would, however, apply to Havana, the result of which is markedly in the opposite direction from that of Kingston.

§ 10. *Time Correlations in Annual World Temperatures.*

Returning to Table VI, it is noticeable that the larger outstanding departures τ do not seem to be scattered at random, but are rather collected in groups of like algebraic sign, as if they were the result of a fluctuation having a period of several years. It would be easy to represent them by the ordinates of a sinuous curve, but a conclusion based on this method would be altogether unreliable. We shall therefore apply the method of time correlation, developed in § 6, which will bring out with numerical exactness any period that may exist, or any periodic tendency. The numerical process is shown in the following lines, the numbers of which are formed as follows: Starting with the departure for 1871, 0.31, which, for our present purpose we call a_0, we form its square, and also its product by the following departures in the order of time to any extent to which we may suspect a correlation. In the present case we have considered it sufficient to form the products through terms of nine years. The nine consecutive products formed by multiplying 0.31 by τ for the years 1871 to 1880 are written in the first line of the following table.

Next we take the year 1872, form the square of its departure, and the products by the departure for the nine years following. These form the second line of the table. We repeat the process for 1873 and subsequent years to the end of the series and write the results in consecutive lines with each initial year of the series. Of course the number of years available will fall off by one for each line in which the initial year is greater than 1895. The series terminating with 1904, we have eight products for 1896, seven for 1887, etc.

TABLE VII.

Time Correlation Among Annual Temperatures.

Initial year	a_0^2	a_0a_1	a_0a_2	a_0a_3	a_0a_4	a_0a_5	a_0a_6	a_0a_7	a_0a_8	a_0a_9
1871	.096	+.003	+.007	−.062	−.025	−.046	+.034	+.037	−.037	−.019
72	.000	+.001	−.002	−.001	−.001	+.001	+.001	−.001	−.001	+.002
73	.014	−.024	−.010	−.018	+.013	+.014	−.014	−.007	+.028	+.024
74	.040	+.016	+.030	−.022	−.024	+.024	+.012	−.046	−.040	−.030
1875	.006	+.012	−.009	−.010	+.010	+.005	−.018	−.016	−.012	+.005
76	.022	−.016	−.018	+.018	−.009	−.035	−.030	−.022	+.009	+.004
77	.012	+.013	−.013	−.007	+.025	+.022	+.016	−.007	−.003	−.011
78	.014	−.014	−.007	+.028	+.024	+.018	−.007	−.004	−.012	−.023
79	.014	+.007	−.028	−.024	−.018	+.007	+.004	+.012	+.023	−.013
1880	.004	−.014	−.012	−.009	+.004	+.002	+.006	+.011	−.007	−.008
81	.053	+.016	+.034	−.014	−.007	−.023	−.044	+.025	+.032	−.030
82	.040	+.030	−.012	−.006	−.020	−.038	+.022	+.028	−.026	−.010
83	.023	−.009	−.005	−.015	−.028	+.017	+.021	−.020	−.008	−.030
84	.004	+.002	+.006	+.011	−.007	−.008	+.008	+.003	+.012	+.014
1885	.002	+.003	+.006	−.003	−.004	+.004	+0.01	+.006	+.007	+.002
86	.010	+.019	−.011	−.014	+.013	+.005	+.020	+.024	+.008	−.002
87	.036	−.021	−.027	+.025	+.010	+.038	+.046	+.015	−.004	−.042
88	.012	+.015	−.014	−.006	−.022	−.026	.009	+.002	+.024	+.022
89	.020	−.018	−.007	−.028	−.034	−.011	−.003	+.031	+.028	−.017
1890	.017	+.007	+.026	+.031	+.010	−.003	−.029	−.026	+.016	+.018
91	.003	+.010	+.012	+.004	−.001	−.011	−.010	+.006	+.007	−.007
92	.040	+.048	+.016	−.004	−.041	−.040	+.024	+.028	−.026	+.002
93	.058	+.019	−.005	−.053	−.048	+.029	+.004	−.031	+.002	−.026
94	.006	−.002	−.018	−.016	+.010	+.014	−.010	+.001	−.009	−.004
1895	.000	+.004	+.004	−.002	−.003	+.003	.000	+.002	+.001	+.001
96	.048	+.044	−.026	−.031	+.029	−.002	+.024	+.011	+.007	
97	.040	−.024	−.028	+.026	−.002	+.022	+.010	+.006		
98	.014	+.017	−.016	+.001	−.013	−.006	−.004			
99	.020	−.018	+.003	−.015	−.007	−.004				
1900	.017	−.001	+.014	+.007	+.004					
01	.000	−.001	−.003	.000						
02	.012	+.006	+.003							
03	.003	+.002								
04	.001									
Σ	.700	+.162	−.080	−.200	−.147	−.031	+.111	+.068	+.019	−.278

It is to the summation found at the bottom of this table that our attention will be especially directed. It must be admitted that the periodicity among the numbers seems to be very well marked, the apparent period being about six years. This is so nearly one-half that of the sun-spot period that, if the result is not purely fortuitous, we may well regard this as an actual period.

Assuming the correlation to be real, the fact brought out may be found by dividing the first sum $[a_0^2]$ into each of the sums following. This is done in Table IX. The second column of the table gives the values of $[a_0a_0]$, $[a_0a_1]$, $\cdots$, $[a_0a_n]$, which are the sums Σ just found. The third column gives the quotients $[a_0a_i] \div [a_0a_0]$. Accepting them as real, the result may be expressed as follows: Whatever the mean annual world departure in any one year, we have had since 1871, as a mean rule, a departure in the same direction of 0.23 of its amount the year following. In the third year following we have had a departure in the opposite direction of 0.30, of its initial amount; in the fourth year of 0.21; in the sixth year a departure, now in the original direction, of 0.16; and in the ninth a departure in the opposite direction, of 0.40 of the initial departure.

To estimate the probability that this periodicity is real we must estimate the probable accumulated amount of the purely fortuitous deviations. We have for this purpose

Standard annual deviation $= \pm 0.11$

The probable mean value of a product of two such deviations will depend upon the law of statistical distribution. Our best result will be derived not by assuming the normal law of distribution, which may not be strictly applicable, but by taking the indiscriminate average, without regard to sign, of the entire 261 products. We thus find

General average $aa = .0155$

The average expected accumulations of 30 such sums, if fortuitous, will be about $\pm .08$. This, then, is the expected average value of a non-systematic $[a_0a_i]$ ($i = 1, 2, 3$, etc.), for the period 1871–1904. The actual average we see to be 0.13. The excess is no greater than might well be the result of chance deviations. But the inference of its reality is strengthened by the evident 6-year periodicity of the sums. On the other hand, the existence of this period as an unbroken one is negatived by the fact that during the last ten years of the series the epoch is practically reversed. The proof of a permanent period half that of the sun-spots therefore falls to the ground. If there is any real periodicity the case is similar to that of the waves of the ocean when, after a series of definite period, a new series sets in with the same period, but not a continuation of the first.

TABLE VIII.

Time Correlations Through Nine-year Terms.

Years 1871–1901			Years 1829–63		
i	$[a_0 a_i]$	Quot.	i	$[a_0 a_i]$	Quot.
0	+0.700	+1.00	0	+4.99	+1.00
1	+0.162	+0.23	1	+1.73	+0.34
2	−0.080	−0.11	2	−1.74	−0.35
3	−0.209	−0.30	3	+1.09	+0.22
4	−0.147	−0.21	4	+0.29	+0.06
5	−0.031	−0.04	5	+0.42	−0.08
6	+0.111	+0.16	6	+1.52	+0.30
7	+0.068	+0.10	7	−0.08	−0.02
8	+0.019	+0.03	8	−0.15	−0.03
9	−0.278	−0.40	9	−0.63	−0.13

The reality of the periodicity can be established only by carrying the investigation back through the years preceding 1871. I have done this with Köpping's table of annual departures already cited, after correction for the sun-spot inequality. The result is found in the second part of Table IX, preceding. There is here not only no periodicity, but, on the contrary, a tendency toward a persistence of the departure in the same direction for as much as six years. The products are, in general, several times larger than those for the modern period, showing wider accidental deviations. We may attribute both this and the systematic character of the correlation products to the imperfections of the older instruments and observations. But this would not be likely to mask entirely a six-year periodicity, if any such existed. We must, therefore, regard the seeming period as unreal, or at least open to serious doubt, notwithstanding the plausibility of the statistical evidence in its favor.

CHAPTER IV.

DISCUSSION OF MONTHLY DEPARTURES.

Since the only period exceeding a month that we can assign *a priori* as probable, that of the sun-spots, has already been investigated in the preceding chapter, the purpose of the present chapter is to determine whether the monthly departures of world-temperature show any systematic character not found in the results of the annual departures. If this result were the only one aimed at, ideal simplicity and perfection would require that we first correct the normal temperatures from which the departures are computed for the fluctuations already derived from the annual means. In other words, our normal temperature should include at least the sun-spot fluctuation. But this has not been done. Consequently, the general departures τ_m affecting all parts of the world simultaneously, may be expected to reappear in the discussion and comparison of the monthly means. But it does not seem objectionable to allow this. We have only to recall the fact in drawing conclusions from any systematic departures that may be found.

The monthly mean departures which have been selected for discussion are partly those of Dove, and partly those specially collected for the present work. Among the latter are included those subsequently given in connection with the ten-day means.

§ 11. *Discussion of Dove's Departures.*

In the *Memoirs* of the Berlin Academy for 1858 Dove gives a great number of tables of observed temperatures at widely separated stations, which are in some points similar in form to those required for the present work. Those best adapted to the present purpose have therefore been used for material. These are found on pp. 364, etc., of the *Memoirs.* A certain number of regions were selected from Dove's tables so far apart that there seemed to be no possibility of a correlation of their monthly temperatures, except from some cosmical cause. It was also necessary to prefer stations and regions where the temperature was least subject to rapid fluctuations, and for reasons already mentioned, regions of low rather than of high latitude. The regions thus selected were :

Eastern Asia ; mean of Nagasaki and Pekin.

Southern Europe ; mean of stations in southern Russia.

United States ; mean of several stations in the southern portion.

Cape of Good Hope ; one station only.

Hobartown ; one station only.

Madras ; one station only.

In taking the means no distinction of weight was made between the different regions or stations.

The mean deviations formed from Dove's tables were tabulated and summed separately for each year. The observations at Hobartown terminated with September, 1848.

The results of the summation of the squares of the deviations for the several years are shown in the following table.

Dove's deviations are given in the Reaumer scale. For convenience these are used without change in the table.

Table IX.

Dove's Simultaneous Monthly Departures of Temperature from the Normal.

	E. Asia	S. Europe	U. S.	Cape	Hobarton	Madras	Σ	r	r²
1845									
Jan.	+1.2	+1.8	+0.9	−1.1	+0.4	0.0	+3.2	+0.53	+0.28
Feb.	+0.3	−2.5	−0.1	−0.9	−0.4	−0.6	−4.2	−0.70	+0.49
Mar.	+0.5	−0.8	−0.1	+0.2	+0.1	−0.8	−0.9	−0.15	+0.02
April	−0.1	0.0	+1.3	−0.3	+0.4	−0.3	+1.0	+0.17	+0.03
May	+0.5	−1.6	−0.4	−0.1	−0.4	−0.1	−2.1	−0.35	+0.12
June	+0.7	+0.4	+0.2	−0.8	−0.1	+0.6	+1.0	+0.17	+0.03
July	0.0	+0.1	+0.5	−0.1	+0.8	+0.3	+1.6	+0.27	+0.07
Aug.	−0.6	−0.8	−0.2	−1.8	+0.2	−0.2	−3.4	−0.57	+0.32
Sept.	−1.0	0.0	0.0	−0.3	+0.9	+0.3	−0.1	−0.02	0.00
Oct.	−0.5	0.0	−0.4	+0.3	+0.7	−0.7	−0.6	−0.10	+0.01
Nov.	−0.6	+1.1	−0.3	−0.2	+0.2	−0.3	−0.7	−0.12	+0.01
Dec.	−2.4	+1.0	−2.3	−0.7	+0.2	−0.6	−4.8	−0.80	+0.64
1846									
Jan.	−0.6	+1.2	−0.3	−0.7	−0.2		−0.6	−0.12	+0.01
Feb.	−0.2	+1.3	−1.0	−0.2	−1.1		−1.2	−0.24	+0.06
Mar.	−0.8	+1.9	+0.1	−0.1	−0.5		+0.6	+0.12	+0.01
April	−0.2	+1.2	−0.6	−0.7	+0.1		−0.2	−0.04	0.00
May	−1.9	+0.9	+0.2	−0.6	+0.5		−0.9	−0.18	+0.03
June	−0.2	+1.5	−0.5	+0.1	+0.1		+1.0	+0.20	+0.04
July	−0.3	+1.2	−0.7	+1.5	−0.4		+1.3	+0.26	+0.07
Aug.	+0.5	+0.7	0.0	−0.7	+0.8		+1.3	+0.26	+0.07
Sept.	+0.9	+0.6	+0.1	+0.8	−0.2		+2.2	+0.44	+0.19
Oct.	+0.7	+0.9	−0.4	+1.1	+0.3		+2.6	+0.52	+0.27
Nov.	−0.3	−0.2	+0.2	+0.2	+0.5		+0.4	+0.08	+0.01
Dec.	+1.1	−1.1	+1.5	+1.1	+0.7		+3.3	+0.66	+0.44
1847									
Jan.	+0.8	−0.1	+0.6	+0.1	−0.2		+1.2	+0.24	+0.06
Feb.	−0.3	−0.9	−0.5	+1.2	−0.2		−0.7	−0.14	+0.02
Mar.	−0.4	−0.6	−1.1	0.0	−0.4		−2.5	−0.50	+0.25
April	+1.1	−0.7	+0.5	−0.4	0.0		+0.5	+0.10	+0.01
May	−0.2	+1.8	−0.8	0.0	−0.8		0.0	0.00	0.00
June	−1.3	−1.8	−0.2	−0.1	−1.0		−4.4	−0.88	+0.77
July	+0.3	−0.2	−0.5	−0.7	+0.1		−1.0	−0.20	+0.04
Aug.	+1.0	0.0	−0.2	−0.8	+0.8		+0.8	+0.16	+0.02
Sept.	−0.9	−0.9	−0.3	0.0	+0.6		−1.5	−0.30	+0.09
Oct.	0.0	−0.8	+0.5	+1.0	−0.3		+0.4	+0.08	+0.06
Nov.	+2.0	−0.7	+1.0	−0.6	−1.2		+0.5	+0.10	+0.01
Dec.	+0.6	−0.4	−1.6	−1.0	+0.5		−1.9	−0.38	+0.14
1848									
Jan.	+0.2	−3.4	+0.9	+0.8	−0.9		−2.4	−0.48	+0.23
Feb.	−0.8	+0.3	+0.3	−0.5	−0.9		−1.6	−0.32	+0.10
Mar.	+0.6	+1.4	+0.1	+0.8	+0.3		+3.2	+0.64	+0.41
April	+0.7	+1.4	−0.5	−0.8	+1.6		+2.4	+0.48	+0.23
May	+0.8	−0.3	+0.3	+0.4	−0.1		+1.1	+0.22	+0.05
June	+0.7	+1.4	0.0	0.0	+0.2		+2.3	+0.46	+0.21
July	+0.8	−0.4	0.0	+0.2	−0.4		+0.2	+0.04	0.00
Aug.	0.0	+0.3	−0.1	−0.4	−0.3		−0.5	−0.10	+0.01
Sept.	+0.1	+0.1	−0.7	0.0	−0.7		−1.2	−0.24	+0.06
Oct.	+0.7	+0.4	+0.5	+0.4	......		+2.0	+0.50	+0.25
Nov.	−0.3	−0.4	−1.8	+0.4	......		−2.1	−0.52	+0.27
Dec.	+1.7	−0.4	+3.5	−0.1	......		+4.7	+1.17	+1.37
1849									
Jan.	+0.3	−0.3	+1.4	+0.2			+1.6	+0.40	+0.16
Feb.	+2.1	+0.7	−1.1	+0.4			+2.1	+0.52	+0.27
Mar.	+1.7	−0.3	+2.0	+0.4			+3.8	+0.95	+0.90
April	+0.6	−1.0	−0.2	0.0			−0.6	−0.15	+0.02
May	−0.6	0.0	+0.3	−0.4			−0.7	−0.17	+0.03
June	−0.5	+1.6	+0.2	+0.2			+1.5	+0.37	+0.14
July	−0.5	−0.3	−0.7	+0.2			−1.3	−0.32	+0.10
Aug.	+0.7	−0.8	+0.8	−0.1			+0.6	+0.15	+0.02
Sept.	+0.7	+0.4	+0.4	+0.1			+1.6	+0.40	+0.16

TABLE IX.—*Continued.*

Dove's Simultaneous Monthly Departures of Temperatures from the Normal.

	E. Asia	S. Europe	U. S.	Cape	Hobarton	Madras	Σ	r	r′
1849									
Oct.	0.0	+0.4	+0.5	−0.2	......		+0.7	+0.17	+0.03
Nov.	−0.3	−0.9	+0.9	−0.5	......		−0.8	−0.20	+0.04
Dec.	0.0	−1.6	+2.9	−0.2	......		+1.1	+0.27	+0.07
1850									
Jan.	−0.4	−2.4	+2.7	−1.0	......		−1.1	−0.27	+0.07
Feb.	0.0	+0.8	−0.4	+0.6	......		+1.0	+0.25	+0.06
Mar.	+0.2	−1.5	+0.8	+0.2	......		−0.3	−0.08	+0.01
April	+1.4	+0.2	−0.1	+0.2	......		+1.7	+0.42	+0.18
May	−1.9	−0.6	−0.5	−0.8	......		−3.8	−0.95	+0.90
June	+0.6	−0.2	−0.9	−0.3	......		−0.8	−0.20	+0.04
July	−0.7	−0.7	+0.4	+0.1	......		−0.9	−0.22	+0.05
Aug.	−0.6	+0.2	+0.9	−0.1	......		+0.4	+0.10	+0.01
Sept.	−0.4	−0.8	+0.1	+0.3	......		−0.8	−0.20	+0.04
Oct.	+0.2	−1.7	−0.6	+0.2	......		−1.9	−0.47	+0.22
Nov.	−1.3	+0.8	+0.3	−1.0	......		−1.2	−0.30	+0.09
Dec.	−0.4	0.0	+1.1	−0.2	......		+0.5	+0.12	+0.01
1851									
Jan.	0.0	+0.9	+0.8	+0.5			+2.2	−0.55	+0.30
Feb.	0.0	−0.2	+1.6	+0.2			+1.6	+0.40	+0.16
Mar.	+0.2	−0.2	0.0	+0.5			+0.5	+0.12	+0.01
April	−1.5	+0.9	0.0	−0.1			−0.7	−0.17	+0.03
May	−0.7	−2.0	+0.1	+0.1			−2.5	−0.62	+0.38
June	−1.1	−0.5	+0.3	+0.4			−1.5	−0.37	+0.14
July	+0.3	−1.1	0.0	−0.3			−1.1	−0.27	+0.07
Aug.	−0.3	−0.7	−0.1	−1.3			−2.4	−0.60	+0.36
Sept.	−1.0	−1.5	−0.6	+0.1			−3.0	−0.75	+0.56
Oct.	−0.6	+0.8	0.0	+0.2			+0.4	+0.10	+0.01
Nov.	+0.2	−2.0	−0.2	0.0			−2.0	−0.50	+0.25
Dec.	−0.9	−1.1	−0.9	+0.3			−2.6	−0.65	+0.42
1852									
Jan.	−0.5	+1.2	−3.8	−0.3	......	0.0	−3.4	−0.68	+0.46
Feb.	−1.2	+0.6	+0.4	−0.7	......	+0.2	−0.7	−0.14	+0.02
Mar.	−2.3	−1.0	+0.9	−0.3	......	+0.4	−2.3	−0.46	+0.21
April	+0.2	−1.5	−0.9	+0.2	......	0.0	−2.0	−0.40	+0.16
May	−0.2	0.0	+0.4	+0.1	......	0.0	+0.3	+0.06	0.00
June	+0.3	−0.1	+0.3	−0.4	......	−0.1	+0.2	+0.04	0.00
July	+0.8	+0.3	−0.2	−0.1	......	−0.2	+0.6	+0.12	+0.01
Aug.	−0.2	+0.1	−0.1	+0.2	......	+0.1	+0.1	+0.02	0.00
Sept.	−0.4	+0.5	−0.2	+0.3	......	+0.4	+0.7	+0.11	+0.02
Oct.	+1.3	−0.2	+0.3	+0.1	......	+0.1	+1.6	+0.32	+0.10
Nov.	−1.0	+2.9	0.0	−0.1	......	+0.4	+2.2	+0.44	+0.19
Dec.	+0.4	+2.5	+1.2	0.0	......	+0.3	+4.4	+0.88	+0.77
1853									
Jan.	−0.2	+1.9	−1.1	+0.7		+0.9	+1.8	+0.36	+0.13
Feb.	−0.9	−0.6	0.0	+0.2		−0.5	−1.8	−0.36	+0.13
Mar.	−1.7	−1.6	+0.3	−0.4		+0.2	−3.2	−0.64	+0.41
April	−0.4	−1.8	+0.4	+0.2		−0.2	−1.8	−0.36	+0.13
May	0.0	−0.4	0.0	−0.2		+0.7	+0.1	+0.02	0.00
June	+0.1	−0.9	−0.4	+0.1		+1.2	+0.1	+0.02	0.00
July	+0.7	+0.6	+0.2	+0.4		+0.5	+2.4	+0.48	+0.23
Aug.	+0.7	+0.2	+0.4	0.0		+0.5	+1.8	+0.36	+0.13
Sept.	+1.2	+0.2	−0.1	−0.2		+0.9	+2.0	+0.40	+0.16
Oct.	−1.3	+0.5	+0.8	−0.7		+0.9	+0.2	+0.04	0.00
Nov.	0.0	+0.2	+1.3	+1.5		0.0	+3.0	+0.60	+0.36
Dec.	−0.6	−1.6	−1.5	+0.8		−0.2	−3.1	+0.62	+0.38
1854									
Jan.	−0.8	+0.9	+0.3	+1.1	......	−0.6	+1.5	+0.30	+0.09
Feb.	−1.6	−1.1	0.0	0.0	......	+0.4	−2.3	−0.46	+0.21
Mar.	+0.6	−0.2	+1.4	−0.4	......	+0.4	+1.8	+0.36	+0.13

TABLE IX.—*Concluded.*

Dove's Simultaneous Monthly Departures of Temperature from the Normal.

	E. Asia	S. Europe	U. S.	Cape	Hobarton	Madras	Σ		τ^2
1854									
April	+0.6	−0.2	+1.5	+0.2		+1.0	+0.4	+0.02	0.00
May	+0.2	+0.4	+0.2	+1.1		+0.8	+2.7	+0.54	+0.29
June	+0.3	−0.8	+0.2	+0.9		+1.3	+1.9	+0.38	+0.14
July	0.4	−0.6	+0.4	−0.3		+0.6	−0.3	−0.06	0.00
Aug.	−0.3	−0.9	−0.1	+0.1		+0.7	−0.5	−0.10	+0.01
Sept.	0.0	−0.9	+0.7	+0.5		+0.4	+0.5	+0.10	+0.01
Oct.	+1.0	+0.1	+0.2	−0.2		−0.4	+1.5	+0.30	+0.09
Nov.	+0.9	−1.2	−1.5	+1.1		+0.6	+0.1	+0.02	0.00
Dec.	+2.6	+2.2	−0.8	+0.4		+0.5	+4.7	+0.94	+0.88
1855									
Jan.	−1.8	−1.3	−0.1	+0.7		+0.2	−2.3	−0.46	+0.21
Feb.	−1.5	−0.6	−2.5	+0.3		+0.1	−4.2	−0.84	+0.70
Mar.	0.0	+0.6	−1.1	+0.7		−2.6	−2.4	−0.48	+0.23
April	+0.4	−0.9	+1.3	−0.1		+0.2	+0.9	+0.18	+0.03
May	−0.2	−0.8	−0.2	+0.6		+1.3	+0.7	+0.14	+0.02
June	+0.3	−0.6	−0.2	+0.3		+0.8	+0.6	+0.12	+0.01
July	0.0	0.0	+0.1	−0.4		+1.1	+0.8	+0.20	+0.04
Aug.	−1.7	+0.2	+0.3	0.0		+1.2	0.0	0.00	0.00
Sept.	−0.2	+0.3	+0.8	+0.1		+0.8	+1.8	+0.36	+0.13
Oct.	......	+2.0	−1.4	+0.6		+0.2	+1.4	+0.35	+0.12
Nov.	......	+0.2	+1.7	+1.7		+0.2	+3.8	+0.95	+0.90
Dec.	......	−2.7	+0.4	+1.2		......	−1.1	−0.37	+0.14
	......	......	......	......		......	......	......	+1.37

The sums of the squares of the deviations which enter into the theory are formed for each year, and shown in the following table. Σe^2 is, in each case, formed from the deviations in the preceding table. $\Sigma_y\tau^2$ is the sum from the last column of that table, which is multiplied, for each year, by n, the number of stations used. As shown in the general theory, the difference, $n^2\Sigma\tau^2 - \Sigma_e e^2$, so far as it is not the result of accidental errors and deviations, measures the correlation among the stations.

Results of Dove's Mean Monthly Deviations.

Year	East Asia	South Europe	U. S.	Cape	Hobarton	Madras	Mean					Equation for τ_0^2	Normal equation
	$\Sigma\tau_1^2$	$\Sigma\tau_2^2$	$\Sigma\tau_3^2$	$\Sigma\tau_4^2$	$\Sigma\tau_5^2$	$\Sigma\tau_6^2$	$\Sigma\tau^2$	$n^2\Sigma\tau^2$	Σe^2	$n-1$	r		
1845	10.3	15.7	9.3	6.7	2.7	2.6	2.13	77	47	5	12	60 $\tau_0^2 = + 4.9$	360 $\tau_0^2 = +30$
46	7.7	15.6	4.7	7.2	3.4	....	1.23	31	30	4	12	48 $\tau_0^2 = - 1.5$	240 $\tau_0^2 = - 8$
47	10.1	10.3	6.9	5.1	4.2	....	1.47	37	37	4	12	48 $\tau_0^2 = - 0.1$	240 $\tau_0^2 = 0$
48	6.8	18.4	17.5	2.9	3.1		1.35	34	31	4	9	36 $\tau_0^2 = + 0.7$	180 $\tau_0^2 = -17$
49	9.7	8.7	18.4	0.9	....	....	2.11	34	37	3	12	36 $\tau_0^2 = - 0.9$	144 $\tau_0^2 = - 3$
1850	9.0	13.8	11.8	3.4	....	....	1.78	28	38	3	12	36 $\tau_0^2 = - 2.4$	144 $\tau_0^2 = -10$
51	6.4	15.8	4.5	2.6	....	....	2.80	45	28	3	12	36 $\tau_0^2 = + 4.0$	144 $\tau_0^2 = +17$
52	10.8	20.2	18.1	1.0	....	0.7	2.00	50	31	4	12	48 $\tau_0^2 = - 0.2$	240 $\tau_0^2 = - 1$
53	8.4	14.0	6.4	4.0	....	5.2	2.13	53	38	4	12	48 $\tau_0^2 = + 3.1$	240 $\tau_0^2 = +15$
54	12.0	11.2	8.1	5.0	....	5.6	1.84	46	43	4	12	48 $\tau_0^2 = + 0.6$	240 $\tau_0^2 = + 3$
1855	8.7	15.7	15.2	6.4		12.6	2.72	68	58	4	12	48 $\tau_0^2 = + 1.9$	240 $\tau_0^2 = +10$
Σ		.....	.....	.....				503	467	42	129	492 $\tau_0^2 = +10.1$	2412 $\tau_0^2 = +36$

By reduction to the centigrade scale the final equation becomes

$$2412\tau_0^2 = 56$$

This equation will be combined with those to be derived from the later material. When taken alone it gives the result

$$\tau_n^2 = .023\,; \qquad \tau_n = \pm 0^\circ.15\ \mathrm{C}.$$

§ 12. *General Discussion of Monthly Departures from 1872 to 1900.*

In pursuance of our general plan we take up the mean simultaneous departures of the temperature in these regions for which I have found observations to be readily available. The results are given in Table X following. In explaining them the object is to facilitate the work of using the departures, rather than to set forth in detail how they were formed. The construction of the table is as follows. The period under discussion, 1872–1900, is divided into periods during each of which the number of stations remain unchanged. This is convenient because our general formulæ, as developed in Chapter I, involve a separate summation for each of these periods.

For the first period the entire United States is taken as a single region, because it is possible that, in the course of a month, a departure of temperature would have time to extend itself across the Rocky mountains from San Diego to Texas. The mean departures found in the table are formed from the ten-day means given in the next chapter. From and after 1874 the West Indian stations are combined with the United States, so as to form one general mean for all of North America. The region South America is practically identical with the Argentine Republic. The data for this region are also given in the ten-day tables.

It will be seen that the Indian stations and Batavia are treated as if completely independent. Whether this is the case cannot be determined in advance of the general discussion. The Australian departures are determined from an extended study and combination of the results given in the publications of the Adelaide Observatory by Sir Charles Todd. For the most part they are formed from the mean of these six stations in which the departures were found to be least subject to fitful fluctuations

The departures at the several stations are numbered e_1, e_2, etc., in accordance with the system followed in Chapter I. These index numbers are therefore the values of i in the equation of § 4–7.

Partly as a check, and partly to facilitate the ulterior discussion, the algebraic sum of the 12 departures for each year are found below the line for December.

The column Σ^2 which terminates the column for each year is the sum of the squares of all the departures for the year at each individual station. From them the steadiness of the temperature may be inferred.

The mean τ, the general world departure so far as it can be inferred from the stations, and its square form the last two columns. These enter into the formulæ of Chapter I, and are summed at the bottom of the columns.

Table X.

Monthly Simultaneous Deviations of Temperature in Widely Separated Regions.

First Period.

Date	U. S. r_1	S. Amer. r_2	India r_3	Batavia r_4	Mean r	Mean r^2	Date	U. S. r_1	S. Am. r_2	India r_3	Batavia r_4	Mean r	Mean r^2
1872							1873						
Jan.	− 0.4	+ 0.3	−0.4	− 1.3	−0.5	0.25	Jan.	+0.2	+0.9	−0.8	− 0.5	−0.1	0.01
Feb.	− 1.1	− 0.2	−0.2	− 1.1	−0.7	0.49	Feb.	−0.2	−0.6	+0.4	− 0.9	−0.3	0.09
Mar.	− 0.6	− 0.3	−0.2	− 0.3	−0.4	0.16	Mar.	+0.5	−1.0	−0.5	− 1.3	−0.6	0.36
April	+ 0.3	+ 0.1	−0.2	+ 0.2	+0.1	0.01	April	−0.1	−0.3	−0.2	− 0.3	−0.2	0.04
May	+ 0.4	− 0.6	−0.1	− 0.2	−0.1	0.01	May	+0.3	+1.5	−0.4	+ 0.1	+0.4	0.16
June	+ 1.2	+ 0.1	−0.3	− 0.2	+0.2	0.04	June	+0.4	+0.8	−0.1	− 0.2	+0.2	0.04
July	+ 0.7	− 0.1	−0.3	− 1.1	−0.2	0.04	July	+0.3	−0.1	+0.3	+ 0.1	+0.2	0.04
Aug.	+ 0.9	+ 0.5	−0.5	− 0.7	+0.1	0.01	Aug.	+0.3	+0.5	−0.1	+ 0.2	+0.2	0.04
Sept.	+ 0.5	+ 0.3	−0.2	+ 0.4	+0.2	0.04	Sept.	+0.4	+0.9	−0.2	+ 0.2	+0.3	0.09
Oct.	− 0.2	+ 0.9	−0.7	+ 0.2	+0.1	0.01	Oct.	−0.6	+0.3	−0.7	− 0.1	−0.3	0.09
Nov.	− 0.8	0.0	−0.2	− 0.7	−0.4	0.16	Nov.	−0.1	+0.5	−0.2	+ 0.3	+0.1	0.01
Dec.	− 1.4	+ 0.1	+0.7	− 0.2	−0.2	0.04	Dec.	+0.2	+0.5	−0.2	− 0.2	+0.1	0.01
Sum	− 0.7	+ 1.1	−2.6	− 5.0	−1.8	1.26	Sum	+1.6	+3.9	−2.7	− 2.6	0.0	0.98
Σ^2	+ 7.6	+ 1.7	+1.6	+ 5.4	......	......	Σ^2	+1.3	+6.6	+1.8	+ 2.9	......	......

Second Period.

Date	N. Am. r_1	S. Am. r_2	India r_3	Batavia r_4	Mean r	Mean r^2	Date	N. Am. r_1	S. Am. r_2	India r_3	Bavaria r_4	Mean r	Mean r^2
1874							1875						
Jan.	+ 0.3	− 0.1	−0.8	− 0.4	−0.2	0.04	Jan.	0.0	−0.2	−0.4	− 0.8	−0.4	0.16
Feb.	+ 0.2	+ 0.2	−0.3	− 0.4	−0.1	0.01	Feb.	−0.2	−0.1	−0.3	− 0.7	−0.3	0.09
Mar.	+ 0.2	− 0.8	−0.4	− 0.3	−0.3	0.09	Mar.	−0.4	−1.3	+0.2	− 1.1	−0.6	0.36
April	− 0.5	0.0	−0.7	0.0	−0.3	0.09	April	−0.9	−0.8	+0.2	− 0.3	−0.4	0.16
May	+ 0.2	− 0.7	−0.8	− 0.8	−0.5	0.25	May	+0.4	−0.4	−0.2	− 0.2	−0.1	0.01
June	+ 0.2	− 0.1	−1.1	− 0.9	−0.5	0.25	June	+0.3	−1.5	+0.1	+ 0.6	−0.2	0.04
July	+ 0.4	− 0.9	−1.0	− 1.3	−0.7	0.49	July	−0.1	−1.0	+0.6	+ 0.3	−0.1	0.01
Aug.	− 0.1	+ 0.4	−0.1	− 1.1	−0.2	0.04	Aug.	+0.9	−0.9	−0.1	+ 0.3	+0.1	0.01
Sept.	− 0.6	0.0	−0.5	− 1.2	−0.6	0.36	Sept.	0.0	−0.1	−0.3	+ 0.7	+0.1	0.01
Oct.	+ 0.1	− 0.5	0.0	− 0.7	−0.3	0.09	Oct.	+0.8	−0.2	−0.7	− 0.4	−0.1	0.01
Nov.	+ 0.2	− 1.1	−0.2	− 0.8	−0.5	0.25	Nov.	+0.5	−0.1	+0.3	+ 0.1	+0.2	0.04
Dec.	+ 0.2	− 0.6	−0.3	− 0.4	−0.3	0.09	Dec.	+1.1	+0.4	+0.3	− 0.6	+0.3	0.09
Sum	+ 0.8	− 4.2	−6.2	− 8.3	−4.5	2.05	Sum	+2.4	−6.2	−0.3	− 2.1	−1.5	0.99
Σ^2	+ 0.9	+ 3.9	+4.3	+ 7.5	......	......	Σ^2	+4.1	+6.7	+1.5	+ 3.1	......	......
1876							1877						
Jan.	+ 1.4	− 0.5	+0.1	0.0	+0.3	0.09	Jan.	−0.1	−0.1	+0.4	− 0.2	0.0	0.00
Feb.	+ 1.1	− 0.7	−0.5	− 0.4	−0.1	0.01	Feb.	+0.3	−0.5	+0.6	− 0.7	−0.1	0.01
Mar.	− 0.5	+ 0.4	+0.4	+ 0.3	+0.2	0.04	Mar.	+0.4	+0.7	−0.2	− 0.4	+0.1	0.01
April	+ 0.3	− 0.5	0.0	+ 0.1	0.0	0.00	April	−0.2	+0.5	−0.4	+ 0.2	0.0	0.00
May	+ 0.1	+ 0.8	+0.2	+ 0.2	+0.3	0.09	May	−0.8	−0.1	−0.6	+ 1.3	0.0	0.00
June	+ 0.6	− 0.1	+0.1	− 0.2	+0.1	0.01	June	+0.5	+0.5	+0.2	+ 0.4	+0.4	0.16
July	+ 0.3	+ 0.9	+0.1	− 0.4	+0.2	0.04	July	+0.7	+2.1	−1.1	+ 0.2	+1.0	1.00
Aug.	− 0.3	− 0.8	+0.1	− 0.2	−0.3	0.09	Aug.	+0.6	+0.1	+0.9	− 0.4	+0.3	0.09
Sept.	− 0.1	+ 0.2	+0.2	− 0.6	−0.1	0.01	Sept.	+0.4	+0.1	+0.4	+ 0.2	+0.3	0.09
Oct.	− 0.5	− 0.4	+0.1	− 0.6	−0.3	0.09	Oct.	+0.3	+0.6	+0.5	+ 1.1	+0.6	0.36
Nov.	− 0.6	− 1.4	−0.4	− 0.3	−0.7	0.49	Nov.	−0.4	+0.7	+0.8	+ 2.8	+1.0	1.00
Dec.	− 1.9	− 1.2	−0.1	− 0.1	−0.8	0.64	Dec.	+0.2	+0.4	+1.4	+ 1.6	+0.9	0.81
Sum	− 0.1	− 3.3	+0.3	− 2.2	−1.2	1.60	Sum	+1.9	+5.0	+5.1	+ 6.1	+4.5	3.53
Σ^2	+ 8.3	+ 6.7	+0.6	+ 1.4	......	......	Σ^2	+2.5	+6.6	+6.2	+14.4	......	......

Table X.—*Continued.*

Monthly Simultaneous Deviations of Temperature in Widely Separated Regions.

Second Period (continued).

Date	N. Am. r_1	S. Am. r_2	India r_3	Batavia r_4	Mean r	Mean r^2
1878						
Jan.	− 0.6	− 0.6	+0.8	+ 2.2	+0.4	0.16
Feb.	+ 0.4	+ 0.8	+1.1	+ 2.4	+1.2	1.44
Mar.	+ 1.0	+ 1.3	+0.8	+ 1.8	+1.2	1.44
April	+ 0.9	+ 0.8	+0.2	+ 1.0	+0.7	0.49
May	+ 0.4	− 0.3	+0.4	+ 1.0	+0.4	0.16
June	+ 0.8	+ 0.5	+1.1	+ 0.2	+0.6	0.36
July	+ 1.0	+ 0.6	−0.3	+ 1.1	+0.6	0.36
Aug.	+ 0.6	− 0.3	−0.1	+ 0.9	+0.3	0.09
Sept.	− 0.1	+ 0.4	0.0	+ 1.3	+0.4	0.16
Oct.	− 0.1	0.0	+0.7	+ 1.8	+0.6	0.36
Nov.	− 0.2	+ 0.8	+0.8	+ 0.2	+0.4	0.16
Dec.	− 1.9	− 0.6	+0.1	0.0	−0.6	0.36
Sum	+ 2.2	+ 3.4	+5.6	+13.9	+6.2	5.54
Σ^2	+ 8.2	+ 5.3	+5.0	+22.7	……	……
1880						
Jan.	+ 1.8	− 0.7	−0.5	− 0.8	−0.1	0.01
Feb.	+ 1.8	− 0.5	−0.6	+ 0.4	+0.3	0.09
Mar.	− 0.4	− 0.3	+0.4	− 0.4	−0.2	0.04
April	+ 0.1	+ 0.2	+0.5	− 0.4	+0.1	0.01
May	+ 0.1	+ 0.9	+0.2	− 0.2	+0.2	0.04
June	+ 0.4	+ 1.9	+0.2	− 1.4	+0.3	0.09
July	+ 0.4	+ 1.0	−0.2	− 1.1	0.0	0.00
Aug.	− 0.3	+ 1.9	0.0	− 0.7	+0.2	0.04
Sept.	− 0.2	− 0.7	−0.5	− 0.9	−0.6	0.36
Oct.	− 0.5	− 1.0	0.0	− 0.7	−0.5	0.25
Nov.	− 1.6	+ 0.3	+0.2	− 0.6	−0.4	0.16
Dec.	− 0.8	+ 0.7	+0.1	− 0.6	−0.2	0.04
Sum	+ 0.8	+ 3.7	−0.2	− 7.4	−0.9	1.13
Σ^2	+10.5	+11.9	+1.2	+ 7.0	……	……
1882						
Jan.	− 0.2	0.0	+0.5	+ 0.1	+0.1	0.01
Feb.	+ 0.5	− 0.6	+0.1	+ 0.7	+0.2	0.04
Mar.	+ 0.6	− 0.2	+0.3	− 0.3	+0.1	0.01
April	+ 0.3	− 1.1	+0.1	+ 0.1	−0.1	0.01
May	0.0	0.0	−0.2	− 0.9	−0.3	0.09
June	+ 0.7	− 0.2	+0.1	− 1.0	−0.1	0.01
July	0.0	− 0.8	−0.7	− 1.0	−0.4	0.16
Aug.	+ 0.1	+ 0.3	0.0	− 0.1	+0.1	0.01
Sept.	0.0	− 0.2	0.0	− 1.0	−0.3	0.09
Oct.	+ 0.2	+ 1.1	−0.5	− 1.3	−0.1	0.01
Nov.	− 0.7	− 0.2	−0.4	− 0.9	−0.6	0.36
Dec.	− 0.7	− 1.4	−0.2	+ 0.3	−0.5	0.25
Sum	+ 0.8	− 3.3	−0.9	− 4.4	−1.9	1.05
Σ^2	+ 2.3	+ 5.5	+1.2	+ 6.0	……	……

Date	N. Am. r_1	S. Am. r_2	India r_3	Batavia r_4	Mean r	Mean r^2
1879						
Jan.	−0.7	−0.4	+0.5	0.0	−0.2	0.04
Feb.	−0.4	−0.4	+0.4	+ 0.2	0.0	0.00
Mar.	+0.8	−0.6	+0.2	− 0.3	0.0	0.00
April	0.0	−0.5	+0.1	0.0	−0.1	0.01
May	+0.3	−0.4	−0.8	− 0.3	−0.3	0.09
June	−0.2	−0.9	−0.8	− 0.7	−0.7	0.49
July	+0.4	+0.5	−0.2	− 0.1	+0.2	0.04
Aug.	−0.1	−0.1	−0.5	− 1.0	−0.4	0.16
Sept.	+0.1	−0.9	+0.2	− 0.4	−0.3	0.09
Oct.	+0.5	−0.7	−0.6	− 0.8	−0.4	0.16
Nov.	−0.2	+0.1	−0.9	0.0	−0.2	0.04
Dec.	+0.1	−0.7	−1.1	+ 0.1	−0.3	0.09
Sum	+0.6	−4.3	−3.6	− 3.0	−2.7	1.21
Σ^2	+1.8	+4.2	+4.4	+ 2.7	……	……
1881						
Jan.	−0.7	0.0	+0.7	− 0.9	−0.2	0.04
Feb.	+0.2	+0.5	+0.4	+ 0.6	+0.4	0.16
Mar.	−1.0	+1.2	+0.2	− 0.2	+0.1	0.01
April	0.0	−0.1	+0.1	+ 0.4	+0.1	0.01
May	+0.9	+0.5	+0.6	+ 0.6	+0.6	0.36
June	+0.9	+0.2	+0.1	+ 0.3	+0.4	0.16
July	+0.2	−0.4	+0.6	+ 0.2	+0.2	0.04
Aug.	0.0	−0.4	0.0	0.0	−0.1	0.01
Sept.	0.0	+0.1	−0.2	0.0	0.0	0.00
Oct.	+0.3	+0.2	+0.3	+ 0.9	+0.4	0.16
Nov.	−0.3	+0.1	−0.1	+ 0.1	−0.1	0.01
Dec.	+0.7	+0.6	+0.1	+ 0.9	+0.6	0.36
Sum	+1.2	+2.5	+2.8	+ 2.9	+2.4	1.32
Σ^2	+3.8	+2.6	+1.6	+ 3.5	……	……

Table X.—*Continued.*

Monthly Simultaneous Deviations of Temperature in Widely Separated Regions.

Third Period.

Date	N. Am. e_1	S. Am. e_2	India e_3	Batavia e_4	Australia e_5	Mean ϵ	Mean ϵ^2
1883							
Jan.	−0.3	−0.1	+0.6	−0.4	+0.4	+0.1	0.01
Feb.	+0.3	+0.1	−0.2	−0.1	−1.1	−0.3	0.09
Mar.	+0.3	+0.7	−0.2	+0.4	+0.2	+0.3	0.09
April	−0.4	−0.4	−0.1	−0.5	+1.3	0.0	0.00
May	−0.2	+0.3	+0.2	−0.3	−0.1	−0.1	0.01
June	+0.7	+0.9	−0.2	+0.9	+1.4	+0.7	0.49
July	+0.1	+0.1	0.5	+0.4	+0.8	+0.2	0.04
Aug.	0.0	1.0	+0.2	−0.1	0.0	−0.2	0.04
Sept.	+0.4	−0.2	+0.1	−0.3	−1.0	−0.2	0.04
Oct.	−0.3	+0.2	0.8	0.6	−0.8	−0.5	0.25
Nov.	+0.1	+0.3	−0.7	−1.1	−0.3	−0.3	0.09
Dec.	+0.3	0.2	−1.4	0.7	0.7	−0.5	0.25
Sum.	+1.3	+1.1	−3.0	−2.4	−0.2	−0.8	1.40
Σ^2	+1.2	+2.7	+3.7	+3.9	+8.1	......	
1885							
Jan.	+0.1	+0.5	−0.1	−0.8	−0.4	−0.1	0.01
Feb.	0.2	0.1	0.8	−0.8	−1.1	0.6	0.36
Mar.	−0.1	−0.6	−0.4	−1.0	−1.4	−0.7	0.49
April	−1.0	+1.4	−0.9	−0.2	−0.2	+0.2	0.04
May	+0.3	+0.4	−0.8	−0.4	+1.4	+0.2	0.04
June	0.0	−0.3	0.0	+0.5	−0.9	−0.1	0.01
July	+0.7	−0.3	+0.1	+0.6	+0.2	+0.3	0.09
Aug.	+0.1	−0.6	+0.3	−0.4	+0.8	+0.2	0.04
Sept.	+0.2	+0.8	+0.3	+0.5	0.0	+0.4	0.16
Oct.	−0.2	+0.2	+0.3	+0.3	+0.9	+0.3	0.09
Nov.	+0.1	+1.1	+0.3	+0.4	−0.1	+0.3	0.09
Dec.	−0.2	+0.1	−0.1	+0.4	+0.7	+0.2	0.04
Sum	+2.1	+2.6	−1.5	−0.9	−0.1	+0.6	1.46
Σ^2	+2.0	+5.2	+2.8	+3.5	+8.1	......	...
1887							
Jan.	0.0	+0.6	−0.3	+0.4	+1.1	+0.4	0.16
Feb.	+1.3	−0.3	−0.5	−0.1	−0.2	+0.1	0.01
Mar	+0.5	−0.3	−0.3	−0.1	+0.2	−0.1	0.01
April	−0.1	−0.6	−0.4	−0.4	−0.1	−0.3	0.09
May	+0.6	−0.5	+0.3	−1.1	−0.8	−0.3	0.09
June	−0.4	+1.6	−0.8	−1.0	−0.9	−0.3	0.09
July	+0.2	−0.3	−0.2	−0.6	0.0	−0.2	0.04
Aug.	−0.1	+2.1	0.6	0.2	0.3	−0.2	0.04
Sept.	0.0	−0.3	−0.7	−1.0	−0.9	+0.6	0.36
Oct.	−0.1	0.0	−0.3	−0.7	0.2	−0.3	0.09
Nov.	+0.2	−0.7	+0.2	−0.9	−1.3	−0.5	0.25
Dec.	−0.4	+0.2	0.0	−0.4	−0.1	−0.1	0.01
Sum	+1.7	+1.5	−2.6	−6.4	−3.9	−2.0	1.24
Σ^2	+2.7	+8.9	+2.3	+5.7	+5.2	......	...
1889							
Jan.	+0.3	−1.0	+0.3	+1.6	+1.1	+0.9	0.81
Feb.	0.5	0.5	−0.3	+1.5	+0.6	+0.5	0.25
Mar.	+0.3	−1.1	+0.3	+1.0	+1.4	+0.8	0.64
April	+0.7	−0.3	+0.1	+1.5	+0.7	+0.7	0.49
May	+0.1	+0.6	+0.4	+1.2	+0.4	+0.5	0.25
June	0.1	−0.5	+0.4	+0.7	+1.0	+0.2	0.04
July	+0.1	+0.3	−0.1	+0.3	0.0	+0.2	0.04
Aug.	+0.1	−0.7	+0.3	−0.9	+0.1	+0.1	0.01
Sept.	0.0	−1.0	+0.2	+0.3	−0.1	−0.1	0.01
Oct.	−0.2	+0.4	−0.2	−0.6	+0.8	0.0	0.00
Nov.	+0.6	−0.3	−0.7	+0.1	+0.5	+0.2	0.04
Dec.	+1.9	+0.8	−0.4	+0.8	−0.3	+0.6	0.36
Sum	+1.0	−3.1	+0.6	+8.9	+5.2	+4.6	2.94
Σ^2	+5.0	+5.6	+1.3	+11.5	+6.2	......	...

Date	N. Am. e_1	S. Am. e_2	India e_3	Batavia e_4	Australia e_5	Mean ϵ	Mean ϵ^2
1884							
Jan.	−0.7	+0.2	−0.9	−0.4	−0.8	+0.1	0.01
Feb.	+0.6	−0.3	−0.7	−0.6	+0.1	−0.3	0.09
Mar.	+0.5	+0.7	−0.3	−0.9	+0.6	+0.3	0.09
April	−0.5	−0.4	−0.6	−0.4	−0.2	0.0	0.00
May	+0.4	−0.9	−0.1	−0.5	+0.1	−0.1	0.01
June	−0.1	−0.8	+0.3	+0.1	+0.1	+0.7	0.49
July	+0.1	−0.1	+0.1	−0.6	−0.7	+0.2	0.04
Aug.	−0.5	+2.4	+0.4	0.0	+1.2	−0.2	0.04
Sept.	0.4	0.4	−0.3	+0.1	+0.2	−0.2	0.04
Oct.	+0.5	−0.3	−0.5	0.0	−0.3	−0.5	0.25
Nov.	+0.1	+0.1	−1.0	−0.3	−0.1	−0.3	0.29
Dec.	+0.8	0.0	−0.5	−0.7	−1.4	−0.5	0.25
Sum	+1.0	+0.2	−4.4	−1.2	−0.9	−0.8	1.40
Σ^2	+2.6	+8.3	+3.8	+2.8	+5.2	......	...
1886							
Jan.	−1.1	+0.6	−0.2	+0.9	+1.1	+0.3	0.09
Feb.	0.0	−0.3	−0.3	−0.1	−1.3	−0.4	0.16
Mar.	−0.6	+0.7	+0.2	0.0	0.0	+0.1	0.01
April	−0.8	+0.1	−0.2	0.0	+0.1	−0.2	0.04
May	+0.2	−0.4	−0.2	+0.2	0.0	0.0	0.00
June	+0.5	−0.6	−0.8	+0.2	−0.3	−0.2	0.04
July	+0.2	−1.0	−0.5	+0.9	+0.7	+0.1	0.01
Aug.	+0.3	−0.9	−0.2	+0.3	+0.3	0.0	0.00
Sept.	+0.5	−0.5	+0.3	+0.5	+1.4	+0.4	0.16
Oct.	−0.4	−0.7	−0.1	−0.2	−1.3	−0.5	0.25
Nov.	1.1	−0.1	+0.3	+0.6	+0.4	0.0	0.00
Dec.	−0.3	+0.3	−0.1	−0.5	−0.3	−0.2	0.04
Sum	−2.5	−2.8	−1.8	+2.8	+0.8	−0.6	0.84
Σ^2	+4.3	+4.2	+4.1	+2.5	+7.6	......	...
1888							
Jan.	−0.9	−0.2	0.0	−1.0	+0.2	−0.4	0.16
Feb.	+1.1	+0.1	+0.3	−0.5	−1.0	+0.1	0.01
Mar.	−0.7	+0.3	+0.3	+0.2	−0.8	−0.1	0.01
April	+0.8	+0.1	+0.3	−0.2	+1.0	+0.4	0.16
May	−0.2	0.0	−0.3	−0.3	+0.5	−0.1	0.01
June	−0.2	−1.2	+0.1	+0.9	−0.8	+0.2	0.04
July	0.0	+0.9	−0.1	+0.1	+0.1	+0.2	0.09
Aug.	−0.3	+0.7	−0.3	+0.7	−0.4	+0.3	0.04
Sept.	+0.3	+1.0	+0.3	+0.7	+0.9	+0.6	0.36
Oct.	+0.1	+1.1	+0.4	+1.1	+0.3	+0.6	0.36
Nov.	0.0	+0.6	+0.8	+1.2	+1.8	+0.9	0.81
Dec.	0.4	+1.2	+0.4	+1.2	+1.2	+0.7	0.49
Sum	+0.9	+4.9	+1.9	+4.4	+4.9	+3.4	2.54
Σ^2	+3.3	+7.0	+1.4	+7.3	+9.3	......	...

TABLE X.—*Continued.*

Monthly Simultaneous Deviations of Temperature in Widely Separated Regions.

FOURTH PERIOD.

Date	N. Am. r_1	S. Am. r_2	India r_3	Batavia r_4	Apia r_5	Australia r_6	Mean r	Mean r^2
1890								
Jan.	+1.4	0.0	+0.1	+1.5	−0.3	+1.0	+0.8	0.64
Feb.	+1.4	+0.1	+0.5	+0.1	0.0	+0.4	+0.4	0.16
Mar.	−0.4	−0.9	+0.6	+0.2	+0.5	+0.5	+0.1	0.01
April	+0.1	−0.3	−0.2	+0.4	−0.4	+0.3	+0.1	0.01
May	+0.3	−0.3	−0.1	−0.5	+0.1	+0.4	0.0	0.00
June	+0.1	−1.7	−1.1	−0.8	+0.1	+1.1	−0.4	0.16
July	+0.3	+0.2	−0.8	−0.9	−0.5	−0.4	−0.3	0.09
Aug.	−0.5	−1.0	−0.9	−0.7	−0.2	−0.3	−0.6	0.36
Sept.	0.5	−0.5	−0.4	−0.8	+0.6	+0.9	−0.1	0.01
Oct.	−0.1	+0.1	−0.1	−1.3	+0.2	−0.3	−0.3	0.09
Nov.	+0.9	+0.6	+0.1	−1.7	+0.1	−1.2	−0.2	0.04
Dec.	+0.5	+0.8	+0.4	−0.3	+0.4	−0.5	+0.2	0.04
Sum	+3.5	−2.3	−1.6	−4.6	+0.6	+2.8	0.3	1.61
Σ²	+5.8	+6.1	+3.6	+9.7	+1.3	+8.3	......	......
1892								
Jan.	−0.9	0.0	−0.9	+0.3	−0.3	−0.7	−0.1	0.01
Feb.	+0.2	+1.6	+1.4	−1.3	+0.4	+0.7	+0.9	0.81
Mar.	−1.0	−1.1	+0.3	+0.2	+0.7	+0.8	0.0	0.00
April	−0.3	−0.7	+1.7	−0.7	+0.2	−1.0	−0.1	0.01
May	−0.2	−1.4	+0.7	−0.1	−0.4	−0.2	−0.3	0.09
June	−0.5	−2.2	−0.3	+0.1	+0.2	+0.4	−0.4	0.16
July	−0.7	−0.3	+0.3	+0.2	−0.1	+0.1	0.0	0.00
Aug.	0.0	−2.3	−0.5	−0.2	+0.2	+0.8	−0.3	0.09
Sept.	−0.2	−1.2	−0.7	0.7	−0.3	−0.1	−0.5	0.25
Oct.	−0.3	+0.2	+0.2	0.0	+0.1	−0.2	0.0	0.00
Nov.	−0.2	−0.2	−0.5	+0.4	−0.7	+0.7	−0.1	0.01
Dec.	−0.5	−1.0	−0.2	+0.5	−0.4	−1.2	−0.5	0.25
Sum	−1.2	−8.6	+3.3	+1.3	−0.4	+0.8	−1.4	1.68
Σ²	+2.0	+18.9	7.4	+3.2	+1.8	+5.1	......	......
1894								
Jan.	+0.7	+0.3	+0.7	−0.8	−0.2	−0.4	0.0	0.00
Feb.	−0.9	+0.4	+1.1	−0.5	−0.1	−1.7	−0.3	0.09
Mar.	+0.1	−1.4	+0.6	−0.4	−0.2	+0.1	−0.2	0.04
April	−0.1	0.0	+0.3	−0.2	+0.5	+0.1	+0.1	0.01
May	0.0	+2.0	+0.1	−0.8	−0.1	−0.9	+0.1	0.01
June	−0.8	−0.7	−0.1	−0.1	+0.3	−0.3	−0.3	0.09
July	−0.3	−0.1	−0.1	+0.4	−0.3	−0.1	−0.1	0.01
Aug.	−0.1	−0.6	+0.3	+0.3	+0.6	−0.2	+0.1	0.01
Sept.	−0.7	−1.2	−0.5	+0.1	+0.5	−1.4	−0.5	0.25
Oct.	−0.1	−1.8	−0.4	0.0	+0.6	−0.5	−0.4	0.16
Nov.	+0.2	+0.4	−0.5	0.0	−0.4	−0.1	−0.1	0.01
Dec.	−0.1	−0.2	−0.3	0.0	−0.1	−0.1	−0.2	0.04
Sum	−1.7	−2.9	+1.2	−2.1	+0.8	−5.8	−1.8	0.66
Σ²	+2.1	+12.0	+3.0	+2.3	+1.8	+6.4	......	......
1896								
Jan.	+0.2	−0.2	+1.1	−0.6	−0.2	+0.2	+0.3	0.09
Feb.	+0.2	−0.2	−0.3	+0.5	−0.4	−0.5	0.0	0.00
Mar.	−0.6	+0.4	+0.5	+0.1	+0.1	+0.2	+0.2	0.04
April	−0.5	+1.1	+1.2	−0.3	−0.2	−0.1	+0.2	0.04
May	+0.1	0.0	+0.8	+0.3	+0.6	−0.6	+0.2	0.04
June	+0.7	−0.2	+0.2	+0.6	−0.4	−1.6	−0.1	0.01
July	0.0	+3.5	+0.1	+0.6	−1.1	−0.8	+0.4	0.16
Aug.	+0.4	+3.9	−0.3	+0.5	0.0	−0.9	+0.6	0.36
Sept.	+0.1	+2.4	+0.9	+0.8	+0.3	−0.9	+0.6	0.36
Oct.	+0.3	+0.7	+1.4	+1.1	+0.6	+0.5	+0.8	0.64
Nov.	+1.1	+0.3	+1.2	+1.8	−0.4	+0.4	+0.7	0.49
Dec.	+0.5	−0.4	+0.9	+0.1	+0.5	−0.3	+0.2	0.04
Sum	+2.5	+11.3	+8.3	+7.3	−0.6	−4.4	+4.1	2.27
Σ²	+2.8	+35.4	+8.6	+7.8	+3.9	+5.9	......	......

Date	N. Am. r_1	S. Am. r_2	India r_3	Batavia r_4	Apia r_5	Australia r_6	Mean r	Mean r^2
1891								
Jan.	0.0	+0.7	+0.1	+0.1	+0.1	−0.7	+0.1	0.01
Feb.	+0.6	+1.4	0.7	−0.1	+0.1	−0.8	+0.1	0.01
Mar.	−0.6	+1.2	−0.4	−0.3	+0.2	−0.6	+0.1	0.01
April	−0.4	+0.4	−0.5	0.0	0.0	0.3	−0.1	0.01
May	−0.4	−0.8	−0.5	+1.0	+0.1	+0.8	+0.1	0.01
June	+0.2	+0.7	+1.0	+0.7	+0.1	−0.7	+0.3	0.09
July	−0.1	−0.1	0.0	+0.2	−0.5	−0.3	−0.2	0.04
Aug.	+0.1	−0.3	+0.3	−0.7	0.1	0.1	−0.2	0.04
Sept.	+0.5	0.3	−0.1	+0.5	0.0	+0.1	+0.1	0.01
Oct.	−0.6	+1.0	+0.3	+1.8	+0.5	0.0	+0.5	0.25
Nov.	+0.1	−0.1	+0.2	+1.4	+0.1	−0.1	+0.2	0.04
Dec.	+0.2	−1.3	+0.3	+0.6	+0.2	0.4	0.1	0.01
Sum	0.1	+1.8	+0.1	+5.5	+0.8	2.2	−0.9	0.53
Σ²	+1.8	+7.9	+2.4	+8.1	+0.8	+3.2		
1893								
Jan.	−1.3	0.0	−0.6	−0.8	−0.7	−0.4	−0.6	0.36
Feb.	+0.1	−4.7	−1.4	−0.6	−0.5	+0.1	−0.5	0.25
Mar.	−0.3	−0.1	−0.7	+0.1	−0.2	+0.9	−0.1	0.01
April	+0.1	−0.6	+0.4	−0.4	−0.8	−0.3	−0.3	0.09
May	−0.2	−1.4	−0.4	−0.3	−0.6	+1.2	−0.3	0.09
June	−0.1	−3.3	−0.7	−0.8	+0.3	−0.1	−0.8	0.64
July	−0.1	+0.1	−0.2	−0.6	−0.1	+0.8	0.0	0.00
Aug.	−0.4	−2.6	0.0	−0.1	−0.1	+0.1	−0.5	0.25
Sept.	−0.1	−3.0	−0.1	−0.3	−0.3	+0.3	−0.6	0.36
Oct.	−0.1	−2.3	−0.4	−0.5	−0.5	+0.5	−0.6	0.36
Nov.	−0.2	−2.1	+0.2	−0.5	0.0	−0.6	−0.5	0.25
Dec.	+0.8	+1.1	+0.2	−0.9	−0.3	0.0	+0.2	0.04
Sum	−1.3	−15.9	−3.7	−6.0	−3.8	+2.5	−4.6	2.70
Σ²	+2.4	+42.9	+4.0	+3.8	+2.2	+4.2	......	......
1895								
Jan.	−0.1	−1.8	−0.4	−0.3	−0.1	−0.8	−0.6	0.36
Feb.	−2.6	+0.6	+0.1	0.5	−1.0	−0.3	−0.6	0.36
Mar.	−0.2	+1.5	+0.4	−0.2	−0.1	−0.3	+0.2	0.04
April	−0.3	+1.5	0.1	+0.3	+0.2	−0.2	+0.2	0.04
May	+0.2	+1.2	−0.2	−0.2	−0.8	0.4	+0.2	0.04
June	−0.1	−3.3	0.0	+0.1	+0.2	+0.3	+0.6	0.36
July	−0.3	+2.0	+0.1	−0.8	+0.4	0.2	+0.2	0.04
Aug.	0.0	+1.5	−0.1	−0.3	−0.2	+0.4	+0.2	0.04
Sept.	+0.6	−0.7	−0.3	+0.9	−0.4	−0.2	0.0	0.00
Oct.	−0.2	−0.9	+0.2	+1.0	0.0	+1.2	+0.2	0.04
Nov.	−0.1	−1.2	+0.0	+0.4	−0.4	−0.7	−0.2	0.04
Dec.	−1.2	−0.6	+0.2	+0.4	+0.1	−0.2	0.0	0.00
Sum	−4.3	+7.6	+0.8	+0.8	−0.2	−1.4	+0.4	1.36
Σ²	+8.8	+28.6	+1.3	+3.3	+2.4	+3.2	......	......
1897								
Jan.	−0.4	−0.5	−0.2	+2.7	−0.3	−1.0	−0.1	0.01
Feb.	+0.6	+0.4	0.3	+1.6	−0.2	+0.4	+0.6	0.36
Mar.	+0.1	+2.7	−0.8	+1.0	+0.3	−1.2	+0.4	0.16
April	0.0	+1.0	+0.2	+0.2	+0.1	+0.8	+0.5	0.25
May	+0.1	+1.6	+0.1	+1.3	−0.1	−0.3	+0.4	0.16
June	−0.3	+0.7	+1.1	+1.3	+0.3	+0.9	+0.7	0.49
July	−0.2	−1.8	+0.3	+0.9	−0.1	+1.2	0.0	0.00
Aug.	0.0	−1.8	+0.5	+0.9	+0.2	−0.4	−0.1	0.01
Sept.	+0.1	−1.0	+0.5	+1.2	−0.5	+0.2	+0.1	0.01
Oct.	−0.9	+1.0	−0.3	+0.5	−0.2	−0.3	+0.4	0.16
Nov.	+0.9	−0.6	−0.5	+0.4	−0.7	+0.9	0.0	0.00
Dec.	+0.5	+0.8	−0.7	+1.0	+0.1	+0.7	+0.6	0.36
Sum	+2.3	+3.4	+0.5	+13.0	−1.1	+1.9	+3.5	1.97
Σ²	+2.5	+23.8	+3.6	+18.7	+1.0	+7.1	......	......

TABLE X.—*Concluded.*

Monthly Simultaneous Deviations of Temperature in Widely Separated Regions.

FOURTH PERIOD (*concluded*).

Date	N. Am. r_1	S. Am. r_2	India r_3	Batavia r_4	Apia r_5	Australia r_6	Mean $\bar{r}$	Mean $\bar{r}^2$
1898								
Jan.	+0.3	+ 0.7	+0.1	+0.2	−0.6	+0.7	+0.3	0.09
Feb.	+0.2	+ 1.4	+0.2	+0.1	−0.6	+1.4	+0.4	0.16
Mar.	−0.1	− 0.8	+0.4	+0.3	−0.8	−0.1	−0.2	0.04
April	0.0	− 1.2	+0.6	+0.4	−0.3	−0.7	−0.2	0.04
May	−0.5	+ 1.4	+0.4	+0.6	−0.3	−1.5	−0.2	0.04
June	+0.1	− 2.4	0.0	+0.5	−0.1	−0.1	+0.5	0.25
July	+0.2	− 1.5	+0.1	+0.3	+0.8	+0.3	0.0	0.00
Aug	+0.2	− 2.1	+0.3	+0.7	0.0	+0.8	0.0	0.00
Sept.	+0.7	− 1.2	0.0	+0.4	+0.2	+0.3	+0.1	0.01
Oct.	0.0	− 2.5	+1.4	−0.6	−0.2	+0.5	−0.2	0.04
Nov.	0.0	− 2.2	+1.2	−0.3	−0.6	−1.1	−0.5	0.25
Dec.	−0.5	− 0.1	+1.0	−0.2	−0.1	+0.9	+0.1	0.01
Sum	−0.6	− 5.7	+6.0	+2.4	−2.6	+1.4	+0.1	0.93
Σ^2	+1.0	+31.3	+5.5	+2.2	+2.0	+8.2	......	......

FIFTH PERIOD.

Date	N. Am. r_1	India r_2	Batavia r_3	Apia r_4	Australia r_5	Mean $\bar{r}$	Mean $\bar{r}^2$
1899							
Jan.	+1.0	−1.1	−0.5	−0.8	− 2.6	−0.8	0.64
Feb.	−1.2	+0.2	−0.6	−0.2	+ 1.3	−0.1	0.01
Mar.	0.0	+0.5	−0.4	−0.2	+ 0.7	+0.1	0.01
April	−0.4	+0.2	−0.3	−0.1	+ 0.3	−0.1	0.01
May	−0.6	+0.3	+0.4	−0.2	− 0.7	−0.2	0.04
June	−0.4	−0.3	−0.3	−0.6	− 0.2	−0.4	0.16
July	+0.1	+0.6	+0.6	+0.3	− 1.3	+0.1	0.01
Aug.	−0.2	+0.8	+0.1	−0.1	− 0.6	0.0	0.00
Sept.	+0.6	+0.7	+0.1	+0.4	− 0.2	+0.3	0.09
Oct.	+0.2	+1.0	+0.4	+0.1	− 0.7	+0.2	0.04
Nov.	+0.9	+0.3	+0.1	+0.4	− 0.4	+0.3	0.09
Dec.	0.0	+0.5	−0.1	−0.1	+ 0.2	+0.1	0.01
Sum	0.0	+4.0	−0.2	−1.1	− 4.2	−0.5	1.11
Σ^2	+4.4	+4.6	+2.0	+1.5	+12.4	......	......

Date	N. Am. r_1	India r_2	Batavia r_3	Apia r_4	Australia r_5	Mean $\bar{r}$	Mean $\bar{r}^2$
1900							
Jan.	+1.0	−0.4	+0.7	+0.5	+0.3	+0.4	0.16
Feb.	−0.2	−0.3	+0.7	+0.5	+0.7	+0.2	0.04
Mar.	+0.4	+0.1	+0.7	−0.3	−0.6	+0.1	0.01
April	−0.3	−0.1	+0.4	0.0	−0.5	−0.1	0.01
May	+0.2	+0.2	+0.1	−0.2	+0.2	+0.1	0.01
June	+0.2	+1.1	+0.5	−0.6	+0.2	+0.3	0.09
July	0.0	+0.9	+0.6	−0.4	−0.2	+0.2	0.04
Aug.	+0.3	+0.2	−0.8	+0.3	−0.2	0.0	0.00
Sept.	+0.4	+0.4	+1.0	+0.5	−0.7	+0.3	0.09
Oct.	+1.1	0.0	+1.0	+0.3	+0.1	+0.5	0.25
Nov.	+1.5	+0.6	+0.6	−0.1	+0.3	+0.6	0.36
Dec.	+1.1	+1.1	+1.1	−0.2	−0.2	+0.6	0.36
Sum	+5.7	+3.8	+6.6	+0.3	−0.4	+3.2	1.42
Σ^2	+6.2	+4.4	+6.5	+1.5	+1.8	......	......

To investigate the correlation among the stations we apply the method and formulæ of § 4, as we have done in the case of the annual deviations. For example, we have for the first period, 1871 and 1872,

$$1871: \quad \Sigma_r r_i^2 = 7.6 + 1.7 + 1.6 + 5.4 = 16.3$$

$$1872: \quad " \quad = 1.3 + 6.6 + 1.8 + 2.9 = 12.6$$

also

$$\Sigma_j \bar{r}^2 = 1.26 + 0.98 = 2.24$$

Thus, this period alone gives

$$\Sigma_{i,j} r^2 = 28.9$$

Since $n = 4$, and r, the number of monthly terms, is 24,

$$n^2 \Sigma_j \tau^2 = 35.8$$

Thus (9) gives the equation

$$288 \tau_p^2 = \Delta = + 6.9$$

Carrying this computation through all the time-terms we have the following results:

Period	n	r	$\frac{\Sigma r'}{n}$	$n \Sigma r'$	Equation for τ_0^2
1872-73	4	24	7.2	9.0	$288 \tau_0^2 = + 7$
1874-82	4	108	47.6	73.7	$1296 \quad + 104$
1883-89	5	84	33.3	58.6	$1680 \quad + 127$
1890-98	6	108	67.5	82.3	$3240 \quad + 89$
1899-00	5	24	9.0	12.7	$480 \quad + 18$
Sum			164.6	236.3	$6984 \tau_0^2 = + 345$

A positive correlation is well shown, leading to the mean result

$$\tau_0^2 = .0493$$
$$\tau_0 = \pm 0.22^\circ \text{ C.} = \pm 0.4^\circ \text{ Fahr.}$$

When we add in the equation from Dove's work the final equation is

$$9396 \tau_0^2 = 401$$

whence

$$\tau_0 = \pm 0^\circ.21$$

The existence of the positive correlation is beyond serious question, but before we accept it as cosmical, we must learn whether it holds between the more distant stations, as well as between those in neighboring great geographic zones.

As no correlation but a cosmical one can exist between the North American and the other regions, we first compare that with the others. The table shows that simultaneous temperatures in North and South America are available from 1872 to 1898, a period of 324 months. Forming the sum of the 324 products $r_1 r_2$ we find the result

$$\Sigma rr' = \Delta = + 15.3$$

Proceeding in the same way with the other stations the collected results are:

North America	— South America;	$r = 324$	$\Sigma rr' =$	+ 15.3
"	— India;	" 348	"	− 2.8
"	— Batavia;	" 348	"	+ 18.4
"	— Australia;	" 216	"	0.0
"	— Apia;	" 132	"	+ 1.0
	Sum			+ 31.9

The South American products being formed in the same way, the results of their summation are :

South America — India ;	$r = 348$	$\Sigma rr' = + 18.$
" " — Australia ;	" 192	" $- 5.$
" " — Apia ;	" 108	" $+ 1.$
" " — Batavia ;	" 327	" $+ 36.$
Sum		$+ 53.$

Next we have

India — Batavia ;	$r = 348$	$\Sigma rr' = + 51.$
" — Apia ;	" 132	" $0.$
" — Australia ;	" 216	" $+ 5.$
Sum		$+ 56.$

Then

Batavia — Australia ;	$r = 216$	$\Sigma rr' = + 26.$
" — Apia ;	" 132	" $+ 2.$
Sum		$+ 28.$

$$\Sigma rr' = + 4$$

It will be seen that, while there seems to be a general tendency toward a positive correlation, the largest part of Δ arises from the two combinations India-Batavia and Batavia-Australia. These pairs being in comparative geographic proximity, we may well throw them out. The remaining pairs give :

Whole number of products, 2924

Sum of all these products + 96

Hence,

$$\text{Mean } rr' = \text{mean } \tau_o^2 = + 0.033$$

$$\text{Mean } \tau_o = \pm 0^\circ.18 \text{ C.} = \pm 0^\circ.32 \text{ Fahr.}$$

It therefore seems that the monthly departures of temperature indicate fluctuations in the general world temperature of which the general amount is about $\pm 0^\circ.18$ C. on each side of the normal mean value. This is scarcely greater than the degree of correlation which we should expect to be shown from our omission to correct the normal tables for the sun-spot inequality, and from the systematic deviations of the annual temperature brought out in § 9. The evidence is therefore rather weak in favor of very minute fluctuations in the sun's radiation for periods greater than one month and less than several years. If they exist, they are too small to produce any noticeable meteorological effect.

CHAPTER V.

STUDY OF TEN-DAY TERMS.

§ 13. *Stations and Material Used.*

The term of ten days was chosen because it has been extensively adopted, especially in the *Dekadenberichte* of the German *Seewarte*. Mean temperatures for this purpose being available in a number of cases, the labor of forming them for the entire work was not necessary. A term of one fourth or one fifth the sun's rotation would have been better adapted to bringing out fluctuations having the period of that rotation; but a lesser period than ten days would be subject to the drawback that small fluctuations in the radiation require time to produce their full effect upon the temperature, so that little indication of their effect could be expected.

Strictly speaking, the period is not ten days but one third of a month. When it was necessary to form independent mean temperatures from daily records, the year was divided into thirty-six parts as nearly equal as possible. There were, therefore, thirty or thirty-one periods of ten days each, and five or six of eleven days in each year. But when the ten-day means had been taken on a different system, the month for example being divided into three parts, I adopted these means without modification, deeming slight defects in coincidence not sufficiently important to be taken account of.

The period chosen for the research commenced with the year 1872, because although observations of the United States Weather Bureau date from 1871, when they were commenced by the Army Signal Service, the data for that year were insufficient. This consideration was paramount in preparing the work because, in first planning the work, it was not intended to include any stations but those for which uniform records were readily obtainable. It was also intended to include as many regions as possible in the investigation, but the circumstances mentioned in § 6 led to the omission of several regions which might have been included had the data been available. It was also believed that definitive results would be obtained by confining the discussion to those regions where the data were easily accessible and undoubted.

The regions and stations finally chosen were as follows:

1. *The United States East of the Rocky Mountains, Called U. S. I.* — In order to lessen the effect of accidental fluctuations at a single point several stations as widely separated as possible are preferable. Guided by the consideration that stations near the tropics were to be preferred, the four finally chosen for this region were Washington, Key West, Galveston and Saint Louis.

2. *The United States West of the Rocky Mountains, or U. S. II.* — The best station in this region was San Diego owing not only to its southern position, but to its compara-

tive steadiness of temperature. The peculiar climate of San Francisco seemed to render it inadvisable to adopt it as a station. The interior points of Salt Lake City and Phoenix, Arizona, were also selected and used as stations, although the observations at each point have suffered some interruption.

3. *The Argentine Republic.*—The main source for this region has been, as mentioned in Chapter II, the publications of the *Oficina Meteorologica Argentina.* The number of stations that could be used was different in different years, and fell off to a single one in 1898.

4. *Samoa.*—The *Deutsche Überseeische Meteorologische Beobachtungen* contain meteorological observations at a number of coast and island stations, but, for the most part, the observations were not pursued continuously through a sufficient period to be well adapted to the present work. The best station for our purpose proved to be Apia, where the record is nearly complete since 1890. The unpublished results for this station up to 1904 were courteously communicated by the director of the *Deutsche Seewarte* at Hamburg.

As no general principle is illustrated by the process of forming means and finding deviations from them by simple subtraction, the writer conceives that the purpose of the present work will be best subserved by omitting these merely routine details. If, as he earnestly hopes, some authority fully equipped with the necessary computing assistance shall in the interest of meteorology reconstruct the work in question, it can now be more thoroughly done than the author has succeeded in doing. Data continually accumulate from year to year and the results of the present work will, it is hoped, be found useful in any such reconstruction. As one of the special purposes now in view is to show the method of determining correlations, that purpose will be best subserved by excluding details not peculiar to the work itself. Some remarks on a few special points may however be made.

After the means were taken for the regions U. S. I, it was found that the accidental deviations at St. Louis were so much larger than at the other stations that the means would be more accordant if this station were omitted entirely. Its weight was therefore reduced to one third and new means taken.

After the definitive means had been formed, it was found that the fluctuations of temperature at Galveston, which were in general quite small, sometimes showed abnormally negative values. When this anomaly was specially noted, and the correctness of the record ascertained, it was too late to modify the work. The most plausible explanation which I can assign for these anomalous temperatures is that they are produced by the "northers" which are known to occasionally come down from the Rocky Mountain region into Texas, but which I did not suppose extended so far south as Galveston. The further examination of this point must be left to meteorologists.

§ 14. *Tabular Exhibit of Ten-day Departures During the Period 1872 to 1904.*

The original departures are shown in the following tables in the form which seemed best adapted to facilitate a critical examination and working out of the results. The means are the unweighted ones of the several regions, and are therefore the values of τ to be used in the formulæ of § 4.

The regions are: Eastern United States, Western United States, Argentina and Apia.

At the bottom of each annual column is given the algebraic sum of the departures, which will be useful in any test to which the work may be submitted. By dividing these terms by 36 we have annual deviations for the different regions, which should not differ much from those used in chapter III.

The comparison of the sum of the means with the mean of the sums may be used to test the accuracy of the computation.

Below each sum is given the sum of the squares of the 36 departures. These are used in the formulæ of § 4.

Table XI.

Simultaneous Departures of Temperature in Regions in °C.

		1872				1873			
		U. S. I	U. S. II	Arg.	Mean	U. S. I	U. S. II	Arg.	Mean
Jan.	*a*	+1.2	−1.2	+0.3	+0.1	−0.6	+1.9	+0.4	+0.6
	b	+0.4	−0.3	−1.4	−0.4	−0.3	+2.1	+1.4	+1.1
	c	−1.1	−1.6	0.0	−1.0	−2.7	+0.5	+0.9	−0.4
Feb.	*a*	−2.8	+0.4	+0.2	−0.7	+0.8	+0.2	−2.1	−0.4
	b	−1.6	+0.3	−0.2	−0.5	+1.0	−2.0	−0.9	−0.6
	c	−0.2	−1.4	−3.5	−1.6	−1.0	−0.4	0.0	−0.5
Mar.	*a*	−2.8	+0.7	+0.6	−0.5	−1.4	+0.1	−1.8	−1.0
	b	−1.4	−0.2	−2.1	−1.2	+1.3	+1.4	+0.3	+1.0
	c	−0.7	+0.3	−3.2	−1.2	0.0	+1.4	−1.7	−0.1
April	*a*	+2.2	−2.0	+1.0	+0.4	+1.5	−0.8	−0.7	0.0
	b	+1.6	−1.5	+3.5	+1.2	−1.6	+1.3	−1.0	−0.4
	c	+1.7	−0.2	−2.6	−0.4	−1.9	+0.9	−0.1	−0.4
May	*a*	+1.0	+0.8	+0.2	+0.7	−1.2	+1.1	+0.9	+0.3
	b	+1.3	−2.5	−2.6	−1.3	+0.2	−0.1	+0.6	+0.2
	c	+1.3	+0.4	+0.6	+0.8	+1.9	+0.1	+1.5	+1.2
June	*a*	+0.9	+0.3	−0.1	+0.1	+1.0	+0.1	+1.2	+0.8
	b	+0.8	+1.0	+4.1	+2.0	+0.7	−0.4	−0.8	−0.2
	c	+1.2	+2.9	−2.2	+0.6	+0.9	+0.2	+2.2	+1.1
July	*a*	+1.4	−0.1	−0.2	−0.4	+0.7	−0.2	−1.5	−0.3
	b	+1.2	+0.5	+2.2	+1.3	+0.5	−0.9	−1.2	−0.5
	c	+1.0	−0.2	−0.6	+0.1	+0.4	+0.9	−0.5	+0.3
Aug.	*a*	+1.2	+0.2	+1.9	+1.1	+0.5	−0.3	−1.1	−0.3
	b	+2.0	−1.2	−0.1	+0.1	−0.1	+0.4	−0.6	−0.1
	c	+1.4	+1.8	0.0	+1.1	+1.0	+0.7	+1.6	+1.1
Sept.	*a*	+1.3	+0.1	−0.1	+0.4	+0.4	−0.3	+2.8	+1.0
	b	−0.1	+0.6	−0.1	+0.1	−0.9	+1.8	+1.2	+0.7
	c	+1.7	−1.0	+0.6	+0.4	+1.0	+0.3	−0.5	+0.3
Oct.	*a*	+0.6	+0.2	+3.0	+1.3	−0.9	−0.8	−0.8	−0.8
	b	−1.1	−0.1	+2.1	+0.2	+0.3	−0.1	+0.5	+0.3
	c	−0.1	−0.6	0.0	−0.2	−2.8	−0.6	+1.1	−0.8
Nov.	*a*	−0.3	−0.4	−0.6	−0.4	−0.3	0.0	+0.9	+0.2
	b	−3.8	+0.9	−1.3	−1.4	−2.3	+2.7	+1.4	+0.6
	c	−1.5	−0.4	0.0	−0.6	−0.7	+0.6	+0.8	+0.2
Dec.	*a*	−0.4	+0.7	0.0	+0.1	+2.6	−0.8	+0.7	+0.8
	b	−1.9	−2.7	−0.5	−1.7	+2.2	−1.7	−0.5	0.0
	c	−4.0	+1.2	−0.4	−1.4	−1.4	+0.3	+1.1	0.0
Sum		−2.6	−4.5	−1.5	−2.6	−1.2	+9.8	+5.7	+5.0
Σe^2		120	41	97	11.42	62	38	48	12.89

		1874				1875			
		U. S. I	U. S. II	Arg.	Mean	U. S. I	U. S. II	Arg.	Mean
Jan.	*a*	+2.3	−0.1	−0.4	+0.7	−2.6	−0.1	+0.3	−0.8
	b	−1.0	+1.4	−1.1	−0.2	−2.4	+0.6	+0.3	−0.4
	c	+2.7	−0.1	−1.2	+0.5	+1.8	−0.1	+0.7	+0.7
Feb.	*a*	−1.2	−0.6	−0.9	−0.9	−2.9	−0.2	+1.6	−0.5
	b	+2.2	−0.8	+0.4	+0.6	−2.2	+0.4	+1.6	−0.1
	c	+2.0	−2.2	+2.0	+0.6	+1.1	−0.1	−1.1	−0.1
Mar.	*a*	+2.0	−2.5	−3.2	−1.2	−1.2	−1.9	−0.2	−1.1
	b	+2.1	−2.4	−2.1	−0.8	0.0	−2.9	−0.7	−1.2
	c	+1.2	−1.3	−0.6	−0.2	+0.6	−1.2	−1.2	−0.6
April	*a*	−0.9	−0.6	−0.5	−0.7	+0.6	−2.8	+0.9	−0.4
	b	−1.0	−2.3	+0.6	−0.9	−3.4	+1.7	−0.3	−0.7
	c	−2.0	+0.8	−1.5	+1.2	−2.8	+1.4	−1.5	−1.0
May	*a*	−1.2	−0.2	+1.3	0.0	−0.3	+1.2	+1.8	+0.9
	b	+0.3	+1.8	−2.1	0.0	−0.7	+1.8	−1.1	0.0
	c	+0.9	+0.9	−2.1	−0.1	+1.0	+0.8	+3.2	+1.7
June	*a*	+1.9	−0.1	+2.3	+1.4	−0.4	+0.3	0.0	0.0
	b	+0.2	+0.6	−1.9	−0.4	−0.3	+1.1	−2.6	−0.6
	c	+1.4	+0.2	+0.5	+0.7	+1.4	+1.2	−3.2	−0.2
July	*a*	+0.4	+2.9	−1.4	+0.6	+0.1	−0.2	+1.5	+0.5
	b	−0.4	+1.3	−0.2	+0.2	+0.2	+0.6	−1.9	−0.4
	c	−0.1	+0.2	+0.3	+0.1	−0.3	+0.3	+0.1	0.0
Aug.	*a*	+0.1	−0.2	+4.1	+1.4	−0.9	+2.8	+0.7	+0.9
	b	+0.8	+0.2	−1.0	0.0	−0.3	+1.3	−1.9	−0.3
	c	−0.8	−0.2	+2.8	+0.6	−1.1	−0.6	+0.2	−0.5
Sept.	*a*	+0.1	−1.0	−0.5	−0.4	+1.4	+1.6	−1.5	+0.5
	b	+0.8	−2.3	+0.6	−0.3	−2.4	+1.3	+2.5	+0.5
	c	−0.4	+0.9	−0.6	0.0	−2.6	+1.6	+1.4	+0.1
Oct.	*a*	−0.4	+1.8	+1.8	+1.1	−0.4	+3.3	0.0	+1.0
	b	−1.8	+1.4	−3.4	−1.3	−2.5	+4.6	+0.8	+1.0
	c	+2.1	+0.4	−2.1	+0.1	+1.1	+1.8	−1.2	+0.6
Nov.	*a*	+1.2	−0.7	−2.8	−0.8	−1.7	+0.5	+0.2	−0.3
	b	+0.4	−0.4	+0.2	+0.1	+1.5	+1.1	+1.4	+1.3
	c	+0.1	+1.7	+0.3	+0.7	+0.5	+1.1	+0.2	+0.6
Dec.	*a*	+0.9	+0.8	+1.2	+1.0	−0.1	+1.8	+1.4	+1.0
	b	+0.6	−1.7	+0.8	−0.1	+0.6	−0.1	−3.3	−0.9
	c	+2.2	−1.4	−0.4	+0.1	+5.5	+1.2	+0.2	+2.3
Sum		+17.9	−3.6	−10.5	+1.2	−14.1	+24.6	−0.5	+3.5
Σe^2		70	64	102	18.15	114	96	81	24.01

TABLE XI.—*Continued.*

Simultaneous Departures of Temperature in Regions in °C.

		1876				1877				1878				1879			
		U. S. I	U. S. II	Arg.	Mean	U. S. I	U. S. II	Arg.	Mean	U. S. I	U. S. II	Arg.	Mean	U. S. I	U. S. II	Arg.	Mean
Jan.	*a*	+4.8	+1.4	+0.5	+2.2	−1.7	+0.8	+1.1	−0.9	−3.8	−2.8	−0.1	−2.2	−5.2	−1.2	−3.2	−3.2
	b	+1.7	−1.0	−1.5	−0.3	+1.4	+0.5	+1.1	+1.0	+1.3	+0.7	−0.6	+0.5	−1.1	−1.7	+0.2	−0.9
	c	+4.2	−0.9	−1.7	+0.5	+1.0	−0.8	+3.2	+1.1	+1.4	+2.4	−3.6	+0.1	+2.6	+1.8	−0.5	+1.3
Feb.	*a*	+0.4	+0.9	−0.8	+0.2	+2.7	+1.2	−0.6	+1.1	0.0	0.0	−1.5	−0.2	−0.9	−1.1	+0.6	−0.5
	b	+2.8	+1.4	−1.1	+1.0	−0.6	+1.2	−0.3	+0.1	+0.3	+1.2	−0.5	+0.3	−1.4	+2.6	−0.5	+0.2
	c	+0.7	+0.1	+1.0	+0.6	−0.7	+2.7	−0.4	+0.5	+2.0	−0.1	+0.2	+0.7	−1.6	+3.5	−1.6	+0.1
Mar.	*a*	+2.0	−1.2	+0.1	+0.3	−0.3	+1.8	+1.3	+0.9	+1.4	−0.4	+2.1	+1.0	+2.0	+2.4	+0.4	+1.6
	b	−0.3	−1.8	−0.5	−0.9	−1.2	+4.0	+2.9	+1.9	+2.5	+3.0	+0.6	+2.0	−0.6	+1.7	−0.1	+0.3
	c	−2.1	−1.2	+2.1	−0.4	−0.7	+3.0	+1.5	+1.3	+1.9	+0.2	−0.4	+0.6	+1.8	+3.4	−0.1	+1.7
April	*a*	−0.5	−0.9	+0.4	−0.3	−0.1	+0.9	−0.7	0.0	+1.2	+1.8	−1.9	+0.4	−1.2	+1.2	−0.7	−0.2
	b	0.0	+0.6	−0.2	+0.1	−0.4	+0.2	+1.7	+0.5	+2.0	−2.4	+0.1	−0.1	−0.8	+0.2	+0.2	−0.1
	c	−0.1	+3.4	−0.2	+1.0	−0.6	−1.3	+1.0	−0.3	+2.0	−0.8	+0.8	+0.7	+1.0	+1.6	+1.0	+1.2
May	*a*	−0.3	+1.3	+2.3	+1.1	−3.3	−0.1	−0.6	−1.3	+0.9	+1.1	+0.1	+0.7	−0.1	+2.2	+0.9	+0.9
	b	+0.3	−0.8	+1.7	+0.4	+0.3	−2.2	−1.2	−1.0	−0.7	0.0	−2.5	−1.1	+1.7	+1.0	+1.2	+1.3
	c	+0.2	+0.6	+0.5	+0.4	+0.1	−0.7	+0.1	−0.2	+0.4	−0.9	+2.9	+0.8	+0.2	−1.7	+0.1	−0.5
June	*a*	+0.6	−0.2	+1.1	+0.5	+0.3	+0.3	+1.6	+0.7	+0.1	+1.0	−0.8	+0.1	−0.3	+1.8	−2.2	−0.2
	b	+0.4	+2.8	−1.8	+0.5	+0.3	+2.0	−1.1	+0.1	−0.3	+1.2	+2.5	+1.1	0.0	−1.4	+2.0	+0.2
	c	+1.0	+1.3	+1.0	+1.1	+0.4	−0.5	+1.9	+0.6	+0.4	+1.4	−3.3	−0.5	−0.3	+0.7	+0.1	+0.2
July	*a*	+1.4	+1.6	+0.6	+1.2	+0.8	+1.5	+2.4	+1.6	+0.9	+1.7	−2.5	0.0	+0.7	−0.1	+1.4	+0.7
	b	+1.3	+0.7	+4.3	+2.1	−0.1	+2.8	+6.4	+3.0	+2.0	+4.0	+1.3	+1.4	+0.7	+0.6	+1.7	+1.0
	c	−0.8	+0.6	+3.1	+1.0	+0.7	+0.2	−2.5	−0.5	+0.8	+0.8	+0.8	+0.8	+0.3	+1.2	+0.7	+0.7
Aug.	*a*	−0.5	−0.1	−0.1	−0.2	+0.5	+0.6	−3.0	−0.6	+1.0	+1.6	+3.0	+1.9	+0.6	+0.6	−1.8	−0.2
	b	+0.5	−0.1	−2.4	−0.7	+0.3	+1.6	+1.8	+1.2	+0.7	+1.7	−2.6	−0.1	−1.2	+1.4	+1.2	+0.5
	c	+0.4	−1.1	+0.7	0.0	+1.4	+0.5	+0.4	+0.8	+0.2	+0.5	−1.5	−0.3	−0.1	−0.1	+2.8	+0.9
Sept.	*a*	+0.6	−0.7	+0.2	0.0	+0.1	+1.0	+1.1	+0.7	+0.9	−1.5	+1.3	+0.2	−0.2	+1.6	−1.7	−0.1
	b	−0.9	−0.3	+0.7	−0.2	+0.7	−0.4	+0.5	+0.3	−0.9	−0.2	−0.1	−0.4	−1.6	+2.1	−0.1	+0.1
	c	−0.3	+1.2	+2.6	+1.2	+0.7	+0.3	−2.0	−0.3	+0.2	−1.2	−0.4	−0.5	−0.1	+1.0	+1.1	+0.6
Oct.	*a*	−2.1	+2.9	+2.1	+1.0	−0.2	+0.4	+1.0	+0.4	+0.6	−0.1	0.0	+0.2	+3.3	−0.3	+2.4	+1.8
	b	−1.6	+0.1	−2.4	−1.3	+1.2	−0.6	+0.3	+0.3	+1.7	−0.6	−0.7	+0.3	+2.7	−0.6	−1.1	+0.3
	c	+0.8	0.0	−1.2	−0.1	+0.8	−1.0	+1.5	+0.4	−1.4	−1.3	−1.0	−1.2	−1.3	+1.3	−2.0	−0.7
Nov.	*a*	+0.1	+0.2	−2.1	−0.6	−1.2	−0.8	−1.1	−1.0	−1.0	+0.5	+0.2	−0.1	−0.4	−0.6	+1.0	0.0
	b	−0.7	+0.3	−2.8	−1.1	+0.5	+0.4	+2.0	+1.0	+0.7	+0.1	+2.1	+1.0	+3.0	−1.4	+1.7	+1.1
	c	−1.5	+0.5	−1.1	−0.7	−0.3	−1.3	−0.2	−0.6	+0.3	−1.0	−0.7	−0.3	0.0	−2.0	−0.2	−0.7
Dec.	*a*	−5.9	+1.0	−1.2	−2.0	−2.2	−2.4	−0.6	−1.7	−0.1	−0.8	−2.2	−1.0	+3.6	−0.7	−1.1	+0.6
	b	−1.6	−2.9	−2.7	−2.4	+3.3	+2.2	+1.8	+2.4	−1.9	−4.4	−0.3	−2.2	+0.7	+1.3	+0.0	+0.7
	c	−3.7	−0.3	−0.6	−1.5	+2.3	−0.4	−0.7	+0.4	−4.5	−3.0	−1.5	−3.0	+1.1	−3.2	+1.0	−0.4
Sum		+1.3	+9.4	+0.6	+3.7	+3.1	+17.6	+21.6	+14.2	+13.2	+1.2	−9.9	+1.6	+8.0	+19.1	+4.8	+10.3
$\Sigma\Delta^2$		124	58	96	37.61	76	81	113	41.18	84	89	97	40.83	101	98	63	32.92

TABLE XI. — *Continued.*

Simultaneous Departures of Temperature in Regions in °C.

		1880				1881				1882				1883			
		U. S. I	U. S. II	Arg.	Mean	U. S. I	U. S. II	Arg.	Mean	U. S. I	U. S. II	Arg.	Mean	U. S. I	U. S. II	Arg.	Mean
Jan.	a	+5.8°	+0.1°	−0.6°	+1.8°	−3.6°	−2.8°	−0.7°	−2.4°	+1.0°	−1.2°	−0.7°	−0.3°	−1.1°	−0.4°	+3.6°	+0.7°
	b	+4.3	+1.6	−1.6	+1.4	−1.3	+0.4	−2.6	−1.2	+2.6	−3.9	+1.1	−0.1	−1.3	−2.9	−1.7	−2.0
	c	+4.0	−1.6	0.0	+0.8	−1.8	−0.7	−0.4	−1.0	+0.9	−2.8	+0.4	−0.5	−0.7	−0.9	−0.9	−0.8
Feb.	a	+0.9	−4.2	+1.1	−1.3	−1.5	+2.9	0.0	+0.5	+2.0	−2.8	−2.3	−1.0	−0.2	−3.9	−0.1	−1.4
	b	+2.3	−3.4	−1.1	−0.7	−1.0	−1.4	+1.4	−0.3	+4.6	−2.0	+0.5	+1.0	+2.6	−1.7	−0.7	+0.1
	c	+3.7	−1.7	−1.3	+0.2	−0.7	+2.7	+1.1	+1.0	+1.6	−1.3	+0.4	+0.2	+0.3	+0.2	+0.7	+0.4
Mar.	a	+3.4	−1.6	−2.2	−0.1	−1.0	−1.1	+0.1	−0.5	+2.6	−2.8	−1.1	−0.4	−0.7	+2.0	+1.6	+1.0
	b	−1.1	−5.0	0.0	−2.0	+0.7	−3.8	+2.7	−0.1	+1.9	−1.0	−0.5	+0.1	−0.1	+1.9	−0.8	+0.3
	c	+0.2	−1.9	+0.3	−0.5	−2.5	+1.8	+0.9	+0.1	+0.9	+1.4	−0.2	+0.7	−2.0	+1.8	+2.0	+0.6
April	a	+1.3	+0.8	+0.7	+0.9	−3.9	+1.9	+0.2	−0.6	+2.9	+0.4	−1.3	+0.7	+1.2	−1.0	+0.6	+0.3
	b	+1.2	−1.8	+0.6	0.0	−1.2	+0.7	−0.6	−0.4	−1.2	−2.6	−1.9	−1.9	+0.9	−2.5	−0.2	−0.6
	c	+0.6	−1.4	−1.5	−0.8	+1.8	+2.7	+1.0	+1.8	−0.2	−0.7	−1.3	−0.7	−1.1	−2.0	−2.6	−1.9
May	a	+1.9	+0.3	+0.2	+0.8	+0.7	+2.1	−0.3	+0.8	+0.2	+0.5	−0.8	0.0	+0.9	−1.6	+1.9	+0.4
	b	+0.9	−0.4	+0.3	+0.3	+1.6	+0.2	+1.3	+1.0	−2.7	+0.8	+0.5	−0.5	−0.4	−1.8	+1.3	−0.3
	c	+1.8	+0.5	+1.0	+1.1	+1.3	+1.3	+0.8	+1.1	−1.2	+0.2	+2.0	+0.3	−1.3	+0.9	−1.0	−0.5
June	a	+0.4	+0.7	+3.4	+1.5	+0.4	+1.0	+0.1	+0.5	−0.6	+1.7	−2.0	−0.3	+0.9	+1.0	+2.1	+1.3
	b	+0.5	+1.0	+1.6	+1.1	+1.4	+0.7	+0.2	+0.8	+0.7	−1.3	0.0	−0.2	+0.8	+0.6	+2.4	+1.3
	c	+0.6	+1.4	+2.0	+1.3	+0.7	+1.0	−1.1	+0.2	+1.6	+0.1	+1.1	+0.9	+0.4	+1.7	−0.7	+0.5
July	a	+0.5	+0.6	+0.3	+0.5	+0.7	+0.1	+0.1	+0.3	−0.5	+1.3	+1.4	+0.7	+0.6	+1.2	+2.1	+1.3
	b	+1.0	−1.4	+2.5	+0.7	+1.0	−0.2	−1.6	−0.3	−0.4	−0.1	−0.2	−0.2	0.0	+0.4	+2.0	+0.8
	c	−0.6	−0.9	−0.6	−0.7	+0.2	−1.0	−1.2	−0.7	−0.1	−0.5	−2.7	−1.1	+0.1	−0.6	−4.2	−1.6
Aug.	a	−1.3	−1.3	+0.4	−0.7	+1.2	0.0	−3.8	−0.9	−0.7	+1.8	+1.5	+0.9	−0.5	−0.6	−0.8	−0.6
	b	−0.2	+0.1	+1.8	+0.6	+0.2	−1.0	−0.3	−0.4	−0.2	+0.2	+0.7	+0.2	−0.1	−0.1	−0.6	−0.3
	c	+1.4	−1.7	+2.3	+0.7	+1.7	−0.9	+3.6	+1.5	−0.1	+0.1	+0.1	0.0	+0.1	+2.0	−0.3	+0.6
Sept.	a	−0.2	+0.1	−0.5	−0.2	+2.8	−2.3	−1.0	−0.2	−0.2	+1.7	−1.9	0.0	−0.9	+2.8	−2.5	−0.2
	b	−0.1	−0.8	−5.8	−2.2	+0.4	+0.4	+0.3	+0.4	+0.8	−1.0	−0.3	−0.5	+0.3	+0.3	+0.2	+0.3
	c	+0.2	−0.5	+1.0	+0.2	+2.1	−2.6	−0.8	−0.4	−0.9	+0.2	+1.8	+0.4	−0.4	+2.6	+0.8	+1.0
Oct.	a	−0.6	−0.1	−2.6	−1.1	+2.7	+1.4	+1.2	+1.8	+1.5	−2.7	+2.2	+0.3	+0.8	−2.0	+2.4	+0.4
	b	−0.1	−2.6	−2.1	−1.6	+2.3	−2.9	+1.6	+0.3	+1.6	−1.0	+1.2	+0.4	+1.3	−2.7	+1.3	0.0
	c	−1.5	+0.8	−1.7	−0.8	+1.3	−1.9	−1.1	−0.6	+1.6	+1.0	+2.8	+1.8	+1.1	−1.7	−2.6	−1.1
Nov.	a	−0.2	−0.8	+1.7	−0.2	+1.4	−2.3	0.0	−0.3	+1.9	+0.6	+0.8	+1.1	+1.6	−0.1	+2.1	+1.2
	b	−3.0	−5.0	−1.2	−3.1	+1.7	−2.7	+1.2	+0.1	−0.5	−3.7	−0.3	−1.5	−2.1	−0.2	−0.7	−1.0
	c	−3.2	−4.3	−0.8	−2.7	−1.0	−2.3	−0.2	−1.2	−2.0	−0.1	+0.2	−0.6	+1.4	−0.8	−0.4	+0.1
Dec.	a	−0.7	−2.3	+2.7	−0.1	+1.8	+0.9	+2.0	+1.6	−1.8	+2.0	−0.3	0.0	+0.7	−0.6	+1.6	+0.6
	b	+0.3	+0.4	+0.4	+0.4	+2.3	−0.3	+1.8	+1.3	−0.7	+2.7	−1.5	+0.2	−0.8	+1.4	+1.5	+0.7
	c	−5.8	+1.6	−0.3	−1.5	+0.2	+0.6	+1.3	+0.7	+0.8	−1.0	−1.5	−0.7	+1.6	+0.6	−0.8	+0.5
Sum		+16.6	−34.7	+0.4	−5.9	+13.3	−7.6	+7.8	+4.3	+17.6	−17.3	−1.9	−0.6	+3.9	−6.7	+8.5	+2.1
$\Sigma\Delta^2$		172	149	109	51.52	104	113	70	31.69	91	114	62	19.76	40	99	108	28.65

TABLE XI.—*Continued.*

Simultaneous Departures of Temperature in Regions in °C.

		1884				1885				1886				1887			
		U. S. I	U. S. II	Arg.	Mean	U. S. I	U. S. II	Arg.	Mean	U. S. I	U. S. II	Arg.	Mean	U. S. I	U. S. II	Arg.	Mean
Jan.	a	−2.3	+1.1	−0.5	−0.6	+0.9	+0.3	+0.1	+0.4	−2.5	−5.0	+2.0	−1.4	−4.4	+1.7	−0.8	−1.2
	b	−1.0	−1.2	+2.7	+0.2	+0.2	+0.2	+0.4	+0.3	−3.2	+0.7	+0.9	−0.5	−0.3	+2.0	+1.6	+1.1
	c	−1.5	+1.0	+2.5	+0.7	−2.2	−1.0	+2.3	−0.3	−1.8	+4.9	+0.5	+1.2	+3.0	+1.2	+1.4	+1.9
Feb.	a	+4.0	+1.0	−0.9	+1.4	+0.5	+2.0	+0.7	+1.1	−4.2	+4.3	−0.3	−0.1	+2.8	−2.3	−0.4	+1.6
	b	+2.2	−3.8	+1.6	0.0	−2.3	+0.4	−1.6	−1.2	−0.4	+2.9	−2.3	+0.1	+3.4	−0.3	−0.2	+1.0
	c	−1.3	+2.2	+0.5	+0.5	−3.5	+1.2	−0.9	−1.1	−1.4	+1.7	+3.2	+1.2	+0.6	−1.4	−0.8	−0.5
Mar.	a	−1.5	+3.1	+1.4	+1.0	−1.1	+1.9	−0.5	+0.1	−2.6	−2.0	+1.6	−1.0	+1.9	+2.5	−0.1	+1.4
	b	+1.2	−0.3	+2.3	+1.1	−2.9	+2.2	0.0	−0.6	+0.8	−1.8	+1.3	+0.1	+0.9	+2.0	+0.9	+1.3
	c	+2.4	−1.9	+2.1	+0.9	−1.9	+1.7	0.0	−0.1	−0.9	−1.1	0.0	−0.7	−2.4	+1.3	+1.4	0.0
April	a	−1.3	+0.6	−2.2	−1.0	+1.0	+3.6	−0.4	+1.4	−2.6	−0.3	+1.4	−0.5	−0.7	+1.1	−0.5	+0.1
	b	−1.3	−0.8	−1.0	−1.0	−0.9	+1.9	+4.2	+1.7	+0.4	−1.3	0.0	−0.3	0.0	−1.8	−1.0	−0.9
	c	−1.4	−1.4	+2.0	−0.3	+1.4	+0.1	−0.1	+0.4	+0.9	−0.9	−1.5	−0.5	−0.4	−0.3	−1.0	−0.6
May	a	+0.6	−0.4	−3.6	−1.1	−0.5	+2.1	0.0	+0.5	0.0	−0.1	−1.4	−0.5	+1.6	+1.0	−2.3	+0.1
	b	+0.4	+1.1	−1.2	+0.1	−0.4	−1.0	−1.6	−1.0	−0.9	0.0	−0.6	−0.5	+0.4	0.0	+0.3	+0.2
	c	−0.2	+0.1	+0.4	+0.1	+0.4	−0.4	−1.0	−0.3	−0.4	+2.8	+2.6	+1.7	+0.1	+1.9	+1.8	+1.3
June	a	+0.4	+0.7	+1.8	+1.0	+0.2	−1.1	+0.3	−0.2	−0.3	+1.1	−0.6	+0.1	−0.6	+0.2	+3.6	+1.1
	b	−0.6	−0.2	−2.3	−1.0	+0.7	−1.2	−4.4	−1.6	+0.3	+1.1	−0.9	+0.2	−0.5	+0.8	+3.8	+1.4
	c	+0.1	+1.2	−4.6	−1.1	−0.1	−0.2	+0.2	0.0	−0.7	+1.3	−0.5	0.0	−1.7	+1.0	+1.1	+0.1
July	a	+0.2	+0.9	0.0	+0.4	+0.3	+0.9	+0.9	+0.7	−0.3	+1.0	−2.6	−0.6	−0.1	+0.8	−1.5	−0.3
	b	−0.4	−0.4	−0.8	−0.5	+0.8	+0.4	−3.5	−0.8	−0.9	+2.2	−1.6	−0.1	+0.8	−1.1	−0.8	−0.4
	c	+0.4	−0.8	−1.4	−0.1	+1.3	−0.1	−3.0	−0.6	+0.4	−0.6	+1.9	+0.6	+0.7	−0.3	+1.9	+0.8
Aug.	a	−0.7	−0.3	+3.6	+0.9	+0.2	−0.4	−3.5	−1.2	−0.4	−0.2	−0.4	−0.3	+0.2	−1.4	+4.9	+1.2
	b	+0.1	−0.8	+2.4	+0.6	−0.2	+2.6	−0.7	+0.6	+0.2	+0.9	−0.7	+0.1	+0.3	0.0	+4.7	+1.7
	c	+0.9	0.0	+3.0	+1.3	+0.4	−0.5	+1.8	+0.6	+0.6	+1.7	+1.0	+1.1	−1.0	−1.2	−0.4	−0.9
Sept.	a	+1.3	−3.7	+1.0	−0.5	−0.3	−0.6	+0.5	−0.1	0.0	+1.7	+2.4	+1.4	−0.3	−1.4	−1.9	−1.2
	b	+0.5	−1.8	+0.3	−0.3	+0.7	+0.3	+2.8	+1.3	+1.0	+0.8	−0.7	+0.4	−0.1	+0.2	−1.4	−0.4
	c	+2.4	−0.6	−1.2	+0.2	−0.1	+1.4	−0.6	+0.2	+0.8	−0.4	−3.2	−0.9	−1.6	+1.6	+1.6	+0.5
Oct.	a	+2.9	−3.1	−0.1	−0.1	−1.1	+2.1	+2.2	+1.1	−1.0	+0.2	−1.1	−0.6	+1.3	+0.2	+1.0	+0.8
	b	+1.5	+1.8	+0.4	+1.2	−0.1	−0.1	−0.3	−0.2	+1.6	−2.0	+0.8	+0.1	−1.2	+0.2	−0.7	−0.6
	c	+1.6	−0.1	−0.8	+0.2	−1.4	+0.8	+0.2	−0.1	−0.2	−1.0	−1.1	−0.8	−2.3	+0.9	−1.7	−1.0
Nov.	a	−0.5	+0.3	−0.1	−0.1	+1.0	+1.0	+3.9	+2.0	+0.6	−2.3	+0.9	−0.3	−0.2	+2.2	−0.6	+0.5
	b	+0.6	+0.3	+0.7	+0.5	+0.8	+1.3	−0.6	+0.5	−0.5	−4.6	−0.3	−1.8	+0.2	+1.3	+0.8	+0.8
		+0.3	+0.6	0.0	+0.3	−1.4	+1.1	+1.9	+0.5	+0.4	−2.7	−0.1	−0.8	+0.2	−0.2	−0.8	−0.3
Dec.	a	+2.3	−1.6	+0.4	+0.4	−1.7	−0.3	+0.3	−0.6	−4.0	−0.7	+1.0	−1.2	+0.9	−0.4	−0.2	+0.1
	b	−1.4	+2.6	+0.6	+0.6	−1.2	−0.8	−0.8	−0.9	−0.9	+1.2	+2.4	+0.9	−0.1	−1.6	+1.2	−0.2
	c	+0.4	+1.4	−0.1	+0.6	+1.5	+4.7	+0.2	+2.1	−0.1	+2.7	+2.1	+1.6	−2.2	−1.4	−1.1	−1.6
Sum		+11.4	−3.0	+8.9	+6.5	−11.9	+26.5	−0.9	+4.6	−22.1	+7.3	+5.9	−2.6	−0.8	+13.7	+13.8	+8.9
Σ Δ²		76	87	115	19.45	64	85	120	29.98	89	154	85	25.40	93	58	119	31.94

TABLE XI. — *Continued.*

Simultaneous Departures of Temperature in Regions in °C.

		1888				1889				1890					1891				
		U. S. I	U. S. II	Arg.	Mo.	U. S. I	U. S. II	Arg.	Mo.	U. S. I	U. S. II	Arg.	Samoa	Mo.	U. S. I	U. S. II	Arg.	Samoa	Mo.
Jan.	a	+1.4	−3.5	+0.5	−0.5	+0.9	−1.6	+1.4	+0.2	+5.9	−2.4	−0.6	......	+1.0	−0.1	+0.6	+1.1	+0.6	+0.6
	b	−2.9	−5.9	+3.1	−1.9	+2.4	+1.3	−0.1	+1.2	+4.4	−3.3	−2.6	......	−0.5	−1.3	−0.3	+0.4	+0.8	−0.1
	c	−1.9	+2.8	+2.5	+1.1	+0.1	−2.9	−0.8	−1.2	+3.4	−0.1	+0.6	−0.3	+0.9	+1.9	+1.7	−0.6	−0.2	+0.7
Feb.	a	+1.1	+1.6	+0.2	+1.0	−1.2	−0.9	−1.0	−1.0	+4.0	+5.0	+1.0	−0.1	+2.5	+2.2	−2.6	+1.1	0.0	+0.2
	b	+0.1	+2.4	+0.5	+1.0	−0.7	−1.4	−0.5	−0.9	+2.2	−0.4	+0.1	+0.2	+0.6	+2.6	−0.6	+1.1	0.0	+0.8
	c	+0.3	+1.7	+1.9	+1.3	−2.9	+2.7	−0.2	−0.1	+1.9	−4.2	−2.1	+0.0	−1.1	+0.2	+0.4	+1.9	+0.3	+0.7
Mar.	a	−1.2	−1.7	0.0	−1.0	−1.6	+3.4	+1.1	+1.0	−2.9	−0.4	−1.0	+0.5	−0.9	−1.1	−1.7	+3.8	−0.1	+0.2
	b	−2.2	+1.0	+1.5	+0.1	+0.3	+1.8	−0.4	+0.8	+0.1	+0.2	−1.3	+0.3	−0.2	−1.4	+1.1	−1.1	+0.5	−0.2
	c	−1.7	−0.3	+0.6	−0.5	−0.5	+2.4	+1.1	+1.0	+2.1	−0.2	−1.3	+0.6	+0.1	−0.8	−1.9	+0.8	+0.3	−0.4
April	a	+2.2	+0.8	+0.7	+1.2	+0.2	+3.0	+1.8	+1.7	+0.9	+0.1	−1.1	−0.7	−0.1	−3.1	−0.7	−1.9	+0.3	−1.4
	b	−0.2	+4.1	+1.6	+1.9	+0.4	+0.1	−3.3	−0.9	−0.1	−0.2	+1.5	−0.8	+0.1	+1.6	−0.7	+1.2	−0.1	+0.5
	c	−0.8	+2.2	+1.2	+0.9	−0.3	+3.1	−0.9	+0.6	−0.6	+0.8	+3.0	+0.2	+0.8	+0.8	+1.4	−0.4	−0.1	+0.4
May	a	+0.1	+0.1	+2.2	+0.8	−0.7	−0.6	+0.9	−0.1	−0.3	+1.2	+1.4	−0.1	+0.6	−0.9	+2.1	−1.4	−0.2	−0.1
	b	−1.6	+1.4	−2.1	−0.8	+0.9	−0.7	−1.9	−0.6	−0.1	+0.4	−2.0	+0.4	−0.4	−1.6	+0.4	−1.8	+0.1	−0.7
	c	−0.5	−0.3	−1.0	−0.6	−0.3	+1.9	+2.3	+1.3	−0.4	+1.1	−1.5	−0.1	−0.2	−1.5	−0.7	+0.8	+0.3	−0.3
June	a	−1.0	+0.4	−2.7	−1.1	−1.6	+0.7	+1.5	+0.2	−0.6	+0.7	0.0	+0.6	+0.2	−1.0	−1.1	0.0	+0.7	−0.4
	b	+0.1	+1.8	−2.7	−0.3	−0.4	+1.2	−2.6	−0.6	+0.3	−0.9	−4.0	−0.2	−1.2	+0.3	−1.3	+1.2	+0.2	+0.1
	c	+0.1	+1.0	−2.2	−0.4	−1.6	+1.0	+0.4	−0.1	+0.7	−1.2	−2.6	0.0	−0.8	+0.4	+1.8	+0.8	−0.7	+0.5
July	a	−0.7	+1.9	+4.1	+1.8	−0.3	+0.3	−2.6	−0.9	+0.1	+1.5	−0.9	+0.4	+0.2	−2.0	−0.1	+1.5	0.0	−0.2
	b	−1.0	−0.2	+1.7	+0.2	0.0	+1.1	−0.9	+0.1	−0.5	+0.4	+0.5	−1.3	−0.2	−0.3	−0.9	−1.2	−0.9	−0.8
	c	−0.7	+0.6	+0.8	+0.2	−0.6	+1.7	+1.4	+0.8	−1.4	+1.7	+2.5	−0.6	+0.6	−0.7	+0.9	−1.0	−0.7	−0.5
Aug.	a	+0.8	−1.0	+4.6	+1.5	−1.3	+1.1	+0.6	+0.1	−0.1	−0.7	−1.6	−0.8	−0.7	−0.2	−0.7	−2.0	−0.2	−0.8
	b	−0.2	−0.5	−1.5	−0.7	−1.3	+1.5	−1.8	−1.5	−0.7	−0.1	−1.7	+0.5	−0.5	0.0	+1.2	−0.3	−0.8	0.0
	c	−0.9	+1.2	+0.7	+0.3	−0.5	+1.4	−1.2	−0.1	−0.8	−0.2	−2.3	−0.2	−0.9	−1.4	+2.2	+1.5	−0.1	+0.6
Sept.	a	−1.3	+1.7	+4.1	+1.5	−0.1	−0.1	−1.9	−0.7	−0.1	−0.8	−1.5	+0.9	−0.4	−1.3	+3.7	−3.8	+0.1	−0.3
	b	−0.2	+2.0	+1.2	+1.0	−0.4	−0.6	+1.3	+0.1	−0.5	+0.8	−2.4	+0.1	−0.5	+1.0	+0.6	−0.2	+0.6	+0.5
	c	−1.9	+2.3	−2.3	−0.6	−2.1	+0.4	−0.4	−0.7	−2.0	+2.5	−0.9	+0.8	+0.1	+1.3	−0.9	+3.1	−0.6	+0.7
Oct.	a	−1.9	+0.6	−0.2	−0.5	−1.9	+2.3	+2.4	+0.9	+1.0	−2.2	+1.2	+0.2	0.0	−0.9	−1.8	+2.6	+0.5	+0.1
	b	−0.8	+0.9	+0.7	+0.3	−1.3	+0.1	+1.4	+0.1	+1.2	−2.0	+1.6	0.0	+0.2	−1.8	−0.1	−0.9	−0.1	−0.7
	c	−0.1	+0.3	+0.3	+0.2	−0.5	+1.2	−0.1	+0.1	−1.8	+2.1	−1.2	+0.5	−0.1	−0.6	+3.0	+1.2	+1.2	+1.2
Nov.	a	+2.7	−1.4	+1.9	+1.1	−0.7	−0.7	−1.1	−0.8	+0.5	+0.8	+1.6	+0.8	+0.9	−0.4	+1.9	−2.8	+0.6	−0.2
	b	+0.2	−0.4	−2.4	−0.9	−0.1	0.0	+0.4	+0.1	+1.9	0.0	−2.3	−0.8	−0.3	−1.0	−0.7	+2.2	+0.6	+0.3
	c	−2.9	+1.2	+0.9	−0.3	+0.4	+2.4	+1.4	+1.4	+0.8	+3.9	+3.5	+0.2	+2.1	−0.3	+2.3	+0.3	−0.8	+0.4
Dec.	a	−1.1	+0.8	+0.5	+0.1	+1.8	+3.0	−1.2	+1.2	−1.0	+1.2	+3.0	+0.1	+0.8	+1.1	−1.6	−1.0	+0.2	−0.3
	b	−0.5	+1.9	+1.6	+1.0	+3.0	+3.4	−1.1	−1.7	−0.6	+3.3	+2.6	+0.5	+1.4	+1.2	−0.9	−1.0	−0.4	−0.3
	c	−0.1	−0.7	+0.7	0.0	+3.2	+0.7	−0.6	+1.8	−0.1	+3.6	+0.8	+0.5	+1.2	+3.1	−2.7	−1.8	+0.7	−0.4
Sum		−19.3	+21.1	+23.2	+8.4	−7.2	+33.7	−8.0	+6.2	+16.5	+12.5	−10.3	+2.3	+5.3	−6.5	+2.6	+2.8	+2.6	+0.4
$\Sigma\Delta^2$		64	131	136	32.24	80	116	93	29.34	126	127	132	7	27.35	63	96	100	5	11.09

TABLE XI.—*Continued.*

Simultaneous Departures of Temperature in Regions in °C.

		1892					1893				
		U.S. I	U.S. II	Arg.	Samoa	Mean	U.S. I	U.S. II	Arg.	Samoa	Mean
Jan.	a	−1.3	+0.1	+0.6	+0.1	−0.1	−2.7	+2.2	+0.6	−0.8	−0.2
	b	−3.0	−1.6	+1.4	−0.8	−1.0	−5.8	−0.2	−1.2	−1.1	−2.1
	c	−0.7	+0.2	−2.0	+0.1	−0.6	−0.1	+0.3	+0.5	−0.2	+0.1
Feb.	a	+1.8	−1.0	+2.8	+0.6	+1.0	+0.5	−1.0	−2.1	−0.2	−0.7
	b	+0.5	−0.3	+1.7	+0.4	+0.6	+0.7	−1.0	−1.5	−0.8	−0.6
	c	+0.2	+1.8	+0.2	−0.2	+0.6	−0.4	−1.8	−1.6	−0.6	−1.1
Mar.	a	−0.9	+1.9	−0.8	+0.7	+0.2	+0.3	−1.6	−0.2	+0.6	−0.2
	b	−4.7	+1.7	−2.0	+0.5	−1.1	−1.0	−2.1	−0.6	−0.8	−1.1
	c	−0.6	−1.3	−0.4	+0.8	−0.5	−0.6	+0.4	+0.4	−0.5	−0.1
April	a	+1.3	−0.5	−0.5	+0.3	+0.2	+2.7	−0.1	−2.8	+0.2	0.0
	b	−1.9	−0.8	−1.5	+0.5	−0.9	−0.1	−2.2	−0.2	−1.1	−0.9
	c	−1.0	−1.0	0.0	−0.1	−0.5	−0.5	−1.3	+1.3	−1.4	−0.5
May	a	+0.8	−2.4	−0.4	−0.7	−0.7	−0.8	+1.1	0.0	−0.8	−0.7
	b	−0.1	−0.3	−1.3	−0.1	−0.4	−0.7	+1.8	0.0	−1.1	0.0
	c	−1.9	+0.9	−2.6	−0.3	−1.0	−0.2	−2.6	−4.2	+0.2	−1.7
June	a	−0.5	−1.2	−1.5	−0.1	−0.8	+0.1	+0.1	−2.9	−0.3	−0.8
	b	+0.3	−1.9	−3.6	+0.6	−1.2	−0.2	+0.5	−3.9	−0.1	−0.9
	c	−0.2	+0.6	−1.5	+0.1	−0.2	−0.9	−0.7	−3.1	+1.3	−0.8
July	a	−2.3	−0.3	0.0	+0.4	−0.6	−0.1	+0.3	−1.8	−0.8	−0.6
	b	−1.1	−0.3	−1.8	−0.6	−1.0	+0.1	0.0	+0.9	+0.4	+0.4
	c	−1.2	−0.6	+1.0	−0.2	−0.2	+0.1	−0.4	+1.1	0.0	+0.2
Aug.	a	−0.1	+0.1	−3.0	−0.5	−0.9	−0.6	0.0	−2.9	+0.1	−0.8
	b	−0.1	+0.7	−1.9	+0.3	−0.2	−0.3	−0.1	−0.6	+0.5	−0.1
	c	+0.8	−0.7	−1.9	+0.8	−0.2	+0.1	−0.2	−4.3	−0.9	−1.3
Sept.	a	−1.3	+0.1	−1.4	−0.9	−0.9	−0.6	0.0	−1.6	−0.6	−0.7
	b	−0.8	+0.8	−0.5	+0.1	−0.1	+1.2	−1.7	−3.6	−0.1	−1.0
	c	+0.7	+2.7	−1.6	0.0	+0.4	−0.3	−1.4	−3.7	−0.1	−1.4
Oct.	a	−0.4	+2.7	+0.1	+0.8	+0.8	+0.9	−0.7	−2.1	−0.9	−0.7
	b	+1.9	−2.7	−1.2	−0.6	−0.7	−0.9	−0.8	−2.3	−0.7	−1.2
	c	−1.4	−0.6	+1.7	0.0	−0.1	−0.1	+0.9	−2.5	0.0	−0.4
Nov.	a	−0.1	+0.3	−1.3	−0.8	−0.5	+0.2	+0.1	−2.8	+0.1	−0.6
	b	−0.5	+1.6	+0.9	−0.9	+0.3	−0.6	−1.5	−2.4	0.0	−1.1
	c	−0.6	−1.6	−0.2	−0.4	−0.7	0.0	+0.1	−1.2	−0.2	−0.3
Dec.	a	+2.0	−1.7	−2.8	−1.0	−0.9	−1.7	+3.4	−1.2	−0.2	+0.1
	b	+0.1	−3.7	−1.4	+0.1	−1.7	+0.9	+1.4	+3.4	−0.3	+1.4
	c	−3.8	+1.4	+1.2	−0.3	−0.3	+3.3	−0.4	+1.2	−0.3	+1.0
Sum		−20.1	−0.5	−25.6	−0.9	−13.9	−8.1	−11.4	−47.0	−11.5	−19.4
$\Sigma\Delta^2$		83	96	97	8	18.49	71	61	187	14	27.02

		1894					1895				
		U.S. I	U.S. II	Arg.	Samoa	Mn.	U.S. I	U.S. II	Arg.	Samoa	Mn.
Jan.	a	+2.7	−3.5	+1.0	+0.2	+0.1	−0.8	+1.3	−1.8	−0.4	−0.4
	b	+3.3	−0.9	−2.2	−0.1	0.0	+0.4	+2.6	−3.4	−0.2	−0.2
	c	−0.4	+1.2	+2.2	−0.7	+0.6	−0.7	−3.0	−0.3	+0.2	−1.0
Feb.	a	+1.5	−2.3	+0.7	−0.6	−0.2	−5.8	−0.9	+1.1	−0.9	−1.6
	b	−0.1	−3.6	+0.7	−0.5	−0.9	−7.5	−2.3	−1.2	−1.0	−3.0
	c	−2.8	−3.3	−0.2	−0.1	−1.6	−1.1	+1.8	+1.9	−1.2	+0.4
Mar.	a	+3.3	−2.4	−1.8	−1.1	−0.5	−0.6	+0.4	+1.4	−0.8	+0.1
	b	+3.2	−0.8	−2.1	+0.2	+0.1	−1.3	−2.6	+0.9	−0.3	−0.8
	c	−2.6	+1.0	−0.4	+0.4	−0.4	+0.3	+0.9	+2.2	+0.7	+1.0
April	a	−0.2	−0.4	+1.0	+0.2	+0.2	−0.2	−0.4	+0.9	+0.2	+0.1
	b	+0.7	−1.2	−0.6	+0.9	0.0	−1.2	+1.0	+2.1	+0.1	+0.5
	c	+1.0	−0.8	−0.4	+0.3	0.0	+0.4	+0.7	+1.5	+0.2	+0.7
May	a	+1.8	−0.7	+4.5	−0.2	+1.3	+1.9	+1.2	−2.1	+0.5	+0.4
	b	+0.5	+0.8	+4.9	−0.1	+1.5	−2.7	+1.4	+1.6	+1.0	+0.3
	c	−1.7	+1.0	−3.5	0.0	−1.0	−0.6	−2.2	+4.0	+0.9	+0.5
June	a	−1.9	+0.1	−0.4	+0.2	−0.5	+0.7	−2.4	+4.2	+0.1	+0.7
	b	−0.1	−2.6	−3.4	+0.4	−1.4	−0.4	−1.6	+5.4	−0.1	+0.8
	c	0.0	−2.0	+1.7	+0.2	0.0	+0.4	+0.1	+0.3	+0.5	+0.4
July	a	−0.4	0.0	+2.2	+0.5	+0.8	−1.0	−1.1	+1.6	+0.8	+0.1
	b	−0.5	−1.4	+0.7	−0.6	−0.4	−0.9	−2.2	+2.1	+0.7	−0.1
	c	−0.6	−0.6	−3.3	−0.9	−1.4	−1.0	−0.8	+2.4	−0.2	+0.1
Aug.	a	−0.9	−1.3	−1.8	+0.6	−0.8	−0.6	−1.2	+6.8	−0.4	+1.2
	b	−0.5	−0.9	+2.0	+0.8	+0.4	+0.7	+0.9	−2.5	+0.1	−0.2
	c	−0.3	+1.7	−2.0	+0.4	0.0	+0.8	−0.6	+0.3	−0.3	0.0
Sept.	a	+1.3	−2.2	−3.1	+0.8	−0.8	+0.6	−0.1	−3.7	−0.5	−0.9
	b	+0.2	−1.1	−1.4	+0.5	−0.4	+1.8	+1.6	−1.2	−0.7	+0.4
	c	+0.1	−0.3	+0.8	+0.2	+0.2	+1.3	−0.6	+2.7	0.0	+0.9
Oct.	a	+0.1	−1.3	−0.8	+0.9	−0.3	−2.0	+0.2	+0.6	+0.3	−0.2
	b	−0.3	+1.2	−2.5	+0.6	−0.2	−1.0	+2.5	−3.8	−0.6	−0.7
	c	+1.4	+0.9	−2.0	+0.4	+0.2	−1.3	+0.9	+0.6	+0.4	+0.2
Nov.	a	−1.0	+0.9	−0.6	−0.2	−0.2	+0.6	−1.4	−4.0	−1.1	−1.5
	b	−1.3	+0.7	+1.1	−0.7	0.0	−0.8	+1.7	+0.2	−0.2	+0.2
	c	+1.6	+1.6	+0.7	−0.4	+0.9	−0.2	−2.0	+0.1	0.0	−0.5
Dec.	a	+1.8	−0.9	−0.8	−1.2	−0.3	−2.5	−0.5	+1.4	+0.2	−0.1
	b	+2.0	−1.0	−1.2	+0.5	+0.1	−0.6	−2.2	+1.2	+0.5	−0.3
	c	−2.3	+0.4	+1.4	+0.4	0.0	+1.8	−4.2	−0.8	+0.4	−0.7
Sum		+8.6	−24.0	−8.9	+2.2	−4.9	−23.1	−12.1	+22.7	−1.1	−3.5
$\Sigma\Delta^2$		191	90	149	7	18.44	136	98	226	8	25.00

TABLE XI. — *Continued.*

Simultaneous Departures of Temperature in Regions in °C.

		1896					1897					1898					1899			
		U.S. I	U.S. II	Arg.	Samoa	Mean	U.S. I	U.S. II	Arg.	Samoa	Mn.	U.S. I	U.S. II	Arg.	Samoa	Mn.	U.S. I	U.S. II	Samoa	Mn.
Jan.	a	−2.0	0.0	−1.9	+0.2	−0.7	+0.6	−0.2	−1.7	−0.4	−0.4	−0.1	+1.8	+0.8	−1.1	+0.4	+0.1	−0.7	−0.4	−0.3
	b	−0.1	+2.3	−0.2	−0.1	+0.5	+1.0	+0.6	+0.3	−0.5	+0.4	+3.0	−3.4	−0.4	−0.5	−0.3	+1.2	+1.6	−1.5	−0.4
	c	+1.1	+2.8	+0.5	−0.6	+0.9	−4.9	+1.6	−0.1	+0.1	−0.8	+1.9	−3.0	+1.7	−0.4	+0.1	−0.6	+3.1	−0.5	+0.7
Feb.	a	+1.6	+0.8	+0.1	−0.4	+0.6	−1.5	+1.3	+0.5	−0.4	0.0	−2.0	+1.5	+1.5	−0.2	+0.2	−4.0	−3.7	0.0	−2.6
	b	−1.6	+2.5	0.0	−0.8	+0.4	+1.2	−1.6	−0.5	−0.6	−0.4	+2.3	+1.0	−0.2	−0.9	+0.6	−7.1	+0.9	−0.7	−2.3
	c	+0.5	+2.4	−0.9	+0.4	+0.5	−0.1	−1.6	+1.2	+0.3	0.0	−0.9	+1.9	+3.0	−0.7	+0.8	+1.1	+0.5	.....	+0.8
Mar.	a	−0.1	−1.8	+2.6	−0.3	+0.1	+2.8	−2.4	+1.7	+0.8	+0.7	0.4	+1.6	+1.7	−0.9	+0.6	−0.6	+1.2	.....	+0.3
	b	−3.7	+1.3	−0.8	+0.3	−0.7	+2.7	−3.7	+3.3	+0.2	+0.6	+4.4	−3.3	−1.6	−0.9	−0.4	+0.8	−1.6	−0.4	−0.4
	c	−0.6	+1.7	−0.6	+0.2	+0.5	+1.6	−3.4	+3.1	0.0	+0.3	+0.5	−3.4	−2.4	−0.7	−1.4	−0.4	−0.6	−0.1	−0.4
April	a	−2.5	+0.6	+1.1	0.0	−0.2	+0.5	−1.3	+1.2	+0.8	+0.3	−2.1	−0.2	+0.4	−0.3	−0.6	−3.1	+0.7	−1.4	−1.3
	b	+3.2	−3.4	−1.9	−0.3	−0.6	−1.3	+2.2	+2.1	−0.1	+0.7	+0.2	+2.2	−2.2	0.0	0.0	−0.6	+1.8	+0.4	+0.4
	c	+1.2	−1.7	+4.1	−0.4	+0.8	+0.2	−0.1	+2.3	−0.4	+0.5	−0.7	+2.5	−1.7	−0.2	−0.2	+0.6	−1.3	+0.7	0.0
May	a	+1.6	−2.6	−3.5	+1.1	+0.9	−0.5	+1.0	+3.6	−0.1	+1.0	−1.7	−0.8	−0.3	−0.6	−0.8	+1.0	−3.1	−0.2	−0.8
	b	+2.3	−3.3	+1.8	+0.4	+0.3	−0.3	+1.9	+3.2	0.0	+1.2	+0.6	−1.0	+1.8	+0.1	+0.4	+0.6	−1.2	0.0	−0.2
	c	+0.7	+1.7	+1.7	+0.3	+1.1	−1.7	+1.9	−2.1	−0.1	−0.5	+0.3	−0.8	+2.8	−0.5	+0.4	−0.1	−2.4	−0.3	−0.9
June	a	+0.3	+0.6	+1.5	+0.1	+0.6	−1.8	+0.2	+3.4	+0.5	+0.6	+0.3	+0.4	+2.1	+0.1	+0.7	+1.7	−2.7	−0.4	−0.5
	b	−0.8	+3.9	−2.8	−0.3	0.0	+0.3	−0.4	+1.7	+0.6	+3.6	−0.1	+0.8	+4.6	−0.5	+1.2	−0.4	+0.8	−0.8	−0.1
	c	+0.1	+1.0	+0.8	−0.9	+0.2	−0.1	−0.5	−3.0	−0.3	−1.0	+0.2	+0.9	+0.5	0.0	+0.4	−0.9	+0.6	−0.7	−0.3
July	a	−0.8	+1.2	+5.2	−1.6	+1.0	+0.6	−1.0	−3.5	−0.3	−1.0	−0.1	0.0	−3.6	+1.1	−0.6	−0.6	+1.2	+0.4	+0.3
	b	−0.6	+0.1	+2.0	−1.9	−0.1	−0.8	−0.3	−0.9	+0.3	−0.4	−0.1	+0.6	−1.4	+1.0	0.0	−0.2	−0.2	+0.4	0.0
	c	+0.3	−1.3	+3.4	+0.1	+0.6	+0.1	−1.5	−1.1	−0.2	−0.7	+0.7	+0.9	+0.4	+0.4	+0.6	−0.2	−0.3	0.0	−0.2
Aug.	a	+1.6	−1.1	+1.9	.....	+0.8	−0.2	−0.4	−0.6	−0.1	−0.3	−0.2	+0.2	−1.2	−0.5	−0.4	+0.1	−2.4	−0.1	−0.8
	b	+0.2	+1.0	+4.8	.....	+2.0	−0.7	−0.3	−2.7	+0.7	−0.8	−0.1	+3.0	−4.3	+0.4	−0.2	+0.1	−1.9	−0.1	−0.6
	c	−0.3	+0.6	+5.1	0.0	+1.4	−0.1	+1.4	−2.0	−0.1	−0.2	+1.3	+0.4	−0.7	+0.1	+0.2	+0.8	−0.1	.....	+0.4
Sept.	a	−0.2	+0.7	+0.7	+0.6	+0.4	+0.3	+0.5	−2.4	−0.7	−0.6	+0.8	+0.9	−1.2	+0.6	+0.3	+0.7	+0.6	+0.8	+0.7
	b	+1.0	+1.3	+1.7	+0.1	+1.0	+1.9	+0.2	+0.7	−0.4	+0.4	0.0	+2.1	−3.0	+0.3	−0.2	−0.3	+0.9	0.0	+0.2
	c	−1.1	−0.7	+4.8	+0.1	+0.8	−1.1	+2.7	−1.4	−0.3	0.0	+1.5	+1.2	+0.7	−0.4	+0.8	−1.6	+2.6	+0.5	+0.5
Oct.	a	−1.6	+1.5	−2.0	+0.4	−0.4	+0.2	+0.5	+3.5	−0.9	+0.8	+2.8	−0.7	−2.4	−0.2	−0.1	−1.7	0.0	+0.1	−0.5
	b	−1.6	+1.6	+2.0	+1.1	+0.8	+2.5	−1.0	+1.2	+0.3	+0.8	−0.7	+0.5	−3.9	−0.3	−1.1	+2.8	−2.8	+0.1	0.0
	c	+1.5	−0.3	+2.2	+0.2	+0.9	+0.7	−1.0	−1.8	0.0	−0.5	−2.8	+1.3	−1.2	−0.2	−0.7	+1.7	+0.3	0.0	+0.7
Nov.	a	+0.8	−1.6	−1.0	−1.1	−0.7	+0.9	−0.7	−2.5	+0.1	−0.6	+0.5	+1.8	−1.3	−1.0	0.0	−1.5	+2.6	+0.8	+0.6
	b	+2.6	+3.2	+0.9	−0.4	+1.6	+0.9	+2.4	+2.0	−1.2	+1.0	−0.1	−0.6	−3.5	−0.3	−1.2	+2.6	+1.8	+1.0	+1.8
	c	+2.1	−1.7	+0.9	+0.5	+0.4	+0.8	+2.1	−1.2	−0.9	+0.2	−2.6	−1.7	−1.7	−0.6	−1.6	+0.7	+1.7	−0.6	+0.6
Dec.	a	−0.3	+0.6	−0.5	+0.2	0.0	+0.5	−1.8	+1.4	+0.3	+0.1	−2.9	−0.2	+0.8	+0.2	−0.5	+0.5	−0.1	−0.4	0.0
	b	+1.1	+1.4	−2.3	+1.0	+0.3	+1.2	−2.5	+0.4	−0.5	−0.4	−2.2	−1.7	−1.4	−0.1	−1.4	+1.7	−1.2	−0.2	+0.1
	c	−0.8	+2.4	+1.5	+0.3	+0.8	−1.0	−2.3	+0.6	+0.5	−0.5	+1.4	−0.8	+0.4	−0.3	+0.2	−2.6	+0.8	+0.2	−0.5
Sum		+5.1	+17.7	+33.9	−2.0	+16.8	+4.4	−7.5	+9.9	−3.0	+1.0	+2.4	+6.2	−16.4	−8.4	−3.8	−7.7	−2.6	−3.4	−4.2
$\Sigma\delta^2$		77	129	296	12	21.04	70	93	148	5	13.70	95	99	163	7	17.00	124	101	8	22.96

TABLE XI.—*Concluded.*

Simultaneous Departures of Temperature in Regions in °C.

		1900				1901			
		U. S. I	U. S. II	Samoa	Mn.	U. S. I	U. S. II	Samoa	Mn.
Jan.	a	−1.0	+3.0	+0.7	−0.9	+1.0	+0.7	+0.5	+0.7
	b	+2.5	+1.3	−0.1	−2.2	+0.7	+2.7	+0.7	+1.1
	c	−0.4	+2.2	+1.0	+0.9	+0.9	+2.9	+0.1	+1.3
Feb.	a	−0.1	+1.5	+0.8	+0.7	−1.4	0.4	+0.6	−0.4
	b	−2.6	+0.1	0.1	−0.9	−1.0	+0.1	−0.4	−0.4
	c	2.8	+2.6	+0.7	+0.2	−1.2	+5.2	+0.3	+0.4
Mar.	a	−0.2	+3.5	0.9	+0.8	−0.6	+2.1	0.0	+0.5
	b	−2.4	+2.9	0.0	+0.2	−0.2	+0.5	+0.6	+0.3
	c	−0.9	+1.6	−0.1	+0.2	+0.7	−2.0	−0.2	−0.5
April	a	−1.0	−1.0	+0.2	−0.6	−1.4	−3.3	+0.8	−1.3
	b	−0.8	+0.4	+0.1	−0.1	−2.4	−0.3	+0.4	−0.8
	c	+0.7	−2.4	−0.2	−0.6	−1.6	+2.3	+1.3	+0.7
May	a	−0.2	+1.4	+0.0	+0.6	−0.1	+0.5	+1.5	+0.7
	b	+0.4	0.0	−0.1	0.0	−0.1	+2.6	0.0	+0.9
	c	−0.6	+1.9	−0.9	+0.1	−2.2	−0.4	−0.2	−0.9
June	a	+0.1	+0.1	+0.2	+0.1	0.9	−0.6	−0.4	−0.6
	b	−1.0	+0.8	−0.8	−0.3	−0.5	−1.7	−0.7	−1.0
	c	+0.1	+3.2	−1.1	+0.8	+1.3	+0.5	+0.5	+0.8
July	a	+0.3	−0.4	−0.1	−0.1	+0.6	+1.0	+1.5	+1.0
	b	+0.1	+0.8	−0.5	+0.1	+0.2	+1.9	−0.2	+0.6
	c	−0.8	+0.7	−0.5	−0.2	+0.2	+0.9	+0.3	+0.5
Aug.	a	+0.1	+0.4	+0.7	+0.4	−0.1	+0.7	+0.7	+0.4
	b	+1.5	−0.8	......	+0.3	+0.4	−0.4	+0.3	+0.1
	c	+1.2	−0.2	+0.1	+0.4	−0.1	+1.4	−1.2	0.0
Sept.	a	+1.8	−0.3	+0.6	+0.9	−0.5	−0.3	+0.2	−0.2
	b	+1.2	−0.7	−0.1	+0.2	−0.6	−0.3	+0.1	−0.1
	c	+2.4	−2.2	+0.9	+0.4	−0.7	−0.7	0.0	−0.3
Oct.	a	+1.9	+0.4	0.0	+0.8	−0.7	+0.2	−0.2	−0.2
	b	+0.4	+1.6	+0.3	+0.8	−0.5	+1.8	−0.5	+0.3
	c	+3.5	−0.5	+0.5	+1.2	+1.3	+2.0	−0.3	+1.0
Nov.	a	+0.9	+3.7	−0.2	+1.5	−0.8	+2.2	+0.5	+0.6
	b	+0.5	+2.8	−0.1	+1.1	−2.1	+1.4	−0.5	−0.4
	c	+2.6	+1.8	+0.1	+1.5	−0.9	+3.8	−0.1	+0.9
Dec.	a	−0.7	+3.3	+1.0	+1.2	−0.6	+2.1	+0.1	+0.5
	b	−0.3	+1.6	−0.3	+0.3	−3.9	+2.6	+0.6	−1.8
	c	+1.3	−0.3	−1.4	−0.1	−0.7	+1.0	+0.4	+0.2
Sum		+8.0	+38.4	+1.3	+15.9	−21.1	+28.1	−7.1	+4.9
$\Sigma\delta^2$		73	13.6	10	21.93	68	131	8	19.90

		1902				1903				1904			
		U. S. I	U. S. II	Samoa	Mn.	U. S. I	U. S. II	Samoa	Mn.	U. S. I	U. S. II	Samoa	Mn.
Jan.	a	−1.0	+3.6	+0.8	+1.1	−1.2	+1.9	+0.8	+0.5	−2.1	−0.8	......	−1.6
	b	−0.8	+2.3	−0.3	+0.4	−1.7	+0.3	+0.6	−0.3	−0.9	+1.6	......	+0.4
	c	−1.7	−3.0	0.0	−1.6	+2.3	+2.7	+0.8	+1.9	−2.2	−1.8	......	−2.0
Feb.	a	−4.6	−0.8	0.0	−1.8	+2.4	+4.4	+0.7	+2.5	+0.1	0.0	−0.1	0.0
	b	−4.9	+3.3	+1.2	+0.2	−1.1	−4.9	+0.4	−1.9	−3.3	+0.7	−0.5	−1.0
	c	−0.1	+0.9	+0.7	+0.5	−0.8	−1.3	+0.3	−0.6	−0.2	+3.3	−0.7	+0.8
Mar.	a	0.5	−0.2	−0.5	−0.4	+2.2	−0.8	+0.2	+0.5	+0.7	+2.3	0.0	+1.0
	b	+0.6	−0.8	+1.2	+0.3	+3.6	−0.1	+0.8	+1.4	+0.6	+0.9	−0.2	+0.4
	c	+2.4	−3.4	0.0	−0.3	+0.3	+1.0	+0.9	+1.0	+1.1	−2.2	−0.4	−0.5
April	a	−1.7	+0.9	−0.3	0.4	+1.3	−0.1	+0.7	+0.6	−0.1	+0.6	−0.4	0.0
	b	−0.8	+1.6	−0.1	+0.2	−0.8	−1.7	+0.2	−0.8	−2.1	+3.0	−0.2	+0.2
	c	+1.5	−0.7	+0.1	+0.3	−1.9	+0.7	−0.4	−0.5	−1.4	−2.3	−0.6	−1.4
May	a	+1.3	+1.2	+0.8	+1.1	−1.9	+0.9	+0.1	−0.3	−0.3	−0.2	+0.6	0.0
	b	+0.7	−0.9	+0.5	+0.1	−0.1	+0.3	+1.1	+0.4	−1.7	+1.0	+0.1	−0.2
	c	+0.3	+0.4	+0.4	+0.4	−0.1	−2.0	−0.7	−0.9	+0.4	−0.1	−0.1	+0.1
June	a	+0.4	+0.7	+0.2	+0.4	−1.4	+1.9	+0.7	+0.4	−0.2	0.0	+0.6	+0.1
	b	+0.6	+0.3	+0.1	+0.3	−3.0	+0.6	+0.6	−0.6	−1.4	+1.8	+0.2	+0.2
	c	−1.7	+1.5	−0.3	−0.2	−1.7	+0.7	+0.4	−0.2	−0.9	+0.2	−1.0	−0.6
July	a	+0.2	−3.5	+0.3	−1.0	+0.2	−0.8	+0.2	−0.1	−1.0	−0.3	−0.2	−0.5
	b	−0.2	+0.2	+0.2	+0.1	−0.9	+0.6	+0.1	−0.1	−0.8	−0.4	−1.1	−0.8
	c	−0.7	+0.2	+0.4	0.0	−0.6	−0.6	+0.2	−0.3	−1.9	−0.8	+0.2	−0.8
Aug.	a	+0.1	+1.0	−0.1	+0.3	−1.4	−0.6	+0.6	−0.5	−1.3	+0.4	−0.7	−0.5
	b	−0.8	−1.0	+0.4	−0.5	−1.3	+1.4	+0.0	0.0	−1.2	+0.4	−0.3	−0.4
	c	−0.2	+0.6	−0.9	−0.2	+0.7	+1.6	+1.0	+1.1	−0.9	+0.3	−0.4	−0.3
Sept.	a	−0.3	+1.6	+0.1	+0.5	−0.2	+1.2	+0.5	+0.5	−0.3	+1.8	−0.3	+0.4
	b	−2.4	+0.1	−0.8	−1.0	+0.4	−2.2	−0.8	−0.9	+0.3	+1.7	−0.4	+0.5
	c	+1.7	−0.6	−0.3	+0.3	−0.8	+0.6	−0.6	−0.3	+0.9	−0.1	0.0	+0.3
Oct.	a	−0.1	−0.1	+0.2	0.0	+0.9	−0.6	+0.7	+0.3	+1.2	+1.7	−0.2	+0.9
	b	+0.9	+1.6	−0.3	+0.7	−0.8	+1.3	0.0	+0.2	+0.2	−0.2	+0.2	+0.1
	c	+1.2	+2.4	+0.3	+1.3	−1.5	+1.4	−0.1	−0.1	−1.7	+1.8	+0.2	+0.1
Nov.	a	+2.0	+2.0	+0.6	+1.5	+0.2	+0.9	−0.5	+0.2	−0.8	+2.4	−0.4	+0.4
	b	+4.0	0.0	+0.2	+1.4	−0.3	+0.8	−0.2	+0.1	−1.5	+1.6	+0.2	+0.1
	c	+1.8	−1.6	+0.6	+0.3	−3.7	+3.1	+0.2	−0.1	+0.3	+3.7	0.0	+1.3
Dec.	a	−0.6	+0.6	−0.5	+0.2	−3.3	−0.6	−0.2	−1.4	−1.3	+0.1	0.0	−0.3
	b	+1.0	−1.8	+0.2	−0.2	−2.4	−0.1	−0.5	−1.0	−3.6	+1.4	−0.1	−0.9
	c	−1.9	+0.9	+1.0	0.0	−0.8	+0.2	+0.2	−0.1	+0.4	−0.1	+0.5	+0.3
Sum		−3.4	+9.5	+7.1	+4.3	−19.2	+13.0	+9.0	+0.6	−27.2	+23.7	−5.5	−4.2
$\Sigma\delta^2$		100	100	7	19.05	99	100	7	25.14	68	88	2	18.27

What we have next to do is to sum all the squares through the whole period of 33 years. This summation, with the partial values of Δ which result from it, is shown in the next table. The most noteworthy circumstance here brought out is the complete absence of any systematic value of the residual Δ. This may be shown by dividing the series into three parts during each of which the stations remained unchanged. The result is as follows:

Summation of Squares for Ten-day Deviations.

$n = 3$

Years	U. S. I Σr_1^2	U. S. II Σr_2^2	Arg. Σr_3^2	Σr^2	$n^2 \Sigma r^2$	Σv^2	Δ
1872	120	44	97	41.4	373	261	+112
73	62	48	48	12.9	116	148	− 32
74	70	64	102	18.2	164	236	− 72
75	114	96	81	24.0	216	291	− 75
76	124	58	96	37.6	338	278	+ 60
77	76	81	113	41.2	371	270	+101
78	84	89	97	40.8	367	270	+ 75
79	101	98	63	32.9	296	262	+ 36
1880	172	149	100	51.5	464	430	+ 36
81	104	113	70	31.7	285	287	− 3
82	99	114	62	19.8	178	267	− 90
83	40	99	108	28.7	258	247	+ 12
84	76	87	115	19.5	176	278	−102
85	64	85	120	30.0	270	269	0
86	80	154	85	25.4	229	319	− 90
87	83	58	119	31.9	287	260	+ 27
88	64	131	136	32.2	290	331	− 39
89	80	116	93	29.3	264	289	− 24
Sum	1605	1674	1714	549.0	4942	4963	− 66

$n = 4$

Years	U. S. I Σr_1^2	U. S. II Σr_2^2	Arg. Σr_3^2	Samoa Σr_4^2	Σr^2	$n^2 \Sigma r^2$	Σv^2	Δ
1890	126	127	132	7	27.4	438	392	+ 48
91	69	96	100	5	11.1	178	270	− 96
92	85	96	97	8	18.5	296	286	+ 8
93	74	64	187	14	27.0	432	333	+100
94	91	90	149	7	18.4	294	337	− 40
95	136	98	226	8	25.0	400	468	− 68
96	77	129	206	12	21.9	350	424	− 72
97	70	93	148	5	13.7	219	316	− 96
1898	95	99	163	7	17.0	272	364	− 92
Sum	820	889	1408	73	180.0	2879	3190	−308

$n = 3$

Years	U. S. I Σr_1^2	U. S. II Σr_2^2	Samoa Σr_3^2	Σr^2	$n\Sigma r^2$	$n^2 \Sigma r^2$	Σv^2	Δ
1899	124	101	8	22.2	67	200	233	−33
1900	73	136	10	21.9	66	197	219	−21
01	68	131	8	19.9	60	179	207	−27
02	100	100	7	19.0	57	171	207	−36
03	90	100	7	26.1	78	235	206	+27
04	68	88	2	18.3	55	165	158	+ 6
Sum	582	656	42	127.4	383	1147	1230	−84

It is not necessary to compute the value of τ_0 from these data because it is evidently evanescent, the mean coming out with an imaginary value. In fact the values of Δ as they come out in the last columns of the table are less than their probable errors by amounts smaller than could be expected, except as the result of chance. There is therefore no evidence of any irregular fluctuation having a period between ten days and several years.

§ 15. *Search for Variations Synchronous with the Sun's Synodic Rotation by the Method of Time-correlation.*

Granting the existence of variations in the solar constant it is extremely improbable, and indeed almost inconsistent with any theory of what is going on in the sun, to suppose them to take place simultaneously over the entire photosphere. We should expect them to be mostly confined in each case to some limited region; then, when this region became visible from the earth, we should experience a change in the solar heat, which would reach its maximum or minimum when, in consequence of the sun's rotation, the meridian of the hot or cool region of the photosphere passed the middle of the sun's disc as seen from the earth. After this the effect would diminish, and would disappear entirely as the region disappeared from our sight on the sun's western limb, to be renewed when it reappeared on the eastern limb. Thus we should have a fluctuation in the terrestrial temperature having the period of the sun's synodic rotation.

Were the period of the rotation a well-defined constant, and were the excess of temperature in any region of one hemisphere permanent, the effect could be determined in the same way that we have determined that of the solar spots, by forming equations of condition for the coefficients expressing the amplitude of the resulting fluctuations. But there are two conditions which would render this method illusory. The first is that, owing to the different periods of rotation in different parallels of solar latitude, there would be no one invariable period of the phenomenon. The other impeding condition is that we must expect such deviations of temperature within any region of the sun to be temporary, lasting only a few weeks or months, and then disappearing, to reappear in some other region of the sun. Then the effect would appear entirely non-periodic if followed during long intervals of time, and could be detected only by the statistical methods already developed. If the change of solar temperature ordinarily disappeared before a rotation was completed, the effect would be entirely irregular and non-periodic. But if it continued through one or more solar rotations, as would probably be the case, then the effect would be temporary fluctuations of temperature having the period of the synodic rotation, but changing their epoch from time to time, and thus annulling each other if we treated them as continuous through long periods of time. We have shown how a phenomenon of this kind can be detected, even if it lasts in each special case through little more than a single rotation of the sun, by the method of time-correlation. The following considerations may guide our course of thought on the subject.

Let us grant that on any occasion a region of the sun extending to, at least near the equator, and hotter than the photosphere in general, is carried past the apparent solar meridian by the sun's rotation. During a period of ten days it will be sufficiently near the meridian to produce a rise in terrestrial temperatures. Then, as it disappears, the temperature will begin to fall until the region reappears on the sun's eastern limb. Then there will be another rise in the temperature, showing a rhythmical movement of the latter. What we have to do is to inquire into the fluctuations of temperature with a view of determining whether there can be found any rythmical tendency among them to recur at the end of about 26 days. This is most completely and rigorously done by searching for correlations between terrestrial temperatures at any one epoch, or through one term, and during the following terms up to 26 days or more. To discover the effect it seems desirable to take terms as short as five days, and to carry their study continuously forward. It is then certain that, if any exceptionally hot or cool region of the photosphere has been carried past our solar meridian, the effect will be at its maximum during at least some one term. A study of the temperatures during the five terms following will then show what changes in terrestrial temperature have taken place while the special region was moving around and returning again to the solar meridian.

I have chosen for this research the temperatures at San Diego because they are fairly steady, and it chanced that the data for 5-day terms were available through a period of more than 30 years, and therefore nearly 400 synodic rotations of the sun. The research was confined to this station more through practical considerations than because it was absolutely the best. If the clearest result is to be brought out, stations in some continental interior, where the temperature is little affected by the ocean, and where the irregular fluctuations are as small as possible, should be preferred. Moreover, as the effect sought for is common to the whole globe, the mean of the largest practical number of such stations should be used. But the writer conceives that a fairly certain result can be derived from San Diego alone.

The method by which the periodicity is to be detected is that developed in § 2. We take the departures of temperature during a number of consecutive five-day terms, as great as we choose. In the present case we have chosen six, making a period of thirty days. The departures during the six terms of this period are designated as

$$a_0,\ a_1,\ a_2,\ a_3,\ a_4,\ a_5$$

Beginning with the first five-day term, we now multiply a_0 into each of the following five departures, and write their products in a horizontal line. A new period is then begun with a_1 of the preceding term so that the departure which appears as a_1 in the first line becomes a_0 in the second, after which it is not used. Thus each individual departure enters into six consecutive periods.

It does not seem necessary to encumber the work by giving the individual departures, 2376 in number, in detail. The following commencement of the table will show how the individual products were formed.

It being usual to designate the ten-day terms of each month as a, b, and c, we designate the five-day terms as a_1, a_2, b_1, etc.

The column a_0 of the table gives the five-day departures of the normal temperature as determined from the records of the Weather Bureau. The method by which the six products in each line are formed will be readily seen, as the factors are all given for the first two lines, and can be readily understood for the lines following.

1872		a_0	a_0^2	a_0a_1	a_0a_2	a_0a_3	a_0a_4	a_0a_5
Jan.	a_1	−3.0	9.0	+4.2	+7.8	−4.5	−0.9	−12.0
	a_2	−1.4	2.0	+3.6	−2.1	−0.4	−5.6	+0.4
	b_1	−2.6	6.8	−3.9	−0.8	−10.4	+0.8	−4.2
	b_2	+1.5	2.2	+0.4	+6.0	−0.4	+2.4	+1.2
	c_1	+0.3	0.1	+1.2	−0.1	+0.5	+0.2	+0.2
	c_2	+4.0	16.0	−1.2	−6.4	+3.2	+2.0	−5.2
Feb.	a_1	−0.3	0.1	−0.5	−0.2	−0.2	+0.4	+0.8

Instead of showing at once the sum total, the addition has been grouped, the period of 33 years being divided into terms of 5 years each, except the last, which includes only 3 years. The results of the separate summations are as follows:

Period	$[a_0]^2$	$[a_0a_1]$	$[a_0a_2]$	$[a_0a_3]$	$[a_0a_4]$	$[a_0a_5]$
1872–76	2029	906	502	333	235	211
1877–81	2810	1506	660	865	807	921
1882–86	2664	1289	652	584	616	500
1887–91	2901	1249	716	416	625	732
1892–96	2790	1032	568	346	313	434
1897–01	2555	1141	673	487	505	547
1902–04	1639	826	570	492	353	273
Sum	17478	7863	4431	3553	3544	3620
r_t		+0.450	+0.254	+0.205	+0.203	+0.207

In the bottom line of the table are given the coefficients of correlation found r_t by dividing the several sums of the products in the last five columns by the sums a_0^2.

The values of r thus found may be regarded as non-periodic. Were there any tendency toward a recurrence at the end of 25 days there should be a marked increase in the values of the 4th and 5th products, because the 5th corresponds to a completion of the sun's synodic rotation. It is true that there is a minute increase of 0.004 between the 4th and 5th terms of the set. But an examination of the several separate sums through which this is formed shows that the increase is too small and uncertain to be regarded as the effect of periodicity.

But a quasi-periodicity is still possible, the persistently positive sign of ε indicating a tendency of the departures to persist through a period of more than 25 days. The exact general fact brought out by the correlation is as follows:

Whatever be the departure of temperature at San Diego during any 5-day term we may expect the subsequent departures to lie in the general average in the same direction for more than a month, the ultimate amount at the end of the month being about one fifth that of the departure taken as the initial one. This persistence certainly seems singular, and it may be that had the correlation period been extended, periodicity would have been brought out.

As a further illustration of the method, without expecting to reach definitive results, I have made a similar time-correlation of the general mean temperatures for each decade as given in Table XI, preceding. The correlation-products were carried through periods of four terms, or 40 days each, counting from the middle of the initial to the middle of the last term. The actual period included is 50 days between extremes. The result, summed by terms of three years, is as follows:

Years	a_0^2	a_0a_1	a_0a_2	a_0a_3	a_0a_4
1872–1874	65.1	+ 13.2	+14.1	+ 8.2	+ 4.2
1875–1877	103.7	+ 36.7	+10.5	+25.8	+11.5
1878–1880	124.7	+ 51.9	+19.0	+26.3	+33.3
1881–1883	80.6	+ 12.2	+ 0.1	− 5.6	− 5.3
1884–1886	75.1	+ 8.5	+ 0.4	+10.9	− 9.4
1887–1889	95.6	+ 29.2	+ 6.2	− 8.8	−10.3
1890–1892	55.5	+ 19.4	+11.3	+10.4	+ 7.3
1893–1895	68.6	+ 25.7	+16.4	+13.6	+12.2
1896–1898	53.4	+ 18.5	+11.4	+16.8	+ 7.7
1899–1901	66.7	+ 25.8	+ 0.1	+ 1.7	+10.1
1902–1904	64.4	+ 12.3	− 0.5	− 2.9	+ 2.2
Sum	854.0	+253.4	+89.3	+96.4	+63.5
ε_i		0.296	0.105	0.113	0.074

A general tendency is here shown in the departures of temperature to continue in the same direction for a period of at least 50 days. The time required for them to disappear entirely can be determined only by continuing the products through a longer period, which requires little more than a work of routine computation.

What is striking in the present case is the small increase of the fourth sum, following the rapid diminution of the first three sums. This is what we should expect from temporary inequalities in the temperature of the two solar photospheres. If this is really the case we may estimate the change in question as affecting terrestrial temperatures by two- or three-hundredths of a degree. A more exhaustive inquiry nto this question certainly seems of scientific interest, but I must, as with the continuation of the present work generally, leave this in other hands. The main point reached is that the influence of any such inequality in the sun upon meteorological phenomena is so nearly evanescent that it can be brought out only by the most refined methods of investigation, and cannot be of practical import.

CHAPTER VII.

Discussion of Results.

§ 16. *Summary of Conclusions.*

The general results of the preceding discussion, so far as concerns fluctuations in the sun's radiant energy, may be summed up in the following propositions.

1. A study of the annual departures of temperature over many regions of the globe in equatorial and middle latitudes shows consistently a fluctuation corresponding in period with that of the solar spots. The maximum fluctuation in the general average is 0°.13 C. on each side of the mean for the tropical regions. The entire amplitude of the change is therefore 0°.26 C., or somewhat less than half a degree of the Fahrenheit scale. As this fluctuation has ample time to produce its entire effect on the earth, we conclude from it that the corresponding fluctuation in the sun's radiation is 0.2 of one per cent. on each side of the mean.

2. Additional to this periodic fluctuation there is some rather inconclusive evidence of changes requiring generally about six years to go through their period, which can be most plausibly attributed to corresponding changes in the sun's radiation. The phenomena may be expressed in the briefest way by saying that, during the years 1871–1901, there seem to have been periods of two, three or four years warmer than the normal, followed by similar periods which were cooler than the normal. But although the general tendency is toward changes in this period of about six years, they show no such correspondence with the solar spots as justified their being attributed to the sun-spot period. Moreover, they do not appear in any marked way before 1871. The average departure from the mean being less than 0°.10 C. prevents a more exact statement of their law, and still leaves open the question whether they are real. This can be settled only by a more complete discussion of meteorological data than the writer has attempted to make.

3. Apart from this regular fluctuation with the solar spots, and this possible more or less irregular fluctuation in a period of a few years, *the sun's radiation is subject to*

no change sufficient to produce any measurable effect upon terrestrial temperatures. The only admissible changes are such as going through their period in 10 days or less, would produce no effect upon 10-day mean departures. Whether any such fluctuations exist, except those arising from the irregular changes of the spots and faculæ, is a question to be judged by the probabilities of the case.

4. There is a certain suspicion, but no conclusive evidence, of a tendency in the terrestrial temperature to fluctuate in a period corresponding to that of the sun's synodic rotation. If the fluctuations are real they affect our temperatures only a small fraction of one tenth of a degree.

5. To facilitate the criticism of the preceding conclusions, and their comparison with those reached by other investigators, we must point out what may be considered a limitation upon their scope. A careful study of the statistical method developed in § 4 will show that the primary intention is not to determine specific fluctuations, and attribute them to changes in the sun's thermal radiation, but only to find a general criterion for determining whether, as a general rule, the fluctuations have any other cause than the accumulation of accidental vicissitudes of temperature in the regions studied. Repeating once more in a condensed form the fundamental principle itself: when we determine the mean temperature of the globe by comparing the actual with the normal temperature at a great number of places through a number of time-terms, — we may determine the general world fluctuation by taking the mean of the departures in the separate regions during this term. This world-departure will have a certain probable deviation, arising from the probable deviations of the individual departures, the magnitude of which is easily computed.

If the world-departures are in general markedly greater than this probable deviation, we should have no difficulty in concluding that at the times of the greater departures the solar radiation was probably greater or less than the normal. Now the statistical method here applied is not intended to solve this easy problem should it arise (which it does not), but the more difficult one which arises when the actual departures do not ordinarily exceed their probable value, and when therefore we must be in doubt as to their arising from a cosmical cause. No sound method of research will enable us to formulate a conclusion on insufficient data, and the logically best method is that which will enable us to formulate all the conclusions that can be drawn. In the present case this is shown to be the probable value, during each time-term, of the square of a certain quantity τ_0 expressive of the increment of the solar radiation during that term. This quantity will have its probable accidental error, and therefore, if its objectively true value is evanescent, may still come out with a certain value, which is then as likely to be negative as positive. Having found this value through all the various terms, if the total sum comes out with a positive value markedly exceeding its probable value, we may infer with a corresponding degree of probability that some at least of the departures are real. If the excess is not great, then what we should conclude is that there is a greater or less probability, in a general way, that the sun's radiation is variable, but not that it had a definite variation at a definite time. To draw the latter conclusion from the data would be fallacious, not from any defect in the method but from the very nature of the case. But, if the well marked excess were a general rule, then we could fairly infer that, as a general rule, the fluctuations of temperature indicated corresponding fluctuations in the solar energy. For example, referring to the column r in Table VI, which shows the residual departure of the annual temperatures after eliminating the effect of the sun-spot period, we may say that the temperature appears to have been above the normal in 1871, again in the years 1881–83 and again in 1896–97. It seems to have been below the normal in 1874–84, 1887 and 1892, and 1893.

Although these fluctuations, even if real, are so small that we cannot expect to trace them in any other meteorological phenomena than the temperature, the question of their reality is of scientific interest. This can be determined only by more extended researches.

To state the limitation in a more condensed form, the proof of general invariability does not positively establish the negative proposition that the sun's heat has never, on any one occasion whatever, undergone a perturbation during the period covered by our researches. In the absence of better positive evidence than is yet available, the assumption of such a perturbation would be a purely gratuitous one, to be refuted by a consideration of its improbability rather than by positive evidence.

§ 17. *Relation Between the Solar Radiation and Meteorological Processes.*

The preceding studies being primarily of fluctuations in the temperature of the air at the earth's surface, the question arises how far, from the steadiness of temperature we have established, we are justified in affirming that the sun's thermal radiation is steady in a corresponding degree. The consideration of this question will be facilitated by calling to mind certain points bearing upon it. A general proposition which, the writer conceives, needs no enforcement, is that so far as our science can show, the earth receives an appreciable supply of heat only from the sun. We may safely assume that the minute amount of heat reaching the earth's surface from the stars or other bodies in the celestial spaces, or by conduction from the earth's interior, is too minute to materially affect the temperature around us. This temperature is determined in a general way by the condition that it is such that the earth shall radiate into space as much heat as it absorbs from the sun's rays.

The radiations which reach the earth or its atmosphere from the sun are of two great classes. We have first *radiance* properly so called by which I understand radiant energy in its ordinary acceptation. This includes not only the rays commonly called *light*, but all other rays of the same class which differ from light only in wave length. It may here be remarked, parenthetically, that the use of the word "light" in physics is rather unfortunate, since the distinction of light and dark rays is not an objective one, but rests only upon the property of affecting the optic nerve. Thus, when we use the word light, we have one word for radiance between certain limits of wave length and no special term for radiance of the same kind of wave length without the visible limits.

Besides radiance as thus defined, we have abundant evidence that the sun sends, at least to the confines of our atmosphere, certain emanations which affect the magnetic needle, and which do not reach us in a steady stream, but fitfully, at irregular intervals. These emanations have, up to the present time, eluded all direct investigation. They are made known only by their effect upon the terrestrial magnetic force, as shown by magnetic storms. It therefore seems probable that those which reach the atmosphere are entirely absorbed in its outer envelopes.

The preceding study is practically limited to radiations of the first class. It is still questionable whether the magnetic or radio-active emanations, whatever they may be, appreciably affect the temperature. The recent researches of Maunder seem to show that they come mainly from the solar spots. Now, it is known that the radiance from the spots is less than from the rest of the photosphere. It follows that, if the emanations in question convey an appreciable amount of thermal energy, it does not reach the earth, but is absorbed in the upper regions of the air, perhaps almost at the surface of the atmosphere itself. But, were this the case, the extreme rarity of the air at high altitudes would result in a proportionately greater rise of temperature through a given radiation of thermal energy. In a word it seems highly improbable that emanations having radiant energy in considerable quantities could be absorbed by so rare a medium as the air at great heights above the earth.

The evidence afforded by the frequency of magnetic storms shows that the emanations in question are greatest at the period of sunspot minimum when the terrestrial temperature is least. This affords an additional ground for believing that the thermal effect of the magnetic radiation is too small to produce any directly observable meteorological effect.

So far as research has yet gone, the balance of evidence would seem to favor the view that the phenomena of atmospheric electricity, especially of thunder storms, so far as they are changeable, arise mainly from terrestrial causes, and are but slightly influenced by solar emanations. Still, the question whether there is any relation between magnetic storms, which afford us the best available evidence of the emanations in question, and thunder storms or other exhibitions of movements of atmospheric electricity, is an interesting one, well worthy of investigation by rigorous statistical methods, and offering no difficulty. The main point to be enforced in the present connection is that our investigation includes the effect of all cosmical causes affecting the terrestrial temperature, and therefore of the emanations in question so far as they produce any thermal effect.

Dropping the consideration of magnetic, electric or radio-active emanations as belonging to another branch of the subject, because they do not cause appreciable fluctuation in terrestrial temperatures, we return to the main question now under consideration — that of the relation between fluctuations in the sun's thermal radiation and the corresponding changes in temperature. Accepting the fourth-power law of radiation, fluctuations in the general temperature of the globe of 0°.2 C. on each side of the mean would produce corresponding changes of 0.3 of one per cent. in the radiation of heat by the earth into space. We have found that the fluctuations of world-temperature, if any at all occur, which is doubtful, do not exceed ± 0°.20 C. We may therefore assign three tenths of one per cent. as the ordinary limit of fluctuation of the sun's radiation in lower periods. But the lag of temperature behind insolation is to be considered in the case of short periods.

Speaking in a general way, it is an observed fact that the maxima and minima of temperature in the temperate regions do not occur until about a month after the maxima and minima of radiation. But, admitting that a month will be required to produce the completed effect through the entire atmosphere and on the surface of the ground and ocean, it does not follow that the effect would be negligible in a shorter period. It is also an observed fact in regions of middle latitude that the rays of the sun between its rising and 2 p. m. elevate the temperature of the air at the earth's surface as read by the thermometer, by an amount ranging from 8° to 10° C. every day. Now, to fix the ideas, suppose that the sun's thermal radiance were increased by one per cent. of its whole amount through ten consecutive days. The result would be that the daily rise would be increased by an amount between 0°.06 and 0°.10. This rise would be in part lost during the night by increased radiation and transmission to the earth and upper air. But, as the earth and air grew warmer day after day the loss would be smaller and smaller, while the gain would continually accumulate. It follows that we should not have to wait more than a week for the change of one per cent. in the sun's energy to produce an effect exceeding that which our study of temperatures shows can be actually found in the world-temperature. But this does not preclude the possibility of much larger fluctuations in shorter periods, because it would take time for temporary increase in the sun's radiation to produce its full effect. The shorter the time that we suppose an increase or decrease to last, the greater it must be. It is mainly a question of judgment and probabilities whether changes of such very short period in the radiation can exist. The probabilities against them are based mainly on the fact that it is scarcely conceivable that any cause affecting the totality of the sun's radiation should act simultaneously over the entire photosphere. The most plausible cause of such fluctuations would be looked for in the faculæ and spots. These, and the phenomena connected with them are mainly local, never covering any important fraction of the sun's disc.

A yet more plausible source of change is found in possible fluctuations in the transparency of the solar envelopes. But these would take a long time to extend themselves over the entire photosphere. By allowing them a period of several weeks to spread over the sun, we bring them within the range of the present studies which then seem to establish their non-existence, except within the limits already several times mentioned.

A collateral question which is not included in the present research is whether the conclusions which have been drawn as to the constancy of the sun's radiation can be applied to other meteorological changes than those of temperature. The writer conceives that fluctuations of temperature are the primary cause of changes in precipitation, rainfall or great movements of the air, and fluctuations of the barometer. Confining ourselves within the limit of reasonable probability, the totality of rainfall must in the long run balance the evaporation. The rate of evaporation is, so far as is known, not influenced by electrical or magnetic conditions of any kind, but dependent solely upon the temperature and physical condition of the evaporating surface, and the temperature and motion of the air in contact with it. If the motions of the air are not affected by changes in the sun's radiation it would therefore follow that the rate of evaporation is determined solely by terrestrial conditions. This being granted it follows also that the total rainfall is determined in the same way. The total mass of the atmosphere being a constant, the integrated barometric pressure through the whole globe must also be a constant. Fluctuations in its amount in any region must therefore be balanced by opposite fluctuations in other regions and must be due to motions of the air which are determined only by conditions of temperature. If these views are correct it follows as the final result of the present investigation that *all the ordinary phenomena of temperature, rainfall and winds are due to purely terrestrial causes and that no changes occur in the sun's radiation which have any influence upon them.*

§ 18. *Comparison with Results of Langley's Work of 1903.*

Although the writer deems it appropriate for the most part to leave the farther discussion of his results, and their comparison with the views of others, to other investigators, an exception may well be made in the case of the very suggestive paper of Langley.[a] It should be premised that Langley does not present his results as conclusive, but only as showing seeming correlations between temperatures and bolometric measurements of the sun's radiation, the results of which should be tested by further researches. He gives the following general summary of his conclusions :

"A series of determinations of the solar radiation outside the atmosphere (the solar constant), extending from October, 1902, to March, 1904, has been made at the Smithsonian Astrophysical Observatory under the writer's direction.

"Care has been exercised to determine all known sources of error which could seriously affect the values relatively to each other, and principally the varying absorption of the Earth's atmosphere. Though uncertainty must ever remain as to the absorption of this atmosphere, different kinds of evidence agree in supporting the accuracy of the estimates made of it and of the conclusions deducted from them.

"The effects due to this absorption having been allowed for, the inference from these observations appears to be that the solar radiation itself fell off by about 10 per cent., beginning at the close of March, 1903. I do not assert this without qualification, but if such a change in solar radiation did actually occur, a decrease of temperature on the Earth, which might be indefinitely less than 7°.5 C., ought to have followed it."

The present writer understands that not only Langley's work with the bolometer, but observations by actinometric methods showed a remarkable diminution of the solar radiation, extending from some time in 1902 through a considerable portion of 1903. But as such observations are made only on the radiation which reaches the earth's surface the results still leave open the question whether the change was in the sun itself or was caused by increased absorption in the earth's atmosphere. The apparent diminution during the period in question has been plausibly attributed to the absorbing matter thrown up by the eruption of Mount Pelée on May 8, 1902. If the diminution of radiation was only apparent, being due to the absorption, we cannot, in the present state of science, decide whether there would be any effect upon terrestrial temperatures. While less heat would reach the earth directly, more would be absorbed in the middle regions of the atmosphere ; and this would apply both to the absorption of the sun's rays and of the heat radiated from the solid earth. The vapors of Mount Pelée, if they had any influence whatever, might, so far as we know,

[a] "On a Possible Variation of the Solar Radiation and Its Probable Effect on Terrestrial Temperatures," *Astrophysical Journal*, June, 1904.

have resulted in either a rise or a fall of the temperature of the earth in general. Hence even if we accept as unquestionable the correctness of the bolometric measures, it does not follow that there would be any corresponding change in the terrestrial temperature.

But Langley has brought forth what seems to be very strong evidence of a correlation between the temperatures in widely separated regions of the globe, using a method identical in principle with that of the present work, but including only the year 1903. His material was derived from the *Dekadenberichte* of the *Deutsche Seewarte* which gives ten-day temperatures in a great number of regions in various parts of the globe. The latter was divided by Langley into seven great regions and the mean departure found in each, on the same general plan that has been followed in the present work. The fluctuations in the seven regions were expressed in the usual way by curves, from a study of which the conclusion that there was a marked synchronism between the curves of temperature *inter se* seems quite plausible. The bolometric measures suffered so many interruptions that the curve representing them is frequently doubtful but, so far as it can be compared, there seems to be some correspondence between it and the temperature curves. Yet, the method of eye estimates through curves is one in which there is too much room for bias, and which does not admit of sufficient precision of determination. The correlation thus exhibited is quite at variance with the general conclusions of the present work, though these would not preclude the possibility of a marked chance correlation through any one year. But even for the special year 1903, it will be seen that the criterion of correlation is only

$$\Delta = 78 - 69 = 9$$

which does not rise above the expected result of chance accumulation of accidental deviations.

In view of the fact that, in the present work, the year 1903 does not show any well-marked correlation among ten-day temperatures, it will be of interest to trace out the cause of the seeming divergence. It would be better that this should be done by another; but some comparisons by the present writer may serve at least as suggestions on the subject.

We remark at the outset that there is no inherent necessity that the fluctuations in the seven regions selected by Langley should show any close relation with those of the three regions chosen in the present work. Such a relation can only be regarded as more or less probable according to circumstances.

The question now presents itself how far the seeming divergence arises from accidental fluctuations in the special data made use of, and how far to differences in the method of investigation. The methods of treatment are different in that the present work includes only regions of low or middle latitudes, while those chosen by Langley include northern regions also, especially Siberia. Thus a seeming discordance in the course of any one year is not surprising. I have not made a careful comparison of the two results except in the most striking case. The most important decade of comparison in the work is the first of 1903. The *Dekadenberichte* show an extraordinary rise of temperature during this term, while by reference to Table XII, 1903, of the present work, it will be found that the general mean deviation here found is only +0°.5. Considering this decade individually the evidence afforded by the *Dekadenberichte* is vastly more complete for the world at large. The positive departure was best marked in European Russia and Siberia, reaching its maximum at Orenburg, where the temperature was 12°.1 C., or more than 20° Fahr. above the normal. But it covered the whole of Europe, Scandinavia excepted. Now, these regions I have mentioned are not included in the present work because the effect of any admissible change in the sun's heat on their temperature would be very slight through a ten-day term, especially in January. Although the general mean for the equatorial region is positive, it is not at all accented as in the wider range of regions used by Langley.

For our present purpose the important question is whether we can attribute this remarkable rise of temperature to an increase of the solar radiation. The reply is that, if there was such an increase during the decade in question, its effect would have been felt mainly in the equatorial regions, and but slightly in northern Europe and Siberia. We therefore conclude only that great fluctuations of temperature occur which we cannot attribute to changes in the sun's radiation, because they do not extend to the regions where such changes would have their greatest effect.

NOTICE

Preceding volumes of the New Series can be obtained at the Hall of the Society. Price, five dollars each.

A few complete sets of the Transactions, New Series, Vols. I—XX, are on sale. Price, one hundred dollars.

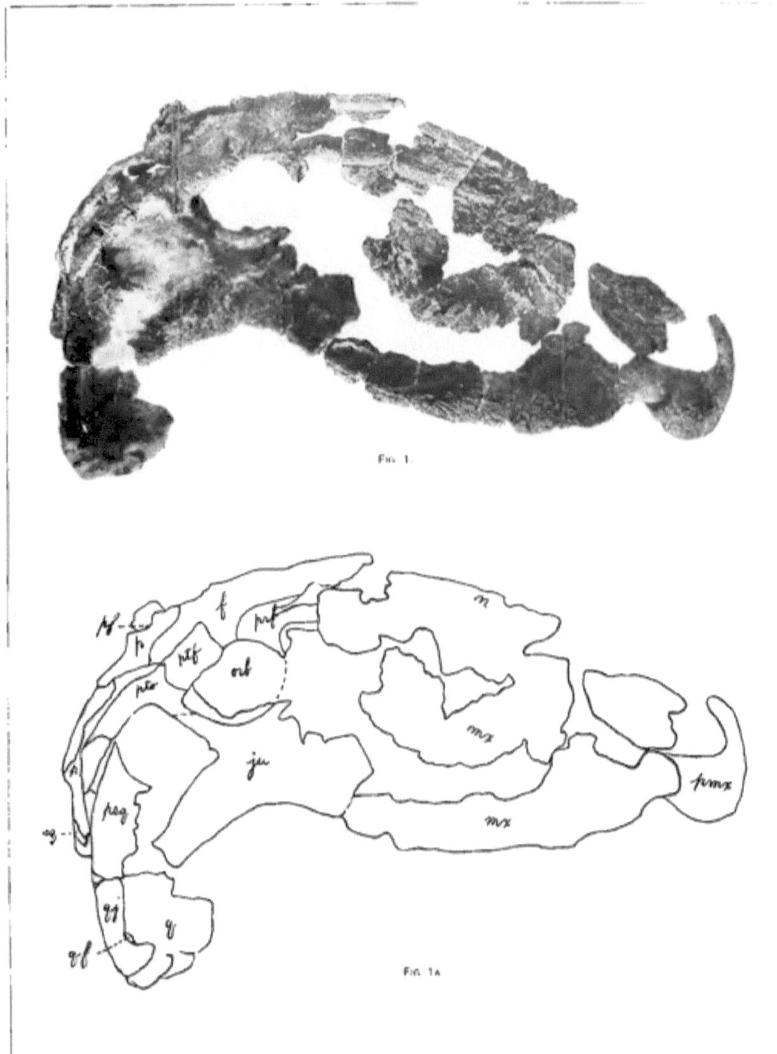

FIG. 1.

FIG. 1A

CASE.—MORPHOLOGY OF SKULL OF PELYCOSAURIAN GENUS DIMETRODON.

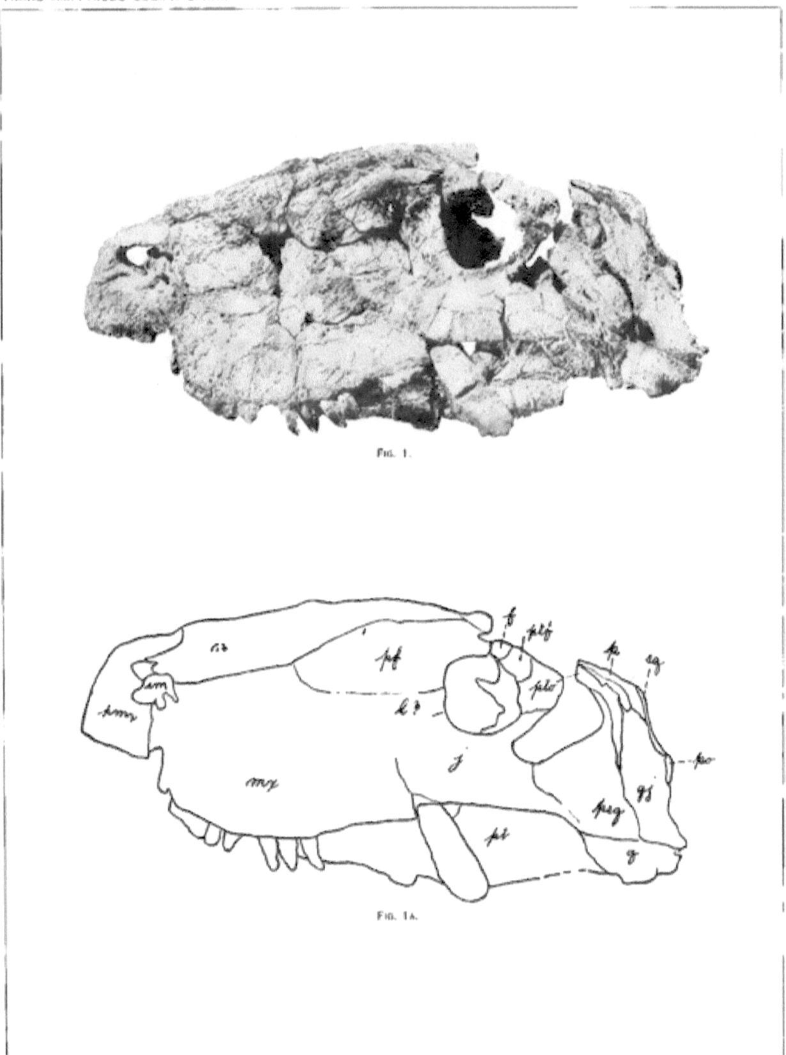

Fig. 1.

Fig. 1a.

Case. Morphology of Skull of Pelycosaurian Genus Dimetrodon.

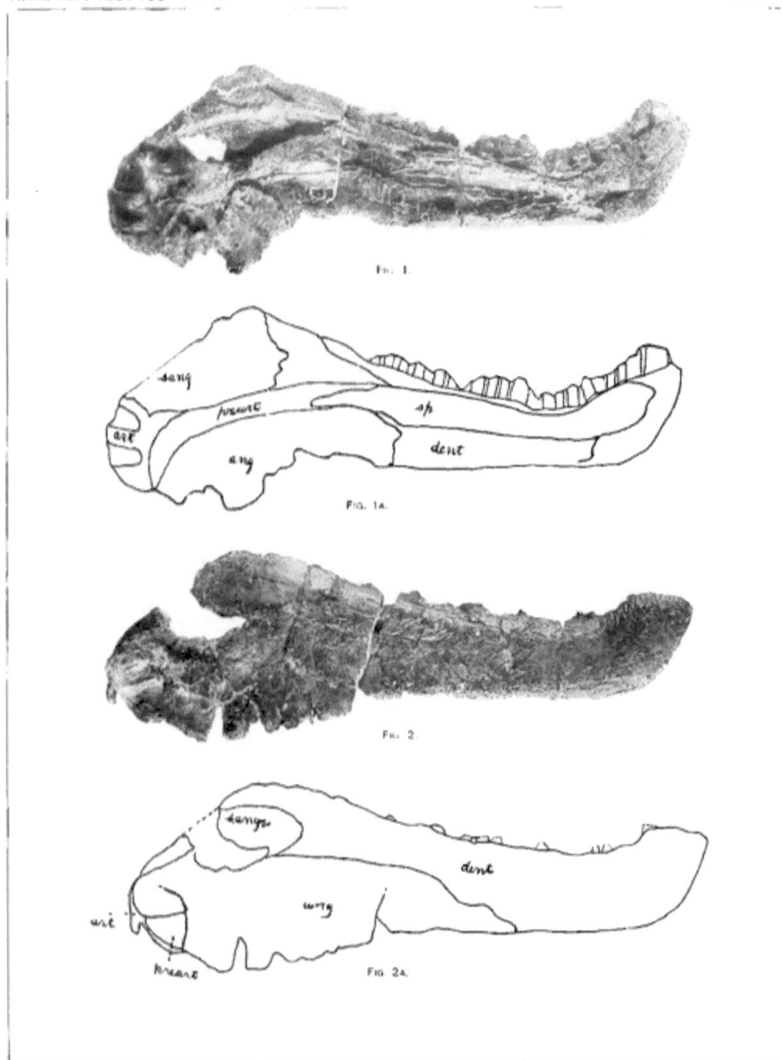

CASE: MORPHOLOGY OF SKULL OF PELYCOSAURIAN GENUS DIMETRODON.

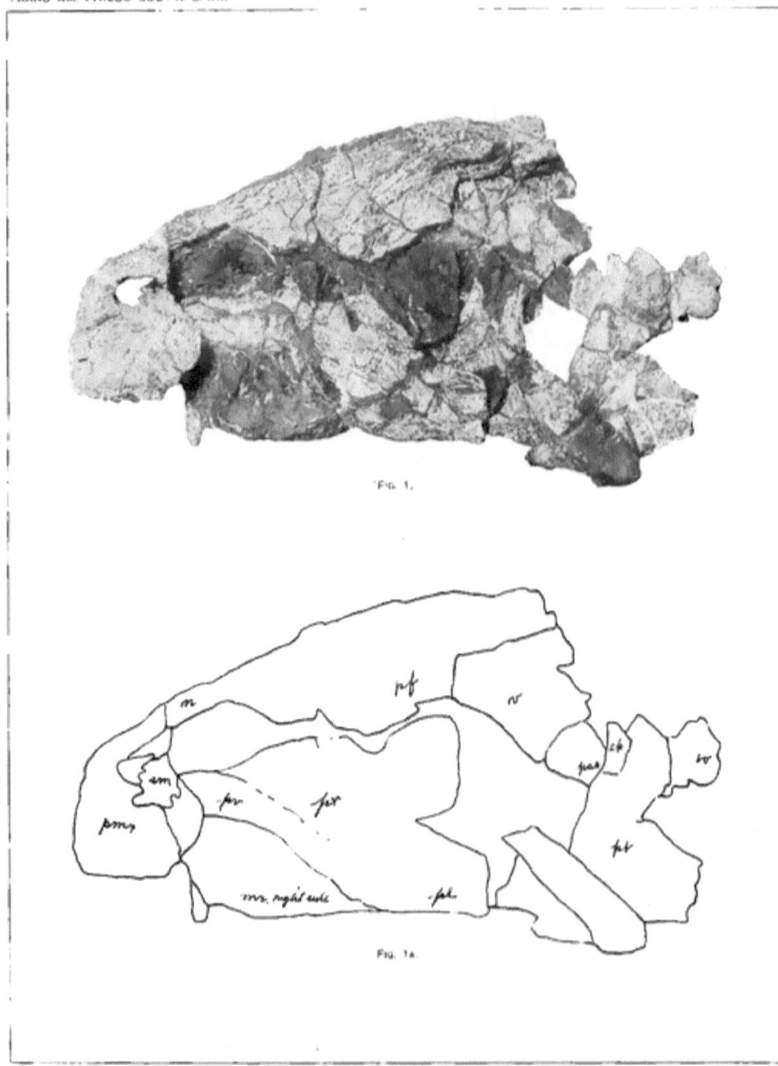

Fig. 1.

Fig. 1a.

Case. Morphology of Skull of Pelycosaurian Genus Dimetrodon.

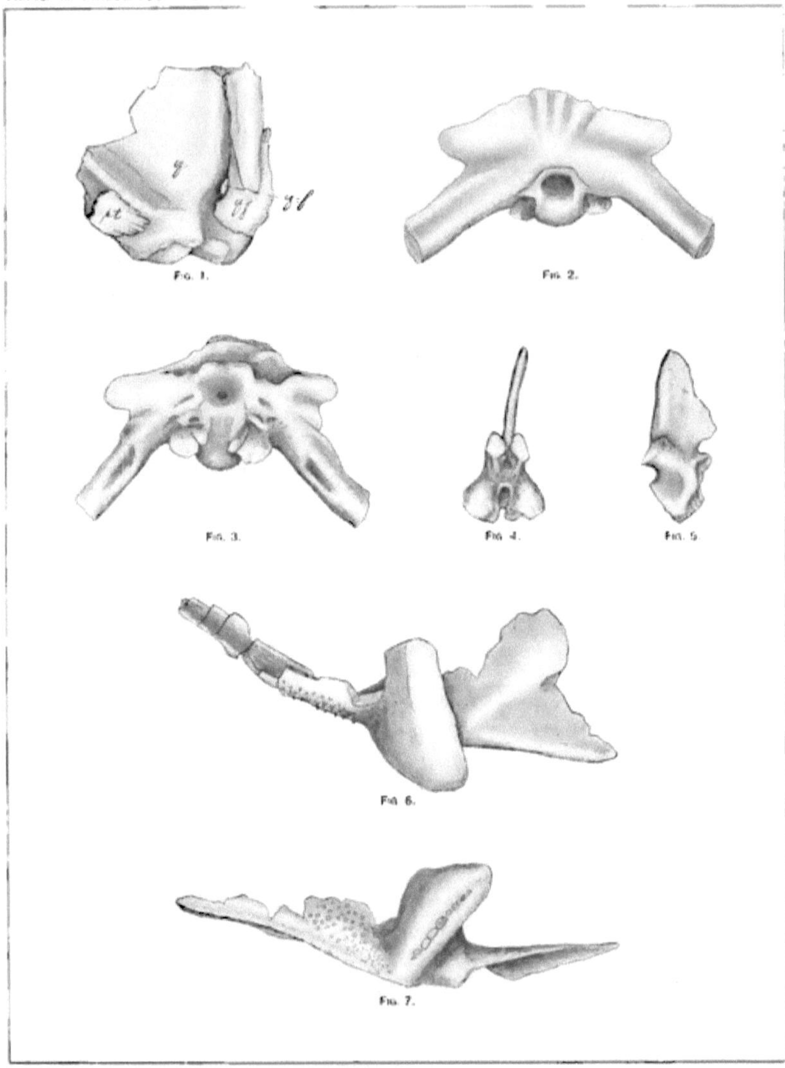

FIG. 1. FIG. 2. FIG. 3. FIG. 4. FIG. 5. FIG. 6. FIG. 7.

CASE.—MORPHOLOGY OF SKULL OF PELYCOSAURIAN GENUS DIMETRODON.

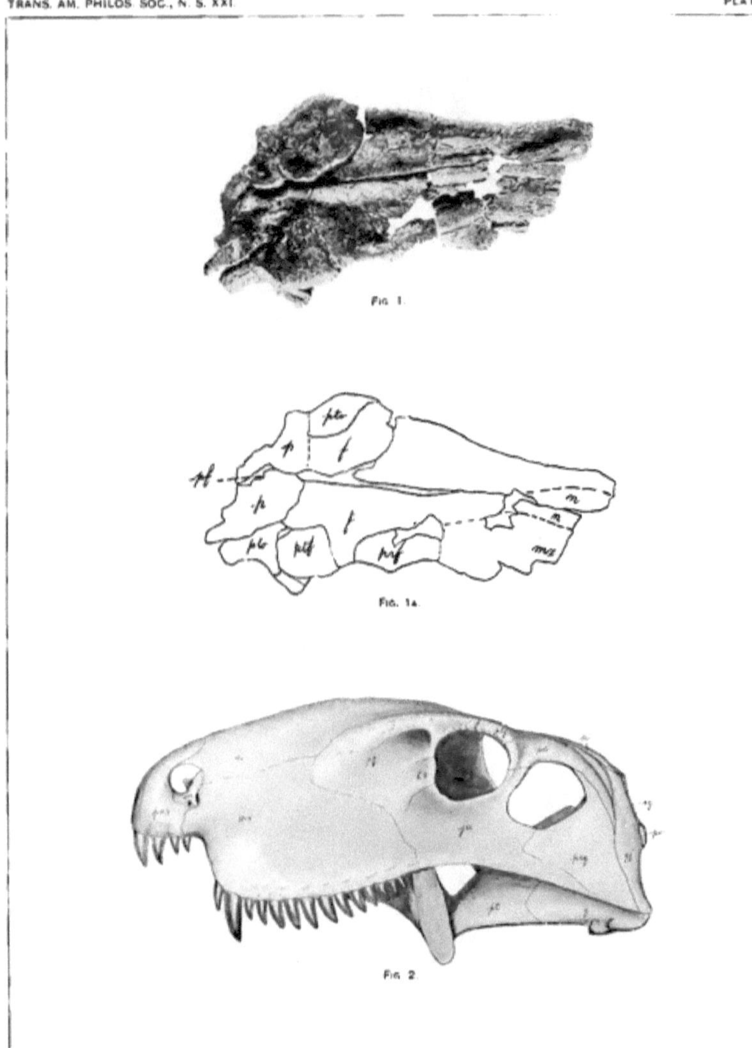

Fig. 1.

Fig. 1a.

Fig. 2.

Case. Morphology of Skull of Pelycosaurian Genus Dimetrodon.

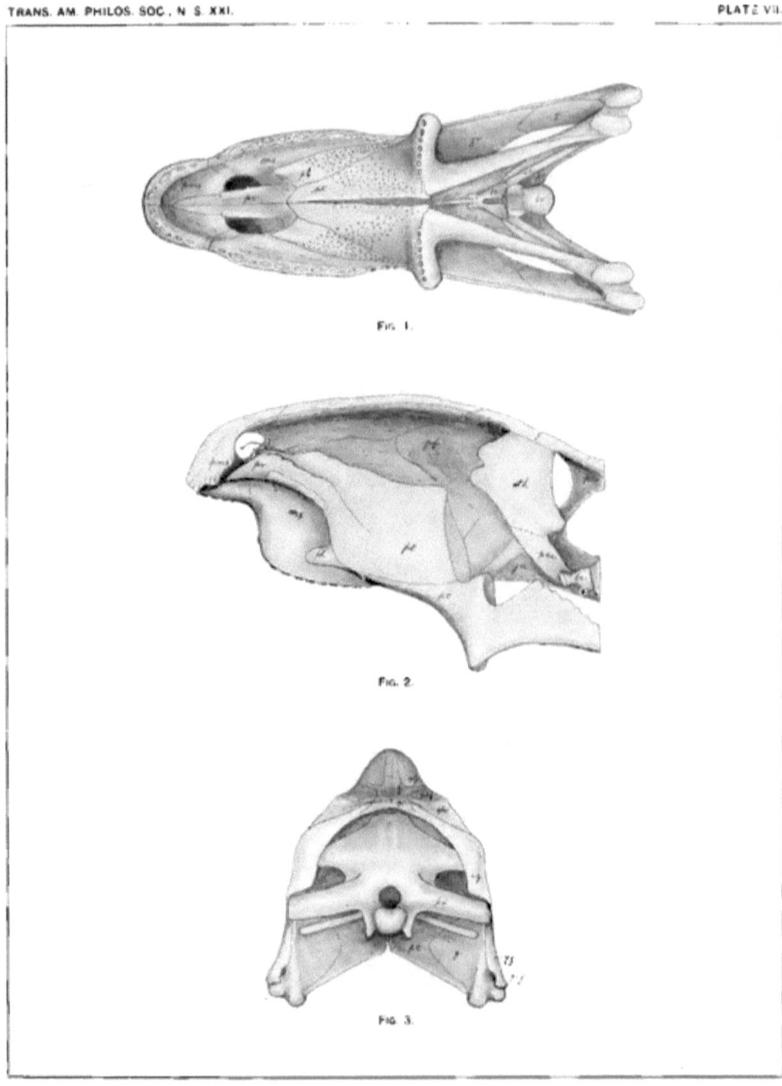

Fig. 1.

Fig. 2.

Fig. 3.

Case.—Morphology of Skull of Pelycosaurian Genus Dimetrodon.

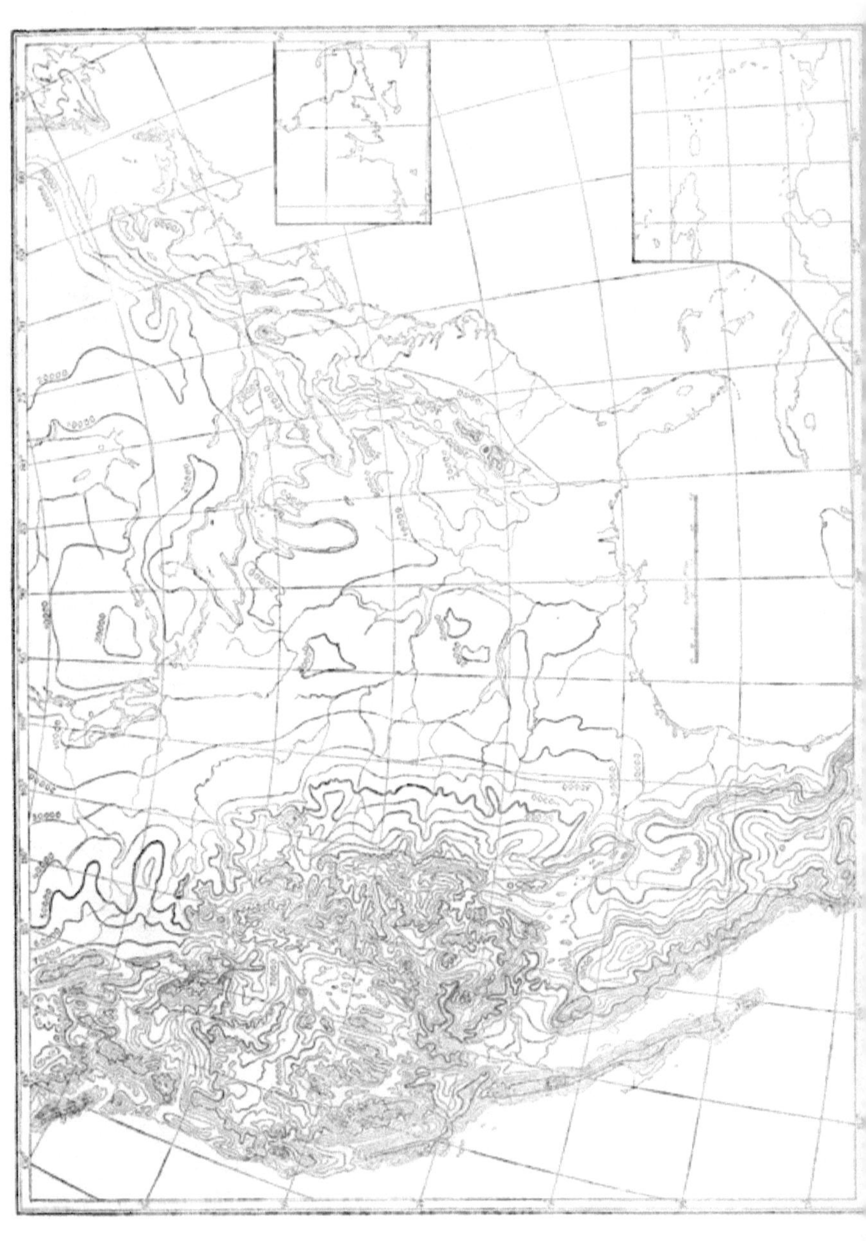

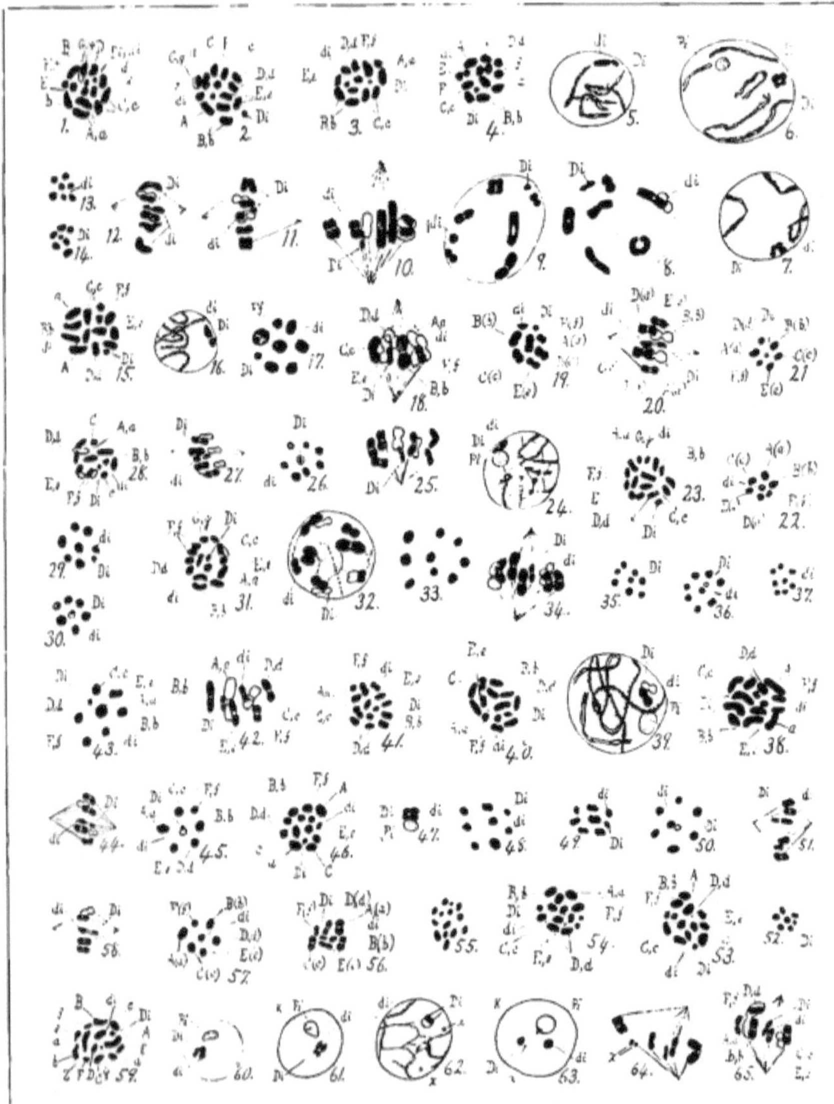

MONTGOMERY.—CHROMOSOMES IN THE SPERMATOGENESIS OF THE HEMIPTERA HETEROPTERA.

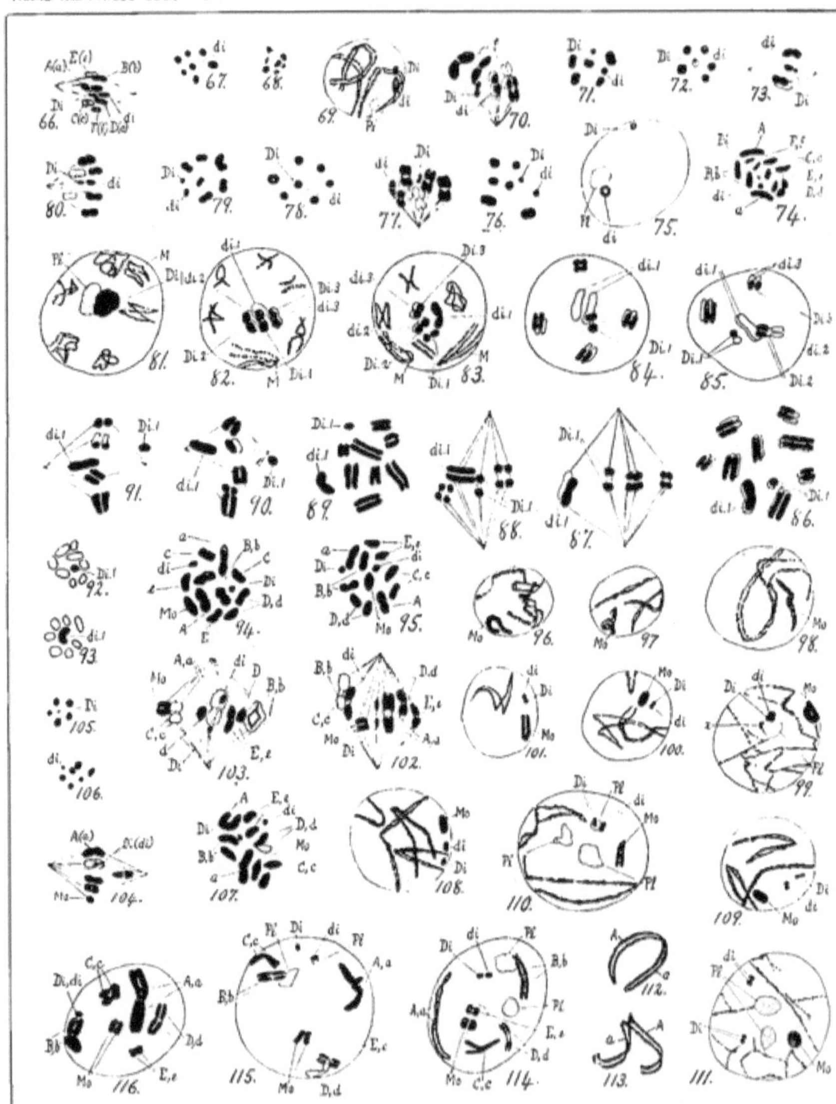

MONTGOMERY. CHROMOSOMES IN THE SPERMATOGENESIS OF THE HEMIPTERA HETEROPTERA.

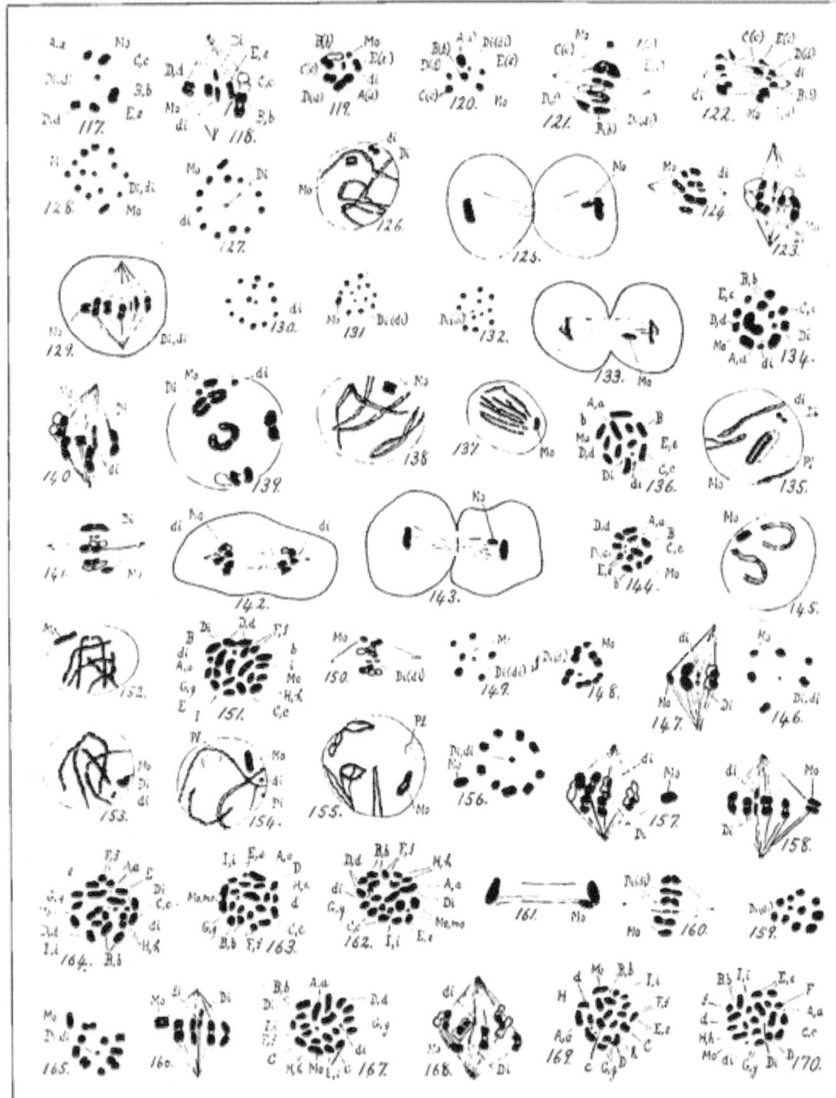

MONTGOMERY.—CHROMOSOMES IN THE SPERMATOGENESIS OF THE HEMIPTERA HETEROPTERA.

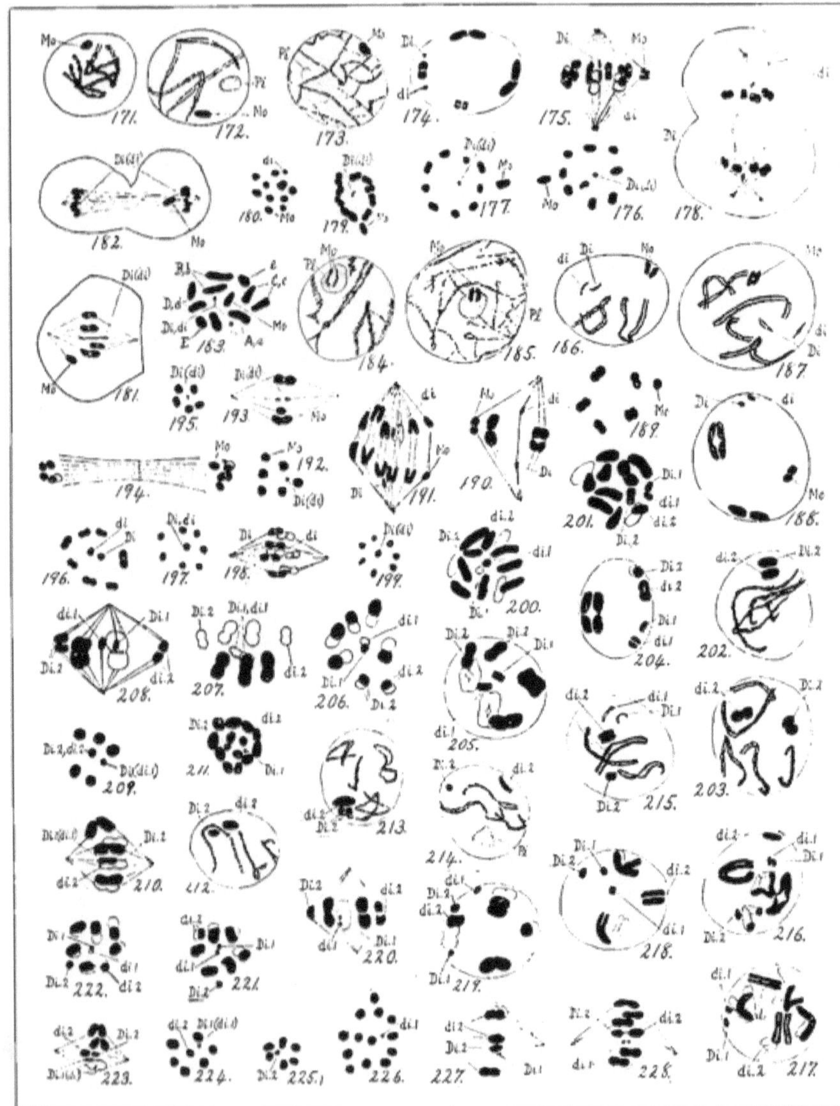

MONTGOMERY. CHROMOSOMES IN THE SPERMATOGENESIS OF THE HEMIPTERA HETEROPTERA.

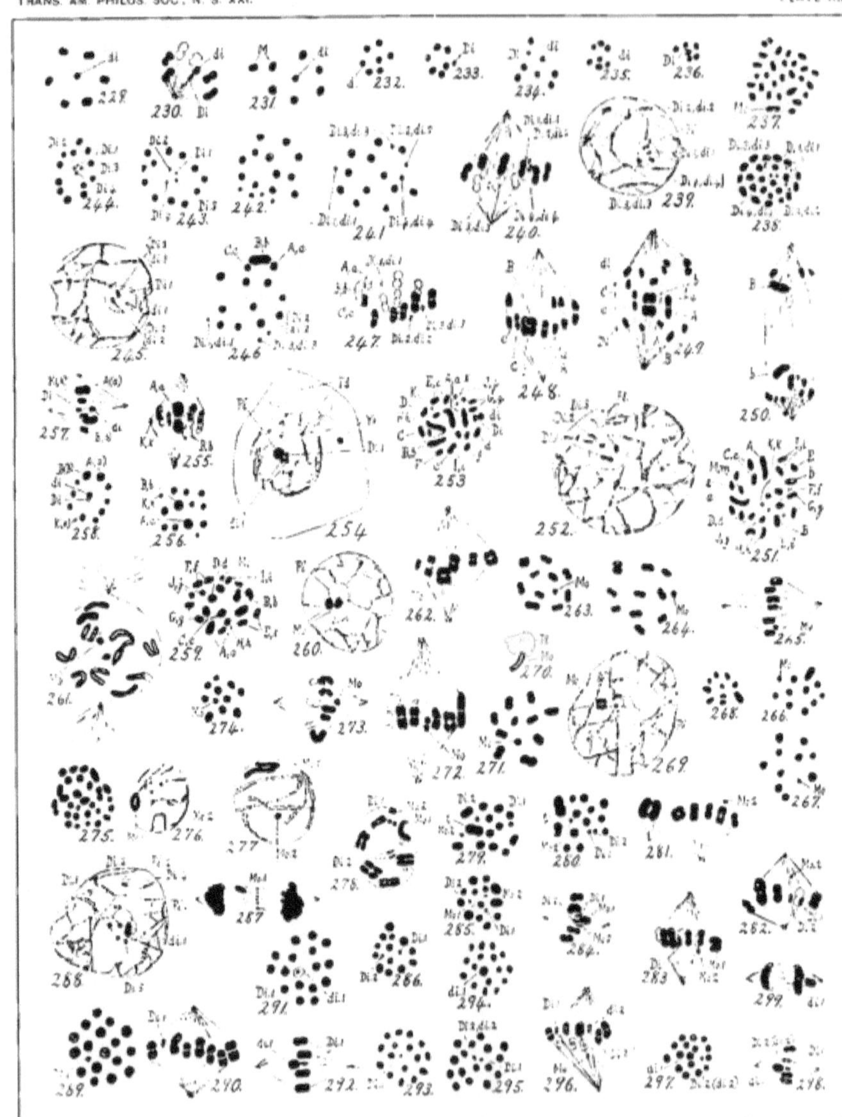

MONTGOMERY. CHROMOSOMES IN THE SPERMATOGENESIS OF THE HEMIPTERA HETEROPTERA.

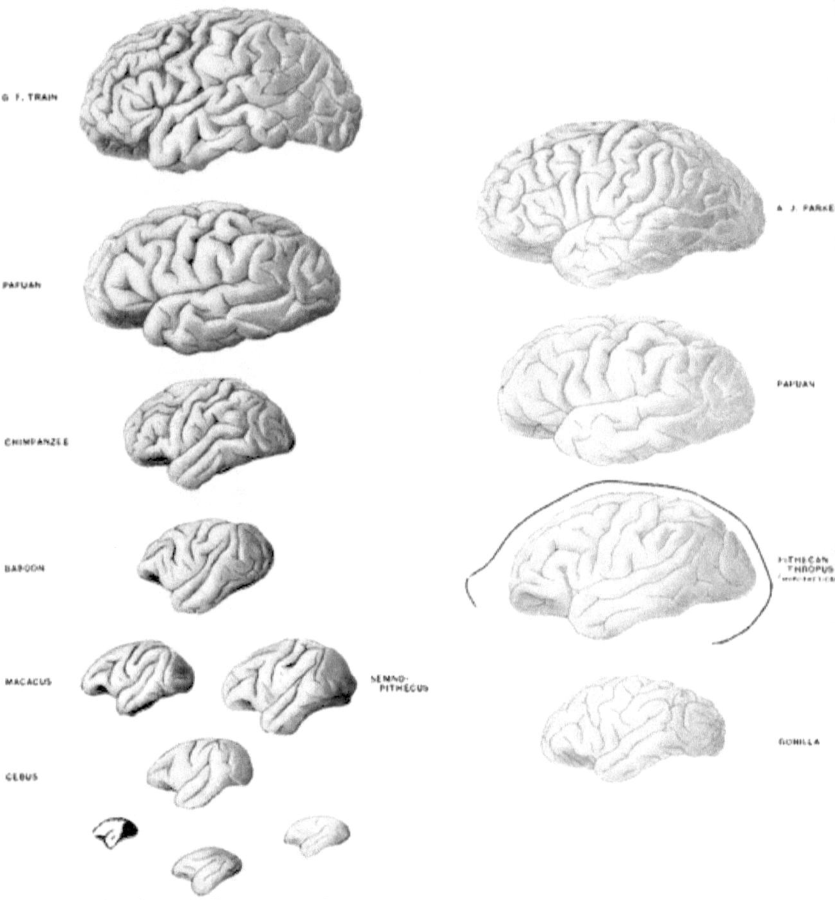

FIG. 3. Brains of Primates arranged in phyletic series.

FIG. 4. The brain of a Papuan and the hypothetical contour of brain of Pithecanthropus (drawn into the cranial outline) interposed tween the brain of a highly intellectual person and that of a gorilla.

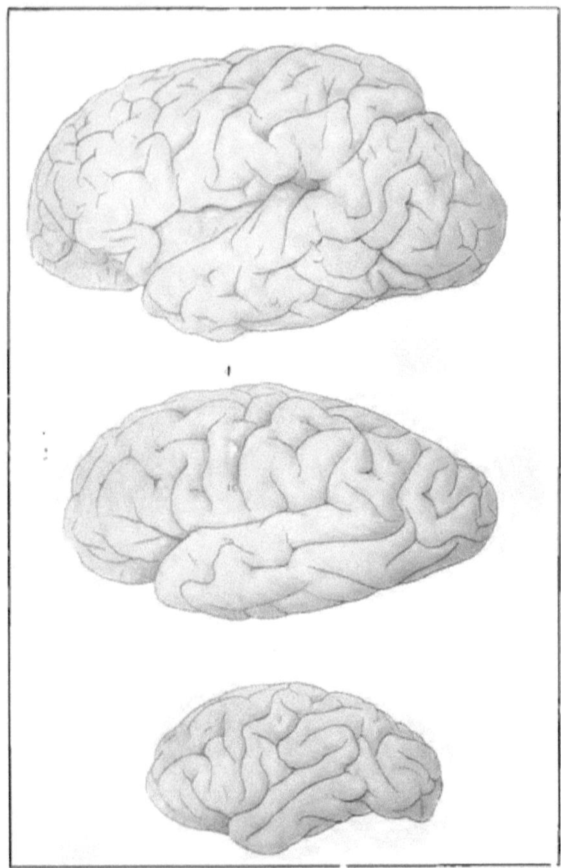

FIG. 11. 1. Brain of Helmholtz (after photo of cast by Hansemann). 2. Brain of Papuan from British New Guinea: specimen in Anatomical Laboratory at Columbia University, New York. 3. Brain of Gorilla (D. 658, Mus. Roy. Coll. Surgeons of England).

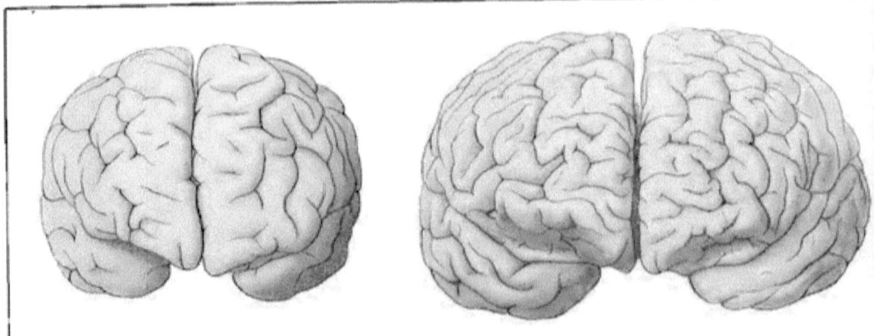

FIG. 12. 1. Frontal Aspect of the Brain of a Papuan of British New Guinea. 2. Frontal Aspect of the Brain of George Francis Train. This is in man[y] respects one of the best developed brains on record.

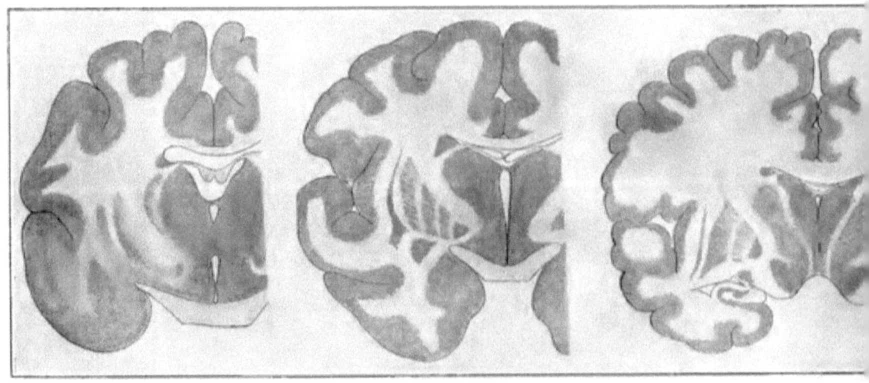

FIG. 13. Cross-sections of the brains of the cat, baboon and man taken at approximately the same plane, and drawn of about the same size to better show the relatively greater mass of white matter in the human brain.

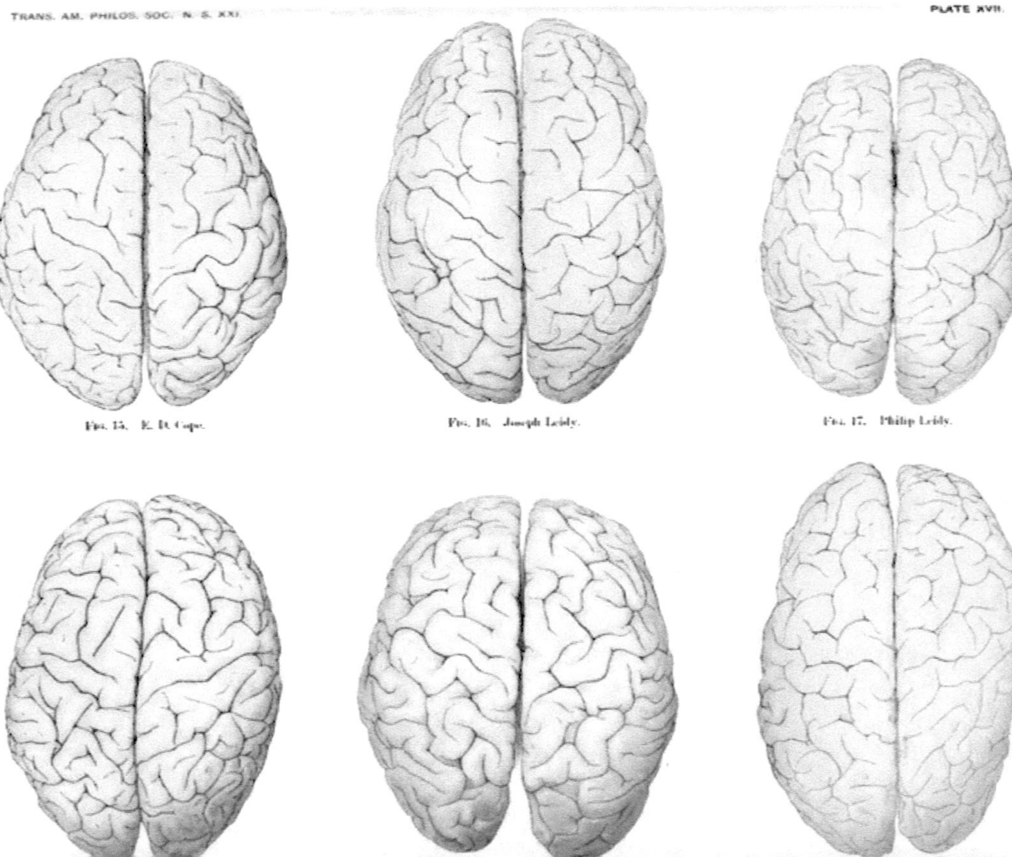

Fig. 15. E. D. Cope.

Fig. 16. Joseph Leidy.

Fig. 17. Philip Leidy.

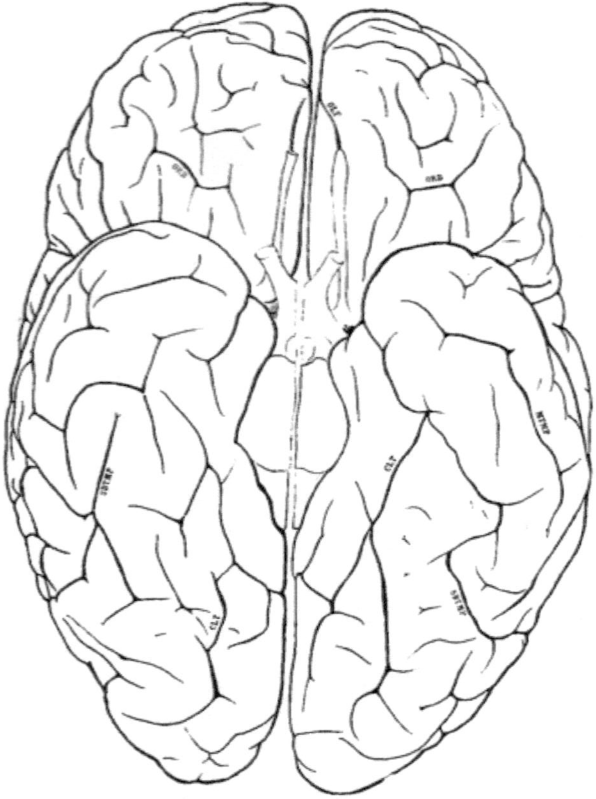

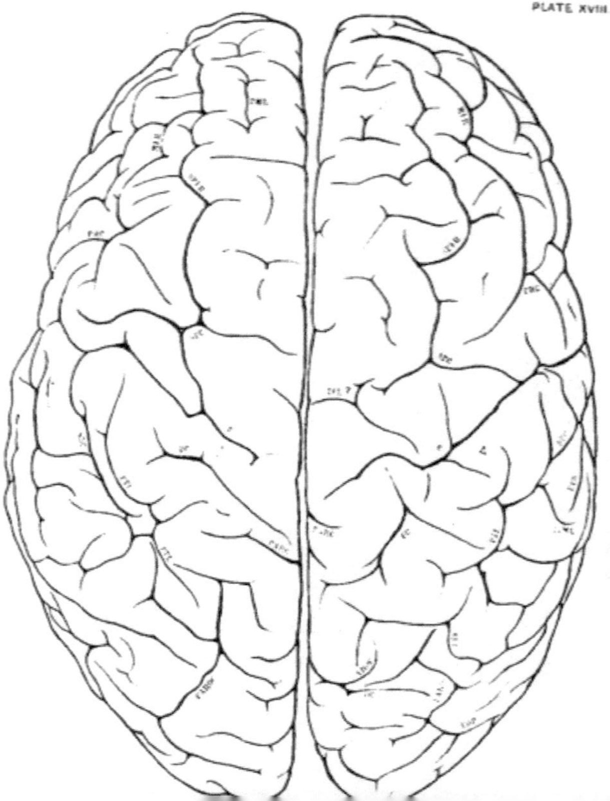

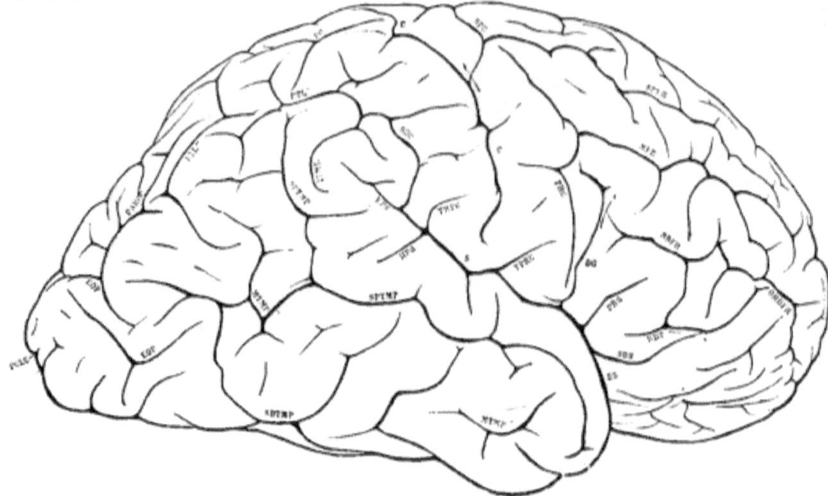

Fig. 25. Lateral aspect of right hemicerebrum.

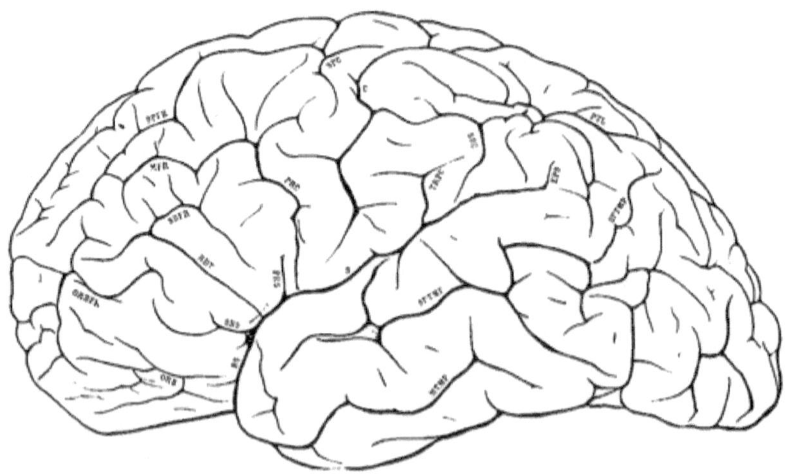

Fig. 26. Lateral aspect of left hemicerebrum.

Brain of Joseph Leidy.

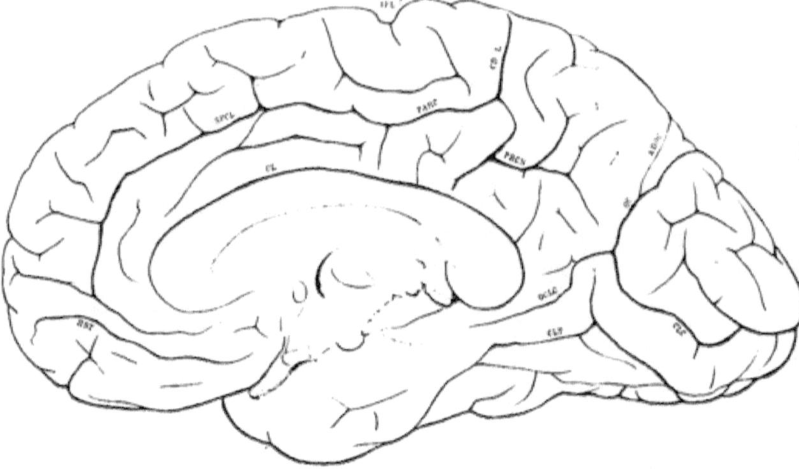

Fig. 27. Mesal aspect of right hemicerebrum.

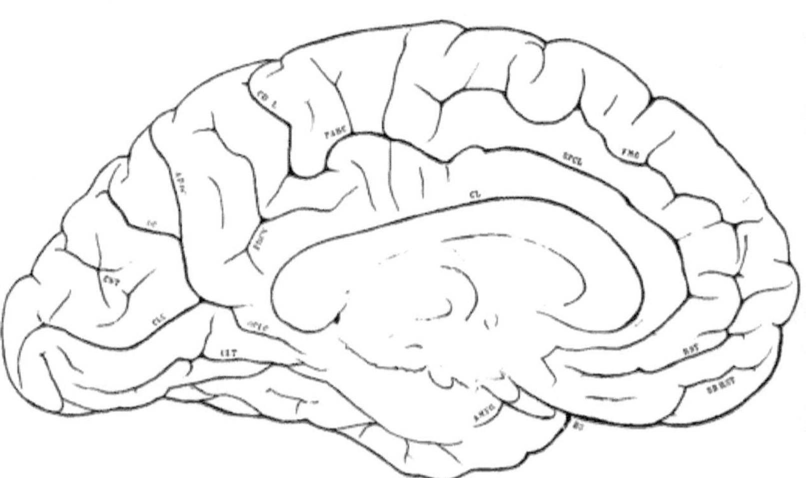

Fig. 28. Mesal aspect of left hemicerebrum.

Brain of Joseph Leidy.

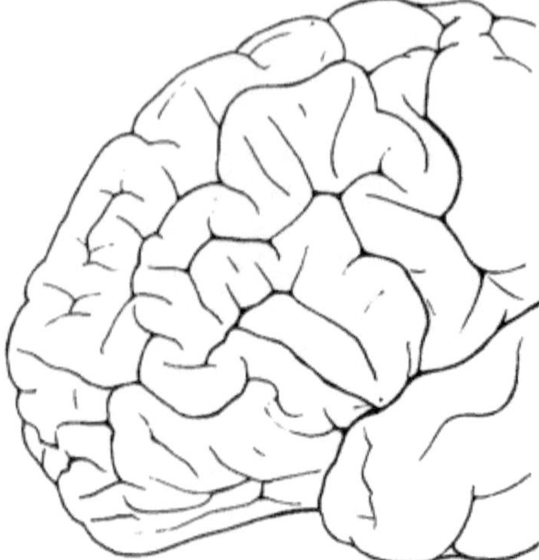

FIG. 29. Left frontal lobe, lateral aspect.

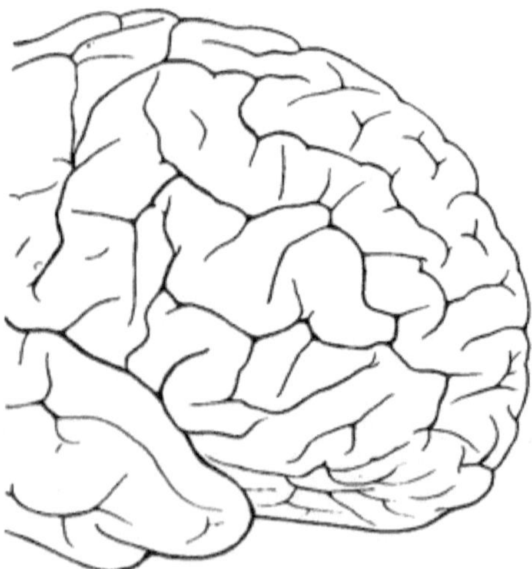

FIG. 30. Right frontal lobe, lateral aspect.

BRAIN OF JOSEPH LEIDY.

A. P. S.—XXI. EE. 2, 11, '07.

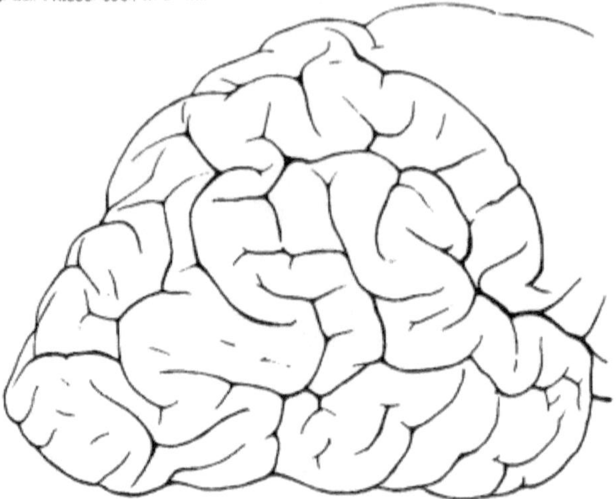

FIG. 31. Lateral aspect of the parieto-occipito-temporal lobes of the right hemicerebrum.

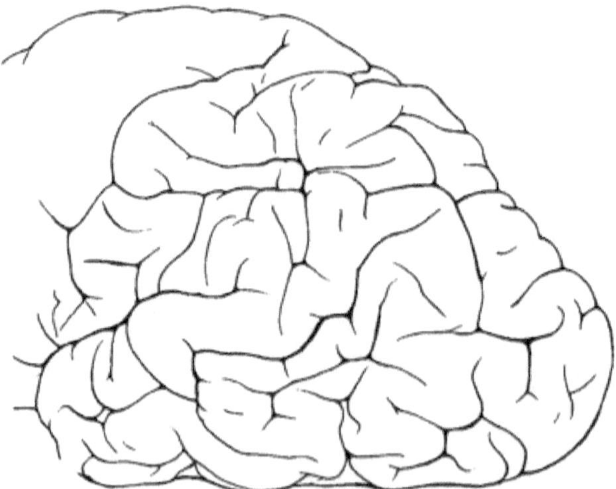

FIG. 32. Lateral aspect of the parieto-occipito-temporal lobes of the left hemicerebrum.

BRAIN OF JOSEPH LEIDY.

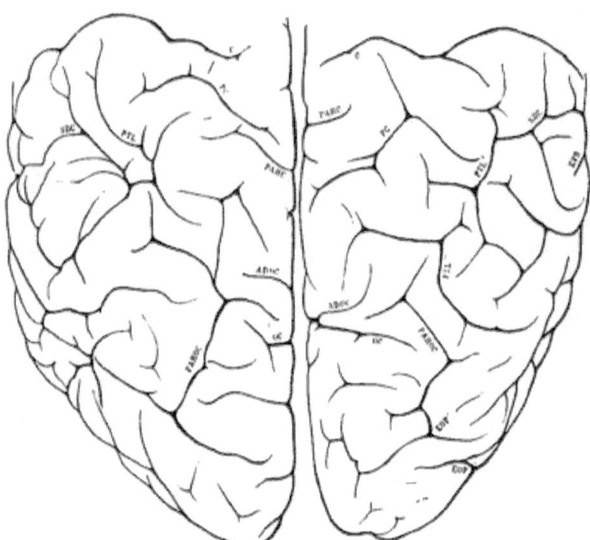

FIG. 33. Dorsocaudal view of the cerebrum.

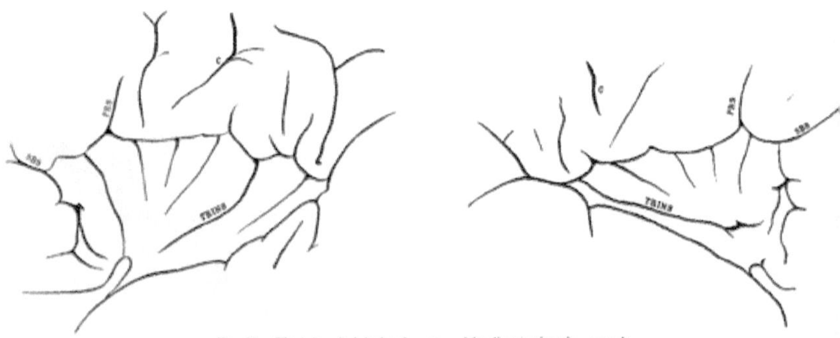

FIG. 34. The left and right insulæ, exposed by divaricating the opercula.

BRAIN OF JOSEPH LEIDY.

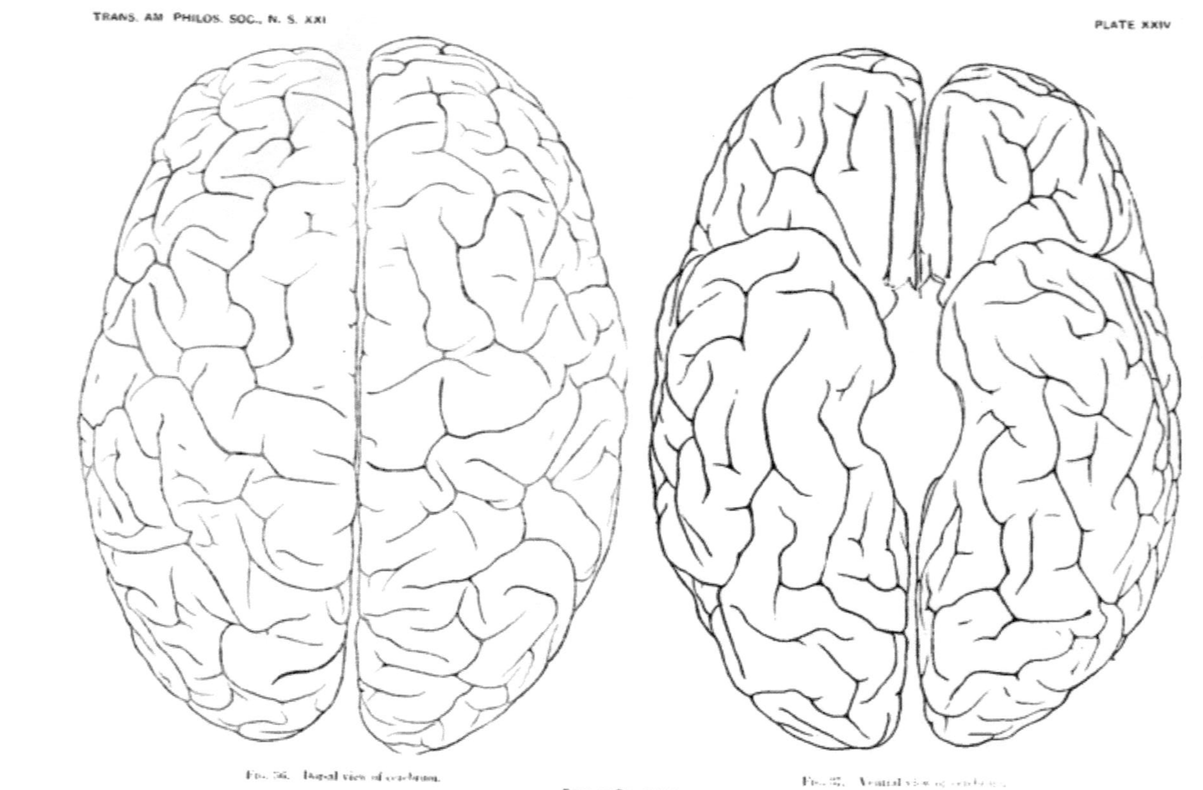

Fig. 56. Dorsal view of cerebrum.

Fig. 57. Ventral view of cerebrum.

Brain of Philip Leidy.

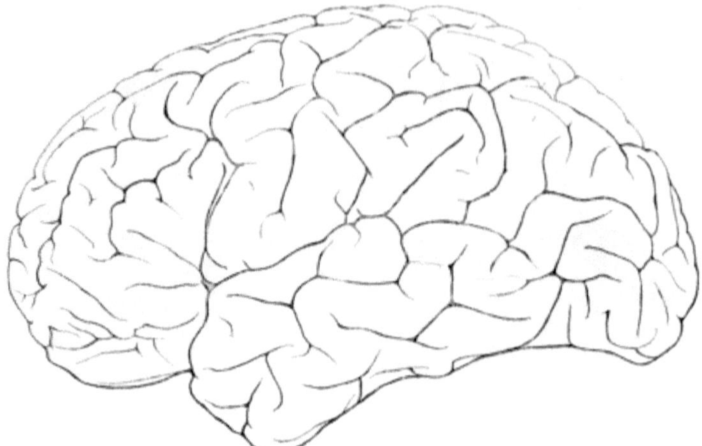

Fig. 38. Lateral view of left hemicerebrum.

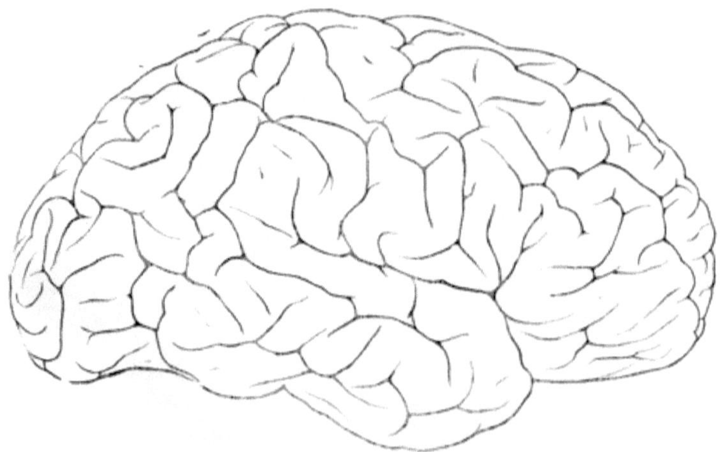

Fig. 39. Lateral view of right hemicerebrum.

BRAIN OF PHILIP LEIDY.

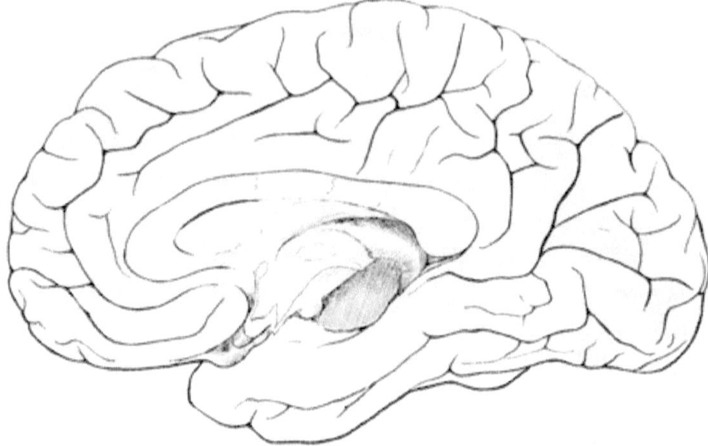

FIG. 40. Mesal view of right hemicerebrum.

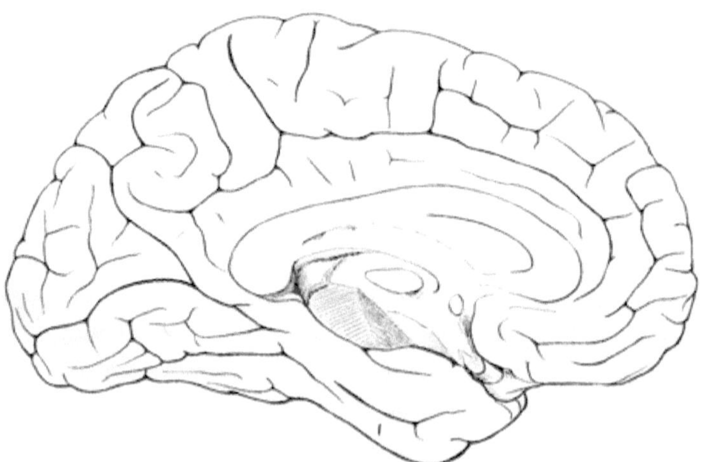

FIG. 41. Mesal view of left hemicerebrum.

BRAIN OF PHILIP LEIDY.

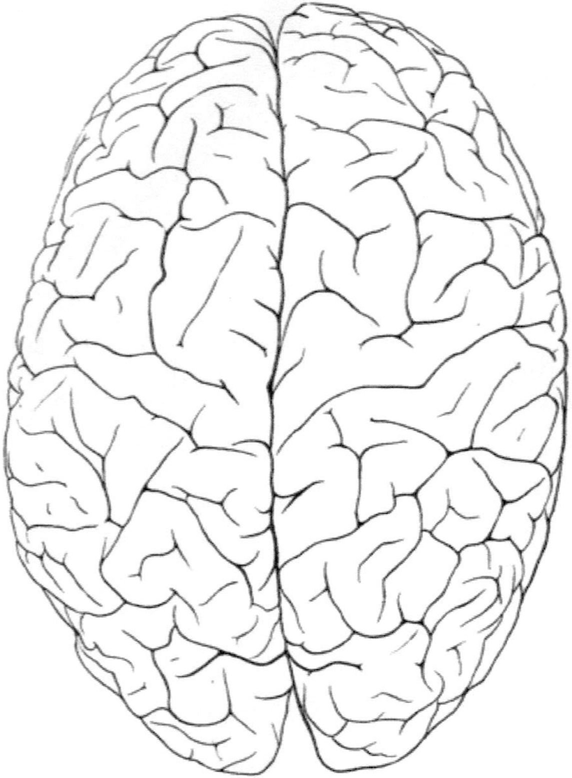

Fig. 42. Dorsal view of the cerebrum.

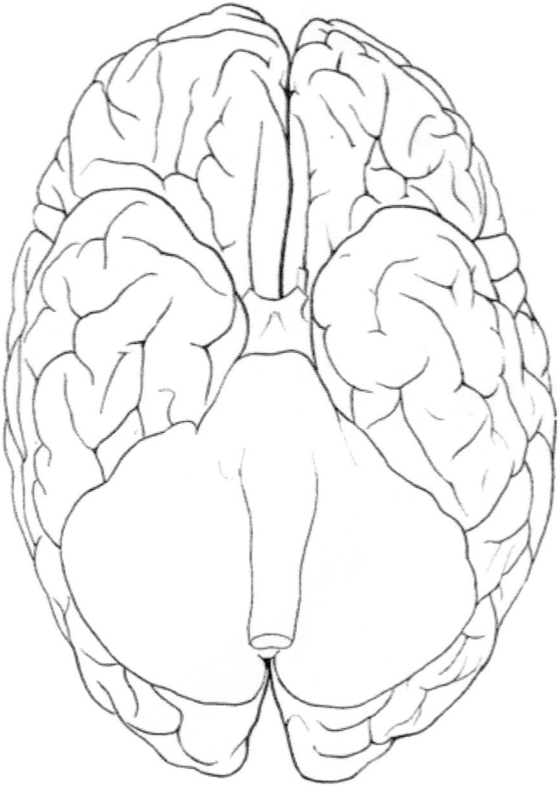

Fig. 43. Ventral view of the brain.

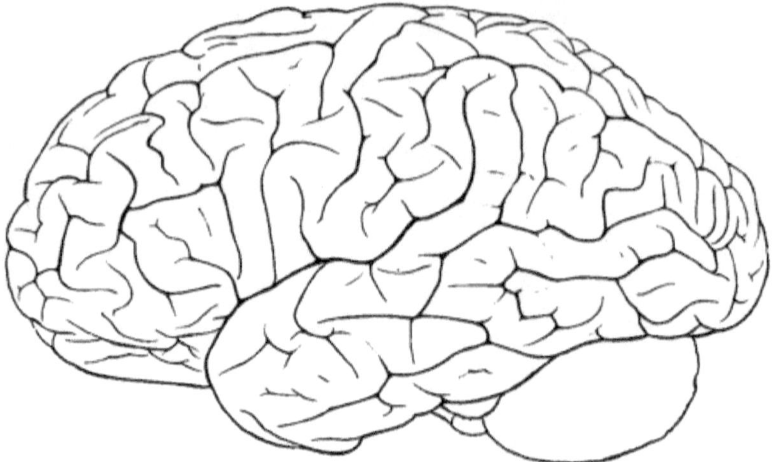

FIG. 44. Lateral view of the left hemicerebrum.

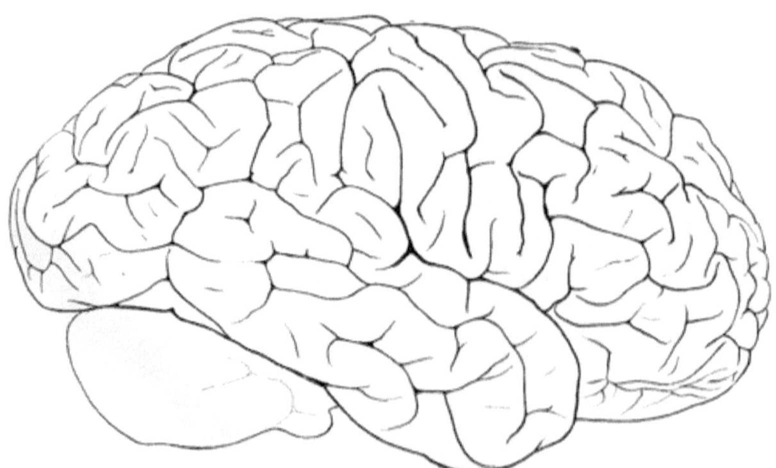

FIG. 45. Lateral view of the right hemicerebrum.

BRAIN OF A. J. PARKER.

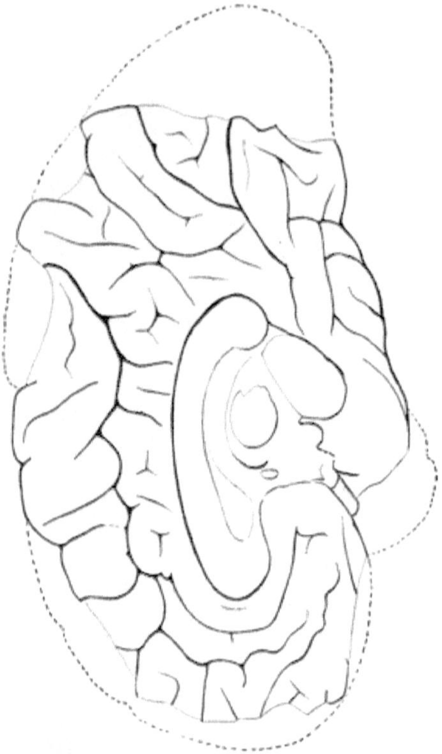

Fig. 46. Mesal view of the right hemicerebrum.

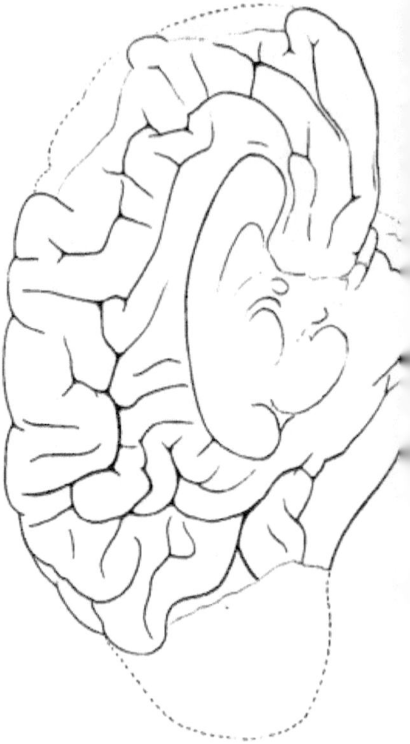

Fig. 47. Mesal view of the left hemicerebrum.

Fig. 48. Left insula.

Fig. 49. Right insula.

Brain of A. J. Parker.

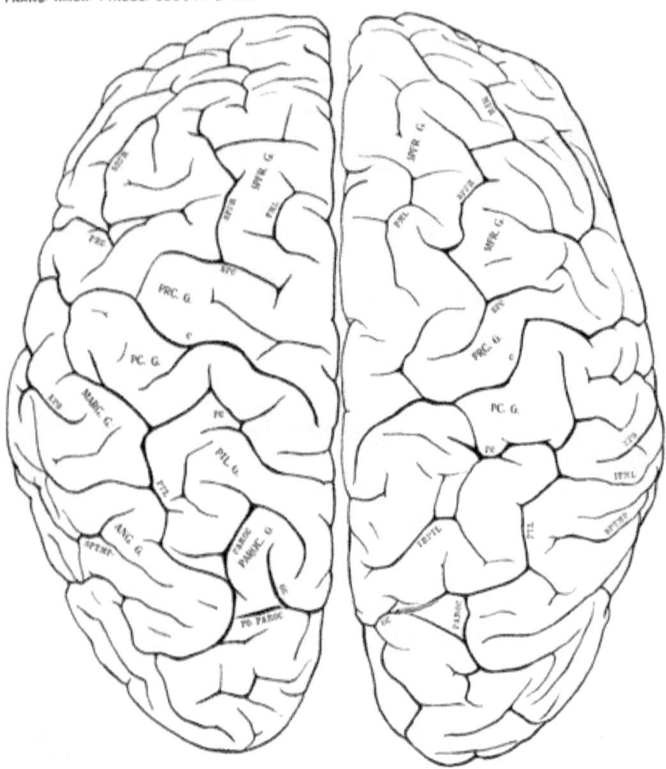

FIG. 51. Dorsal view of cerebrum.

BRAIN OF HARRISON ALLEN.

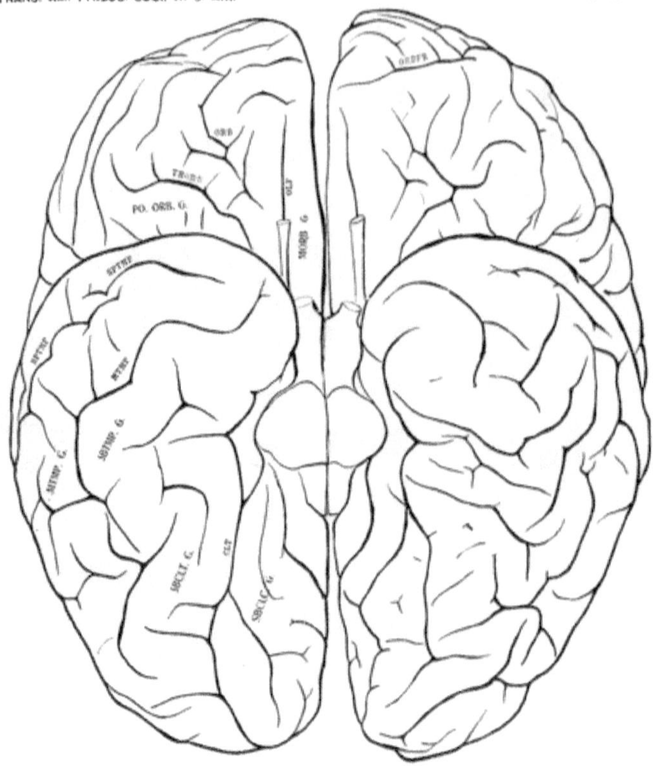

Fig. 52. Ventral view of cerebrum.

Brain of Harrison Allen.

A. P. S.—XXI. JJ. 5, 11, '07.

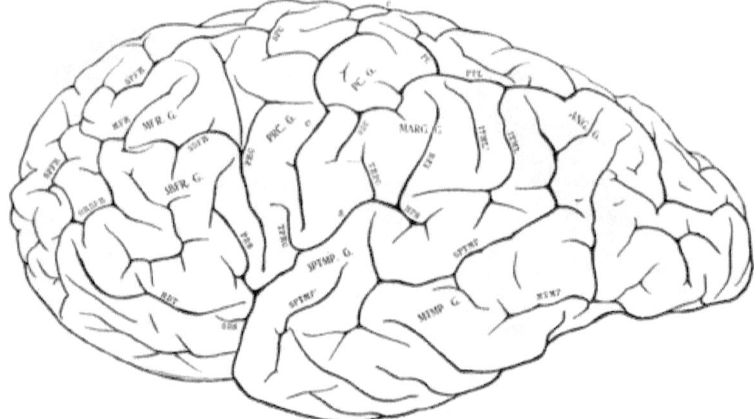

Fig. 53. Lateral view of left hemicerebrum.

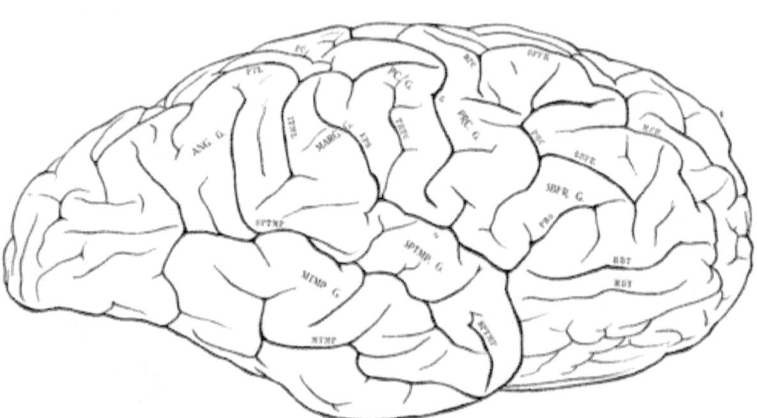

Fig. 54. Lateral view of right hemicerebrum.

Brain of Harrison Allen.

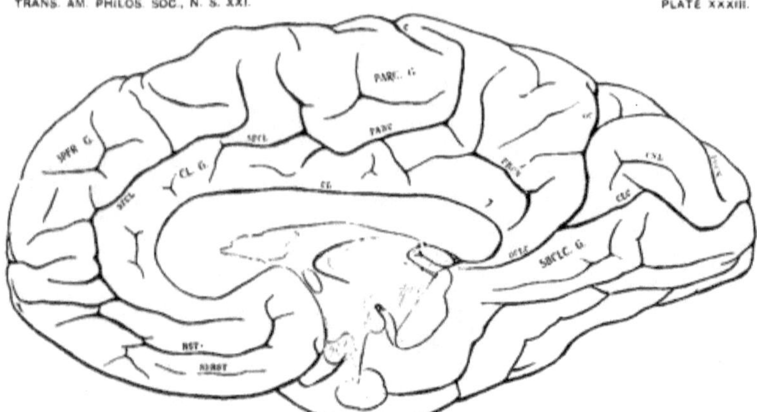

Fig. 55. Mesal view of right hemicerebrum.

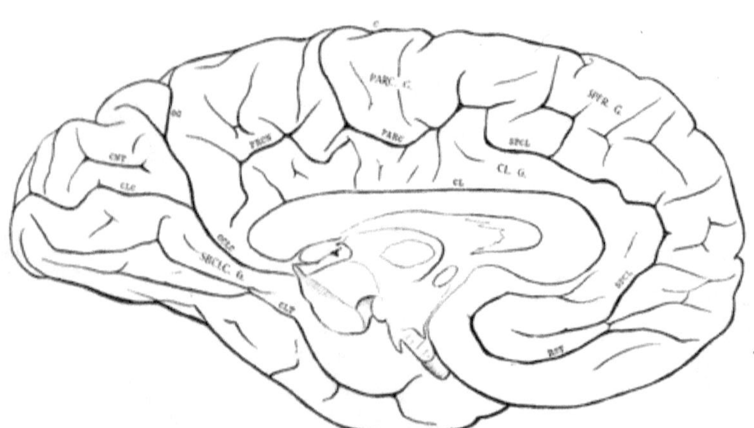

Fig. 56. Mesal view of left hemicerebrum.

Brain of Harrison Allen.

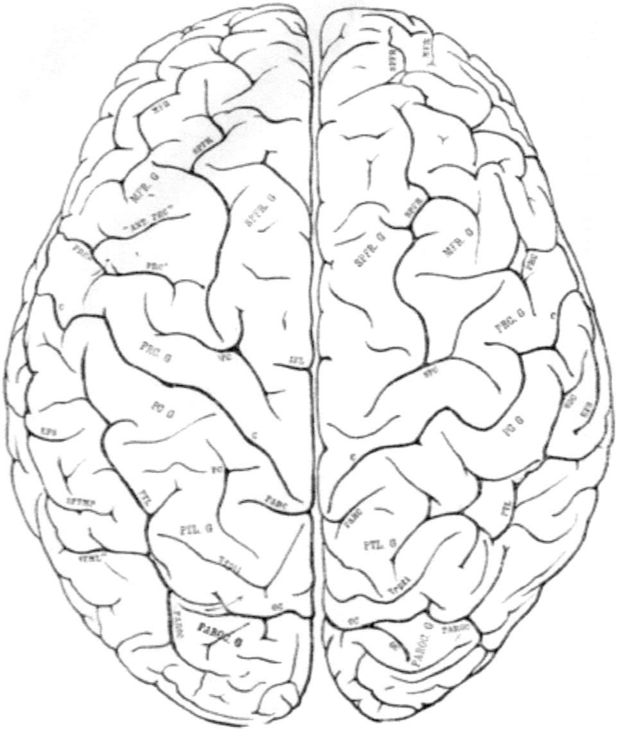

Fig. 57. Dorsal view of cerebrum.

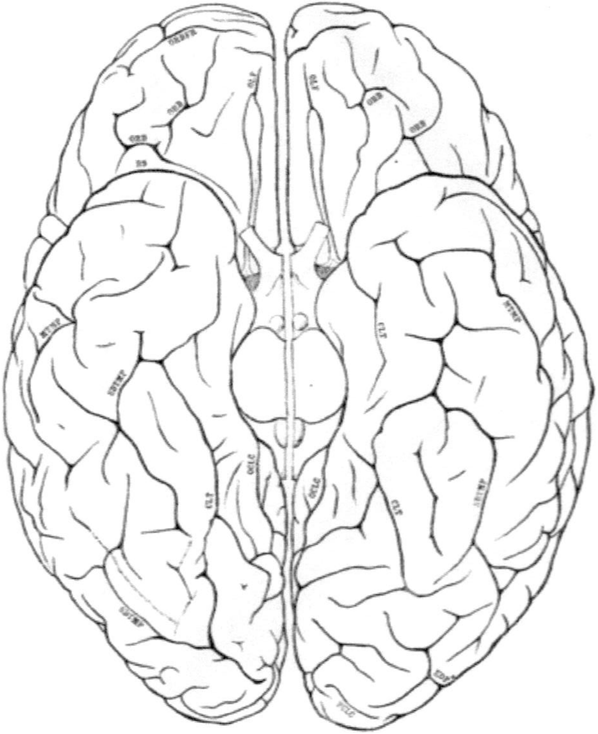

Fig. 58. Ventral view of cerebrum.

BRAIN OF E. D. COPE

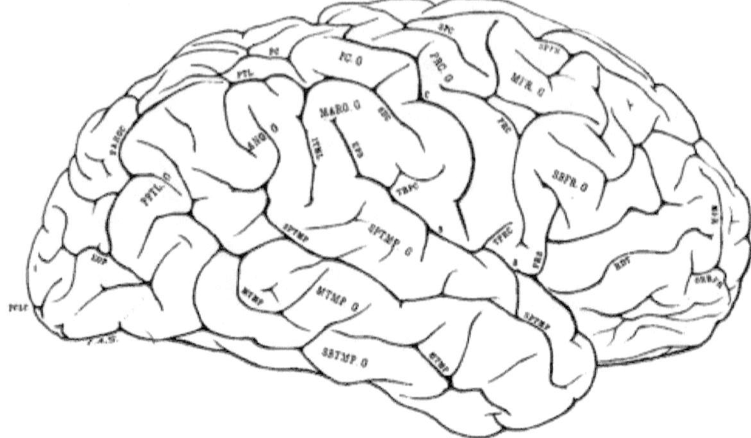

FIG. 59. Lateral view of right hemicerebrum.

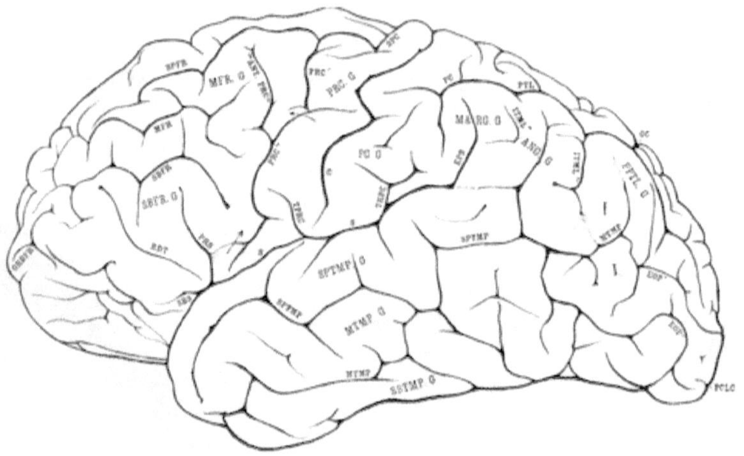

FIG. 60. Lateral view of left hemicerebrum.

BRAIN OF E. D. COPE.

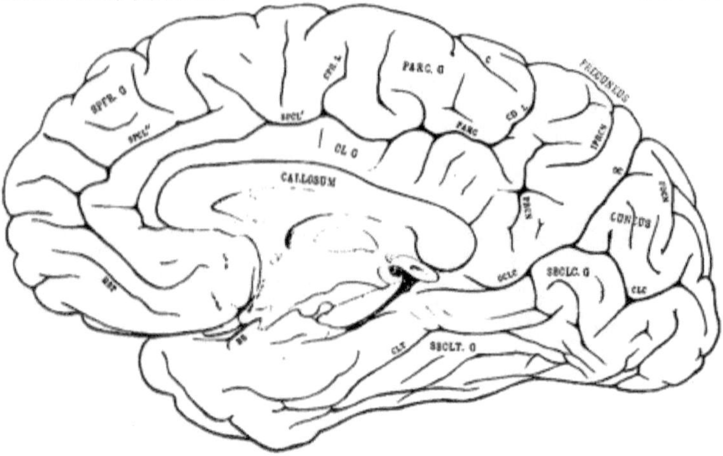

FIG. 61. Mesal view of right hemicerebrum.

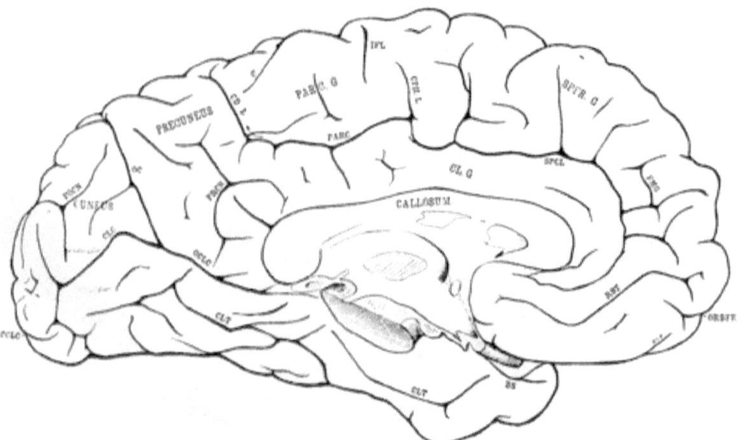

FIG. 62. Mesal view of left hemicerebrum.

BRAIN OF E. D. COPE.

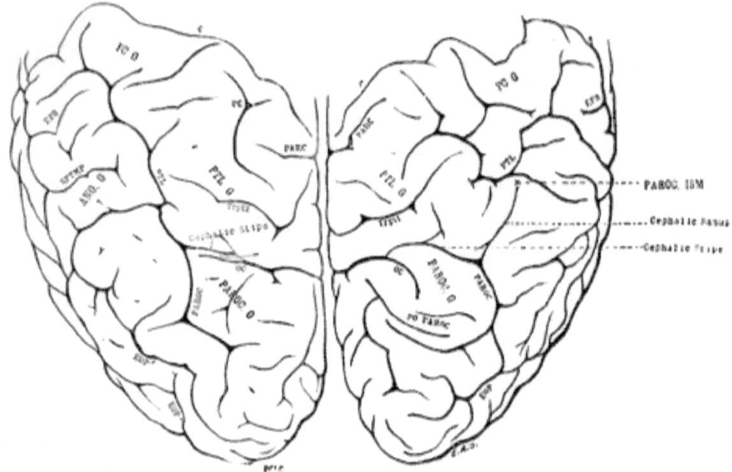

Fig. 63. Dorso-caudal view of the cerebrum.

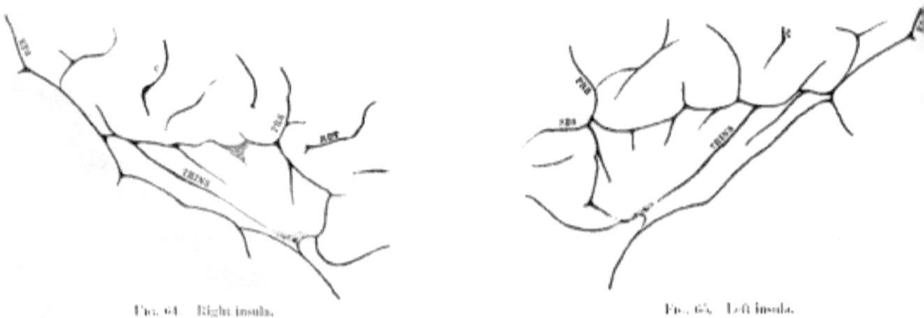

Fig. 64. Right insula.

Fig. 65. Left insula.

BRAIN OF E. D. COPE

A. P. S.—XXI. LL 8, 11, '07.

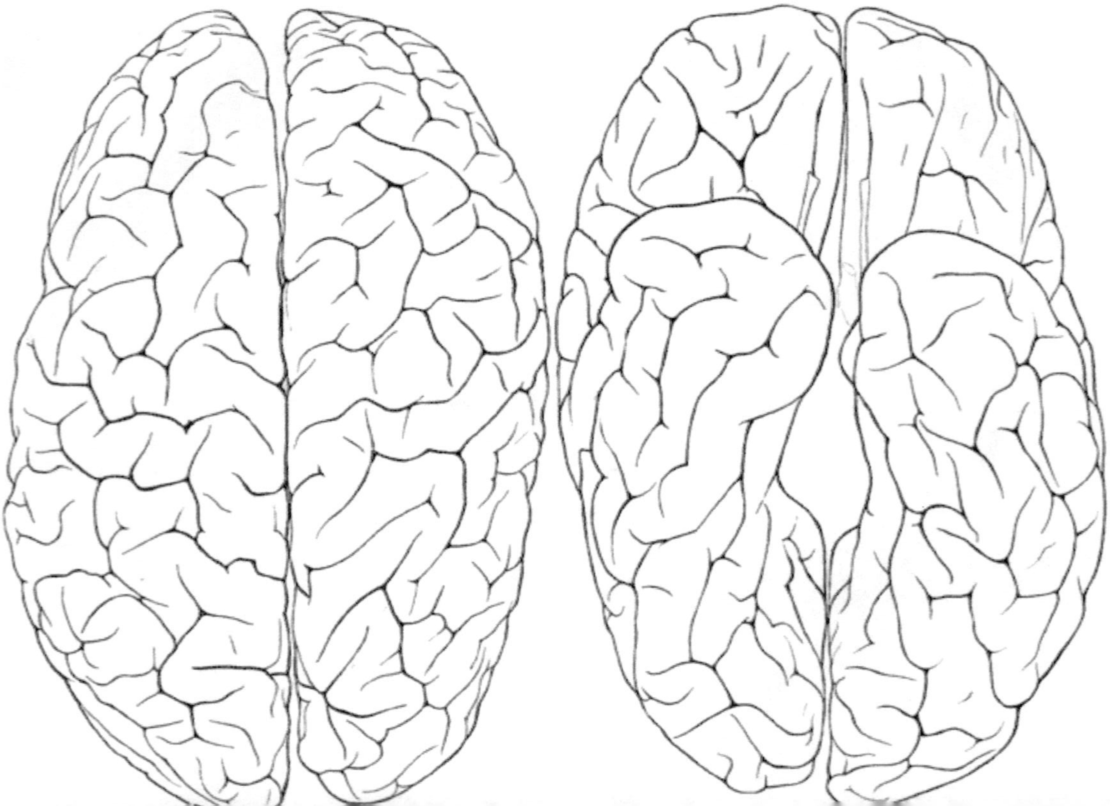

A. P. S.—XXI. NN. 8, 11, '07.

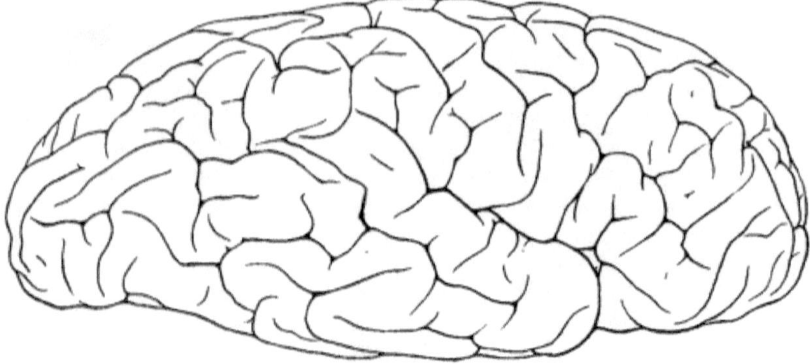

FIG. 68. Lateral view of the right hemicerebrum.

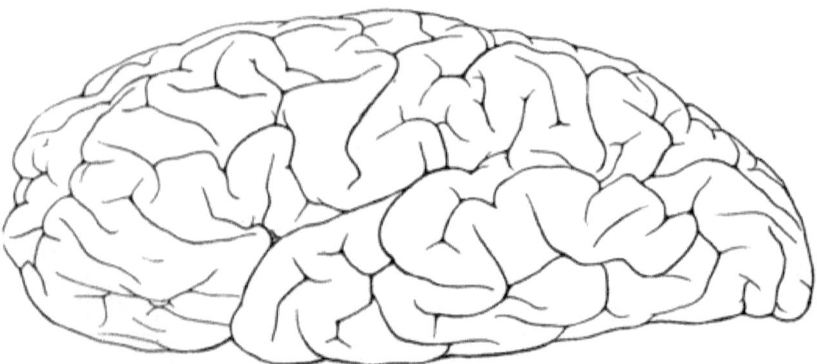

FIG. 69. Lateral view of the left hemicerebrum.

BRAIN OF WILLIAM PEPPER.

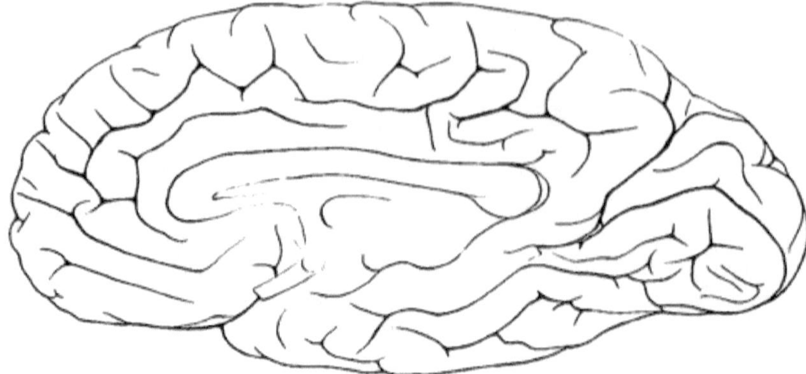

Fig. 70. Mesal view of right hemicerebrum.

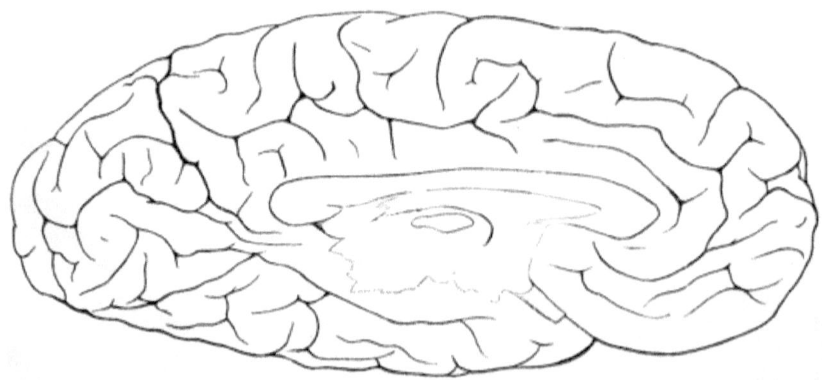

Fig. 71. Mesal view of left hemicerebrum.

Brain of William Pepper

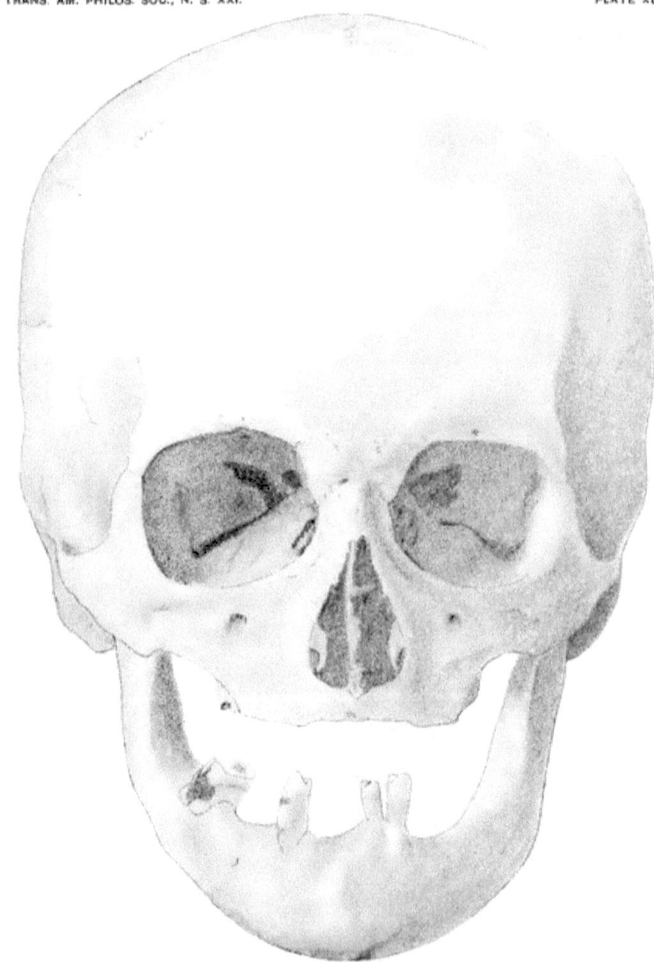

FIG. 72.
SKULL OF E. D. COPE.

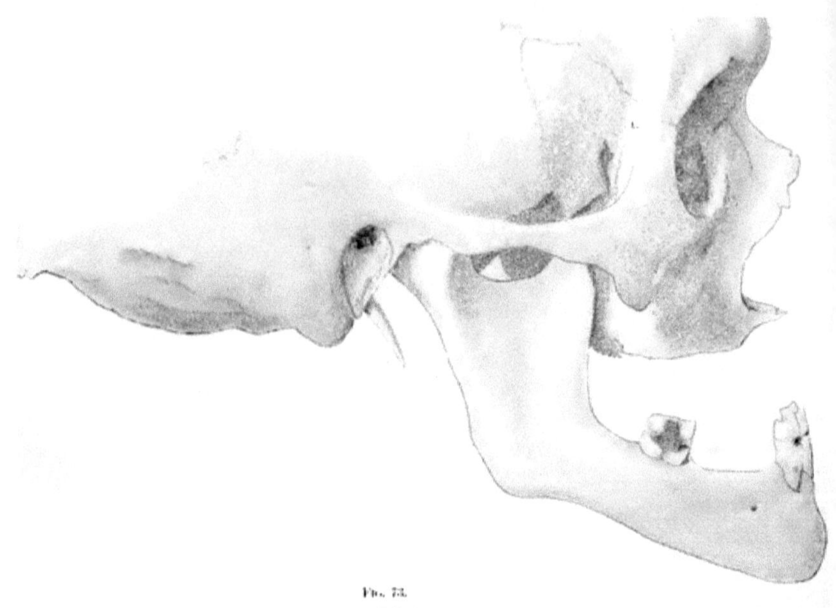

Fig. 73.

Skull of E. D. Cope.

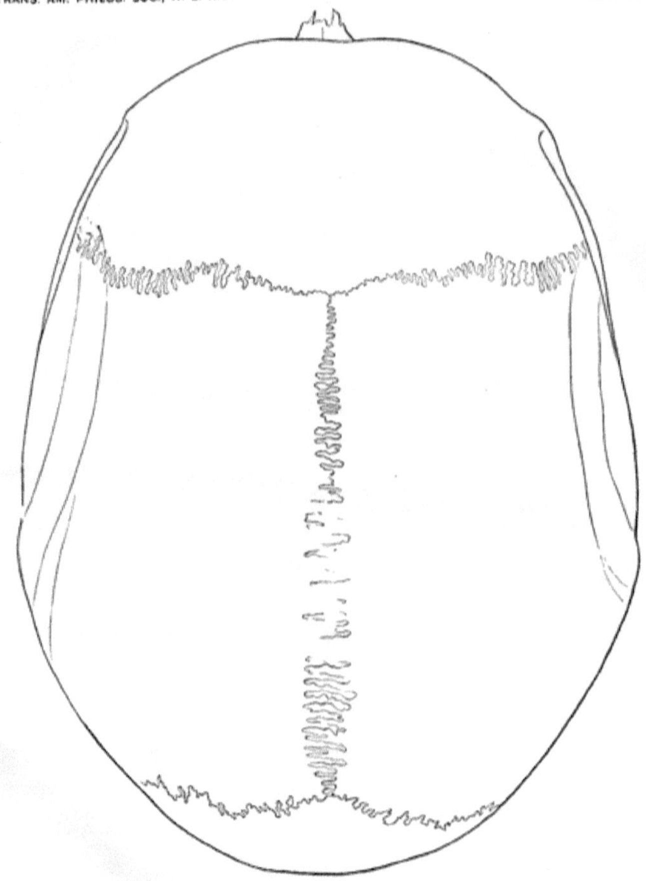

FIG. 74.

SKULL OF E. D. COPE.